D1595519

ANTENNAS AND RADIOWAVE PROPAGATION

McGraw-Hill Series in Electrical Engineering

ANTENNAS AND RADIOWAVE PROPAGATION

Robert E. Collin

Case Western Reserve University

McGraw-Hill, Inc.
New York St. Louis San Francisco Auckland Bogotá
Caracas Lisbon London Madrid Mexico City Milan
Montreal New Delhi San Juan Singapore
Sydney Tokyo Toronto

This book was set in Times Roman.
The editors were Sanjeev Rao and David A. Damstra;
the production supervisor was Phil Galea.
The cover was designed by Mark Wieboldt.
The drawings were done by J & R Services, Inc.
Braun-Brumfield Inc., was printer and binder.

ANTENNAS AND RADIOWAVE PROPAGATION

4 5 6 7 8 9   BRBBRB   9 3 9 8 7 6 5 4 3 2 1 0

ISBN 0-07-011808-6

Library of Congress Cataloging in Publication Data

Collin, Robert E.
   Antennas and radiowave propagation.

   (McGraw-Hill series in electrical engineering)
   Bibliography: p.
   Includes indexes.
   1. Antennas (Electronics)   2. Radio wave propagation.
I. Title.   II. Series.
TK7871.6.C62   1985   621.3841'1   84-17108
ISBN 0-07-011808-6

CONTENTS

Part 2 Propagation

PREFACE

This book is the outgrowth of class notes developed for a course on antennas and radio-wave propagation that has been offered as an elective course for juniors and seniors at Case Institute of Technology, Case Western Reserve University, for a number of years. The objective of the course is to provide an introduction to the fundamental principles of antennas and propagation for communications-oriented electrical engineers. The book differs from currently available texts on antennas in that there is more emphasis on the communications aspects. For example, a whole chapter on the receiving properties of antennas and communication-link evaluations is included.

In the text fundamental principles are stressed. The treatment in detail of specific antenna types is based on the need to illustrate the application of basic principles and to introduce the properties of a reasonable variety of commonly used antennas. The text extends considerably beyond the needs of a single, specific, one-semester course. There are two compelling reasons for this—the first being the need for flexibility in the structure of a course which might be based on this text, the second being the desire for a degree of completeness that makes the text a useful reference for practicing engineers who need occasionally to refer to basic equations in the course of their work. The result is a text that should, in many ways, fulfill the needs for an introductory course on antennas alone, at either the senior-year or first-year-graduate level, for a course with a mixture of antenna and propagation topics, or even for a short introductory course on radio-wave propagation.

The first chapter is a brief introduction to antennas and propagation, with a number of illustrations of real antenna systems. The second chapter develops the basic principles of radiation and introduces typical antenna concepts such as gain, directivity, and radiation patterns. The last part of the second chapter introduces the theory for impedance determination for cylindrical dipole antennas based on the Hallén integral equation and the method of moments. This subject has been treated with more care than usual in order to put into proper perspective the significance of various approximations that are commonly made in the practical application of the theory. The fact that the usual approximate integral equation that many authors adopt does not have an exact solution is not ignored. An explanation is given for the reason approximate solutions of a nonsolvable integral equation yield useful results for the antenna impedance.

The application of transmission-line concepts to dipole and wire antennas provides a useful insight into how these antennas function. Chapter 3 exploits these concepts in order to develop an understanding of the behavior of short dipole antennas and of folded dipoles, the use of loading coils and of capacitive end loading, and the impedance properties of antennas. Many of the topics are classical and might be considered outdated in a modern text. However, it is the author's experience that these topics precisely treat those antenna configurations with which many students have become acquainted through their involvement in amateur radio work and which spark a considerable amount of interest on the part of many students. This chapter also develops the principles of array antennas and treats several useful techniques and concepts for array synthesis. The chapter concludes with a discussion of long-wire antennas such as the rhombic and vee antennas.

Chapter 4 is devoted to a treatment of aperture-type antennas, among which are open waveguides, horns, reflectors, and slotted waveguide arrays and microstrip antennas. The planar aperture theory is based on Fourier transform theory and is also developed using field-equivalence principles. The parabolic reflector antenna is such a widely used and practical antenna, particularly in satellite communications, that the theory and properties of this type of antenna are developed in more detail than that found in most texts. Aperture efficiency, cross-polarization properties, offset parabolic reflectors, and cassegrain and gregorian systems are among the topics treated. New material on feeds with low cross-polarization properties is included. The practicing antenna engineer will find most of this material useful, since much of it is not available in convenient textbook form. The last part of Chap. 4 provides an introduction to slot antennas, slotted waveguide arrays, and microstrip antennas.

The receiving properties of antennas are treated in detail in Chap. 5. The concepts of effective area, polarization mismatch, effective complex length, impedance mismatch, and antenna-noise temperature are all developed from fundamental principles. The evaluation of communication systems, taking into account antenna noise, lossy transmission-line noise, and receiver noise, is carried out. Various examples of link evaluations are included to illustrate the application of the theory to line-of-sight microwave links, radar systems, and satellite communication systems. This material will be useful to the communications engineer whose interests relate to systems evaluation and planning.

The last chapter is a rather long one that treats a broad spectrum of topics related to radio-wave propagation. The primary objective of this chapter is to introduce the communications engineer to most of the propagation phenomena likely to be encountered in practice and to present fundamental principles so that an appreciation of the underlying physical phenomena is obtained. This chapter serves to introduce and orient the reader to those aspects of propagation that must be considered in the planning and evaluation of a communication system of a given type and frequency of operation.

The literature on radio-wave propagation is vast and highly specialized. It is not possible to give a detailed account of the many varied phenomena that affect the propagation of radio waves in a general introductory text. Nevertheless an awareness, general overview, and understanding of propagation phenomena are necessary for communications engineers if they are to communicate in an effective manner with the propagation specialist and be able to pursue specialized papers and books with an informed perspective.

The following topics are covered: interference effects for antennas located over a flat earth and a spherical earth, low- and medium-frequency surface-wave propagation, ionospheric propagation phenomena, microwave attenuation and scattering by atmospheric constituents, tropospheric scatter propagation, very low frequency propagation in the earth-ionosphere waveguide, and, briefly, ducting and propagation into seawater. A number of examples illustrating the application of the theory to the evaluation of communication links are included.

The treatment of scattering from rain and tropospheric scattering is based on an application of the reciprocity principle. This method gives an expression for the received open-circuit voltage caused by the scattered field in terms of the interaction of the antenna radiation field with the random currents induced in the scattering medium. The advantage of this method is that the polarization properties of the scattered field are retained and the resultant polarization mismatch at the receiving antenna is accounted for. Theories based on scalar scattering cross section per unit volume do not account for the polarization properties of the scattered field.

Any general text draws very heavily on the work of many engineers and scientists. It is not possible to include references to the whole body of published work in the field. For the most part only those books and papers that were consulted in the preparation of the manuscript are referenced, along with selected references that are appropriate for the reader to obtain more detail and breadth.

Several of the author's colleagues have provided valuable comments and suggestions for improving the treatment of various topics. In particular, I would like to acknowledge the critical review of many parts of the manuscript by Georg Karawas. Subsequent discussions with him led to a clearer presentation of several topics.

This book is dedicated to my wife, Kathleen, for her love, understanding, and patience. Her encouragement provided the necessary motivation to complete the project.

I am also most grateful to Susan F. Sava who typed the manuscript, corrected my grammar and spelling errors, and assisted me with the proofreading and the preparation of the index. Her expertise, friendship, and good sense of humor made the overall task a pleasant one.

Robert E. Collin

ANTENNAS AND RADIOWAVE PROPAGATION

PART
ONE

ANTENNAS

COMMUNICATION WITH RADIO WAVES

Communication by electrical means began with the introduction of telegraphy in 1844, followed by telephony in 1878. In these systems electrical signals are sent over two-wire transmission lines that connect the sender and recipient. During the same time period that these systems were being developed the theoretical foundation for electromagnetic radiation was being laid by Maxwell and others. However, it was not until 1897 that Marconi first patented a complete wireless telegraphy system based on the use of electromagnetic radiation (radio waves) that had been predicted theoretically by Maxwell 43 years earlier. The early transmitters were of the spark-gap variety and served the purpose of sending the on-off pulses characteristic of telegraphy. The actual transmission of voice by means of electromagnetic radiation did not occur before the invention of the vacuum tube amplifier and oscillator in the period from 1904 to 1915. With these inventions all phases of communication began to develop at a much more rapid pace, a pace that seems to show no sign of slowing down.

The engineer who wants to specialize in the communication field needs to have a basic understanding of the roles of electromagnetic radiation, antennas, and related propagation phenomena in modern communication systems, in addition to knowledge of communication systems utilizing various forms of transmission lines, such as twisted pairs and coaxial cable. The objective of this text is to provide this basic background. The intent is not to delve very deeply into the intricate details of a great variety of antenna types. The objective is to develop enough of the basic concepts to give a reasonable understanding of antenna fundamentals and of the basic limitations of antennas, of how antennas are characterized and of how communication systems incorporating antennas are evaluated, and finally to introduce the more common phenomena affecting the propagation of electromagnetic waves and the influence this effect has on the performance of a communication system.

1.1 TYPES OF COMMUNICATION SYSTEMS

There are two broad categories of communication systems: those that utilize transmission lines in an interconnected network and those that rely on electromagnetic radiation with an antenna at both the transmitting and receiving sites. In cities where the population density is high and in systems where the required signal bandwidth is small, as in voice communication, it is economically viable to interconnect the many users with simple, low-cost, twisted-pair transmission lines. Such lines will introduce an attenuation of around 2 to 3 dB/km at frequencies around 10 kHz. The twisted pair is not suitable for high-frequency use, so it is generally limited to the telephone service and low-data-rate digital transmissions.

In populated areas it is also fairly common to transmit television video signals over coaxial transmission lines, and the loss is around 4 to 5 dB/km. A fundamental characteristic of transmission lines is that the attenuation is exponential in its behavior. Thus a loss of 5 dB/km becomes a loss of 100 dB over a 20-km path. If the path is doubled to 40-km an additional loss of 100 dB is suffered. When it is recalled that a 100-dB loss is a reduction in received signal power by a factor of 10^{-10}, it is readily appreciated that the exponential attenuation law ultimately places a severe restriction on the distance over which communication can take place without the use of repeater amplifiers.

In communication systems using electromagnetic radiation, the signal power is radiated into a substantial angular region of space by the transmitting antenna and only a small fraction of this radiated power is intercepted by the receiving antenna. There is thus a very significant coupling loss between the transmitting and receiving antennas. On the other hand, the loss incurred versus distance is algebraic in behavior rather than exponential. The reason for this is as follows: For many communication links the radiated power per unit area incident on the receiving antenna decreases as the inverse square of the distance between the transmitting and receiving antennas. Every doubling of the distance decreases the received power by a factor of 4 or 6 dB. If in a particular system the total loss is 100 dB for a 20-km path, a doubling of this distance would add only an additional 6 dB of loss instead of the 100-dB loss that occurs with a transmission line system as discussed above. It is apparent then that beyond a certain distance the loss in a communication system using electromagnetic radiation will become increasingly less than with transmission lines. The relative costs of the two systems depend in a complex way on the number of users, type of service, and distances involved.

The attenuation and cost factors are not the only ones that dictate the choice between transmission lines and electromagnetic radiation. In any mobile communication service such as ship-to-shore, between aircraft and control centers, between mobile land vehicles, and in satellite systems, transmission lines obviously cannot be used. In many other cases as well it is not economically feasible to install transmission lines because of the hostile terrain and environment. Antennas are clearly essential components in communication systems for many and varied reasons. Consequently, the communication engineer should have an appreciation and understanding of antenna fundamentals and be able to evaluate the performance of a communication system utilizing this basic knowledge.

1.2 ANTENNA SYSTEMS

The commonly used "whip" antennas on cars, "rabbit ears" on television receivers, single-turn loop antennas for UHF (ultrahigh frequency) television reception, roof-mounted log-periodic TV antennas, and satellite paraboloidal-reflector receiving antennas are so prevalent that most readers are clearly aware of the need for antennas in the support of our daily communication needs. These commonly occurring antennas represent only a small segment of the antenna systems that have been developed. For specialized and high-performance communication links, radar systems, navigational systems, and scientific studies, highly complex antenna systems are needed. In order to give an impression of the physical characteristics of some of these complex antenna systems a number of photographs are included in this section. These should help the reader to appreciate the creativity of the antenna engineer in having developed the necessary theory, design methodology, and manufacturing techniques needed to put such complex systems into use.

Figure 1.1 shows a microwave relay tower on which are mounted two inclined flat-plate reflectors. These reflectors direct the incoming radiation to a ground-based amplifier which amplifies the signal and retransmits it up to the second reflector. The latter redirects the signal on to the next relay station. Figure 1.2 shows a microwave relay tower on which are mounted several paraboloidal-reflector antennas enclosed in plastic radome housings. Relay stations of this type are in widespread use by the telephone companies, public and private utility companies, and various private corporate communication links.

The next series of five figures shows several antenna systems and feed systems that are typical of those used for satellite communications. Figure 1.3 is an artist's rendition of a satellite and shows the large outlying solar panels and two dual-reflector antenna systems with multihorn feed systems. Figure 1.4 is an artist's rendition of a cassegrain dual-reflector antenna used for satellite signal reception. In Fig. 1.5 a dual-mode conical horn is illustrated. This horn was designed to be used in an array of many horns (Fig. 1.6) with a reflector system to provide "trunking" beams in a satellite communication system. The next two photographs, Figs. 1.6 and 1.7, show multibeam antenna (MBA) feed

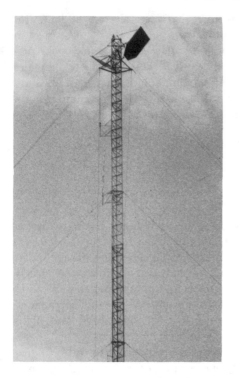

Figure 1.1 A microwave relay system using two inclined flat reflectors.

Figure 1.2 A microwave relay tower on which are mounted several radome-enclosed paraboloidal reflector antennas.

systems consisting of arrays of conical or pyramidal horns. In order to provide multibeam capability very complex waveguide coupling arrangements are required, as is apparent from the photographs. These feed systems were designed by TRW, Inc., for NASA for use in a 20- to 30-GHz communication satellite.

The last two photographs, Figs. 1.8 and 1.9, are of the antenna facilities at the M.I.T. Haystack Observatory. These antennas are used for scientific studies. A more detailed description is given in the figure captions.

1.3 PROPAGATION OF ELECTROMAGNETIC WAVES

The performance of a communication link depends not only on the antennas used but also on a variety of phenomena that affect the propagation of electromagnetic waves. In the standard AM broadcast band (0.55 to 1.6 MHz) ground-based vertical towers are generally used for the transmitting antennas. The reason for this is that an antenna cannot be much shorter than a quarter wavelength and radiate with high efficiency. Consequently, at the long

Figure 1.3 Artist's rendition of a satellite showing two dual-reflector antenna systems with multihorn arrays used for primary illumination of the reflectors. (*Photo courtesy of J. Smetana, NASA-Lewis Research Center, Cleveland, Ohio.*)

Figure 1.4 Artist's rendition of a cassegrain dual-reflector satellite receiving antenna. (*Photo courtesy of J. Smetana, NASA-Lewis Research Center, Cleveland, Ohio.*)

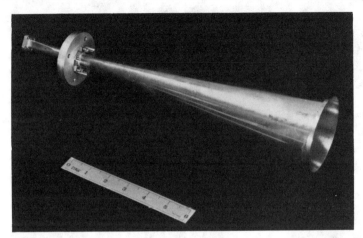

Figure 1.5 A dual-mode conical horn designed for use in a feed array such as shown in Fig. 1.6. (*Photo courtesy of J. Smetana, NASA-Lewis Research Center, Cleveland, Ohio.*)

wavelengths only simple antennas with low gain are used, and these antennas are located on the ground because of their large physical size. For ground-based antennas the ground has a strong influence on the propagation of the signal. The mode of propagation is called a *surface wave*, and it attenuates approximately as the inverse fourth power of the distance. In addition to the

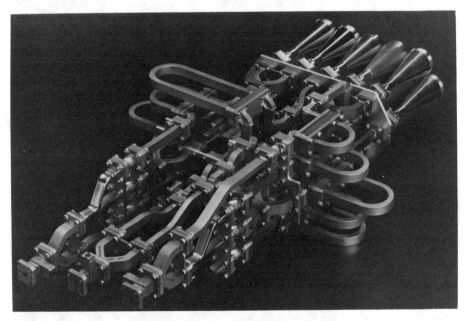

Figure 1.6 An array of conical dual-mode horns for use in a multibeam trunk-beam feed system to illuminate a reflector antenna for satellite communications. (*Photo courtesy of J. Smetana, NASA-Lewis Research Center, Cleveland, Ohio.*)

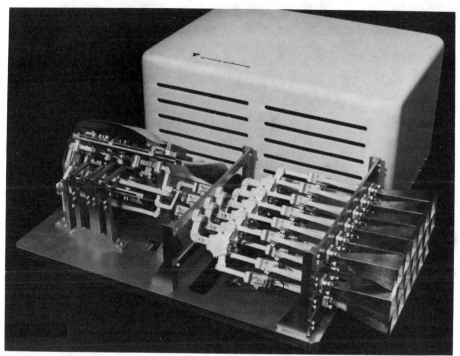

Figure 1.7 An array of pyramidal horns for a multibeam antenna used to illuminate a reflector for satellite communications. (*Photo courtesy of J. Smetana, NASA-Lewis Research Center, Cleveland, Ohio.*)

attenuation there is a high level of atmospheric noise in the AM broadcast band as well as human-induced electrical interference that is picked up by the receiving antenna. Thus, in practice, large transmitter power must be used in order to provide an adequate signal-to-noise ratio. Transmitter powers of 50 kW are quite common, and some stations operate with powers as large as 500 kW. The useful coverage distance is typically only a few hundred miles because of the large attenuation and high noise level.

The attenuation of the surface wave increases rapidly with an increase in frequency so that, above 20 MHz, communication is generally not by means of the surface wave. Fortunately above 10 MHz or so the wavelength is only 30 m or less, and it becomes practical to build larger antenna arrays with higher gain and to mount these on towers above the surface of the ground. Communication then takes place by means of direct line-of-sight propagation plus radiation reflected from the ground midway between the transmitting and receiving sites. In communication links of this type the antenna heights must be chosen with some care in order that the direct line-of-sight propagated field will add in phase with the wave reflected from the ground. Whenever there are two or more paths that waves can propagate along to reach the receiving antenna,

Figure 1.8 An aerial view of the antennas used for radio/radar astronomy and atmospheric research at M.I.T.'s Haystack Observatory, Westford, Mass. The geodesic radome in the foreground houses a steerable 120-ft antenna that retains its paraboloidal shape to within a few millimeters. In the center are a fixed 220-ft dish and a steerable 150-ft dish that are used for probing the atmosphere and the ionosphere at 440 MHz. The smaller antenna near the right-hand top is an 84-ft dish used for deep-space probing at L band by the Lincoln Laboratory. The smaller radome houses a facility for very long baseline interferometry. (*Photo by permission of Lincoln Laboratory, M.I.T.*)

interference effects occur. If the propagation path is not a stable one, fading will occur, and this manifests itself in large variations in signal power taking place over time intervals typically measured in seconds or minutes. The instability in the propagation path is caused by variations in the index of refraction of the atmosphere, which in turn are caused by temperature and humidity fluctuations. Variations in the index of refraction cause the phase angle of the signal arriving at the receiving site to vary in a random way. Thus signals arriving along different paths combine with more or less random phases and at times tend to cancel one another, which results in fading. In communication systems designed for very high reliability some form of diversity is generally incorporated to overcome the effects of fading. A typical system could consist of several spaced receiving antennas with the signals combined in such a fashion that a useful signal is received with high probability at all times. With spaced antennas it is unlikely that deep fades will occur at all sites simultaneously, and hence system reliability is improved by the use of space diversity.

Figure 1.9 A close-up view of the fixed 220-ft antenna (foreground) and the fully steerable 150-ft antenna used for incoherent-scatter radar studies of the ionosphere at 440 MHz. The steerable antenna is used for studying the morphology of the ionosphere over a very wide geographical region. This radar is also used for monitoring motions in the stratosphere and troposphere. (*Photo by permission of Lincoln Laboratory, M.I.T.*)

In the frequency range from a few megahertz up to 30 to 40 MHz, it is possible to achieve very long distance communication by ionospheric refraction of the radio wave back toward the ground. The resulting skip distance can be several thousand kilometers. The international shortwave broadcast service utilizes this mode of communication. The refractive properties of the ionosphere are dependent on the electron density as produced by solar radiation. Electron density varies on a daily basis as well as throughout the year and in accordance with general solar activity, i.e., sun spots. The refractive properties are also frequency-dependent so that generally above 40 MHz the radiated wave will penetrate through the ionosphere and not be refracted back to earth at all. There is considerable fading associated with the ionospheric propagation path, so again some form of diversity, such as several spaced antennas or broadcasting on several frequencies simultaneously, is utilized in high-reliability links.

At frequencies above 40 MHz, communication is essentially limited to line-of-sight paths. A typical line-of-sight link is that used for television broadcasting. Another example is the line-of-sight microwave link used in the telephone service.

In order for an antenna to radiate into a small angular region and thereby provide a higher concentration of power at the receiving site it must be physically large in terms of wavelength. In the microwave band where the wavelength is in the range of 3 to 30 cm, large reflector antennas with gains as large as 40 to 50 dB are quite common. With the large available antenna gain, the transmitter power can be reduced accordingly. It is not unusual to use transmitter powers of a few watts or even as low as a few hundred milliwatts in the microwave band. There is also much less atmospheric noise at the higher frequencies so smaller signal levels can be used.

As one moves up into the millimeter wavelength region, atmospheric attenuation as well as attenuation by rain becomes a serious limiting factor in the separation between the transmitting and receiving antennas. This attenuation is exponential in character and is in addition to the inverse square of the distance attenuation. As such it can severely limit the useful propagation distance.

The discussion above has briefly touched on a few of the factors that affect wave propagation at different frequencies. It points out the necessity to consider propagation phenomena in the design of a communication link. Propagation effects are generally analyzed by assuming average typical values for those physical parameters that characterize the propagation path. The results of the analysis serve to describe the effects that occur. However, in the real physical situation it must be remembered that the relevant physical parameters change with time in a generally unpredictable manner so that the design of a communication link should be carried out on a statistical basis. The level of reliability required, i.e., the percentage of time that a signal of sufficient strength will be received, will be dependent on the type of service involved.

1.4 FREQUENCY BANDS

In Table 1.1 we summarize the frequency band designations that are in common use, along with the typical services provided on each band.

The microwave and millimeter frequency bands cover the range from 500 MHz to 40 GHz and up. This range of frequencies is broken down into several bands designated by letters. In Table 1.2 the band designations are listed. Note that the old letter designations do not coincide with the new lettering. The older designation was established during the mid-nineteen forties and is still in common use.

1.5 OVERVIEW

This text is divided into two major parts. Part I discusses antennas and radiation, and Part II covers propagation phenomena. Part I consists of four

Table 1.1 Frequency band designation

Frequency band	Designation	Typical service
3–30 kHz	Very low frequency (VLF)	Navigation, sonar
30–300 kHz	Low frequency (LF)	Radio beacons, navigational aids
300–3000 kHz	Medium frequency (MF)	AM broadcasting, maritime radio, Coast Guard communication, direction finding
3–30 MHz	High frequency (HF)	Telephone, telegraph, and facsimile; shortwave international broadcasting; amateur radio; citizen's band; ship-to-coast and ship-to-aircraft communication
30–300 MHz	Very high frequency (VHF)	Television, FM broadcast, air traffic control, police, taxicab mobile radio, navigational aids
300–3000 MHz	Ultrahigh frequency (UHF)	Television, satellite communication, radiosonde, surveillance radar, navigational aids
3–30 GHz	Superhigh frequency (SHF)	Airborne radar, microwave links, common-carrier land mobile communication, satellite communication
30–300 GHz	Extremely high frequency (EHF)	Radar, experimental

chapters covering radiation fundamentals, simple antennas, basic antenna characteristics, antenna arrays, long-wire antennas, aperture-type antennas such as horns and paraboloids, and finally the properties of an antenna when used to receive electromagnetic radiation. Chapter 5 on receiving antennas also deals with the evaluation of communication links, including the effects of antenna and receiver noise.

Part II of the text provides an introduction to propagation phenomena. Among the topics covered are low-frequency surface-wave propagation, interference effects in line-of-sight communication links, coverage diagrams, the influence of the ionosphere on shortwave broadcasting in the 1- to 30-MHz frequency range, atmospheric and rain attenuation in the microwave and millimeter bands, scattering by atmospheric constituents, and an introduction to tropospheric scatter communication systems. Propagation phenomena is a diverse and extensive subject that cannot be covered in great depth in an

Table 1.2 Microwave frequency band designation

Frequency	Microwave band designation	
	Old	New
500–1000 MHz	VHF	C
1–2 GHz	L	D
2–3 GHz	S	E
3–4 GHz	S	F
4–6 GHz	C	G
6–8 GHz	C	H
8–10 GHz	X	I
10–12.4 GHz	X	J
12.4–18 GHz	Ku	J
18–20 GHz	K	J
20–26.5 GHz	K	K
26.5–40 GHz	Ka	K

introductory text. Thus we are limiting the discussion to those aspects that are broadly applicable to communication systems operating at frequencies of a megahertz or less up through the microwave band with frequencies as high as 30 GHz or more. The problem of statistical evaluation of communication links and fading phenomena is not dealt with.

TWO

FUNDAMENTALS OF ELECTROMAGNETIC RADIATION, ANTENNAS, AND ANTENNA IMPEDANCE

An antenna is a structure, usually made from a good conducting material, that has been designed to have a shape and size such that it will radiate electromagnetic power in an efficient manner. It is a well-established fact that time-varying currents will radiate electromagnetic waves. Thus an antenna is a structure on which time-varying currents can be excited with a relatively large amplitude when the antenna is connected to a suitable source, usually by means of a transmission line or waveguide. There is an almost endless variety of structural shapes that can be used for an antenna. However, from a practical point of view those structures that are simple and economical to fabricate are the ones most commonly used. In order to radiate efficiently, the minimum size of the antenna must be comparable to the wavelength. A very common antenna is the half-wavelength dipole antenna, which consists of two conducting rods. Each of the rods are one-quarter wavelength long and are placed end to end with a small spacing at the center at which point a transmission line is connected. The properties of this antenna are discussed in a later section of this chapter.

If the current density **J** excited on the antenna structure is known, there is no great difficulty in calculating the radiated field. The difficult problem is the one of determining the current density **J** on the antenna such that the resultant field will satisfy the required boundary conditions on the antenna. Fortunately it is often possible to estimate the actual current distribution with sufficient accuracy to obtain an excellent approximation to the radiated field. However, in order to calculate the impedance properties of the antenna the current distribution must generally be known with greater accuracy. The boundary-value problem that must be solved is quite complex.

Maxwell's equations are linear, so if the radiation from a short filament of current—say $I\,dl$—is known, then the principle of superposition may be used to find the radiated field from an arbitrary distribution of current by superimposing the field produced by each differential element of current. This is the approach that is generally used to determine the radiated field from an antenna.

In this chapter, Maxwell's equations are reviewed, and the vector and scalar potentials, which form a convenient mathematical tool for solving Maxwell's equations for a given set of sources, are introduced. The radiation from a short current filament is then found.

Many of the fundamental characteristics of an antenna, such as the radiation pattern, beam width, directivity, and radiation resistance, can be introduced in connection with the radiation from a short filament of current. Hence, this is a basic problem that serves very well to introduce the subject of antennas and is exploited in this chapter.

The last part of the chapter looks at the radiation from a small loop of wire with a current I flowing in it and the radiation from a half-wave dipole antenna. The latter problem illustrates the use of superposition as applied to the calculation of radiation fields. The chapter concludes with a discussion of antenna impedance.

2.1 MAXWELL'S EQUATIONS AND BOUNDARY CONDITIONS

Throughout this book we will deal primarily with sinusoidal time-varying fields. Thus, we follow the usual phasor type of analysis and generally will not show explicitly the time-dependent factor $e^{j\omega t}$. The currents and fields are expressed as vector functions of the spatial coordinates, and each component is, in general, a complex function with a real and imaginary part. For example, the electric field is expressed in the form

$$\mathbf{E}(\mathbf{r}) = E_x(\mathbf{r})\mathbf{a}_x + E_y(\mathbf{r})\mathbf{a}_y + E_z(\mathbf{r})\mathbf{a}_z \tag{2.1}$$

in rectangular coordinates. Each component, such as E_x, is a complex function of the form $E_{xr} + jE_{xi}$ where E_{xr} is the real part and E_{xi} is the imaginary part. If the real physical electric field is required, it may be obtained by multiplying $\mathbf{E}(\mathbf{r})$ by $e^{j\omega t}$ and taking the real part, that is,

$$\mathscr{E}(\mathbf{r}, t) = \operatorname{Re} \mathbf{E}(\mathbf{r})e^{j\omega t} \tag{2.2a}$$

which gives

$$\mathscr{E}_x(\mathbf{r}, t) = E_{xr}(\mathbf{r}) \cos \omega t - E_{xi}(\mathbf{r}) \sin \omega t \tag{2.2b}$$

for the x component of the physical field.

The four field quantities of interest are the electric field $\mathbf{E(r)}$, the magnetic intensity $\mathbf{H(r)}$, the electric displacement field $\mathbf{D(r)}$, and the magnetic flux field $\mathbf{B(r)}$. These fields, along with the source terms—current density $\mathbf{J(r)}$ and charge density $\rho(\mathbf{r})$—are related by Maxwell's equations as follows:

$$\nabla \times \mathbf{E} = -j\omega\mathbf{B} \qquad \text{(Faraday's law)} \qquad (2.3a)$$

$$\nabla \times \mathbf{H} = j\omega\mathbf{D} + \mathbf{J} \qquad \text{(generalized Ampere's law)} \qquad (2.3b)$$

$$\nabla \cdot \mathbf{D} = \rho \qquad \text{(Gauss' law)} \qquad (2.3c)$$

$$\nabla \cdot \mathbf{B} = 0 \qquad \text{(continuity of magnetic flux)} \qquad (2.3d)$$

$$\nabla \cdot \mathbf{J} = -j\omega\rho \qquad \text{(continuity law)} \qquad (2.3e)$$

In a free-space environment (vacuum) the constitutive relations are

$$\mathbf{D} = \epsilon_0\mathbf{E} \qquad (2.4a)$$

$$\mathbf{B} = \mu_0\mathbf{H} \qquad (2.4b)$$

where $\epsilon_0 = 10^{-9}/36\pi$ farad per meter is the permittivity of free space and $\mu_0 = 4\pi \times 10^{-7}$ henry per meter is the permeability of free space. In a lossy dielectric medium with permittivity ϵ and conductivity σ, a conduction current $\mathbf{J}_c$ given by $\mathbf{J}_c = \sigma\mathbf{E}$ will flow, and $\mathbf{D} = \epsilon\mathbf{E}$. If we include $\mathbf{J}_c$ in addition to the impressed current $\mathbf{J}$, the relation (2.3b) will become

$$\nabla \times \mathbf{H} = (j\omega\epsilon + \sigma)\mathbf{E} + \mathbf{J}$$

$$= j\omega\left(\epsilon + \frac{\sigma}{j\omega}\right)\mathbf{E} + \mathbf{J} \qquad (2.5)$$

Thus $\epsilon + \sigma/j\omega$ may be viewed as a complex permittivity. In general, a dielectric material exhibits polarization damping losses in addition to a possible finite conductivity, so even though σ may be zero, ϵ is still complex and of the form $\epsilon' - j\epsilon''$. When it is necessary to deal with a lossy dielectric medium we will simply use a complex permittivity and include any conduction loss as part of the imaginary component ϵ''.

It is often necessary to find solutions to Maxwell's equations in non-homogeneous regions, that is, in regions where there are boundaries separating media with different constitutive parameters. The following situations are of particular interest to us: the boundary at a perfect conductor, the boundary at an imperfect conductor, and the boundary between two different dielectric media. We will present the appropriate boundary conditions to apply for each of these situations without going through the detailed derivations which may be found in most texts covering electromagnetic theory.†

---

† The derivation of the boundary conditions given here may be found in R. E. Collin, *Foundations for Microwave Engineering*, McGraw-Hill Book Company, New York, 1966.

Boundary of a Perfect Conductor

Figure 2.1 shows a perfect conductor ($\sigma = \infty$) with a unit normal **n** at the surface. In the conductor the electromagnetic field is zero. At the surface the tangential component of the electric field is continuous across the boundary and hence equals zero (Why?); thus

$$\mathbf{n} \times \mathbf{E} = 0 \tag{2.6a}$$

Likewise, the normal component of **H** must be zero, since no magnetic flux penetrates into the conductor; hence

$$\mathbf{n} \cdot \mathbf{H} = 0 \tag{2.6b}$$

On the conductor a surface current of density $\mathbf{J}_s$ A/m will flow and is given by

$$\mathbf{J}_s = \mathbf{n} \times \mathbf{H} \tag{2.6c}$$

The current density equals the tangential magnetic field in magnitude but is oriented at right angles to it. The surface charge density ρ_s on the conductor is given by

$$\rho_s = \mathbf{n} \cdot \mathbf{D} \tag{2.6d}$$

The flux lines of **D** terminate on the charge since there is no field within the conductor.

Boundary of an Imperfect Conductor

A perfectly conducting metal does not exist, so it is only an approximation, and usually a very good one, to treat a metal as a perfect conductor. In an actual conductor, the electromagnetic field will penetrate, but its amplitude falls off exponentially according to the relation e^{-z/δ_s}, where z is the distance into the conductor, as shown in Fig. 2.2, and δ_s is the skin depth given by

$$\delta_s = \left(\frac{2}{\omega \mu_0 \sigma}\right)^{1/2} \tag{2.7}$$

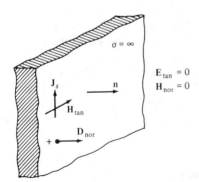

Figure 2.1 Boundary conditions at a perfect conductor.

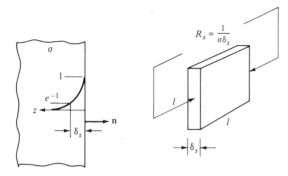

Figure 2.2 Boundary of an imperfect conductor showing the exponential decay law. The surface resistance equals the dc resistance of a square of metal of thickness δ_s.

For copper with $\sigma = 5.8 \times 10^7$ S/m, the skin depth equals only 6.6×10^{-3} cm at 1 MHz and is extremely small at 1000 MHz, where it equals 2.1×10^{-4} cm. For most practical purposes, the field can be considered as not penetrating into a good conductor such as metal.

The fact that a metal has a finite conductivity implies that there will be some dissipation or ohmic loss in the metal. When it is necessary to account for this loss, the following approximate procedure, which is widely used to find the attenuation of transmission lines, waveguides, etc., may be applied. First the electromagnetic field is found assuming perfect conductivity. From the magnetic field **H** the surface current density $\mathbf{J}_s$ is then found using Eq. (2.6c). The actual electric field tangent to the surface is related to this current density by the relationship:

$$\mathbf{n} \times \mathbf{E} = Z_s \mathbf{n} \times \mathbf{J}_s \tag{2.8}$$

where Z_s, the surface impedance of the conductor, is given by

$$Z_s = \frac{1+j}{\sigma \delta_s} \text{ ohms per square} \tag{2.9}$$

The resistive part $1/\sigma\delta_s$ is the equivalent static or dc resistance of a square sheet of metal of a thickness equal to the skin depth δ_s and with conductivity σ as shown in Fig. 2.2. There is an equal inductive component due to the magnetic field penetration.

The power loss that occurs per unit area is given by the real part of the complex Poynting vector flux normal to the surface and is

$$P = -\tfrac{1}{2} \operatorname{Re} \mathbf{n} \cdot \mathbf{E} \times \mathbf{H}^*$$

$$= -\tfrac{1}{2} \operatorname{Re} \mathbf{n} \times \mathbf{E} \cdot \mathbf{H}^*$$

$$= -\tfrac{1}{2} \operatorname{Re} Z_s \mathbf{n} \times \mathbf{J}_s \cdot \mathbf{H}^*$$

$$= \tfrac{1}{2} \operatorname{Re} Z_s \mathbf{J}_s \cdot \mathbf{n} \times \mathbf{H}^*$$

$$= \tfrac{1}{2} \operatorname{Re} Z_s \mathbf{J}_s \cdot \mathbf{J}_s^* = \tfrac{1}{2} \frac{|\mathbf{J}_s|^2}{\sigma \delta_s} \tag{2.10}$$

The minus sign at the beginning is due to the normal **n** being directed outwards. The asterisk denotes the complex-conjugate value.

As σ tends to infinity, the skin depth, surface impedance, and power loss vanish. A measure of how small the surface impedance is can be obtained by comparing it with the intrinsic impedance $Z_0 = (\mu_0/\epsilon_0)^{1/2} = 377\,\Omega$ of free space. For copper at 1 MHz, $Z_s = 2.6 \times 10^{-4}(1+j)\,\Omega$. The small relative value of Z_s means that copper is very nearly a short circuit or zero-impedance surface at 1 MHz, and at other frequencies as well.

The above relations may be applied to any good conductor, i.e., metal, as long as the radius of curvature at the surface is several skin depths or more. For a very thin wire of diameter only one or two skin depths in value or less, the results do not apply.

Example 2.1 AC impedance of a wire Find the ac impedance per unit length for a copper wire of diameter 0.4 cm at 1 MHz, as shown in Fig. 2.3.

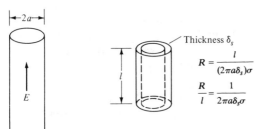

$$R = \frac{l}{(2\pi a \delta_s)\sigma}$$

$$\frac{R}{l} = \frac{1}{2\pi a \delta_s \sigma}$$

Figure 2.3 A round conductor with an applied electric field.

The diameter is more than 66 skin depths so the wire can be described by a surface impedance Z_s. The current density on the wire will be

$$J_s = \frac{E}{Z_s}$$

where E is the axial electric field along the wire. The total current is $I = 2\pi a J_s$ and the voltage drop per unit length along the wire equals E in value. Hence, the ac impedance per unit length is E/I or $Z_s/2\pi a$. Numerically,

$$Z = \frac{2.6 \times 10^{-4}(1+j)}{2\pi \times 2 \times 10^{-3}} = 0.0207(1+j) \qquad \Omega/\text{m} \qquad \blacksquare$$

Boundary between Two Dielectric Media

Figure 2.4 shows the boundary between two dielectric media with permittivities ϵ_1 and ϵ_2. At this boundary the tangential field components are equal on adjacent sides so that

$$\mathbf{n} \times \mathbf{E}_1 = \mathbf{n} \times \mathbf{E}_2 \qquad (2.11a)$$

$$\mathbf{n} \times \mathbf{H}_1 = \mathbf{n} \times \mathbf{H}_2 \qquad (2.11b)$$

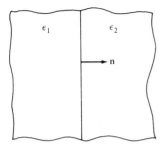

Figure 2.4 Boundary between two dielectric media.

In addition, the normal electric flux is continuous, so we also have the relation:

$$\mathbf{n} \cdot \mathbf{D}_1 = \mathbf{n} \cdot \mathbf{D}_2 \qquad (2.11c)$$

2.2 VECTOR AND SCALAR POTENTIALS

By taking the curl of Eq. (2.3a), using Eq. (2.3b) and the constitutive relations (2.4), it will be found that

$$\nabla \times \nabla \times \mathbf{E} = k_0^2 \mathbf{E} - j\omega\mu_0 \mathbf{J} \qquad (2.12)$$

where $k_0 = \omega(\mu_0\epsilon_0)^{1/2}$ is the free-space wave number. This is the equation that must be solved to find the electric field directly in terms of the specified current source $\mathbf{J}$. In practice a simpler equation to solve is obtained by introducing the vector potential $\mathbf{A}$ and scalar potential Φ.

Since the divergence of $\mathbf{B}$ is identically zero, $\mathbf{B}$ can be expressed as

$$\mathbf{B} = \nabla \times \mathbf{A} \qquad (2.13)$$

because $\nabla \cdot \nabla \times \mathbf{A} \equiv 0$. $\mathbf{A}$ is called the *vector potential.* By using Eq. (2.13) in Eq. (2.3a), we obtain

$$\nabla \times (\mathbf{E} + j\omega\mathbf{A}) = 0$$

Any function with zero curl can be expressed as the gradient of a scalar function; thus we can assume that

$$\mathbf{E} + j\omega\mathbf{A} = -\nabla\Phi \qquad (2.14)$$

In order that Eq. (2.3b) will hold, we require

$$\nabla \times \mu_0\mathbf{H} = \nabla \times \nabla \times \mathbf{A}$$

$$= j\omega\mu_0\epsilon_0\mathbf{E} + \mu_0\mathbf{J}$$

$$= j\omega\mu_0\epsilon_0(-j\omega\mathbf{A} - \nabla\Phi) + \mu_0\mathbf{J}$$

We can now use the expansion $\nabla \times \nabla \times \mathbf{A} = \nabla\nabla \cdot \mathbf{A} - \nabla^2\mathbf{A}$ to obtain, after a rearrangement of terms,

$$\nabla^2\mathbf{A} + k_0^2\mathbf{A} = -\mu_0\mathbf{J} + \nabla(\nabla \cdot \mathbf{A} + j\omega\mu_0\epsilon_0\Phi)$$

So far only the curl of **A** is fixed by the relation (2.13). Thus, we are still free to specify the divergence of **A**. In order to simplify the equation for **A** we choose

$$\nabla \cdot \mathbf{A} = -j\omega\mu_0\epsilon_0\Phi \tag{2.15}$$

which is known as the *Lorentz condition*. Our equation for **A** now becomes the inhomogeneous Helmholtz equation:

$$\nabla^2\mathbf{A} + k_0^2\mathbf{A} = -\mu_0\mathbf{J} \tag{2.16}$$

If Eqs. (2.14) and (2.15) are used in Eq. (2.3c), it will be found that Φ satisfies a similar equation, namely,

$$\nabla^2\Phi + k_0^2\Phi = -\frac{\rho}{\epsilon_0} \tag{2.17}$$

However, the charge is not an independent source term for time-varying fields, since it is related to the current by the continuity equation (2.3e), and it is not necessary to solve for the scalar potential Φ. By using the Lorentz condition in Eq. (2.14), we can find the electric field in terms of the vector potential **A** alone by means of the relation:

$$\mathbf{E} = -j\omega\mathbf{A} + \frac{\nabla\nabla \cdot \mathbf{A}}{j\omega\mu_0\epsilon_0} \tag{2.18}$$

The simplification obtained by introducing the vector potential **A** may be appreciated by considering the case of a z-directed current source $\mathbf{J} = J_z\mathbf{a}_z$ in which case $\mathbf{A} = A_z\mathbf{a}_z$ and A_z is a solution of the scalar equation

$$(\nabla^2 + k_0^2)A_z = -\mu_0 J_z \tag{2.19}$$

The equation satisfied by the electric field is a vector equation even when the current has only a single component.

2.3 RADIATION FROM A SHORT CURRENT FILAMENT

Figure 2.5 shows a short, thin filament of current located at the origin and oriented along the z axis. For this source the vector potential has only a z component and is a solution of Eq. (2.19), that is,

$$(\nabla^2 + k_0^2)A_z = -\mu_0 J_z$$

where $J_z = I/dS$ and dS is the cross-sectional area of the current filament of length dl. The volume $dV = dS\,dl$ occupied by the current is of infinitesimal size so the source term can be considered as located at a point. There is spherical symmetry in the source distribution, so A_z will be a function only of the radial distance r away from the source. A_z will not be a function of the polar angle θ or the azimuth angle ϕ shown in Fig. 2.5. For values of r not

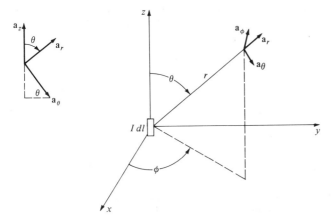

Figure 2.5 The short current filament and the spherical coordinate system.

equal to zero, A_z satisfies the equation

$$\frac{1}{r^2}\frac{\partial}{\partial r}r^2\frac{\partial A_z'}{\partial r} + k_0^2 A_z = 0 \qquad (2.20)$$

as obtained by expressing the Laplace operator ∇^2 in spherical coordinates and dropping the derivatives with respect to θ and ϕ. If we make the substitution $A_z = \psi/r$, then $dA_z/dr = r^{-1}\, d\psi/dr - r^{-2}\psi$, and the equation obtained from Eq. (2.20) for ψ becomes

$$\frac{d^2\psi}{dr^2} + k_0^2\psi = 0 \qquad (2.21)$$

This is a simple harmonic-motion equation with solutions $C_1\, e^{-jk_0 r}$ and $C_2\, e^{jk_0 r}$, where C_1 and C_2 are constants. If we choose the first solution and restore the time factor we obtain

$$\psi(r, t) = C_1\, e^{-jk_0 r + j\omega t}$$

Now $k_0 = \omega/c$, where $c = (\mu_0\epsilon_0)^{-1/2}$ is the speed of light in free space, so

$$\psi(r, t) = C_1\, e^{j\omega(t - r/c)} \qquad (2.22)$$

This is a wave solution corresponding to an outward propagating wave, since the phase is retarded by the factor $k_0 r$ and the corresponding time delay is r/c. The other solution with the constant C_2 corresponds to an inward propagating spherical wave and is not present as part of the solution for radiation from a current element located at $r = 0$. Our solution for A_z is now seen to be of the form

$$A_z = C_1\frac{e^{-jk_0 r}}{r} \qquad (2.23)$$

In order to relate the constant C_1 to the source strength, we integrate both sides of Eq. (2.19) over a small spherical volume of radius r_0. We note that $\nabla^2 A_z = \nabla \cdot \nabla A_z$, so upon using the divergence theorem we obtain

$$\int_V \nabla^2 A_z \, dV = \int_V \nabla \cdot \nabla A_z \, dV$$

$$= \oint_S \nabla A_z \cdot \mathbf{a}_r r_0^2 \sin \theta \, d\theta \, d\phi$$

$$= -k_0^2 \int_V A_z \, dV - \mu_0 \int_V J_z \, dV$$

Now $dV = r^2 \sin \theta \, d\theta \, d\phi \, dr$ and A_z varies as $1/r$; consequently, if we choose r_0 vanishingly small the volume integral of A_z, which is proportional to r_0^2, vanishes. The volume integral of J_z gives $J_z \, dS \, dl = I \, dl$, which is the total source strength. Also

$$\nabla A_z \cdot \mathbf{a}_r = \frac{\partial A_z}{\partial r} = -(1 + jk_0 r) C_1 \frac{e^{-jk_0 r}}{r^2}$$

so

$$\lim_{r_0 \to 0} \int_0^{2\pi} \int_0^\pi -(1 + jk_0 r_0) C_1 \, e^{-jk_0 r_0} \sin \theta \, d\theta \, d\phi = -4\pi C_1 = -\mu_0 I \, dl$$

Our final solution for the vector potential is

$$\mathbf{A} = \mu_0 I \, dl \, \frac{e^{-jk_0 r}}{4\pi r} \, \mathbf{a}_z \tag{2.24}$$

The vector potential is an outward propagating spherical wave with an amplitude that decreases inversely with distance. The surfaces of constant phase or constant time delay are spheres of fixed radius r centered on the source. The phase velocity of the wave is the speed of light c, or 3×10^8 m/s. The distance that corresponds to a phase change of 2π is the wavelength λ_0 and may be found from the relationship $k_0 \lambda_0 = 2\pi$; thus

$$\lambda_0 = \frac{2\pi}{k_0} = \frac{c}{\omega/2\pi} = \frac{c}{f} \tag{2.25}$$

From our solution for the vector potential we can readily find the electromagnetic field by using Eqs. (2.13) and (2.18). This evaluation is best done in spherical coordinates, so we first express $\mathbf{A}$ in terms of components in spherical coordinates by noting that (see Fig. 2.5)

$$\mathbf{a}_z = \mathbf{a}_r \cos \theta - \mathbf{a}_\theta \sin \theta$$

and consequently

$$\mathbf{A} = \frac{\mu_0 I \, dl}{4\pi r} e^{-jk_0 r} (\mathbf{a}_r \cos\theta - \mathbf{a}_\theta \sin\theta) \tag{2.26}$$

We now use Eq. (2.13) to obtain

$$\mathbf{H} = \frac{1}{\mu_0} \nabla \times \mathbf{A} = \frac{I \, dl \sin\theta}{4\pi} \left(\frac{jk_0}{r} + \frac{1}{r^2} \right) e^{-jk_0 r} \mathbf{a}_\phi \tag{2.27}$$

and use Eq. (2.18) to obtain

$$\mathbf{E} = -j\omega \mathbf{A} + \frac{\nabla\nabla \cdot \mathbf{A}}{j\omega\mu_0\epsilon_0}$$

$$= -\frac{jZ_0 I \, dl}{2\pi k_0} \cos\theta \left(\frac{jk_0}{r^2} + \frac{1}{r^3} \right) e^{-jk_0 r} \mathbf{a}_r$$

$$- \frac{jZ_0 I \, dl}{4\pi k_0} \sin\theta \left(-\frac{k_0^2}{r} + \frac{jk_0}{r^2} + \frac{1}{r^3} \right) e^{-jk_0 r} \mathbf{a}_\theta$$

$$= E_r \mathbf{a}_r + E_\theta \mathbf{a}_\theta \tag{2.28}$$

When r is large relative to the wavelength λ_0, the only important terms are those that vary as $1/r$. These terms make up the far zone, or radiation field, and are

$$\mathbf{E} = jZ_0 I \, dl \, k_0 \sin\theta \frac{e^{-jk_0 r}}{4\pi r} \mathbf{a}_\theta \tag{2.29a}$$

$$\mathbf{H} = jI \, dl \, k_0 \sin\theta \frac{e^{-jk_0 r}}{4\pi r} \mathbf{a}_\phi \tag{2.29b}$$

We note that in the far zone the radiation field has transverse components only; that is, both $\mathbf{E}$ and $\mathbf{H}$ are perpendicular to the radius vector as well as perpendicular to each other. The ratio of E_θ to H_ϕ equals the intrinsic impedance $Z_0 = (\mu_0/\epsilon_0)^{1/2}$ of free space. This is a general feature of the radiation field from any antenna. In vector form, one always finds that the radiation field in the far-zone region satisfies the relations

$$\mathbf{E} = -Z_0 \mathbf{a}_r \times \mathbf{H} \tag{2.30a}$$

$$\mathbf{H} = Y_0 \mathbf{a}_r \times \mathbf{E} \tag{2.30b}$$

where $Y_0 = Z_0^{-1}$. This spatial relationship is illustrated in Fig. 2.6.

We also note that both E_θ and H_ϕ vary as $\sin\theta$. Thus the radiated field is not a spherically symmetric outward-propagating wave as was found for the vector potential. This is also a general feature of all radiation fields—the electromagnetic radiation field can never have complete spherical symmetry.

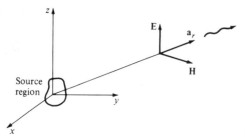

Figure 2.6 Spatial relationship for the electric and magnetic fields in the radiation zone.

The complex Poynting vector for the radiation field is

$$\tfrac{1}{2}\mathbf{E} \times \mathbf{H}^* = II^* Z_0 (dl)^2 \, k_0^2 \sin^2 \theta \, \frac{\mathbf{a}_r}{32\pi^2 r^2} \qquad (2.31)$$

and is pure real, and directed radially outward. The radiated power per unit area decreases as $1/r^2$, as expected because of the spreading out of the field as it propagates radially outward. This is the inverse-square-law attenuation behavior discussed in Chap. 1.

Before we proceed any further with the discussion of the radiation field we return to an examination of the other terms in Eqs. (2.27) and (2.28). These terms, varying as $1/r^2$ and $1/r^3$, will become predominant when $r < \lambda_0$ and make up the near-zone reactive field. It is a reactive field because the near-zone magnetic and electric fields have a pure imaginary Poynting vector, indicating reactive power rather than real radiated power. If $k_0 r$ is very small—so that we can replace $e^{-jk_0 r}$ by unity—then the near-zone fields become

$$\mathbf{H} = \frac{I \, dl \sin \theta}{4\pi r^2} \, \mathbf{a}_\phi \qquad (2.32a)$$

$$\mathbf{E} = \frac{I \, dl \, Z_0}{4\pi} \left[\frac{2 \cos \theta}{r^2} \left(1 + \frac{1}{jk_0 r} \right) \mathbf{a}_r \right.$$

$$\left. + \frac{\sin \theta}{r^2} \left(1 + \frac{1}{jk_0 r} \right) \mathbf{a}_\theta \right] \qquad (2.32b)$$

For $k_0 r \ll 1$ we can also replace $1 + 1/jk_0 r$ by $1/jk_0 r$. We also note that the charge Q at the end of the current filament must change according to $j\omega Q = I$ since current is the rate of change of charge. Hence

$$\frac{IZ_0}{jk_0} = \frac{j\omega Q (\mu_0/\epsilon_0)^{1/2}}{j\omega (\mu_0 \epsilon_0)^{1/2}} = \frac{Q}{\epsilon_0}$$

and Eq. (2.32b) becomes

$$\mathbf{E} = \frac{Q \, dl}{4\pi\epsilon_0} \left(\frac{2 \cos \theta}{r^3} \, \mathbf{a}_r + \frac{\sin \theta}{r^3} \, \mathbf{a}_\theta \right) \qquad (2.32c)$$

The results given by Eqs. (2.32a) and (2.32c) can be recognized as the static field distributions from a short current filament and an electric dipole, respectively.

Although the near-zone fields do not contribute to the radiated power, they do represent a storage of electric and magnetic energy in the space immediately surrounding the antenna and account for the reactive part of the impedance seen looking into the antenna terminals. Thus, except for impedance calculations, the near-zone fields are not of great interest.

We could obtain the complete complex Poynting vector $\frac{1}{2}\mathbf{E} \times \mathbf{H}^*$ by using the complete expressions for the fields. If this is done, it will be discovered that the real part, the part that will give rise to radiated power, involves only the radiation field and is given by our earlier expression [Eq. (2.31)].

2.4 SOME BASIC ANTENNA PARAMETERS

Radiation from a short current filament is commonly called *dipole radiation*. Since a short current filament may be viewed as an elementary antenna, it has associated with it a number of basic characteristics described by parameters used to characterize antennas in general. In this section we will introduce these parameters and illustrate them using the short current filament as an example.

Radiation Pattern

The relative distribution of radiated power as a function of direction in space is the radiation pattern of the antenna. For the elementary dipole the radiated power varies according to $\sin^2 \theta$, as Eq. (2.31) shows. The radiation pattern is similar to the figure 8 revolved about an axis, as shown in Fig. 2.7a. It is common practice to show planar sections of the radiation pattern instead of the complete three-dimensional surface. The two most important views are those of the principal E-plane and H-plane patterns. The E-plane pattern is a view of the radiation pattern obtained from a section containing the maximum value of the radiated field and in which the electric field lies in the plane of the chosen sectional view. Similarly, the H-plane pattern is a sectional view in which the H field lies in the plane of the section, and again the section is chosen to contain the maximum direction of radiation. The E- and H-plane patterns for the dipole antenna are shown in Fig. 2.7b and 2.7c.

The half-power beam width is usually given for both the principal E- and H-plane patterns and is the angular width between points at which the radiated power per unit area is one-half of the maximum. For the dipole the E-plane half-power beam width is 90°, while the H plane does not show a half-power beam width, since the pattern is a constant circular pattern in the H plane.

Directivity and Gain

An antenna does not radiate uniformly in all directions. The variation of the intensity with direction in space is described by the directivity function $D(\theta, \phi)$

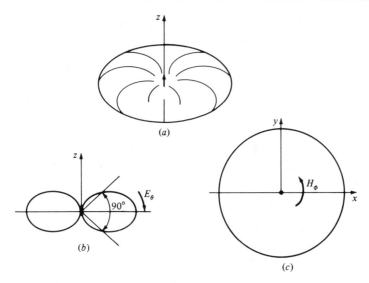

Figure 2.7 (*a*) Power radiation pattern for short current filament. (*b*) Principal *E*-plane pattern. (*c*) Principal *H*-plane pattern.

for the antenna. The intensity of radiation is the power radiated per unit solid angle, and this is obtained by multiplying the Poynting vector flux density by r^2. For the dipole we obtain

$$\frac{dP_r}{d\Omega} = \tfrac{1}{2}r^2 \, \text{Re} \, \mathbf{E} \times \mathbf{H}^* \cdot \mathbf{a}_r = II^* Z_0 (dl)^2 \, k_0^2 \frac{\sin^2 \theta}{32\pi^2} \tag{2.33}$$

for the power radiated per unit solid angle. The definition of the directivity function $D(\theta, \phi)$ is

$$D(\theta, \phi) = \frac{\text{power radiated per unit solid angle}}{\text{average power radiated per unit solid angle}}$$

$$= \frac{dP_r/d\Omega}{P_r/4\pi} = 4\pi \frac{dP_r/d\Omega}{P_r} \tag{2.34}$$

where P_r is the total radiated power. For the dipole we can compute the total radiated power by integrating the Poynting-vector power flux through a closed spherical surface surrounding the dipole. This is equivalent to integrating the intensity over the solid angle of a sphere; thus from Eq. (2.33),

$$P_r = \frac{II^* Z_0 \, (dl)^2 \, k_0^2}{32\pi^2} \int_0^{2\pi} \int_0^{\pi} \sin^2 \theta \, \sin \theta \, d\theta \, d\phi$$

since $d\Omega = \sin \theta \, d\theta \, d\phi$. The integration is readily done after replacing $\sin^2 \theta$ by $1 - \cos^2 \theta$ to give

$$P_r = \frac{II^* Z_0 (k_0 \, dl)^2}{12\pi} \tag{2.35}$$

It is now found that by using Eqs. (2.33) and (2.34)

$$D(\theta, \phi) = 1.5 \sin^2 \theta \qquad (2.36)$$

The maximum directivity is 1.5 and occurs in the $\theta = \pi/2$ plane.

The *maximum directivity*, which often is referred to simply as the *directivity*, is a measure of the ability of an antenna to concentrate the radiated power in a given direction. For the same amount of radiated power, the dipole produces 1.5 times the power density in the $\theta = \pi/2$ direction that an isotropic radiator would produce. An *isotropic radiator or antenna* is a fictitious antenna that radiates uniformly in all directions and is commonly used as a reference.

The gain of an antenna is defined in a manner similar to that for the directivity, except that the total input power to the antenna rather than the total radiated power is used as the reference. The difference is a measure of the efficiency of the antenna; that is,

$$P_r = \eta P_{in} \qquad (2.37)$$

where η is the efficiency, P_{in} is the total input power, and P_r is the total radiated power. Most antennas have an efficiency close to unity. The gain of an antenna may be stated as follows:

$$G(\theta, \phi) = 4\pi \, \frac{\text{power radiated per unit solid angle}}{\text{input power}}$$

$$= 4\pi \, \frac{dP_r/d\Omega}{P_{in}} = \eta D(\theta, \phi) \qquad (2.38)$$

The maximum gain, or simply gain, of an antenna is a more significant parameter in practice than the directivity, even though the two are closely related.

The gain of an antenna is often incorporated into a parameter called the *effective isotropic radiated power*, or *EIRP*, which is the product of the input power and the maximum gain. Its significance is that an antenna with a gain of 10 and 1 W of input power is just as effective as an antenna with a gain of 2 and an input power of 5 W. Both have the same 10 W of effective isotropic radiated power. Thus input power can be reduced by using an antenna with a higher gain. In later chapters we will find that the gain of an antenna is proportional to its cross-sectional area measured in wavelengths squared. Thus, very high gain antennas are usually found only in the microwave band, where a wavelength is a few centimeters or less.

Radiation Resistance

The radiation resistance of an antenna is that equivalent resistance which would dissipate the same amount of power as the antenna radiates when the current in that resistance equals the input current at the antenna terminals. For the dipole antenna the radiation resistance R_a is found from the relation

$\frac{1}{2}|I|^2 R_a = P_r$. When we use Eq. (2.35) for P_r we find that

$$R_a = \frac{Z_0(k_0\,dl)^2}{6\pi} = 80\pi^2\left(\frac{dl}{\lambda_0}\right)^2 \qquad (2.39)$$

upon using $Z_0 = 120\pi$, $k_0 = 2\pi/\lambda_0$. As an example, consider $dl = 1$ m and $\lambda_0 = 300$ m, corresponding to a frequency of 1 MHz. The radiation resistance equals $0.0084\,\Omega$, which is very small. Although the dipole is not a practical antenna, the above example does illustrate the general result that the radiation resistance of an antenna that is a small fraction of a wavelength long is very small. Such antennas usually also exhibit a very high reactance and a very poor efficiency, which in turn means very low gain. In small antennas most of the input power is dissipated in ohmic losses instead of being radiated. An efficient antenna must be comparable to a wavelength in size. It is for this reason that antennas at low frequencies are of necessity simple structures such as the very high towers used in the radio broadcast band 500 to 1500 kHz, where the wavelength ranges from 600 down to 200 m.

2.5 RADIATION FROM A SMALL CURRENT LOOP

Figure 2.8 shows a small current loop of radius r_0, area πr_0^2, and with a current I. The axis of the loop is oriented in the z direction. For $r_0 \ll \lambda_0$ the loop may be treated as a point source. A small loop of current is called a *magnetic dipole*, and its magnetic dipole moment equals the product of the area with the current; thus

$$\mathbf{M} = \pi r_0^2 I \mathbf{a}_z \qquad (2.40)$$

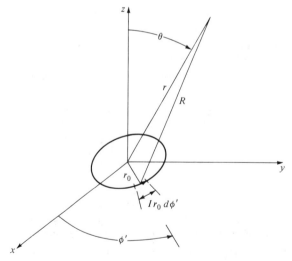

Figure 2.8 A small current loop in the xy plane.

The field radiated by a small magnetic dipole is the dual of that radiated by a small electric dipole, i.e., the short current filament. The roles of electric and magnetic fields are interchanged so the radiation field has an E_ϕ and an H_θ component only.

With reference to Fig. 2.8, consider the current filament at ϕ', which has the vector orientation $-\mathbf{a}_x \sin \phi' + \mathbf{a}_y \cos \phi' = \mathbf{a}_{\phi'}$. The contribution of the current filament of strength $Ir_0 \, d\phi'$ to the total vector potential may be found by using the fundamental solution [Eq. (2.24)] derived earlier. Thus from $Ir_0 \, d\phi'(-\mathbf{a}_x \sin \phi' + \mathbf{a}_y \cos \phi')$ we obtain a contribution given by

$$\frac{\mu_0 Ir_0 \, d\phi'}{4\pi R}(-\mathbf{a}_x \sin \phi' + \mathbf{a}_y \cos \phi') \, e^{-jk_0 R}$$

where $R = [(x - r_0 \cos \phi')^2 + (y - r_0 \sin \phi')^2 + z^2]^{1/2}$. The total vector potential is obtained by integrating over the current loop; thus

$$\mathbf{A} = \frac{\mu_0 Ir_0}{4\pi} \int_0^{2\pi} \frac{e^{-jk_0 R}}{R}(-\mathbf{a}_x \sin \phi' + \mathbf{a}_y \cos \phi') \, d\phi' \qquad (2.41)$$

This integral is difficult to evaluate unless we make certain approximations in the expression for R. We are primarily interested in the far-zone radiation field, so we can assume that $r \gg r_0$. We have already assumed that $r_0 \ll \lambda_0$, so $k_0 r_0 \ll 1$. By imposing the above conditions we can replace R by r in the amplitude factor $1/R$. With reference to a spherical coordinate system $x = r \sin \theta \cos \phi$, $y = r \sin \theta \sin \phi$, and $r^2 = x^2 + y^2 + z^2$, so the expression for R can be rewritten in the form

$$R = [r^2 + r_0^2 - 2rr_0 \sin \theta(\cos \phi \cos \phi' + \sin \phi \sin \phi')]^{1/2}$$

We now drop r_0^2 relative to r^2 and use the binomial expansion $(1 + u)^{1/2} \approx 1 + u/2$ for $|u| \ll 1$ to obtain

$$R \approx r - r_0 \sin \theta(\cos \phi \cos \phi' + \sin \phi \sin \phi')$$

In the exponential function $e^{-jk_0 R}$ we will have a term involving $k_0 r_0$ when we substitute our approximate expression for R. But $k_0 r_0 \ll 1$, so we can use the approximation $e^u \approx 1 + u$ for $|u| \ll 1$ to obtain the following simplified form:

$$e^{-jk_0 R} \approx e^{-jk_0 r}[1 + jk_0 r_0 \sin \theta(\cos \phi \cos \phi' + \sin \phi \sin \phi')]$$

By using these approximations the integral [Eq. (2.41)] for $\mathbf{A}$ becomes

$$\mathbf{A} = \frac{\mu_0 Ir_0}{4\pi R} e^{-jk_0 r} \int_0^{2\pi} (-\mathbf{a}_x \sin \phi' + \mathbf{a}_y \cos \phi')$$

$$\times [1 + jk_0 r_0 \sin \theta(\cos \phi \cos \phi' + \sin \phi \sin \phi')] \, d\phi'$$

The only terms that do not integrate to zero are the $\cos^2 \phi'$ and $\sin^2 \phi'$ terms, both of which give a factor of π. Hence the final expression for the vector potential becomes

$$\mathbf{A} = \frac{jk_0\mu_0(\pi r_0^2 I)}{4\pi r}\sin\theta\, e^{-jk_0 r}\mathbf{a}_\phi \qquad (2.42)$$

where we have also put $-\mathbf{a}_x \sin\phi + \mathbf{a}_y \cos\phi = \mathbf{a}_\phi$.

We can find the magnetic intensity $\mathbf{H}$ by using Eq. (2.13), which gives

$$\mathbf{H} = \frac{1}{\mu_0}\nabla\times\mathbf{A} = -\frac{1}{\mu_0 r}\frac{\partial}{\partial r}(rA_\phi)\mathbf{a}_\theta$$

$$= -\frac{Mk_0^2\sin\theta}{4\pi r}e^{-jk_0 r}\mathbf{a}_\theta \qquad (2.43)$$

where $M = \pi r_0^2 I$ and is the dipole moment of the small current loop. In the radiation zone the electric field is related to $\mathbf{H}$ by the simple expression (2.30a), which gives

$$\mathbf{E} = -Z_0\mathbf{a}_r \times \mathbf{H} = \frac{MZ_0k_0^2\sin\theta}{4\pi r}e^{-jk_0 r}\mathbf{a}_\phi \qquad (2.44)$$

These expressions show that the role of the electric and magnetic fields for magnetic dipole radiation have been interchanged from their role in electric dipole radiation. However, the radiation pattern and directivity have not changed.

The total radiated power is given by

$$P_r = \tfrac{1}{2}\text{Re}\int_0^{2\pi}\int_0^\pi E_\phi H_\theta^* r^2 \sin\theta\, d\theta\, d\phi$$

$$= \frac{M^2 Z_0 k_0^4}{32\pi^2}\int_0^{2\pi}\int_0^\pi \sin^2\theta \sin\theta\, d\theta\, d\phi$$

$$= \frac{M^2 Z_0 k_0^4}{12\pi} \qquad (2.45)$$

The radiation resistance of the loop may be found by equating $\tfrac{1}{2}|I|^2 R_a$ to P_r. After simplification we find that

$$R_a = 320\pi^6\left(\frac{r_0}{\lambda_0}\right)^4 \qquad (2.46)$$

As an example, consider a loop with $r_0 = 10$ cm at 1 MHz. For this loop, $R_a = 3.80 \times 10^{-9}\ \Omega$.

It is obvious that a small loop antenna is a very poor radiator. If N turns of wire are used, the radiation resistance is increased by a factor of N^2. Small loop antennas are often used as receiving antennas for portable radios. Although they are very inefficient, they do give an acceptable performance because of the large available signal level. In a later chapter we will find that at low frequencies atmospheric noise is often the limiting factor, so a more efficient antenna does not necessarily give better reception. Of course, a small loop antenna would not be used for transmitting purposes unless very short distances were involved and the poor gain could be tolerated. The gain of a small loop antenna is very low because the ohmic resistance of the wire is generally much greater than the radiation resistance.

2.6 RADIATION FROM ARBITRARY CURRENT DISTRIBUTIONS

In this section we will present some useful formulas for calculating the far-zone radiation field from an arbitrary distribution of current. Consider a volume V with a current distribution $\mathbf{J}(\mathbf{r'})$, as shown in Fig. 2.9. The current element $\mathbf{J}(\mathbf{r'}) \, dV'$ will contribute an amount

$$\frac{\mu_0 \mathbf{J}(\mathbf{r'}) \, dV'}{4\pi R} e^{-jk_0 R}$$

to the total vector potential where $R = |\mathbf{r} - \mathbf{r'}|$. In the far-zone region $|\mathbf{r}| \gg |\mathbf{r'}|$ for all $\mathbf{r'}$ in V. Thus all rays from the various current elements to the far-zone field point can be considered to be parallel to each other, as shown in Fig. 2.9. Thus a useful approximation for R is

$$R \approx r - \mathbf{a}_r \cdot \mathbf{r'} \tag{2.47}$$

We can replace R by r in the amplitude term for the vector potential, since this has a negligible effect on the amplitude of each elementary contribution when $r \gg r'$. Hence in the far zone we obtain

$$\mathbf{A}(\mathbf{r}) = \frac{\mu_0 e^{-jk_0 r}}{4\pi r} \int_V \mathbf{J}(\mathbf{r'}) \, e^{jk_0 \mathbf{a}_r \cdot \mathbf{r'}} \, dV' \tag{2.48}$$

This equation superimposes the effects of each current element and takes into

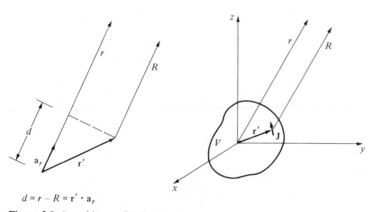

$$d = r - R = \mathbf{r'} \cdot \mathbf{a}_r$$

Figure 2.9 An arbitrary distribution of current.

account the relative phase angle or path-length phase delay of each contribution. Since the current elements do not, in general, contribute in phase, interference effects are produced that may be exploited to control the shape of the radiation pattern. In the next chapter we will examine the use of such interference effects to produce high-gain directive radiation beams.

We can find the fields **E** and **H** from Eq. (2.48) by using the relations (2.13) and (2.18). When only the terms varying as $1/r$ are retained, it is found that

$$\mathbf{E(r)} = \frac{jk_0Z_0\,e^{-jk_0r}}{4\pi r} \int_V [\mathbf{a}_r \cdot \mathbf{J(r')}\mathbf{a}_r - \mathbf{J(r')}]\,e^{jk_0\mathbf{a}_r \cdot \mathbf{r'}}\,dV' \qquad (2.49a)$$

$$\mathbf{H} = Y_0\mathbf{a}_r \times \mathbf{E} \qquad (2.49b)$$

The form of the integrand in this expression shows that in a given direction, as specified by the unit vector $\mathbf{a}_r$, it is only the current perpendicular to $\mathbf{a}_r$ that contributes to the radiation field. The reason for this is that the radiation field along the axis of a current element is zero.

When the current is a line current I along a contour C, then Eq. (2.49a) can be expressed in the form

$$\mathbf{E(r)} = \frac{jk_0Z_0\,e^{-jk_0r}}{4\pi r} \int_C [(\mathbf{a}_r \cdot \mathbf{a})\mathbf{a}_r - \mathbf{a}]I(l')\,e^{jk_0\mathbf{a}_r \cdot \mathbf{r'}}\,dl' \qquad (2.50)$$

where $\mathbf{a}$ is a unit vector along C in the direction of the current.

From Eqs. (2.49a) and (2.50) we see that the electric field has the form

$$\mathbf{E(r)} = \frac{jk_0Z_0\,e^{-jk_0r}}{4\pi r}\,\mathbf{f}(\theta, \phi) \qquad (2.51)$$

where $\mathbf{f}(\theta, \phi)$, which is given by the integral, describes the radiation amplitude pattern or the angular dependence of the radiation distribution in space. The other factor $e^{-jk_0r}/4\pi r$ is the outward-propagating spherical wave function.

2.7 HALF-WAVE DIPOLE ANTENNAS

One of the simplest practical antennas is the half-wave dipole antenna shown in Fig. 2.10. It is usually fed from a two-wire transmission line. Each arm of the antenna is very nearly one-quarter wavelength long. It has been found both theoretically and experimentally that the current distribution on a thin half-wave dipole antenna is closely approximated by a sinusoidal standing wave of the form

$$I = I_0 \cos k_0z \qquad -\frac{\lambda_0}{4} \le z \le \frac{\lambda_0}{4} \qquad (2.52)$$

The current is, of necessity, zero at the ends where $z = \pm\lambda_0/4$. We can find the far-zone radiated field from the half-wave dipole antenna by using Eq. (2.50), given in the previous section.

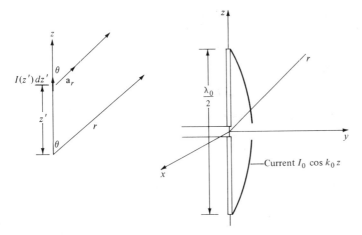

Figure 2.10 The half-wave dipole antenna.

With reference to Fig. 2.10, it is seen that the unit vector $\mathbf{a} = \mathbf{a}_z$, $\mathbf{r}' = z'\mathbf{a}_z$, and $\mathbf{a}_r \cdot \mathbf{a}_z = \cos\theta$. Hence Eq. (2.50) gives

$$\mathbf{E} = \frac{jk_0 I_0 Z_0}{4\pi r} e^{-jk_0 r} \int_{-\lambda_0/4}^{\lambda_0/4} (\mathbf{a}_r \cos\theta - \mathbf{a}_z) \cos k_0 z' \, e^{jk_0 z' \cos\theta} \, dz'$$

We now note that $\mathbf{a}_z = \mathbf{a}_r \cos\theta - \mathbf{a}_\theta \sin\theta$, so $\mathbf{a}_r \cos\theta - \mathbf{a}_z = \mathbf{a}_\theta \sin\theta$. Thus we find that

$$\mathbf{E} = E_\theta \mathbf{a}_\theta$$

$$= \frac{jk_0 I_0 Z_0}{4\pi r} e^{-jk_0 r} \mathbf{a}_\theta \sin\theta \int_{-\lambda_0/4}^{\lambda_0/4} \frac{e^{jk_0 z'} + e^{-jk_0 z'}}{2} e^{jk_0 z' \cos\theta} \, dz'$$

$$= \frac{jI_0 Z_0}{2\pi r} e^{-jk_0 r} \frac{\cos\left(\dfrac{\pi}{2} \cos\theta\right)}{\sin\theta} \mathbf{a}_\theta \qquad (2.53)$$

The magnetic field is given by Eq. (2.49b) and is

$$\mathbf{H} = H_\phi \mathbf{a}_\phi = \frac{jI_0}{2\pi r} e^{-jk_0 r} \frac{\cos\left(\dfrac{\pi}{2} \cos\theta\right)}{\sin\theta} \mathbf{a}_\phi \qquad (2.54)$$

The power flux per unit area is given by

$$\tfrac{1}{2} \operatorname{Re} \mathbf{E} \times \mathbf{H}^* \cdot \mathbf{a}_r = \tfrac{1}{2} E_\theta H_\phi^*$$

$$= \frac{|I_0|^2 Z_0}{8\pi^2 r^2} \left[\frac{\cos\left(\dfrac{\pi}{2} \cos\theta\right)}{\sin\theta} \right]^2 \qquad (2.55)$$

The total radiated power is obtained by integrating this expression over the surface of a sphere of radius r; thus

$$P_r = \frac{|I_0|^2 Z_0}{8\pi^2} \int_0^{2\pi} \int_0^{\pi} \left[\frac{\cos\left(\frac{\pi}{2}\cos\theta\right)}{\sin\theta} \right]^2 \sin\theta \, d\theta \, d\phi \qquad (2.56)$$

This integral can be evaluated in terms of the cosine integral[†]

$$\text{Ci } x = -\int_x^{\infty} \frac{\cos u}{u} \, du$$

The values of this integral are tabulated.[‡] The result of carrying out the integration is

$$P_r = 36.565 |I_0|^2 \qquad (2.57)$$

When we equate this expression to $\frac{1}{2}|I_0|^2 R_a$, we find that the radiation resistance of the half-wave dipole is 2×36.56, or $73.13\ \Omega$. The transmission line that feeds the half-wave dipole should have a characteristic impedance of $73.13\ \Omega$ for maximum power transfer.

The directivity function for the half-wave dipole is obtained by using Eq. (2.55) multiplied by r^2 and Eq. (2.57) in the defining relation (2.34) and is

$$D(\theta, \phi) = 1.64 \left[\frac{\cos(\pi/2 \cos\theta)}{\sin\theta} \right]^2 \qquad (2.58)$$

The maximum directivity is 1.64, which is only a modest increase over the value of 1.5 for the short current filament. The radiation pattern in the E plane is shown in Fig. 2.11. The half-power beam width is 78°, which is only a small amount less than the 90° for the short current filament. The most important difference between the short electric dipole and the half-wave dipole antenna is that the latter has a radiation resistance of $73.13\ \Omega$, which is much larger than the ohmic resistance would be for most practical antenna structures. Thus the

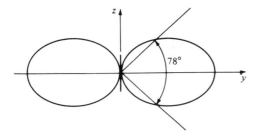

Figure 2.11 Principal E-plane radiation pattern for a half-wavelength dipole antenna.

[†] See J. A. Stratton, *Electromagnetic Theory*, McGraw-Hill Book Company, New York, 1941, Sec. 8.7.

[‡] E. Jahnke and F. Emde, *Tables of Functions*, Dover Publications, New York, 1945.

gain is also very nearly equal to 1.64. It also turns out that when the dipole is a half-wavelength long (actually a few percent less) the input reactance is zero, so the input impedance is essentially equal to the radiation resistance.

2.8 ANTENNA IMPEDANCE: EXPERIMENTAL

The impedance seen looking into the terminals of an antenna is an important parameter that needs to be known in order to design a network that will provide a conjugate impedance match to the transmission line. The latter is necessary in order to obtain maximum power transfer from the source genera-tor to the antenna. Ideally the input impedance should be a constant resistance equal to the radiation resistance, in which case the antenna can be connected directly to a transmission line with a characteristic impedance Z_c equal to the radiation resistance. This ideal condition is essentially achieved for the resonant half-wave dipole antenna over a band width of a few percent.

Let the antenna impedance be Z_a and let the antenna be coupled to a signal source by means of a transmission line with characteristic impedance Z_c, as shown in Fig. 2.12. At the antenna terminals a reflection coefficient Γ given by

$$\Gamma = \frac{Z_a - Z_c}{Z_a + Z_c} \tag{2.59}$$

is produced. This mismatch results in a partial standing wave on the trans-mission line, with a voltage standing wave ratio (VSWR) given by

$$\text{VSWR} = \frac{1 + |\Gamma|}{1 - |\Gamma|} \tag{2.60}$$

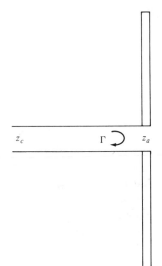

Figure 2.12 A half-wave dipole antenna coupled to a transmission line.

The impedance match is usually considered acceptable if the VSWR is less than 1.5. A VSWR of 1.5 corresponds to a reflection coefficient $|\Gamma|$ of 0.2 or a power reflection coefficient of 0.04, or 4 percent, which is acceptable.

The calculation of antenna impedance is difficult because it requires accurate expressions for the current excited on the antenna and the resultant near-zone reactive fields. The radiation resistance can be found quite easily and is not a sensitive function of the current distribution. However, an accurate evaluation of the reactive component does require an accurate expression for the current distribution. In the next section the theoretical evaluation of the antenna impedance is outlined.

The antenna impedance is related to the radiated power, dissipated power, and stored reactive energy in the following way:†

$$Z_a = \frac{P_r + P_d + 2j\omega(W_m - W_e)}{\frac{1}{2}I_0 I_0^*} \qquad (2.61)$$

where P_r is the radiated power, P_d is the power dissipated in ohmic losses, W_m is the average magnetic energy, W_e is the average electric energy stored in the near-zone reactive field, and I_0 is the input current at the antenna terminals. When the stored magnetic and electric energy are equal, a condition of resonance exists, and the reactive part of Z_a vanishes. For a thin dipole antenna this occurs when the antenna length is close to a multiple of a half wavelength.

We can calculate the ohmic resistance by finding the power dissipated in the skin-effect resistance using the results given in Sec. 2.1. Consider a half-wave dipole made of a copper rod with radius r_0. The total current on the antenna is $I_0 \cos k_0 z$, so the surface current density is $(I_0/2\pi r_0) \cos k_0 z$. The power dissipated is given by (we assume that I_0 is real)

$$P_d = \frac{1}{2}\int_0^{2\pi} r_0 \, d\phi \int_{-\lambda_0/4}^{\lambda_0/4} \left(\frac{I_0}{2\pi r_0}\right)^2 \frac{\cos^2 k_0 z}{\sigma \delta_s} \, dz$$

$$= 2\pi r_0 \frac{\lambda_0}{8}\left(\frac{I_0}{2\pi r_0}\right)^2 \frac{1}{\sigma \delta_s} = \frac{1}{2}I_0^2 R$$

Thus the ohmic resistance R is given by

$$R = \frac{\lambda_0}{8\pi r_0 \sigma \delta_s} \qquad (2.62)$$

As an example, let $r_0 = 0.5$ cm and let $\lambda_0 = 3$ m (100 MHz). The skin depth in copper at 100 MHz is $\delta_s = 6.6 \times 10^{-6}$ m. We then find that $R = 0.062\ \Omega$, which is negligible relative to the radiation resistance of 73.13 Ω. If the current on the antenna were uniform, the ohmic resistance would be $l/(2\pi r_0 \sigma \delta_s) = \lambda_0/(4\pi r_0 \sigma \delta_s)$, according to Example 2.1. The reason Eq. (2.62) is a factor of $\frac{1}{2}$

† See, for example, Collin, op. cit., Sec. 4.2.

less is due to the cosinusoidal current variation. The average value of $\cos^2 k_0 z$ reduces the dissipation by this factor of $\frac{1}{2}$ and hence makes the effective ohmic resistance also less by this same amount.

The general behavior of the input impedance of a dipole antenna of total length l made from a cylindrical rod of diameter d is shown in Figs. 2.13 and 2.14. These curves are based on actual measurements carried out by Brown and Woodward.[†]

It is seen that when $l/\lambda_0 \approx 0.48$ the reactance is zero. This is the first resonant length and is the length at which $R_a \approx 73\ \Omega$. At resonance there are equal amounts of reactive energy stored in the near-zone electric and magnetic fields, that is, $W_e = W_m$. Another resonance occurs at l/λ_0 in the range 0.8 to 0.9. At this point the radiation resistance is large because the current at the feed point is very small, since the current standing wave on the antenna now has a minimum instead of a maximum at the input terminals. If the antenna is

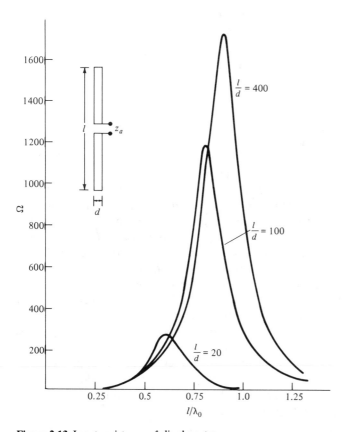

Figure 2.13 Input resistance of dipole antenna.

† G. H. Brown, and O. M. Woodward, Jr., "Experimentally Determined Impedance Characteristics of Cylindrical Antennas," *Proc. IRE*, vol. 33, 1945, pp. 257–262.

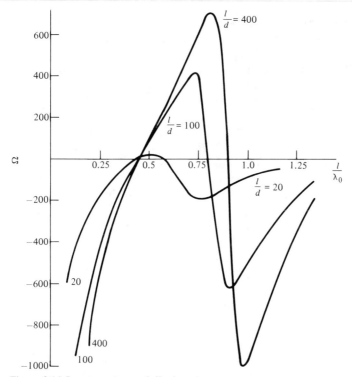

Figure 2.14 Input reactance of dipole antenna.

made thinner, this second resonance point moves closer to $l/\lambda_0 = 1$, and the radiation resistance can reach values of several thousand ohms. For a thicker antenna the reactance and resistance are more nearly uniform, with changes in l/λ_0, a feature which is desirable if the antenna is to be operated over a band of frequencies. Additional resonances occur with each increase in l by $\lambda_0/2$. Note also that an antenna with l/λ_0 much less than $\frac{1}{2}$ has a very small radiation resistance and a large capacitive reactance. The antenna can be tuned to resonance with an inductor at the feed point, but the additional ohmic loss in the inductor reduces the efficiency. The bandwidth is also reduced whenever the antenna has a large input reactance that must be tuned out.

It should be kept in mind that the input impedance is influenced in a nonnegligible way by the capacitance associated with the physical junction where the transmission line is connected to the antenna. The structure used to support the antenna, if any, will also influence the input impedance. Consequently, the curves given in Figs. 2.13 and 2.14 should be viewed as representative of typical behavior only.

2.9 ANTENNA IMPEDANCE: THEORETICAL CONSIDERATIONS

The theoretical calculation of antenna impedance has been studied by many authors, and a large number of specialized papers and several books deal extensively with this subject. The books by King and Schelkunoff provide comprehensive discussions.† The evaluation of antenna impedance is also discussed in many of the general references given at the end of this text.

The input impedance of an antenna is dependent, to some extent, on the manner in which the transmission-line feed is connected to the antenna. In order to avoid the complications associated with the feed line the usual procedure followed by most authors is to construct an idealized version of a dipole antenna that is easier to analyze but yet represents a close approximation to a real antenna.‡ The model to be examined here is shown in Fig. 2.15a. It consists of a circular rod of radius a and length $2l_0 = l$. The antenna is excited by a uniform applied electric field of strength E_g acting over

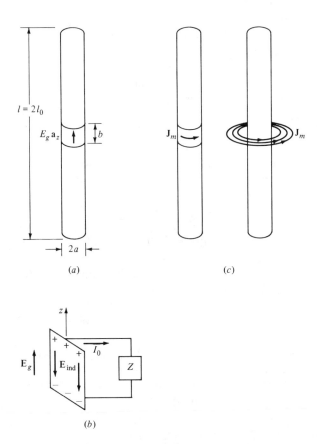

Figure 2.15 (a) Dipole antenna with applied electric field E_g over a small circular band of length b. (b) Simple circuit used to explain antenna model. (c) Excitation of dipole antenna by a small loop of "magnetic" current.

† R. W. P. King, *Theory of Linear Antennas*, Harvard University Press, Cambridge, Mass., 1956; S. A. Schelkunoff, *Advanced Antenna Theory*, John Wiley & Sons, Inc., New York, 1952.
‡ Various dipole antenna models are discussed in App. III.

a centered circular band of length b along the antenna axis. The radius a is assumed to be very small relative to the wavelength λ_0 and the length l_0. Under these conditions the near-zone field, and in particular the field at the surface of the rod, can be found with sufficient accuracy by replacing the circumferentially uniform current on the rod by a line current of equal total strength located at the center of the rod. There are, however, fundamental limitations associated with this assumption, and these are discussed later on. The current is an unknown quantity and is to be found such that the resultant tangential electric field cancels the applied field over the band of length b and equals zero along the rest of the surface of the perfectly conducting rod. The general nature of this model may be understood by considering the system shown in Fig. 2.15b.

The system shown in Fig. 2.15b consists of a thin, flat, perfectly conducting plate to which an electric circuit with impedance Z is connected. A uniform electric field $E_g \mathbf{a}_z$ is applied to the plate. This will cause a charge displacement along the plate and a current I_0 to flow. The charge displacement and current will produce an induced electric field (scattered field) that will cancel the applied field on the surface of the plate, since the total tangential electric field must be zero. The voltage acting across Z equals $I_0 Z$ and is also given by the line integral of the applied field taken from the bottom to the top of the plate, that is, by $E_g b = V_g$. The circuit impedance equals V_g/I_0. The action of the assumed applied field acting on the dipole antenna is similar. Even though this is not a practical way to excite the antenna, it is, nevertheless, a useful model for impedance calculations. The length b of the band over which the applied field acts is not critical as long as it is short relative to the antenna length. Later on in the analysis it will be convenient to make the bandlength b vanishingly small. The capacitive effects associated with the transmission line-dipole junction in a real antenna system is not dealt with when using the above model. This means that the theoretical values computed for the antenna impedance will not necessarily agree with measured values. In practice it is found that the mathematical model leads to impedance values that are surprisingly close to typical measured values. The mathematical model gives the impedance of the dipole antenna itself, while measured values include the effects of the input region circuit.

A somewhat different model for the dipole antenna excitation is shown in Fig. 2.15c. In this model the antenna is driven by a small "magnetic" current loop either in the form of a band of length b or a disk of radius b. In either case the impressed electric field is highly peaked near the loop but does extend to some extent along the antenna. However, this has a rather small effect on the computed value of impedance, so we will discuss only the simpler model.

The steps involved in calculating the input impedance are as follows:

1. Assume an unknown current distribution $I(z')$, with $I(0)$ being the value of $I(z')$ at $z' = 0$, that is, at the input, and with $I(z')$ equal to zero at $z = \pm l_0$.
2. Find the z component of the vector potential and electric field in terms of $I(z')$.

3. Impose the boundary conditions

$$E_z = -E_g \qquad -\frac{b}{2} < z < \frac{b}{2} \qquad r = a$$

$$= 0 \qquad \frac{b}{2} < |z| < l_0 \qquad r = a$$

on the electric field and solve the resultant integral equation for the unknown current $I(z')$

4. The applied voltage that excites the antenna is $V_g = E_g b$ and the input impedance is given by

$$Z_a = \frac{E_g b}{I(0)}$$

The formal solution for the vector potential $A_z(x, y, z)$ may be found from a superposition of the contribution from each current-filament element $I(z') \, dz'$ using Eq. (2.24), and is

$$A_z(x, y, z) = \frac{\mu_0}{4\pi} \int_{-l_0}^{l_0} \frac{e^{-jk_0 R}}{R} I(z') \, dz' \qquad (2.63)$$

where $R = [r^2 + (z - z')^2]^{1/2}$ and r is the cylindrical radial coordinate $(x^2 + y^2)^{1/2}$. The z component of the electric field is given by

$$E_z = -j\omega A_z + \frac{1}{j\omega\epsilon_0\mu_0} \frac{\partial^2 A_z}{\partial z^2} = \frac{1}{j\omega\epsilon_0\mu_0} \left(k_0^2 + \frac{\partial^2}{\partial z^2} \right) A_z \qquad (2.64)$$

The integral equation for $I(z')$ is obtained by using Eq. (2.63) in Eq. (2.64) and imposing the boundary conditions on E_z; thus

$$\left(k_0^2 + \frac{\partial^2}{\partial z^2} \right) \int_{-l_0}^{l_0} I(z') \frac{e^{-jk_0 R}}{4\pi R} \, dz' = \begin{cases} -j\omega\epsilon_0 E_g & -\frac{b}{2} < z < \frac{b}{2} \\ 0 & \frac{b}{2} < |z| < l_0 \end{cases} \qquad (2.65)$$

where R is set equal to $[a^2 + (z - z')^2]^{1/2}$ on the surface of the rod. This integral equation was first derived by Pocklington in 1897. A modification of this equation was introduced by Hallén in 1938 and is simpler to deal with from a numerical-computation point of view. Hallén's integral equation is derived by first solving the differential equation

$$\left(\frac{d^2}{dz^2} + k_0^2 \right) A_z = j\omega\epsilon_0\mu_0 E_z = \begin{cases} -j\omega\epsilon_0\mu_0 E_g & -\frac{b}{2} < z < \frac{b}{2} \\ 0 & \frac{b}{2} < |z| < l_0 \end{cases} \qquad (2.66)$$

When b is very small, and in particular as b tends to zero, we can express the applied electric field as a voltage pulse across a band of infinitesimal length; thus let

$$\lim_{b \to 0} bE_g = V_g \tag{2.67a}$$

and let

$$E_g = V_g \delta(z) \tag{2.67b}$$

where $\delta(z)$ is the Dirac delta function, which has the properties that

$$\delta(z) = 0 \qquad z \neq 0 \tag{2.68a}$$

$$\int_{-z}^{z} \delta(z')\, dz' = 1 \tag{2.68b}$$

The delta function used here is the same as that used in circuit theory, except the argument is z instead of the time t.

With the above idealization to a band of infinitesimal length the vector potential A_z is a solution of the homogeneous equation

$$\left(\frac{d^2}{dz^2} + k_0^2\right)A_z = 0 \qquad z \neq 0 \tag{2.69a}$$

for all z not equal to zero. In order that at $z = 0$ we get

$$\left(\frac{d^2}{dz^2} + k_0^2\right)A_z = -j\omega\epsilon_0\mu_0 V_g \delta(z) \tag{2.69b}$$

the potential A_z must be continuous, and the first derivative of A_z, namely, dA_z/dz, should have a step change of amount $-j\omega\epsilon_0\mu_0 V_g$ at $z = 0$, so that the second derivative will have an impulse of the same strength. The behavior of A_z in the vicinity of $z = 0$ is shown in Fig. 2.16.

The general solution to the homogeneous equation over the interval

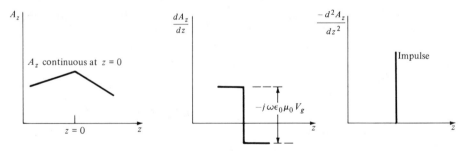

Figure 2.16 Behavior of the vector potential function A_z in the vicinity of the input region of the antenna.

$-l_0 < z < l_0$ is

$$A_z = C_1 \cos k_0 z + C_2 \sin k_0 z \qquad z < 0$$

$$= C_3 \cos k_0 z + C_4 \sin k_0 z \qquad z > 0$$

where C_1 through C_4 are constants. In order that A_z will be continuous at $z = 0$ we require that $C_1 = C_3$. The derivative of A_z evaluated between $z = 0_+$ and $z = 0_-$ is

$$\left. \frac{dA_z}{dz} \right|_{0_-}^{0_+} = k_0 C_4 - k_0 C_2 = -j\omega\epsilon_0\mu_0 V_g$$

Since the antenna is symmetrical about $z = 0$, both A_z and E_z will be even functions of z; hence $C_4 = -C_2$ and then we find that

$$C_2 = \frac{j\omega\mu_0\epsilon_0}{2k_0} V_g = \frac{j}{2} Y_0 \mu_0 V_g$$

upon using $\omega\mu_0\epsilon_0 = k_0 Y_0 \mu_0$. The solution for A_z along the antenna surface is thus

$$A_z = -\frac{j}{2} Y_0 \mu_0 V_g \sin k_0 |z| + C_1 \cos k_0 z \qquad (2.70)$$

where C_1 is still an unknown constant.

Hallén's integral equation is now obtained by expressing A_z in terms of the current $I(z')$ and is

$$\frac{1}{4\pi} \int_{-l_0}^{l_0} I(z') \frac{e^{-jk_0 R}}{R} \, dz' = -\frac{j}{2} Y_0 V_g \sin k_0 |z| + C \cos k_0 z \qquad (2.71)$$

where $R = [a^2 + (z - z')^2]^{1/2}$ and $C = C_1/\mu_0$. The solution to Eq. (2.71) may be found numerically using the method of moments, for which there are several variations.† The constant C must be determined so that $I(z)$ will equal zero at the ends of the antenna, that is, at $z = \pm l_0$.

The relationship between Pocklington's and Hallén's equations may be established in a more definitive way. We can express Eq. (2.65) in the form

$$\left(k_0^2 + \frac{\partial^2}{\partial z^2} \right) Q(z) = j\omega\epsilon_0 E_z \qquad (2.72)$$

where

$$Q(z) = \int_{-l_0}^{l_0} \frac{e^{-jk_0 R}}{4\pi R} I(z') \, dz'$$

The equation for $Q(z)$ may be solved by first solving the Green's function

---

† See R. F. Harrington, *Field Computation by Moment Methods*, available from Krieger Publishing Company, Inc., Melbourne, Fla.

problem:†

$$\left(k_0^2 + \frac{\partial^2}{\partial z^2}\right)G(z, z') = -\delta(z - z') \tag{2.73}$$

which is the field from a point source at z'. When G is known we can find $Q(z)$ as follows: We first multiply Eq. (2.72) by G and Eq. (2.73) by Q and subtract the two equations to obtain

$$G\frac{\partial^2 Q}{\partial z^2} - Q\frac{\partial^2 G}{\partial z^2} = \frac{\partial}{\partial z}\left(G\frac{\partial Q}{\partial z} - Q\frac{\partial G}{\partial z}\right)$$

$$= j\omega\epsilon_0 E_z G + Q\delta(z - z')$$

We now interchange z and z' and integrate over z' from $-l_0$ to l_0; thus

$$\int_{-l_0}^{l_0} \frac{\partial}{\partial z'}\left(G\frac{\partial Q}{\partial z'} - Q\frac{\partial G}{\partial z'}\right) dz' = j\omega\epsilon_0 \int_{-l_0}^{l_0} E_z(z')G(z', z)\, dz'$$

$$+ \int_{-l_0}^{l_0} Q(z')\delta(z - z')\, dz'$$

This expression reduces to the following:

$$Q(z) = -j\omega\epsilon_0 \int_{-l_0}^{l_0} E_z(z')G(z', z)\, dz' + \left(G\frac{\partial Q}{\partial z'} - Q\frac{\partial G}{\partial z'}\right)\Bigg|_{-l_0}^{l_0} \tag{2.74}$$

The solution for Q is seen to be given by a superposition integral plus boundary terms.

A solution for G may be found by using an approach similar to that used in the derivation of Hallén's equation. G must satisfy the homogeneous equation when $z \neq z'$, must be continuous at $z = z'$, and must have a discontinuous first derivative at $z = z'$; that is,

$$\frac{\partial G}{\partial z}\Bigg|_{z'_-}^{z'_+} = -1$$

This will make $\partial^2 G/\partial z^2$ behave like $-\delta(z - z')$. In view of these properties we choose (other forms are possible; see Prob. 2.11)

$$G = C_1 \sin k_0 |z - z'|$$

We now require

$$\frac{\partial G}{\partial z}\Bigg|_{z'_-}^{z'_+} = -1 = 2k_0 C_1$$

---

† A unique solution to Eq. (2.73) requires boundary conditions for G to be specified at $z = \pm l_0$. For the purpose of discussion in the text we only need to find one particular solution for G.

Hence a solution for the Green's function is

$$G(z, z') = -\frac{\sin k_0|z - z'|}{2k_0} \tag{2.75}$$

When we apply the boundary condition $E_z = -V_g\delta(z)$ we find, from Eq. (2.74), that

$$Q(z) = -\frac{j\omega\epsilon_0 V_g}{2k_0} \sin k_0|z| - \frac{1}{2k_0} \frac{\partial Q(z')}{\partial z'} \sin k_0|z' - z|\Big|_{-l_0}^{l_0}$$

$$+ \frac{1}{2k_0} Q(z') \frac{\partial}{\partial z'} \sin k_0|z' - z|\Big|_{-l_0}^{l_0}$$

Since $I(z')$ is assumed to be an even function of z', the vector potential $Q(z')$ will be an even function and $\partial Q/\partial z'$ will be an odd function of z'. By using these symmetry properties and replacing $\omega\epsilon_0/k_0$ by Y_0 we obtain

$$Q(z) = \int_{-l_0}^{l_0} \frac{e^{-jk_0 R}}{4\pi R} I(z') \, dz' = -j\frac{Y_0 V_g}{2} \sin k_0|z|$$

$$+ Q(l_0) \cos k_0 l_0 \cos k_0 z - \frac{1}{k_0} \frac{\partial Q(z')}{\partial z'}\Big|_{l_0} \sin k_0 l_0 \cos k_0 z \tag{2.76}$$

This is Hallén's integral equation and shows that the constant C which occurs in Eq. (2.71) is given by

$$C = Q(l_0) \cos k_0 l_0 - \frac{1}{k_0} Q'(l_0) \sin k_0 l_0$$

where Q' means $\partial Q/\partial z'$. When the dipole antenna is $\lambda_0/2$ long, $k_0 l_0 = \pi/2$ and C depends only on $Q'(l_0)$. For an antenna λ_0 long, C depends only on $Q(l_0)$. When the applied field acts over a finite length b the first term on the right-hand side of Eq. (2.76) becomes

$$-j\frac{Y_0 V_g}{k_0 b}\left(1 - \cos k_0 \frac{b}{2} \cos k_0 z\right) \simeq -j\frac{Y_0 V_g}{2k_0 b} k_0^2\left(\frac{b^2}{4} + z^2\right) \qquad |z| \le b$$

$$-j\frac{Y_0 V_g}{2} \frac{\sin k_0(b/2)}{k_0(b/2)} \sin k_0|z| \qquad |z| \ge b$$

and comes from the integration of the product of the applied field with the Green's function.

Hallén's integral equation as given above actually gives the vector potential on the surface $r = a$ due to a filament of current on the z axis and extending from $-l_0$ to l_0. The electric field derived from this potential will be continuous with continuous derivatives and zero divergence everywhere on the surface $r = a$. We therefore cannot make this radiated field cancel an arbitrary impressed field on the surface $r = a$. At the ends of the antenna where $z = \pm l_0$, $r = a$, the field from the line source will be finite. However, it is a well-known fact that the electric field normal to the surface must become infinite at the edge. As a result of these required edge conditions, it follows that the approximate integral equation cannot have an exact solution.

The exact integral equation has the same form as the approximate integral equation does, except that the integration over the current distribution is taken over the actual surface of the antenna (see Prob. 2.13). For the exact integral equation the antenna input current will increase logarithmically if the applied field is approximated by a delta function. If the applied field extends over a finite band the input current remains finite.

In spite of these limitations it turns out that approximate solutions to the approximate integral equation give results that are in close agreement with measured data. The reasons for this somewhat unusual situation are explained more fully in Sec. 2.12. In that section it will be shown that for thin antennas with l_0/a greater than 50 the approximate integral equation will yield good results, provided the current can be adequately approximated by a finite Fourier series of no more than 25 to 30 terms. Fortunately this turns out to be adequate. For thick antennas with l_0/a less than about 10, the approximate solutions to the approximate integral equation become unsatisfactory, but there is a way to correct these solutions, as explained in Sec. 2.12.

As a preliminary step to obtaining an approximate numerical solution of Hallén's equation we will present some relevant material pertaining to the method-of-moments technique

2.10 METHOD OF MOMENTS†

A typical integral equation that occurs in practice (a Fredholm equation of the first kind) and that may be solved numerically by the method of moments is

$$\int_0^1 G(u, u')I(u')\, du' = f(u) \tag{2.77}$$

where $G(u, u')$ is a known kernel, or Green's function, $f(u)$ is a known function, and $I(u)$ is the unknown function to be determined. The first step is to choose a set of basis functions in which to expand $I(u')$. These may be, for example, the Fourier series sine and cosine functions, the unit height-pulse functions shown in Fig. 2.17a, or the overlapping triangular functions shown in Fig. 2.18a. We will let $\Phi_n(u)$ denote the nth basis function and approximate

† Early work on the method of moments was carried out by N. M. Krylov in the period 1925–1926. See L. V. Kantorovich and V. I. Krylov, *Approximate Methods of Higher Analysis*, Interscience Publishers, Inc., New York, 1958.

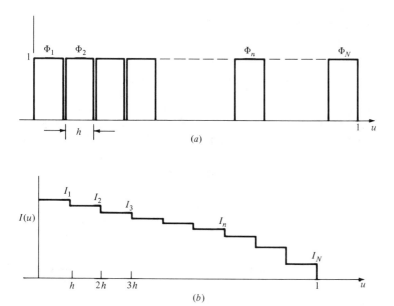

Figure 2.17 (*a*) Rectangular pulse basis functions. (*b*) Approximation of $I(u)$ by a series of pulse functions.

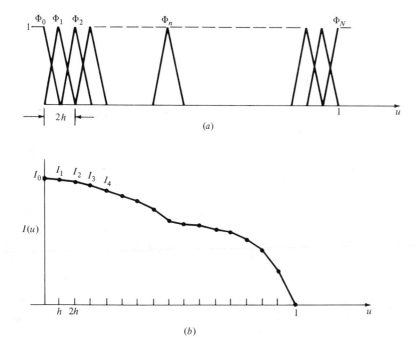

Figure 2.18 (*a*) Triangular basis functions. (*b*) Approximation of $I(u)$ by a series of triangular functions.

$I(u)$ by the expansion

$$I(u') = \sum_{n=1}^{N} I_n \Phi_n(u')$$

where I_n are unknown amplitude constants to be determined. When the Φ_n are the pulse functions shown in Fig. 2.17a the approximation to $I(u)$ is a staircase approximation, as shown in Fig. 2.17b. If the triangular basis functions are used, the approximation is a linear interpolation of $I(u)$ between sample points represented by the coefficients I_n, as shown in Fig. 2.18b. The latter gives a smoother approximation, and for a given numerical accuracy fewer terms are needed using triangular basis functions than if rectangular pulse functions are used. Many other sets of basis functions that are useful in practice also exist.†
The number of terms used in the expansion of $I(u)$ is dictated by the numerical accuracy required and the desire to keep the cost of computing as low as possible.

When the expansion for $I(u)$ is substituted into the integral equation we obtain

$$\sum_{n=1}^{N} I_n \int_0^1 G(u, u')\Phi_n(u')\, du' = f(u)$$

$$= \sum_{n=1}^{N} I_n G_n(u) \qquad (2.78)$$

where

$$G_n(u) = \int_0^1 G(u, u')\Phi_n(u')\, du'$$

The latter integral can be viewed as the moment of $G(u, u')$ with respect to Φ_n.

The integral equation [Eq. (2.77)] has been approximated by a new equation [Eq. (2.78)], and for a finite N, the left-hand side of Eq. (2.78) can equal $f(u)$ only in an approximate sense. The objective now is to choose the coefficients I_n such that Eq. (2.78) will be satisfied as closely as possible. There are N unknown constants I_n, so a system of N equations must be obtained that will allow these unknown constants to be determined. One procedure is to equate both sides of Eq. (2.78) at N different values of u, usually equally spaced by increments of $h = 1/(N-1)$. This point-matching procedure gives the system of equations below:

$$\sum_{n=1}^{N} G_{mn} I_n = \sum_{n=1}^{N} I_n G_n(mh) = f(mh) = f_m \qquad m = 0, 1, 2, \ldots, N-1 \quad (2.79)$$

---

† When the basis and testing functions are powers of u, the integrals are the classical Chebyshev moments. This appears to be the origin for the name *method of moments*.

where $G_{mn} = G_n(mh)$. In matrix form we can write

$$[G_{mn}][I_n] = [f_m] \qquad (2.80a)$$

and

$$[I_n] = [G_{mn}]^{-1}[f_m] \qquad (2.80b)$$

where $[G_{mn}]^{-1}$ is the inverse matrix. There are standard computer programs that will solve a linear system, so the solution of Eq. (2.80b) for the I_n can be readily carried out.

In the general method-of-moments procedure a set of N testing or weighting functions, say, $\psi_m(u)$, $m = 1, 2, \ldots, N$, are chosen and Eq. (2.78) is multiplied by these in turn and integrated from 0 to 1. This procedure gives the system of equations:

$$\sum_{n=1}^{N} G_{mn}I_n = f_m \qquad m = 1, 2, \ldots, N \qquad (2.81)$$

where now

$$G_{mn} = \int_0^1 \psi_m(u)G_n(u)\, du = \int_0^1 \int_0^1 \psi_m(u)G(u, u')\Phi_n(u')\, du'\, du$$

$$f_m = \int_0^1 \psi_m(u)f(u)\, du$$

The above procedure is also called the *method of weighted residuals* since the residual error

$$\left[\sum_{n=1}^{N} I_n G_n(u) - f(u) \right]$$

is weighted by $\psi_m(u)$, integrated, and equated to zero. The point-matching method corresponds to using delta functions $\delta(u - mh)$ as testing (weighting) functions. When the ψ_m are the same functions as the Φ_n, the method is called *Galerkin's method*.

The method-of-moments procedure outlined above may be given a geometrical interpretation that provides a useful insight to the problem. The function $f(u)$ can be thought of as a vector in an infinite dimensional vector space and the $\psi_m(u)$ can be viewed as analogous to unit vectors in this space. The vector components of $f(u)$ are then the projections along the unit vectors $\psi_m(u)$, the mth component being given by

$$f_m = \int_0^1 f(u)\psi_m(u)\, du$$

The $\psi_m(u)$ can always be normalized such that

$$\int_0^1 \psi_m^2(u)\, du = 1$$

and thereby made to correspond to unit basis vectors. When the ψ_m are an orthogonal set of functions, that is,

$$\int_0^1 \psi_m(u)\psi_n(u)\,du = 0 \qquad n \neq m$$

they correspond to a set of orthogonal or mutually perpendicular unit vectors. In order to represent $f(u)$ exactly we must find all of its components, which generally requires an infinite number of the ψ_m functions (a complete set). When a finite number of the ψ_m are used such that $f(u)$ is approximated by

$$f(u) \simeq \sum_{m=1}^{N} f_m\psi_m(u)$$

it is equivalent to finding the projection of the vector f onto an N dimensional subspace spanned by the N functions (unit vectors) $\psi_m(u)$, $m = 1, 2, \ldots, N$.

The method of moments can now be seen to correspond to finding the projections of the vector $f(u)$ and the vectors $I_n G_n(u)$ onto a finite N dimensional subspace and adjusting the lengths of the $I_n G_n(u)$ vectors, i.e., choosing the I_n so that the projected components are equal. When the testing functions are arbitrarily chosen, the solution does not have any particular optimum properties in general. If a bad choice is made for the N testing functions (vectors), it may very well turn out that both $\sum_{n=1}^N I_n G_n(u)$ and $f(u)$ have large and very different components that are perpendicular to the subspace on which the projection is made. In order to get a good approximation, the ψ_m must be chosen so that the $N\psi_m$ will give a good representation of both $f(u)$ and $\sum_{n=1}^N I_n G_n(u)$. The optimum choice is not always easy to determine a priori.

The following vector problem will illustrate many of the concepts discussed above. We will assume that we have a problem of the form

$$LI = f = (2-j)\mathbf{a}_x - (1+j)\mathbf{a}_y + (4+3j)\mathbf{a}_z \qquad (2.82)$$

where L is a known operator, I is the unknown, and the expression on the far right is the complex vector representing f. The unknown I is expanded as $I = I_1\Phi_1 + I_2\Phi_2$ and the result of the application of the operator L upon Φ_1 and Φ_2 is assumed to give

$$L\Phi_1 = \mathbf{k}_1 = (1+j)\mathbf{a}_x + (2-j)\mathbf{a}_y$$

$$L\Phi_2 = \mathbf{k}_2 = \mathbf{a}_x + j\mathbf{a}_y + (3+2j)\mathbf{a}_z$$

Our approximate equation corresponding to Eq. (2.82) is

$$I_1\mathbf{k}_1 + I_2\mathbf{k}_2 = \mathbf{f} \qquad (2.83)$$

The equation can hold in an approximate sense only, since we did not use a complete set of functions (basis vectors) to expand the unknown I. We now project both sides onto a two-dimensional space and match projections in this space. We can use the space spanned by $\mathbf{a}_x, \mathbf{a}_y$ or $\mathbf{a}_x, \mathbf{a}_z$ or $\mathbf{a}_y, \mathbf{a}_z$ or some other pair of noncollinear vectors. A priori we do not know which pair will be the best. We will choose $\mathbf{a}_x$ and $\mathbf{a}_y$ as the test vectors; thus

$$I_1\mathbf{k}_1 \cdot \mathbf{a}_x + I_2\mathbf{k}_2 \cdot \mathbf{a}_x = \mathbf{f} \cdot \mathbf{a}_x$$

$$I_1\mathbf{k}_1 \cdot \mathbf{a}_y + I_2\mathbf{k}_2 \cdot \mathbf{a}_y = \mathbf{f} \cdot \mathbf{a}_y$$

The equations that result from this testing procedure are

$$I_1(1+j) + I_2 = 2 - j$$

$$I_1(2-j) + I_2j = -(1+j)$$

We may solve for the unknowns I_1 and I_2 and can then compute the error vector

$$\mathbf{f} - (I_1\mathbf{k}_1 + I_2\mathbf{k}_2)$$

which is found to be equal to $(1+j)\mathbf{a}_z$ with a magnitude of 1.414. Note that the error vector is perpendicular to the subspace on which the projection was made, since the projected components were made equal.

At this point it should be clear that an optimum objective would be to minimize the error vector. This will give the closest approximation to Eq. (2.83). Hence, we should choose I_1 and I_2 so as to minimize the magnitude of the error vector, that is, to minimize

$$E = |I_1\mathbf{k}_1 + I_2\mathbf{k}_2 - \mathbf{f}|^2$$

$$= (I_1\mathbf{k}_1 + I_2\mathbf{k}_2 - \mathbf{f}) \cdot (I_1^*\mathbf{k}_1^* + I_2^*\mathbf{k}_2^* - \mathbf{f}^*)$$

where the $*$ denotes the complex conjugate. The minimization is obtained by setting the partial derivatives of E with respect to the real and imaginary parts of I_1 and I_2 equal to zero.

Let $I_1 = I_{1r} + jI_{1i}$ and $I_2 = I_{2r} + jI_{2i}$, where r and i refer to the real and imaginary components. Since

$$\frac{\partial}{\partial I_{1r}} = \frac{\partial}{\partial I_1}\frac{\partial I_1}{\partial I_{1r}} = \frac{\partial}{\partial I_1} \quad \text{and} \quad \frac{\partial}{\partial I_{1i}} = \frac{\partial}{\partial I_1}\frac{\partial I_1}{\partial I_{1i}} = j\frac{\partial}{\partial I_1}$$

and similarly for I_2 and I_1^*, I_2^*, we can take the partial derivatives with respect to the I_1, I_2, I_1^*, and I_2^*. The derivatives with respect to I_1^* and I_2^* are the complex conjugates of those with respect to I_1 and I_2, so only the second (or first) pair are needed. We now readily find that

$$\frac{\partial E}{\partial I_1^*} = \mathbf{k}_1^* \cdot (I_1\mathbf{k}_1 + I_2\mathbf{k}_2 - \mathbf{f}) = 0 \tag{2.84a}$$

$$\frac{\partial E}{\partial I_2^*} = \mathbf{k}_2^* \cdot (I_1\mathbf{k}_1 + I_2\mathbf{k}_2 - \mathbf{f}) = 0 \tag{2.84b}$$

These equations simply state that we should use $\mathbf{k}_1^*$ and $\mathbf{k}_2^*$ as the optimum test vectors to test the system described by Eq. (2.83). When we solve the above for I_1 and I_2 the error vector is found to be $(0.0864 - 0.0578j)\mathbf{a}_x +$

$(-0.1826 - 0.3366j)\mathbf{a}_y + (0.6922 - 0.3078j)\mathbf{a}_z$, with a magnitude of 0.855. Clearly the error vector is smaller than it was in the previous case. In the minimization procedure we work in the complete vector space instead of in a subspace and adjust the lengths I_1 and I_2 of $\mathbf{k}_1$ and $\mathbf{k}_2$ to get a vector that is as close to being equal to $\mathbf{f}$ as possible.

When the above minimization is applied to the method-of-moments equation (2.78) the optimum test functions are found to be $G_m^*(u)$. If we test Eq. (2.78) with these we find that

$$\sum_{n=1}^{N} G_{mn}I_n = f_m \tag{2.85}$$

where now

$$G_{mn} = \int_0^1 G_m^*(u)G_n(u)\,du$$

$$f_m = \int_0^1 G_m^*(u)f(u)\,du$$

and

$$G_n(u) = \int_0^1 G(u, u')\Phi_n(u')\,du'$$

The I_n determined this way minimizes the expression

$$\int_0^1 \left| \sum_{n=1}^{N} I_nG_n(u) - f(u) \right|^2 du$$

which corresponds to matching the two sides of Eq. (2.78) so as to obtain a minimum mean square error. The method is often called the *method of least squares*.

Numerical Integration

Many of the integrals that occur in the equations to which the method of moments is applied cannot be done analytically. It is then necessary to compute these integrals numerically. One well-known numerical integration algorithm is *Simpson's rule*. Consider a function $g(u)$ and divide the interval of integration $0 \le u \le 1$ into an even number of subdivisions of length h, as in Fig. 2.19a. Over each subdivision of length $2h$ we approximate $g(u)$ by a quadratic function; thus over $0 \le u \le 2h$ let $g(u)$ be approximated by $A_1 + B_1u + C_1u^2$. We now match the two functions at $u = 0$, h, and $2h$. If we let $g_0 = g(0)$, $g_1 = g(h)$, $g_2 = g(2h)$, etc., we find that

$$A_1 = g_0 \qquad B_1 = \frac{4g_1 - 3g_0 - g_2}{2h} \qquad C_1 = \frac{g_0 + g_2 - 2g_1}{2h^2}$$

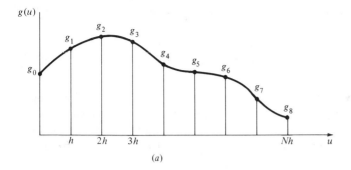

(a)

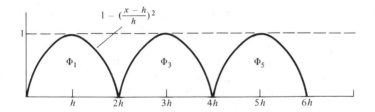

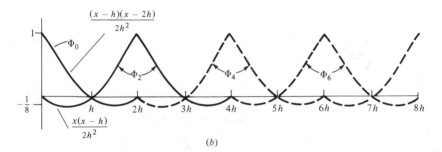

(b)

Figure 2.19 (a) Illustration for Simpson's rule. (b) The Lagrange polynomials basis functions.

For the nth section we approximate $g(u)$ by

$$A_n + B_n[u - 2(n-1)h] + C_n[u - 2(n-1)h]^2$$

The coefficients are given by the formulas above with g_0, g_1, g_2 replaced by g_{2n-2}, g_{2n-1}, and g_{2n}, respectively. The integral of $g(u)$ from 0 to $2h$ is now approximated by the area under the quadratic curve from 0 to $2h$; thus

$$\int_0^{2h} g(u)\,du \simeq A_1(2h) + \tfrac{1}{2}B_1(2h)^2 + \tfrac{1}{3}C_1(2h)^3$$

$$= \frac{h}{3}(g_0 + 4g_1 + g_2) \tag{2.86}$$

When we repeat this procedure for the remaining sections and sum the results we obtain Simpson's rule:

$$\int_0^1 g(u)\, du \simeq \frac{h}{3} \sum_{n=0}^{N} S_n g_n \qquad (2.87)$$

where the Simpson weights S_n are equal to $1, 4, 2, 4, 2, 4, \ldots, 4, 1$. An interesting feature of Simpson's quadratic rule is that it gives the exact answer for the integral of any cubic polynomial even though $g(u)$ is approximated by quadratic polynomials. For example, the integral of $C_0 + C_1 u + C_2 u^2 + C_3 u^3$ from 0 to $2h$ is

$$C_0(2h) + \tfrac{1}{2}C_1(2h)^2 + \tfrac{1}{3}C_2(2h)^3 + \tfrac{1}{4}C_3(2h)^4$$

Simpson's rule gives exactly the same result, as may readily be shown by using Eq. (2.86).

The quadratic approximation corresponds to the use of Lagrange polynomials of order 2 for the basis functions.[†] The odd-numbered basis functions are parabolas of unit height that span an interval $2h$, while the even-numbered ones correspond to two parabolic segments that span an interval of length $4h$, as shown in Fig. 2.19b. The expansion of $g(u)$ is given by

$$g(u) = \sum_{n=0}^{N} a_n \Phi_n(u) = \sum_{n=0}^{N} g_n \Phi_n(u)$$

since at each point $u = nh$ only the nth basis function is nonzero and equal to unity and thus makes a_n equal to $g(nh) = g_n$.

We can also use higher-degree polynomial approximations. If we divide the interval 0 to 1 into subintervals of length h such that the total interval consists of an integer number of sections of length $3h$—that is, Nh is divisible by 3—then over the interval 0 to $3h$ we can approximate $g(u)$ by $A + Bu + Cu^2 + Du^3$. When we solve for the constants by matching at $u = 0$, h, $2h$, and $3h$, the area under the cubic curve is found to be given by

$$\frac{3h}{8}(g_0 + 3g_1 + 3g_2 + g_3) \simeq \int_0^{3h} g(u)\, du$$

which is *Newton's 3/8 rule.*

Newton's 3/8 rule will give almost the correct result for the integral of any polynomial function of degree 4. For a function such as

$$C_0 + C_1 u + C_2 u^2 + C_3 u^3 + C_4 u^4$$

the integral from 0 to $3h$ is

$$C_0(3h) + \tfrac{1}{2}C_1(3h)^2 + \tfrac{1}{3}C_2(3h)^3 + \tfrac{1}{4}C_3(3h)^4 + \tfrac{1}{5}C_4(3h)^5$$

Newton's 3/8 rule gives the same first four terms but gives $(11/54)C_4(3h)^5$

[†] The author is indebted to Georg Karawas for bringing this to his attention.

instead of $(11/55)C_4(3h)^5$ for the last term. However, this is normally a small error. For the interval 0 to 1 Newton's 3/8 rule approximates the integral of $g(u)$ by the following series:

$$\int_0^1 g(u)\, du \simeq \frac{3h}{8} \sum_{n=0}^{N} S_n g_n \tag{2.88}$$

where now the weights S_n are 1, 3, 3, 2, 3, 3, 2, ..., 3, 3, 1.

The number of subdivisions that must be used depends on how rapidly the function $g(u)$ varies. For slowly varying functions only a few subdivisions are needed to obtain three-figure accuracy.

2.11 DIPOLE IMPEDANCE: NUMERICAL SOLUTION

We will now apply the least-squares method-of-moments procedure to Hallén's integral equation, along with numerical integration using Simpson's quadratic rule, in order to find the input current and hence the impedance of a dipole antenna. The integral equation to be solved is given by Eq. (2.71) and is repeated below

$$\int_{-l_0}^{l_0} \frac{e^{-jk_0 R}}{R} I(z')\, dz' = -j2\pi Y_0 V_g \sin k_0 |z| + 4\pi C \cos k_0 z$$

where $R = [(z - z')^2 + a^2]^{1/2}$. We will simplify this equation by introducing the following normalized variables:

$$u = z/l_0 \qquad u' = z'/l_0 \qquad k_0 l_0 = \theta \qquad a/l_0 = \alpha$$

The integral from $-l_0$ to 0 is also converted to an integral from 0 to l_0 by changing z' to $-z'$ in that part of the integral and using the symmetry property $I(-z') = I(z')$ for the unknown current. The resultant integral equation is

$$\int_0^1 \left(\frac{\cos \theta R_1 - j \sin \theta R_1}{R_1} + \frac{\cos \theta R_2 - j \sin \theta R_2}{R_2} \right) I(u')\, du'$$

$$= -j2\pi Y_0 V_g \sin \theta u + 4\pi C \cos \theta u \tag{2.89}$$

where $R_1 = [(u - u')^2 + \alpha^2]^{1/2}$ and $R_2 = [(u + u')^2 + \alpha^2]^{1/2}$. The function $(\sin \theta R_1)/R_1$ equals $(\sin \theta \alpha)/\alpha \simeq \theta$ when $u = u'$, but $(\cos \theta R_1)/R_1$ equals $(\cos \theta \alpha)/\alpha$, which is a large number, when $u = u'$. Thus the $(\cos \theta R_i)/R_i$ are highly peaked functions when $u' = u$ or $-u$. These rapidly varying functions would require dividing the interval 0 to 1 into many subintervals of small length h in order to carry out an accurate numerical integration. In order to avoid such a fine division we can integrate the singular terms by writing the integral of those terms in the following form:

$$\int_0^1 \left[\frac{\cos \theta R_1}{R_1} I(u') - \frac{\cos \theta \alpha}{R_1} I(u) \right] du'$$

$$+ \int_0^1 \left[\frac{\cos \theta R_2}{R_2} I(u') - \frac{\cos \theta \alpha}{R_2} I(u) \right] du'$$

$$+ I(u) \cos \theta \alpha \int_0^1 \left[\frac{1}{R_1} + \frac{1}{R_2} \right] du' \qquad (2.90)$$

The first two integrals are now well behaved at $R_1 = \alpha$ and $R_2 = \alpha$, since the numerator vanishes. The third integral can be done analytically and is given by

$$\int_0^1 \left(\frac{1}{R_1} + \frac{1}{R_2} \right) du' = \ln \frac{[1 - u + \sqrt{\alpha^2 + (1-u)^2}][1 + u + \sqrt{\alpha^2 + (1+u)^2}]}{\alpha^2}$$

$$(2.91)$$

All of the integrals that remain to be carried out can be evaluated using Simpson's rule and relatively large values of h.

The integral equation [Eq. (2.89)] is of the form

$$\int_0^1 G(u, u')I(u') \, du' = f(u)$$

A suitable expansion for $I(u')$ can be made in terms of second-degree polynomials over each subinterval of length $2h$. Thus over the nth subinterval we let [the basis functions are Lagrange polynomials, which we denote by $\Phi_n(u')$]

$$I(u') = A_n + B_n[u' - 2(n-1)h] + C_n[u' - 2(n-1)h]^2$$

$$= I_{2n-2}\Phi_{2n-2}(u') + I_{2n-1}\Phi_{2n-1}(u') + I_{2n}\Phi_{2n}(u')$$

where A_n, B_n, and C_n are unknown but can be expressed in terms of I_{2n-2}, I_{2n-1}, and I_{2n}. When these quadratic functions are used and the integral is evaluated using Simpson's rule, we obtain

$$\sum_{n=0}^N I_n \frac{H}{3} \sum_{j=0}^J G_j(u) S_j \Phi_n(jH) = f(u) \qquad (2.92)$$

where $G_j(u) = G(u, jH)$, $H = 1/J$, and J is the number of divisions the interval $0 \le u' \le 1$ is divided into in order to carry out the numerical integration. For convenience let

$$\psi_m(u) = \frac{H}{3} \sum_{j=0}^J G_j(u) S_j \Phi_m(jH)$$

The optimum testing functions that will give a minimum mean square error for the solution to Eq. (2.92) are the functions $\psi_m^*(u)$. When Eq. (2.92) is tested with these and the integrals are evaluated using Simpson's rule and a subinterval length H', we obtain

$$\sum_{n=0}^{N} I_n \frac{H'}{3} \sum_{i=0}^{J'} \psi_n(iH')\psi_m^*(iH')S_i = \frac{H'}{3} \sum_{i=0}^{J'} f(iH')\psi_m^*(iH')S_i$$

This system of equations may be written as

$$\sum_{i=0}^{J'} S_i \psi_m^*(iH') \left[\sum_{n=0}^{N} I_n \psi_n(iH') - f(iH') \right] = 0 \qquad m = 0, 1, 2, \ldots, N$$

If we choose $J' = N$ this general result simplifies considerably, for there will then be exactly $N + 1$ values of i at which each term is evaluated. The resultant system of equations is readily seen to have the solution specified by requiring that (note that $H' = h = 1/N$)

$$\sum_{n=0}^{N} I_n \psi_n(ih) = f(ih) \qquad i = 0, 1, 2, \ldots, N$$

This result is interesting in that it does not depend on the choice of testing functions used; it is simply the result obtained by point matching Eq. (2.92) at the points $u = ih$. In essence, the numerical integration limits the knowledge of $\psi_n(u)$ and $f(u)$ to the sample points $u = ih$, and clearly if Eq. (2.92) holds exactly at these points the error is zero at these points. Since no other information about $\psi_n(u)$ and $f(u)$ is used, this is the optimum solution for this choice of H'.

According to the above, the equations to be solved are

$$\sum_{n=0}^{N} I_n \frac{H}{3} \sum_{j=0}^{J} G_j(ih)S_j \Phi_n(jH) = f(ih) \qquad i = 0, 1, 2, \ldots, N$$

A further simplification of the above equations occurs if we choose $J = N$ so that $H = h$ also, because if the basis functions are local functions that span an interval $2h$ and have the property that $\Phi_n(nh) = 1$, $\Phi_n(nh \pm h) = 0$ the system of equations reduces to

$$\frac{h}{3} \sum_{n=0}^{N} G_{mn} S_n I_n = f_m \qquad m = 0, 1, 2, \ldots, N \qquad (2.93)$$

where $G_{mn} = G(mh, nh)$ and $f_m = f(mh)$. This result is independent of the choice of local basis functions used and is simply the result of evaluating the integral in the integral equation numerically and then using point matching. Although the derivation appears to be sound, the end result gives a solution for the I_n that depends on the choice of the numerical integration algorithm that is used (see Prob. 2.16). Thus the numerical results obtained are not, in general, reliable.

In the integral equation for the current on a dipole antenna the dominant part of the kernel was integrated exactly. The remainder is a relatively small correction and hence may be treated in an approximate manner without introducing a large error (see Probs. 2.21 and 2.22). Thus we will use Eq. (2.93) in spite of its limitations, since it is a numerically very simple and efficient procedure. The results obtained compare very favorably with those based on alternative numerical procedures or approximate analytical solutions. The attractive feature of this method is that the matrix elements are known—they are simply the values of the kernel function at the sample points multiplied by the Simpson weights. The method appears to converge quite rapidly with increasing N, and this is due to the fact that the dominant part of the kernel was extracted and integrated exactly.

The algebraic equations that will determine the current on the dipole antenna are obtained by using the final expression (2.93) derived above, after substituting Eq. (2.91) into Eq. (2.90) and adding the remaining terms from Eq. (2.89). It is found that the system of equations to be solved is

$$
\begin{aligned}
\frac{h}{3} \sum_{n=0}^{N} S_n & \left[\frac{(\cos\theta\sqrt{(n-m)^2h^2+\alpha^2} - j\sin\theta\sqrt{(n-m)^2h^2+\alpha^2})I_n - I_m\cos\theta\alpha}{\sqrt{(n-m)^2h^2+\alpha^2}} \right. \\
& \left. + \frac{(\cos\theta\sqrt{(n+m)^2h^2+\alpha^2} - j\sin\theta\sqrt{(n+m)^2h^2+\alpha^2})I_n - I_m\cos\theta\alpha}{\sqrt{(n+m)^2h^2+\alpha^2}} \right] \\
& + I_m \cos\theta\alpha \ln \frac{[1-mh+\sqrt{\alpha^2+(1-mh)^2}][1+mh+\sqrt{\alpha^2+(1+mh)^2}]}{\alpha^2} \\
& = -j2\pi Y_0 V_g \sin\theta mh + 4\pi C \cos\theta mh \quad m = 0,1,2,\ldots,N \quad (2.94)
\end{aligned}
$$

Note that $I(l_0) = I_N$ must be equal to zero. The constant C may be found from the equation obtained for $m = 0$. After the constant C has been eliminated, the equations that result can be expressed in the following matrix form:

$$
\begin{bmatrix}
R_{10} & R_{11} & R_{12} & \cdots & R_{1,N-1} \\
R_{20} & R_{21} & R_{22} & \cdots & R_{2,N-1} \\
\multicolumn{5}{c}{\cdots\cdots\cdots\cdots\cdots} \\
R_{N0} & R_{N1} & R_{N2} & \cdots & R_{N,N-1}
\end{bmatrix}
\begin{bmatrix}
I_0 \\ I_1 \\ \vdots \\ I_{N-1}
\end{bmatrix}
= -j\frac{6\pi}{h} Y_0 V_g
\begin{bmatrix}
\sin\theta h \\ \sin 2\theta h \\ \vdots \\ \sin N\theta h
\end{bmatrix}
\quad (2.95)
$$

where the matrix elements R_{mn} are given by

$$
R_{mn} = S_n \left[\frac{\cos\theta\sqrt{\alpha^2+(n-m)^2h^2}}{\sqrt{\alpha^2+(n-m)^2h^2}} + \frac{\cos\theta\sqrt{\alpha^2+(n+m)^2h^2}}{\sqrt{\alpha^2+(n+m)^2h^2}} \right.
$$

$$
\left. - 2\cos\theta mh \frac{\cos\theta\sqrt{\alpha^2+n^2h^2}}{\sqrt{\alpha^2+n^2h^2}} \right]
$$

$$
+ \delta_{mn} \cos\theta\alpha \left\{ \frac{3}{h} \ln \frac{[1-nh+\sqrt{\alpha^2+(1-nh)^2}][1+nh+\sqrt{\alpha^2+(1+nh)^2}]}{\alpha^2} \right.
$$

$$-\sum_{j=0}^{N} S_j \left[\frac{1}{\sqrt{\alpha^2 + (j+n)^2 h^2}} + \frac{1}{\sqrt{\alpha^2 + (j-n)^2 h^2}} \right] \Bigg\}$$

$$- \delta_{0n} \cos\theta\alpha \cos\theta mh \left[\frac{6}{h} \ln \frac{1 + \sqrt{1+\alpha^2}}{\alpha} - \sum_{j=0}^{N} \frac{2S_j}{\sqrt{\alpha^2 + (jh)^2}} \right]$$

$$- jS_n \left[\frac{\sin\theta\sqrt{\alpha^2 + (n-m)^2 h^2}}{\sqrt{\alpha^2 + (n-m)^2 h^2}} + \frac{\sin\theta\sqrt{\alpha^2 + (n+m)^2 h^2}}{\sqrt{\alpha^2 + (n+m)^2 h^2}} \right]$$

$$- 2\cos\theta mh \frac{\sin\theta\sqrt{\alpha^2 + (nh)^2}}{\sqrt{\alpha^2 + (nh)^2}} \right] \tag{2.96}$$

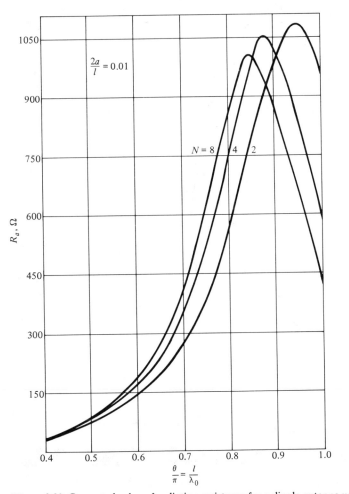

Figure 2.20 Computed value of radiation resistance for a dipole antenna using different values of N, $2a/l = 0.01$.

with $\delta_{mn} = 0$ for $n \neq m$ and $\delta_{nn} = 1$. The input impedance $Z_a = R_a + jX_a$ is given by V_g/I_0.

The simplest approximation that can be made is to choose $N = 2$, which corresponds to approximating the current on the antenna by a polynomial of degree 2. The numerical results for R_a and X_a with this approximation are shown in Figs. 2.20 and 2.21 for the case $a/l_0 = 0.01$. For comparison, the more accurate results obtained by using $N = 4$ and $N = 8$ are also shown.† The results for $N = 2$ predict the general behavior of Z_a and its dependence on the antenna radius quite well, with the exception that the curves are displaced to

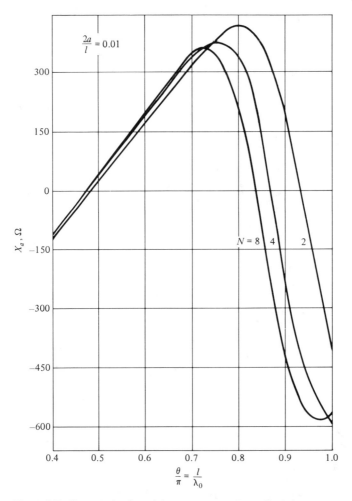

Figure 2.21 Computed value of input reactance for a dipole antenna using different values of N, $2a/l = 0.01$.

† The author is indebted to John Silvestro for the numerical computations.

the right relative to the more accurate results obtained using $N = 8$. In Figs. 2.22 and 2.23 results for R_a and X_a using $N = 2$, 8, and 12 are given for $\alpha = 0.001$. Figures 2.24 and 2.25 give corresponding results for $\alpha = 0.05$. These curves agree reasonably well with the measured values given in Figs. 2.13 and 2.14. In Figs. 2.26 and 2.27 the computed values of R_a and X_a using $N = 8$ and 12 for $\alpha = 0.0135$ are compared with the results of the King-Middleton improved second-order theory.† The King-Middleton theory has been shown to agree very well with measured data obtained by Mack‡. Since the numerical

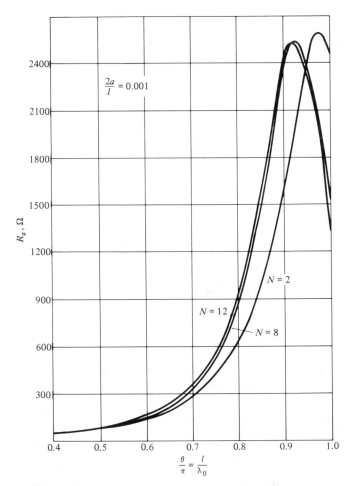

Figure 2.22 Computed value of radiation resistance for a dipole antenna with $2a/l = 0.001$.

† R. W. P. King, "Cylindrical Antennas and Arrays," Chap. 9 in R. E. Collin and F. J. Zucker (eds.), *Antenna Theory*, Pt. I, McGraw-Hill Book Company, New York, 1969.

‡ R. B. Mack, *A Study of Circular Arrays*, Cruft Laboratory Tech. Rept. Nos. 381–386, Harvard University, Cambridge, Mass., 1963.

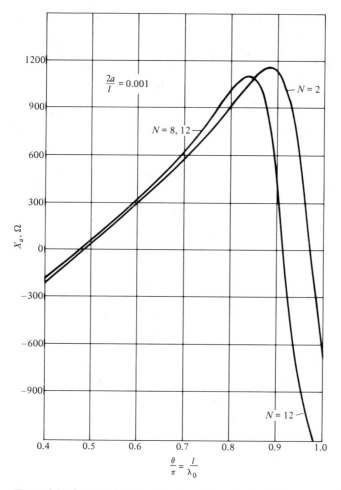

Figure 2.23 Computed value of input reactance for a dipole antenna with $2a/l = 0.001$.

results for $N = 8$ or 12 also agree quite closely it appears that for practical purposes it is not necessary to use a larger value of N.

For reference purposes some specific values of Z_a are tabulated in Table 2.1. In Table 2.2 the numerical values obtained using $N = 8$ and 12 are compared with those from the King-Middleton theory.

The effect of a finite-length band over which the applied electric field acts is very small for thin antennas ($\alpha < 0.01$) as far as the computed values of impedance are concerned. As long as $k_0 b$ is small, a finite-length source region can be accounted for by replacing the source terms in Eq. (2.95) by $\sin \theta m h - \theta \alpha (b/4a) \cos \theta m h$. This change comes from solving for the constant C in Hallén's equation by matching at $z = 0$ and using the result given after Eq. (2.76), that is, $-jY_0 V_g k_0 b/8$, for the source term at $z = 0$. The contribution to C from this term can then be absorbed with the source term $-(jY_0 V_g/2) \sin k_0|z|$

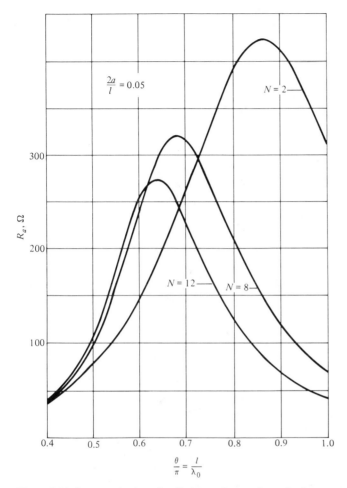

Figure 2.24 Computed value of radiation resistance for a dipole antenna with $2a/l = 0.05$.

in Eq. (2.71). Some typical values of Z_a using $N = 2$, $b = 2a$, and $\alpha = 0.01$ are given in Table 2.3. These show a negligible change for l/λ_0 less than 0.5. The changes at the larger values of l/λ_0 are actually caused by a shift in the peak values of R_a and X_a toward smaller values of l/λ_0 and are not due to any significant change in the peak values. For a thicker antenna the effect would be larger if it is assumed that b is made proportional to a.

Since the integral equation that is solved is an approximate one without an exact solution there is little justification in refining the numerical solution much beyond that corresponding to using $N = 12$. Figure 2.28 (page 68) shows the convergence property of the numerical solutions for R_a and X_a for a dipole antenna $\lambda_0/2$ long and for various values of $\alpha = 2a/l$. These curves indicate that very little further change in R_a or X_a would occur by increasing N beyond 12.

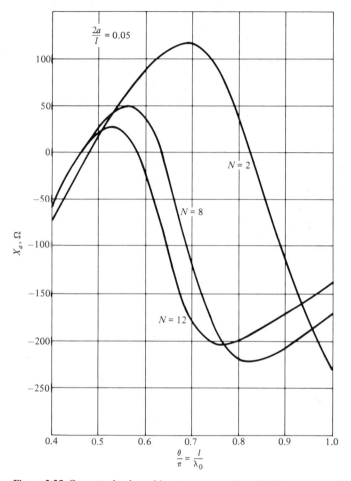

Figure 2.25 Computed value of input reactance for a dipole antenna with $2a/l = 0.05$.

Neff, Siller, and Tillman have used a trigonometric function expansion of the antenna current, of the form

$$I(z) = \sum_{n=1}^{N} I_n \sin \frac{n\pi}{2l_0} (l_0 - |z|)$$

along with point matching to compute the dipole impedance. They report that good results are obtained using five terms.† The analytical evaluation of the

† H. P. Neff, C. A. Siller, and J. D. Tillman, "Simple Approximation to the Current on the Surface of an Isolated Thin Cylindrical Center-Fed Dipole Antenna of Arbitrary Length," *IEEE Trans., Antennas Prop.*, vol. AP-18, 1970, pp. 399–400. See also "A Trigonometric Approximation to the Current in the Solution of Hallén's Equation," *IEEE Trans., Antennas Prop.*, vol. AP-17, 1969, pp. 805–806.

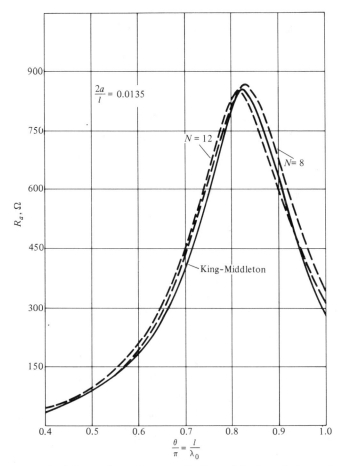

Figure 2.26 Comparison of computed values of dipole radiation resistance with the results of the King-Middleton theory.

input impedance using the induced electromotive-force (EMF) method, the variational method, and a discussion of the King-Middleton iteration method may be found in the text by Elliott.† This text also discusses numerical solutions. The numerical solution of Pocklington's equation is treated by Stutzman and Thiele in their recent text.‡ Harrington and Mautz have carried out extensive computations of the dipole antenna impedance using triangle expansion functions and point matching.§

---

† R. S. Elliott, *Antenna Theory and Design*, Prentice-Hall, Inc., Englewood Cliffs, N.J., 1981.
  ‡ W. L. Stutzman and G. A. Thiele, *Antenna Theory and Design*, John Wiley & Sons., Inc., New York, 1981.
  § R. F. Harrington and J. Mautz, *Computations for Linear Wire Antennas and Scatterers*, Tech. Rept. No. RADC-TR-66-351, vol. II, Rome Air Development Center, Griffis Air Force Base, Rome, N.Y., DDC No. AD639745, Aug. 1966.

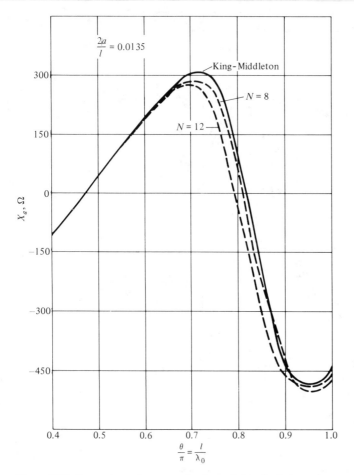

Figure 2.27 Comparison of computed values of the dipole input reactance with the results of the King-Middleton theory.

Table 2.1

N	α	$Z_a, l = 0.45\lambda_0$	$Z_a, l = 0.5\lambda_0$	$Z_a, l = 0.55\lambda_0$
8	0.0010	$57.49 - j82.02$	$79.98 + j38.82$	$111.5 + j161.80$
8	0.0100	$60.20 - j37.9$	$86.25 + j38.1$	$124.4 + j115$
8	0.0135	$60.90 - j32.2$	$88.00 + j37.66$	$128.0 + j107.9$
8	0.0500	$67.58 - j11.47$	$105.70 + j24.88$	$163.5 + j48$
12	0.0010	$57.64 - j80.6$	$80.43 + j40.34$	$112.6 + j163.86$
12	0.0135	$61.50 - j29.99$	$89.96 + j39.97$	$132.8 + j110.8$
12	0.0500	$69.35 - j11.46$	$114.50 + j18.87$	$182.3 + j24.51$

Table 2.2

l/λ_0	Z_a, $\alpha = 0.0135$, $N = 8$	Z_a, $\alpha = 0.0135$, $N = 12$	King-Middleton theory
0.45	$60.9 - j32.2$	$61.5 - j30.0$	$60.9 - j32.4$
0.50	$88.0 + j37.65$	$89.96 + j39.97$	$85.3 + j39.5$
0.60	$188.6 + j178.6$	$199.15 + j181.8$	$181 + j187$
0.75	$620.7 + j254.8$	$669.5 + j205.8$	$603 + j281$
1.00	$343.0 - j482.6$	$287.9 - j460.8$	$283 - j449$

2.12 ASYMPTOTIC BEHAVIOR OF SOLUTIONS TO HALLÉN'S INTEGRAL EQUATION

In this section we will compare the solutions of Hallén's approximate integral equation with those of the exact integral equation. The general behavior of the solutions to the approximate and exact integral equations have been investigated by many authors. A comprehensive and detailed discussion has been given by Wu.†

The model that we will examine consists of a hollow conducting tube of radius a and length $2l_0$. The walls are assumed to have negligible thickness. When the applied field acts uniformly around the antenna the induced current is entirely in the z direction, and the vector potential will have a z component only. The applied field is assumed to be highly concentrated at the center of the antenna. For the mathematical model we will assume that this applied field is constant and equal to V_g/b over the band $-b/2 \leq z \leq b/2$ at the surface of the antenna, as shown in Fig. 2.29. Since the incident field does not vary with the angle ϕ, the induced current $J(z')$ on the antenna surface is a function of z'

Table 2.3

l/λ_0	Z_a, $N = 2$, $b = 0$, $\alpha = 0.01$	Z_a, $N = 2$, $b = 2a$
0.25	$13 - j451$	$13.0 - j453$
0.50	$77.1 + j21.5$	$77 + j21.6$
0.75	$391.6 + j382.5$	$397.6 + j385.4$
1.00	$966 - j395$	$943 - j424$

† T. T. Wu, "Introduction to Linear Antennas," chap. 8 in R. E. Collin and F. J. Zucker (eds.), *Antenna Theory*, McGraw-Hill Book Company, New York, 1969. See also T. T. Wu and R. W. P. King, "The Thick Tubular Transmitting Antenna," *Radio Sci.*, vol. 2, 1967, pp. 1061–1065; R. H. Duncan and F. A. Hinckey, "Cylindrical Antenna Theory," *NBS Jour. of Res.*, vol. 64D, no. 5, Sept.–Oct. 1960, pp. 569–584; and W. A. Imbriale and P. G. Ingerson, "On Numerical Convergence of Moment Solutions of Moderately Thick Wire Antennas Using Sinusoidal Basis Functions," *IEEE Trans.*, vol. AP-21, May 1973, pp. 363–366.

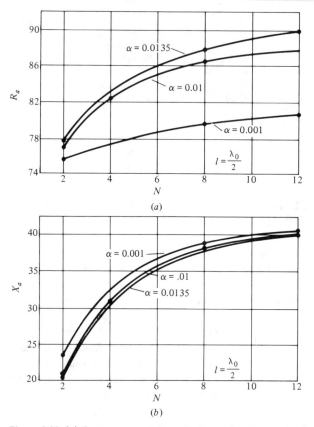

Figure 2.28 (*a*) Convergence of the radiation resistance as a function of *N*. (*b*) Convergence of the input reactance as a function of *N*.

only. $J(z')$ represents the total current on the exterior and interior surfaces. Since the field will not penetrate very far into the tube at the ends when $a \ll \lambda_0$, the total current at $z = 0$ is essentially just the current on the outer surface. Hence the input current is $2\pi a J(0)$, and the input impedance is $V_g/2\pi a J(0)$. The exact integral equation for the current $J(z')$ is the same as Eq. (2.71), except that

$$R = [(x - x')^2 + (y - y')^2 + (z - z')^2]^{1/2} = [(z - z')^2 + 2a^2 - 2a^2 \cos(\phi - \phi')]^{1/2}$$

since both x, x' and y, y' lie on the surface $r = a$. In addition, the right-hand side of Eq. (2.71) is replaced by the expression given after Eq. (2.76), when the applied field extends over a finite band of length b.

Instead of dealing directly with the integral equation we will consider the differential equation for the vector potential A_z, which is

$$\frac{1}{r}\frac{\partial}{\partial r}r\frac{\partial A_z}{\partial r} + \frac{\partial^2 A_z}{\partial z^2} + k_0^2 A_z = -\mu_0 J(z)\delta(r - a) \qquad (2.97)$$

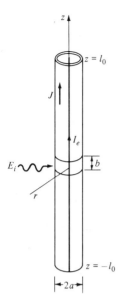

Figure 2.29 The tubular cylindrical antenna.

We can eliminate the dependence on z by taking a Fourier transform with respect to z. Thus if we let

$$\hat{J}(w) = \int_{-l_0}^{l_0} J(z)\, e^{jwz}\, dz \tag{2.98a}$$

$$\hat{A}_z(r, w) = \int_{-\infty}^{\infty} A_z(r, z)\, e^{jwz}\, dz \tag{2.98b}$$

we find that $\hat{A}_z$ is a solution of

$$\frac{1}{r}\frac{\partial}{\partial r}r\frac{\partial \hat{A}_z}{\partial r} + (k_0^2 - w^2)\hat{A}_z = -\mu_0 \hat{J}(w)\delta(r - a) \tag{2.99}$$

The solution for $\hat{A}_z(r, w)$ in the region $r < a$ must remain finite at the origin and hence is

$$\hat{A}_z(r, w) = C_1 J_0(r\sqrt{k_0^2 - w^2}) \tag{2.100a}$$

where J_0 is the Bessel function of order zero. For $r > a$ the solution must represent outward-propagating cylindrical waves and therefore must be

$$\hat{A}_z(r, w) = C_2 H_0^2(r\sqrt{k_0^2 - w^2}) \tag{2.100b}$$

where H_0^2 is the Hankel function of the second kind. The constants C_1 and C_2 are determined by the conditions that $\hat{A}_z$ is continuous at $r = a$ and that the scattered magnetic field is discontinuous by an amount equal to the current density at $r = a$; thus

$$\hat{H}_\phi(r, w)\Big|_{a_-}^{a_+} = \hat{J}(w) = \frac{1}{\mu_0}\frac{\partial \hat{A}_z(r, w)}{\partial r}\Big|_{a_-}^{a_+}$$

It is readily found, upon using the Wronskian relationship,

$$J_0(x)\frac{dH_0^2(x)}{dx} - H_0^2(x)\frac{dJ_0(x)}{dx} = -\frac{2j}{\pi x}$$

that the solution for $\hat{A}_z(r, w)$ is

$$\hat{A}_z(r, w) = -j\frac{\mu_0}{4}2\pi a\hat{J}(w)J_0(r_<\sqrt{k_0^2 - w^2})H_0^2(r_>\sqrt{k_0^2 - w^2}) \quad (2.101)$$

where $r_<$ is the smaller of r, a and $r_>$ is the greater of r, a. We can express $\hat{J}(w)$ in terms of $\hat{A}_z(a, w)$ as follows:

$$2\pi a\hat{J}(w) = \frac{4j\hat{A}_z(a, w)}{\mu_0 J_0(a\sqrt{k_0^2 - w^2})H_0^2(a\sqrt{k_0^2 - w^2})} \quad (2.102)$$

The approximate integral equation is obtained when the total antenna current $2\pi aJ(z')$ is assumed to be concentrated on the z axis. Instead of making this assumption we will look for an *equivalent line current* $I_e(z')$ that will produce the same vector potential function A_z at $r = a$. The relationship between I_e and the total antenna current $2\pi aJ = I$ can then be established. In the Fourier transform domain it is readily found that for the equivalent line current we obtain

$$\hat{I}_e(w) = \frac{4j\hat{A}_z(a, w)}{\mu_0 H_0^2(a\sqrt{k_0^2 - w^2})} \quad (2.103)$$

This result may be obtained by replacing $2\pi a\hat{J}$ by $\hat{I}_e$ in Eq. (2.101) and then letting a equal zero, which makes the J_0 function equal to unity. A comparison of Eqs. (2.102) and (2.103) shows that

$$\hat{I}_e(w) = 2\pi a\hat{J}(w)J_0(a\sqrt{k_0^2 - w^2}) \quad (2.104)$$

For $a \ll \lambda_0$ and $|w| \le k_0$ the J_0 function is very nearly equal to unity. For these values of w we see that $\hat{I}_e(w) = 2\pi a\hat{J}(w)$, and hence the low spatial-frequency content of the equivalent line current is the same as for the total antenna current. On the other hand when w is real and large we have $(k_0^2 - w^2)^{1/2} \approx -j|w|$ and by using the asymptotic formula for J_0, that is,

$$J_0(a\sqrt{k_0^2 - w^2}) \approx J_0(-j|w|a)$$

$$\sim \sqrt{\frac{-2}{\pi j|w|a}}\cos\left(-j|w|a - \frac{\pi}{4}\right)$$

$$\sim \sqrt{\frac{1}{2\pi|w|a}}e^{|w|a}$$

we find that the asymptotic behavior of $\hat{I}_e(w)$ for large w is

$$\hat{I}_e(w) = \frac{e^{|w|a}}{\sqrt{2\pi|w|a}} \, 2\pi a \hat{J}(w) \qquad (2.105)$$

Consequently, the high spatial-frequency content of the equivalent line current grows exponentially. This is the *fundamental reason* why the approximate integral equation does not have a solution.

A line current that varies rapidly with z (large w) produces a field that rapidly decays exponentially in the radial direction. Thus if the high spatial-frequency components of the field are to make a significant contribution on the surface $r = a$, the corresponding line current must have exponentially growing high spatial-frequency components.

The antenna current $J(z)$ can be expanded in a Fourier series of the form

$$J(z) = \sum_{n=1,3,\ldots}^{\infty} J_n \cos \frac{n\pi z}{2l_0} \qquad (2.106a)$$

The equivalent line source has a similar expansion

$$I_e(z) = \sum_{n=1,3,\ldots}^{\infty} I_{en} \cos \frac{n\pi z}{2l_0} \qquad (2.106b)$$

The Fourier series coefficients J_n and I_{en} can be related to the sample values of the corresponding Fourier transforms at the points $w = n\pi/2l_0$, as we show below.

The Fourier transform of Eq. (2.106a) is

$$\hat{J}(w) = \sum_{n=1,3,\ldots}^{\infty} J_n \int_{-l_0}^{l_0} e^{jwz} \cos \frac{n\pi z}{2l_0} \, dz$$

$$= \sum_{n=1,3,\ldots}^{\infty} J_n \left[\frac{\sin(w + n\pi/2l_0)l_0}{w + n\pi/2l_0} + \frac{\sin(w - n\pi/2l_0)l_0}{w - n\pi/2l_0} \right]$$

If we now let w approach $m\pi/2l_0$, where m is an odd integer, then every term in the sum vanishes except the term $n = m$ in the second series which gives

$$l_0 J_m = \hat{J}\left(\frac{m\pi}{2l_0}\right) \qquad (2.107a)$$

and is the desired result. In a similar way we find that

$$l_0 I_{em} = \hat{I}_e\left(\frac{m\pi}{2l_0}\right) \qquad (2.107b)$$

It is now seen that the Fourier series coefficients are also related by the expressions (2.104) and (2.105), that is,

$$I_{en} = 2\pi a J_n J_0[a\sqrt{k_0^2 - (n\pi/2l_0)^2}] \qquad (2.108a)$$

$$I_{en} \sim 2\pi a J_n \frac{e^{n\pi a/2l_0}}{\sqrt{n\pi^2 a/l_0}} \qquad n \text{ large} \qquad (2.108b)$$

The Fourier coefficients for the high-order harmonics of the equivalent line current must grow exponentially. This exponential growth takes over when $n\pi a/2l_0$ is of order 2, that is, when $n > 4l_0/\pi a$. For a thin antenna with $l_0/a = 100$, this growth manifests itself when n becomes larger than about $400/\pi$ or 130. For a thick antenna with $l_0/a = 10$, the exponential growth would show up for n greater than 13.

The above result shows quite clearly why approximate solutions to the approximate integral equation, which is really the integral equation for the equivalent line source, are often very good. As long as the antenna current can be approximated by a finite Fourier series with terms up to n of order $4l_0/\pi a$, then the corresponding equivalent line current has the same Fourier series. However, if the solution to the approximate integral equation is carried out to a higher order of accuracy than this, the solution will ultimately diverge since the Fourier coefficients for the equivalent line source must grow exponentially for large n. For thin antennas as many as 100 harmonics or more can be used, so the approximate solutions to the approximate integral equation for thin antennas are generally very good. For a thick antenna the Fourier coefficients begin to grow exponentially for much smaller values of n, and thus the approximate solutions may not be very accurate at all. However, we may still determine the I_{en} for a thick antenna from solutions of the approximate integral equation and then use Eq. (2.108a) to find the Fourier coefficients of the actual antenna current. The antenna input impedance is then given by

$$Z_a \approx \frac{V_g}{\displaystyle\sum_{n=1,3,\dots}^{N} 2\pi a J_n} = \frac{V_g}{\displaystyle\sum_{n=1,3,\dots}^{N} I_{en}/J_0[a\sqrt{k_0^2 - (n\pi/2l_0)^2}]} \qquad (2.109)$$

It is also possible to establish the asymptotic behavior of the Fourier coefficients J_n for large n from a knowledge of the behavior of the applied electric field at the input region and that of the scattered electric field at the two edges $z = \pm l_0$, $r = a$.

The scattered electric field component along z is given by

$$j\omega\epsilon_0\mu_0 E_z(r, z) = \left(k_0^2 + \frac{\partial^2}{\partial z^2}\right)A_z(r, z) \qquad (2.110a)$$

The Fourier transform of this equation is

$$j\omega\epsilon_0\mu_0 \hat{E}_z(r, w) = (k_0^2 - w^2)\hat{A}_z(r, w) \qquad (2.110b)$$

At $r = a$ and $|z| \le l_0$ the scattered field must cancel the applied field E_i. For $|z| \ge l_0$ let the scattered electric field at $r = a$ be $\psi(z)$. When z approaches $\pm l_0$, $r = a$, the edge condition requires that $\psi \sim (z^2 - l_0^2)^{-1/2}$.† As a result the Fourier transform $\hat{\psi}(w)$ behaves like $w^{-1/2}$ for large values of w. In the Fourier

---

† R. E. Collin, *Field Theory of Guided Waves*, McGraw-Hill Book Company, New York, 1960, pp. 18, 421.

transform domain the boundary condition on the scattered electric field $\hat{E}_z(a, w)$ at the antenna surface and on the surface $r = a$, $|z| \geq l_0$ becomes

$$\hat{E}_z(a, w) = -\hat{E}_i(w) + \hat{\psi}(w) \qquad (2.111)$$

With this condition we can use Eq. (2.110b) to express $\hat{J}(w)$ in Eq. (2.102) as follows:

$$2\pi a \hat{J}(w) = 4k_0 Y_0 \frac{\hat{E}_i(w) - \hat{\psi}(w)}{(k_0^2 - w^2)J_0(a\sqrt{k_0^2 - w^2})H_0^2(a\sqrt{k_0^2 - w^2})} \qquad (2.112)$$

For w real and large, the asymptotic behavior is

$$2\pi a \hat{J}(w) \sim -j4k_0 a \pi Y_0 \frac{\hat{E}_i(w) - Kw^{-1/2}}{|w|} \qquad (2.113)$$

where K is a suitable constant. When $E_i(z)$ is a constant V_g/b over the band $-b/2 \leq z \leq b/2$, its Fourier transform is

$$\hat{E}_i(w) = \frac{V_g \sin(wb/2)}{wb/2}$$

For this case the Fourier coefficients for large n behave like

$$J_n \sim \frac{-4jk_0 Y_0}{\pi} \left[\frac{V_g \sin(n\pi b/4l_0)}{n(n\pi b/4l_0)} - \frac{K}{n^{3/2}} \left(\frac{2l_0}{\pi} \right)^{1/2} \right] \qquad (2.114)$$

The Fourier series in this case is uniformly convergent since the J_n decrease faster than $1/n$.

If the applied field is a delta function $V_g \delta(z)$ with a Fourier transform V_g, the first Fourier series arising from Eq. (2.113) would give a contribution $J_1(z)$ to $J(z)$ that behaves asymptotically like

$$2\pi a J_1(z) \sim j8k_0 a Y_0 V_g \sum_{n=1,3,\dots}^{\infty} \frac{\cos n\pi z/2l_0}{n}$$

The series may be summed to give†

$$2\pi a J_1(z) \sim -j4k_0 a Y_0 V_g \ln \tan \frac{\pi z}{4l_0} \qquad (2.115)$$

From this result we find that for a delta-function applied field the total antenna input current must grow logarithmically at the input. Hence even the exact integral equation cannot yield a finite solution for the input impedance for a delta-function applied field.

It is interesting to note that for an applied constant field over a band of length b [$\sin(wb/2)$]/$(wb/2)$ does not depart much from unity before wb is of order π which corresponds to n of order $2l_0/b$. When b equals the diameter $2a$,

† Ibid., p. 580.

this occurs for $n > l_0/a$. It follows that the Fourier series coefficients J_n for a delta-function applied field are essentially the same as those for a uniform applied field over a band of length $2a$ for the harmonics up to order $n = l_0/a$, which is a large number for a thin antenna. It is for this reason that approximate solutions using a delta-function applied field are satisfactory as long as only low-order Fourier coefficients up to n of order l_0/a give a good approximation for the antenna current. The logarithmic growth in the input current begins for values of n in the same range as the exponential growth of the Fourier coefficients for the equivalent line source begins.

On the basis of the analysis given above, the qualitative behavior of the equivalent line source current and the total antenna current $I = 2\pi aJ$ at the input, as a function of the number of terms used in the Fourier series expansion, can be expected to be as shown in Fig. 2.30. Initially there is a region of rapid convergence as the number of harmonics used is increased. This is followed by a stable region in which the input current changes very slowly and is nearly equal to the converged result. As the number of harmonics is increased beyond $n = 4l_0/\pi a$, the Fourier coefficients for the equivalent line source current will begin to grow exponentially. If the applied field is a delta function the logarithmic growth in the actual antenna current will also begin at this point. For a thin antenna the stable region is quite wide, and this accounts for the success of the approximate solutions to the approximate integral equation. For a thick antenna the stable region is very narrow or may not exist. Thus for a thick antenna the delta-function applied field should be avoided. The approximate integral equation may be used, provided the Fourier coefficients are corrected as explained earlier.

For a solid cylindrical antenna, the edge condition requires that $\psi(z)$ behave like $(z^2 - l_0^2)^{-1/3}$ at $z = \pm l_0$, $r = a$, in which case $\hat{\psi}(w)$ behaves like $w^{-2/3}$ for large w. The second Fourier series in Eq. (2.114) will now have coefficients that vary, like $n^{-5/3}$. For the solid antenna the radial current on the caps must be included to obtain the correct edge behavior. The axial current also does not

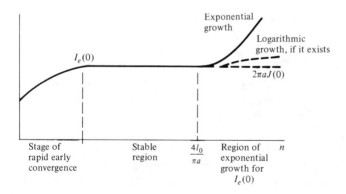

Figure 2.30 Qualitative behavior of the equivalent line current $I_e(0)$ and the total antenna current $2\pi aJ(0)$ as a function of the number of harmonics used in the Fourier series expansion.

have to vanish at $z = \pm l_0$ but may flow over the edge onto the end caps. A constant z-directed current at $z = l_0$ makes E_z behave like $(l_0 - z)^{-1}$ near the edge, but this singularity is cancelled by the finite radial current at $r = a$ on the end cap.† For a thin antenna the current can be assumed to be zero at $z = \pm l_0$, with negligible error.

2.13 MUTUAL IMPEDANCE

When two dipole antennas are located in close proximity to each other, the current distribution on one is affected by the field radiated from the other one. In order to determine the current distributions, and from these the self-impedance and the mutual impedance, a pair of coupled integral equations must be solved. In this section we will provide an introductory treatment of the mutual impedance problem.

Figure 2.31 shows two parallel dipoles of radius a and lengths $2l_1$ and $2l_2$. They are separated by a perpendicular distance d and are driven by delta-function applied fields $V_1\delta(z_1)$ and $V_2\delta(z_2)$, respectively. The coordinates z_1' and z_2' measure positions along the axis of each dipole, while z_1 and z_2 are positions along the surface of each respective dipole.

Let $A_{11}(z_1)$ be the vector potential along z_1 due to the current $I_1(z_1')$ and let $A_{12}(z_1)$ be the vector potential along z_1 due to the current $I_2(z_2')$. The scattered electric field along the z direction and on the surface of dipole 1 is then given

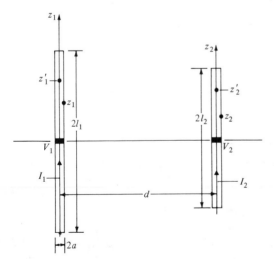

Figure 2.31 Two parallel dipole antennas with mutual coupling.

† R. E. Collin, "Equivalent Line Current for Cylindrical Antennas and Its Asymptotic Behavior," *IEEE Trans.*, vol. AP-32, Feb. 1984, pp. 200–204.

by

$$\left(k_0^2 + \frac{\partial^2}{\partial z_1^2}\right)[A_{11}(z_1) + A_{12}(z_1)] = j\omega\epsilon_0\mu_0 E_1(z_1)$$

$$= -j\omega\epsilon_0\mu_0 V_1\delta(z_1) \qquad (2.116a)$$

where the last equality comes from the boundary condition that must hold. On the surface of dipole 2 we must have a similar equation; thus

$$\left(k_0^2 + \frac{\partial^2}{\partial z_2^2}\right)[A_{21}(z_2) + A_{22}(z_2)] = j\omega\epsilon_0\mu_0 E_2(z_2)$$

$$= -j\omega\epsilon_0\mu_0 V_2\delta(z_2) \qquad (2.116b)$$

This pair of equations may be solved, or integrated, in the same manner as Hallén's equation was derived and gives

$$A_{11}(z_1) + A_{12}(z_1) = \frac{-jk_0 Y_0\mu_0}{2} V_1 \sin k_0|z_1| + C_1 \cos k_0 z_1 \qquad (2.117a)$$

A similar equation holds on the surface of dipole 2, that is,

$$A_{21}(z_2) + A_{22}(z_2) = \frac{-jk_0 Y_0\mu_0}{2} V_2 \sin k_0|z_2| + C_2 \cos k_0 z_2 \qquad (2.117b)$$

The constants C_1 and C_2 must be found such that $I_1(\pm l_1) = I_2(\pm l_2) = 0$. The vector potential functions are given by

$$A_{ij}(z_i) = \frac{\mu_0}{4\pi}\int_{-l_j}^{l_j} \frac{e^{-jk_0 R_{ij}}}{R_{ij}} I_j(z_j')\,dz_j' \qquad i,j = 1,2 \qquad (2.118)$$

where

$$R_{11} = [(z_1 - z_1')^2 + a^2]^{1/2}$$
$$R_{12} = [(z_1 - z_2')^2 + d^2]^{1/2}$$
$$R_{21} = [(z_2 - z_1')^2 + d^2]^{1/2}$$
$$R_{22} = [(z_2 - z_2')^2 + a^2]^{1/2}$$

The approximation of placing the total antenna current on the axis for the purpose of evaluating the vector potential has been made. This approximation is valid for thin antennas, as explained in Sec. 2.12. We have also approximated the perpendicular distance from the axis of one dipole to the surface of the other dipole by d in R_{12} and R_{21}.

In principle, the pair of integral equations given in Eq. (2.117) can be solved, using the method of moments, in a manner similar to that for a single dipole. The final result can be expressed in the form

$$V_1 = I_1(0)Z_{11} + I_2(0)Z_{12}$$
$$V_2 = I_1(0)Z_{21} + I_2(0)Z_{22} \qquad (2.119)$$

The reciprocity principle requires that $Z_{21} = Z_{12}$. In general the self-impedances Z_{11} and Z_{22} are somewhat different from the corresponding input impedances of the isolated dipoles. This is caused by the interaction between the two dipoles, even if one dipole is open-circuited at the center, since this does not force the current to be zero everywhere along the dipole even though it is zero at the center. Z_{12} is the mutual impedance.

For thin dipoles around $\lambda_0/2$ long and spaced by $\lambda_0/5$ or more, the self-impedances can be approximated by the isolated-dipole input impedances. An approximate expression for the mutual impedance Z_{12} can be obtained directly from Eq. (2.116), as will be shown below.

The reciprocity principle, which is derived in Chap. 5, shows that the interaction of the electric field E_{z21} radiated by $I_1(z_1)$ with $I_2(z_2)$ must equal the interaction of the field E_{z12} radiated by $I_2(z_2)$ with $I_1(z_1)$, that is,

$$\int_{-l_2}^{l_2} E_{z21}(z_2)I_2(z_2)\,dz_2 = \int_{-l_1}^{l_1} E_{z12}(z_1)I_1(z_1)\,dz_1$$

In terms of the vector potential functions we have

$$\int_{-l_2}^{l_2} I_2(z_2)\left(k_0^2 + \frac{\partial^2}{\partial z_2^2}\right)A_{21}(z_2)\,dz_2 = \int_{-l_1}^{l_1} I_1(z_1)\left(k_0^2 + \frac{\partial^2}{\partial z_1^2}\right)A_{12}(z_1)\,dz_1$$

This result suggests that we should multiply Eq. (2.116a) by $I_1(z_1)$ and integrate over z_1, and similarly multiply Eq. (2.116b) by $I_2(z_2)$ and integrate over z_2. The result of this operation on Eq. (2.116a) gives

$$-jk_0 Y_0 V_1 \int_{-l_1}^{l_1} \frac{I_1(z_1)}{I_1(0)} \delta(z_1)\,dz_1 = -jk_0 Y_0 V_1$$

$$= I_1(0) \int_{-l_1}^{l_1}\int_{-l_1}^{l_1} \frac{I_1(z_1)I_1(z_1')}{I_1(0)I_1(0)} \left(k_0^2 + \frac{\partial^2}{\partial z_1^2}\right) \frac{e^{-jk_0 R_{11}}}{4\pi R_{11}}\,dz_1'\,dz_1$$

$$+ I_2(0) \int_{-l_1}^{l_1}\int_{-l_2}^{l_2} \frac{I_1(z_1)I_2(z_2')}{I_1(0)I_2(0)} \left(k_0^2 + \frac{\partial^2}{\partial z_1^2}\right) \frac{e^{-jk_0 R_{12}}}{4\pi R_{12}}\,dz_2'\,dz_1$$

$$(2.120)$$

A similar equation is obtained from Eq. (2.116b), with the same mutual coupling term since $R_{21} = R_{12}$. We now assume that the normalized current distributions $I_1(z_1)/I_1(0)$ and $I_2(z_2)/I_2(0)$ are not changed by interaction between the dipoles; that is, $I_2(z_2)/I_2(0)$ is independent of $I_1(0)$ and vice versa. With this assumption, the integrals in Eq. (2.120) are not dependent on the amplitudes of the input current, since the currents are normalized. Hence $I_1(0)$ and $I_2(0)$ in Eq. (2.120) can be regarded as independent variables. When we compare Eq. (2.120) with Eq. (2.119) we find that

$$Z_{12} = \frac{j}{4\pi k_0 Y_0} \int_{-l_1}^{l_1}\int_{-l_2}^{l_2} \frac{I_1(z_1)I_2(z_2)}{I_1(0)I_2(0)} \left(k_0^2 + \frac{\partial^2}{\partial z_1^2}\right) \frac{e^{-jk_0 R_{12}}}{R_{12}}\,dz_2\,dz_1 \qquad (2.121)$$

where we have dropped the prime on z_2', and

$$R_{12} = [(z_1 - z_2)^2 + d^2]^{1/2}$$

The corresponding equation that can be derived from Eq. (2.116b) would have given $Z_{21} = Z_{12}$ because $R_{12} = R_{21}$.

The mutual impedance Z_{12} is not critically dependent on the current distributions. Hence for dipoles approximately $\lambda_0/2$ long we may assume that the normalized current distributions are

$$\frac{\sin k_0(l_1 - |z_1|)}{\sin k_0 l_1} \quad \text{and} \quad \frac{\sin k_0(l_2 - |z_2|)}{\sin k_0 l_2}$$

The second term in Eq. (2.121) may be integrated by parts twice with respect to z_1. By using the relations $I_1(\pm l_1) = 0$ and

$$\frac{d}{dz_1} \sin k_0(l_1 - |z_1|) = -k_0 sgz_1 \cos k_0(l_1 - |z_1|)$$

where $sgz_1 = 1$ for $z_1 > 0$ and -1 for $z_1 < 0$, and

$$\frac{d^2}{dz_1^2} \sin k_0(l_1 - |z_1|) = -k_0^2 \sin k_0(l_1 - |z_1|) - 2k_0 \delta(z_1) \cos k_0 l_1$$

The equation for Z_{12} reduces to

$$Z_{12} = \frac{jZ_0}{4\pi \sin k_0 l_1 \sin k_0 l_2} \int_{-l_2}^{l_2} \left(\frac{e^{-jk_0 R_1}}{R_1} + \frac{e^{-jk_0 R_2}}{R_2} \right.$$
$$\left. - 2 \cos k_0 l_1 \frac{e^{-jk_0 R_0}}{R_0} \right) \sin k_0(l_2 - |z_2|) \, dz_2 \qquad (2.122)$$

where $R_1 = [(l_1 - z_2)^2 + d^2]^{1/2}$

$R_2 = [(l_1 + z_2)^2 + d^2]^{1/2}$

$R_0 = (z_2^2 + d^2)^{1/2}$

The integrals in Eq. (2.122) may be expressed in terms of cosine and sine integrals or carried out numerically.

Figure 2.32 shows typical results for $Z_{12} = R_{12} + jX_{12}$ for two parallel dipoles $\lambda_0/2$ long as a function of the spacing d. If V_2 is zero, then

$$I_2(0) = \frac{-Z_{12} I_1(0)}{Z_{22}(0)}$$

and the input impedance for dipole 1 will be

$$Z_{in,1} = \frac{V_1}{I_1(0)} = Z_{11} + \frac{Z_{12}}{Z_{22}} \frac{I_2(0)}{I_1(0)} = Z_{11} - \frac{Z_{12}^2}{Z_{22}}$$

which shows that mutual coupling can have a strong influence on the input impedance for closely spaced dipoles, since Z_{12} is then quite large.

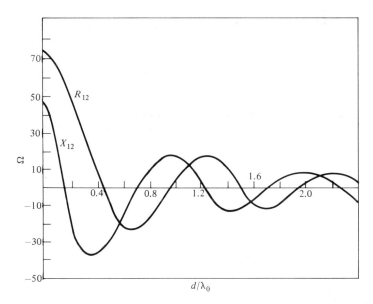

Figure 2.32 Variation of mutual impedance between two parallel dipoles $\lambda_0/2$ long as a function of the separation d/λ_0.

A more complete treatment of the mutual coupling problem has been given by King,† who finds that for a two-element array of dipoles λ_0 long the self-admittance differs by 10 to 20 percent from that of an isolated dipole for spacings in the range $0.2\lambda_0$ to $0.8\lambda_0$. Thus the dipole interaction in changing the current distribution is not entirely negligible.

PROBLEMS

2.1 If magnetic currents $\mathbf{J}_m$ and magnetic charge ρ_m existed, Maxwell's equations would be

$$\nabla \times \mathbf{E} = -j\omega \mathbf{B} - \mathbf{J}_m \qquad \nabla \times \mathbf{H} = j\omega \mathbf{D}$$

$$\nabla \cdot \mathbf{B} = \rho_m \qquad \nabla \cdot \mathbf{D} = 0 \qquad \nabla \cdot \mathbf{J}_m = -j\omega\rho_m$$

Let $\mathbf{D} = -\nabla \times \mathbf{A}_m$ and follow the general procedure of Sec. 2.2 to show that the magnetic vector potential $\mathbf{A}_m$ and magnetic scalar potential Φ_m satisfy the equations

$$(\nabla^2 + k_0^2)\mathbf{A}_m = -\epsilon_0 \mathbf{J}_m$$

$$(\nabla^2 + k_0^2)\Phi_m = -\frac{\rho_m}{\mu_0}$$

and that

$$\mathbf{H} = -j\omega \mathbf{A}_m + \frac{\nabla\nabla \cdot \mathbf{A}_m}{j\omega\mu_0\epsilon_0}$$

† R. W. P. King, "Cylindrical Antennas and Arrays," op. cit.

In antenna theory these relationships are useful whenever the field can be expressed as that from equivalent magnetic sources. In Chap. 4 the results are used in connection with radiation from aperture-type antennas.

2.2 On a dipole antenna of total length l the current distribution is $I_0 \sin k_0(|z| - l/2)/\sin(k_0 l/2)$. When $l \leq 0.2\lambda_0$ this can be approximated by $I = I_0(1 - 2|z|/l)$, as shown in Fig. P2.2. Find the radiated electric field, the radiated power, and the radiation resistance. Note that $k_0 l/2$ is small enough that $\cos(k_0 z' \cos \theta) \approx 1$, an approximation that may be used to simplify the integration. Show that the radiation resistance is proportional to the square of the area under the current-distribution curve.

2.3 Find the radiation field from a full-wave dipole antenna, as shown in Fig. P2.3, with current $I = I_0|\sin k_0 z|$, $-\lambda_0/2 \leq z \leq \lambda_0/2$. Sketch the radiation pattern.

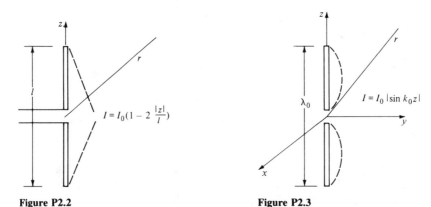

$$I = I_0\left(1 - 2\,\frac{|z|}{l}\right)$$

$$I = I_0\,|\sin k_0 z|$$

Figure P2.2   **Figure P2.3**

2.4 Find the radiation field, total radiated power, and radiation resistance for the quarter-wave antenna above an infinite ground plane, as shown in Fig. P2.4. The current on the antenna is $I = I_0 \cos k_0 z$. *Hint:* By image theory the field above the ground plane is the same as for the half-wave antenna. The field below the ground plane is zero.

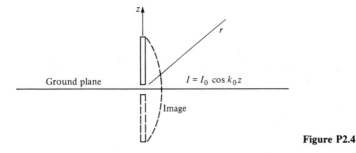

Ground plane

$I = I_0 \cos k_0 z$

Image

Figure P2.4

2.5 A small coil of radius $r_0 = 5$ cm and with $N = 10$ turns is used as a receiving antenna. This antenna is located 10 km away from a half-wave dipole and oriented for maximum magnetic flux penetration, as shown in Fig. P2.5. Find the induced open-circuit voltage $-j\omega B_\phi N(\pi r_0^2)$ in the loop when the input power to the half-wave dipole antenna is 5 W. The frequency of operation is 27 MHz.

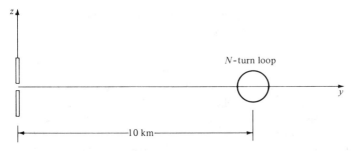

Figure P2.5

2.6 Figure P2.6 shows a small electric dipole antenna located along the bisector of a large 90° corner reflector. Use image theory to find the resultant radiated electric field in the xy plane. Sketch the radiation pattern. *Hint*: Each dipole will radiate the same field as a dipole at the origin, except for a difference in phase according to the factor $e^{jk_0\mathbf{a}_r \cdot \mathbf{r}_i}$, where $\mathbf{r}_i$ is the position vector of the ith dipole. Note that the sign of each image source must also be taken into account. The scalar products between unit vectors in rectangular and spherical coordinates are given in App. I.

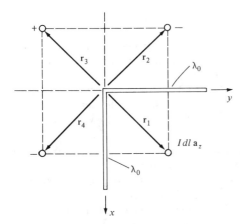

Figure P2.6

2.7 A plane wave $\mathbf{E} = E_0 \mathbf{a}_z e^{jk_0 x}$ is incident on a small dielectric sphere at the origin, as shown in Fig. P2.7. The sphere has a radius $r_0 \ll \lambda_0$ and permittivity ϵ. Since $r_0 \ll \lambda_0$ the sphere is essentially immersed in a constant uniform field $E_0 \mathbf{a}_z$. The induced dielectric polarization in the sphere is the same as in the static case, so the polarization density is

$$p = 3\left(\frac{\epsilon - \epsilon_0}{\epsilon + 2\epsilon_0}\right)\epsilon_0 E_0$$

The total induced dipole moment is

$$4\pi r_0^3 \left(\frac{\epsilon - \epsilon_0}{\epsilon + 2\epsilon_0}\right)\epsilon_0 E_0 \mathbf{a}_z = \mathbf{P}$$

Find the far-zone field radiated by this equivalent electric dipole. This is the field scattered by the dielectric sphere. Find the total scattered power. The scattering cross section σ_s is defined as the total scattered power divided by the incident power per unit area. Show that the scattering cross section is given by

$$\sigma_s = \frac{128}{3} \pi^4 (\pi r_0^2) \left(\frac{\epsilon - \epsilon_0}{\epsilon + 2\epsilon_0}\right)^2 \left(\frac{r_0}{\lambda_0}\right)^4$$

Note that the scattering cross section varies as λ_0^{-4}, which is known as the *Rayleigh scattering law*. Can you use this law to explain why the sky appears blue and why a sunset appears red? *Hint*: Since the charge at the end of a current filament is given by $j\omega Q = I$ then $I\,dl = j\omega Q\,dl = j\omega P$, where $P = Q\,dl$ is the dipole moment. Thus $I\,dl$ can be replaced by $j\omega P$ in the formulas for radiation from a short current filament.

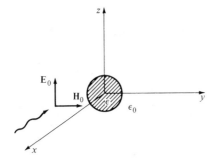

Figure P2.7

2.8 Figure 2.14 shows that a dipole antenna with length to diameter ratio $l/d = 100$ is resonant when $l = 0.458\lambda_0$. This antenna is connected to a transmission line with characteristic impedance $Z_c = 73\ \Omega$. The frequency is now increased so that at the new wavelength $\lambda_0' < \lambda_0$ the antenna length $l = 0.5\lambda_0'$ (about an 8 percent increase in frequency). By using the data from Figs. 2.13 and 2.14, find the input reflection coefficient, the VSWR, and the power reflection coefficient. At the new frequency the figures give $Z_a \approx 100 + j80\ \Omega$.

2.9 Let a small single-turn loop be located at $x = z = 0$ and $y = r_1$ and with its axis along the x direction, as in Fig. P2.9. The loop radius is r_0. A small current filament $I_d\,dl\ \mathbf{a}_z$ is located at the origin. Find the induced open-circuit voltage in the loop and denote it by V_l. When the current in the loop is I_l find the electric field impressed along the current filament. (Note that the current filament is in the far-zone region and oriented to receive the maximum electric field radiated by the loop.) By multiplying the impressed electric field by dl the open-circuit induced voltage V_d along the current filament is obtained. Show that $V_d I_d = V_l I_l$, which is an example of the reciprocity theorem applied to antennas.

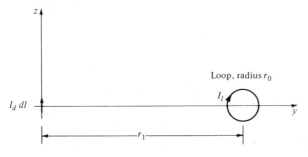

Figure P2.9

2.10 Use the reciprocity relation obtained in Prob. 2.9 to derive the expression for the electric field radiated by a small loop antenna located at the origin. *Hint*: Consider electric dipoles located at various positions in space and with orientations that produce a maximum magnetic flux in the loop.

2.11 Show that a Green's function that satisfies Eq. (2.73) and vanishes at $z' = \pm l_0$ is

$$G = -\frac{\sin k_0(z_> - l_0) \sin k_0(z_< + l_0)}{k_0 \sin 2k_0 l_0}$$

where $z_> = z$ for $z > z'$ and z' for $z' > z$, and $z_< = z$ for $z < z'$ and z' for $z' < z$; that is, $z_>$ is the greater of z and z' and $z_<$ is the smaller of z and z'. *Hint*: Assume that $G = C_1 \sin k_0(z - l_0)$, $z > z'$ and $G = C_2 \sin k_0(z + l_0)$, $z < z'$. At $z = z'$ make G continuous and make the first derivative be discontinuous by amount -1.

2.12 When the Green's function in Prob. 2.11 is used to integrate Pocklington's equation, show that the resultant Hallén's equation is

$$Q(z) = -j\frac{Y_0 V_g}{2} \sin k_0 |z| + \frac{jY_0 V_g}{2} \tan k_0 l_0 \cos k_0 z + Q(l_0)\frac{\cos k_0 z}{\cos k_0 l_0}$$

Hint: Note that $Q(-l_0) = Q(l_0)$ and that

$$\sin k_0(|z| - l_0) = \sin k_0 |z| \cos k_0 l_0 - \sin k_0 l_0 \cos k_0 z$$

$$\sin 2k_0 l_0 = 2 \cos k_0 l_0 \sin k_0 l_0$$

2.13 Let the current on a dipole antenna be $J_z(z')$ on the surface $r = a$. Show that the integral in Hallén's integral equation will then be given by

$$\frac{1}{2\pi a} \int_0^{2\pi} \int_{-l_0}^{l_0} I(z') \frac{e^{-jk_0 R}}{4\pi R} a \, d\phi' \, dz'$$

where $2\pi a J_z(z') = I(z')$

$$R^2 = (x - x')^2 + (y - y')^2 + (z - z')^2$$

$$= 2a^2 - 2a^2 \cos(\phi - \phi') + (z - z')^2$$

$$= 4a^2 \sin^2\frac{\phi - \phi'}{2} + (z - z')^2$$

In the latter expression ϕ may be set equal to zero when the applied field is independent of ϕ. When this expression is used, the resultant integral equation will have an exact solution.

2.14 Derive the expression given by Eq. (2.122) for the mutual impedance using the steps outlined in the text.

2.15 Consider the Fredholm integral equation of the first kind

$$\int_0^1 K(x, y)I(y) \, dy = f(x)$$

Use Simpson's rule with a subinterval $h = 1/N$ to carry out a numerical integration over y. By point matching at the points $x = mh$, $m = 0, 1, 2, \ldots, N$ show that the system of equations to be solved for the sample values $I_n = I(nh)$ of the unknown function $I(y)$ is

$$\frac{h}{3} \sum_{n=0}^{N} K_{mn} S_n I_n = f_m \qquad m = 0, 1, 2, \ldots, N$$

where $K_{mn} = K(mh, nh)$, $f_m = f(mh)$, and the S_n are the Simpson weights.

Show that the same system of equations is obtained if $I(y)$ is expanded in a set of subdomain or local basis functions $\Phi_n(y)$, that is,

$$I(y) = \sum_{n=0}^{N} I_n \Phi_n(y)$$

that have the property that $\Phi_n(nh) = 1$ and $\Phi_n(jh) = 0$, $j \neq n$.

2.16 The trapezoidal rule for numerical integration is

$$\int_0^1 g(x)\, dx \approx \frac{h}{2} \sum_{n=0}^{N} \bar{S}_n g_n$$

where $g_n = g(nh)$ and the weights $\bar{S}_n$ equal $1, 2, 2, 2, 2, \ldots, 2, 1$. If this integration algorithm is used, show that for the procedure described in Prob. 2.15 now

$$\frac{h}{2} \sum_{n=0}^{N} K_{mn} \bar{S}_n \bar{I}_n = f_m \qquad m = 0, 1, 2, \ldots, N$$

By comparing this system with that in Prob. 2.15, it is clear that

$$\frac{S_n I_n}{3} = \frac{\bar{S}_n \bar{I}_n}{2}$$

and consequently the two different numerical integration algorithms give significantly different solutions for the values of $I(y)$ at the sample points $y = nh$. Increasing the number of basis functions, that is, reducing h, does not change this result. Consequently, the numerical solution of the Fredholm integral equation of the first kind must be handled carefully if a valid solution is to be obtained.

2.17 Consider the Fredholm integral equation of the first kind

$$\int_0^1 K(x, y) I(y)\, dy = f(x)$$

Let $I(y)$ be approximated by a finite expansion in terms of the basis functions $\Phi_n(y)$:

$$I(y) = \sum_{n=0}^{N} I_n \Phi_n(y)$$

Use Simpson's rule with a subinterval $h = 1/J$ to obtain

$$\frac{h}{3} \sum_{n=0}^{N} I_n \sum_{j=0}^{J} K(x, jh) \Phi_n(jh) S_j = f(x)$$

Let

$$\psi_m(x) = \sum_{j=0}^{J} K(x, jh) \Phi_m(jh) S_j$$

The optimum testing functions that will give a minimum mean square error are the $\psi_m^*(x)$. Test the above equations with these and evaluate the integrals using Simpson's rule with a subinterval $H = 1/T$; show that the system of equations to determine the I_n is

$$\int_0^1 \psi_m^*(x) \left[\sum_{n=0}^N \frac{h}{3} I_n \psi_n(x) - f(x) \right] dx$$

$$= \frac{H}{3} \sum_{t=0}^T S_t \psi_m^*(tH) \left[\sum_{n=0}^N \frac{h}{3} I_n \psi_n(tH) - f(tH) \right]$$

$$= 0 \qquad m = 0, 1, 2, \ldots, N$$

Show that these equations may be expressed as

$$\sum_{n=0}^N I_n \left[\sum_{i=0}^J \sum_{j=0}^J \sum_{t=0}^T S_i S_j S_t \Phi_n(jh) \Phi_m(ih) K(tH, jh) K^*(tH, ih) \right]$$

$$- \frac{3}{h} \sum_{t=0}^T \sum_{i=0}^J S_i S_t \Phi_m(ih) f(tH) K^*(tH, ih)$$

$$= 0 \qquad m = 0, 1, 2, \ldots, N$$

The sums over i and j will contain only a few terms if the basis functions are local functions that span an interval only a few increments h in length.

2.18 As a special case of Prob. 2.17 choose a subinterval $H = 1/N$ in the numerical integration for the testing procedure. Show that the system of equations for determining the I_n has a solution determined by solving the system

$$\frac{h}{3} \sum_{n=0}^N I_n \psi_n(tH) = \frac{h}{3} \sum_{n=0}^N I_n \sum_{j=0}^J K(tH, jh) \Phi_n(jh) S_j$$

$$= f(tH) \qquad t = 0, 1, 2, \ldots, N$$

With this particular choice for the subinterval length H, the choice of testing functions has no effect on the solution for the I_n. In order that the testing functions should influence the numerical values of the I_n the number of intervals T must be greater than the number N of basis functions used.

2.19 As a further special case of Probs. 2.17 and 2.18, let the $\Phi_n(y)$ be a set of subdomain basis functions such as the triangle functions, the Lagrange polynomials, or any other set that individually span an interval $2h$ and have the property $\Phi_h(nh) = 1$, $\Phi_n(jh) = 0$, $j \neq n$. Show that the equations for determining the I_n now become (assume also that $H = h$)

$$\frac{h}{3} \sum_{n=0}^N I_n K(mh, nh) S_n = f(mh) \qquad m = 0, 1, 2, \ldots, N$$

which is independent of the particular subdomain basis functions that are used. This problem shows that the interval $2h$ used in Simpson's rule must be smaller than the span over which the subdomain basis function is nonzero if the properties of the basis functions are to influence the numerical solution.

2.20 Consider a kernel function $K(x - y)$ that has a dominant singular part that can be represented by a delta function $\delta(x - y)$, that is,

$$K(x - y) = G(x - y) + \delta(x - y)$$

Show that for this kernel the Fredholm integral equation of the first kind becomes a Fredholm integral equation of the second kind, that is,

$$I(x) + \int_0^1 G(x - y)I(y)\, dy = f(x)$$

Whenever the integral represents a small correction, the numerical solution of this equation has much better convergence properties than an integral equation of the first kind. An integral equation of the first kind does not always have a solution.

2.21 For $N = 2$ the solution of Eq. (2.95) for the antenna impedance Z_a is given by

$$Z_a = \frac{R_{10}R_{21} - R_{11}R_{20}}{R_{21}f_1 - R_{11}f_2} V_g$$

where R_{mn} is given by Eq. (2.96). Find Z_a for the case where $\alpha = 0.01$, $\theta = \pi/4$.

Answer: $R_{10} = -38.4176 - j0.07949$
$R_{21} = -2.04035 - j1.19556$
$R_{11} = 40.362 - j0.3132$
$R_{20} = -30.8172 - j0.303478$
$Z_a = 12.97 - j451$

2.22 Compute Z_a for $N = 2$, $\alpha = 0.01$, $\theta = \pi/4$ using the trapezoidal integration rule instead of Simpson's rule. (Replace $h/3$ by $h/2$ and use $S_0 = S_2 = 1$, $S_1 = 2$ in place of the weights 1, 4, 1.)

Answer: $R_{10} = -26.2275 - j0.07949$
$R_{21} = -1.020177 - j0.59778$
$R_{11} = 27.1572 - j0.1566$
$R_{20} = -21.4879 - j0.303478$
$Z_a = 12.996 - j468$

By comparing these results with those in Prob. 2.21, it is seen that Eq. (2.95) is relatively independent of the numerical integration algorithm used.

THREE

DIPOLES, ARRAYS, AND LONG-WIRE ANTENNAS

This chapter begins with further discussion on dipole antennas. The dipole antenna is similar in many respects to an open-circuited transmission line. One particular dipole antenna, the biconical antenna, is readily analyzed as a transmission line. This structure is therefore examined for the additional insight it provides into the operation of a dipole antenna. Additional topics of practical importance in connection with dipole antennas are then taken up. These include the folded dipole, which has a radiation resistance of 292.5 Ω and a broader band of operation than a conventional half-wave dipole, the short dipole antenna and the use of loading coils and of capacitive loading to improve the current distribution, and related quarter-wave antennas.

In order to produce a more concentrated beam of radiation and a larger antenna gain, several half-wave dipole antennas may be arranged in an array. Thus the basic properties of arrays are of importance and are discussed. An important principle, that of pattern multiplication, is introduced as a useful tool in array analysis. Some final topics on arrays address the problem of array synthesis to produce certain desirable radiation pattern characteristics. Special arrays, such as the frequency-independent log-periodic antenna, are also covered.

The chapter concludes with a discussion of long-wire antennas, which are useful at the lower frequencies where it is impractical to build arrays.

3.1 BICONICAL ANTENNAS

The biconical antenna is shown in Fig. 3.1 and consists of two cones with half angle θ_0. It is excited at the center, between two spherical caps, by a sinusoidal voltage source. An extensive study of the biconical antenna has been made by Schelkunoff, and the material presented here is based on that work.[†]

† S. A. Schelkunoff, *Advanced Antenna Theory*, John Wiley & Sons, Inc., New York, 1952.

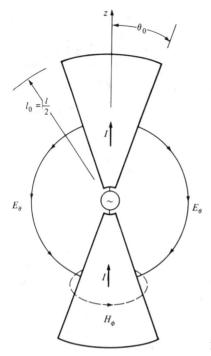

Figure 3.1 The biconical antenna.

The biconical structure will support a transverse spherical (TEM) electro-magnetic wave analogous to that on a conventional transmission line. The field pattern of the TEM mode is also shown in Fig. 3.1. The in-line orientation of the two cones in the biconical antenna is such that at $r = l_0$ ideal open-circuit conditions do not exist, even though the cones terminate at this point. In the space $r > l_0$, electromagnetic radiation is produced, and the presence of this field beyond the terminating sphere of radius l_0 results in an effective terminat-ing impedance Z_t for the biconical transmission line that is very large but not infinite, as it would be for an ideal open-circuit termination. If Z_t can be evaluated, then ordinary transmission-line theory can be used to find the input impedance at the terminals located at $r = r_0$. Of course, in practice the additional impedance, usually capacitance, introduced by the terminal con-nections to the feed transmission line will modify the value computed by considering only the biconical transmission line driven by an ideal voltage source impressed across the spherical gap of radius r_0.

In order to analyze the TEM wave on a biconical antenna we will begin with the assumptions that the TEM wave has only E_θ and H_ϕ components and that these are functions of r and θ only. It will turn out that a solution to Maxwell's equations with these restrictions can be found, so our assumptions will be justified. Obviously we are making use of the work of previous authors and known results to provide this starting point for the analysis. Without that knowledge, it is not necessarily obvious that such assumptions should be made—but we do not want to "reinvent the wheel" at this point.

With the assumptions made above, Maxwell's curl equations

$$\nabla \times \mathbf{E} = -j\omega\mu_0\mathbf{H} \qquad \nabla \times \mathbf{H} = j\omega\epsilon_0\mathbf{E}$$

reduce to the following (see App. I):

$$\frac{\mathbf{a}_\phi}{r}\frac{\partial}{\partial r}(rE_\theta) = -j\omega\mu_0 H_\phi \mathbf{a}_\phi \tag{3.1a}$$

$$\frac{\mathbf{a}_r}{r\sin\theta}\frac{\partial}{\partial\theta}(\sin\theta H_\phi) - \frac{\mathbf{a}_\theta}{r}\frac{\partial}{\partial r}(rH_\phi) = j\omega\epsilon_0 E_\theta \mathbf{a}_\theta \tag{3.1b}$$

Clearly Eq. (3.1b) is inconsistent unless the term with the factor $\mathbf{a}_r$ is zero, since we have assumed that E_r is zero. Hence we require that

$$H_\phi = \frac{Cf(r)}{\sin\theta} \tag{3.2}$$

where C is a constant and $f(r)$ is as yet an unknown function. The form (3.2) makes $\sin\theta H_\phi$ independent of θ, as required in order to make the factor multiplied by $\mathbf{a}_r$ in Eq. (3.1b) vanish. By using Eq. (3.2) we are able to rewrite Eq. (3.1a) and (3.1b) as follows:

$$\frac{\partial}{\partial r}(rE_\theta) = -j\omega\mu_0\frac{Crf(r)}{\sin\theta} \tag{3.3a}$$

$$C\frac{\partial}{\partial r}\frac{rf(r)}{\sin\theta} = -j\omega\epsilon_0 rE_\theta \tag{3.3b}$$

We now differentiate Eq. (3.3a) with respect to r and substitute from Eq. (3.3b) on the right-hand side; thus

$$\frac{\partial^2}{\partial r^2}(rE_\theta) = -k_0^2 rE_\theta \tag{3.4}$$

This simple harmonic motion equation has the solution

$$rE_\theta = C_1(\theta)\,e^{-jk_0 r} + C_2(\theta)\,e^{jk_0 r}$$

where C_1 and C_2 are functions of θ only. Now we note that the right-hand side of Eq. (3.3a) varies as $1/\sin\theta$, so E_θ must then also have this same dependence on θ. Hence our fundamental solution for E_θ is

$$E_\theta = C^+\frac{e^{-jk_0 r}}{r\sin\theta} + C^-\frac{e^{jk_0 r}}{r\sin\theta} \tag{3.5}$$

which consists of radially outward- and inward-propagating spherical waves with amplitudes C^+ and C^-. By using Eq. (3.1a) we find that H_ϕ is given by

$$H_\phi = C^+ Y_0 \frac{e^{-jk_0 r}}{r \sin \theta} - C^- Y_0 \frac{e^{jk_0 r}}{r \sin \theta} \tag{3.6}$$

where $Y_0 = (\epsilon_0/\mu_0)^{1/2}$ is the intrinsic admittance of free space. We see that H_ϕ also consists of a pair of spherical waves. The reversal in sign in the second term reflects the reversal in direction of power flow, as given by $\frac{1}{2}\mathrm{Re}\, E_\theta H_\phi^*$ in the radial direction. The inward-propagating wave must have its Poynting vector in the $-\mathbf{a}_r$ direction.

The field found above is a TEM wave, since both $\mathbf{E}$ and $\mathbf{H}$ lie on spherical surfaces, that is, are transverse to the radial coordinate. The voltage between the cones is given by the line integral of E_θ from θ_0 to $\pi - \theta_0$ and is

$$V = \left(C^+ \frac{e^{-jk_0 r}}{r} + C^- \frac{e^{jk_0 r}}{r} \right) \int_{\theta_0}^{\pi - \theta_0} \frac{r\, d\theta}{\sin \theta}$$

$$= (C^+ e^{-jk_0 r} + C^- e^{jk_0 r}) \ln \tan \frac{\theta}{2} \Big|_{\theta_0}^{\pi - \theta_0}$$

$$= V^+ e^{-jk_0 r} + V^- e^{jk_0 r} \tag{3.7}$$

where we have used $\ln \tan[(\pi - \theta_0)/2] = \ln \cot(\theta_0/2)$ and $-\ln \tan(\theta_0/2) = \ln \cot(\theta_0/2)$ and put $2C^\pm \ln \cot(\theta_0/2)$ equal to $V^\pm$. Equation (3.7) expresses the total voltage as the sum of two voltage waves.

The current density on the cones is related to H_ϕ by $\mathbf{J}_s = \mathbf{a}_\theta \times \mathbf{H}$ on the upper cone and by $-\mathbf{a}_\theta \times \mathbf{H}$ on the lower cone. Thus we find that

$$J_s = C^+ Y_0 \frac{e^{-jk_0 r}}{r \sin \theta_0} - C^- Y_0 \frac{e^{jk_0 r}}{r \sin \theta_0}$$

on both cones, and the direction of J_s is along the z direction. The total current on each cone equals I with $I = 2\pi r \sin \theta_0 J_s$, since the radius of the cross section is $r \sin \theta_0$. We can now write, after substituting for C^+ and C^-,

$$I = I^+ e^{-jk_0 r} - I^- e^{jk_0 r} = Y_c(V^+ e^{-jk_0 r} - V^- e^{jk_0 r}) \tag{3.8}$$

for the current waves and where the characteristic admittance of the biconical transmission line is given by

$$Y_c = \frac{\pi Y_0}{\ln \cot \theta_0/2} \tag{3.9}$$

The characteristic impedance is the reciprocal of Y_c and is given by

$$Z_c = \frac{Z_0}{\pi} \ln \cot \frac{\theta_0}{2} = 120 \ln \cot \frac{\theta_0}{2} \tag{3.10}$$

When θ_0 is small, say less than 0.5, then

$$Z_c \approx \frac{Z_0}{\pi} (\ln 2 - \ln \theta_0) = 120(\ln 2 - \ln \theta_0) \tag{3.11}$$

If the surface at $r = l_0$ is an ideal open circuit then at $r = l_0$ the current I will be zero, which requires that $V^- e^{jk_0l_0} = V^+ e^{-jk_0l_0}$. In this case

$$I = V^+ Y_c (e^{-jk_0r} - e^{-2jk_0l_0+jk_0r})$$
$$= 2jV^+ Y_c e^{-jk_0l_0} \sin k_0(l_0 - r) \qquad (3.12)$$

Because of the termination of the cones at $r = l_0$, a perturbing field is excited in the region $r < l_0$ corresponding to other non-TEM-type modes as well as a radiated field in the region $r > l_0$. The currents induced on the cone by all of the modes is such that the TEM-mode current by itself does not need to vanish. The effect this has on the TEM mode is to produce an effective terminating impedance Z_t at $r = l_0$ that is different from an ideal open circuit. The additional modes excited at $r = l_0$ decay in amplitude as r decreases, so that at the input where $r = r_0$ they produce only a small effect. Consequently, the antenna input impedance is given quite closely by the usual transmission-line formula (see App. II):

$$Z_a = Z_c \frac{Z_t + jZ_c \tan k_0l_0}{Z_c + jZ_t \tan k_0l_0} \qquad (3.13)$$

which for $l_0 = \lambda_0/4$, corresponding to a half-wave dipole, is

$$Z_a = \frac{Z_c^2}{Z_t} = \frac{Z_0^2}{\pi^2 Z_t} \left(\ln \cot \frac{\theta_0}{2} \right)^2 \qquad (3.14)$$

When the cone half-angle θ_0 is very small, the characteristic impedance Z_c becomes very large. In his book Schelkunoff shows that the terminating impedance Z_t becomes large also as θ_0 approaches zero and, in actual fact, increases in value faster than the logarithmic growth of Z_c. Consequently, in the limit of an infinitely thin cone, an ideal open-circuit condition is achieved, and the current distribution becomes a pure sinusoidal standing wave. Thus the biconical antenna theory provides a theoretical basis for assuming a sinusoidal current distribution on thin-wire antennas.

The cylindrical dipole antenna shown in Fig. 3.2 is quite similar to the thin biconical antenna. Consequently, the dominant field in the region $r < l_0$ should be very nearly that of a standing spherical TEM wave. The main difference is that the boundaries do not coincide with those of a cone with fixed half-angle θ_0. In essence, the cylindrical dipole antenna is analogous to a transmission line whose characteristic impedance changes gradually along its length. For the cylindrical antenna the equivalent cone angle at the position z is given by $\tan \theta_0 = a/z \approx \theta_0$, as Fig. 3.2 shows. When we replace $\cot \theta_0/2$ by $2/\theta_0$ the expression for the characteristic impedance of the thin cylindrical antenna at the point z is

$$Z_c(z) = \frac{Z_0}{\pi} \ln \frac{2}{\theta_0(z)} = 120 \ln \frac{2z}{a} \qquad (3.15)$$

For a thin antenna $Z_c(z)$ varies slowly with z, so that as a first approximation

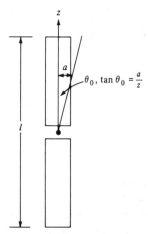

Figure 3.2 The cylindrical antenna.

the average value of Z_c may be used. This average value is given by

$$Z_c = \frac{120}{l/2} \int_0^{l/2} \ln \frac{2z}{a}\, dz = \frac{240}{l} \int_0^{l/2} \left(\ln z + \ln \frac{2}{a}\right) dz$$

$$= \frac{240}{l} \left(z \ln z - z + z \ln \frac{2}{a}\right)\Big|_0^{l/2}$$

$$= 120\left(\ln \frac{l}{a} - 1\right) \tag{3.16}$$

The average characteristic impedance, along with the assumption of open-circuit terminal conditions and the transmission-line formula for an open-circuited line,

$$Z_{\text{in}} = -jZ_c \cot k_0 l/2$$

may be used to estimate the input reactance for a *short* cylindrical dipole antenna. For a short dipole, $\cot k_0 l/2 \approx 2/k_0 l$, so we obtain

$$jX_a \approx -j\frac{240}{k_0 l}\left(\ln \frac{l}{a} - 1\right) = -j\frac{240c}{\omega l}\left(\ln \frac{l}{a} - 1\right) \tag{3.17}$$

where c is the speed of light. As expected, the input reactance is capacitive. The input resistance may be found in terms of the radiation resistance by using a triangular current distribution and is (see Prob. 2.2)

$$R_a = 20\pi^2\left(\frac{l}{\lambda_0}\right)^2 \tag{3.18}$$

Although Eq. (3.17) is not very accurate it does provide a useful estimate for the input reactance when other information is not available.

The evaluation of the terminating impedance Z_t has been carried out by

Schelkunoff for thin cones and may be used to find the input impedance for the biconical antenna with the aid of formula (3.13). In practice, there is no advantage in using a thin biconical antenna in preference to a cylindrical antenna, which is easier to fabricate. However, the wide-angle biconical antenna has a fairly large bandwidth of operation and is used in practice. For example, for a half-cone angle of 30° Brown and Woodward found experimentally that for $\lambda_0/2 < l < 3\lambda_0/2$ the reactance does not exceed $50\,\Omega$ in magnitude, and the input resistance remains between 130 and $200\,\Omega$.† This antenna, when fed with a transmission line having a characteristic impedance of $158\,\Omega$, which is the characteristic impedance of the biconical structure, has an acceptable impedance match over more than a 3-to-1 frequency band. This property of the wide-angle biconical antenna is also found for the thick cylindrical antenna, as shown in Figs. 2.13 and 2.14. However, the biconical antenna is somewhat better than the cylindrical antenna in its impedance behavior over a broad band.

A simple approximation to the wide-angle biconical antenna is the triangular, or "bow-tie," antenna shown in Fig. 3.3. The impedance properties of this antenna are not as good as those of the biconical antenna but are acceptable for use as a simple antenna to cover the UHF television channels 14 to 83 (frequency of 450 to 900 MHz). The bow-tie antenna is preferably made from a sheet of copper or aluminum but may also be made from wire, although the latter has a poorer performance. The dimensions shown in Fig. 3.3 are suitable for use on the UHF television band with a $300\,\Omega$ feed line. Further information on this antenna may be found in the paper by Brown and Woodward.

3.2 FOLDED DIPOLE ANTENNAS

The folded dipole antenna is shown in Fig. 3.4. It consists of two conductors of length l connected together at each end. One conductor is split at the center and connected to the transmission line. The folded dipole antenna has a

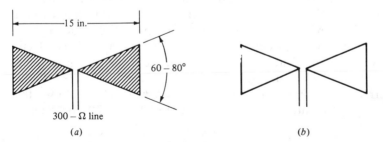

Figure 3.3 Bow-tie antenna. (*a*) Solid metal construction. (*b*) Wire construction.

† G. H. Brown and O. M. Woodward, Jr., "Experimentally Determined Radiation Characteristics of Conical and Triangular Antennas," *RCA Review*, vol. 13, no. 4, Dec. 1952, p. 425.

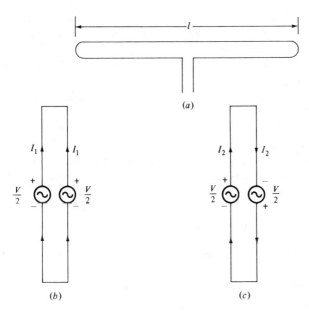

Figure 3.4 (*a*) The folded dipole antenna. (*b*) Even excitation. (*c*) Odd excitation.

radiation resistance of 292 Ω and is therefore useful with transmission feeder lines having a nominal characteristic impedance of 300 Ω, which is the most common impedance level used for television receivers. The folded dipole antenna, by virtue of its construction, has an equivalent transmission-line tuning stub that compensates for some of the variation of the antenna input impedance with frequency. Thus the useful frequency band of operation for the folded dipole antenna is larger than that of a conventional dipole antenna of equivalent thickness.

At the resonant length where $l \approx \lambda_0/2$ the current on each conductor is the same, provided these conductors have the same diameter. The reason for this is the strong mutual coupling between the two closely spaced conductors. The current on each conductor can be approximated by $I_0 \cos k_0 z$. Since the conductors are spaced by a very small fraction of a wavelength there is negligible phase difference in the field radiated from each conductor. Consequently, the radiated field is twice as strong as that from a single conductor with current $I_0 \cos k_0 z$. The radiated power P_r is thus four times as great. Since the input current supplied by the transmission line is only I_0, the radiation resistance referred to the input terminals is increased by a factor of 4 over that of a conventional dipole antenna. That is, in place of Eq. (2.57), the radiated power is given by

$$P_r = 4 \times 36.56 |I_0|^2$$

and

$$\tfrac{1}{2} R_a |I_0|^2 = P_r = 4 \times 36.56 |I_0|^2$$

so

$$R_a = 4 \times 73.13 = 292.5 \ \Omega \qquad (3.19)$$

In order to understand the impedance-compensating feature of the folded dipole antenna, its operation may be viewed as a superposition of the effects obtained by driving it as an antenna and as a transmission line. Figure 3.4b and 3.4c shows two ways of driving the structure. The excitation in Fig. 3.4b will excite equal currents on both conductors and will function as a conventional dipole antenna. The excitation in Fig. 3.4c will produce oppositely directed currents in each conductor or, in other words, will make the structure function as two series-connected short-circuited transmission lines. Since the transmission line currents are oppositely directed and closely spaced, the radiation from the two is almost completely cancelled. When the effects of the two methods of exciting the structure are superimposed, the resultant driving voltage for one conductor becomes V and is reduced to zero for the other. The input current may be found by adding together the currents in the driven conductor due to the two separate excitations.

Figure 3.5a shows the equivalent dipole antenna problem for which the current $2I_1$ is given by

$$2I_1 = \frac{V}{2} Y_1 \qquad (3.20)$$

where Y_1 is the input admittance of a dipole antenna made from two parallel conductors connected together at each end and at the center, as shown. The equivalent transmission-line problem is shown in Fig. 3.5b, from which it is seen that $I_2 = Y_{in} V/2$ and thus

$$\frac{I_2}{V} = -j \frac{Y_2}{2} \cot k_0 \frac{l}{2} \qquad (3.21)$$

where Y_2 is the characteristic admittance of the two-wire transmission line consisting of the two conductors that make up the folded dipole antenna.

When the two excitations shown in Fig. 3.5a and 3.5b are superimposed we obtain the original excitation shown in Fig. 3.5c. The input admittance seen at the terminals is

$$Y_a = \frac{I_1 + I_2}{V} = \frac{Y_1}{4} - j \frac{Y_2}{2} \cot k_0 \frac{l}{2} \qquad (3.22)$$

as may be found by using Eqs. (3.20) and (3.21). Note that the antenna dipole admittance is reduced by a factor of 4, and a compensating admittance $-j(Y_2/2) \cot k_0 l/2$ is added in parallel. When $l = \lambda_0/2$ the compensating admittance vanishes, since $k_0 l/2 = \pi/2$. For very thin conductors the antenna is also resonant when $l = \lambda_0/2$ and $Y_1 = (73.13)^{-1} \Omega$, so $Z_a = R_a = 292.5 \ \Omega$. For $k_0 l/2 \ne \pi/2$ we have $Y_1 = G_1 + jB_1$ with B_1 positive or capacitive for $k_0 l/2 < \pi/2$, and hence $(-jY_2/2) \cot k_0 l/2$ is a compensating inductive admittance for $l <$

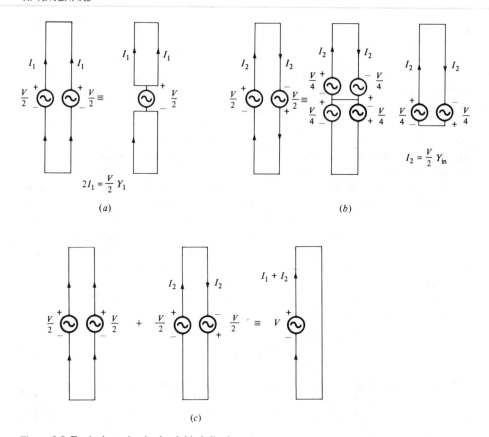

Figure 3.5 Equivalent circuits for folded dipole antenna.

$\lambda_0/2$. For $l > \lambda_0/2$ the antenna susceptance B_1 is negative, but $\cot k_0 l/2$ also changes sign, so again compensation takes place. With a proper choice of the dimensions of the folded dipole the bandwidth of operation can be increased over that of a conventional dipole antenna of equivalent thickness by a substantial amount. In a practical folded dipole antenna the resonant length is a few percent less than $\lambda_0/2$, and hence the antenna and transmission-line resonant frequencies do not coincide exactly.

A folded dipole antenna is not limited to a structure with two equal-diameter conductors. By varying the ratio of conductor diameters, the impedance step-up ratio can be varied from less than 2 to 20 or more. It is also possible to use three or more conductors connected in parallel, with one conductor driven. For three identical conductors, the input impedance is increased by a factor of 9. A summary of useful formulas for folded dipoles may be found in the book edited by Jasik.†

† H. Jasik, *Antenna Engineering Handbook*, McGraw-Hill Book Company, New York, 1961.

A two-wire transmission line with a characteristic impedance of less than $100\,\Omega$ is not very practical because of the close spacing required for the conductors. For antennas that must be driven by a two-wire line the much higher impedance of a folded dipole antenna is a useful feature for this reason alone. In certain types of antenna arrays the dipole antenna impedance is reduced considerably because of the mutual coupling with neighboring elements. The higher impedance of the folded dipole antenna helps to offset this decrease and thus to keep the required impedance of the feed line within reasonable bounds.

3.3 SHORT DIPOLE ANTENNAS

At the lower frequencies where the wavelength is large, space limitations often do not permit the use of a dipole antenna a full half-wavelength long. As a consequence the radiation resistance is reduced considerably, and some means must be employed to tune out the large capacitive reactance. The latter is usually accomplished by means of one or more inductors connected in series with the antenna. The additional losses in these tuning coils reduce the antenna efficiency and gain. A simple tuning arrangement is shown in Fig. 3.6.

If the tuning coils are moved to the center of each arm of the antenna, as shown in Fig. 3.7, then a more nearly uniform distribution of current on the antenna is obtained, and this increases the radiation resistance. For a short dipole the current distribution is triangular (see Prob. 2.2), and the radiated power is proportional to the area under the current-distribution curve squared. If a uniform current distribution could be achieved, an increase in the radiation resistance by a factor of 4 over that for a triangular distribution would be obtained.

In order to see how tuning coils arranged as in Fig. 3.7 can improve the current distribution, the antenna is modeled as a loaded open-circuited transmission line, as shown in Fig. 3.8. The inductance of the coils should be chosen so as to make the antenna resonant. This is equivalent to making the transmission-line model effectively a quarter-wavelength long, which means that the input impedance in the transmission line model should vanish. Just to the left of the coils the input impedance is $-jZ_c \cot k_0 l/4 + j\omega L_0$. This impedance is transformed to the following value at the input:

$$Z_{\text{in}} = Z_c \frac{-jZ_c \cot k_0 \frac{l}{4} + j\omega L_0 + jZ_c \tan k_0 \frac{l}{4}}{Z_c + \left(j\omega L_0 - jZ_c \cot k_0 \frac{l}{4}\right) j \tan k_0 \frac{l}{4}}$$

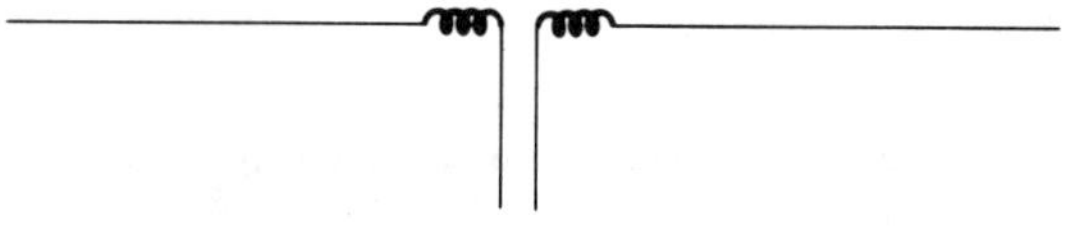

Figure 3.6 Short dipole antenna with tuning coils at the input.

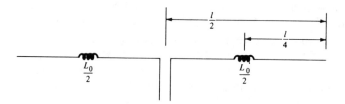

Figure 3.7 Center-loaded short dipole antenna.

The input impedance will vanish when the numerator in the above expression vanishes; thus

$$\omega L_0 = Z_c \left(\cot k_0 \frac{l}{4} - \tan k_0 \frac{l}{4} \right) \qquad (3.23)$$

which determines the required inductance.

We will now use the transmission line equations given in App. II to find the voltage and current standing waves on the transmission line. On the left-hand section we can write

$$V = V_1 \sin k_0 z \qquad (3.24a)$$

$$I = I_1 \cos k_0 z \qquad (3.24b)$$

since the zero input impedance conditions require the input voltage standing wave to have a node at $z = 0$ and the current standing wave must then have a maximum. The relationship between V_1 and I_1 is obtained by using $dV/dz =$

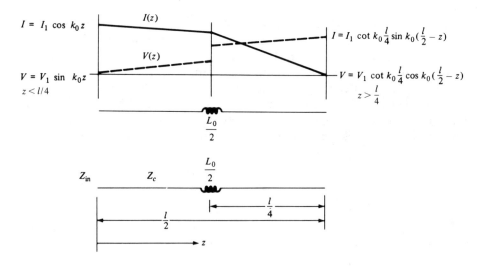

Figure 3.8 Transmission-line model of a center-loaded dipole and the voltage and current standing waves.

$-j\omega LI$ to obtain

$$k_0 V_1 \cos k_0 z = -j\omega L I_1 \cos k_0 z$$

or

$$V_1 = \frac{-j\omega L}{k_0} I_1 = \frac{-jL}{\sqrt{LC}} I_1 = -jZ_c I_1 \tag{3.25}$$

upon using $k_0 = \omega\sqrt{LC}$ and $Z_c = \sqrt{L/C}$, which are relationships that hold for a transmission line.

In the section to the right of the coils, the current standing wave must vanish at $z = l/2$, and the voltage standing wave will have a maximum value. Thus we can write

$$V = V_2 \cos k_0\left(\frac{l}{2} - z\right) \tag{3.26a}$$

$$I = I_2 \sin k_0\left(\frac{l}{2} - z\right) \tag{3.26b}$$

where again $V_2 = -jZ_c I_2$. At $z = l/4$ the current is continuous through the coils; hence

$$I_1 \cos k_0 \frac{l}{4} = I_2 \sin k_0 \frac{l}{4} \tag{3.27}$$

The voltage drop across L_0 is $j\omega L_0 I_1 \cos k_0 l/4$, and this requires that the voltage on the transmission line be discontinuous, so

$$V_1 \sin k_0 \frac{l}{4} - V_2 \cos k_0 \frac{l}{4} = j\omega L_0 I_1 \cos k_0 \frac{l}{4}$$

or

$$-jZ_c I_1 \sin k_0 \frac{l}{4} + jZ_c I_2 \cos k_0 \frac{l}{4} = j\omega L_0 I_1 \cos k_0 \frac{l}{4} \tag{3.28}$$

after expressing the voltages in terms of the currents. When the relation (3.23) is used, Eq. (3.28) gives

$$I_2 = I_1 \cot k_0 \frac{l}{4} \tag{3.29}$$

which is consistent with the relation (3.27).

For an antenna with $l \leq \lambda_0/4$ we can approximate $\sin k_0(l/2 - z)$ by $k_0(l/2 - z)$ and $\cos k_0 z$ by unity, since the maximum value of the argument is only $k_0 l/4 = \pi l/2\lambda_0 \leq \pi/8$. In this approximation the current is uniform and equal to I_1 for z up to $l/4$ and then decreases linearly to zero at $z = l/2$. The current and voltage variations are shown in Fig. 3.8 in the general case. For the approximation made here, the area under the current-distribution curve is

$2(I_1l/4 + I_1l/8) = 3I_1l/4$ instead of $I_1l/2$ for a triangular distribution. Thus the radiation resistance is increased by a factor of $(1.5)^2$, or 2.25, which demonstrates the advantage gained by placing the tuning coils in the center of each antenna arm, as in Fig. 3.7, instead of at the input, as shown in Fig. 3.6.

Another method used to provide a more uniform current distribution on a short dipole antenna is to provide capacitive loading at the two ends. One method that may be used is to connect four or more radially oriented conductors of length l_1 at each end, as shown in Fig. 3.9. The current does not need to vanish at $z = \pm l/2$, since it can divide and flow into the radial arms. At the ends of each radial arm the current must go to zero. The overall effect is a lengthening of the antenna by an amount $2l_1$, and this will make the current distribution on the antenna proper more nearly uniform. The current will be nearly equal to $I_0 \sin k_0(l/2 + l_1 - |z|)/\sin k_0(l/2 + l_1)$ up to $z = \pm l/2$. If the antenna is short, this current distribution may be approximated by the expression

$$I(z) = I_0\left(1 - \frac{|z|}{l/2 + l_1}\right) \qquad |z| \le \frac{l}{2} \tag{3.30}$$

The area under this current distribution curve is

$$2I_0\int_0^{l/2}\left(1 - \frac{z}{l/2 + l_1}\right)dz = \frac{4l_1 + l}{2l_1 + l}\frac{lI_0}{2} \tag{3.31}$$

The improvement over a triangular distribution is $(4l_1 + l)/(2l_1 + l)$. If $l_1 = l/4$ this is a factor of 4/3 and will increase the radiation resistance by a factor of 16/9, or 1.78.

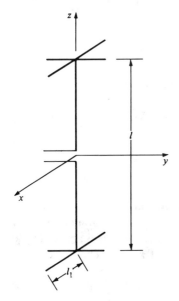

Figure 3.9 A capacitively loaded short dipole antenna.

The capacitively loaded dipole antenna may also be modeled by a transmission line with a terminating capacitance, as shown in Fig. 3.10. The current standing wave on this line may be determined in a straightforward manner and is (see Prob. 3.6)

$$I(z) = \frac{I_0}{\sin \alpha} \sin(\alpha - k_0 z) \qquad (3.32)$$

where

$$\alpha = k_0 \frac{l}{2} + \tan^{-1} \frac{Z_c}{X_c} \qquad (3.33)$$

and X_c is the capacitive reactance added at the end. This relation shows that the antenna is lengthened by an amount $2l_1' = 2k_0^{-1} \tan^{-1}(Z_c/X_c)$ or $\tan k_0 l_1' = Z_c/X_c$. The transmission-line model is, of course, not exact, but it does predict the general expected effect of capacitive end loading. For a short antenna the current distribution given by Eq. (3.32) can be approximated by

$$I(z) = I_0 \left(1 - \frac{2|z|}{l + 2Z_c/k_0 X_c}\right) \qquad (3.34)$$

where we have also made use of the approximation $\tan^{-1}(Z_c/X_c) = Z_c/X_c$, which is normally true in practice since the amount of capacitive loading that can be obtained is quite small; that is, X_c is large.

For the antenna shown in Fig. 3.9 the currents in the radial arms are oppositely directed and hence produce only a small change in the radiation pattern from that of a similar antenna without capacitive loading.

One of the reasons for introducing the biconical antenna and its transmission-line features was to establish a basis for looking at a dipole as an open-circuited transmission line. This point of view is very helpful in providing an insight into the various effects that are produced by loading an antenna with series coils or using capacitive end loading.

Multiband dipole antennas are sometimes constructed from long dipole

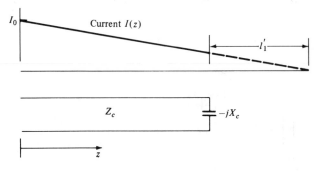

Figure 3.10 Transmission-line model for a capacitively loaded antenna.

structures with parallel-tuned resonant circuits located at suitable points along the antenna in order to make it function as a shorter dipole antenna at a given high frequency and yet function as a longer dipole antenna at a given lower frequency. One structure of this type is shown in Fig. 3.11. The L_1C_1 circuit is chosen to be resonant at the frequency where $l_1 = \lambda_0/2$. The resonant circuit provides a very high impedance to the current and effectively isolates the outer portions of the dipole from the inner section at this frequency. At some desired lower frequency the L_1C_1 circuit has a net inductive reactance and forms a loading coil to tune the dipole antenna of length l to resonance at this lower frequency. This antenna may also be analyzed as a transmission-line circuit in order to establish its main operating characteristics. An approximate analysis of this antenna is called for in Prob. 3.7.

3.4 MONOPOLE ANTENNAS

A monopole antenna consists of one-half of a dipole antenna mounted above the earth or a ground plane. It is normally one-quarter wavelength long, except where space restrictions or other factors dictate a shorter length. The vertical monopole antenna is used extensively for commercial broadcasting in the AM band (500 to 1500 kHz), in part because it is the shortest efficient antenna to use at these long wavelengths (200 to 600 m) and also because vertical polarization suffers less propagation loss than horizontal polarization does at these frequencies. The monopole antenna is also widely used for the land mobile-communication service. Figure 3.12 shows a typical vertical tower used for AM broadcasting. The support wires are broken up into sections no longer than one-eighth wavelength by means of insulators in order to keep the induced currents in these guy wires small. The base of the tower is insulated from the ground, and the system is fed by a coaxial transmission line, with the outer conductor connected to ground. Figure 3.13 shows a monopole antenna mounted on a tower above a ground plane consisting of four radial rods approximately 0.3 wavelengths long. These rods simulate a large ground plane sufficiently well that the radiation pattern and gain are very close to those of a half-wave dipole antenna. This antenna is a typical base station antenna used in mobile communications.

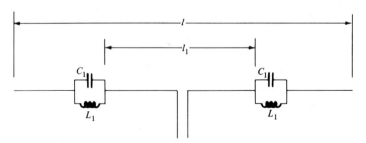

Figure 3.11 A dual-band dipole antenna.

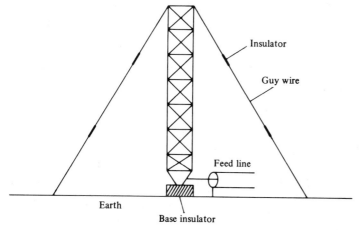

Figure 3.12 A vertical quarter-wavelength tower for broadcasting on the lower frequencies (below 2 MHz).

An ideal quarter-wave antenna mounted above a perfectly conducting large ground screen has a radiation resistance of 36.56 Ω. Practical quarter-wave antennas mounted above a suitable ground screen have a radiation resistance close to this value. For quarter-wave antennas mounted above the earth the poor conductivity of the soil results in excessive power loss from the induced currents in the soil. This dissipation reflects itself as an increase in the input resistance of the antenna and a large decrease in efficiency. The effect of poor ground conductivity is overcome by installing a ground screen, which usually consists of approximately 120 radial wires extending outward from the antenna base for a distance of about $\lambda_0/3$, as shown in Fig. 3.14. The screen is

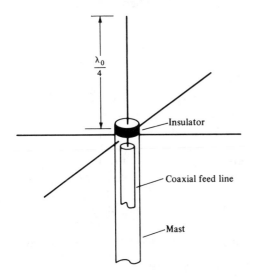

Figure 3.13 A monopole antenna with a four-radial-arm ground screen.

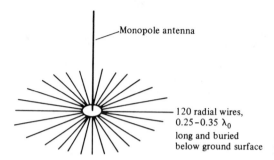

Monopole antenna

120 radial wires,
0.25–0.35 λ_0
long and buried
below ground surface

Figure 3.14 A radial ground screen.

normally buried several inches below the surface of the ground. A ground system of this type will keep the additional resistance added to the radiation resistance at a nominal value of around 2 Ω which represents an efficiency of around 95 percent.

For economic reasons it may not be possible to build a tower one-quarter wavelength high at the lower frequencies in the AM broadcast band and below. In this case a base-loading coil or some other form of matching network must be used to tune the antenna to resonance. Capacitive top loading is sometimes also employed.

Quarter-wave antennas are widely used in mobile communications, with the vehicle itself providing the required ground plane. In the 27-MHz citizen band, a quarter-wavelength monopole antenna is 2.77 m long. Many citizen-band users find an antenna of this length undesirable. Consequently antennas for the citizen band are often only 1 to 1.5 m (3 to 5 ft) long and use either base loading or center loading to tune the antenna to resonance. The overall efficiency will not be as great as for the full-length antenna, since the radiation resistance is reduced quite markedly, and the unavoidable dissipative losses in the tuning coil, ground screen, and the antenna itself will consume a significant fraction of the input power.

3.5 BALUNS

A *balun* is a device used to couple a balanced system to an unbalanced system.† A dipole antenna fed by a two-wire transmission line is balanced with respect to the ground, provided the two halves of the dipole have the same orientation and placement with respect to the ground. In the balanced mode the two halves of the dipole are at potentials V and $-V$ with respect to ground. If the dipole is connected to a coaxial transmission line, which is an unbalanced drive system, then the outer conductor and one arm of the dipole will be at a different potential level with respect to the ground than that of the center conductor of the coaxial line and the other arm of the dipole. The result is that currents are excited on the outside of the outer conductor of the coaxial line,

---

† The word *balun* is derived from the word combination balanced-unbalanced.

and the current in the two halves of the dipole antenna will not be the same. The radiation from the current on the outside of the coaxial line will interfere with the radiation from the dipole antenna, with a resultant modification of the radiation pattern. The change in the radiation pattern, which is not readily predicted, and the modification of the antenna input impedance because of the unbalanced currents are undesirable effects. Therefore, when a coaxial feed line is used, some form of balun is necessary to convert the unbalanced feed system to a balanced system before connection to the antenna is made. Baluns are constructed in a variety of ways, depending on the frequency band involved. A description of several types of baluns is given in Chap. 31 of Jasik's book.†

A particular type of balun that is useful at the higher frequencies is shown in Fig. 3.15a. It consists of a sleeve one-quarter wavelength long placed around the coaxial line at the position of the antenna. The end farthest away from the antenna is connected to the coaxial line outer conductor, and the other end is left unconnected. This sleeve functions as a short-circuited transmission line one-quarter wavelength long and hence presents a very high impedance at the input end. This high impedance prevents currents from flowing on the coaxial line and is said to "choke off" the currents. For this reason this balun is sometimes referred to as a *quarter-wave choke.*

A very common type of balun that is used in television antenna systems is shown in Fig. 3.15b through 3.15e. It consists of two lengths of transmission line with characteristic impedance Z_c, with the load Z_L equal to $2Z_c$ connected in series, and with the input terminals connected in parallel. The input impedance equals $Z_L/4$, so a standard coaxial line with characteristic impedance of 75 Ω may be used at the input when a folded dipole with radiation resistance of 292 Ω is used for the antenna. This type of balun thus allows an unbalanced coaxial line to be used to connect the antenna to the receiver and provides an impedance match as well.

The operation of this balun may be understood by referring to the series of Fig. 3.15b through 3.15e. In Fig. 3.15b the two transmission lines are excited in balanced modes with respect to ground. From the symmetry of the excitation, the midpoint a of the load and the point b can be seen to be at zero potential. Thus these points can be connected together and $Z_L/2$ then becomes the terminating impedance for each line and should be equal to the characteristic impedance Z_c of the transmission lines. Hence the matched load impedance equals $2Z_c$. In Fig. 3.15c all input terminals are driven with the same potential V with respect to ground. The four conductors are equivalent to a single conductor, and the input current will be small, since the load impedance now is the stray capacitance between the antenna and ground. The inductance of the four conductors in parallel also presents a high impedance to the current. In Fig. 3.15d the two modes of excitation are superimposed. The result is that the terminals 1 and 4 are at a potential $2V$ and terminals 2 and 3 are at zero

† Ibid.

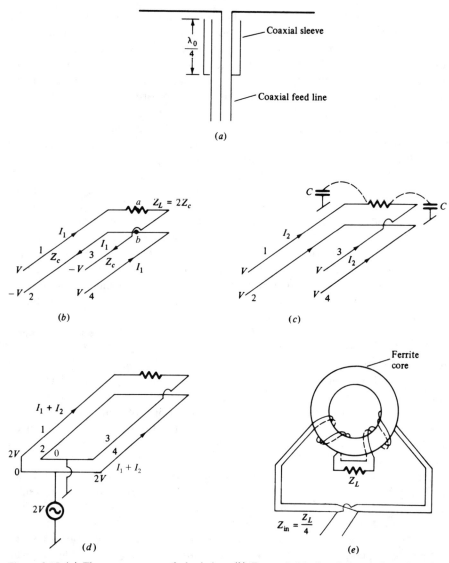

Figure 3.15 (*a*) The quarter-wave choke balun. (*b*) Transmission line balun, balanced mode. (*c*) Transmission line balun, unbalanced mode. (*d*) Transmission line balun, superposition of balanced and unbalanced modes. (*e*) Transmission line balun wound on ferrite core to suppress unbalanced mode currents.

potential. These pairs of terminals may be connected together and driven by a single voltage source with one end connected to ground; that is, the input source can be unbalanced with respect to ground.

Let I_1 be the input current for the balanced mode in Fig. 3.15*b* and let I_2 be the input current for the unbalanced mode shown in Fig. 3.15*c*. The input impedance for the connection shown in Fig. 3.15d will be

$$Z_{in} = \frac{2V}{2(I_1 + I_2)} \approx \frac{V}{I_1} = \frac{Z_c}{2} = \frac{Z_L}{4}$$

since I_2 is very small and $Z_c = 2V/I_1$, as Fig. 3.15b shows. In order to increase the impedance to the flow of the current I_2, the transmission lines are often wound on a ferrite toroidal core, thereby increasing the inductance of the four parallel conductors (see Fig. 3.15e). This has little effect on the balanced mode current, since this is a transmission-line mode with equal and opposite currents in each pair of conductors, and therefore does not produce any magnetization in the ferrite core.

3.6 INTRODUCTION TO ANTENNA ARRAYS

The dipole antenna is a very simple antenna suitable for use when a nearly omnidirectional pattern is required. However, its gain is low. In many communication systems one is interested in point-to-point communication, and a much more highly directive beam of radiation can be used to advantage. By arranging several dipoles (or other elementary radiators) into an array, a directive beam of radiation can be obtained. A more directive beam means that the antenna will also have a higher gain. Simple arrays are readily built that will give gains of 10 to 15 dB over that of a half-wave dipole. An increase in the gain by a factor of 10 permits the transmitter power to be reduced tenfold for the same signal strength at the receiving site. If, in addition, the receiving antenna also has a gain of 10 dB, a further tenfold reduction in power can be afforded for the same relative performance. It is apparent that increasing the gain of the antenna has significant advantages.

   In order to establish the basic method used in analyzing arrays, consider the general array shown in Fig. 3.16. This array consists of N identical antennas with the same orientation but excited with relative amplitudes C_i and phase α_i for the ith antenna. The position of the ith antenna is given by the position vector r_i. For reference purposes we let the electric field radiated by a reference antenna located at the origin and with an excitation coefficient of unity be

$$\mathbf{E}(\mathbf{r}) = \mathbf{f}(\theta, \phi) \frac{e^{-jk_0 r}}{4\pi r} \tag{3.35}$$

where $\mathbf{f}(\theta, \phi)$ describes the electric-field radiation pattern of the elementary antenna used in the array. In the far zone or radiation region where $|\mathbf{r}| \gg r_i$, the rays from all of the antennas in the array are essentially parallel. Thus the distance from the ith antenna to the far-field point of interest is $R_i = r - \mathbf{a}_r \cdot r_i$. The distant field produced by the ith antenna will suffer a propagation-phase delay by an amount $k_0 \mathbf{a}_r \cdot r_i$ smaller than that of the reference antenna at the

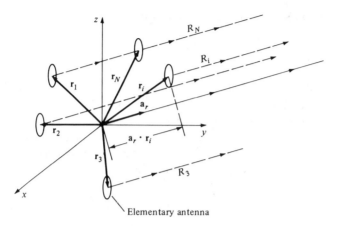

Figure 3.16 A general N-element array.

origin. (This antenna is not necessarily present in the array; it serves as a reference to which the radiated field of the antennas in the array can be compared.) When the different propagation-phase delays and the different amplitudes and phases of excitation are taken into account the resultant field from all the antennas in the array can be expressed in the following form:

$$\mathbf{E}(\mathbf{r}) = \sum_{i=1}^{N} C_i e^{j\alpha_i} \mathbf{f}(\theta, \phi) \frac{e^{-jk_0 r + jk_0 \mathbf{a}_r \cdot \mathbf{r}_i}}{4\pi r}$$

$$= \mathbf{f}(\theta, \phi) \frac{e^{-jk_0 r}}{4\pi r} \sum_{i=1}^{N} C_i e^{j\alpha_i + jk_0 \mathbf{a}_r \cdot \mathbf{r}_i} \tag{3.36}$$

In this expression we have used the approximation $R_i \approx r$ in the amplitude factor $1/r$. Note that even though R_i and r may differ by less than one part in a thousand, this could still represent a distance of several wavelengths, so the approximation of putting R_i equal to r cannot be used in the exponential function. A path difference of one wavelength corresponds to a phase change of 360°. These phase differences due to different path lengths from the various antennas in the array are of fundamental importance in controlling the interference effects that enable a directive beam of radiation to be formed.

Principle of Pattern Multiplication

If the expression (3.36) is examined, it will be seen to be the product of the radiation field from the reference antenna and the array factor $F(\theta, \phi)$ given by

$$F(\theta, \phi) = \sum_{i=1}^{N} C_i e^{j\alpha_i + jk_0 \mathbf{a}_r \cdot \mathbf{r}_i} \tag{3.37}$$

The radiation pattern and directivity is proportional to $16\pi^2 r^2 |\mathbf{E}|^2$ and hence

$$D(\theta, \phi) \propto |\mathbf{f}(\theta, \phi)|^2 \left| \sum_{i=1}^{N} C_i e^{j\alpha_i + jk_0 \mathbf{a}_r \cdot \mathbf{r}_i} \right|^2$$

$$= |\mathbf{f}(\theta, \phi)|^2 |F(\theta, \phi)|^2 \tag{3.38}$$

This relation expresses the very important *principle of pattern multiplication, which states that the radiation pattern of an array is the product of the pattern function of the individual antenna with the array pattern function.* The latter is a function of the location of the antennas in the array and their relative complex amplitudes of excitation. We will have several occasions to apply this principle in this chapter.

The derivation of the principle of pattern multiplication rests on the assumption that all antennas in the array have the same radiation pattern. This assumption is generally not correct, because the current distribution on an antenna is affected by mutual coupling effects with nearby objects, that is, the other antennas in the array. Thus the elements near the sides of the array will be influenced in a different manner from those in the center of the array. However, the modification in the radiation pattern of the individual antennas is often small enough that it can be neglected. The general behavior of arrays can be predicted with good accuracy by assuming that the principle of pattern multiplication is valid, so we will proceed on that basis in the discussion that follows.

In the study of arrays it is usual to focus attention on the array factor alone, since in an array with high directivity the individual antennas usually have a very broad pattern, and most of the directivity is contributed by the array factor. For the most part we will follow this procedure in the discussion of various antenna arrays.

Uniform One-Dimensional Arrays

Figure 3.17 shows a line array of $N + 1$ elements, which for convenience we

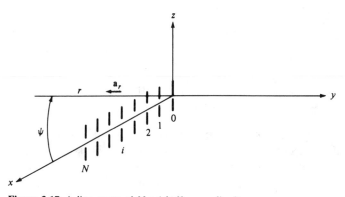

Figure 3.17 A line array of $N + 1$ half-wave dipoles.

assume to be half-wave dipoles, spaced by a distance d. Each antenna is excited with the same constant amplitude $C = I_0$ but with a progressive phase change αd from element to element, so that $\alpha_n = n\alpha d$. For this array direct application of Eq. (3.37) gives

$$F(\theta, \phi) = I_0 \sum_{n=0}^{N} e^{jn\alpha d + jk_0 nd \cos \psi}$$

where ψ is the angle between the radius vector $\mathbf{a}_r$ and the array axis, which is the x axis in this case. Note that $\mathbf{r}_n = nd\mathbf{a}_x$ so that $\mathbf{a}_r \cdot \mathbf{r}_n = nd \cos \psi = nd \sin \theta \cos \phi$, a relation that will display the θ, ϕ dependence of $F(\theta, \phi)$. The above expression is a geometric series that may be summed using the known relation

$$\sum_{n=0}^{N} w^n = \frac{1 - w^{N+1}}{1 - w} \tag{3.39}$$

Thus we find that

$$F = I_0 \frac{1 - e^{j(N+1)(\alpha + k_0 \cos \psi)d}}{1 - e^{j(\alpha + k_0 \cos \psi)d}}$$

$$= I_0 e^{j(N/2)(\alpha + k_0 \cos \psi)d} \frac{\sin\{[(N+1)/2](\alpha + k_0 \cos \psi)d\}}{\sin[(\alpha + k_0 \cos \psi)d/2]} \tag{3.40}$$

The array *field pattern* $|F|$ is given by

$$|F| = I_0 \left| \frac{\sin\{[(N+1)/2](\alpha + k_0 \cos \psi)d\}}{\sin[(\alpha + k_0 \cos \psi)d/2]} \right| \tag{3.41}$$

In order to study the array factor it is convenient to introduce the new variable u given by

$$u = k_0 d \cos \psi \tag{3.42}$$

and also the variable u_0 given by

$$u_0 = \alpha d \tag{3.43}$$

The array factor can now be expressed as

$$|F(u)| = I_0 \left| \frac{\sin\{[(N+1)/2](u + u_0)\}}{\sin[(u + u_0)/2]} \right| \tag{3.44}$$

This function behaves very much like the well-known function $(\sin u)/u$, except that it is periodic. In Fig. 3.18 the array factor given by Eq. (3.44) is shown as a function of u. Note that major maxima occur when $u = -u_0$ and whenever $(u + u_0)/2 = m\pi$, where m is an integer. These maxima have a peak value of $(N + 1)I_0$ corresponding to an in-phase addition of the radiated field from all

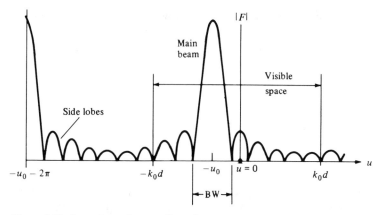

Figure 3.18 Array factor for a uniform line array.

$N + 1$ dipoles. The intervening smaller maxima are called *side lobes*, with the largest one occurring a distance

$$\Delta u = \frac{\pm 3\pi}{2(N + 1)/2} = \frac{\pm 3\pi}{N + 1}$$

away from $-u_0$. These first side lobes have an amplitude equal to $2/3\pi$, or 0.21, of that of the main lobe when N is large (eight or more). There are $N - 1$ minor lobes between adjacent major lobes.

As a function of u the array pattern repeats every 2π units along the u axis. We now note that since

$$u = k_0 d \cos \psi$$

the range of u corresponding to physical space or the *visible region* is $-k_0 d \leq u \leq k_0 d$ since $\cos \psi$ lies between -1 and 1. Thus the visible region corresponds to a value of u equal to $\pm 2\pi d/\lambda_0$ on either side of $u = 0$. In practice we normally want only one main lobe to occur in physical space, and this requires that we choose the spacing d small enough so that the region a distance of $\pm 2\pi d/\lambda_0$ on either side of $u = 0$ does not include another major lobe, as shown in Fig. 3.18. Two special cases of importance are the broadside array and the end-fire array, which we discuss below.

Broadside Arrays. When we put $\alpha = 0$ then $u_0 = 0$, and the major lobe maximum occurs at $u = 0$ or $\cos \psi = 0$, which gives $\psi = \pi/2$. Thus maximum radiation occurs broadside to the array axis, as intuition would tell us should be the case with all elements fed in phase. If we examine Fig. 3.18 we see that, provided we keep the spacing d between elements somewhat less than λ_0, additional major lobes will not occur in visible space since the closest other major lobes are $\pm 2\pi$ away from the lobe at $u = 0$. The visible region extends from $-k_0 d$ to $k_0 d$ and this will lie within the interval $-2\pi < u < 2\pi$, provided $d < \lambda_0$.

It is of interest to determine the angular width of the main lobe between zeros, since this is a measure of the beam concentration achieved. The nulls for the main beam occur when the argument of the sine function in the numerator in Eq. (3.44) equals $\pm\pi$; thus

$$\frac{N+1}{2} k_0 d \cos \psi = \pm\pi$$

or

$$\cos \psi = \frac{\pm 2\pi}{(N+1)k_0 d} = \frac{\pm\lambda_0}{(N+1)d}$$

For N large, $\cos \psi$ is small, so ψ is close to $\pi/2$. Hence if we let $\psi = \pi/2 \pm \Delta\psi$ we can replace $\cos(\pi/2 \pm \Delta\psi) = \pm \sin \Delta\psi$ by $\pm\Delta\psi$. Consequently the beam width BW is given by

$$\text{BW} = 2\Delta\psi = \frac{2\lambda_0}{(N+1)d} = \frac{2\lambda_0}{L} \tag{3.45}$$

where $L = (N+1)d$ is essentially the length of the array. Equation (3.45) expresses the general property of a broadside line array that the beam width is inversely proportional to the array length measured in wavelengths. For a beam width of 6^0, or about 0.1 rad, an array about 20 wavelengths long is required. This is quite feasible at high frequencies, but at 1 MHz, where $\lambda_0 = 300$ m, the array length would be 6 km, which might prove to be impractical. (It certainly would be costly to build 20 or more towers $\lambda_0/4$ tall and to purchase the large tract of land required for the installation.) The array amplitude pattern factor shown in Fig. 3.18 can be easily shown as a function of θ and ϕ, as in Fig. 3.19a. If the array consists of half-wave dipoles, then the overall resultant pattern is the product of the array pattern with the dipole pattern, as shown in Fig. 3.19c. Note that the null along the z axis for the dipole pattern results in two fan beams along the $\pm y$ directions, together with the minor lobes or side lobes.

It is generally quite difficult to calculate the absolute value of the directivity for an array because the complex pattern makes it difficult to evaluate the total radiated power. In the present case it would require evaluation of the following integral:

$$\int_0^{2\pi} \int_0^{\pi} \left(\frac{\cos(\pi/2 \cos \theta)}{\sin \theta} \frac{\sin\{[(N+1)/2]k_0 d \sin \theta \cos \phi\}}{\sin[(k_0 d/2) \sin \theta \cos \phi]} \right)^2 \sin \theta \, d\theta \, d\phi$$

A reasonable estimate of the directivity may be obtained by dividing 4π by the solid angle occupied by the main beam and approximating this by the product of the principal E- and H-plane half-power beam widths. For the array under discussion, the E-plane half-power beam width is that of the half-wave dipole antenna and is $78°$, or 1.36 rad. The H-plane half-power beam width is determined by the array factor. This may be obtained by equating Eq. (3.44) to

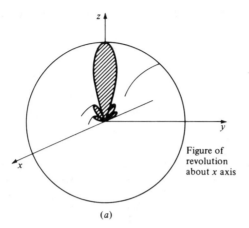

(a)

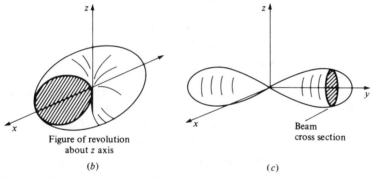

Figure of revolution
about z axis

(b)

Beam
cross section

(c)

Figure 3.19 (a) Array pattern. (b) Half-wave dipole pattern. (c) Resultant pattern obtained by pattern multiplication but with side lobes not shown.

$(N + 1)I_0/\sqrt{2}$; thus

$$\sin^2\left(\frac{N+1}{2}u\right) = \frac{1}{2}\left(\frac{u}{2}\right)^2 (N+1)^2$$

In this expression $\sin u/2$ was replaced by $u/2$ since the denominator in Eq. (3.44) varies much more slowly than the numerator and u is close to zero. The solution for u may be found with adequate accuracy by approximating the remaining sine function by the first two terms in its series expansion; thus

$$\sin\left(\frac{N+1}{2}\right)u \approx (N+1)\frac{u}{2} - \tfrac{1}{6}(N+1)^3\left(\frac{u}{2}\right)^3 = \frac{u(N+1)}{2\sqrt{2}}$$

which gives

$$u_{1/2} = \frac{2.65}{N+1}$$

Now $u_{1/2} = k_0 d \cos(\pi/2 - \Delta\psi_{1/2}) \approx k_0 d \, \Delta\psi_{1/2}$, so the half-power beam width is given by

$$BW_{1/2} = 2 \, \Delta\psi_{1/2} = \frac{2.65 \times 2}{(N+1)k_0 d} = \frac{2.65\lambda_0}{(N+1)\pi d} \tag{3.46}$$

The directivity is now readily found to be

$$D \approx \frac{4\pi}{2 \times 1.36 \times BW_{1/2}} = 5.48 \frac{(N+1)d}{\lambda_0} \tag{3.47}$$

where the extra factor of 2 in the denominator accounts for the presence of two beams. As an example, consider a 21-element array with $N = 20$, $d = 0.9\lambda_0$. We then find that $BW_{1/2} = 0.045$ rad, or 2.54°. The estimate for the directivity is (there are two beams)

$$D \approx \frac{4\pi}{2 \times 1.36 \times 0.045} = 103 \qquad \text{or } 20.1 \text{ dB}$$

Thus a 21-element array has a very substantial directivity and also a large gain since the losses would normally be quite small.

If the array elements were isotropic radiators instead of half-wave dipoles, the pattern would have rotational symmetry about the array axis. In place of the factor 1.36, which is the half-power beam width of the dipole antenna, we must now use an angular width of 2π in the formula for D and also delete the extra factor 2 in the denominator. Hence, for a uniform line array of $N + 1$ isotropic-radiating elements the estimate for the directivity becomes

$$D \approx \frac{4\pi}{2\pi BW_{1/2}} = \frac{2\pi}{2.65} \frac{(N+1)d}{\lambda_0} = 2.37 \frac{(N+1)d}{\lambda_0}$$

A theoretical formula for the directivity of a line array of isotropic radiators can be derived quite readily and will provide a useful check on the estimate given above. For isotropic radiators the radiated electric field is proportional to

$$E \propto \sum_{n=0}^{N} I_n e^{jn(\alpha d + k_0 d \cos \psi)}$$

The directivity is given by

$$D = \frac{4\pi |E_{max}|^2}{\int_0^{2\pi} \int_0^{\pi} |E(\theta, \phi)|^2 \sin \theta \, d\theta \, d\phi}$$

We can choose the array axis as the z axis and then, since E depends only on the polar angle ψ, we obtain

$$D = \frac{4\pi |E_{max}|^2}{2\pi \int_0^{\pi} |E(\psi)|^2 \sin \psi \, d\psi}$$

If we now change variables by letting $u = \alpha d + k_0 d \cos \psi$, $du = -k_0 d \sin \psi \, d\psi$, and with limits on u from $(\alpha + k_0)d$ to $(\alpha - k_0)d$ we obtain

$$D = \frac{2|\Sigma_{n=0}^N I_n|^2 k_0 d}{\Sigma_{n=0}^N \Sigma_{m=0}^N I_n I_m^* \int_{(\alpha-k_0)d}^{(\alpha+k_0)d} e^{j(n-m)u} \, du}$$

$$= \frac{k_0 d|\Sigma_{n=0}^N I_n|^2}{\Sigma_{n=0}^N \Sigma_{m=0}^N I_n I_m^* e^{j(n-m)\alpha d}[\sin(n-m)k_0 d]/(n-m)} \tag{3.48}$$

For the second special case of a uniform array with all $I_n = I_0$ and $d = \lambda_0/2$, this expression becomes

$$D = \frac{k_0 d(N+1)^2}{\Sigma_{n=0}^N \Sigma_{m=0}^N [\sin(n-m)\pi]/(n-m)}$$

$$= \frac{k_0 d(N+1)^2}{(N+1)\pi} = 2(N+1)\frac{d}{\lambda_0} = N+1$$

since all terms in the denominator vanish except the $N+1$ terms corresponding to $n = m$, each of which equals π. When we compare this exact expression with our earlier estimate we find that in place of the factor 2.37 we have a factor of 2, so our estimate was about 18 percent too large.

In general, for a uniformly excited array of $N + 1$ isotropic radiators, the expression for D simplifies to the form

$$D = \frac{N+1}{1 + 1/k_0 d \, \Sigma_{s=1}^N [(N+1-s)/(N+1)s] \cos s\alpha d \sin sk_0 d} \tag{3.49}$$

This form is obtained by introducing a new summation index $s = n - m$ in Eq. (3.48) and noting that there are $(N + 1) \, s = 0$ terms; $Ns = \pm 1$ terms; $(N-1) \, s = \pm 2$ terms; or, in general, $(N+1) - |s|$ terms in $\pm s$. When the $\pm s$ terms are combined to give the $\cos s\alpha d$ factor, Eq. (3.49) is obtained.

End-fire Arrays. If u_0 is chosen equal to $-k_0 d$, a beam maximum is formed when $u = -u_0 = k_0 d = k_0 d \cos \psi$ or at $\psi = 0$, which is along the array axis. The progressive phase change αd along the array is then $-k_0 d$, an amount that just offsets the propagation-phase advance from element to element in the x direction. An array that is phased to produce a beam along its axis is called an *end-fire array*. If u_0 is chosen equal to $k_0 d$ then the beam is formed in the $-x$ direction.

The array factor and resultant array pattern are shown in Fig. 3.20. From this figure it is seen that a spacing d of somewhat less than $\lambda_0/2$ is now required to avoid having a second beam appear in visible space. The second beam first begins to appear along the $-x$ direction when d approaches $\lambda_0/2$. The array pattern is again a figure of revolution about the array axis.

For the end-fire array the array factor is

$$|F| = I_0 \left| \frac{\sin\{[(N+1)/2]k_0 d(\cos \psi - 1)\}}{\sin[(k_0 d/2)(\cos \psi - 1)]} \right| \tag{3.50}$$

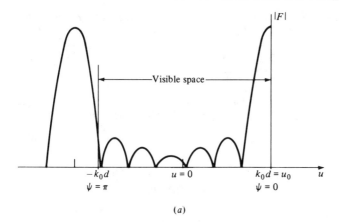

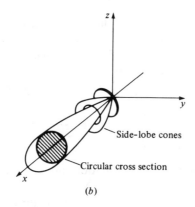

Figure 3.20 Array factor and array pattern for an end-fire array.

The main beam nulls occur when

$$\frac{N+1}{2} k_0 d(\cos \psi - 1) = \pm \pi$$

For N large, the value $\Delta\psi$ of ψ at the nulls is small, so that $\cos \Delta\psi \approx 1 - (\Delta\psi)^2/2$ and we obtain

$$\frac{(\Delta\psi)^2}{2} = \frac{2\pi}{(N+1)k_0 d}$$

or

$$\text{BW} = 2 \, \Delta\psi = 2\left(\frac{2\lambda_0/d}{N+1}\right)^{1/2} = 2\left(\frac{2\lambda_0}{L}\right)^{1/2} \tag{3.51}$$

where $L = (N+1)d$ is essentially the array length. We see that for an end-fire array the beam width is inversely proportional to the square root of the array length measured in wavelengths. The beam is not as narrow in a given plane as for the broadside array, but this narrowing occurs in two planes. The greater beam width is compensated by a narrowing of the pattern in both the E plane and H plane. For a long array the multiplication of the array pattern by the half-wave dipole pattern has little effect, since the latter is almost constant over the angular region occupied by the array pattern.

We may estimate the directivity by finding the half-power beam width. When we equate Eq. (3.50) to $(I_0/\sqrt{2})(N+1)$, approximate $\cos \Delta\psi_{1/2} - 1$ by $(\Delta\psi_{1/2})^2/2$, use a two-term expansion of the sine function in the numerator, and approximate the denominator by $k_0 d(\Delta\psi_{1/2})^2/4$, we find that

$$\Delta\psi_{1/2} = 1.63\left[\frac{\lambda_0}{\pi d(N+1)}\right]^{1/2} \tag{3.52}$$

The solid angle of a conical beam of width $\Delta\psi_{1/2}$ is given by

$$\Omega = \int_0^{2\pi} \int_0^{\Delta\psi_{1/2}} \sin\theta \, d\theta \, d\phi = 2\pi(1 - \cos\Delta\psi_{1/2}) \approx \pi(\Delta\psi_{1/2})^2$$

The approximate expression for the directivity is thus

$$D = \frac{4\pi}{\Omega} = 4.73\frac{(N+1)d}{\lambda_0} \tag{3.53}$$

Table 3.1 compares the estimated values of D from Eq. (3.53) with the exact values computed from Eq. (3.49) from some representative cases of end-fire arrays with $\alpha d = -k_0 d$. It can be seen that the approximate formula does give a good estimate.

A greater directivity can be obtained by making the total progressive phase delay along the array π rad greater than $Nk_0 d$. Thus, instead of choosing $N\alpha d$ equal to $-Nk_0 d$, we choose $N\alpha d = -Nk_0 d - \pi$, or

$$\alpha d = u_0 = -k_0 d - \frac{\pi}{N} \tag{3.54}$$

which is known as the *Hansen-Woodyard condition*. This choice makes the main lobe maximum occur where $u = -u_0 = k_0 d + \pi/N$ or where $k_0 d \cos\psi = k_0 d + \pi/N$, which is in invisible space since it requires $\cos\psi > 1$. What has happened is shown in Fig. 3.21 and corresponds to shifting the array factor pattern to the right by a small amount π/N. The portion of the main lobe that

Table 3.1

$N+1$	d/λ_0	D from Eq. (3.53)	D from Eq. (3.49)
6	0.4	11.35	12.17
12	0.4	22.7	26.7
6	0.3	8.51	7.85
12	0.3	17.03	16.04

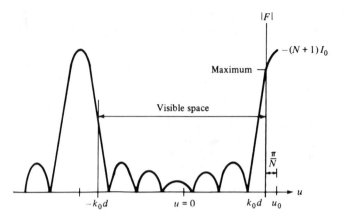

Figure 3.21 Illustration of the Hansen-Woodyard condition.

remains in visible space is now a narrower lobe with a smaller maximum value. It may seem a contradiction that reducing the maximum value achieved by the main lobe in visible space should lead to an increase in directivity. The anomaly is resolved by recalling that the directivity is proportional to the maximum power density divided by the total radiated power. The latter is proportional to the area under the curve representing the square of the array factor shown in Fig. 3.21. For a small shift of the main lobe into the invisible region, this area decreases faster than the square of the resultant maximum of $|F|$ in visible space and hence results in increased directivity. By means of a graphical evaluation, Hansen and Woodyard arrived at the condition given by Eq. (3.53) as the optimum choice for u_0 to give maximum directivity.

Uniform Two-Dimensional Arrays

A two-dimensional array of half-wave dipoles is shown in Fig. 3.22. It consists of $N + 1$ dipoles along x and $M + 1$ dipoles along z, or a total of $(N + 1)(M + 1)$ dipoles. The dipoles are assumed to have the same amplitude of excitation but with a progressive phase change along both the x and z directions. Thus the phase of the current in the mnth element is given by $e^{jn\alpha d + jm\beta d}$.

The array described may be viewed as an array of $M + 1$ linear arrays. Thus by using the principle of pattern multiplication, the two-dimensional array factor is the product of the array factor for the $M + 1$ antennas arrayed along z with the array factor for the $N + 1$ elements arrayed along x. Thus we have

$$|F(\theta, \phi)| = I_0 \left| \frac{\sin\{[(N + 1)/2](k_0 d \sin \theta \cos \phi + \alpha d)\}}{\sin[(d/2)(k_0 \sin \theta \cos \phi + \alpha)]} \right|$$

$$\times \left| \frac{\sin\{[(M + 1)/2](k_0 d \cos \theta + \beta d)\}}{\sin[(d/2)(k_0 \cos \theta + \beta)]} \right| \qquad (3.55a)$$

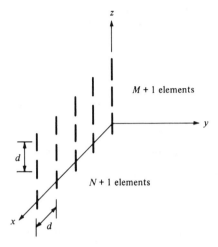

Figure 3.22 A two-dimensional array.

where we have used $\mathbf{a}_r \cdot \mathbf{a}_x = \sin \theta \cos \phi$ and $\mathbf{a}_z \cdot \mathbf{a}_r = \cos \theta$. It is convenient to let

$$u = k_0 d \sin \theta \cos \phi \qquad u_0 = \alpha d$$

$$v = k_0 d \cos \theta \qquad v_0 = \beta d$$

and rewrite Eq. (3.55a) as

$$|F| = I_0 \left| \frac{\sin\{[(N + 1)/2](u + u_0)\} \sin\{[(M + 1)/2](v + v_0)\}}{\sin[(u + u_0)/2] \sin(v + v_0)/2} \right| \qquad (3.55b)$$

The array factor has its first principal maximum when $u = -u_0$, $v = -v_0$, which defines the direction in space of the main radiation beam. If $\alpha = \beta = 0$ this direction is perpendicular to the plane of the array, that is, along $\pm y$. For suitable values of α and β the beam can be directed in any desired direction. If the element phasing is controlled by phase changers in each element's feed line, control of the beam direction can be obtained electronically so the beam can be made to scan any desirable angular sector. Arrays of this type are called *phased arrays*.

In the case of a broadside array the angular width of the lobe in the xy and yz planes is obtained by setting

$$\frac{N + 1}{2} u = \pm \pi \qquad \text{and} \qquad \frac{M + 1}{2} v = \pm \pi$$

as was done for the line array. It is readily found that

$$(\text{BW})_{xy} = \frac{2\lambda_0}{(N + 1)d} \qquad (3.56a)$$

$$(\text{BW})_{yz} = \frac{2\lambda_0}{(M + 1)d} \qquad (3.56b)$$

The beam width in each plane is inversely proportional to the array length in that plane. In a similar way the half-power beam widths can be found and are given by expressions like Eq. (3.46); thus

$$(\text{BW}_{1/2})_{xy} = \frac{2.65\lambda_0}{(N+1)\pi d} \tag{3.57a}$$

$$(\text{BW}_{1/2})_{yz} = \frac{2.65\lambda_0}{(M+1)\pi d} \tag{3.57b}$$

The directivity is approximately given by (note that there are two beams)

$$D \approx \frac{4\pi}{2(\text{BW}_{1/2})_{xy}(\text{BW}_{1/2})_{yz}} = \frac{8.83(N+1)(M+1)d^2}{\lambda_0^2}$$

$$= 8.83\frac{A}{\lambda_0^2} \tag{3.58}$$

where we have replaced $(N+1)(M+1)d^2$ by the area A occupied by the array. We see that the directivity of the antenna is proportional to the area measured in wavelengths squared, a property that is characteristic of all antennas.

It is interesting to examine how the beam width changes as the beam is scanned away from the direction normal to the array. If we assume that $\beta = 0$ and choose αd equal to $-k_0 d \cos \psi_0$, then the beam direction is at the angle ψ_0 relative to the x axis and in the xy plane. For values of ϕ close to ψ_0 we can use a Taylor series expansion of

$$k_0 d(\cos \phi - \cos \psi_0)$$

to obtain (we expand the function of ϕ about ψ_0)

$$k_0 d(\cos \phi - \cos \psi_0) \approx (-k_0 d \sin \psi_0)(\phi - \psi_0)$$

Thus when we put $(N+1)(u-u_0)/2$ equal to $\pm\pi$ to find the beam width we obtain

$$\frac{N+1}{2}(-k_0 d \sin \psi_0)(\phi - \psi_0) = \pm\pi$$

and hence

$$2|\phi - \psi_0| = 2\,\Delta\phi = \frac{4\pi}{(N+1)k_0 d \sin \psi_0} = \frac{2\lambda_0}{(N+1)d \sin \psi_0} \tag{3.59}$$

which is the desired result. It is seen that the beam width is increased by the factor $1/\sin \psi_0$. We now note that $(N+1)d \sin \psi_0$ is the projected width of the array in the direction of the beam, and since the projected width is less than the true width, the beam width is broadened, that is, it varies inversely with the projected width.

The two-dimensional, or curtain, array produces a single beam on each side of the array plane, provided the element spacing d is less than λ_0 for broadside radiation and is reduced to less than $\lambda_0/2$ for edgeside radiation. If the element spacing is too large, several beams will be formed in visible space on each side of the array plane. The extra beams formed with large element spacings are often referred to as *grating lobes*, a term that comes from the theory of optical diffraction gratings.

3.7 ARRAY PATTERN SYNTHESIS

The preceding discussion was limited to arrays with equal amplitude excitation. Narrow beams were found to be formed, provided the phasing of each element was chosen properly. The relative phasing controls the interference between the radiation produced by each element so as to permit a beam of radiation to be formed. If the excitation amplitudes are also varied from element to element, it then turns out that considerable control can be exercised on the shape and width of the main beam and on the locations and amplitudes of the side lobes. Thus it is possible to actually synthesize an array to produce a radiation pattern that closely approximates an a priori specified pattern. This synthesis is called *array pattern synthesis* or simply *array synthesis*.

Different methods have been developed for array synthesis and are too great in number for discussion in this text.† Instead we will look at some of the fundamental aspects of array synthesis and discuss a few selected methods only. We will consider only one-dimensional arrays, but the methods may be applied to two-dimensional arrays, since for the latter the array factor is the product of the two one-dimensional array factors, and each array factor may be synthesized separately.

Fourier Series Method

Consider the line array with $2N+1$ elements, as shown in Fig. 3.23. Let the excitation of each element be proportional to C_n for the nth element. For in-phase excitation the array factor is

$$F = \sum_{n=-N}^{N} C_n e^{jk_0 nd \cos \theta} \tag{3.60}$$

If we choose $C_n = C_{-n}$ we can write

$$F(k_0 d \cos \theta) = F(u) = C_0 + \sum_{n=1}^{N} 2C_n \cos nu \tag{3.61}$$

which is a finite Fourier cosine series with $N+1$ unknown amplitudes. By proper choice of the C_n, this series can be used to approximate various desired radiation patterns $F_d(u)$. Note that $0 \le \theta \le \pi$ so the range $-k_0 d \le u \le k_0 d$ is

† Synthesis methods are reviewed in R. E. Collin and F. J. Zucker, *Antenna Theory*, vol. I, McGraw-Hill Book Company, New York, 1969, Chaps. 5, 7.

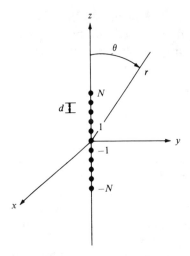

Figure 3.23 A line array with $2N + 1$ elements.

the range of u that corresponds to physical space. However, the pattern must be specified over the complete period $-\pi \le u \le \pi$. As an example, let $F_d(u)$ be the rectangular pattern shown in Fig. 3.24. A least-mean-square error fit to this pattern is obtained by choosing the C_n as the usual Fourier series coefficients, that is,

$$C_n = \frac{1}{2\pi} \int_{-\pi}^{\pi} F_d(u) \cos nu \, du = \frac{1}{2\pi} \int_{-k_0d/2}^{k_0d/2} \cos nu \, du \qquad (3.62)$$

For the rectangular pattern we find that

$$C_n = \frac{1}{n\pi} \sin\left(n \frac{k_0d}{2}\right)$$

The pattern obtained for $d = \lambda_0/2$ and using only the coefficients $C_0 = 1/2$, $2C_1 = 2/\pi$, $2C_2 = 0$, $2C_3 = -2/3\pi$ is also shown in Fig. 3.24. If we use a very

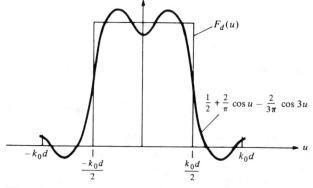

Figure 3.24 A desired pattern and the approximation obtained with a seven-element array but with elements -2, 2 having zero excitation.

large array, then F as given by Eqs. (3.61) and (3.62) will be a good approximation to the desired pattern. On the other hand, for a small array with very few elements, the approximation will be poor in general because of the few terms in the Fourier series. The Fourier series method is one approach to array pattern synthesis that is easy to apply and yields a least-mean-square error approximation to the desired pattern.

Binomial Arrays

The array factor for an array of $2N + 1$ elements can be chosen to be

$$F(u) = (e^{j(k_0 d/2)\cos\theta} + e^{-j(k_0 d/2)\cos\theta})^{2N}$$
$$= (e^{j(u/2)} + e^{-j(u/2)})^{2N}$$
$$= 2^{2N}\left(\cos\frac{u}{2}\right)^{2N} = e^{-jNu}\sum_{n=0}^{2N} C_n^{2N} e^{jnu} \qquad (3.63)$$

upon using the binomial expansion. The $C_n^{2N} = (2N)!/n!(2N-n)!$ are the binomial coefficients, and the last form was obtained by factoring out $e^{-ju/2}$ as the e^{-jNu} factor. Now $C_n^{2N} = C_{2N-n}^{2N}$, so Eq. (3.63) is a series of the same form as Eqs. (3.60) and (3.61), that is,

$$F(u) = (C_0^{2N} e^{-jNu} + C_{2N}^{2N} e^{jNu}) + [C_1^{2N} e^{-j(N-1)u} + C_{2N-1}^{2N} e^{j(N-1)u}] + \cdots$$
$$= 2C_0^{2N} \cos Nu + 2C_1^{2N} \cos(N-1)u + \cdots + C_N^{2N}$$

The binomial array pattern is characterized by the complete absence of side lobes. The pattern $|F(u)| = 2^{2N}(\cos u/2)^{2N}$ has $2N$ zeros at $\cos u/2 = 0$ or $u = \pm\pi$ and thus is maximally flat at these points. To make the visible region correspond to $-\pi \le u \le \pi$ we must choose $k_0 d = \pi$ or $d = \lambda_0/2$ since $u = \pm k_0 d$ when $\theta = 0, \pi$, respectively. The radiation pattern of the binomial array is shown in Fig. 3.25. The disadvantage with the binomial array is that the

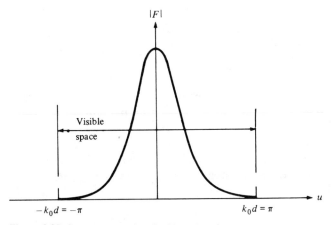

Figure 3.25 Array pattern for the binomial array.

half-power beam width is broader than that of a uniform array and the directivity is lower. Both of these features are caused by the inefficient use of the available array length 2*Nd*, since the excitation amplitudes are made proportional to the binomial coefficients (this is the origin of the name *binomial array*), and hence the elements near each end of the array are weakly excited. The small contribution to the total field from the elements near the ends of the array is equivalent to a reduction in the effective length of the array, which results in the decreased directivity and larger beam width noted above.

The Array Polynomial

Let us consider an array of $N + 1$ elements spaced by equal amounts d along the z axis (as in Fig. 3.23 but with no elements along $-z$). The phasing between elements is αd. For this array the array factor is

$$|F| = \left| \sum_{n=0}^{N} C_n e^{jn(u+u_0)} \right| \tag{3.64}$$

where $u = k_0 d \cos \theta$, $u_0 = \alpha d$. We now let the complex variable Z be defined as

$$Z = e^{j(u+u_0)} \tag{3.65}$$

The array factor can be expressed in terms of this new variable as an Nth degree polynomial:

$$|F| = \left| \sum_{n=0}^{N} C_n Z^n \right| \tag{3.66}$$

This polynomial representation was introduced by Schelkunoff.[†] It has the advantage that the properties of a polynomial can be related to properties of the array factor, and thus it provides a guide to the synthesis of a desirable pattern, even though it is not a true synthesis method.

Any polynomial of degree N has N zeros, so Eq. (3.66) can be written in factored form as

$$|F| = |C_N(Z - Z_1)(Z - Z_2)\ldots(Z - Z_N)| \tag{3.67}$$

Each factor such as $Z - Z_i$ can be interpreted as the array factor for a two-element array. Thus we have the theorem:

1. The array factor of an $(N + 1)$-element array is the product of the array factor of N two-element arrays superimposed to produce nulls at the zeros of F, as given by Eq. (3.67).

Another basic theorem is:

2. The array factor of an $(N + 1)$-element array is a polynomial of degree N, and conversely any polynomial of degree N can be interpreted as an $(N + 1)$ element array factor.

[†] S. A. Schelkunoff, "A Mathematical Theory of Linear Arrays," *Bell Syst. Tech. J.*, vol. 22, no. 1, 1943, pp. 80–107.

Since the product of two polynomials is also a polynomial, the following theorem holds:

3. The product of two polynomials is the array factor for an array whose pattern is the product of the patterns associated with each polynomial by itself.

Visible space corresponds to $-k_0 d \le u \le k_0 d$, and since $|Z| = 1$ for all real values of u and u_0, visible space corresponds to a portion of the unit-circle circumference extending from $-k_0 d + u_0$ to $k_0 d + u_0$ in angle measure, as shown in Fig. 3.26. When $d = \lambda_0/2$ a full 360° is covered, while if $d = \lambda_0/4$ a range of 180° is covered. For spacing greater than $\lambda_0/2$, a portion of the unit circle is covered twice. As θ increases from 0 to π, the point on the unit circle moves from an angular position $k_0 d + u_0$, in a clockwise sense, to the angular position $-k_0 d + u_0$. If the coefficients C_n are complex, the additional phase of each C_n is added to the progressive phase $n\alpha d$ for each element's excitation. The zeros Z_n correspond to zeros in the radiation pattern whenever they lie on that part of the unit circle representing visible space.

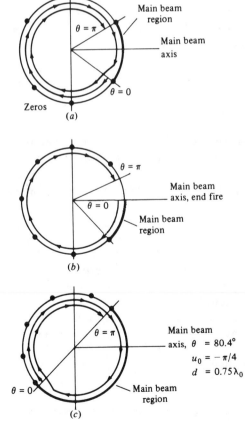

(a)

(b)

Main beam
axis, θ = 80.4°
$u_0 = -\pi/4$
$d = 0.75\lambda_0$

(c)

Figure 3.26 (a) Visible space on unit circle for element spacing greater than $\lambda_0/2$, $u_0 = 0$, angular extent $2k_0 d$, θ increasing. (b) Visible space for element spacing less than $\lambda_0/2$, end-fire array. (c) Visible space for $d = 3\lambda_0/4$, $u_0 = -\pi/4$, all zeros located in overlapping region.

In order to appreciate how the polynomial representation may be used as a guide to array design we can imagine $|F|$ to be a stretched rubber band at some height h above a plane surface. We now imagine pinning this rubber band to the surface at the points u_n corresponding to the zeros Z_n. The band will rise above the surface at the in-between points. If we place the zeros close together we can keep the band close to the surface over the intervening region, and this corresponds to low side lobes. If double zeros are used, then $|F|$ and its derivative are both zero, and this helps to keep the adjacent side lobes small. Along those intervals where there are no zeros the side-lobe level will be large, corresponding to a section where the rubber band is not pinned down.

An example that we have already discussed is the binomial array. For an array with $N + 1$ elements, $u_0 = 0$, and $d = \lambda_0/2$, let us place all of the N available zeros at $u = \pi$, that is, at $Z = -1$. This corresponds to the point $\theta = 0$ and π. The array factor is

$$|F| = C_n|(Z + 1)^N|$$

When this is expanded we obtain

$$(Z + 1)^N = Z^N + C_1^N Z^{N-1} + C_2^N Z^{N-2} + \cdots C_N^N$$

where the C_n^N are the binomial coefficients. Hence we arrive at the same result obtained earlier for the excitation coefficients. This approach to the binomial array demonstrates the additional insight to array behavior obtained with the polynomial representation.

As a second example, consider a uniform five-element array with array polynomial

$$|F| = |1 + Z + Z^2 + Z^3 + Z^4|$$

For this array the first side lobe is approximately 13.5 dB below the main lobe. Let us now replace all the single zeros with double zeros, which will reduce the side-lobe level considerably. This is readily accomplished by squaring the array factor for the uniform array, since every factor $Z - Z_n$ will then appear twice. Thus for the new array we choose

$$|F| = |(1 + Z + Z^2 + Z^3 + Z^4)^2| \qquad (3.68)$$

The array pattern is the square of that for the uniform array so the first side lobe is now 27 dB below the main lobe maximum. The patterns of the two arrays are shown in Fig. 3.27. Note that if $d = \lambda_0/2$, the unit circle in the Z plane is covered once by visible space, and four pattern nulls occur. When d approaches λ_0 the unit circle is covered twice and eight pattern nulls occur. In addition, grating lobes along the array axis, along with the main lobe at broadside, will appear when $d = \lambda_0$.

When Eq. (3.68) is expanded it becomes

$$|F| = |1 + 2Z + 3Z^2 + 4Z^3 + 5Z^5 + 3Z^6 + 2Z^7 + Z^8|$$

which represents a nine-element array, with the excitation coefficients having

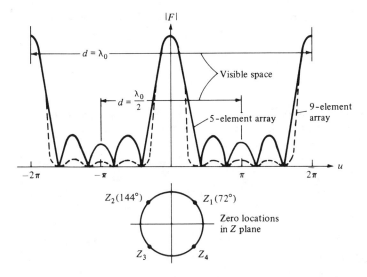

Figure 3.27 Array factor for a uniform five-element array and for a nine-element array with double zeros.

the triangular distribution

$$1: 2: 3: 4: 5: 4: 3: 2: 1$$

It should be noted that the array with triangular current distribution will have a broader beam width and smaller directivity than a uniform array of the same total number of elements but will have much lower side lobes. The tapering of the excitation of the elements of an array towards zero as the ends of the array are approached generally results in reduced side-lobe levels and a broader radiation pattern and lower directivity. The decrease in directivity and increase in beam width may be viewed as caused by the inefficient use of the available array length, as discussed earlier in connection with the binomial array. In general, reduced side-lobe levels are obtained at the expense of a decrease in directivity and a broader main beam.

For a broadside array with the maximum allowed element spacing, almost two complete circuits around the unit circle corresponds to visible space. Thus a broadside array with $N + 1$ elements will have $2N$ nulls or zeros in its radiation pattern, since the N zeros of the array polynomial are encountered twice, as shown in Fig. 3.26a. For an end-fire array the spacing is restricted to less than $\lambda_0/2$, so less than one complete circuit around the unit circle corresponds to visible space. Hence an end-fire array with $N + 1$ elements can have at most N nulls, or zeros, in its radiation pattern (see Fig. 3.26b). For an array with the beam pointed away from the array axis, visible space has a portion of the unit circle traversed twice, and the available N zeros can all be placed in this region, as shown in Fig. 3.26c. However, this is generally not an optimum choice, since it leaves a large region without zeros and thus results in a broad asymmetrical main lobe. The placement of the pattern zeros controls the pattern shape and side-lobe level and must be done in an appropriate manner.

Chebyshev Arrays

One design criterion that is often chosen is that which will produce the narrowest possible beam width for a given side-lobe level or conversely that will produce the smallest side-lobe level for a given beam width. If we had a polynomial with these properties it would be easy to determine the required current distribution in the elements of the array. Fortunately there exists a series of polynomials known as the *Chebyshev polynomials* that can be adapted to the design of optimum arrays according to the criterion given above. The method was first introduced by Dolph, so this type of array is also called a *Dolph-Chebyshev array.*[†] The theory of the Chebyshev array is readily developed by using the Fourier series representation of the array factor. Before presenting this theory we will summarize the basic properties of the Chebyshev polynomials.

The Chebyshev polynomials are defined by the following relations:

$$T_1(x) = x$$
$$T_2(x) = 2x^2 - 1$$
$$T_3(x) = 4x^3 - 3x \qquad (3.69)$$
$$T_4(x) = 8x^4 - 8x^2 + 1$$
$$T_n(x) = 2xT_{n-1} - T_{n-2}$$

These polynomials also satisfy the relationship

$$T_n(\cos \gamma) = \cos n\gamma \qquad (3.70a)$$

and when γ is complex

$$T_n(\cosh \gamma) = \cosh n\gamma \qquad (3.70b)$$

The Chebyshev polynomials oscillate between ± 1 for x in the range -1 to 1 and have all n zeros in this interval. For $|x| > 1$ the polynomials increase monotonically, as shown in Fig. 3.28. The zeros of the Chebyshev polynomials are given by

$$\cos n\gamma = 0 \qquad \text{or} \qquad \gamma = \frac{1+2m}{2n}\pi \qquad m = 0, 1, 2, \ldots, n-1 \qquad (3.71)$$

The corresponding values of x are

$$x_m = \cos \gamma_m = \cos \frac{1+2m}{2n}\pi \qquad m = 0, 1, 2, \ldots, n-1 \qquad (3.72)$$

[†] C. L. Dolph, "A Current Distribution for Broadside Array Which Optimizes the Relationship Between Beamwidth and Sidelobe Level," *Proc. IRE.*, vol. 34, no. 6, 1946, p. 335.

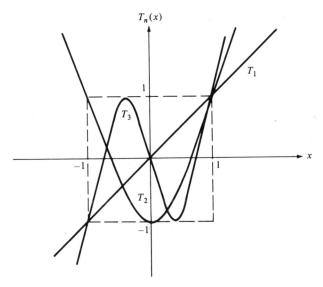

$T_n(x)$

T_1

T_3

T_2

Figure 3.28 The first three Chebyshev polynomials.

Let us now consider the function $T_2(a + b \cos u) = 2(a + b \cos u)^2 - 1$ upon using Eq. (3.69). When we expand this and use $2 \cos^2 u = \cos 2u + 1$ we obtain

$$T_2(a + b \cos u) = (2a^2 + b^2 - 1) + 4ab \cos u + b^2 \cos 2u \qquad (3.73)$$

which is a finite cosine Fourier series up to the term in $\cos 2u$. Similarly, upon using $4 \cos^3 u = 3 \cos u + \cos 3u$ we find that

$$T_3(a + b \cos u) = 4(a + b \cos u)^3 - 3(a + b \cos u)$$
$$= (4a^3 + 6ab^2 - 3a) + (12a^2b + 3b^3 - 3b) \cos u$$
$$+ 6ab^2 \cos 2u + b^3 \cos 3u \qquad (3.74)$$

which is also a finite Fourier series. In general, $T_N(a + b \cos u)$ is a finite Fourier series with terms up to $\cos Nu$ and may therefore be identified as an array factor for an array with $2N + 1$ elements.

For a symmetrical broadside array with $2N + 1$ elements, the array factor is given by Eq. (3.61), which we repeat here for convenience

$$F(u) = C_0 + 2 \sum_{n=1}^{N} C_n \cos nu \qquad (3.75)$$

This series may be equated to the Chebyshev polynomial of degree N, since $T_N(a + b \cos u)$ is also a series of the same form as Eq. (3.75). The constants a and b are chosen to make the visible range of u correspond to values of x in $T_N(x)$ that range from $x = -1$ up to $x = x_1$, where $x_1 > 1$. The value of $T_N(x_1)$ corresponds to the maximum value of $F(u)$, which is greater than 1, and the side lobes correspond to $-1 \le x \le 1$ and are of unit amplitude. There are two cases that require separate treatment. When the element spacing d is given and is less than or equal to $\lambda_0/2$, the parameter $x = a + b \cos u$ reaches its smallest value $a + b \cos k_0d$ for $\theta = 0, \pi$. The design formulas for this case are given first. For spacings d greater than $\lambda_0/2$, a narrower beam width for a given side-lobe level can be achieved by optimizing the spacing. The design formulas for this case are given later.

As θ varies from 0 to $\pi/2$ to π, the variable $u = k_0d \cos \theta$ varies from k_0d to zero to $-k_0d$. The variable $a + b \cos u = x$ then varies from $a + b \cos k_0d$ to $a + b$ and then back to $a + b \cos(-k_0d) = a + b \cos k_0d$. These relationships are illustrated in Fig. 3.29. We see that $x = a + b = x_1$ is the value of x for the beam maximum and $x = a + b \cos k_0d$ should equal -1 to yield the farthest-out side lobes at $\theta = 0, \pi$. Hence we require $a + b = x_1$, $a + b \cos k_0d = -1$ or

$$a = -\frac{1 + x_1 \cos k_0d}{1 - \cos k_0d} \tag{3.76a}$$

$$b = \frac{1 + x_1}{1 - \cos k_0d} \tag{3.76b}$$

If $d = \lambda_0/2$ these constants become

$$a = \frac{x_1 - 1}{2} \tag{3.77a}$$

$$b = \frac{x_1 + 1}{2} \tag{3.77b}$$

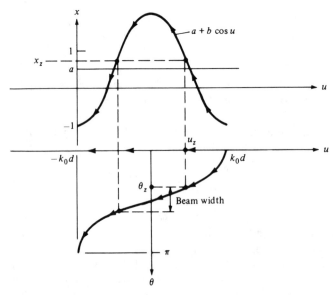

Figure 3.29 Illustration of relationship between θ, u, and x.

If we specify the ratio of the main-beam maximum to the side-lobe level to be R, we require $T_N(x_1) = R$. We can use Eq. (3.70b) to give $x_1 = \cosh \gamma_1$, $T_N(x_1) = \cosh N\gamma_1 = R$, and hence $\gamma_1 = N^{-1} \cosh^{-1} R$ and then

$$x_1 = \cosh \gamma_1 = \cosh\left(\frac{1}{N}\cosh^{-1} R\right) \tag{3.78}$$

The constants a and b can now be found explicitly.

In some designs the beam width is given. The main beam extends from the last zero of $T_N(x)$ before x reaches the value of 1 up to x_1. If the beam null is placed at θ_z, then the corresponding value of u is $u_z = k_0 d \cos \theta_z$ and x_z is given by

$$x_z = a + b \cos u_z = a + b \cos(k_0 d \cos \theta_z) \tag{3.79}$$

Now x_z, the zero closest to one, is also given by Eq. (3.72) as

$$x_z = \cos \frac{\pi}{2N} = a + b \cos u_z \tag{3.80}$$

This equation, along with the requirement that $a + b \cos k_0 d = -1$, can be solved for a and b to give

$$a = -\frac{\cos u_z + x_z \cos k_0 d}{\cos u_z - \cos k_0 d} \tag{3.81a}$$

$$b = \frac{1 + x_z}{\cos u_z - \cos k_0 d} \tag{3.81b}$$

The beam-maximum-to-side-lobe-level ratio R can be found from

$$T_N(x_1) = T_N(a + b) = R = \cosh[N \cosh^{-1}(a + b)] \tag{3.82}$$

since at $u = 0$ we have $x = x_1 = a + b$.

In the design of a Chebyshev array we can specify the side-lobe ratio parameter R, in which case the beam width is fixed and can be found from the known value of x_1 and the value of x_z given by Eq. (3.80). The value of θ_z at the null is given by Eq. (3.79) using Eqs. (3.76) or (3.77) for a and b. The alternative choice is to specify the beam width θ_z, in which case there is no choice available for the parameter R. In this latter case we must find a and b using Eq. (3.81) and can find R by using Eq. (3.82). The array excitation coefficients are determined by expanding $T_N(a + b \cos u)$ into a Fourier series and comparing it with Eq. (3.75). A variety of designs have been worked out, so in practice the computation does not need to be repeated.†

We will illustrate the design theory by considering two examples.

† R. J. Stegen, "Excitation Coefficients and Beamwidths of Chebyshev Arrays," *Proc. IRE.*, vol. 41, Nov. 1952, pp. 1671–1674.

Example 3.1: Five-element array with 20-dB side lobes A broadside array of five elements, with spacing $d = \lambda_0/2$ and with side-lobe amplitudes that are 10 percent of the main-beam maximum, is required (side lobes 20 dB below the main lobe). The parameter $R = 10$ and Eq. (3.78) with $N = 2$ (there are $2N + 1 =$ five elements) gives

$$x_1 = \cosh(\tfrac{1}{2}\cosh^{-1} 10) = 2.3452$$

From Eq. (3.77) we obtain $a = 0.6726$, $b = 1.6726$. We now use Eq. (3.73) to obtain $F(u) = T_2(a + b\cos u) = 2.7 + 4.5\cos u + 2.8\cos 2u$. Thus the current in element number 0 is $2.7I_0$, that in elements -1 and 1 is $2.25I_0$, and that in elements -2 and 2 is $1.4I_0$.

At the beam null Eq. (3.80) gives $x_z = \cos \pi/4 = 0.707$ and $\cos u_z = (0.707 - a)/b = .0206$, so $u_z = 1.5501$. But $u_z = k_0d \cos \theta_z - \pi \cos \theta_z$, so $\theta_z = \cos^{-1}(u_z/\pi) = 1.054$ rad $= 60.43°$. Hence the beam width is $2(90 - 60.43) = 59.13°$. The array factor is illustrated in Fig. 3.30. ∎

Example 3.2: Five-element array with a 40° beam width The array of the preceding example is to be modified to give a 40° beam width. For this beam width $\theta_z = 90° - 20° = 70°$ and $u_z = \pi \cos \theta_z = 1.074$. From the first example, $x_z = 0.707$, so upon using Eq. (3.81) we get $a = 0.156$, $b = 1.156$. From Eq. (3.82) we find that $R = 2.44$. We note that reducing the beam width from 59.13 to 40° (about a 32 percent reduction) raises the side-lobe level from 20 to 7.75 dB. The resultant array design is not a very good one. The excitation coefficients can be found by using Eq. (3.73), as in the previous example. ∎

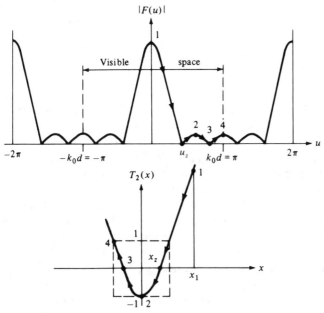

Figure 3.30 A five-element Chebyshev array with 20-dB side lobes.

Superdirective Arrays

We have found [see Eq. (3.45)] that for a uniform line array the beam width is inversely proportional to the array length measured in wavelengths. In principle it is possible to design arrays with a fixed length L to have as narrow a beam width and as high a directivity as desired. Any array with a directivity significantly greater than that of a uniform array is called a *superdirective* or *supergain array*. In practice, it turns out that these superdirective arrays are not practical for several reasons which we will discuss later.

If we have an array of fixed length L and use $2N + 1$ elements the spacing $d = L/2N$. There are $2N$ zeros available, and if we locate all of these in visible space we can keep the side-lobe level as small as possible and still achieve a narrow beam and high directivity. We will illustrate a superdirective design with u_0 chosen equal to zero for simplicity. The major lobe peak will be chosen to occur at $u = 0$, or $\theta = \pi/2$. The visible space corresponds to $-k_0 d \leq u \leq k_0 d$, or in view of the restriction placed on d,

$$-\frac{k_0 L}{2N} \leq u \leq \frac{k_0 L}{2N}$$

We will design the array as a Chebyshev array and restrict the array length L to equal $\lambda_0/4$ and use seven elements. The side lobes will be made equal to 0.1 of the main lobe (20 dB down).

The required element spacing is such that $k_0 d = k_0 L/6$, or $d = \lambda_0/24$. If we follow the procedure in Example 3.1 we obtain $a = -73.01544219$, $b = 74.55587192$, and $x_1 = 1.54042973$. The relative values of the currents in the elements are

$$-3.99200886 \times 10^6 \quad \text{element no. 0}$$
$$3.006383214 \times 10^6 \quad \text{elements no. 1 and } -1$$
$$-1.2175861 \quad \times 10^6 \quad \text{elements no. 2 and } -2$$
$$2.072123161 \times 10^5 \quad \text{elements no. 3 and } -3$$

In the broadside direction of the main lobe the field is proportional to the algebraic sum of all the currents, since they all contribute in phase. This sum equals 10.0002 in spite of the very large currents (millions of amps) in each element and is due to cancellation effects because the currents alternate in sign. The beam width can be determined as in Example 3.1 and is 69.7°. It is thus seen that even though the array length was restricted to $\lambda_0/4$ a beam width of 69.7° could be obtained with side lobes 20 dB down. The array factor is shown in Fig. 3.31. Note the small visible region, which does contain six nulls, and the very large value that $|F(u)|$ reaches in invisible space (1.28×10^7 versus 10 for the main lobe).

This example of a superdirective array illustrates very clearly why these antennas are not practical. The required current in each element is very large

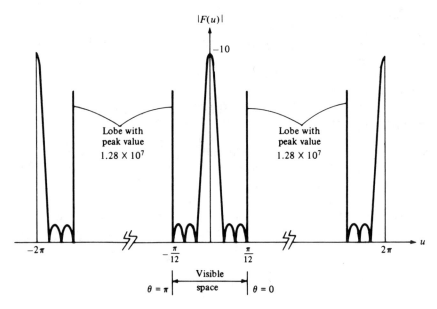

Figure 3.31 Array factor for a seven-element supergain array $\lambda_0/4$ long (side lobes 20 dB down).

and results in large ohmic losses. The effective current, producing radiation in the direction of the beam maximum, is very small because the currents in adjacent elements are of opposite sign. Thus relative to the input currents in each element, the radiated power is very small, and hence the radiation resistance is small—usually much smaller than the ohmic resistance. The required tolerance on the current is severe. A change in the current in one element by ten parts in several million could reduce the main lobe amplitude to zero. The reactive field is related in amplitude to the value of the array factor $F(u)$ in the invisible region and is large (due to the large currents), and hence the input reactance of the antenna is very large and the band width of operation is vanishingly small. These effects are so severe that in practice only a very small amount of supergaining could be incorporated into the antenna design. A gain greater than that obtained with a uniform array using $\lambda_0/2$ element spacing is difficult to achieve. The term *supergain* is inappropriate in as much as the superdirective arrays have a vanishing gain because of the high ohmic losses relative to the radiated power. Nevertheless, superdirective antennas are interesting from the mathematical viewpoint and have been the subject of a large number of papers.[†]

Chebyshev Arrays with $d > \lambda_0/2$

The narrowest main beam for a given side-lobe level is achieved by crowding as many side lobes as possible into the visible range of u. When d is allowed to be

---

[†] A. Bloch et al., "Superdirectivity," *Proc. IRE.*, vol. 48, 1960, p. 1164. This article contains 31 references.

greater than $\lambda_0/2$ the spacing d can be optimized to achieve the narrowest possible beam width. When $d > \lambda_0/2$, $k_0 d$ is greater than π. Thus $x = a + b \cos u$ will reach a minimum value of $a - b$ when $k_0 d \cos \theta = \pi$ and will then increase in value as θ moves further toward the value π, as shown in Fig. 3.32. We can allow x to vary from x_1 (beam maximum) to -1 and back to 1, and this will repeat the side lobes in $-1 < x < 1$ twice in the visible range of u. By referring to Fig. 3.32 we see that we need to choose

$$x_1 = a + b \cos(k_0 d \cos \theta) = a + b \qquad \theta = \pi/2 \qquad (3.83a)$$

$$-1 = a - b \qquad k_0 d \cos \theta = \pm \pi \qquad \text{or} \qquad \theta = \cos^{-1} \pm \frac{\lambda_0}{2d} \qquad (3.83b)$$

$$1 = a + b \cos k_0 d \qquad \theta = 0, \pi \qquad (3.83c)$$

The first two equations may be solved for a and b to give

$$a = \frac{x_1 - 1}{2} \qquad (3.84a)$$

$$b = \frac{x_1 + 1}{2} \qquad (3.84b)$$

while the third equation gives the optimum spacing d, that is,

$$\cos k_0 d = \frac{1 - a}{b} = \frac{3 - x_1}{1 + x_1} \qquad \pi < k_0 d < 2\pi \qquad (3.84c)$$

Equation (3.82) for the beam-maximum-to-side-lobe ratio R is still applicable. When the beam width θ_z is given, we require $u_z = k_0 d \cos \theta_z$ and

$$a + b \cos u_z = x_z = \cos \frac{\pi}{2N} \qquad (3.85)$$

where x_z is the first zero of $T_N(x)$ to the left of $x = 1$, as given by Eq. (3.80). In

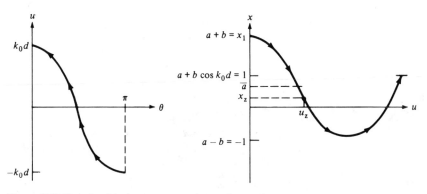

Figure 3.32 Relationship between u and θ and x and u for a Chebyshev array with optimum spacing d.

addition, Eq. (3.83*b*) and (3.83*c*) must hold, so the required design formulas are

$$a = \frac{x_z - \cos u_z}{1 + \cos u_z} \tag{3.86a}$$

$$b = \frac{1 + x_z}{1 + \cos u_z} \tag{3.86b}$$

$$\cos k_0 d = \frac{1 + 2 \cos u_z - x_z}{1 + \cos u_z} \tag{3.86c}$$

Example 3.3: Five-element array with optimum spacing This example is similar to Example 3.1, except that the spacing d is also optimized. For 20-dB side lobes $R = 10$ and $x_1 = 2.3452$. Hence, from Eq. (3.84), we obtain $a = 0.6726$, $b = 1.6726$, and the optimum spacing ($k_0 d$ is greater than π)

$$\frac{d}{\lambda_0} = \frac{1}{2\pi} \cos^{-1} \frac{3 - x_1}{1 + x_1} = 0.781$$

The beam width may be found from θ_z. The first zero to the left of 1 for $T_2(x)$ is at $x = 0.707$ so $u_z = 1.55$, as in Example 3.1. Thus we obtain $\theta_z = \cos^{-1}(u_z/k_0 d) = \cos^{-1} 1.55/(2\pi \times 0.781) = 71.59°$, which corresponds to a beam width of $2(90 - 71.59) = 36.82°$. This is considerably less than the 59.13° beam width obtained by using $d = \lambda_0/2$. The reduction in beam width is a result of making the overall array longer by increasing the spacing d to the maximum possible value without allowing a second major lobe to occur in visible space. The array pattern is shown in Fig. 3.33. ∎

In the discussion of Schelkunoff's polynomial representation of the array factor it was pointed out that for an array with $2N + 1$ elements a total of $2N$ zeros could be placed in visible space when the element spacing is less than $\lambda_0/2$. For element spacings approaching λ_0 the zeros are repeated, so a total of

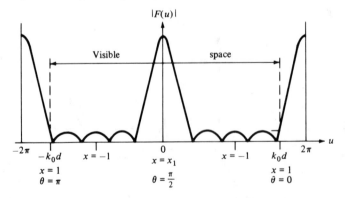

Figure 3.33 Array factor for a five-element Chebyshev array with optimum spacing (compare with Fig. 3.30).

4*N* zeros can be placed in visible space. The design procedures described above do result in the full use of the maximum available number of zeros.

The transformation $x = a + b \cos u$ was introduced by Riblet and is applicable to arrays with an odd number of elements only.† It may also be applied to end-fire arrays, and the design formulas may be found in a paper by DuHamel.‡

In the original paper by Dolph, the transformation $x = b \cos(u + u_0)/2$ was used. A function such as $\cos N\alpha$ can be expressed as a polynomial in $\cos \alpha$ of degree N and contains only even or odd powers in accordance with whether N is even or odd. This property is readily verified by repeated application of the formula

$$\cos N\alpha = 2 \cos \alpha \cos(N - 1)\alpha - \cos(N - 2)\alpha$$

The array factor for an array with an odd number of elements and with symmetrical excitation has the form

$$F_o = I_0 + \sum_{n=1}^{N} 2I_n \cos 2n\left(\frac{u + u_0}{2}\right)$$

while an array with an even number of elements has an array factor of the form

$$F_e = \sum_{n=1}^{N} 2I_n \cos \frac{2n - 1}{2}(u + u_0)$$

These array factors can be expressed as polynomials of the form

$$F_o = C_0 + \sum_{n=1}^{N} C_n\left(\cos \frac{u + u_0}{2}\right)^{2n}$$

$$F_e = \sum_{n=1}^{N} C_n\left(\cos \frac{u + u_0}{2}\right)^{2n-1}$$

where the C_n are suitable constants. Since the Chebyshev polynomial $T_M[b \cos(u + u_0)/2]$ is a polynomial of degree M in $\cos(u + u_0)/2$ and contains only even or odd powers in accordance with the parity of M, it follows that for both cases the array factor can be represented by a Chebyshev polynomial of degree one less than the number of elements in the array.

For the broadside array case, Dolph's method will not yield optimum designs if the spacing is less than $\lambda_0/2$, since it will not allow the full number of available zeros to be utilized. However, for the end-fire array and also for the broadside array with optimized spacing, Dolph's method gives optimum designs. The optimized designs for broadside arrays using either Dolph's

† H. J. Riblet, Discussion on "A Current Distribution for Broadside Arrays Which Optimizes the Relationship Between Beam Width and Sidelobe Level," *Proc. IRE*, vol. 35, May 1947, pp. 489–492.

‡ R. H. DuHamel, "Optimum Patterns for Endfire Arrays," *Proc. IRE*, vol. 41, May 1953, pp. 652–659.

transformation or Riblet's transformation are identical. The design formulas using Dolph's transformation $x = b \cos(u + u_0)/2$ are summarized below for arrays with N elements and an array factor $T_{N-1}[b \cos(u + u_0)/2]$.

Broadside Array with Optimum Spacing

1. Side-lobe ratio R specified:

$$b = \cosh\left(\frac{1}{N-1} \cosh^{-1} R\right) \tag{3.87a}$$

$$\cos \frac{k_0 d \cos \theta_z}{2} = \frac{\cos[\pi/2(N-1)]}{b} \tag{3.87b}$$

$$BW = \pi - 2\theta_z \tag{3.87c}$$

2. Beam width $(\pi - 2\theta_z)$ specified:

$$b = \frac{\cos[\pi/2(N-1)]}{\cos[(k_0 d \cos \theta_z)/2]} \tag{3.88a}$$

$$R = \cosh[(N-1)\cosh^{-1} b] \tag{3.88b}$$

For both cases the optimum spacing is determined by the relation

$$\cos \frac{k_0 d}{2} = -\frac{1}{b} \tag{3.89}$$

End-fire Arrays

1. Side-lobe ratio R specified:

$$x_1 = \cosh\left(\frac{1}{N-1} \cosh^{-1} R\right) \tag{3.90a}$$

$$b = \frac{[(1 + x_1^2) + 2x_1 \cos k_0 d]^{1/2}}{\sin k_0 d} \tag{3.90b}$$

$$u_0 = -2 \tan^{-1} \frac{(x_1 + 1)\cot(k_0 d/2)}{x_1 - 1} \tag{3.90c}$$

$$k_0 d \cos \theta_z = -u_0 - 2\cos^{-1}\left[\frac{1}{b}\cos\frac{\pi}{2(N-1)}\right] \tag{3.90d}$$

Beam width $= \theta_z$

The spacing must satisfy the condition

$$k_0 d \le 2 \tan^{-1}\left(\frac{x_1 + 1}{x_1 - 1}\right)^{1/2}$$

2. Beam width θ_z specified:

$$\cos\left(\frac{-u_0}{2}\right) = \frac{x_z \sin(k_0 d/2) - \sin[(k_0 d \cos \theta_z)/2]}{\{x_z^2 + 1 + 2x_z \cos[k_0 d(1 + \cos \theta_z)/2]\}^{1/2}} \qquad (3.91a)$$

where $x_z = \cos \dfrac{\pi}{2(N-1)}$ $\qquad\qquad (3.91b)$

$b = -\sec \dfrac{u_0 - k_0 d}{2}$ $\qquad\qquad\qquad (3.91c)$

$x_1 = b \cos \dfrac{k_0 d + u_0}{2}$ $\qquad\qquad\qquad (3.91d)$

$R = \cosh[(N-1)\cosh^{-1} b]$ $\qquad\qquad (3.91e)$

For the end-fire array the design is optimum for all values of $d < \lambda_0/2$.

The end-fire array design produces the unexpected result that for a given side-lobe level the beam width becomes smaller as the spacing is reduced. However, very small spacing results in a superdirective array, along with high currents and ohmic losses, as explained earlier.

3.8 FEED NETWORKS FOR ARRAYS

The design of a transmission-line network that will provide input currents having a prescribed amplitude and phase at each element can be very complicated, because the input impedance for each element is affected by the mutual impedance with all neighboring elements. In particular, the input impedance of the elements in the central portion of the array will be different from that of the elements near the sides of the array. The problem is further complicated in the case of nonuniformly excited elements because of the need to use some form of low-loss power-splitting circuit element to achieve different amplitude levels at the various elements. It is usually necessary to match each element to the transmission line feeding it in order to obtain acceptable performance from the array over a band of frequencies. In typical feed networks the various elements are usually grouped into smaller subgroups or bays according to the overall symmetry in the array. Similar bays are then fed from symmetrical feed networks. As an example, Fig. 3.34 shows a nine-element array arranged into three bays consisting of three elements each. Each bay is fed by a single transmission line, which is brought back to the main input transmission line. The symmetrical arrangement of the feed network ensures that the excitation of the overall array will also have a high degree of symmetry independent of impedance mismatches and mutual impedance effects. In the array of Fig. 3.34, elements 1, 3, 7, and 9 will have the same excitation as will elements 2 and 8 and also elements 4 and 6. By maintaining

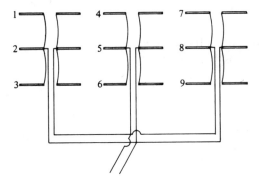

Figure 3.34 Nine-element array grouped into three bays to obtain a high degree of symmetry in the excitation of the elements.

symmetry in the feed network the problem of achieving the correct amplitude and phase of excitation for each element is greatly simplified.†

One useful method of feeding an element in an array that will force the current in the element to be related directly both in phase and amplitude to the voltage on a main feed line is to couple the element to the feed line through a section of transmission line one-quarter wavelength long, as shown in Fig. 3.35a. Let Z_f be the characteristic impedance of the main line and let Z_a be the characteristic impedance of the quarter-wave section. Also, let the antenna element input impedance be $Z_{a,in}$. If the voltage at the input to the quarter-wave section is V_f, then transmission-line theory requires that the current at the input to the quarter-wave section be $I_a = I_a^+ - I_a^-$ and that $V_f = Z_a(I_a^+ + I_a^-)$, where I_a^+ and I_a^- are the incident and reflected current waves on the quarter-wave section. At the antenna element these current waves are delayed and

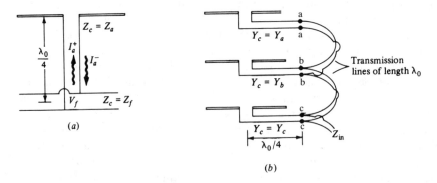

Figure 3.35 (a) A dipole fed through a quarter-wave section. (b) A three-element array fed through quarter-wave sections to produce currents proportional to Y_a, Y_b, and Y_c.

† The feed arrangement shown in Fig. 3.34 is often called a *corporate feed* by analogy with the typical management organization in a corporation. If the radiating elements are small horns, waveguides are used in place of transmission lines.

advanced by 90° and become

$$I_{in} = I_a^+ e^{-j\pi/2} - I_a^- e^{j\pi/2} = -j(I_a^+ + I_a^-)$$

$$= \frac{-jV_f}{Z_a} = -jY_a V_f$$

It is seen that I_{in} is related to V_f/Z_a independent of the antenna element input impedance and the characteristic impedance of the main line.

In Fig. 3.35b the above principle is applied to excite three elements with in-phase currents proportional to Y_a, Y_b, and Y_c. Since the length of the transmission line between each quarter-wave section is λ_0, the voltage at each point $a - a$, $b - b$, $c - c$, is the same, so the antenna element currents are proportional to the characteristic admittances of each $\lambda_0/4$ section. Transmission lines $\lambda_0/2$ can also be used by reversing the connection to element b to compensate for the 180° phase difference in the voltage at this point relative to that for elements a and c. The input impedance seen on the main line is the parallel combination of $Z_a^2/Z_{a,in}$, $Z_b^2/Z_{b,in}$, and $Z_c^2/Z_{c,in}$. If each element is matched to its quarter-wave section, then Z_{in} equals the parallel combination of Z_a, Z_b, and Z_c.

Butler Matrix

It is sometimes desirable to feed an array through a feed system that will have a number of input ports, with each input port exciting the array so as to produce one of many different beams all offset from each other by a finite angle. Such feed systems are known as *beam-forming matrices* and the best-known type is the Butler matrix.† Beam-forming matrices use a combination of hybrid junctions and fixed-phase shifters to achieve the desired results. A simple example of a Butler beam-forming matrix is shown in Fig. 3.36b. The feed system uses a hybrid junction such as the waveguide magic tee shown in Fig. 3.36a and a 90° fixed-phase shifter. The hybrid junction has the property that ports 1 and 4 as well as ports 2 and 3 are uncoupled. The transmission from port 1 to ports 2 and 3 is equal, while transmission from port 4 to ports 2 and 3 differs in phase by 180°. Consider now the effect of exciting port 1. The signal delivered to element A in the array will be $-90°$ out of phase with the signal delivered to element B. The beam is thus formed in the direction that will make the path length l from element B $\lambda_0/4$ longer than that from element A (Fig. 3.36d) in order to compensate for the $-90°$ phasing of element A. This direction is 45° to the left of the centerline, as shown in Fig. 3.36c. When port 4 is excited, the phase of element A will be advanced by 90° relative to that of element B and thus produces a beam at an angle of 45° on the right side of the centerline. Since ports 1 and 4 are uncoupled, these beams are independent

---

† See J. L. Butler, "Digital, Matrix, and Intermediate Frequency Scanning," in R. C. Hansen (ed.), *Microwave Scanning Arrays*, Academic Press, New York, 1966, Chap. 3.

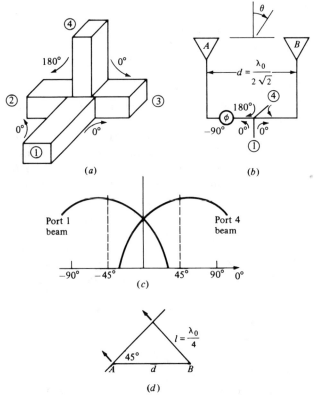

Figure 3.36 (*a*) Magic tee hybrid junction. (*b*) Two-element array with beam-forming matrix. (*c*) Beams formed by exciting ports 1 and 4. (*d*) Path-length delay *l* for maximum beam direction for port 1 beam.

and may exist separately or simultaneously. The principle involved in this two-element array may be extended to arrays with many elements and will result in a number of independent uncoupled input ports, each of which produces a single beam using the full gain capability of the array. The number of elements in the array must equal a power of 2 in order to construct the beam-forming matrix using hybrid junctions.

A Butler beam-forming matrix for a four-element array is shown in Fig. 3.37*a*. This matrix uses 90° phase-lag hybrid junctions with the transmission properties shown in Fig. 3.37*b*. By tracing the signal from the four input ports to the array elements, the reader can readily verify that the following aperture relative phase distributions are established:

Port 1:	0°	−135°	−270°	−405°
Port 2:	0°	−45°	−90°	−135°
Port 3:	0°	45°	90°	135°
Port 4:	0°	135°	270°	405°

The system produces four separate beams.

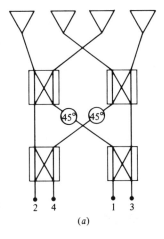

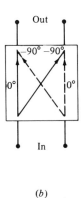

(a)

(b)

Figure 3.37 (a) A Butler beam-forming matrix for a four-element array. (b) Transmission phase relationships for a 90° phase-lag hybrid junction.

3.9 PARASITIC ARRAYS

Arrays in which not all of the elements are driven are called *parasitic arrays*. The nondriven, or parasitic, elements are excited by mutual impedance coupling with the driven elements, as well as with the other parasitic elements. Parasitic arrays have usually been designed by experimental methods because of the difficulty of calculating the mutual impedances, the element lengths, and the optimum spacings, since these parameters are all interrelated in a complex nonlinear way. The best-known parasitic array is the Yagi-Uda array.[†]

The simplest parasitic array is the two-element array, which is shown in Fig. 3.38a and which consists of a driven element and a reflector element. It is an end-fire array with maximum radiation along the array axis. We can view this two-element array as a two-terminal pair network. Since element 1, the reflector, is not driven, its terminal voltage is zero. Thus we can write

$$0 = Z_{11}I_1 + Z_{12}I_2 \tag{3.92a}$$

$$V_2 = Z_{12}I_1 + Z_{22}I_2 \tag{3.92b}$$

We can solve for the currents I_1 and I_2 to obtain

$$I_1 = \frac{-Z_{12}V_2}{Z_{11}Z_{22} - Z_{12}^2} \tag{3.93a}$$

$$I_2 = \frac{Z_{11}V_2}{Z_{11}Z_{22} - Z_{12}^2} \tag{3.93b}$$

[†] Some computer-generated design data for Yagi-Uda arrays is available; see P. Viezbickie, "Yagi Antenna Design," NBS Tech. Note 688, U.S. Government Printing Office, Dec. 1976.

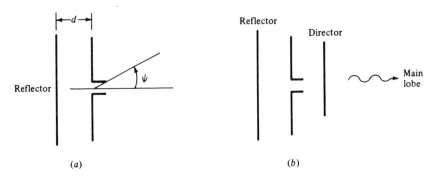

Figure 3.38 (*a*) A two-element parasitic array. (*b*) A three-element parasitic array.

The ratio of I_1 to I_2 is $-Z_{12}/Z_{11}$. If we let this ratio be $-|Z_{12}/Z_{11}| e^{j\alpha d}$, then the array factor will be

$$F(u) = 1 - \left|\frac{Z_{12}}{Z_{11}}\right| e^{j\alpha d - jk_0 d \cos \psi} \tag{3.94}$$

where ψ is the angle relative to the array axis. In order to obtain maximum radiation in the $\psi = 0$ direction, we require $\alpha d - k_0 d = \pm\pi$ or $d = \mp\pi/(k_0 - \alpha)$. If the radiation in the backwards direction $\psi = \pi$ is required to be zero, then we also need $\alpha d + k_0 d = 0$ or 2π and $|Z_{12}/Z_{11}| = 1$. It is generally not feasible to make $|Z_{12}/Z_{11}|$ equal unity so only a minimum and not a null can be obtained in the backward direction. The phase angle of Z_{11} can be varied by varying the element length. When the element is shorter than the resonant length, Z_{11} has a capacitive reactance, and when its length is greater than the resonant length the reactance is inductive. The mutual impedance Z_{12} depends on the spacing d. In practice it is found that the reflector-element length must be greater than the resonant length, and the spacing d should be around $0.15\lambda_0$ for the best approximation to the desired goals given above. Ideally we should have $d = \lambda_0/4$, $\alpha d = -\pi/2$ and $|Z_{12}/Z_{11}| = 1$. A spacing d equal to $\lambda_0/4$ results in a small value of Z_{12} and hence a small induced current. Thus a spacing smaller than $\lambda_0/4$ is better, even though the exact theoretically required value of the phase αd can generally not be obtained. With the optimum choice of spacing and element length a directivity of around 3 can be achieved.

If the parasitic element is made shorter than its resonant length it acts as a director, and maximum radiation occurs in the direction of the director element. Further improvement in directivity can be obtained by using both reflector and director parasitic elements, as shown in Fig. 3.38*b*. This array is the simplest form of the Yagi-Uda array.

A serious shortcoming of parasitic arrays is the small value of radiation resistance seen from the terminals of the driven element. The reduction in radiation resistance with a spacing of 0.1 wavelength for a single parasitic element is by a factor of about 0.15, and at a spacing of $0.5\lambda_0$ it is reduced by a factor of about 0.3. For a standard half-wave dipole the radiation resistance in the presence of a parasitic element would typically be 20 Ω or less. This value can be increased by a factor of 4 by using a folded dipole. In addition to the decrease in radiation resistance, the frequency band of operation usually does not exceed 2 or 3 percent because of the required critical tuning of the parasitic elements for optimum results.

A typical Yagi-Uda array is an end-fire array with one driven element, one reflector element, and several director elements, as shown in Fig. 3.39. With reference to Fig. 3.39 let Z_{ij} be the mutual impedance between elements i and j, let Z_{ii} be the self-impedance of element i, and, noting that all terminal voltages are zero except V_0 for the driven element, we can write the following circuit equations:

$$0 = Z_{-1-1}I_{-1} + Z_{-10}I_0 + Z_{-11}I_1 + \cdots Z_{-1N}I_N$$

$$V_0 = Z_{0-1}I_{-1} + Z_{00}I_0 + \cdots \cdots \cdots \cdots Z_{0N}I_N$$

$$\cdots\cdots\cdots\cdots\cdots\cdots\cdots\cdots\cdots\cdots\cdots\cdots\cdots\cdots\cdots$$

$$0 = Z_{N-1}I_{-1} + Z_{N0}I_0 + \cdots\cdots\cdots\cdots Z_{NN}I_N \qquad (3.95)$$

If we knew all of the Z_{ij} we could determine the currents I_i and then calculate the radiated field. The design problem requires that we choose the spacings d_i and element lengths l_i (which control the Z_{ii}) such that the currents I_i will have the proper phase to provide in-phase addition to the radiated field in the forward direction. Since the adjustable parameters are all interrelated, it is difficult to get good design data. Over the years a number of designs have been developed, mostly by experimental methods, and these are used to design Yagi-Uda arrays. With typical arrays of 8 to 10 elements, gains of around 14 dB are obtained. Because of the critical length of each element, the Yagi-Uda array is a narrow-band antenna and could be expected to operate satisfactorily over a bandwidth of a few percent only. Its popularity is due to its simple structure.†

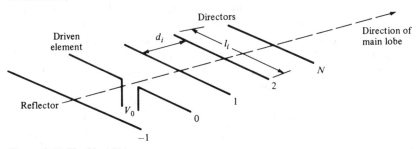

Figure 3.39 The Yagi-Uda array.

† Useful design information for Yagi-Uda arrays and for parasitic arrays in general may be found in the following references, in addition to the technical note by Viezbickie, which was cited earlier:

A.R.R.L. Antenna Handbook, American Radio Relay League, Inc., West Hartford, Conn., 1956.

A. B. Bailey, *TV and Other Receiving Antennas*, J. F. Rider, Publisher, Inc., New York, 1950.

R. M. Fishenden and E. R. Wiblin, "Design of Yagi Aerials," *Proc. IEEE, Pt. III*, vol. 96, Jan. 1949, p. 5.

S. Uda and Y. Mushiake, *Yagi-Uda Antenna*, Maruzen Co., Ltd., Tokyo, 1954 (in English).

3.10 LOG-PERIODIC ARRAYS

A significant advance in antenna design was achieved with the development of the log-periodic antennas. These antennas are truly broadband devices and can be built to operate over essentially any frequency band desired. Operation over a 3-to-1 frequency band or more is quite common in log-periodic antennas designed for television reception. The log-periodic antenna was developed by D. E. Isbell at the University of Illinois and was part of an extensive research program on frequency-independent antennas.[†]

The underlying concept in log-periodic antenna design is that of building a structure that scales into itself periodically as the frequency, and hence wavelength, changes. A given antenna that operates satisfactorily at a wavelength λ_1 will perform equally well at a wavelength λ_2 if its dimensions are changed by the factor λ_2/λ_1. Many of the central concepts on which frequency-independent antennas are based were originated by Professor V. H. Rumsey.[‡]

Consider the infinite array of dipoles shown in Fig. 3.40a, with the nth dipole of length l_n, a distance x_n from the apex, spaced d_n from element x_{n+1}, and having a radius a_n. All dimensions are related as follows:

$$\frac{x_{n+1}}{x_n} = \frac{l_{n+1}}{l_n} = \frac{d_{n+1}}{d_n} = \frac{a_{n+1}}{a_n} = \tau \tag{3.96}$$

The array is completely defined by any two of the parameters τ, $\sigma = d_n/2l_n$, or the angle α.

If we multiply all dimensions of this array by τ it scales into itself with element n becoming element $n + 1$, element $n + 1$ becoming element $n + 2$, etc. This self-scaling property implies that the array will have the same radiating properties at all frequencies that are related by a factor τ, that is, at $f_1, f_2 = \tau f_1$, $f_3 = \tau^2 f_1$, $f_4 = \tau^3 f_1$, etc. We note that $\ln f_2/f_1 = \ln \tau$, $\ln f_3/f_1 = \ln \tau^2 = 2 \ln \tau$, etc.; hence τ is called the *log period*, from which the array gets its name.

In order to obtain radiation from the array it must be excited by a feed system. It has been found experimentally that it is necessary to introduce a 180° phase reversal between elements, and this is accomplished by using a twisted transmission line feed, as shown in Fig. 3.40b. It has also been found that at a given frequency the currents in all elements except those that are close to one-half wavelength long are small because of the highly reactive impedance of nonresonant elements. In addition, the current along the feed line decreases

[†] E. C. Jordan et al., "Developments in Broadband Antennas," *IEEE Spectrum*, vol. 1, April 1964, pp. 58–71. The invention of the log-periodic dipole antenna was an evolutionary process stimulated by earlier work by J. Dyson and R. H. DuHamel on spiral antennas, log-periodic toothed structures, and trapezoidal log-periodic structures at the antenna laboratory of the University of Illinois. The evaluation of the log-periodic dipole array and the compilation of design data were carried out by R. L. Carrel.

[‡] V. H. Rumsey, "Frequency Independent Antennas," *IRE Nat'l Conv. Record*, 1957, pp. 114–118.

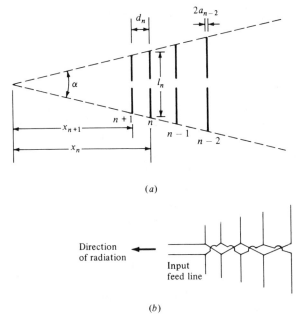

(a)

(b)

Figure 3.40 (a) Basic log-periodic dipole array. (b) Log-periodic antenna feed system.

rapidly beyond the resonant elements. These properties make it possible to terminate the array a few elements beyond those that resonate at the lowest frequency of interest and also at the front end a few elements before those that resonate at the highest frequency of interest. Over the frequency band thus defined the antenna has essentially the same properties at each frequency $\tau^n f$ and will have nearly the same performance at the frequencies between $\tau^n f$ and $\tau^{n+1} f$ when τ is close to 1.

Theoretical design information for the log-periodic dipole array is not available. However, a computer study of this antenna has been carried out by R. L. Carrel and design data based on this study is available.[†] It has been found that as τ varies from 0.96 to 0.8 the optimum value of σ varies linearly from 0.18 to 0.14. For τ close to 0.96, a gain of 12 dB is obtained, while for $\tau = 0.8$ the gain drops to 8 dB.

In addition to the log-periodic dipole array discussed above, other similar types of log-periodic structures have also been developed. Some of these predate the type of array considered here. Antennas based on the equiangular spiral configuration and having circular polarization are also among the class of frequency-independent antennas, since spirals are defined on the basis of an

---

[†] This data is summarized in W. L. Weeks, *Antenna Engineering*, McGraw-Hill Book Company, New York, 1968. See also R. L. Carrel, "Analysis and Design of the Log Periodic Dipole Antenna," *Univ. Ill. Antenna Lab. Tech. Rept.* 52, 1961.

angle and not a characteristic length. A discussion of these other antennas may be found in the literature.†

3.11 OTHER TYPES OF ARRAYS

The discussion so far is intended to provide a background on the basic principles involved in antenna arrays. It is, by no means, a complete discussion of arrays as currently used in practice. Antenna arrays are characterized by one important feature: The signal input (or output) of each element is separately available. This feature opens up the possibility of a variety of signal processing schemes that may be implemented in order to enhance the versatility and performance of the antenna system for different applications. A few of these special types of arrays are briefly described below.

Phased Arrays

Large antenna systems are difficult to mechanically scan in a rapid fashion, and because of this electronically scanned arrays have been developed. These arrays, which may have several thousand elements, are scanned by incorporating either ferrite or diode phase shifters in each feed line. The electronic control of these phase shifters to produce incremental changes in phase allows very fast scanning of the beam direction in space. Large phased arrays typically use open waveguides, small horns, or slots for the radiating elements. (These basic antennas are described in Chap. 4.) The array may have a planar aperture, or it may be made conformal to fit around cylindrical structures such as the fuselage of an aircraft. The applications for large phased arrays are mostly in advanced radar systems and in radio astronomy. Smaller phased arrays and beam-forming arrays are used as feed systems to illuminate a reflector in satellite communication systems when it is necessary to provide several spot beams, scanning beams, and/or wide-angle coverage beams from the one-antenna system.

The reader is referred to the papers by Stark and Mailloux for a discussion of large phased arrays and the associated problems and solutions that have been developed.‡ Arrays are also discussed in several specialized books and these are listed in the general bibliography at the end of this text.

Retrodirective or Self-Focusing Arrays

A retrodirective array is an array that will receive a signal from any direction in space and return a signal, usually after suitable modulation and amplification,

† Jordan et al., op. cit.

‡ L. Stark, "Microwave Theory of Phased-Array Antennas—A Review," *Proc. IEEE*, vol. 62, Dec. 1974, pp. 1661–1701; R. J. Mailloux, "Phased Array Theory and Technology," *Proc. IEEE*, vol. 70, Mar. 1982, pp. 246–291.

back to the source. The returned signal can be at a different carrier frequency if desired. A retrodirective array can be effectively used in a mobile communication system such as from a ground station to a moving aircraft or satellite. In this type of application the array would be used to receive a pilot signal in order to establish the direction of the source. The pilot signal would then be amplified, translated by a small increment in frequency, and modulated with the information to be sent to the moving aircraft or satellite. The basic principle of operation of a retrodirective array is illustrated in Fig. 3.41. Let the incoming signal received by element n in the array be $A_n \cos(\omega_1 t - \phi_n)$. The phase ϕ_n is a measure of the relative time delays from the source to the various elements in the array. In order to send a signal back to the source such that the signals from all the elements in the array will arrive with the same phase it is necessary to change the phase from ϕ_n to $-\phi_n$ for transmission. This reversal of the phase is equivalent to providing the proper time advance to the transmitted signals so that they will arrive at the source in phase.

The phase reversal may be accomplished by mixing the signal with a common local oscillator having a frequency equal to twice that of the incoming signal plus the desired offset $\Delta\omega$. For the signal at the nth element the mixing operation gives

$$A_n \cos(\omega_1 t - \phi_n) \cos[(2\omega_1 + \Delta\omega)t] = \frac{A_n}{2} \cos[(\omega_1$$

$$+ \Delta\omega)t + \phi_n] + \frac{A_n}{2} \cos[(3\omega_1 + \Delta\omega)t - \phi_n]$$

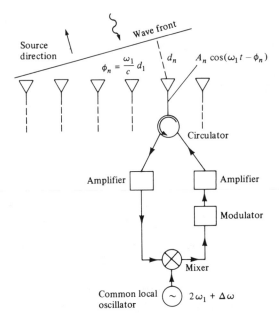

Figure 3.41 A retrodirective array. Each element has the same electronic circuit.

The lower sideband signal is the desired one, since it has the reversed phase. This signal is selected by an appropriate filter and then modulated with the information to be transmitted. A circulator is used to separate the incoming and outgoing signal paths. The frequency offset must be kept small since it results in some shift in the beam direction from that of the incoming wave. That this is the case can be seen by considering the factor $k_0 d \cos \psi + \alpha d$ that occurs in the array factor and establishes the beam direction, which is $\psi_0 = \cos^{-1}(-\alpha/k_0)$. Clearly a change in $k_0 = \omega/c$ will change the beam direction ψ_0, but the change will be small if the change in ω is small.

Adaptive Arrays

Adaptive arrays are arrays that will self-adapt to various incoming signal conditions so as to maximize the signal from a particular source or to null out interfering signals. A variety of configurations are possible. For illustration we will consider the self-phasing array, shown in Fig. 3.42, which is designed to bring all the signals received by the various elements from a particular source into phase. The basic principle that is utilized is to mix all of the incoming signals with separate local oscillators whose phases are adjusted so that all of the signals at the intermediate frequency are in phase and may be added together in a summing amplifier. These objectives are achieved by using

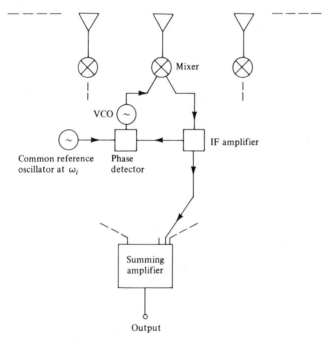

Figure 3.42 A self-phasing adaptive array. Each element has its own VCO, IF amplifier, and phase detector. A common oscillator provides the phase reference signal.

phase-locked loop principles. Each local oscillator is a voltage-controlled oscillator (VCO) whose instantaneous phase is controlled by an applied voltage. The phase of the mixed signal at the intermediate frequency is compared with that of a fixed reference oscillator operating at the intermediate frequency ω_i. A phase detector produces an error voltage $V(\phi)$ with a magnitude proportional to the phase error and with a sign that causes the phase of the voltage-controlled oscillator to change so as to reduce the phase error to zero. The voltage-controlled oscillators are thus forced to track with the frequency ω_i above (or below) the signal frequency and with a phase offset such that the intermediate frequency signal has the same phase as that of the reference oscillator.

Other types of signal-processing arrays and adaptive arrays are described by Bickmore[†] and in a special issue of the *IEEE Transactions*.[‡]

There are also arrays that employ nonlinear signal processing, such as multiplying or correlating the signals received on two different arrays. Arrays of this type find application in radio astronomy and are described in detail by Ksienski.[§]

3.12 LONG-WIRE ANTENNAS

In the frequency band from 2 to 30 MHz long wires (several wavelengths in length) supported by suitable towers may be used as efficient antennas. The best-known types are the horizontal V antenna, the horizontal rhombic antenna, the vertical V and sloping rhombic antennas, the vertical inverted V or half-rhombic antenna, and the single-horizontal-wire antenna. Illustrations of these antennas are shown in Fig. 3.43. Most long-wire antennas can be operated as resonant antennas, in which case the current on the wire will be a standing wave with the characteristic sinusoidal variation. These antennas usually operate satisfactorily only at a particular frequency and harmonics of this frequency. The input impedance will be highly frequency-sensitive, so only narrow-band operation is possible. Most long-wire antennas can also be operated as traveling-wave or nonresonant structures by terminating the far end of the wire (or wires) in a suitable resistance having a value equal to the characteristic impedance of the antenna viewed as a transmission line. In this mode of operation the useful frequency band can be quite large, with an acceptable impedance match over the whole range of frequencies.

Various types of long-wire antennas are used for commercial shortwave transmission in the frequency range from 2 to 30 MHz when propagation is by means of ionospheric reflection. For these applications the optimum angle of

† R. W. Bickmore, "Adaptive Antenna Arrays," *Spectrum*, vol. 1, Aug. 1964, pp. 78–88.

‡ *IEEE Trans. Antennas Propag.*, vol. AP-12, March 1964.

§ A. A. Ksienski, "Signal Processing Antennas," Chap. 27 in R. E. Collin and F. J. Zucker (eds.), *Antenna Theory*, Part II, McGraw-Hill Book Company, New York, 1969.

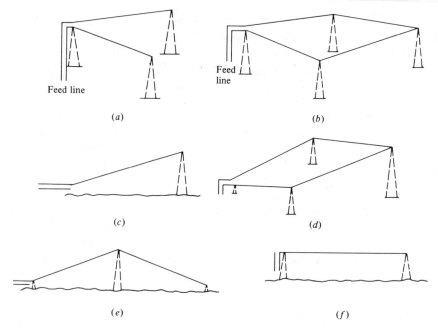

Figure 3.43 Long-wire antennas. Dashed lines represent support towers. (*a*) Horizontal V. (*b*) Horizontal rhombic. (*c*) Vertical V. (*d*) Sloping rhombic. (*e*) Inverted V. (*f*) Horizontal straight wire.

radiation is usually from 10 to 30° relative to the horizontal line in the direction of the receiving station.

Since long-wire antennas are located in the presence of the ground, the latter has an important effect on the radiation pattern and must be taken into account in the design of the antenna configuration. In general, the design problem is one of obtaining a directive beam at the desired angle relative to the ground for optimum long-distance communication via reflection from the ionosphere (ionospheric propagation is discussed in Chap. 6), along with acceptable input impedance characteristics that will facilitate matching the antenna to its feed line.

In this section we will first examine some of the radiation characteristics of typical long-wire antennas in free space. The effect the ground has on the radiation pattern will then be introduced by applying the principle of pattern multiplication from array theory. From the results thus obtained it will be possible to predict the main features associated with long-wire antennas in the presence of the ground.

Radiation from a Resonant Long-Wire Antenna

Figure 3.44 shows a long-wire antenna of length $l = n\lambda_0/2$ with a current distribution $I(x) = I_0 \sin k_0 x$. It will be convenient to use the angle ψ as the

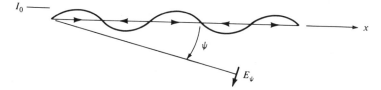

Figure 3.44 Straight-wire antenna with sinusoidal current distribution.

polar angle relative to the direction of the wire and to express the radiated electric field as E_ψ. The field may be found in the same manner as used for the half-wave dipole antenna in Chap. 2; it is given by

$$E_\psi = \frac{jk_0 I_0 Z_0}{4\pi r} \sin\psi \int_0^{n\lambda_0/2} \sin k_0 x' \, e^{-jk_0 r + jk_0 x' \cos\psi} \, dx'$$

$$= \frac{I_0 Z_0}{2\pi r} e^{-jk_0 r + j(n\pi/2)(1+\cos\psi)} \left\{ \begin{array}{ll} \dfrac{\sin(n\pi/2)\cos[(n\pi/2)\cos\psi]}{\sin\psi} & n,\ \text{odd} \\[2ex] \dfrac{\cos(n\pi/2)\sin[(n\pi/2)\cos\psi]}{\sin\psi} & n,\ \text{even} \end{array} \right.$$

$$= \frac{-I_0 Z_0}{2\pi r} e^{-jk_0 r + j(n\pi/2)(1+\cos\psi)} (-1)^n \frac{\sin[n\pi \sin^2(\psi/2)]}{\sin\psi} \qquad (3.97)$$

The last expression is obtained by replacing $\cos\psi$ by

$$1 - 2\sin^2(\psi/2)$$

and expanding the trigonometric functions. The resultant radiation patterns for $n = 2$, 3, and 4 are shown in Fig. 3.45. The patterns shown should be revolved around the axis of the wire to get the three-dimensional radiation patterns, which are then seen to consist of several cones of radiation. In general, the number of lobes or cones formed is equal to n. The pattern is symmetrical with respect to the plane that is perpendicular to the midpoint of the wire. When n is even, there is a null in the direction $\psi = \pi/2$, that is, perpendicular to the wire. As n increases, the lobes become sharper. The first major lobe makes a smaller angle with respect to the wire axis as n increases in value. As the length of the antenna increases, the maximum directivity increases along with the radiation resistance referred to the current maximum, that is, $\frac{1}{2}I_0^2 R_a = P_r$. Table 3.2 lists representative values for the directivity and radiation resistance.

The long-wire antenna may be fed at one end, as shown in Fig. 3.46a and b. However, because of the unsymmetrical arrangement the currents in the transmission line will not be balanced, and some radiation will occur from the feed line itself. A more satisfactory feed arrangement is to connect the transmission line at the center of a current loop as close to the midpoint of the antennas as possible, as in Fig. 3.46b. A $\lambda_0/4$ transformer can be used to

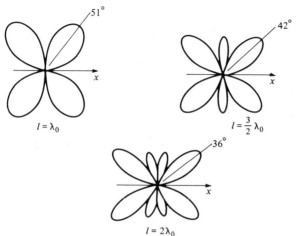

Figure 3.45 Radiation patterns for the long-wire antenna with sinusoidal current distribution.

transform the radiation resistance to the commonly used 600-Ω two-wire transmission line. The required characteristic impedance of the matching section is given by $Z_c = \sqrt{600 R_a}$.

Radiation from a V Antenna

The V antenna shown in Fig. 3.47 consists of two straight-wire antennas arranged so as to subtend an angle ψ_0. The radiation is the superposition of that from each straight-wire section. The objective in the design of a V antenna is to choose the angle ψ_0 so as to align the two lobes produced by each straight-wire section. If a maximum in the direction of the V antenna and in the plane of the V antenna is desired, then the optimum value for the angle ψ_0 is twice the angle that the radiation lobe makes with the wire axis for a straight-wire antenna. If each arm of the V antenna is $3\lambda_0/2$ long, this optimum angle is 84°, as reference to Fig. 3.45 shows. For $l = 2\lambda_0$, the optimum angle is approximately 72°. The currents on the two arms of the V antenna are out of phase, but this is just the condition required for the electric field E_ψ radiated by each arm to be in phase in the direction of maximum radiation. The resultant radiation pattern of the V antenna will have a maximum lobe in both the forward and backward directions. Smaller minor lobes will occur in between.

For a horizontal V antenna designed to radiate with a maximum at an

Table 3.2

$2l/\lambda_0$	1	2	3	4	5	6	7	8
D	1.64	1.8	2	2.1	2.5	2.7	2.9	3.3
R_a	73	94	105	114	121	126	131	135

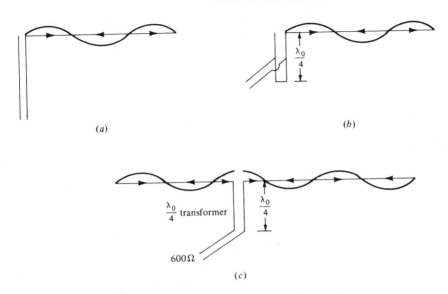

(a)

(b)

$\dfrac{\lambda_0}{4}$ transformer

$\dfrac{\lambda_0}{4}$

$600\,\Omega$

(c)

Figure 3.46 Methods of feeding a long-wire antenna. (a) End feed using a resonant feed line. (b) End feed using a matching section. (c) Feed at current maximum near midpoint of wire.

angle γ relative to the horizontal plane, the angle ψ_0 must be reduced to bring the lobes into alignment. That this is the case may be seen by recalling that the pattern from a single wire is a cone of radiation, so that in order to bring the points labeled P_1 and P_2 in Fig. 3.48 into coincidence, the V angle ψ_0 must be reduced. An alternative procedure is to slope the V antenna upwards by the required elevation angle γ.

The discussion above applies in general to the rhombic antenna also. The design objective is to choose the angular orientation of each straight-wire section so as to align the radiation lobes from the four individual sections in

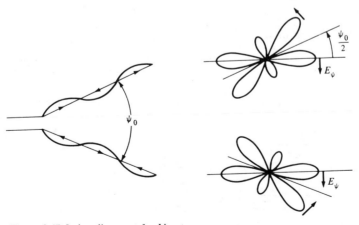

Figure 3.47 Lobe alignment for V antenna.

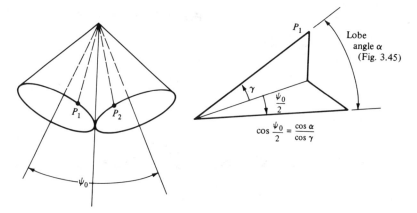

Figure 3.48 Radiation cone alignment for V antenna.

one common direction. In addition, the length of each arm must be chosen so as to obtain in-phase addition of the field radiated by each straight-wire section.

Radiation from a Long-Wire Antenna with Traveling Wave Current

If the far end of the straight-wire antenna is terminated in a matched resistance, as shown schematically in Fig. 3.49, the current distribution on the antenna can be approximated as a traveling wave of the form $I = I_0 e^{-jk_0 x}$. The resultant radiation pattern is given by

$$E_\psi = \frac{jk_0 I_0 Z_0}{4\pi r} \sin \psi \, e^{-jk_0 r} \int_0^l e^{-jk_0 x'(1-\cos \psi)} \, dx'$$

$$= \frac{jI_0 Z_0}{4\pi r} e^{-jk_0[r+(l/2)(1-\cos \psi)]} \sin \psi \, \frac{\sin[k_0 l \sin^2(\psi/2)]}{\sin^2(\psi/2)} \tag{3.98}$$

The lobe maxima are determined by

$$\frac{\tan \beta}{\beta} = 2 - \frac{2\beta}{k_0 l} \tag{3.99}$$

where $\beta = k_0 l \sin^2(\psi/2)$. For $k_0 l \gg 1$ the solution is $\beta = 1.165$. For other values

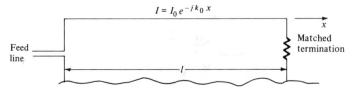

Figure 3.49 Traveling-wave antenna.

of $k_0 l$, this value can be used for β on the right-hand side in Eq. (3.99) to obtain a corrected value for β. A somewhat more realistic approximation for the current is $I_0 e^{-jk_0x-\alpha x}$, where the attenuation constant α accounts for radiation loss from the antenna as the current wave propagates along the wire. The attenuation factor α is small and produces only a small change in the radiation pattern, so we are neglecting this effect.

The radiation pattern for the traveling-wave antenna is shown in Fig. 3.50 for two different antenna lengths l. The main feature exhibited by these patterns is a major cone of radiation in the forward direction and the absence of a major cone of radiation in the backward direction. As the length of the antenna is increased, the angle of the major cone decreases. If $l = n\lambda_0$ there will be a total of $2n$ lobes.

The V antenna can be converted to a traveling-wave antenna by terminating each arm in a matched resistance. The optimum V angle is chosen to align the radiation cones from each arm in the one common desired direction. The principles involved are the same as those for the resonant V antenna.

The rhombic antenna can also be made into a traveling-wave antenna by inserting a suitable resistance at the vertex farthest away from the feed end. The current on each wire in the rhombus will then be a traveling current wave analogous to that on a transmission line terminated in a matched load. The nominal input resistance of the rhombic antenna is in the range of 700 to 800 Ω.

The traveling-wave antennas have the advantage that the input impedance is mostly resistive and relatively independent of frequency. Thus these antennas will operate over a fairly broad frequency band. The limiting factor is primarily the misalignment of the lobes that takes place as the frequency is changed.

Ground Interference Effects

Consider the long-horizontal-wire antenna shown in Fig. 3.51. For radiation at

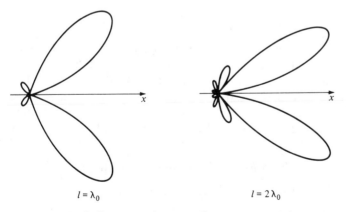

$l = \lambda_0$ $l = 2\lambda_0$

Figure 3.50 Radiation pattern for a traveling-wave antenna.

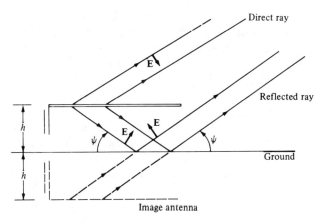

Figure 3.51 Illustration of ground reflection.

the angle ψ, the field has a contribution from the direct radiation from the antenna and from radiation reflected from the ground at the angle ψ. The reflected radiation undergoes a propagation-phase delay equivalent to that from the image of the antenna in the ground. If the field radiated by the antenna in free space is

$$E = f(\psi)\frac{e^{-jk_0r}}{4\pi r}$$

the total field obtained by taking the reflected field into account will be

$$E = f(\psi)\frac{e^{-jk_0r}}{4\pi r}(1 + \rho\, e^{j\alpha - j2k_0h\, \sin\psi}) \qquad (3.100)$$

where $\rho\, e^{j\alpha}$ is the reflection coefficient at the ground and $2h \sin \psi$ is the extra propagation distance introduced when the antenna is at a height h. This expression is seen to be of the same form as that occurring in array theory, with the array factor being

$$F(\psi) = 1 + \rho\, e^{j\alpha - 2jk_0h\, \sin\psi} \qquad (3.101)$$

The reflection coefficient depends on the conductivity of the ground, on the grazing angle ψ, and on whether the field is vertically or horizontally polarized. For these reasons no simple universal evaluation of Eq. (3.101) is possible. It is often possible to assume that the ground acts as a perfectly conducting surface without serious error. In this case $\rho = 1$ and $\alpha = \pi$ for horizontal polarization and $\alpha = 0$ for vertical polarization.[†] With these idealized conditions the array factor becomes

$$|F(\psi)| = 2|\sin(k_0h\, \sin\psi)| \qquad \text{horizontal polarization}$$

$$|F(\psi)| = 2|\cos(k_0h\, \sin\psi)| \qquad \text{vertical polarization}$$

[†] When the grazing angle is only a few degrees or less, the reflection coefficient can be approximated by -1 for both polarizations (see Sec. 6.1).

For a horizontal wire the reflected field is out of phase with the direct radiation, as shown in Fig. 3.51; that is, the image current is out of phase with the antenna current, so the appropriate array factor to use is $2|\sin(k_0 h \sin \psi)|$, which is approximately equal to $2|\sin k_0 h \psi|$ for the range of angles ψ of interest in practice. The array factor is shown in Fig. 3.52 for values of h corresponding to $\lambda_0/4$, $\lambda_0/2$, and λ_0. It is readily seen that the reflection from the ground will reduce the far field significantly at low elevation angles unless the antenna height is large enough so that the array factor itself will exhibit a lobe maximum in the desired direction. For example, for a maximum at $\psi = 20°$ we require $k_0 h \psi = 90°$ or $h = 2.25\lambda_0/\pi = 0.72\lambda_0$. With this height the free-space field is doubled in value by the reflected field adding in phase. With an actual ground the reflection coefficient ρ will be less than unity; nevertheless a significant reinforcement of the direct radiation will occur when the antenna height is appropriately chosen.

In a later chapter where propagation at frequencies below 2 MHz is discussed it is shown that the dominant mode of propagation is by means of the surface wave. For this mode of propagation horizontally polarized fields are attenuated much more rapidly than vertically polarized fields. For this reason horizontally oriented long-wire antennas are normally not used below 2 MHz. In the shortwave band from 2 to 30 MHz, where propagation is via ionospheric reflection, long-wire antennas are effective and because of their simple structure are commonly used. Rhombic and V antennas also find some applications at frequencies from 30 to 60 MHz.

A considerable amount of design data for long-wire antennas has been worked out, and the reader is referred to the literature for this information.†

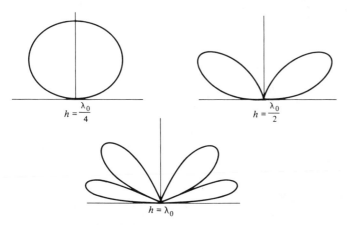

Figure 3.52 Array factor for horizontal antenna above a perfect ground.

† *A.R.R.L. Antenna Handbook*, op. cit.
Jasik, op. cit.
A. E. Harper, *Rhombic Antenna Design*, D. Van Nostrand Co., Inc., Princeton, N.J., 1941.
D. Foster, "Radiation from Rhombic Antennas," *Proc. IRE*, vol. 25, Oct., 1937, p. 1327.

PROBLEMS

3.1 Let a transmission line have inductance L and capacitance C per unit length. Then the following relations hold:

$$k_0 = \omega(\mu_0\epsilon_0)^{1/2} = \omega(LC)^{1/2}$$

$$Z_c = (L/C)^{1/2}$$

Use these relations, along with Eq. (3.10), to show that for a biconical antenna

$$L = (\mu_0\epsilon_0)^{1/2}Z_c = \frac{\mu_0}{\pi}\ln\cot\frac{\theta_0}{2}$$

$$C - (\mu_0\epsilon_0)^{1/2}Y_c = \frac{\pi\epsilon_0}{\ln\cot(\theta_0/2)}$$

3.2 A biconical antenna has an input impedance of $130 + j40\ \Omega$ and is connected to a transmission line with characteristic impedance of $158\ \Omega$. Find the power reflection coefficient and the VSWR on the input transmission line.

3.3 Find the radiation pattern of a dipole antenna of total length $3\lambda_0/2$. The antenna is located along the z axis between $-3\lambda_0/4$ and $3\lambda_0/4$. The current on the antenna is given by $I_0 \cos k_0 z$. Sketch the radiation pattern and compare the field strength in the $\theta = \pi/2$ plane with that produced by a dipole $\lambda_0/2$ long. Give a physical reason why the longer antenna does not produce a larger field strength.

3.4 Find the maximum field strength along the x axis for the V-shaped dipole antenna shown in Fig. P3.4. Consider the two cases when $l_0 = \lambda_0/4$ and $l_0 = 3\lambda_0/4$. Compare the field strength for the two cases with that obtained in Prob. 3.3 when $\alpha = 30$ and $45°$. *Hint*: Show that on the x axis E_θ is given by

$$E_\theta = j\omega A_z = \frac{jk_0Z_0}{4\pi x}e^{-jk_0x}2I_0\cos\alpha\int_0^{l_0}\cos k_0u\,e^{jk_0u\,\sin\alpha}\,du$$

The current is $I_0 \cos k_0 u$.

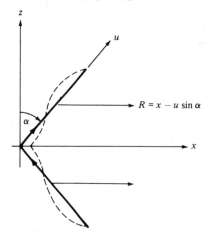

Figure P3.4

3.5 A two-wire transmission line is required to have a characteristic impedance of 73 Ω. The conductors have a diameter of 0.5 in. Find the required spacing D. See Fig. II-2 in Appendix II. Is this a practical transmission line?

3.6 For the transmission line circuit shown in Fig. 3.10 let $I(z) = I_0 \sin(\alpha - k_0 z)/\sin \alpha$. Use $\partial I/\partial z = -j\omega C_0 V$ to find $V(z)$. At $z = l/2$ the terminal condition $I = j\omega C V$ must hold. Use these results to derive Eq. (3.33) where $X_c = 1/\omega C$.

3.7 The transmission-line model of the dual-band dipole antenna shown in Fig. 3.11 is like that shown in Fig. 3.8 but with $L_0/2$ replaced by the parallel resonant $L_1 C_1$ circuit. It is desired to operate this antenna at a frequency f_1 and also at $f_2 = 1.5f_1$. Find the required lengths l_1, l and the parameters L_1, C_1 when $f_1 = 50$ MHz and the antenna characteristic impedance Z_c equals 600 Ω. A practical value to use for $\sqrt{L_1/C_1}$ is 600 Ω. *Hint*: The input impedance in the transmission-line model must vanish at both frequencies. At f_2 the resonant circuits have infinite (in practice, very large) impedance.

3.8 A uniform line array of five elements has a spacing of $d = 0.4\lambda_0$. Find the phasing in order to produce a beam at 45° to the array axis, that is, at $\psi = \pi/4$. Plot the array factor $|F|$ and show the visible region. Sketch the main lobe radiation pattern.

3.9 A line array is required that will produce beams at $\psi = 0$, $\pi/2$, and π. Find the required spacing d and the phase of excitation of each element.

3.10 An antenna produces a field $E_\theta = C \cos^3 \theta(e^{-jk_0 r}/4\pi r)$ where C is a constant. The pattern consists of beams along the $\pm z$ axis.

    (*a*) Find the total radiated power.
    (*b*) Find the directivity D at $\theta = 0$.
    (*c*) Find the half-power beam width.
    (*d*) Find the solid angle occupied by the beam up to the half-power angle. This is given by the area intercepted by the beam on a sphere of unit radius.
    (*e*) Estimate the directivity by dividing 4π by the solid angle of the two beams up to the half-power angle and compare with the exact result obtained in (*b*).

3.11 Consider the two-element array, shown in Fig. P3.11, consisting of half-wave dipoles at $x = 0$, $x = d$ on the x axis. The current in the two dipoles is I_0 and $I_0 e^{j\alpha d}$. Find α and the spacing d so that zero radiation occurs in the $-x$ direction and maximum radiation occurs in the $+x$ direction. Sketch the radiation pattern in the xy plane.

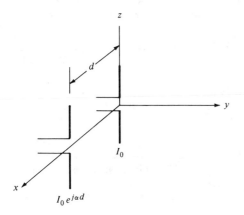

$I_0 e^{j\alpha d}$ **Figure P3.11**

3.12 Use the Fourier series method to find a seven-element array that will produce a least-mean-square error approximation to the array factor F_d shown in Fig. P3.12. Sketch the approximate pattern. Assume $d = \lambda_0/2$.

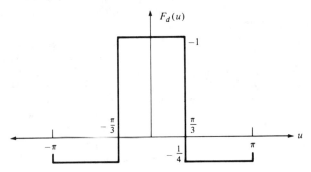

Figure P3.12

3.13 Use the array polynomial method to design a six-element broadside array with a radiation pattern having nulls at $\theta = 0$, $\pi/6$, $\pi/3$, $2\pi/3$, $5\pi/6$ and π. Choose $d = \lambda_0/2$ and find the relative values of the required current in each element. Sketch the array factor. Note that the zeros at $\theta = 0$, π both correspond to $Z = -1$.

3.14 Design a seven-element broadside array having double zeros in its radiation pattern at $\theta = 0$, $\pi/4$, $3\pi/4$, and π. Assume that $d = \lambda_0/2$. Find the relative value of the required current in each element. Sketch the array factor. Note that the zeros at $\theta = 0$, π both correspond to $Z = -1$. Repeat the design when $d = \lambda_0/3$ and nine elements are used.

3.15 Design a seven-element Chebyshev array with $d = \lambda_0/2$ having side lobes 26 dB below the main lobe. Find the excitation coefficients and the beam width. Sketch the array factor $|F(u)|$.

3.16 Find the excitation coefficients and side-lobe level for a five-element broadside Chebyshev array with element spacing $d = \lambda_0/2$ and having a beam width of 55°.

3.17 Find the currents for a five-element superdirective array of length $L = \lambda_0/4$ and with side lobes 20 dB down. Find the beam width. Sketch the array factor. Find the effective radiating current in the direction of the main lobe. You will need six-figure accuracy in the computations.

3.18 Repeat Prob. 3.17 but use an array length $L = \lambda_0$. What is the peak value of $F(u)$ in the invisible region? This occurs when $x = a + b \cos u = a + b \cos \pi = a - b$ and may be found from $T_2(x)$ for this value of x.

3.19 Design a five-element optimum Chebyshev array having the specifications given in Example 3.3. Use the design formulas given by Eq. (3.87). Note that the same results as in Example 3.3 are obtained.

3.20 Design an optimum end-fire array with five elements using the design formulas given by Eq. (3.90). Carry out the design for the three cases—$k_0d = 0.6\pi$, 0.4π, and 0.1π—and compare the beam widths in the three cases. The smaller spacings result in a supergain design with extreme values for the currents. The side lobe ratio $R = 10$.

Answer: The beam widths are 56.3, 50.6, and 47.5°. For $k_0d = 0.01\pi$ the beam width is 47.34°.

3.21 For the four-element array driven through the Butler beam-forming matrix shown in Fig. 3.37 verify that the relative aperture phase distributions are as given in the text. If the element spacing d equals $\lambda_0/2$, find the directions in space of the four beams.

3.22 Consider the two-element array shown in Fig. P3.22. This array is fed through a 90° phase-lag hybrid junction, and a −90° phase shifter is incorporated in one feed line. The element spacing $d = 3\lambda_0/4$. Find the directions of the beams that are formed by exciting ports 1 and 2.

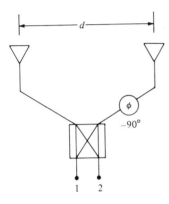

Figure P3.22

3.23 Find the optimum angle ψ_0 for a V antenna, having arms $2\lambda_0$ long, which will produce maximum radiation at an elevation angle of 10°.

3.24 For the inverted V antenna shown in Fig. P3.24 find the optimum angle ψ_0 in order to obtain maximum radiation at an elevation angle of 0°. Each leg of the antenna is $3\lambda_0/2$ long. Can the lobes be aligned for maximum radiation at a finite elevation angle γ?

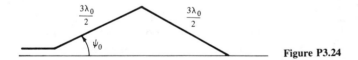

Figure P3.24

3.25 Carry out the basic design of a traveling-wave rhombic antenna with arms that are $4\lambda_0$ long. Specify the angles that will align the lobes in the plane of the rhombus. Will this angle cause the field radiated from each arm of the rhombus to add in phase in the desired direction? Find the angles that will result in the correct phase. *Hint*: Consider the relative propagation delay from the middle of each wire. The electric field in the aligned lobes is oppositely oriented corresponding to a relative phase of π radians. Since $l = 4\lambda_0$, the current at the center of each leg is in phase. Thus the center of the forward leg should be $n\lambda_0 + \lambda_0/2$ ahead of the center of the leg at the feed end. Change the rhombus angle to obtain correct phasing. Plot the resultant pattern.

FOUR

APERTURE-TYPE ANTENNAS

All of the antennas discussed so far could be analyzed in terms of the current distribution on the antenna. There is another broad class of antennas, more conveniently viewed as *aperture antennas*, in which the radiation is considered to occur from an aperture. Two common antennas in this class are the paraboloidal reflector antenna and the horn antenna. An aperture-type antenna must have an aperture length and width of at least several wavelengths in order to have a high gain. Thus it is no surprise that aperture-type antennas find their most important applications in the microwave frequency band where the wavelength is only a few centimeters.

In the first part of this chapter we will develop the necessary theory for calculating the radiation field in terms of an assumed known field distribution over the aperture of the antenna. This theory is the counterpart of the theory used to calculate the radiation field in terms of an assumed current distribution.

After the basic theory has been developed, we will apply it to analyze some of the more important features associated with open waveguide and horn antennas, lenses, and paraboloidal reflector antennas; radiation from slots and waveguide slot arrays; and microstrip antennas.

4.1. RADIATION FROM A PLANAR APERTURE: THE FOURIER TRANSFORM METHOD

The first approach that we will use to find the field radiated from a planar aperture will be based on Fourier transforms. The importance of this method is that it shows that the radiation-field pattern is the Fourier transform of the aperture field. This enables one to use many of the known properties of Fourier transform pairs to predict the performance of aperture-type antennas.

In Fig. 4.1 we show an aperture S_a located in the $z = 0$ plane. We assume that we know the tangential components of the electric field on this aperture surface and let $\mathbf{E}_a$ denote this field. We wish to determine the radiated field in the region $z > 0$. We can imagine that the aperture field is somehow established by means of suitable sources in the region $z < 0$. We do not need to know these sources since the field $\mathbf{E}_a$ on the aperture will uniquely determine the field in the half space $z > 0$.

If we have a function of x, say, $w(x)$, its Fourier transform is

$$W(k_x) = \int_{-\infty}^{\infty} w(x)\, e^{jk_x x}\, dx \tag{4.1a}$$

and the inverse relation is

$$w(x) = \frac{1}{2\pi} \int_{-\infty}^{\infty} W(k_x)\, e^{-jk_x x}\, dk_x \tag{4.1b}$$

The variables k_x and x play the same role as time t and radian frequency ω in the Fourier analysis of time signals. In a similar manner, if we have a function of both x and y, say, $u(x, y)$, we can apply the Fourier transform to both variables; thus

$$U(k_x, k_y) = \int\!\!\int_{-\infty}^{\infty} u(x, y)\, e^{jk_x x + jk_y y}\, dx\, dy \tag{4.2a}$$

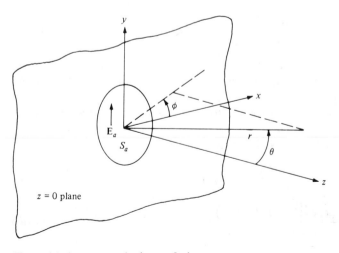

Figure 4.1 An aperture in the $z = 0$ plane.

for which the inverse relation is

$$u(x, y) = \frac{1}{4\pi^2} \int\limits_{-\infty}^{\infty}\!\!\int U(k_x, k_y)\, e^{-jk_x x - jk_y y}\, dk_x\, dk_y \tag{4.2b}$$

These are the basic formulas we will use.

In Chap. 2 it was shown that the electric field satisfied the following equation [Eq. (2.12)]:

$$\nabla \times \nabla \times \mathbf{E} - k_0^2 \mathbf{E} = -j\omega\mu_0 \mathbf{J}$$

Now $\nabla \times \nabla \times \mathbf{E} = \nabla\nabla \cdot \mathbf{E} - \nabla^2\mathbf{E}$, and in the region $z > 0$ both $\mathbf{J}$ and ρ are zero, so $\nabla \cdot \mathbf{E} = 0$, and the equation satisfied by $\mathbf{E}$ becomes

$$\nabla^2\mathbf{E} + k_0^2\mathbf{E} = 0 \tag{4.3a}$$

$$\nabla \cdot \mathbf{E} = 0 \tag{4.3b}$$

For the conventional Fourier transform we have the operational property that

$$\mathscr{F}_t \frac{ds(t)}{dt} = j\omega \mathscr{F}_t s(t) \tag{4.4}$$

that is, the Fourier transform of the time derivative of a function equals $j\omega$ times the Fourier transform of the function. In a similar manner we will have

$$\mathscr{F}_x \frac{\partial u(x, y)}{\partial x} = -jk_x \mathscr{F}_x u(x, y) \tag{4.5a}$$

$$\mathscr{F}_x \frac{\partial^2 u(x, y)}{\partial x^2} = (-jk_x)^2 \mathscr{F}_x u(x, y) \tag{4.5b}$$

$$\mathscr{F}_{yx} \frac{\partial^2 u(x, y)}{\partial x^2} = -k_x^2 \mathscr{F}_{yx} u(x, y) \tag{4.5c}$$

and so forth. In the above the script letter $\mathscr{F}$ with a subscript is a symbolic way of indicating that the Fourier transform is to be taken with respect to the variable corresponding to the subscript. The minus sign occurs in Eq. (4.5a) and not Eq. (4.4) because x corresponds to ω, and k_x corresponds to t in the basic relation given by Eq. (4.1a).

Equation (4.3) can be expressed in the form

$$\left(\frac{\partial^2}{\partial x^2} + \frac{\partial^2}{\partial y^2} + \frac{\partial^2}{\partial z^2} + k_0^2\right)\mathbf{E}(x, y, z) = 0 \tag{4.6a}$$

$$\frac{\partial E_x(x, y, z)}{\partial x} + \frac{\partial E_y(x, y, z)}{\partial y} + \frac{\partial E_z(x, y, z)}{\partial z} = 0 \tag{4.6b}$$

If we Fourier transform both of these equations with respect to x and y we obtain

$$\left[\frac{\partial^2}{\partial z^2} + (k_0^2 - k_x^2 - k_y^2)\right] \mathbf{E}(k_x, k_y, z) = 0 \qquad (4.7a)$$

$$k_x E_x(k_x, k_y, z) + k_y E_y(k_x, k_y, z) + j \frac{\partial}{\partial z} E_z(k_x, k_y, z) = 0 \qquad (4.7b)$$

where $\mathbf{E}(k_x, k_y, z)$ is the Fourier transform of the electric field with respect to x and y. We are using the same symbol $\mathbf{E}$, but the arguments are shown explicitly to remind us that $\mathbf{E}(k_x, k_y, z)$ *is an entirely different function* from $\mathbf{E}(x, y, z)$.
If we let

$$k_z^2 = k_0^2 - k_x^2 - k_y^2 \qquad (4.8)$$

then Eq. (4.7a) becomes

$$\frac{\partial^2 \mathbf{E}(k_x, k_y, z)}{\partial z^2} + k_z^2 \mathbf{E}(k_x, k_y, z) = 0 \qquad (4.9)$$

which has solutions of the form $e^{\pm jk_z z}$. Since the field should consist of waves propagating outwards along z from the aperture, only the function $e^{-jk_z z}$ will be valid. Thus the general solution to Eq. (4.9) is

$$\mathbf{E}(k_x, k_y, z) = \mathbf{f}(k_x, k_y) e^{-jk_z z} \qquad (4.10)$$

where $\mathbf{f}(k_x, k_y)$ is still to be found.
When we use Eq. (4.10) in Eq. (4.7b) we find that

$$k_x f_x + k_y f_y + k_z f_z = 0 \qquad (4.11a)$$

or

$$\mathbf{k} \cdot \mathbf{f} = 0 \qquad (4.11b)$$

where $\mathbf{k}$ is the vector with components k_x, k_y, k_z. Equation (4.11) tells us that only two components of the vector $\mathbf{f}$ are independent, and this reflects the corresponding restriction on the electric field imposed by the vanishing of the divergence as expressed by Eqs. (4.3b) and (4.6b).
When we use the inverse Fourier transform relations, our solution for the electric field can be expressed as

$$\mathbf{E}(x, y, z) = \frac{1}{4\pi^2} \int\int_{-\infty}^{\infty} \mathbf{f}(k_x, k_y) e^{-j\mathbf{k}\cdot\mathbf{r}} \, dk_x \, dk_y \qquad (4.12)$$

where we have introduced the compact notation $\mathbf{k} \cdot \mathbf{r} = k_x x + k_y y + k_z z$. This equation states that an arbitrary electric field in the half space $z > 0$ can be represented as a spectrum of plane waves since $\mathbf{f}(k_x, k_y) e^{-j\mathbf{k}\cdot\mathbf{r}}$ is a plane wave with vector amplitude $\mathbf{f}$ propagating in the direction of the propagation vector $\mathbf{k}$. Note that the definition of k_z is such that $|\mathbf{k}| = k_0$. For $k_x^2 + k_y^2 > k_0^2$ the propagation constant k_z is imaginary, and the plane waves in this part of the spectrum are exponentially decaying or evanescent in the z direction. These evanescent waves make up the near-zone field in front of the aperture. Only those plane waves that come from the part of the spectrum corresponding to values of $k_x^2 + k_y^2$ inside the circle of radius k_0 in the $k_x - k_y$ plane contribute to the radiation field, since only these waves are outward-propagating waves.

When $z = 0$ our solution for the x and y components of the electric field must equal the assumed known aperture tangential field. Thus if we let $\mathbf{f}_t$ denote the x and y components of $\mathbf{f}$ we must have

$$\mathbf{E}_a(x, y) = \mathbf{E}_{\tan}(x, y, 0)$$

$$= \frac{1}{4\pi^2} \int\int_{-\infty}^{\infty} \mathbf{f}_t(k_x, k_y)\, e^{-jk_x x - jk_y y}\, dk_x\, dk_y \qquad (4.13)$$

This expression can be recognized as a two-dimensional Fourier transform, and thus from Eq. (4.2a) we see that

$$\mathbf{f}_t(k_x, k_y) = \int\int_{S_a} \mathbf{E}_a(x, y)\, e^{jk_x x + jk_y y}\, dx\, dy \qquad (4.14)$$

so $\mathbf{f}_t$ is given in terms of the Fourier transform of the aperture field. From Eq. (4.11b) we can find f_z, and it is given by

$$f_z = \frac{-\mathbf{k}_t \cdot \mathbf{f}_t}{k_z} = \frac{-k_x f_x - k_y f_y}{\sqrt{k_0^2 - k_x^2 - k_y^2}} \qquad (4.15)$$

We have now found a formal solution for the electric field everywhere in the region $z > 0$, provided we can evaluate the integral in Eq. (4.12). In general this is difficult to do except in the radiation zone where r is large compared with λ_0, i.e., $k_0 r$ is large. Since we are primarily interested in the radiation field the asymptotic value of Eq. (4.12) as r tends to infinity is all we need to know. This asymptotic evaluation is carried out in the appendix to this chapter, and the result is

$$\mathbf{E}(\mathbf{r}) \sim \frac{jk_0 \cos \theta}{2\pi r}\, e^{-jk_0 r} \mathbf{f}(k_0 \sin \theta \cos \phi, k_0 \sin \theta \sin \phi) \qquad (4.16)$$

where θ and ϕ are the spherical coordinate angles shown in Fig. 4.1. This rather remarkable result shows that the far-zone radiation field, which is the diffraction pattern of the aperture field, is simply related to the Fourier transform of the aperture field with k_x put equal to $k_0 \sin \theta \cos \phi$, and k_y set equal to $k_0 \sin \theta \sin \phi$. These are the appropriate components of the propagation vector for a wave propagating radially outwards along r in the direction specified by the angles θ and ϕ. In the evaluation of $\mathbf{f}_t$ the integrals over x and y are taken over all portions of the $z = 0$ plane on which nonzero values of the tangential electric field exist. If S_a is an opening cut in a perfectly conducting screen, then everywhere outside S_a there will be zero tangential electric field.

For an aperture that is large in terms of wavelength, $\mathbf{f}_t$ is highly peaked in the forward direction along the z axis, and in this direction f_z is very small and $\cos \theta \approx 1$. Thus the radiated field is given very nearly by $\mathbf{f}_t$ in this region and is related directly to the Fourier transform of the aperture field.

Since $\nabla \cdot \mathbf{E} = 0$, $\mathbf{k} \cdot \mathbf{f} = 0$ and hence $\mathbf{f}$ does not have a component in the direction of observation, which is the direction of the propagation vector $\mathbf{k}$. Thus the field is a TEM field in the radiation zone. Along the z axis $\cos \theta = 1$ and $\mathbf{E}(\mathbf{r})$ has only x and y components proportional to f_x and f_y, which are the *Fourier transforms* of the aperture electric field. For other directions of observation it is convenient to express the field in terms of its spherical components; thus we have

$$\mathbf{E}(\mathbf{r}) = jk_0 \frac{e^{-jk_0 r}}{2\pi r} \left[\mathbf{a}_\theta (f_x \cos \phi + f_y \sin \phi) + \mathbf{a}_\phi \cos \theta (f_y \cos \phi - f_x \sin \phi) \right]$$

$$(4.17a)$$

The magnetic field in the radiation zone is given by

$$\mathbf{H} = Y_0 \mathbf{a}_r \times \mathbf{E} \qquad (4.17b)$$

We will now consider several examples that will illustrate the use of Eqs. (4.16) and (4.17) and will also show the similarity between aperture radiation and radiation from arrays.

Radiation from a Rectangular Aperture

A rectangular aperture of dimensions $2a$ along x and $2b$ along y and located in the $z = 0$ plane is shown in Fig. 4.2a. We will assume that the field in the aperture is uniform and is given by

$$\mathbf{E}_a = E_0 \mathbf{a}_x \qquad |x| \le a \qquad |y| \le b$$
$$= 0 \qquad \text{otherwise}$$

We then have

$$\mathbf{f}_t = E_0 \mathbf{a}_x \int_{-a}^{a} \int_{-b}^{b} e^{jk_x x + jk_y y} \, dy \, dx$$

$$= 4ab E_0 \mathbf{a}_x \frac{\sin k_x a}{k_x a} \frac{\sin k_y b}{k_y b}$$

$$= 4ab E_0 \mathbf{a}_x \frac{\sin(k_0 a \sin \theta \cos \phi)}{k_0 a \sin \theta \cos \phi} \frac{\sin(k_0 b \sin \theta \sin \phi)}{k_0 b \sin \theta \sin \phi}$$

$$= 4ab E_0 \mathbf{a}_x \frac{\sin u}{u} \frac{\sin v}{v} \qquad (4.18)$$

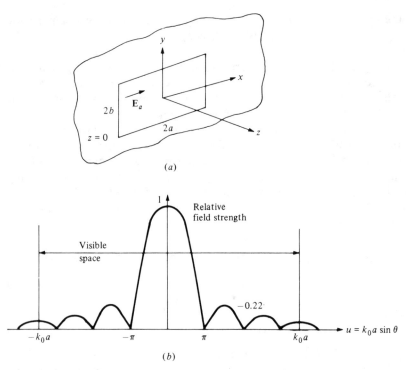

Figure 4.2 (*a*) Rectangular aperture with a uniform field. (*b*) Radiation-field pattern.

where $u = k_0 a \sin \theta \cos \phi$, $v = k_0 b \sin \theta \sin \phi$. The radiated electric field is given by Eq. (4.17*a*) and is

$$\mathbf{E}(\mathbf{r}) = \frac{jk_0 4abE_0}{2\pi r} e^{-jk_0 r} \frac{\sin u}{u} \frac{\sin v}{v} (\mathbf{a}_\theta \cos \phi - \mathbf{a}_\phi \sin \phi \cos \theta) \qquad (4.19)$$

This expression is similar to that given by Eq. (3.55) for the broadside array, and indeed the radiation patterns are nearly identical in the visible region of *uv* space, which extends over $|u| \leq k_0 a$ and $|v| \leq k_0 b$. For an array the pattern repeats periodically, while for an aperture the side-lobe pattern continues to decrease as *u* and *v* move into the invisible region. For a large array the range of *u* and *v* to cover visible space is small enough that the sin *u*/2 sin *v*/2 term in the denominator of the array factor can be replaced by *uv*/4, in which case the pattern for a uniform two-dimensional array of dipoles becomes identical with the pattern from a uniformly illuminated aperture. Note, however, that for an array we defined *u* to be equal to $k_0 d \sin \theta \cos \phi$ [see Eq. (3.55)] where *d* is the element spacing. A one-to-one correspondence with the aperture problem would require defining *u* as $k_0 [(N + 1)/2]d \sin \theta \cos \phi$ for the array. But this is simply a change in scale for *u* and does not change the pattern. The above remarks also apply to the variable *v*.

In a principal plane, say, $\phi = 0$, we have

$$\mathbf{E} = jk_0 \frac{e^{-jk_0 r}}{2\pi r} \mathbf{a}_\theta 4abE_0 \frac{\sin(k_0 a \sin \theta)}{k_0 a \sin \theta} \qquad (4.20)$$

A sketch of $|\mathbf{E}|$ is given in Fig. 4.2*b* as a function of *u*. The main diffraction lobe has an angular width $\Delta\theta$ given by

$$BW = \Delta\theta = 2 \sin^{-1} \frac{\pi}{k_0 a} = 2 \sin^{-1} \frac{\lambda_0}{2a} \approx \frac{\lambda_0}{a} \qquad \text{for } a \gg \lambda_0$$

Thus the diffraction lobe has an angular width *inversely proportional* to the aperture width measured in wavelengths, which was also found to be the case for an array.

Radiation from a Circular Aperture

Figure 4.3*a* shows a circular aperture of radius *a* in the $z = 0$ plane. A linearly

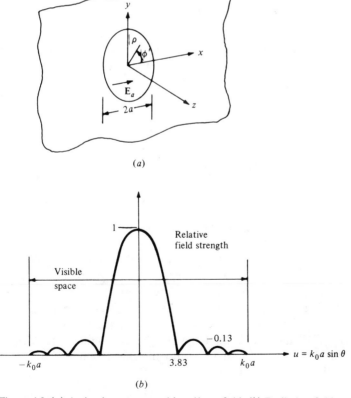

(a)

(b)

Figure 4.3 (*a*) A circular aperture with uniform field. (*b*) Radiation-field pattern.

polarized uniform electric field given by

$$\mathbf{E}_a = E_0\mathbf{a}_x \qquad x^2 + y^2 \le a^2$$
$$= 0, \text{ otherwise}$$

will be assumed for the aperture field. We then have

$$\mathbf{f}_t = E_0\mathbf{a}_x \iint\limits_{S_a} e^{jk_xx + jk_yy} \, dx \, dy$$

In order to evaluate this integral we introduce cylindrical coordinates ρ, ϕ' with $\rho = \sqrt{x^2 + y^2}$; thus $x = \rho \cos \phi'$, $y = \rho \sin \phi'$. We also have $k_x = k_0 \sin \theta \cos \phi$, $k_y = k_0 \sin \theta \sin \phi$. Hence

$$\mathbf{f}_t = E_0\mathbf{a}_x \int_0^a \int_0^{2\pi} e^{jk_0\rho \sin \theta \cos(\phi - \phi')} \rho \, d\phi' \, d\rho$$

We now note that

$$e^{jw \cos(\phi - \phi')} = J_0(w) - 2[J_2(w) \cos 2(\phi - \phi') - J_4(w) \cos 4(\phi - \phi') + \cdots]$$
$$+ 2j[J_1(w) \cos(\phi - \phi') - J_3(w) \cos 3(\phi - \phi') + \cdots]$$

where $J_n(w)$ is a Bessel function of the first kind and order n. By using this expansion the ϕ' integration is readily done. All terms integrate to zero except the term involving the J_0 function. The remaining integral over ρ can be done and gives

$$\mathbf{f}_t = E_0\mathbf{a}_x \int_0^a 2\pi J_0(k_0\rho \sin \theta)\rho \, d\rho$$

$$= 2\pi a^2 E_0\mathbf{a}_x \frac{J_1(k_0a \sin \theta)}{k_0a \sin \theta} \qquad (4.21)$$

upon using

$$\int_0^z u^\nu J_{\nu-1}(u) \, du = z^\nu J_\nu(z)$$

The Bessel function $J_1(x)$ is similar to a damped sinusoid and for large values of x equals $(2/\pi x)^{1/2} \sin(x - \pi/4)$. In the $\phi = 0$ plane the radiated field is proportional to f_x, as Eq. (4.17a) shows. The diffraction or radiation pattern described by Eq. (4.21) is shown in Fig. 4.3b. It is similar to the radiation pattern from a rectangular aperture, except that the decaying behavior of the J_1 function makes the side lobes smaller. The main lobe goes to zero at $k_0a \sin \theta = 3.832$, which is the first zero for the Bessel function J_1. Thus the angular width of the main lobe is

$$\text{BW} = \Delta\theta = 2 \sin^{-1} \frac{3.832}{k_0a} \approx \frac{3.832}{\pi} \frac{\lambda_0}{a} \qquad (4.22)$$

The first side lobe has an amplitude of 0.13 (-17.6 dB) relative to the main lobe.

Uniform Aperture Field with a Linear Phase Variation

We will now reconsider the rectangular aperture problem shown in Fig. 4.2 but assume that the aperture field has a linear phase variation; that is,

$$\mathbf{E}_a = E_0 \mathbf{a}_x e^{-j\alpha x - j\beta y} \qquad |x| \le a \qquad |y| \le b \tag{4.23}$$

For this aperture distribution

$$\mathbf{f}_t = E_0 \mathbf{a}_x \int_{-a}^{a} \int_{-b}^{b} e^{j(k_x - \alpha)x + j(k_y - \beta)y} \, dy \, dx$$

which shows that the only modification in the pattern is that brought about by replacing k_x and k_y by $k_x - \alpha$ and $k_y - \beta$. Hence if we call $\alpha a = u_0$, $\beta b = v_0$, we obtain by direct analogy with Eq. (4.19)

$$\mathbf{E}(\mathbf{r}) = \frac{jk_0 4abE_0}{2\pi r} e^{-jk_0 r} \frac{\sin(u - u_0)}{u - u_0} \frac{\sin(v - v_0)}{v - v_0} (\mathbf{a}_\theta \cos \phi - \mathbf{a}_\phi \sin \phi \cos \theta) \tag{4.24}$$

In uv space the pattern is the same as before, except for a shift of the maximum from $u = v = 0$ to $u = u_0$, $v = v_0$. In physical space this means that the radiation lobe is no longer along the z axis but instead occurs at the angles specified by

$$k_0 a \sin \theta \cos \phi = u_0 = \alpha a$$

$$k_0 b \sin \theta \sin \phi = v_0 = \beta b$$

These relations can also be expressed in the form

$$\tan \phi = \frac{\beta}{\alpha} \tag{4.25a}$$

$$\sin \theta = \frac{(\alpha^2 + \beta^2)^{1/2}}{k_0} \tag{4.25b}$$

The beam can be scanned or positioned in any desired direction by controlling the linear phase variation of the aperture field in a manner analogous to what was found for the two-dimensional array.

If $\beta = 0$, then the direction of maximum radiation is in the $\phi = 0$ or xz plane at an angle $\theta = \theta_0$ given by $\sin^{-1}(\alpha/k_0) = \sin^{-1}(\alpha \lambda_0/2\pi)$. The beam nulls occur where $u - u_0 = \pm\pi$ or at $u = u_0 \pm \pi = k_0 a \sin \theta \approx k_0 a[\sin \theta_0 + \cos \theta_0 (\theta - \theta_0)]$ upon using a Taylor series expansion of $\sin \theta$ about θ_0, the position of the maximum as given by $k_0 a \sin \theta_0 = u_0$. The beam width between nulls is thus given by

$$\text{BW} = 2(\theta - \theta_0) = \frac{2\pi}{k_0 a \cos \theta_0} = \frac{\lambda_0}{a \cos \theta_0} \tag{4.26}$$

We find that when the beam is scanned away from the normal to the aperture the beam width is increased inversely with the reduced or projected width of the aperture in the direction of the main lobe. This same result was also found for the array.

Tapered Aperture Field

In many applications of antennas it is desired to have very low side-lobe levels in order to reduce interference effects. A strong interfering signal incident on a receiving antenna in a direction corresponding to a side lobe will interact with a weaker desired signal incident along the direction of the main lobe. It is often necessary to reduce the side-lobe level to 30 dB or more below the main lobe. For a rectangular aperture with a uniform field the first side lobe is down by only 13 dB. For a uniformly illuminated circular aperture the first side lobe is about 17.6 dB below the main lobe, which is only a modest amount better. In the study of arrays it was found that the side-lobe level could be reduced by tapering the element excitations toward the ends of the array. This same technique works with apertures as well. A tapered aperture-field distribution will generally result in a reduction of the side-lobe level. The penalty paid is an increase in the beam width and a reduction in the directivity brought about by a reduced efficiency of utilization of the available aperture area.

In order to illustrate the effect of a tapered aperture field we will consider the rectangular aperture with a triangular aperture-field distribution of the form

$$\mathbf{E} = E_0\mathbf{a}_x\left(1 - \frac{|x|}{a}\right) \qquad |x| \le a \qquad |y| \le b \qquad (4.27)$$

For this aperture field

$$\mathbf{f}_t = E_0\mathbf{a}_x \int_{-a}^{a}\int_{-b}^{b}\left(1 - \frac{|x|}{a}\right)e^{jk_xx+jk_yy}\,dy\,dx$$

$$= 4bE_0\mathbf{a}_x\,\frac{\sin k_yb}{k_yb}\int_0^a\left(1 - \frac{x}{a}\right)\cos k_xx\,dx$$

$$= 4bE_0\mathbf{a}_x\,\frac{\sin k_yb}{k_yb}\,\frac{1 - \cos k_xa}{k_x^2a}$$

$$= 2abE_0\mathbf{a}_x\,\frac{\sin k_yb}{k_yb}\left[\frac{\sin k_x(a/2)}{k_x(a/2)}\right]^2 \qquad (4.28)$$

The radiated electric field is thus

$$\mathbf{E(r)} = \frac{jk_0abE_0}{\pi r}e^{-jk_0r}\,\frac{\sin v}{v}\left(\frac{\sin u/2}{u/2}\right)^2 \cdot (\mathbf{a}_\theta\cos\phi - \mathbf{a}_\phi\sin\phi\cos\theta) \qquad (4.29)$$

We note that the maximum field strength at $u = v = 0$ is $abE_0k_0/r\pi$ in place of

$2abE_0k_0/r\pi$ for a uniformly illuminated aperture. This reduction is due to using a triangular aperture field. The pattern function along u now involves the square of $(\sin u/2)/(u/2)$ in place of the function $(\sin u)/u$ and this means that the beam width between nulls has been doubled, but at the same time the first side lobe has been reduced from 13 to 26 dB below the main lobe. It is clear from this example that tapering the aperture field can have a pronounced effect on the side-lobe level. The radiation pattern along u has double zeros and is similar to that shown in Fig. 3.27 for the array with triangular current distribution.

Although the Fourier transform theory provides a convenient formulation for calculating the radiated field from a known aperture field on a plane surface, it cannot be applied directly to the case of an aperture cut in a curved surface such as on a cylinder or sphere. Therefore it is necessary to develop a more general approach to aperture radiation, and this is the topic taken up in the next two sections.

4.2 ELECTRIC AND MAGNETIC SOURCES AND FIELD-EQUIVALENCE PRINCIPLES

We will show shortly that it is convenient and useful to introduce fictitious magnetic currents and charges as a technique to aid in the analysis of the radiation from an aperture. Magnetic currents $\mathbf{J}_m$ and charges ρ_m can be introduced into Maxwell's equations, by analogy with the way electric currents $\mathbf{J}_e$ and electric charge ρ_e enter into these equations, in the following way:

$$\nabla \times \mathbf{E} = -j\omega\mathbf{B} - \mathbf{J}_m \qquad (4.30a)$$

$$\nabla \times \mathbf{H} = j\omega\mathbf{D} + \mathbf{J}_e \qquad (4.30b)$$

$$\nabla \cdot \mathbf{B} = \rho_m \qquad (4.30c)$$

$$\nabla \cdot \mathbf{D} = \rho_e \qquad (4.30d)$$

When both types of sources are present the resultant field is a superposition of that produced by the electric sources $\mathbf{J}_e$, ρ_e and the magnetic sources $\mathbf{J}_m$, ρ_m acting separately. The field produced by the electric sources is readily found using the electric-type vector potential, which we now denote by $\mathbf{A}_e$ instead of $\mathbf{A}$, as shown in Chap. 2. By means of a similar development, the field radiated by magnetic sources can be found using a magnetic-type vector potential $\mathbf{A}_m$, as shown in Prob. 2.1.† The total field is thus determined by solving

$$(\nabla^2 + k_0^2)\mathbf{A}_e = -\mu_0\mathbf{J}_e \qquad (4.31a)$$

$$(\nabla^2 + k_0^2)\mathbf{A}_m = -\epsilon_0\mathbf{J}_m \qquad (4.31b)$$

† We have adopted the use of the words *electric type* and *magnetic type* in referring to the vector potentials so as to be descriptive of the type of source involved and consistent with the terminology used for the closely related hertzian potentials. Many authors use the opposite terminology; e.g., $\mathbf{A}_e$ is called a *magnetic vector potential*.

$$\mathbf{E} = -j\omega \mathbf{A}_e + \frac{\nabla\nabla \cdot \mathbf{A}_e}{j\omega\mu_0\epsilon_0} - \frac{1}{\epsilon_0}\nabla \times \mathbf{A}_m \qquad (4.31c)$$

$$\mathbf{H} = -j\omega \mathbf{A}_m + \frac{\nabla\nabla \cdot \mathbf{A}_m}{j\omega\mu_0\epsilon_0} + \frac{1}{\mu_0}\nabla \times \mathbf{A}_e \qquad (4.31d)$$

In the radiation zone the solutions for $\mathbf{A}_e$ and $\mathbf{A}_m$ are [see Eq. (2.48)]

$$\mathbf{A}_e(\mathbf{r}) = \frac{\mu_0}{4\pi r} e^{-jk_0 r} \int_V \mathbf{J}_e(\mathbf{r}') e^{jk_0\mathbf{a}_r \cdot \mathbf{r}'} \, d\mathbf{r}' \qquad (4.32a)$$

$$\mathbf{A}_m(\mathbf{r}) = \frac{\epsilon_0}{4\pi r} e^{-jk_0 r} \int_V \mathbf{J}_m(\mathbf{r}') e^{jk_0\mathbf{a}_r \cdot \mathbf{r}'} \, d\mathbf{r}' \qquad (4.32b)$$

where $d\mathbf{r}'$ stands for an element of volume dV'. The corresponding expression for the electric and magnetic fields in the *radiation zone* are

$$E_\theta = -j\omega A_{e\theta} - j\omega Z_0 A_{m\phi} \qquad (4.33a)$$

$$E_\phi = -j\omega A_{e\phi} + j\omega Z_0 A_{m\theta} \qquad (4.33b)$$

$$H_\theta = -Y_0 E_\phi \qquad (4.33c)$$

$$H_\phi = Y_0 E_\theta \qquad (4.33d)$$

The application of these equations will be deferred until later.

Field-Equivalence Principles

In order to introduce some basic concepts in connection with what are called field-equivalence principles we will consider an elementary electrostatic field problem. A point charge q at the origin, as in Fig. 4.4a, will produce an electric field given by

$$\mathbf{E} = \frac{q}{4\pi\epsilon_0 r^2} \mathbf{a}_r$$

Let us now focus attention on the field outside the spherical surface of radius r_0. We can maintain the same field $\mathbf{E}$ in the region $r > r_0$ by removing the point charge q and placing a surface density of charge $\rho_s = q/4\pi r_0^2$ on the surface $r = r_0$, as in Fig. 4.4b. The charge density ρ_s provides the proper termination of the lines of force associated with $\mathbf{E}$ at the surface $r = r_0$. This new source produces a null field interior to the surface $r = r_0$. The new source placed on $r = r_0$ is equivalent to the original point charge q as far as the field outside the surface $r = r_0$ is concerned. This is an example of what is called a *field-equivalence principle*.

We can modify the above problem in the following way without affecting the field for $r > r_0$. Let us postulate the existence of a uniform field $\mathbf{E}_1 = E_0\mathbf{a}_x$ in the interior $r < r_0$, as shown in Fig. 4.4c. The field for $r > r_0$ is to remain unchanged. Thus on the surface $r = r_0$ we must place the charge density $q/4\pi r_0^2$

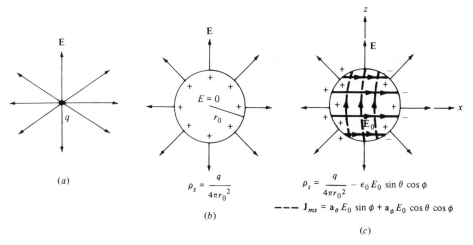

(a)

(b) $\rho_s = \dfrac{q}{4\pi r_0^2}$

(c) $\rho_s = \dfrac{q}{4\pi r_0^2} - \epsilon_0 E_0 \sin\theta\cos\phi$

$--- \mathbf{J}_{ms} = \mathbf{a}_\theta E_0 \sin\phi + \mathbf{a}_\phi E_0 \cos\theta\cos\phi$

Figure 4.4 Equivalent charge and magnetic current distributions needed to support a field $E\mathbf{a}_r$ in $r > r_0$ and a field $E_0\mathbf{a}_x$ in $r < r_0$.

to support the field $\mathbf{E}$ for $r > r_0$ and also place a charge density $-\epsilon_0\mathbf{a}_r \cdot E_0\mathbf{a}_x = -\epsilon_0 E_0 \sin\theta\cos\phi$ to terminate the normal component of the field $\mathbf{E}_1$ at the surface $r = r_0$ so that it will not contribute to the field in $r > r_0$.

We must also place a static magnetic current sheet on the sphere to terminate the tangential electric field in the interior. A surface on which an electric current sheet of density $\mathbf{J}_{es}$ flows results in a discontinuous change in the tangential magnetic field according to the relation $\mathbf{n} \times (\mathbf{H}_2 - \mathbf{H}_1) = \mathbf{J}_{es}$. The corresponding relationship for the discontinuity in the tangential electric field across a magnetic current sheet of density $\mathbf{J}_{ms}$ is

$$-\mathbf{n} \times (\mathbf{E}_2 - \mathbf{E}_1) = \mathbf{J}_{ms}$$

Hence we require a magnetic current sheet $\mathbf{J}_{ms} = \mathbf{a}_r \times \mathbf{a}_x E_0 = \mathbf{a}_\theta E_0 \sin\phi + \mathbf{a}_\phi E_0 \cos\theta\cos\phi$ on the surface $r = r_0$ in addition to the layer of electric charge.

In essence we can place on the surface $r = r_0$ an equivalent layer of charge and magnetic current that will produce the original field from the point charge q outside of $r = r_0$ and that will terminate any arbitrary source-free field that we wish to postulate for the interior region. The charge and field configuration that we have set up is indeed a solution to Maxwell's equations, since everywhere except at $r = r_0$ both $\nabla \times \mathbf{E}$ and $\nabla \cdot \mathbf{E}$ vanish, as does $\nabla \times \mathbf{E}_1$ and $\nabla \cdot \mathbf{E}_1$ by hypothesis. At the surface, $r = r_0$, $\epsilon_0\mathbf{a}_r \cdot (\mathbf{E} - \mathbf{E}_1) = \rho_s$, and $-\mathbf{a}_r \times (\mathbf{E} - \mathbf{E}_1) = \mathbf{J}_{ms}$ by construction. Hence Maxwell's equations and the required boundary conditions are satisfied. When we choose $\mathbf{E}_1$ to be zero we can place a conducting spherical shell just inside the surface $r = r_0$ without affecting the exterior field.

The conclusion to be drawn from this example is that there are many equivalent-source distributions that may be placed on a closed surface surrounding the original sources and that will produce the same field outside of this surface as the original sources produced. The concepts involved can also be applied to a time-varying electromagnetic field as we now show.

Let a system of electric sources $\mathbf{J}_e$, ρ_e contained in a volume V_1 bounded by a closed surface S radiate a field $\mathbf{E}$, $\mathbf{H}$, as in Fig. 4.5a. We now remove the sources $\mathbf{J}_e$, ρ_e and postulate the existence of an arbitrary source-free field $\mathbf{E}_1$, $\mathbf{H}_1$ inside S and the original field $\mathbf{E}$, $\mathbf{H}$ in V_2 outside of S, as in Fig. 4.5b. The postulated total fields are a valid solution only if they are properly joined across the common boundary S. This is accomplished by offsetting the discontinuity in the tangential field components by surface currents given by

$$\mathbf{J}_{es} = \mathbf{n} \times (\mathbf{H} - \mathbf{H}_1) \qquad (4.34a)$$

$$\mathbf{J}_{ms} = -\mathbf{n} \times (\mathbf{E} - \mathbf{E}_1) \qquad (4.34b)$$

Equation (4.34a) is just the boundary condition for the magnetic field across a current sheet. In order that we can have a discontinuous change in the tangential electric field we must postulate the existence of an equivalent layer of magnetic surface current $\mathbf{J}_{ms}$. It is this requirement that motivated the introduction of magnetic sources in the beginning of this section. The fields $\mathbf{E}_1$, $\mathbf{H}_1$ in V_1 and $\mathbf{E}$, $\mathbf{H}$ in V_2, along with the currents on S, are a valid solution to the generalized Maxwell's equations everywhere. Since the solution is unique, when all boundary conditions are satisfied the currents given by Eq. (4.34) must radiate the postulated fields. Hence, as far as the fields in V_2 are concerned, the currents given by Eq. (4.34) are fully equivalent to the original set of sources. Furthermore, $\mathbf{E}_1$, $\mathbf{H}_1$ are arbitrary, so we may choose this as a null field. Thus

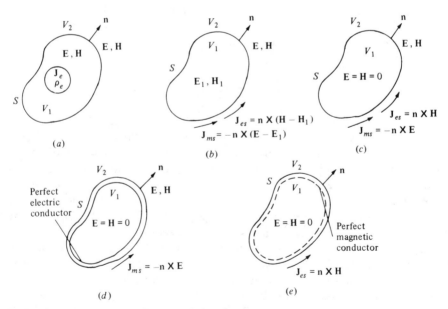

Figure 4.5 Equivalent sources for the field $\mathbf{E}$, $\mathbf{H}$ outside S.

surface currents given by

$$\mathbf{J}_{es} = \mathbf{n} \times \mathbf{H} \qquad (4.35a)$$

$$\mathbf{J}_{ms} = -\mathbf{n} \times \mathbf{E} \qquad (4.35b)$$

placed on S will radiate the original field outside S and a null field inside S, as in Fig. 4.5c. This is the mathematical statement of Huygen's principle and is known as *Love's field-equivalence principle*. The currents specified in Eqs. (4.34) and (4.35) radiate in a free-space environment, and the field may be found using the vector potential functions $\mathbf{A}_e$ and $\mathbf{A}_m$.

If we choose a null field in V_1 then we can replace S by a perfect electric conductor, as in Fig. 4.5d. In this case the current $\mathbf{J}_{es}$ is short-circuited and does not radiate. Hence the field $\mathbf{E}$, $\mathbf{H}$ in V_2 can be found from magnetic currents $\mathbf{J}_{ms} = -\mathbf{n} \times \mathbf{E}$ placed on a perfect electric conducting surface S. We could also replace S by a perfect magnetic conductor (a surface on which $\mathbf{n} \times \mathbf{H} = 0$), as in Fig. 4.5e, in which case $\mathbf{E}$, $\mathbf{H}$ in V_2 can be found from electric currents $\mathbf{J}_{es} = \mathbf{n} \times \mathbf{H}$ placed on a perfect magnetic conducting surface S. The fields radiated by the equivalent surface currents $\mathbf{J}_{ms}$ alone or $\mathbf{J}_{es}$ alone must, of course, be found such that the boundary conditions on the enclosed perfect electric and magnetic conductors are satisfied.

It is not necessary to impose any boundary conditions on the normal components of the fields at the surface S since, if the tangential field components are properly matched by suitable current sheets, Maxwell's equations ensure that the normal components will have the proper behavior at the surface S. The reader wishing to pursue field-equivalence principles in further depth is referred to the literature.† For our purpose the relations needed to formulate the problem of radiation from an aperture are either the set (4.34) or (4.35), depending on how we wish to specify $\mathbf{E}_1$, $\mathbf{H}_1$. In the next section we show how these field equivalence principles may be applied to aperture radiation.

4.3 APPLICATION OF FIELD-EQUIVALENCE PRINCIPLES TO APERTURE RADIATION

Consider again the aperture in a conducting screen shown in Fig. 4.1. Let $\mathbf{E}_a$, $\mathbf{H}_a$ be the tangential fields on the $z = 0$ plane, which we assume that we have somehow determined. Note that $\mathbf{E}_a = 0$ outside the aperture opening, but

---

† S. A. Schelkunoff, "Some Equivalence Theorems of Electromagnetics and Their Applications to Radiation Problems," *Bell Systems Tech. Jour.*, vol. 15, 1936, pp. 92–112.

S. A. Schelkunoff, "Kirchhoff's Formula, Its Vector Analogue and Other Field Equivalence Theorems," *Commun. Pure Appl. Math.*, vol. 4, June 1951, pp. 43–59.

R. F. Harrington, *Time Harmonic Electromagnetic Fields*, McGraw-Hill Book Company, New York, 1961.

B. B. Baker, and E. R. Copson, *The Mathematical Theory of Huygen's Principle*, Oxford University Press, New York, 1939.

$\mathbf{H}_a$ is not zero in general. The radiation field may be found from the currents $\mathbf{J}_{es} = \mathbf{n} \times \mathbf{H}_a$, $\mathbf{J}_{ms} = -\mathbf{n} \times \mathbf{E}_a$ using Eqs. (4.32) and (4.33). These currents are considered radiating into a free-space environment.

We could also replace the whole $z = 0$ plane by a perfect conductor and find the fields from a magnetic current distribution $\mathbf{J}_{ms} = -\mathbf{a}_z \times \mathbf{E}_a$ alone. If we use image theory we can remove the screen and find the total field from a current source $2\mathbf{J}_{ms} = -2\mathbf{a}_z \times \mathbf{E}_a$ on $z = 0$ and considered as radiating into a free-space environment. Alternatively we can replace the $z = 0$ plane by a perfect magnetic conductor and find the field for $z > 0$ from $\mathbf{J}_{es} = \mathbf{n} \times \mathbf{H}_a$ alone, or use image theory and find the field from a current source $2\mathbf{J}_{es} = 2\mathbf{n} \times \mathbf{H}_a$ on $z = 0$ considered as radiating into free space.

We will work out the result in detail only for the case where we use the equivalent source $2\mathbf{J}_{ms} = -2\mathbf{a}_z \times \mathbf{E}_a$ radiating in free space. From Eq. (4.32b) the solution for $\mathbf{A}_m$ is

$$\mathbf{A}_m(\mathbf{r}) = \frac{-\epsilon_0 e^{-jk_0 r}}{2\pi r} \mathbf{a}_z \times \iint_{S_a} \mathbf{E}_a(x', y') e^{jk_0 \mathbf{a}_r \cdot (\mathbf{a}_x x' + \mathbf{a}_y y')} \, dx' \, dy'$$

Now $\mathbf{a}_r \cdot \mathbf{a}_x = \sin\theta \cos\phi$, $\mathbf{a}_r \cdot \mathbf{a}_y = \sin\theta \sin\phi$, and the integrand may be recognized as $\mathbf{f}_t(k_0 \sin\theta \cos\phi, k_0 \sin\theta \sin\phi)$ by comparing it with the definition of $\mathbf{f}_t$ given by Eq. (4.14). If we now use Eq. (4.33) and note that

$$\mathbf{a}_z \times \mathbf{a}_x = \mathbf{a}_y = \mathbf{a}_r \sin\theta \sin\phi + \mathbf{a}_\theta \cos\theta \sin\phi + \mathbf{a}_\phi \cos\phi$$

and

$$\mathbf{a}_z \times \mathbf{a}_y = -\mathbf{a}_x = -\mathbf{a}_r \sin\theta \cos\phi - \mathbf{a}_\theta \cos\theta \cos\phi + \mathbf{a}_\phi \sin\phi$$

we find that

$$\mathbf{E}(\mathbf{r}) = \frac{jk_0}{2\pi r} e^{-jk_0 r} [\mathbf{a}_\theta(f_x \cos\phi + f_y \sin\phi) + \mathbf{a}_\phi(f_y \cos\phi - f_x \sin\phi) \cos\theta]$$

where we have also put $\omega\epsilon_0 Z_0 = k_0$. This solution is the same as that obtained using Fourier transforms and given by Eq. (4.17a).

The solution using the other two possible equivalent sources $2\mathbf{J}_{es}$ or $\mathbf{J}_{es}$ and $\mathbf{J}_{ms}$ may be derived in a similar way. The results are summarized below. The function $\mathbf{g}_t$ is defined as the *Fourier transform of the tangential magnetic field in the aperture plane* and is

$$\mathbf{g}_t(k_x, k_y) = \int\int_{-\infty}^{\infty} \mathbf{H}_a(x', y') e^{jk_x x' + jk_y y'} \, dx' \, dy' \tag{4.36}$$

In terms of the equivalent sources $\mathbf{J}_{es}$, $\mathbf{J}_{ms}$; $2\mathbf{J}_{es}$; or $2\mathbf{J}_{ms}$ we then find that the electric field is given by

$\mathbf{J}_{es}$ and $\mathbf{J}_{ms}$

$$E_\theta = \frac{jk_0}{4\pi r} e^{-jk_0 r}[f_x \cos\phi + f_y \sin\phi + Z_0 \cos\theta(g_y \cos\phi - g_x \sin\phi)]$$

$$(4.37a)$$

$$E_\phi = \frac{jk_0}{4\pi r} e^{-jk_0 r}[\cos\theta(f_y \cos\phi - f_x \sin\phi) - Z_0(g_y \sin\phi + g_x \cos\phi)]$$

$$(4.37b)$$

$2\mathbf{J}_{es}$

$$E_\theta = \frac{jk_0 Z_0 \cos\theta}{2\pi r} e^{-jk_0 r}(g_y \cos\phi - g_x \sin\phi) \qquad (4.38a)$$

$$E_\phi = \frac{-jk_0 Z_0}{2\pi r} e^{-jk_0 r}(g_y \sin\phi + g_x \cos\phi) \qquad (4.38b)$$

$2\mathbf{J}_{ms}$

$$E_\theta = \frac{jk_0}{2\pi r} e^{-jk_0 r}(f_x \cos\phi + f_y \sin\phi) \qquad (4.39a)$$

$$E_\phi = \frac{jk_0 \cos\theta}{2\pi r} e^{-jk_0 r}(f_y \cos\phi - f_x \sin\phi) \qquad (4.39b)$$

We have already seen that Eq. (4.39) agrees with the results obtained earlier by using Fourier transforms. The solution given by Eq. (4.37) is the average of Eqs. (4.38) and (4.39). If the correct aperture fields are known, all three of the above procedures give identical results. However, when approximate aperture fields $\mathbf{E}_a$, $\mathbf{H}_a$ are used, the three formulations generally disagree. There is some advantage in using Eq. (4.38) or (4.39) alone, since only one of $\mathbf{E}_a$ or $\mathbf{H}_a$ needs to be specified. On a curved surface, image theory cannot, of course, be used. In that case we must use Eqs. (4.32) and (4.33) directly.

Obviously the above theory is of little use unless one is able to find a satisfactory estimate of either the aperture electric field or aperture magnetic field. For many practical antennas it is possible to use the geometrical ray optics theory or other means to find approximate solutions for the aperture fields. Some of these techniques will be explored in the remaining sections of this chapter.

Magnetic sources do not have a physical existence, but they may, nevertheless, be introduced as part of the equivalent system of sources needed to produce the same field in a restricted region of space as some other real physical sources do. It is in this context that magnetic sources are used, and for this purpose they provide a convenient mathematical artifice to aid in the calculation of fields radiated by aperture-field distributions.

The steps leading to the result of Eq. (4.39), which is the same as given by Eq. (4.17a) and obtained by using Fourier transforms, are an independent way of finding the asymptotic value of the integral (4.12) for the total field as $k_0 r$ becomes large.

If we refer to Eqs. (4.32) and (4.35) we see that an element of area dS, with unit normal $\mathbf{n}$ and on which the tangential fields are $\mathbf{E}_a(\mathbf{r}')$, $\mathbf{H}_a(\mathbf{r}')$, will contribute to the vector potentials in the following way:

$$d\mathbf{A}_e(\mathbf{r}) = \frac{\mu_0}{4\pi r} e^{-jk_0 r} \mathbf{n} \times \mathbf{H}_a(\mathbf{r}') e^{jk_0 \mathbf{a}_r \cdot \mathbf{r}'} \, dS \qquad (4.40a)$$

$$d\mathbf{A}_m(\mathbf{r}) = -\frac{\epsilon_0}{4\pi r} e^{-jk_0 r} \mathbf{n} \times \mathbf{E}_a(\mathbf{r}') e^{jk_0 \mathbf{a}_r \cdot \mathbf{r}'} \, dS \qquad (4.40b)$$

The evaluation of the radiation from an aperture in a conducting enclosure such as a cylinder or a sphere is more difficult to carry out than that of an aperture in a conducting plane. The formulation that is usually used is to close the aperture by a perfect conductor and place a magnetic current sheet $\mathbf{J}_{ms} = -\mathbf{n} \times \mathbf{E}$ in front. The radiated field may be found from this magnetic current source but must be determined so that $\mathbf{n} \times \mathbf{E}$ will vanish on the conducting surface. The magnetic current cannot be considered as radiating in a free-space environment. If a good estimate for $\mathbf{J}_{ms}$ cannot be made, then $\mathbf{J}_{ms}$ must be treated as an unknown quantity. The boundary-value problem requires that the total electromagnetic field both inside and outside the enclosure be found such that the tangential components are continuous across the aperture opening. The free-space formulas (4.40) can only be applied if we know both $\mathbf{n} \times \mathbf{H}_a$ and $\mathbf{n} \times \mathbf{E}_a$ over the *total* surface enclosing the structure of interest.

4.4 OPEN WAVEGUIDES AND HORN ANTENNAS

An open rectangular or circular waveguide is not normally used as an antenna by itself because of its low directivity. However, waveguides are frequently used as the primary feed to illuminate a paraboloidal reflector, so it is of some interest to examine their radiation characteristics.

Rectangular Waveguides

Figure 4.6a shows a rectangular waveguide of dimensions $a \times b$, with the aperture located in the $z = 0$ plane. The dominant propagating mode in the rectangular waveguide is the TE_{10} (transverse electric) mode, which has a y component of electric field and x and z components of magnetic field. The x and y field components are given by

$$E_y = E_0 \cos \frac{\pi x}{a} e^{-j\beta z} \qquad (4.41a)$$

$$H_x = -E_0 Y_w \cos \frac{\pi x}{a} e^{-j\beta z} \qquad (4.41b)$$

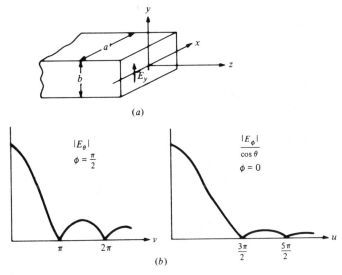

Figure 4.6 (*a*) Open rectangular waveguide. (*b*) Radiation-field pattern.

where the propagation constant $\beta = (k_0^2 - \pi^2/a^2)^{1/2}$ and the wave admittance Y_w for the mode is given by $Y_w = \beta Y_0/k_0$. At $z = 0$ the dominant mode fields are

$$E_y = E_0 \cos \frac{\pi x}{a} \tag{4.42a}$$

$$H_x = - Y_w E_0 \cos \frac{\pi x}{a} \tag{4.42b}$$

With the guide terminated at $z = 0$, a reflected dominant mode plus higher-order modes of small amplitude are excited near the open end. If these are neglected and if we also assume that outside the aperture on the $z = 0$ plane the x and y components of the field are negligible, then Eq. (4.42) may be considered to specify the aperture fields on the $z = 0$ plane. This approximation, in practice, gives a reasonably good estimate of the main radiation lobe even though it does not give a very accurate estimate of the side lobes in the radiation pattern. In the application of waveguides as feeds for paraboloidal reflectors we are mainly interested in the characteristics of the main lobe, so the assumptions made above are usually acceptable for this purpose.

In order to calculate the radiation field it is simpler to use a single current source, which we choose to be the magnetic current source

$$\mathbf{J}_{ms} = -\mathbf{n} \times \mathbf{E}_a = -\mathbf{a}_z \times \mathbf{a}_y E_0 \cos \frac{\pi x}{a}$$

$$= \mathbf{a}_x E_0 \cos \frac{\pi x}{a} \tag{4.43}$$

The radiated far-zone field is given by Eq. (4.39), with $f_x = 0$ and

$$f_y = E_0 \int_{-b/2}^{b/2} \int_{-a/2}^{a/2} \cos \frac{\pi x}{a} \, e^{jk_x x + jk_y y} \, dx \, dy$$

$$= 2\pi ab E_0 \frac{\sin[k_y(b/2)]}{k_y(b/2)} \frac{\cos[k_x(a/2)]}{\pi^2 - (k_x a)^2} \qquad (4.44)$$

where $k_x = k_0 \sin \theta \cos \phi$ and $k_y = k_0 \sin \theta \sin \phi$.

In the $\phi = \pi/2$ plane, i.e., the yz plane, the radiated field E_θ is proportional to $f_y = (2/\pi)ab E_0 \sin[k_0(b/2) \sin \theta]/[k_0(b/2) \sin \theta]$ which is the characteristic pattern associated with uniform illumination of the aperture along the y direction. In the xz plane where $\phi = 0$ the radiated field E_ϕ is described by the factor

$$\frac{\cos[k_0(a/2) \sin \theta]}{\pi^2 - (k_0 a \sin \theta)^2} \cos \theta$$

which is the pattern associated with a cosinusoidal aperture field. The two principal plane patterns are shown in Fig. 4.6b, without the $\cos \theta$ factor for E_ϕ, as functions of $u = k_0(a/2) \sin \theta$ and $v = k_0(b/2) \sin \theta$. Note from Eq. (4.39b) that, because of the $\cos \theta$ factor, E_ϕ vanishes on the $z = 0$ plane, and hence the far-zone radiation field does not have an x or y component on the $z = 0$ plane. This, of course, must be the case since we made this assumption in specifying the aperture field, and the theory should be self-consistent.

The aperture of a rectangular waveguide is small in terms of wavelength. For example, at X band (8 to 12 GHz) the wavelength ranges from 3.75 to 2.5 cm, while the standard WR-90 waveguide has dimensions $a = 0.9$ in = 2.29 cm and $b = 0.4$ in = 1.02 cm. Consequently, the beam width is quite large and the directivity is small. If we assume $\lambda_0 = 3$ cm, then the beam width in the $\phi = \pi/2$ plane (E plane) is not defined, since b is too small for a null to occur in visible space; that is, the first null occurs where $v = (k_0 b/2) \sin \theta = \pi = (\pi b/\lambda_0) \sin \theta$, which requires $\sin \theta > 1$ and hence is in invisible space. In the $\phi = 0$ plane (H plane) the null occurs where $(k_0 a/2) \sin \theta = 3\pi/2$ or for $\sin \theta = 3\lambda_0/2a$, and this also does not occur in visible space unless $\lambda_0 < 2a/3$.

The total power radiated may be found from the integral of the complex Poynting vector over the aperture when we assume that the aperture fields are known and are given by Eq. (4.42). For this aperture field we obtain

$$P_r = \frac{1}{2} \int_{-a/2}^{a/2} \int_{-b/2}^{b/2} E_0^2 Y_w \cos^2 \frac{\pi x}{a} \, dy \, dx = \frac{ab}{4} Y_w E_0^2$$

From Eq. (4.39), along with Eq. (4.44), we find that the maximum radiated power per unit solid angle along the z axis is

$$\frac{r^2}{2} Y_0 |E_\theta|^2 = \frac{k_0^2 Y_0}{8\pi^2} \left(\frac{2\pi ab E_0}{\pi^2} \right)^2 = \frac{k_0^2 Y_0 E_0^2 (ab)^2}{2\pi^4}$$

Hence the directivity is given by

$$D = 4\pi \frac{r^2 Y_0 |E_\theta|^2}{2P_r} = \frac{64}{\beta\lambda_0} \frac{ab}{\lambda_0^2} \tag{4.45}$$

For $\lambda_0 = 3$ cm and a WR-90 waveguide $D = 3.5$.

If the radiated field is calculated from both $\mathbf{J}_{es}$ and $\mathbf{J}_{ms}$ using Eq. (4.37), it is found that E_θ is modified by a factor $(k_0 + \beta \cos \theta)/2k_0$ and E_ϕ is modified by a factor $(k_0 \cos \theta + \beta)/2k_0$, and the directivity D is thus found to differ from that given by Eq. (4.45) by a factor $(k_0 + \beta)^2/4k_0^2$. For the example given above this would give $D = 3.07$. The difference is due to the fact that the assumed aperture fields are only approximately correct.

Circular Waveguides

For a circular waveguide of radius a as shown in Fig. 4.7 the dominant mode is the TE_{11} mode for which the electric field distribution over the cross section is

$$E_\rho = \frac{2 \sin \phi}{\rho} J_1\left(1.84 \frac{\rho}{a}\right)$$

$$E_\phi = \frac{2a \cos \phi}{1.84} \frac{dJ_1(1.84\rho/a)}{d\rho}$$

where J_1 is the Bessel function of the first kind and order 1 and ρ is the cylindrical radial coordinate shown in Fig. 4.7. In rectangular coordinates the expressions for the field distribution are given by

$$E_x = E_\rho \cos \phi - E_\phi \sin \phi$$

$$E_y = E_\rho \sin \phi + E_\phi \cos \phi$$

If the following Bessel function recurrence relations are used:

$$\frac{dJ_m(u)}{du} = \tfrac{1}{2}[J_{m-1}(u) - J_{m+1}(u)]$$

$$\frac{m}{u} J_m(u) = \tfrac{1}{2}[J_{m-1}(u) + J_{m+1}(u)]$$

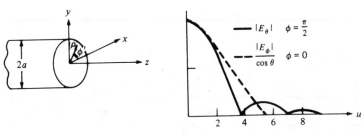

Figure 4.7 Open circular waveguide and typical principal-plane radiation-field patterns.

it is readily found that

$$E_x = J_2\left(1.84\frac{\rho}{a}\right)\sin 2\phi \tag{4.46a}$$

$$E_y = J_0\left(1.84\frac{\rho}{a}\right) - J_2\left(1.84\frac{\rho}{a}\right)\cos 2\phi \tag{4.46b}$$

If we assume that the aperture field can be approximated by these expressions, then it is relatively easy to derive the corresponding radiation field.

In order to find f_x and f_y an integration over the circular aperture is required. The exponential factor involved is $e^{jk_x x' + jk_y y'}$. Now

$$k_x x' + k_y y' = k_0\rho \sin \theta(\cos \phi \cos \phi' + \sin \phi \sin \phi')$$
$$= k_0\rho \sin \theta \cos(\phi - \phi')$$

By using the same expansion for $\exp[jk_0\rho \sin \theta \cos(\phi - \phi')]$ as was used in Sec. 4.1 for the uniformly illuminated circular aperture, along with the Lommel integral formula

$$\int_0^u uJ_n(\alpha u)J_n(\beta u)\,du = \frac{u}{\alpha^2 - \beta^2}\left[J_n(\alpha u)\frac{dJ_n(\beta u)}{du} - J_n(\beta u)\frac{dJ_n(\alpha u)}{du}\right]$$

it is possible to evaluate f_x and f_y. Thus we find, after a considerable amount of algebraic manipulation, that

$$E_\theta = \frac{jk_0}{r} e^{-jk_0 r} 2a^2 \sin \phi \frac{J_1(1.84)}{1.84}\frac{J_1(u)}{u} \tag{4.47a}$$

$$E_\phi = \frac{jk_0}{r} e^{-jk_0 r} 2a^2 \cos \phi \cos \theta \left[\frac{1.84 J_1(1.84)}{1.84^2 - u^2}\frac{dJ_1(u)}{du}\right] \tag{4.47b}$$

where $u = k_0 a \sin \theta$.

It is seen that in the $\phi = \pi/2$ plane (E plane) the pattern is the same as for a uniformly illuminated aperture [see Eq. (4.21)]. In the H plane where $\phi = 0$ the pattern is quite similar to that for the H-plane pattern of the rectangular waveguide. Typical principal-plane patterns are shown in Fig. 4.7b.

The directivity may be found in the same way as for the rectangular waveguide and is†

$$D = \frac{66}{\beta\lambda_0}\frac{\pi a^2}{\lambda_0^2} \tag{4.48}$$

where $\beta = [k_0^2 - (1.84/a)^2]^{1/2}$ and is the propagation constant for the TE$_{11}$ mode

---

† S. Silver (ed.), *Microwave Antenna Theory and Design*, McGraw-Hill Book Company, New York, 1949. Silver uses both electric and magnetic currents, so his expression for D differs by a factor $(k_0 + \beta)^2/4k_0^2$. See also comments made after Eq. (4.45) for the directivity of the rectangular waveguide.

in a circular waveguide. This expression is very nearly the same as that for the rectangular waveguide except for the difference in the formulas for the area of the aperture.

It is possible to solve the problem of radiation from a circular waveguide exactly, and thus a comparison of the approximate theory given above with the exact results can be made. This comparison is given in a later section covering feeds with low cross-polarization properties.

H-Plane Horns

In order to obtain a sharper beam and higher directivity than that given by a simple open waveguide radiator, the waveguide may be flared into a horn with a much larger aperture opening. If the width a of the rectangular waveguide is increased to a' by flaring the waveguide in the H plane, the H-plane horn shown in Fig. 4.8 is obtained. The field launched in the horn from the input waveguide is a cylindrical wave with a circular constant-phase front. In order that the aperture field will be nearly in-phase over the aperture, the flare angle must be small. The gain and radiation pattern are very close to those for a constant-phase aperture field, provided the phase error does not exceed $\pm\pi/4$ at the sides of the aperture. With reference to Fig. 4.8 this restriction on phase error can be stated as

$$k_0(R_2 - R_1) \leq \frac{\pi}{4}$$

From Fig. 4.8 it is seen that $R_1 = R_2 \cos \psi/2$ and $a' = 2R_2 \sin \psi/2$. Hence

$$\frac{2\pi}{\lambda_0} R_2\left(1 - \cos\frac{\psi}{2}\right) = \frac{\pi}{\lambda_0} a' \csc\frac{\psi}{2}\left(1 - \cos\frac{\psi}{2}\right) \leq \frac{\pi}{4}$$

which gives

$$\tan\frac{\psi}{4} \leq \frac{\lambda_0}{4a'} \tag{4.49}$$

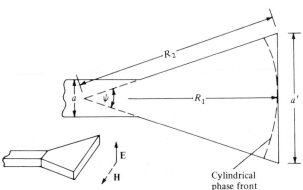

Cylindrical
phase front

Figure 4.8 H-plane horn.

The maximum value of ψ that satisfies this equation is plotted as a function of a'/λ_0 in Fig. 4.9. It should be apparent from this figure that in order to have a large aperture opening the flare angle will be small, resulting in a very long and bulky horn. This feature has limited the application of horns to those instances where only a modest gain is needed, such that the aperture is usually less than 10 wavelengths in width. Even for $a' = 10\lambda_0$ the horn will be close to 100 wavelengths long.

When the phase variation in the aperture field can be neglected the aperture-field distribution may be assumed to be the same as for the dominant TE_{10} mode in the input waveguide; that is,

$$\mathbf{E}_a = \mathbf{a}_y E_0 \cos\frac{\pi x}{a'} \qquad |x| \le \frac{a'}{2} \qquad |y| \le \frac{b}{2} \qquad (4.50)$$

The radiated field is thus given by the same formulas as for the rectangular waveguide, with a replaced by a', and hence upon using Eqs. (4.39) and (4.44) we obtain

$$E_\theta = \frac{jk_0 a' b E_0}{4r} e^{-jk_0 r} \sin\phi \frac{\sin v}{v} \frac{\cos u}{(\pi/2)^2 - u^2} \qquad (4.51a)$$

$$E_\phi = \frac{jk_0 a' b E_0}{4r} e^{-jk_0 r} \cos\phi \cos\theta \frac{\sin v}{v} \frac{\cos u}{(\pi/2)^2 - u^2} \qquad (4.51b)$$

where $v = (k_0 b/2)\sin\theta \sin\phi$ and $u = (k_0 a'/2)\sin\theta \cos\phi$. The directivity is given by Eq. (4.45) with $\beta = (k_0^2 - \pi^2/a'^2)^{1/2} \approx k_0$; so

$$D = 10.2 \frac{a'b}{\lambda_0^2} \qquad (4.52)$$

The gain of the horn antenna is essentially equal to the directivity since the losses are normally negligible.

If the horn length is fixed, a larger gain can be obtained by increasing the

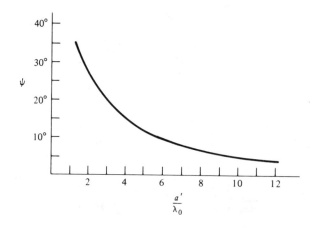

Figure 4.9 Flare angle ψ as a function of a'/λ_0 for the H-plane horn in Fig. 4.8.

flare angle somewhat and allowing a larger phase error, since the increased aperture width more than compensates for the decrease in gain brought about by the larger phase error. By analyzing the effects of phase error on gain it is found that for a *fixed length* the maximum gain is obtained by increasing the aperture width a' until a phase error of around 0.75π occurs. This optimum value of gain or directivity is a factor of about 1.3 less than that given by Eq. (4.52) and illustrates the effect a phase error has on antenna gain.

E-Plane Horns

If a rectangular waveguide is flared in the E plane, as shown in Fig. 4.10, an E-plane horn is obtained. The same considerations regarding phase error and flare angle apply to the E-plane horn as to the H-plane horn. Thus the flare angle versus aperture height b' is given in Fig. 4.9, with b' replacing a'. The radiated field and directivity are given by Eqs. (4.51) and (4.52), with b replaced by b' and a' replaced by a.

If the horn length is fixed, the maximum gain is obtained by increasing b' until a phase error of around 0.5π occurs. The tolerable phase error for the H-plane horn is larger, because the aperture field goes to zero at the sides of the aperture in the H plane, while for the E-plane horn the aperture field is constant in the E plane. For the optimum-gain horn the effect of the phase error reduces the directivity from that given by Eq. (4.52) by a factor of about 1.25.

Pyramidal Horns

For a given length of horn the greatest gain is obtained by flaring the waveguide in both the H plane and E plane to obtain the pyramidal horn shown in Fig. 4.11. In order to have a negligible phase error the flare angle in both planes should satisfy the condition (4.49). The radiated field and directivity are given by Eqs. (4.51) and (4.52), with b replaced by b'.

For a horn of *fixed length* the maximum gain is obtained by increasing the flare angles to allow a phase error of around 0.75π in the H plane and 0.5π in the E plane. For a horn designed according to this criterion, the directivity as

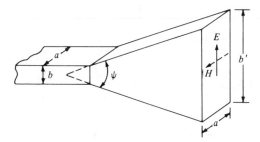

Figure 4.10 The E-plane horn.

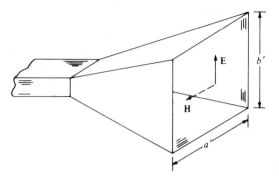

Figure 4.11 The pyramidal horn.

given by Eq. (4.52) should be multiplied by a factor of 0.63 to give

$$D = 6.4 \frac{a'b'}{\lambda_0^2} \qquad \text{optimum-gain horn} \qquad (4.53)$$

The design of pyramidal horns is discussed in the book by Jasik.† A common use for a pyramidal horn is as a standard-gain horn for determining the gain of other antennas by comparison. Small pyramidal horns are also used as feed horns for paraboloidal reflectors.

4.5 RAY OPTICS

At optical frequencies lenses and reflectors are designed on the basis of geometrical or ray optics. The success of this method is due to the large dimensions of the lenses and reflectors used relative to the wavelength, which is only a few micrometers (10^{-6} meters) or less. The same techniques are applicable to the design of lenses and reflectors in the microwave frequency band, since again these structures are usually large in terms of wavelength, which is only a few centimeters. Geometrical or ray optics has a theoretical foundation based on Maxwell's equations and results from an asymptotic solution to these equations as the frequency ω tends to infinity. The basic elements of this theory are given in App. IV. For our purpose we will summarize in this section the results that we will need to analyze reflector antennas.

According to ray optics the electromagnetic field everywhere is locally a plane wave and propagates in straight lines, i.e., along straight rays, in homogeneous media. At a boundary between two different media the rays are reflected or refracted at the tangent plane according to Snell's law, and the Fresnel reflection coefficients hold. The power is viewed as flowing in flux tubes, and if a flux tube is reflected from a perfectly conducting surface the power in the reflected flux tube equals that in the incident flux tube. If the

† H. Jasik, *Antenna Engineering Handbook*, McGraw-Hill Book Company, New York, 1961.

reflecting surface is a plane, the solid angle of the incident and reflected flux tubes are the same. If the reflecting surface is curved, the rays forming the boundary of the reflected flux tube may have a greater divergence than those of the incident flux tube or they may converge, depending on whether the surface is convex or concave. The electric and magnetic fields are transported along the flux tubes, and their polarization or orientation in space does not change except upon reflection or refraction at a boundary. The electric and magnetic fields are mutually perpendicular and orthogonal to the rays.

Figure 4.12 shows a flux tube with bounding rays emanating from a common point P and incident on a plane reflecting surface. The reflected rays make an angle θ_r with the normal $\mathbf{n}$ to the reflector that is equal to the angle of incidence θ_i. The reflected rays appear to come from the image P′ of the point P in the reflector, as shown.

If $\mathbf{s}_i$ is a unit vector along the incident ray and $\mathbf{s}_r$ is a unit vector along the reflected ray, then Snell's law of reflection can be stated as

$$\mathbf{s}_r = \mathbf{s}_i - 2(\mathbf{n} \cdot \mathbf{s}_i)\mathbf{n} \tag{4.54}$$

since only the normal component of the incident ray unit vector is reversed in direction upon reflection.

At the reflector surface the tangential electric field must vanish. Thus if $\mathbf{E}_i$ is the incident field and $\mathbf{E}_r$ is the reflected field we must have

$$\mathbf{n} \times (\mathbf{E}_i + \mathbf{E}_r) = 0 \tag{4.55a}$$

where $\mathbf{n}$ is the unit normal at the surface. The normal component of the electric field in the reflected wave equals the normal component in the incident wave, since the total electric field must be perpendicular to the ray; thus

$$\mathbf{n} \cdot \mathbf{E}_r = \mathbf{n} \cdot \mathbf{E}_i \tag{4.55b}$$

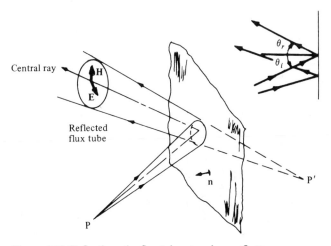

Figure 4.12 Reflection of a flux tube at a plane reflector.

We can rewrite the condition (4.55a) as

$$\mathbf{E}_r - (\mathbf{n} \cdot \mathbf{E}_r)\mathbf{n} = -\mathbf{E}_i + (\mathbf{n} \cdot \mathbf{E}_i)\mathbf{n}$$

When we make use of Eq. (4.55b) we find that

$$\mathbf{E}_r = -\mathbf{E}_i + 2(\mathbf{n} \cdot \mathbf{E}_i)\mathbf{n} \qquad (4.56a)$$

which can also be expressed in the form

$$\mathbf{E}_r = (\mathbf{n} \cdot \mathbf{E}_i)\mathbf{n} + \mathbf{n} \times (\mathbf{n} \times \mathbf{E}_i) \qquad (4.56b)$$

The relations (4.55a) and (4.55b) show that the normal components of $\mathbf{E}_i$ and $\mathbf{E}_r$ as well as the corresponding tangential components are equal in magnitude. Thus we also have

$$|\mathbf{E}_r| = |\mathbf{E}_i| \qquad (4.56c)$$

Only the direction of the electric field is changed upon reflection. The above equations determine the electric field at the input end of the reflected flux tube. As the field propagates along the flux tube its amplitude decreases inversely with the square root of the cross-sectional area of the flux tube, since the power in a flux tube is conserved.

In general, the rays in the incident flux tube will not come from a common point P. They may come from a line or other focal surface. Figure 4.13 shows a flux tube in which the wave front, which is the surface that is everywhere normal to the rays, is not part of a spherical surface. Let OP be a line from a point O that passes through the wave front at P and that coincides with the normal unit vector $\mathbf{n}$ to the surface at P. For any smooth surface there are two mutually orthogonal curves C_1 and C_2 that can be drawn that have a maximum radius of curvature R_1 and a minimum radius of curvature R_2. All rays in the plane containing C_1 appear to come from a point a distance R_1 from P on the line OP, while those rays in the plane containing C_2 appear to come from a

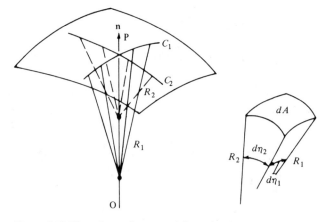

Figure 4.13 Wave front of a general flux tube showing the two principal radii of curvature.

point a distance R_2 from P and again lying on the line OP. For other curves C drawn on the wave-front surface the radius of curvature R will be between R_1 and R_2 in value and the corresponding rays will appear to come from a point on OP a distance R from P. If $d\eta_1$ and $d\eta_2$ are the angular separations of the rays in the two principal planes, as shown in Fig. 4.13, then $dA = R_1 R_2 \, d\eta_1 \, d\eta_2$ is the cross-sectional area of the flux tube. The power density is inversely proportional to dA and hence inversely proportional to $R_1 R_2$, since $d\eta_1 \, d\eta_2$ does not vary along the flux tube. The reciprocal of the product of the maximum and minimum radii of curvature is called the *gaussian curvature of the wave-front surface.*

When an arbitrary flux tube is incident on a curved reflector, it is generally difficult to calculate the principal radii of curvature for the reflected flux tube. In the special case when the incident rays all come from a common point O so that the wave front is spherical, then it can be shown that the gaussian curvature $K'(P)$ of the reflected flux tube at the point P on the surface of the reflector is given by†

$$K'(P) = \frac{1}{R'_1 R'_2}$$
$$= \frac{(4R^2 + R_u R_v)\cos\theta_i + 2R(R_u \sin^2\gamma_1 + R_v \sin^2\gamma_2)}{R^2 R_u R_v \cos\theta_i} \qquad (4.57)$$

where θ_i is the angle between the incident central ray and the normal **n** to the reflector surface at P, γ_1 and γ_2 are the angles between the incident central ray and the two principal directions on the reflector surface shown as the curves u and v in Fig. 4.14, R_u and R_v are the principal radii of curvature of the

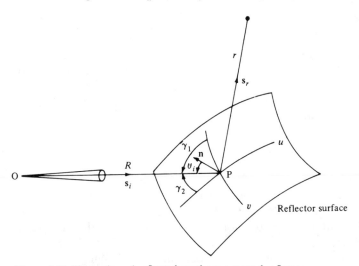

Figure 4.14 Illustration of reflected ray from a curved reflector.

† Silver, op. cit., p. 143.

reflector surface at P (these are positive for a convex surface and negative for a concave surface), R is the radius of curvature of the incident wave front at P, and $K'(P)$ is the gaussian curvature of the reflected wave front.

The two principal radii of curvature R_1' and R_2' for the reflected flux tube are in general not equal. However, at a long distance r from the point P along the central ray of the reflected flux tube the two radii of curvature $R_1' + r$ and $R_2' + r$ of the reflected wave front will be essentially the same and equal to r. Since the power density per unit area is proportional to the gaussian curvature of the wave front, the reflected power density $P_r(r)$ at r is related to that at the point P on the reflector surface as follows:

$$P_r(r) = P_r(P) \frac{R_1' R_2'}{r^2} = \frac{P_r(P)}{r^2 K'(P)} \tag{4.58}$$

The gaussian curvature $K'(P)$ of the reflected wave front at the point P on the reflector surface multiplied by R^2 is the reciprocal of the divergence factor of the surface. The latter is denoted by the symbol $D(P)$, thus

$$D(P) = \frac{1}{R^2 K'(P)} \tag{4.59}$$

where $K'(P)$ is given by Eq. (4.57). When D is introduced, Eq. (4.58) becomes

$$P_r(r) = \frac{R^2}{r^2} D(P) P_r(P) \tag{4.60}$$

The reflected field at r is then obtained by using Eq. (4.56b) and noting that the field strength is proportional to $[P_r(r)]^{1/2}$ so that

$$\mathbf{E}_r(\mathbf{r}) = \frac{R}{r} D^{1/2} e^{-jk_0 r} [(\mathbf{n} \cdot \mathbf{E}_i)\mathbf{n} + \mathbf{n} \times (\mathbf{n} \times \mathbf{E}_i)] \tag{4.61}$$

In practice, for many reflectors of interest the relationship between the incident and reflected flux tubes is simple enough that it is not necessary to evaluate the reflector-surface divergence factor. As an example in illustrating the application of ray optics, we will apply the concepts to a microwave lens to find the aperture-field distribution.

Microwave Lens

Figure 4.15 shows a typical microwave lens made from dielectric material with dielectric constant κ. The index of refraction n equals $\sqrt{\kappa}$. A point source is located at O a distance f, called the *focal length*, from the rear surface as shown. We want to find the equation of the rear surface so that the rays emerging from the front surface are all parallel. The front surface of the lens is thus an equiphase surface. The propagation constant in the lens medium is $\omega\sqrt{\mu_0\varepsilon} = nk_0$. The optical path length is equal to the physical path length multiplied by the index of refraction n. In order that the front surface of the

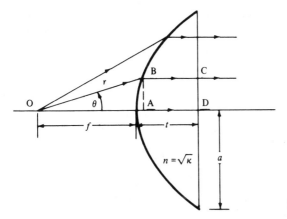

Figure 4.15 A microwave lens.

lens coincides with an equiphase wave front the optical path length from O to any point on the front surface must be the same for all rays (the same propagation-phase delay, which equals k_0 times the optical path length). With reference to Fig. 4.15 it is seen that we require

$$f + nt = r + n\overline{BC}$$

Since the two paths $\overline{BC}$ and $\overline{AD}$ are equal we can write

$$f + n(r \cos \theta - f) = r$$

which can be put in the form

$$r = \frac{(n-1)f}{n \cos \theta - 1} \tag{4.62}$$

This equation describes a hyperboloid surface (hyperbola of revolution), which is the required surface for the back surface of the lens. If the lens diameter $2a$ is small relative to the focal length f, the maximum value of θ is small and the portion of the hyperboloid surface involved can be approximated by a spherical surface. Although this approximation frequently holds for optical lenses it rarely applies for a microwave lens. The maximum angle θ is that which makes $n \cos \theta = 1$ so $\cos \theta_{max} = 1/n$. A typical dielectric material might have $n = 1.6$, in which case $\theta_{max} = 51.3°$. In practice the angle would be limited to about $30°$ for this value of n. For a given θ_{max} the lens radius is given by $a = r \sin \theta_{max}$, and upon using Eq. (4.62) for r,

$$2a = \frac{2(n-1)f \cos \theta_{max}}{n \sin \theta_{max} - 1} \tag{4.63}$$

The F number for the lens is $f/2a$. With $n = 1.6$ and $\theta_{max} = 30°$, the F number is 0.64, which is quite small compared to values usually encountered in optics. A small F number is desirable from the point of view of having a large lens diameter for a given focal length.

In order to find the field distribution over the aperture it is necessary to know the field radiated by the feed antenna located at the point O. A suitable feed antenna for a microwave lens is an open circular waveguide that has a radiation pattern given by [see Eq. (4.47)]

$$E_\theta = jk_0 \frac{2r_0^2}{r} e^{-jk_0 r} \sin \phi \, \frac{J_1(1.84)}{1.84} \frac{J_1(k_0 r_0 \sin \theta)}{k_0 r_0 \sin \theta} \qquad (4.64a)$$

$$E_\phi = jk_0 \frac{2r_0^2}{r} e^{-jk_0 r} \cos \phi \, \cos \theta \frac{1.84 J_1(1.84)}{1.84^2 - (k_0 r_0 \sin \theta)^2} \frac{dJ_1(k_0 r_0 \sin \theta)}{d(k_0 r_0 \sin \theta)} \qquad (4.64b)$$

where r_0 now stands for the radius of the circular waveguide.

With reference to Fig. 4.16 the incident field at some point on the lens surface is given by Eq. (4.64), with r having the value specified by Eq. (4.62). Part of the incident field is reflected from the surface. There is also reflection from the front surface and multiple reflections within the lens from the two surfaces. These reflections will seriously degrade the performance of the lens, since the aperture field will no longer be a constant-phase field. In practice, it is necessary to match the lens surfaces to free space to prevent reflection at the surface. (In optics this is known as *lens blooming* because of the characteristic color associated with a coated lens.) The front surface of the lens can be matched by a quarter-wave layer having an index of refraction n_1 given by $n_1 = \sqrt{n}$ and a thickness equal to one-quarter wavelength $(\lambda_0/4n_1)$ in the matching medium. A matching layer of this type is analogous to a quarter-wave transformer. The rear surface can be matched in a similar way but requires an index of refraction and a thickness that depends on both the angle of incidence

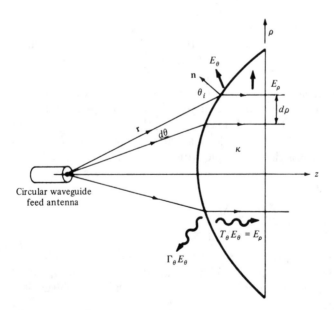

Figure 4.16 Reflection and transmission at the surface of a lens.

and the polarization of the incident electric field. Since the incident field has both a θ and a ϕ component a perfect match for both polarizations cannot be achieved. For the purpose of discussion here we will assume that only the front surface of the lens is matched.

The θ component of the incident electric field is in the plane of incidence, which is the plane containing the radius vector **r** and the unit normal **n** (not to be confused with the index of refraction n) for which the Fresnel reflection and transmission coefficients are given by (this is the parallel polarization case)†

$$\Gamma_\theta(\theta) = \frac{\kappa \cos \theta_i - \sqrt{\kappa - \sin^2 \theta_i}}{\kappa \cos \theta_i + \sqrt{\kappa - \sin^2 \theta_i}} \tag{4.65a}$$

$$T_\theta(\theta) = (1 - \Gamma_\theta) \frac{n \cos \theta_i}{\sqrt{\kappa - \sin^2 \theta_i}} \tag{4.65b}$$

where θ_i is the angle of incidence shown in Fig. 4.16. The transmitted electric field in the lens and also at the front surface of the lens is in the ρ direction, where ρ is the cylindrical radial coordinate $(x^2 + y^2)^{1/2}$. Thus apart from an irrelevant phase the electric field in the aperture, at a distance $\rho = r \sin \theta$ from the lens axis, due to E_θ is given by

$$E_\rho = \frac{2k_0 r_0^2}{r} \sin \phi T_\theta(\theta) \frac{J_1(1.84)}{1.84} \frac{J_1(k_0 r_0 \sin \theta)}{k_0 r_0 \sin \theta} \tag{4.66}$$

where in this expression we must put $r = (n-1)f/(n \cos \theta - 1)$ from Eq. (4.62) and evaluate T_θ according to Eq. (4.65b). The unit normal to the lens surface is given by

$$\mathbf{n} = \frac{(1 - n \cos \theta)\mathbf{a}_r + n \sin \theta \mathbf{a}_\theta}{\sqrt{\kappa + 1 - 2n \cos \theta}} \tag{4.67}$$

and hence

$$\cos \theta_i = -\mathbf{a}_r \cdot \mathbf{n} = \frac{n \cos \theta - 1}{\sqrt{\kappa + 1 - 2n \cos \theta}} \tag{4.68}$$

This is sufficient information to find E_ρ. A convenient way to proceed is to find E_ρ as a function of θ first and then convert this to a function of ρ by using $\rho = r \sin \theta = (n-1)f \sin \theta/(n \cos \theta - 1)$.

The field component E_ϕ becomes an E_ϕ component on the aperture surface. For E_ϕ, which corresponds to perpendicular polarization, the reflection and transmission coefficients are

$$\Gamma_\phi = \frac{\cos \theta_i - \sqrt{\kappa - \sin^2 \theta_i}}{\cos \theta_i + \sqrt{\kappa - \sin^2 \theta_i}} \tag{4.69a}$$

$$T_\phi = 1 + \Gamma_\phi \tag{4.69b}$$

† Most texts on electromagnetic fields give a derivation of these formulas.

The aperture field E_ϕ is given by multiplying Eq. (4.64b) by T_ϕ and in order to correspond to Eq. (4.66) the phase factor $j e^{-jk_0 r}$ should be dropped.

The above analysis is quite complex, so in practice a simpler, but less accurate, method is sometimes used. If the back surface of the lens is reasonably well matched and we let $g(\theta, \phi)/r^2$ be the power per unit area radiated by the feed, then the power incident in an angular sector $d\phi \, d\theta$ is proportional to

$$r^2 \sin \theta \, d\theta \, d\phi \, \frac{g(\theta, \phi)}{r^2} = g(\theta, \phi) \sin \theta \, d\theta \, d\phi$$

This power must also flow through the annular ring of radius $\rho = r \sin \theta$ and width $d\rho$, as shown in Fig. 4.16. Hence if $P(\rho, \phi)$ is the power density per unit area in the aperture we must have

$$P(\rho, \phi) r \sin \theta \, d\rho \, d\phi = g(\theta, \phi) \sin \theta \, d\theta \, d\phi$$

and thus

$$P(\rho, \phi) = g(\theta, \phi) \frac{1}{r} \frac{d\theta}{d\rho}$$

Since $\rho = r \sin \theta = (n - 1)f \sin \theta/(n \cos \theta - 1)$, upon using Eq. (4.62) we find that

$$\frac{d\rho}{d\theta} = \frac{(n - 1)f(n - \cos \theta)}{(n \cos \theta - 1)^2}$$

By using this result the expression for the power density in the aperture becomes

$$P(\rho, \phi) = g(\theta, \phi) \frac{(n \cos \theta - 1)^3}{(n - \cos \theta)(n - 1)^2 f^2} \tag{4.70}$$

with ρ given in terms of θ by the expression given earlier. The aperture-field amplitude will be proportional to the square root of $P(\rho, \phi)$. This approach neglects the polarization properties of the aperture field. Usually if the feed is linearly polarized the aperture field can be assumed, without serious error for the purpose of calculating the radiation pattern, to be linearly polarized also.† The aperture-field amplitude variation is shown in Fig. 4.17 for a typical case when $n = 1.5$ and $g(\theta, \phi)$ is a constant. The natural tapering of the field amplitude is due to each segment $d\theta$ of the incident flux tube mapping into a ring of increasing width $d\rho$ as θ increases, along with the decrease in the incident power density due to the $1/r^2$ factor.

A solid dielectric lens is heavy and bulky, so microwave lenses are usually designed with a stepped surface or by using an artificial dielectric medium. A variety of special lenses have been developed for use in scanning antenna

---

† This approximation cannot be made if the cross-polarized radiation pattern is to be found. Cross polarization is discussed in Sec. 4.7.

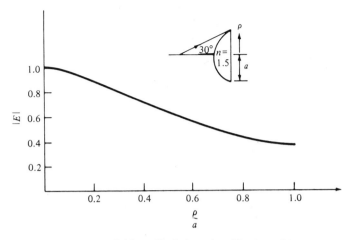

Figure 4.17 Aperture-field amplitude for a lens illuminated by an isotropic point source.

systems.† Microwave lenses are not widely used except in specialized applications, since for most communications purposes the paraboloidal reflector antenna is simpler and more economical.

4.6 PARABOLOIDAL REFLECTOR ANTENNAS

At microwave frequencies the paraboloidal reflector antenna is perhaps the most useful and widely used antenna for communications purposes. The majority of satellite communication links use paraboloidal reflector antennas. The paraboloidal reflector has a surface generated by revolving the parabolic curve shown in Fig. 4.18 about the axis and is given by

$$r = \frac{2f}{1 + \cos \theta} = f \sec^2 \frac{\theta}{2} \tag{4.71}$$

The reflector is commonly illuminated by a small feed horn located at the prime focus a distance f from the vertex.

The paraboloid surface has the property that all rays originating from the focus are reflected from the surface parallel to the axis. This would imply, if ray optics were an exact solution, that the radiated beam would have zero beam width. The analysis of the diffracted field may be carried out by using ray optics to find the field on the aperture plane, which is the circular disk just in front of the paraboloid as shown in Fig. 4.18, and applying the formulas given earlier for calculating the radiated field from a known aperture-field distribution. An alternative procedure is to determine the surface currents on the paraboloidal

---

† Jasik, op. cit., Chap. 14.

R. E. Collin and F. J. Zucker (eds.), *Antenna Theory*, Part II, McGraw-Hill Book Company, New York, 1969, Chap. 18.

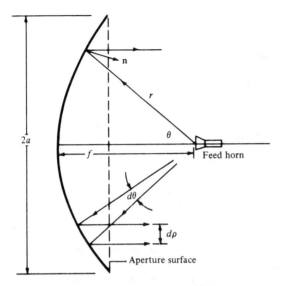

Figure 4.18 Paraboloidal reflector antenna.

surface and then find the radiated field from these by using the same basic formula as used for the dipole antenna. The induced-current method is described in Sec. 4.8. Both methods yield results that are essentially the same for the principal polarized radiation pattern and agree quite well with experimental results as long as the aperture is large in terms of wavelength.

   In some radio astronomy applications the prime-focus feed system is not used because the radiation pattern of the feed does not go to zero at the edge of the reflector; with the reflector pointed toward the sky the feed is pointed toward the ground and will receive thermal noise from the ground, which reduces the sensitivity of the system. An alternative feed system that generally has a better performance in this respect is the cassegrain system shown in Fig. 4.19. In this system the primary feed is located at the vertex and is used to illuminate a subreflector located between the focus and main reflector. This

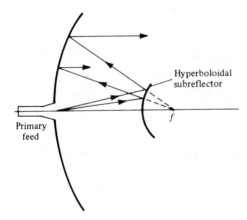

Figure 4.19 The cassegrain feed system.

subreflector provides illumination of the paraboloidal reflector. The required surface for the subreflector is a hyperboloid surface.

Aperture Efficiency

In order to establish some of the important factors involved in the design of a paraboloidal antenna system we will let $g(\theta, \phi)$ be the power-radiation pattern of the feed located at the focus. The power incident on the reflector in the flux tube of angular width $d\theta \, d\phi$ is given by

$$P_i(\theta, \phi) = g(\theta, \phi) \sin \theta \, d\theta \, d\phi$$

This same power must appear in the reflected flux tube of width $d\rho$ on the aperture surface, as shown in Fig. 4.18, and hence

$$P(\rho, \phi) r \sin \theta \, d\phi \, d\rho = g(\theta, \phi) \sin \theta \, d\theta \, d\phi$$

or

$$P(\rho, \phi) = g(\theta, \phi) \frac{1}{r} \frac{d\theta}{d\rho} \tag{4.72}$$

where $P(\rho, \phi)$ is the power density per unit area on the aperture surface. This relation is the same as that found for the microwave lens. By using Eq. (4.71) we find that

$$\rho = r \sin \theta = \frac{2f \sin \theta}{1 + \cos \theta} \qquad \frac{d\rho}{d\theta} = \frac{2f}{1 + \cos \theta}$$

$$\cos \theta = \frac{4f^2 - \rho^2}{4f^2 + \rho^2}$$

and hence

$$P(\rho, \phi) = g(\theta, \phi) \frac{(1 + \cos \theta)^2}{4f^2} = g(\theta, \phi) \frac{16f^2}{(4f^2 + \rho^2)^2} \tag{4.73}$$

If $g(\theta, \phi)$ is a constant then $P(\rho, \phi)$ is proportional to $(1 + \cos \theta)^2 = 4 \cos^4(\theta/2)$. If we wish to have a uniform aperture power distribution the feed power-radiation pattern would be required to vary proportional to $\sec^4(\theta/2)$. For $g(\theta, \phi)$ equal to a constant, Eq. (4.73) gives the aperture-field taper as a function of ρ. For a paraboloidal reflector with an angular aperture of ψ (twice the maximum value of θ) the normalized aperture field $[P(\rho)/P(0)]^{1/2}$ is shown in Fig. 4.20. For later use we note that the half-angular aperture of the paraboloidal reflector is given by $\psi/2$, where

$$\rho = a = \frac{2f \sin \psi/2}{1 + \cos \psi/2} = 2f \tan \frac{\psi}{4} \tag{4.74}$$

When the radiation pattern of the feed is also taken into account, the effect

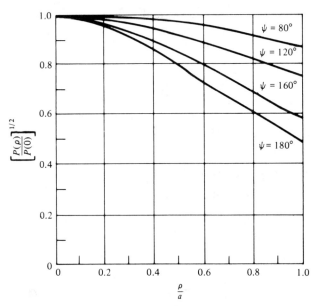

Figure 4.20 Amplitude of aperture field for a paraboloid illuminated by an isotropic feed for various angular apertures ψ.

is to increase the amplitude taper in the aperture field, which leads to a lowering of the aperture illumination efficiency. This tapering reduces the directivity of the antenna and increases the beam width, both of which are undesirable effects. On the other hand, a tapered aperture-field distribution generally results in lower side-lobe amplitudes, which is desirable since it reduces interference effects in a communication system.

There is some power lost, and hence a reduction in antenna gain, because of radiation from the feed that is not intercepted by the reflector. This loss, which is called *spillover loss*, is given by integrating the power pattern of the feed over the angular region outside of that subtended by the reflector. The efficiency factor η_s due to spillover is the ratio of the power intercepted by the reflector to the total power radiated by the feed and is given by

$$\eta_s = \frac{\int_0^{2\pi} \int_0^{\psi/2} g(\theta, \phi) \sin \theta \, d\theta \, d\phi}{\int_0^{2\pi} \int_0^{\pi} g(\theta, \phi) \sin \theta \, d\theta \, d\phi} \tag{4.75a}$$

The expression for the spillover efficiency can be written in a simpler form by introducing the directivity D_f of the feed. The feed directivity is equal to $4\pi g(0,0)$ divided by the total power radiated by the feed. Consequently, Eq. (4.75a) can be reexpressed in the form

$$\eta_s = D_f \int_0^{2\pi} \int_0^{\psi/2} \frac{g(\theta, \phi)}{4\pi g(0, 0)} \sin \theta \, d\theta \, d\phi \tag{4.75b}$$

The loss in gain due to a tapered aperture-field distribution, nonconstant phase for the aperture field, and the presence of unwanted cross-polarized fields is expressed by a factor called the *aperture efficiency*. This parameter is described below.

Let the aperture electric field be expressed in terms of its rectangular components; thus

$$\mathbf{E}_a(\rho, \phi) = E_x(\rho, \phi)\mathbf{a}_x + E_y(\rho, \phi)\mathbf{a}_y$$

The total radiated power *from the aperture* is given approximately by the following expression:

$$P_a = \frac{Y_0}{2} \int_0^{2\pi} \int_0^a (|E_x|^2 + |E_y|^2)\rho \, d\rho \, d\phi$$

$$= \int_0^{2\pi} \int_0^a P(\rho, \phi)\rho \, d\rho \, d\phi$$

when we assume that the aperture field is nearly that of a plane wave for which $Y_0|\mathbf{E}_a|^2/2$ is the power density on the aperture surface (this approximation is examined more carefully later on). Along the z axis the radiated electric field is given by Eq. (4.16) along with Eq. (4.14) using $k_x = k_y = 0$. This radiated field has a magnitude given by

$$|\mathbf{E}| = \frac{k_0}{2\pi r} \left| \int_0^{2\pi} \int_0^a \mathbf{E}_a(\rho, \phi)\rho \, d\rho \, d\phi \right|$$

The resultant radiation intensity, that is, power density per unit solid angle, will be

$$\tfrac{1}{2}Y_0 r^2 |\mathbf{E}|^2 = \frac{k_0^2 Y_0}{8\pi^2} \left| \int_0^{2\pi} \int_0^a \mathbf{E}_a(\rho, \phi)\rho \, d\rho \, d\phi \right|^2$$

If the total radiated power P_a from the aperture were distributed uniformly over the aperture with a density $P_a/\pi a^2$, the resultant aperture electric field would be $E_a = (2P_a/\pi a^2 Y_0)^{1/2}$, provided the field is linearly polarized and has a constant phase. This field would produce a power density per unit solid angle, on the z axis, of amount $k_0^2 \pi a^2 P_a/4\pi^2$. Usually only one polarization is desired and we will choose this to be the y-polarized field. The aperture efficiency η_A is the ratio of the on-axis radiation intensity from the desired polarization to that which would be produced from a uniform, linearly polarized, constant-phase aperture field radiating the same total power. Hence we have

$$\eta_A = \frac{\dfrac{k_0^2 Y_0}{8\pi^2} \left| \int_0^{2\pi} \int_0^a E_y(\rho, \phi)\rho \, d\rho \, d\phi \right|^2}{[(k_0^2 \pi a^2)/4\pi^2]P_a}$$

$$= \frac{\left| \int_0^{2\pi} \int_0^a E_y(\rho, \phi)\rho \, d\rho \, d\phi \right|^2}{\pi a^2 \int_0^{2\pi} \int_0^a (|E_x|^2 + |E_y|^2)\rho \, d\rho \, d\phi} \tag{4.76}$$

upon substituting for P_a from the expression given earlier.

The aperture efficiency can be expressed as a product of three terms that account for loss due to nonuniform illumination $(1 - \eta_i)$, loss due to nonconstant phase of the aperture field $(1 - \eta_p)$, and cross-polarization loss $(1 - \eta_x)$; thus $\eta_A = \eta_i \eta_p \eta_x$. The factoring of η_A into the above form depends on how the various losses are defined. Suitable definitions for these efficiency factors are given below. (Other definitions can be used, but the ones adopted in this text are felt by the author to be the most appropriate ones.†)

The on-axis gain of the antenna can be expressed as

$$G = \frac{I}{P_{in}/4\pi} = 4\pi \frac{I}{P_{in}}$$

where I is the radiation intensity in watts per unit solid angle for the desired polarization and P_{in} is the input power to the feed. The power radiated by the feed is $P_T = \eta_f P_{in}$, where η_f is the efficiency of the feed. The power intercepted by the aperture is $\eta_s P_T = P_a$ from the definition of spillover efficiency. We can thus express G in the form

$$G = 4\pi \frac{I}{P_a} \frac{P_a}{P_T} \frac{P_T}{P_{in}} = \eta_s \eta_f 4\pi \frac{I}{P_a}$$

Let E_y be the desired aperture-field polarization, which we will call the *copolarized* field. The x component E_x of the aperture field is then the *cross-polarized field* (co- and cross-polarized fields are defined more carefully in Sec. 4.7). The power radiated by the copolarized and cross-polarized aperture fields will be denoted by P_{co} and P_x, respectively. The sum of these powers equals the total power radiated from the aperture because the two polarizations are orthogonal. The desired term is P_{co}, so the cross-polarization efficiency will be defined by the relationship

$$\frac{P_a - P_x}{P_a} = \frac{P_{co}}{P_a} = \eta_x$$

We now obtain

$$G = \eta_s \eta_f 4\pi \frac{I}{P_{co}} \frac{P_{co}}{P_a} = \eta_s \eta_f \eta_x 4\pi \frac{I}{P_{co}}$$

The desired aperture field $E_y(x, y)$ can be separated into even and odd functions of x and y. The part that is an even function of x is

$$E_{yex} = \tfrac{1}{2}[E_y(x, y) + E_y(-x, y)]$$

while the part that is an odd function of x is

$$E_{yox} = \tfrac{1}{2}[E_y(x, y) - E_y(-x, y)]$$

---

† For a discussion of other definitions see A. C. Ludwig, "Antenna Feed Efficiency," *Space Programs Summary 37–26*, vol. IV, Jet Prop. Lab., C.I.T., Pasadena, Calif., 1965, pp. 200–208.

Each of these functions may be further split into functions that are even and odd with respect to y. Only that part of E_y that is even in both x and y will contribute to the on-axis radiated field for a symmetric aperture, since the other contributions integrate to zero. The complete even function is E_{ye} and is given by

$$E_{ye} = \tfrac{1}{4}[E_y(x, y) + E_y(-x, y) + E_y(x, -y) + E_y(-x, -y)]$$

We now adopt the following definition for phase-error efficiency: the phase-error efficiency is the ratio of the on-axis intensity I produced by the even part E_{ye} of the copolarized aperture field to the maximum radiation intensity I_{max} that would be obtained when E_{ye} has a constant phase. This ratio is given by

$$\eta_p = \frac{I}{I_{max}} = \frac{|\int_0^{2\pi} \int_0^a E_{ye}(\rho, \phi)\rho \, d\rho \, d\phi|^2}{[\int_0^{2\pi} \int_0^a |E_{ye}(\rho, \phi)|\rho \, d\rho \, d\phi]^2}$$

where cylindrical coordinates have been introduced to carry out the integration. We can now express G in the form

$$G = \eta_f \eta_s \eta_x \eta_p 4\pi \frac{I_{max}}{P_{co}}$$

If the total copolarized power P_{co} were radiated by a constant-amplitude, constant-phase, linearly polarized aperture field, the resultant on-axis radiation intensity would be $I_0 = k_0^2 \pi a^2 P_{co}/4\pi^2$. The ratio I_{max}/I_0 gives the illumination efficiency η_i. We now obtain our final factored form for G:

$$G = \eta_f \eta_s \eta_x \eta_p \eta_i 4\pi \frac{I_0}{P_{co}}$$

$$= \eta_f \eta_s \eta_x \eta_p \eta_i \left(4\pi \frac{k_0^2 \pi a^2}{4\pi^2}\right)$$

$$= \eta_f \eta_s \eta_x \eta_p \eta_i \left(\frac{4\pi}{\lambda_0^2} \pi a^2\right) \tag{4.77}$$

The product of the three factors $\eta_x \eta_p \eta_i$ is the aperture efficiency η_A given in Eq. (4.76). The explicit expressions for η_x, η_p, and η_i are [note that E_y can be replaced by E_{ye} in Eq. (4.76)]

$$\eta_x = \frac{\int_0^{2\pi} \int_0^a |E_{ye}(\rho, \phi)|^2 \rho \, d\rho \, d\phi}{\int_0^{2\pi} \int_0^a (|E_x|^2 + |E_y|^2)\rho \, d\rho \, d\phi} \tag{4.78a}$$

$$\eta_p = \frac{|\int_0^{2\pi} \int_0^a E_{ye}(\rho, \phi)\rho \, d\rho \, d\phi|^2}{[\int_0^{2\pi} \int_0^a |E_{ye}(\rho, \phi)|\rho \, d\rho \, d\phi]^2} \tag{4.78b}$$

$$\eta_i = \frac{1}{\pi a^2} \frac{[\int_0^{2\pi} \int_0^a |E_{ye}(\rho, \phi)|\rho \, d\rho \, d\phi]^2}{\int_0^{2\pi} \int_0^a |E_{ye}(\rho, \phi)|^2 \rho \, d\rho \, d\phi} \tag{4.78c}$$

The reader can readily verify that the product of these three factors equals η_A, as given in Eq. (4.76).

When we assume that the aperture field has a constant phase and is linearly polarized, the phase-error efficiency and cross-polarization efficiency both equal unity. The aperture efficiency for this case is equal to the illumination efficiency and can be expressed in the form

$$\eta_i = \frac{1}{\pi a^2} \frac{[\int_0^{2\pi} \int_0^a [P(\rho, \phi)]^{1/2} \rho \, d\rho \, d\phi]^2}{\int_0^{2\pi} \int_0^a P(\rho, \phi) \rho \, d\rho \, d\phi}$$

Since the gain function $g(\theta, \phi)$ for the feed is usually known, the integrals are best carried out by transforming back to the variable θ using Eq. (4.73) and the relations preceding Eq. (4.73); that is,

$$\rho \, d\rho = \frac{4f^2 \sin \theta \, d\theta}{(1 + \cos \theta)^2}$$

We then find that

$$\eta_i = \frac{4f^2}{\pi a^2} \frac{[\int_0^{2\pi} \int_0^{\psi/2} [g(\theta, \phi)]^{1/2} \tan(\theta/2) \, d\theta \, d\phi]^2}{\int_0^{2\pi} \int_0^{\psi/2} g(\theta, \phi) \sin \theta \, d\theta \, d\phi} \tag{4.79}$$

In order to have a uniform aperture distribution, $g(\theta, \phi) = \sec^4(\theta/2)$, as noted earlier. In this case

$$\eta_i = \frac{4f^2}{\pi a^2} 2\pi \frac{[\int_0^{\psi/2} \sec^2(\theta/2) \tan(\theta/2) \, d\theta]^2}{\int_0^{\psi/2} \sec^4 \frac{\theta}{2} \sin \theta \, d\theta}$$

$$= \frac{4f^2}{a^2} \tan^2 \frac{\psi}{4} = 1$$

upon using Eq. (4.74). This, of course, is the expected result in view of the definition of η_i.

Aperture Directivity

For a uniform constant-phase aperture field with linear polarization, the radiated field is given by Eq. (4.17a) along with Eq. (4.21), from which we find that on the z axis [note that $J_1(u)/u$ equals $1/2$ when $u = 0$]

$$\mathbf{E} = \frac{jk_0 E_0}{2\pi r} e^{-jk_0 r} \pi a^2 \mathbf{a}_\theta$$

The power density per unit solid angle is

$$\frac{r^2}{2} Y_0 |E_\theta|^2 = \frac{1}{8} k_0^2 E_0^2 Y_0 a^4$$

The total radiated power may be found from an integral of the complex

Poynting vector over the aperture. This is given approximately by

$$P_a = \frac{1}{2} \int_0^{2\pi} \int_0^a Y_0 E_0^2 \rho \, d\rho \, d\phi = \frac{1}{2}\pi a^2 Y_0 E_0^2$$

The directivity D_A of the aperture is thus

$$D_A = 4\pi \frac{\frac{1}{8}k_0^2 Y_0 a^4 E_0^2}{\frac{1}{2}\pi a^2 Y_0 E_0^2} = \frac{4\pi}{\lambda_0^2}(\pi a^2) \qquad (4.80)$$

The maximum directivity obtainable from an aperture antenna with a constant-phase field equals $4\pi/\lambda_0^2$ times the aperture area. For a paraboloidal antenna with an aperture efficiency η_A, the aperture directivity is reduced by the factor η_A. For a paraboloidal antenna with a spillover efficiency η_s, the directivity is smaller by the factor $\eta_s\eta_A$, and hence

$$D = \frac{4\pi}{\lambda_0^2}(\pi a^2)\eta_s\eta_A \qquad (4.81)$$

It is seen that in order to achieve maximum directivity the product $\eta_s\eta_A$ must be maximized.

The aperture efficiency can be increased by using a reflector with a small angular aperture, as Fig. 4.20 shows, along with a feed having a radiation-power pattern that is as nearly proportional to $\sec^4 \theta/2$ as possible over the angle subtended by the reflector. The latter requirement cannot be met without a large spillover loss, so a compromise between high aperture-illumination efficiency and low spillover efficiency must be sought such that the product $\eta_s\eta_i$ is maximized. Some insight into the relationships between these parameters may be obtained by considering the family of feed radiation patterns†:

$$g(\theta) = 2(n + 1) \cos^n \theta \qquad 0 \le \theta \le \pi/2$$
$$= 0 \qquad \theta > \pi/2$$

The constant $2(n + 1)$ is a normalization factor chosen to make the total power radiated by the feed equal to 4π; that is,

$$\int_0^{2\pi} \int_0^{\pi/2} g(\theta) \sin \theta \, d\theta \, d\phi = 4\pi = 4\pi(n + 1) \int_0^{\pi/2} \cos^n \theta \sin \theta \, d\theta$$

With this normalization $g(\theta)$ becomes the directivity function for the feed antenna and $D_f = 2(n + 1)$.

By using Eq. (4.75b) we find that the spillover efficiency η_s is given by

$$\eta_s = (n + 1) \int_0^{\psi/2} \cos^n \theta \sin \theta \, d\theta = 1 - \left(\cos\frac{\psi}{2}\right)^{n+1} \qquad (4.82)$$

† Silver, op. cit.

The aperture illumination efficiency, as given by Eq. (4.79), is

$$\eta_i = \frac{4f^2}{a^2} 2(n+1)\left[\int_0^{\psi/2} (\cos\theta)^{n/2} \tan\frac{\theta}{2}\, d\theta\right]^2$$

where Eq. (4.82) has been used to evaluate the denominator in Eq. (4.79). Now $\cos\theta = 2\cos^2\theta/2 - 1$, and if we assume that n is even and put $n/2 = m$ we obtain

$$\eta = \eta_s\eta_i = \frac{8f^2(n+1)}{a^2}\left[\int_0^{\psi/2}\left(2\cos^2\frac{\theta}{2} - 1\right)^m \frac{\sin\theta/2}{\cos\theta/2}\, d\theta\right]^2$$

The integral can be evaluated and yields

$$\eta = \eta_s\eta_i = \cot^2\frac{\psi}{4}\begin{cases} 24\left(\sin^2\dfrac{\psi}{4} + \ln\cos\dfrac{\psi}{4}\right)^2 & n = 2 \\[2ex] 40\left(\sin^4\dfrac{\psi}{4} + \ln\cos\dfrac{\psi}{4}\right)^2 & n = 4 \\[2ex] 14\left[\tfrac{1}{2}\sin^2\dfrac{\psi}{2} + \tfrac{1}{3}\left(1 - \cos\dfrac{\psi}{2}\right)^3 + 2\ln\cos\dfrac{\psi}{4}\right]^2 & n = 6 \\[2ex] 18\left[\tfrac{1}{2}\sin^2\dfrac{\psi}{2} + \tfrac{1}{3}\left(1 - \cos\dfrac{\psi}{2}\right)^3 + 2\ln\cos\dfrac{\psi}{4} - \tfrac{1}{4}\left(1 - \cos^4\dfrac{\psi}{2}\right)\right]^2 & n = 8 \end{cases} \quad (4.83)$$

where we have replaced $2f/a$ by $\cot\psi/4$ from Eq. (4.74). In Fig. 4.21 the overall efficiency $\eta_s\eta_i$ is shown as a function of the angular aperture ψ. It is seen that an efficiency of greater than 80 percent can be achieved with the optimum choice of angular aperture for a given feed pattern. Figure 4.22 shows the spillover efficiency, which is seen to approach 100 percent more rapidly for the larger values of n. This is to be expected, since the larger values of n correspond to a higher-gain feed and hence a narrower radiation beam for the feed, with a consequent smaller amount of power spillover.

In a paraboloidal antenna system there will be additional losses due to cross-polarized radiation, scattering from the feed-support structure, partial blocking of the radiation from the paraboloid by the feed, and, of course, feed-radiation patterns that do not coincide with those assumed to obtain the results shown in Figs. 4.21 and 4.22. For paraboloids fed by small horns or open waveguides typical values of overall efficiency realized in practice usually fall in the range of 50 to 65 percent. With optimum feed design efficiencies as high as 75 percent or more can be achieved.

For the optimum angular aperture obtained from Fig. 4.21 the normalized value of the feed-radiation pattern at the edge of the reflector is given by $\cos^n\psi/2$. The corresponding value of the aperture power density is [Eq. (4.73)],

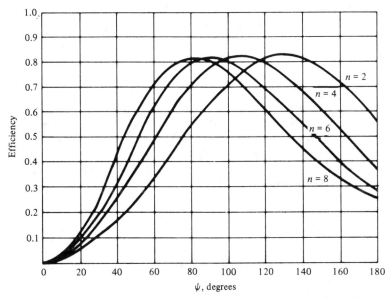

Figure 4.21 Efficiency factor $\eta_s\eta_i$ as a function of angular aperture.

$$P(a) = \cos^n \frac{\psi}{2} \frac{(1 + \cos \psi/2)^2}{4f^2} 2(n + 1)$$

The aperture-field amplitude at the edge is proportional to $\sqrt{P(a)}$ and, when

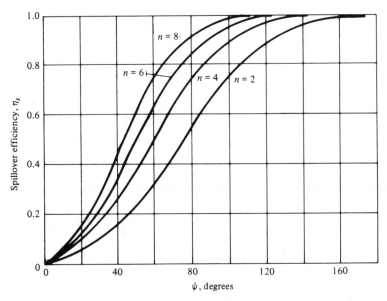

Figure 4.22 Spillover efficiency for a paraboloid as a function of the angular aperture.

normalized to its value at the center, is given by $\frac{1}{2}(\cos \psi/2)^{n/2}(1 + \cos \psi/2)$. The variation of the normalized amplitude of the aperture field at the edge of the reflector as a function of n is shown in Fig. 4.23 and is seen to be essentially constant at a value of 0.3. This corresponds to a level of 10.5 dB below the field at the center of the aperture. Hence for optimum gain, approximately 10 dB of taper should be employed in the aperture-field distribution. The corresponding taper in the feed-radiation pattern is between 7.5 and 9.5 dB, as shown in Fig. 4.23. It should be recalled however, that it may be desirable to use a greater amount of amplitude taper in order to achieve a lower side-lobe level.

The effect that tapering the amplitude distribution has on the beam width and side-lobe level may be assessed by considering the family of linearly polarized aperture fields given by

$$\mathbf{E}_a = E_0 \mathbf{a}_y \left[(1 - A) + A \left(1 - \frac{\rho^2}{a^2} \right)^n \right]$$

where A is a parameter that determines the relative value of the field at the edge of the aperture. This relative value is $(1 - A)E_0$. For the above aperture field $f_x = 0$ and f_y is given by

$$f_y = \int_0^{2\pi} \int_0^a e^{jk_0\rho \sin \theta \cos(\phi - \phi')} E_0 \left[(1 - A) + A \left(1 - \frac{\rho^2}{a^2} \right)^n \right] \rho \, d\rho \, d\phi'$$

where we have expressed $k_x x + k_y y$ in cylindrical coordinates, as was done in Sec. 4.1 for the circular aperture. The integral over ϕ' is the same as that encountered in the circular aperture problem and gives $2\pi J_0(k_0\rho \sin \theta)$. Hence we

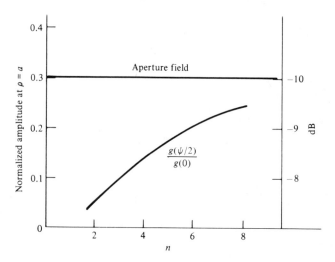

Figure 4.23 Aperture field at reflector edge for the optimum angular aperture and the relative feed gain in dB.

have

$$f_y = 2\pi E_0 \int_0^a J_0(k_0\rho \sin \theta) \left[(1 - A) + A \left(1 - \frac{\rho^2}{a^2} \right)^n \right] \rho \, d\rho$$

The integral involving the constant factor $(1 - A)$ gives the uniform aperture field result $[2\pi a^2 E_0(1 - A)J_1(u)]/u$ where $u = k_0 a \sin \theta$. For the other term we use the result that

$$\int_0^a J_0(k_0\rho \sin \theta) \left(1 - \frac{\rho^2}{a^2} \right)^n \rho \, d\rho = a^2 \int_0^1 J_0(ux)(1 - x^2)^n x \, dx$$

$$= \frac{a^2}{2} \frac{2^n n! J_{n+1}(u)}{u^{n+1}}$$

where J_{n+1} is the Bessel function of the first kind and order $n + 1$. Our final result is

$$f_y = \pi a^2 E_0 \left[2(1 - A) \frac{J_1(u)}{u} + A2^n n! \frac{J_{n+1}(u)}{u^{n+1}} \right] \tag{4.84}$$

By using Eq. (4.39) we can find the radiated field, which is

$$\mathbf{E} = \frac{jk_0 e^{-jk_0 r}}{2\pi r} \pi a^2 E_0 \left[2(1 - A) \frac{J_1(u)}{u} + A2^n n! \frac{J_{n+1}(u)}{u^{n+1}} \right] (\mathbf{a}_\theta \sin \phi + \mathbf{a}_\phi \cos \phi \cos \theta) \tag{4.85}$$

For a high-gain antenna the radiation pattern is essentially that given by Eq. (4.84) in both the $\phi = 0$ and $\phi = \pi/2$ planes, since $\cos \theta$ varies slowly and can be considered constant for angles that include the main lobe and the near-in side lobes. A typical pattern is shown in Fig. 4.24 for $A = 0.9$, $n = 2.5$, which corresponds to a 20-dB taper. For comparison, the uniform aperture-field pattern is also shown ($A = 0$). It is seen that with a 20-dB taper the main lobe is almost twice as broad as that for a uniform aperture field. However, the side-lobe level is reduced to below the -40-dB level, whereas for the uniform aperture field the first side lobe is only 17.6 dB below the main lobe.

The parameter A governs the edge illumination level, while the parameter n controls the rate at which the aperture field decreases with ρ. For the same value of A the larger values of n result in lower side-lobe levels, larger beam widths, and lower aperture illumination efficiency. Figure 4.25 shows the dependence of side-lobe level and aperture illumination efficiency on the parameters A and n.

Up to this point the general properties of a paraboloidal reflector antenna have been examined in terms of various assumed aperture-field distributions without reference to any particular feed antenna. The actual aperture field that is obtained in practice is dependent on the type of feed antenna used. When the feed antenna has been chosen, the aperture field can be found using ray optics principles. From the aperture field thus determined the radiation field from the paraboloidal reflector can be found by the methods already described.

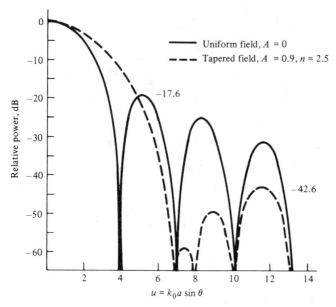

Figure 4.24 Radiation patterns for circular aperture.

In order to illustrate the procedure we will assume that the feed is a pyramidal horn of dimensions a' by b' and with an aperture field $E_0 \mathbf{a}_y \cos \pi x/a'$. For this horn the radiation field of the horn is given by Eq. (4.51) and is (the polar axis is directed toward the center of the reflector, as in Fig. 4.18)

$$\mathbf{E}_i = \frac{jk_0 \, e^{-jk_0 r}}{2\pi r} f_y (\mathbf{a}_\theta \sin \phi + \mathbf{a}_\phi \cos \phi \cos \theta) \qquad (4.86)$$

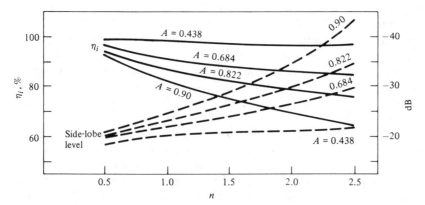

Figure 4.25 Aperture illumination efficiency and maximum side-lobe level for aperture field $(1 - A) + A(1 - \rho^2/a^2)^n$.

where $f_y = \dfrac{a'b'E_0}{4}\dfrac{\sin v}{v}\dfrac{\cos u}{(\pi/2)^2 - u^2}$

$v = (k_0 b'/2)\sin\theta\sin\phi$

$u = (k_0 a'/2)\sin\theta\cos\phi$

This is the field incident on the reflector.

In order to find the reflected field using Eq. (4.56a) we need to know the unit normal **n** to the reflector surface. The equation for the reflector surface is given by relation (4.71) as $r - f\sec^2\theta/2 = 0$. The gradient of this function is normal to the surface and has the value

$$\mathbf{a}_r - \frac{f}{r}\mathbf{a}_\theta \frac{\partial}{\partial\theta}\sec^2\frac{\theta}{2} = \mathbf{a}_r - \frac{f}{r}\sec^2\frac{\theta}{2}\tan\frac{\theta}{2}\mathbf{a}_\theta = \mathbf{a}_r - \tan\frac{\theta}{2}\mathbf{a}_\theta$$

The unit inward normal to the surface is then seen to be

$$\mathbf{n} = -\mathbf{a}_r\cos\frac{\theta}{2} + \mathbf{a}_\theta\sin\frac{\theta}{2} \tag{4.87}$$

At the reflector surface the reflected electric field, as given by Eq. (4.56a), is

$$\mathbf{E}_r = 2(\mathbf{n}\cdot\mathbf{E}_i)\mathbf{n} - \mathbf{E}_i$$

When we make use of Eqs. (4.86) and (4.87) we find that

$$\mathbf{E}_r = \frac{jk_0 e^{-jk_0 r}}{2\pi r}f_y\left[2\sin\phi\sin\frac{\theta}{2}\left(\mathbf{a}_\theta\sin\frac{\theta}{2} - \mathbf{a}_r\cos\frac{\theta}{2}\right) - (\mathbf{a}_\theta\sin\phi + \mathbf{a}_\phi\cos\phi\cos\theta)\right]$$

This expression can be simplified by using

$$2\sin\frac{\theta}{2}\cos\frac{\theta}{2} = \sin\theta$$

$$2\sin^2\frac{\theta}{2} = 1 - \cos\theta$$

and noting that $\mathbf{a}_y = (\mathbf{a}_r\sin\theta + \mathbf{a}_\theta\cos\theta)\sin\phi$. By means of these relations the expression for $\mathbf{E}_r$ can be written as

$$\mathbf{E}_r = \frac{-jk_0 e^{-jk_0 r}}{2\pi r}f_y(\mathbf{a}_y + \mathbf{a}_\phi\cos\phi\cos\theta) \tag{4.88}$$

At the reflector surface we also have

$$\frac{\cos\theta}{r} = \frac{\cos\theta(1 + \cos\theta)}{2f} = \frac{4f(4f^2 - \rho^2)}{(4f^2 + \rho^2)^2} \tag{4.89}$$

as obtained by using $\rho = r\sin\theta$, the equation for the reflector surface, and solving for $\cos\theta$ in terms of the radial coordinate ρ. In place of Eq. (4.88) we now obtain

$$\mathbf{E}_r = \frac{-jk_0\,e^{-jk_0r}}{\pi}\,2ff_y\,\frac{(4f^2+\rho^2)\mathbf{a}_y+(4f^2-\rho^2)\cos\phi\,\mathbf{a}_\phi}{(4f^2+\rho^2)^2} \tag{4.90}$$

Since the reflected field propagates as a plane wave to the aperture surface, Eq. (4.90) also gives the field on the aperture plane if the phase term $-j\,e^{-jk_0r}$ is replaced by $-j\,e^{-jk_0(r+d)}$, where d is the distance to the aperture surface from the reflector. The phase term is the same for all rays, so it may be ignored. Thus we may take the aperture field to be given by

$$\mathbf{E}_a = \frac{k_0fa'b'E_0}{2}\frac{\sin v}{v}\frac{\cos u}{(\pi/2)^2-u^2}\frac{(4f^2+\rho^2)\mathbf{a}_y+(4f^2-\rho^2)\cos\phi\,\mathbf{a}_\phi}{(4f^2+\rho^2)^2}=\frac{k_0fa'b'E_0}{2}\frac{\sin v}{v}$$

$$\times\frac{\cos u}{(\pi/2)^2-u^2}\frac{[2(4f^2+\rho^2)+(4f^2-\rho^2)(1+\cos 2\phi)]\mathbf{a}_y-(4f^2-\rho^2)\sin 2\phi\,\mathbf{a}_x}{2(4f^2+\rho^2)^2} \tag{4.91}$$

In this expression v and u must be expressed in terms of ρ by using $\sin\theta=\rho/r=\rho(1+\cos\theta)/2f=4f\rho/(4f^2+\rho^2)$. This completes the derivation of the aperture field as a function of the aperture coordinates ρ and ϕ.

The component of the field along $\mathbf{a}_x$ represents the cross-polarized component. A sketch of the aperture field is shown in Fig. 4.26. From this figure it can be seen that, because of the antisymmetrical distribution, the cross-polarized component will not contribute to the radiated field along the z axis. The major effect of the cross-polarized component is to produce cross-polarized lobes that have maxima in the planes that are located $\pm45°$ from the principal E and H planes. There is also a small loss in gain due to a finite amount of power radiated by the cross-polarized field. The principal E- and H-plane patterns are also not affected by the cross-polarized aperture field component, as may be seen from the antisymmetrical distribution of the cross-polarized field on the aperture plane.

In general it is difficult to analytically evaluate the radiated field from the aperture field given by Eq. (4.91) because of its complex dependence on ρ and

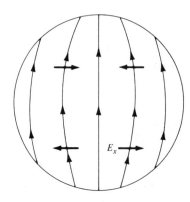

Figure 4.26 Illustration of aperture-field polarization for a paraboloid with pyramidal-horn feed.

ϕ. However, numerical integration can be used to evaluate the radiated field for any particular case.

Aperture Radiated Power: Exact Equations

In the preceding discussion it was assumed that the power radiated from the aperture could be found from an integral of $|\mathbf{E}_a|^2/2Z_0$ over the aperture surface. In the case of a large aperture and with $\mathbf{E}_a$ having constant phase and varying slowly over a distance of one wavelength, the aperture magnetic field $\mathbf{H}_a$ is very nearly equal to $(\mathbf{a}_z \times \mathbf{E}_a)/Z_0$, so $|\mathbf{E}_a|^2/2Z_0$ is then equal to the Poynting-vector power flux on the aperture surface. It is of some interest to compare this method of determining the radiated power with an exact method that is based on the use of the exact expression for the complex Poynting vector at the aperture surface.

In Sec. 4.1 the tangential electric field on the aperture was expressed in the form

$$\mathbf{E}_a(x, y) = \frac{1}{(2\pi)^2} \int\limits_{-\infty}^{\infty} \int \mathbf{f}_t(k_x, k_y)\, e^{-j\mathbf{k}_t \cdot \mathbf{r}}\, dk_x\, dk_y \qquad (4.92)$$

The Fourier transform of Maxwell's equation $\nabla \times \mathbf{E} = -j\omega\mu_0\mathbf{H}$ gives

$$\mathbf{H}(k_x, k_y) = \frac{\mathbf{k} \times \mathbf{E}(k_x, k_y)}{k_0 Z_0} = \frac{\mathbf{k} \times \mathbf{f}}{k_0 Z_0}$$

Consequently at $z = 0$ we can express $\mathbf{H}(x, y)$ in the form

$$\mathbf{H}(x, y) = \frac{1}{(2\pi)^2} \frac{1}{k_0 Z_0} \int\limits_{-\infty}^{\infty} \int \mathbf{k}' \times \mathbf{f}(k'_x, k'_y)\, e^{-j\mathbf{k}'_t \cdot \mathbf{r}}\, dk'_x\, dk'_y \qquad (4.93)$$

The complex Poynting vector in the z direction is $\mathbf{E}(x, y) \times \mathbf{H}^*(x, y) \cdot \mathbf{a}_z$ and involves the quantity

$$\mathbf{f}_t(k_x, k_y) \times [\mathbf{k}' \times \mathbf{f}(k'_x, k'_y)]^* \cdot \mathbf{a}_z = \mathbf{f}_t(k_x, k_y) \cdot \mathbf{f}^*_t(k'_x, k'_y)(k'_z)^* - \mathbf{f}_t(k_x, k_y) \cdot \mathbf{k}'_t f^*_z(k'_x, k'_y)$$

Since $k_z f_z = -\mathbf{k}_t \cdot \mathbf{f}_t$, this expression is real for $k_t^2 = k_x^2 + k_y^2 \le k_0^2$ and imaginary for $k_t > k_0$, since for the latter condition k_z is pure imaginary. When we use the above result we find that the total radiated power from the aperture is given by

$$P_a = \frac{1}{2k_0 Z_0 (2\pi)^4} \int_{S_a} \int\int\limits_{k_t \le k_0} \int\int\limits_{k'_t \le k_0} [\mathbf{f}_t(k_x, k_y) \cdot \mathbf{f}^*_t(k'_x, k'_y) k'_z$$

$$+ \mathbf{f}_t(k_x, k_y) \cdot \mathbf{k}'_t \mathbf{k}'_t \cdot \mathbf{f}^*_t(k'_x, k'_y)(k'_z)^{-1}\, e^{-j\mathbf{k}_t \cdot \mathbf{r} + j\mathbf{k}'_t \cdot \mathbf{r}}\, dk'_x\, dk'_y\, dk_x\, dk_y\, dx\, dy \qquad (4.94)$$

The integral over x gives $2\pi\delta(k_x - k'_x)$, while that over y gives $2\pi\delta(k_y - k'_y)$ where $\delta(k_x - k'_x)$ is the Dirac delta function. The aperture field is defined over the whole

xy plane and is taken to be zero outside the actual physical aperture, thus allowing the integration over x and y to go from minus to plus infinity. The integrals over k'_x, k'_y can be performed and simply result in the replacement of k'_x, k'_y by k_x, k_y. Consequently the expression for the total radiated power reduces to the following:

$$P_a = \frac{1}{2k_0 Z_0} \frac{1}{(2\pi)^2} \iint_{k_t \leq k_0} [|\mathbf{f}_t(k_x, k_y)|^2 + |f_z(k_x, k_y)|^2] k_z \, dk_x \, dk_y \qquad (4.95)$$

If we started with the expression $\mathbf{E}_a(x, y) \cdot \mathbf{E}_a^*(x, y)$, a similar derivation would show that

$$\frac{1}{2Z_0} \iint_{S_a} |\mathbf{E}_a(x, y)|^2 \, dx \, dy = \frac{1}{2Z_0} \frac{1}{(2\pi)^2} \iint_{-\infty}^{\infty} |\mathbf{f}_t(k_x, k_y)|^2 \, dk_x \, dk_y \qquad (4.96)$$

This expression is a statement of Parseval's theorem for Fourier transforms.

Equation (4.96) is the approximate expression used earlier for the radiated power. The exact expression is given by Eq. (4.95). However, for a large aperture with a slowly varying constant-phase aperture field, $\mathbf{f}_t$ is highly peaked near $k_t = 0$. For $k_t > k_0$, $\mathbf{f}_t$ is very small. Furthermore, for $k_t \approx 0$, $k_z \approx k_0$ and f_z is very small. When these approximations hold we can drop the term $|f_z|^2$ in Eq. (4.95), replace k_z by k_0, and extend the integration over the whole k_x, k_y plane. The result is then identical to that given by Eq. (4.96).

4.7 CROSS POLARIZATION

There is considerable interest in the development of the 12-GHz-band television broadcast system using satellites in a geostationary orbit. There is only one geostationary orbit, the equatorial orbit, and hence it is anticipated that the demand for satellite positions in this orbit will continue to increase. In order to achieve a high utilization of this orbit it is necessary to space the satellites as closely as possible.† This will require the ground receiving antennas to have very low side-lobe levels in order to keep interfering signals below the level at which they cause objectionable interference with the desired signal. A side-lobe level 35 dB below the main lobe is desirable. In addition, if the cross-polarized radiation can be kept below this level also, then signals may be received on opposite polarizations without serious cross interference. These stringent requirements have resulted in considerable effort to develop feed antennas that will give the required low side-lobe levels and cross polarization and yet produce a high aperture efficiency with low spillover loss. Considerable

† The new FCC regulations will require 2° spacing between satellites launched in the future.

progress has been achieved in this direction with the development of corrugated horns and dual-mode horns and coaxial waveguide feeds. A discussion of cross polarization and some of these newer feeds is given in this section. An excellent survey of work in this area is available in a recent review paper on the subject, and the interested reader is referred to this paper for a more detailed coverage.†

Consider a paraboloidal reflector antenna system that radiates an electromagnetic field that has both an E_x and an E_y component of electric field along the z axis or bore-sight direction. If a small dipole antenna is used as a receiving antenna and is oriented with its axis parallel to E_y, then the received signal will not have any contribution from the cross-polarized component E_x. The power radiated in the cross-polarized field is wasted, and this reduces the effective gain of the system. If the desired polarization is in the y direction along the axis of the paraboloidal antenna, then for directions off-axis the two field components E_θ and E_ϕ must have a particular relationship to each other in order that the resultant field will correspond to a pure, linearly polarized field having the optimum orientation in space. The required relationship can be established by considering the antenna system shown in Fig. 4.27. We will assume that on-axis the radiated field is in the y direction, which is thus the desired polarization. This field may be received by a small dipole antenna having its axis parallel to the y axis. When we move the dipole off axis in any direction but do not rotate it, i.e., if it is always kept oriented parallel to the yz plane, then it receives the component of the radiated field that is called the *copolarized field*. The field component that is perpendicular to this polarization is called the *cross-polarized field*.‡ Insteady of moving the dipole off-axis we can keep the dipole fixed and rotate the transmitting antenna such that its bore-sight axis moves along a great circle at some particular angle ϕ. Let the radiated field at the point P specified by the angles θ and ϕ be $\mathbf{E}(\theta, \phi) = E_\theta(\theta, \phi)\mathbf{a}_\theta + E_\phi(\theta, \phi)\mathbf{a}_\phi$. When the point P is rotated so it coincides with the z axis the field $\mathbf{E}(\theta, \phi)$ can be resolved into x and y components, which, from Fig. 4.27b, are readily seen to be given by

$$E_x = E_\theta \cos \phi - E_\phi \sin \phi \qquad (4.97a)$$

$$E_y = E_\theta \sin \phi + E_\phi \cos \phi \qquad (4.97b)$$

E_x is the cross-polarized field, and E_y is the desired copolarized field. In order that the cross-polarized field be zero we see that the radiated field must have the property that

$$E_\theta(\theta, \phi) \cos \phi = E_\phi(\theta, \phi) \sin \phi \qquad (4.98)$$

† P. J. B. Clarricoats and G. T. Poulton, "High-Efficiency Microwave Reflector Antennas—A Review," *Proc. IEEE*, vol. 65, Oct. 1977, pp. 1470–1504.

‡ Other definitions of co- and cross-polarized radiation are possible. However, the one used in this text is generally the most useful one and corresponds to Ludwig's definition three. See A. C. Ludwig, "The Definition of Cross-Polarization, "*IEEE Trans.*, vol. AP-21, Jan. 1973, pp. 116–119.

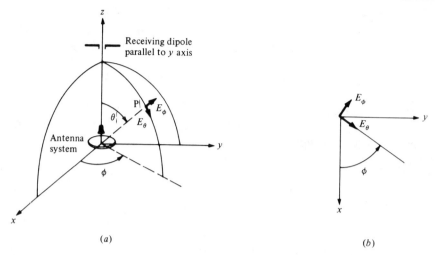

Figure 4.27 Illustration of field components radiated by an antenna system.

for all values of θ and ϕ. A sufficient condition for this relation to hold is that the field have the following form:

$$E_\theta(\theta, \phi) = e(\theta) \sin \phi \qquad (4.99a)$$

$$E_\phi(\theta, \phi) = e(\theta) \cos \phi \qquad (4.99b)$$

If these relations hold then $E_x = 0$, and the cross-polarized field is zero in all directions, while the copolarized field equals $e(\theta)(\sin^2 \phi + \cos^2 \phi) = e(\theta)$ in all directions. The copolarized field is oriented along the unit vector $\mathbf{a}_1$ given by

$$\mathbf{a}_1 = \mathbf{a}_\theta \sin \phi + \mathbf{a}_\phi \cos \phi \qquad (4.100a)$$

and the cross-polarized unit vector, which is perpendicular to $\mathbf{a}_1$, is

$$\mathbf{a}_2 = \mathbf{a}_\theta \cos \phi - \mathbf{a}_\phi \sin \phi \qquad (4.100b)$$

It should be apparent that $\mathbf{a}_1 \cdot \mathbf{E}$ gives the copolarized field while $\mathbf{a}_2 \cdot \mathbf{E}$ gives the cross-polarized field. [Compare these scalar products with the expressions in Eq. (4.97).]

When the relations given in Eq. (4.99) hold, the radiation pattern of the antenna exhibits rotational symmetry about the axis. The E-plane pattern would be measured by rotating the antenna along the $\phi = \pi/2$ arc, and the measured pattern would be $E_\theta(\theta, \pi/2) = e(\theta)$. The H-plane pattern would be measured by rotating the antenna along the $\phi = 0$ arc and would be $E_\phi(\theta, 0) = e(\theta)$. Thus the E- and H-plane patterns are identical, as are the patterns in any other plane as well.

In order for a paraboloidal reflector antenna to produce a radiated field with negligible cross polarization, it must be illuminated by a feed whose radiation pattern also has no cross polarization. That this is the case will be established in the next section where radiation from a paraboloidal reflector is analyzed in terms of the induced currents on the reflector surface.

4.8 RADIATION FROM PARABOLOIDAL REFLECTORS: INDUCED CURRENT METHOD

A feed with equal E- and H-plane amplitude and phase patterns and which satisfies the relation (4.99) has zero cross polarization. Such a feed when used to illuminate a paraboloid results in an antenna with very small cross polarization, as will be shown below.

Circular waveguide coaxial feeds excited by a mixture of TE_{1m} (transverse electric) and TM_{1m} (transverse magnetic) modes produce a feed primary pattern of the form

$$\mathbf{E}_f(\theta', \phi', r') = \frac{e^{-jk_0\rho}}{\rho}[e_{\theta'}(\theta')\sin\phi'\mathbf{a}_{\theta'} + e_{\phi'}(\theta')\cos\phi'\mathbf{a}_{\phi'}] \qquad (4.101)$$

where $e_{\theta'}(\theta')$ and $e_{\phi'}(\theta')$ depend on the particular feed and excitation used. In the discussion below we assume that the feed pattern has this form. The coordinate system used is shown in Fig. 4.28. The polar axis for describing the feed pattern is directed toward the reflector, while that used to describe the radiated field is directed away from the reflector. In rectangular coordinates the feed field is given by

$$\mathbf{E}_f = \frac{e^{-jk_0\rho}}{\rho}[\mathbf{a}_x(e_\theta\cos\theta\cos\phi\sin\phi - e_\phi\sin\phi\cos\phi)$$
$$+ \mathbf{a}_y(e_\theta\cos\theta\sin^2\phi + e_\phi\cos^2\phi) - \mathbf{a}_z e_\theta\sin\theta\sin\phi] \qquad (4.102)$$

Note that $\phi = -\phi'$ and $\theta = \pi - \theta'$, as shown in Fig. 4.28. Now assume that at $\theta = 0$ the field is polarized along y, then $e_\theta = e_\phi$ at $\theta = 0$. In the $\phi = 0$ plane or H plane the feed pattern is proportional to $\mathbf{a}_y e_\phi = e_\phi\mathbf{a}_\phi$, while in the $\phi = \pi/2$ or E plane the pattern is proportional to $\mathbf{a}_y e_\theta\cos\theta - \mathbf{a}_z e_\theta\sin\theta = e_\theta\mathbf{a}_\theta$. The E- and

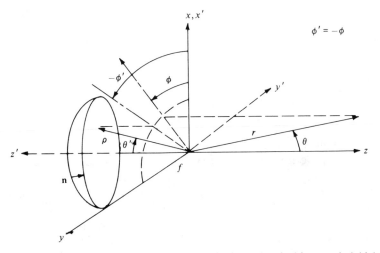

Figure 4.28 Coordinates used to describe a field associated with a paraboloidal antenna.

H-plane patterns will be equal if $e_\theta(\theta) = e_\phi(\theta)$ for all values of θ. The cross-polarized pattern will then also be zero for all values of θ and ϕ.

The incident magnetic field on the paraboloid is $\mathbf{H}_f = Y_0 \mathbf{a}_\rho \times \mathbf{E}_f$, where $\mathbf{E}_f$ is given by Eq. (4.101) in terms of the variables θ', ϕ', ρ. On the paraboloid surface $\rho = 2f/(1 + \cos\theta') = f\sec^2(\theta'/2)$. If each portion of the paraboloid is treated as a flat reflecting surface, then the surface current produced on the paraboloid is given by

$$\mathbf{J}_s = 2\mathbf{n} \times \mathbf{H}_f = 2Y_0 \mathbf{n} \times (\mathbf{a}_\rho \times \mathbf{E}_f)$$

$$= \frac{2\,e^{-jk_0\rho}}{Z_0\rho}\left[\cos\frac{\theta'}{2}(e_{\theta'}\sin\phi'\mathbf{a}_{\theta'} + e_{\phi'}\cos\phi'\mathbf{a}_{\phi'})\right.$$

$$\left. + \sin\frac{\theta'}{2}\,e_{\theta'}\sin\phi'\mathbf{a}_\rho\right] \tag{4.103}$$

upon using $\mathbf{n} = -\mathbf{a}_\rho \cos(\theta'/2) + \mathbf{a}_{\theta'}\sin(\theta'/2)$. In terms of this current, which is called the *physical optics current*, the radiated electric field is found to be

$$\mathbf{E}(\mathbf{r}) = \frac{-jk_0 Z_0}{4\pi r}e^{-jk_0 r}\int_S [\mathbf{J}(\mathbf{r}') - \mathbf{a}_r \cdot \mathbf{J}(\mathbf{r}')\mathbf{a}_r]e^{jk_0\mathbf{a}_r \cdot \mathbf{r}'}\,dS \tag{4.104}$$

where $\mathbf{r}'$ is the position vector to a point on the paraboloid (see Sec. 2.6). By using Eq. (4.103) in Eq. (4.104) and carrying out the integration over ϕ we obtain

$$\mathbf{E}(\mathbf{r}) = \frac{jk_0 f\,e^{-jk_0 r}}{r}\int_0^{\theta_0}\left[(e_{\theta'} + e_{\phi'})J_0(v_1)(\mathbf{a}_\theta\cos\theta\sin\phi + \mathbf{a}_\phi\cos\phi)\right.$$

$$- (e_{\theta'} - e_{\phi'})J_2(v_1)(\mathbf{a}_\theta\cos\theta\sin\phi - \mathbf{a}_\phi\cos\phi)$$

$$\left. - 2jJ_1(v_1)e_{\theta'}\sin\theta\sin\phi\tan\frac{\theta'}{2}\mathbf{a}_\theta\right]\left(e^{-jv_2}\tan\frac{\theta'}{2}\right)d\theta' \tag{4.105}$$

where $v_1 = 2k_0 f\sin\theta\tan\dfrac{\theta'}{2}$

$$v_2 = 2k_0 f\frac{1 + \cos\theta\cos\theta'}{1 + \cos\theta'}$$

J_n = Bessel function of order n

and $2\theta_0 = \psi$ is the angular aperture of the paraboloid with focal length f.

In the aperture-field method the reflected field at the aperture surface is first found from the relation

$$\mathbf{E}_r = -\mathbf{E}_f + 2\mathbf{n} \cdot \mathbf{E}_f\mathbf{n} \tag{4.106}$$

This field is assumed to propagate as a plane wave to the aperture surface, which will be taken as the $z = 0$ plane. The total path length is $2f$, and hence we find that the x and y components of the aperture field are

$$\mathbf{E}_a = \frac{e^{-j2k_0f}}{\rho} [\mathbf{a}_x(e_{\phi'} - e_{\theta'}) \sin \phi' \cos \phi' + \mathbf{a}_y e_{\phi'} \cos^2 \phi' + \mathbf{a}_y e_{\theta'} \sin^2 \phi'] \quad (4.107)$$

When $e_{\theta'} = e_{\phi'}$ the aperture field is linearly polarized in the y direction. In terms of the aperture electric field alone, the radiated electric field is given by

$$\mathbf{E(r)} = \frac{jk_0f\,e^{-jk_0r-2jk_0f}}{r} \int_0^{\theta_0} [(e_{\theta'} + e_{\phi'})J_0(v_1) (\mathbf{a}_\theta \sin \phi + \mathbf{a}_\phi \cos \theta \cos \phi) - (e_{\theta'} - e_{\phi'})$$

$$\times J_2(v_1)(\mathbf{a}_\theta \sin \phi - \mathbf{a}_\phi \cos \theta \cos \phi)] \tan \frac{\theta'}{2} d\theta' \quad (4.108)$$

If the radiated field is determined in terms of the tangential magnetic field alone on the aperture surface, then it is found that

$$\mathbf{E(r)} = \frac{jk_0f\,e^{-jk_0r-2jk_0f}}{r} \int_0^{\theta_0} [(e_{\theta'} + e_{\phi'})J_0(v_1)$$

$$\times (\mathbf{a}_\theta \cos \theta \sin \phi + \mathbf{a}_\phi \cos \phi) - (e_{\theta'} - e_{\phi'})$$

$$\times J_2(v_1)(\mathbf{a}_\theta \cos \theta \sin \phi - \mathbf{a}_\phi \cos \phi)] \tan \frac{\theta'}{2} d\theta'$$

$$(4.109)$$

If a formulation in terms of both electric and magnetic fields on the aperture surface is used, the result is the average of Eqs. (4.108) and (4.109). The latter formulation is commonly used. The various formulations give very nearly the same results for the copolarized radiation field but show a more pronounced difference for the cross-polarized radiated field, as will be seen later.

In the region close to the axis, that is, θ small, the use of the approximation $\cos \theta = 1$ makes v_2 in Eq. (4.105) equal to $2k_0f$. With this approximation, Eqs. (4.105) and (4.109) will agree, with the exception of the small term involving $J_1(v_1)$ in Eq. (4.105). This latter term vanishes at $\theta = 0$ and remains small since it is multiplied by $\sin \theta$. It is due to the z component of current on the paraboloid.

The difference in the phase function in the surface-current formulation and that in the aperture-field method is due to the difference in path lengths, as shown in Fig. 4.29. In the aperture-field method propagation from the paraboloid surface to the aperture surface is along a path parallel to the z axis in accordance with the geometrical optics theory that is used to determine the aperture field. The difference in phase between the two methods is

$$2k_0f - v_2 = 2k_0f \frac{(1 - \cos \theta) \cos \theta'}{1 + \cos \theta'}$$

For a paraboloid with $f = 18\lambda_0$ and $\theta = 10°$ this phase difference varies from

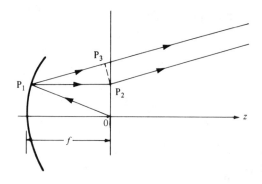

Figure 4.29 Path lengths OP_1P_2 for aperture-field method and OP_1P_3 for surface-current method of computing radiation from a paraboloid.

0.547π at $\theta' = 0°$ to 0.365π at $\theta' = 60°$, or a total variation of 0.18π ($32.4°$) over the aperture. This amount of phase variation does not produce a significant change in the radiated pattern in the region $\theta \leq 10°$.

All of the above formulas show that low cross-polarization is achieved by making $e_{\theta'} = e_{\phi'}$. As long as $\cos \theta$ can be approximated by unity the radiated electric field will then satisfy the relationship given by Eq. (4.99), provided the small term involving $J_1(v_1)$ in the expression for E_θ in Eq. (4.105) is neglected. This approximation will be good for values of θ up to at least 10°, where $\cos \theta = 0.985$ and hence the cross polarization will be small over the region of interest for paraboloids with diameters exceeding 50 wavelengths. It is thus concluded that the desirable feed pattern should be of the form given by Eq. (4.101) with $e_{\theta'} = e_{\phi'}$. This type of feed pattern also leads to small cross-polarization loss in a paraboloidal antenna. The objective in coaxial waveguide feed design is to excite the proper combination of TE_{1m} and TM_{1m} modes in the aperture of the feed so as to obtain a pattern of the desired form as given by Eq. (4.101). The paraboloidal antenna side-lobe level is determined by the amplitude taper over the paraboloid, and this is directly related to the directivity of the feed pattern.

With reference to Eq. (4.101) it is seen that the dominant part of the radiated field comes from the terms multiplied by $J_0(v_1)$. The radiated field can be resolved as components along the unit vectors $\mathbf{a}_1 = (\mathbf{a}_\theta \sin \phi + \mathbf{a}_\phi \cos \phi)$ and $\mathbf{a}_2 = (\mathbf{a}_\theta \cos \phi - \mathbf{a}_\phi \sin \phi)$, which define the copolarized and cross-polarized fields. It is then found that the copolarized field in the $\phi = \pi/4$ plane is given by

$$E_{co} = \frac{jk_0 f}{r} e^{-jk_0 r} \int_0^{\theta_0} \left[(e_{\theta'} + e_{\phi'}) J_0(v_1) \left(\frac{\cos \theta + 1}{2} \right) \right.$$
$$\left. - (e_{\theta'} - e_{\phi'}) J_2(v_1) \left(\frac{\cos \theta - 1}{2} \right) - j J_1(v_1) e_{\theta'} \sin \theta \, \tan \frac{\theta'}{2} \right] \left(e^{-jv_2} \tan \frac{\theta'}{2} \right) d\theta'$$

$$(4.110)$$

The term multiplied by J_0 is the contribution from the copolarized feed pattern, the term multiplied by J_2 comes from the feed cross-polarized pattern, and the last term multiplied by $J_1 \sin \theta$ comes from the z component of the induced current on the reflector.

The cross-polarized field is given by the scalar product of Eq. (4.105) with the unit vector $\mathbf{a}_2$; thus

$$E_{\text{cross}} = \frac{jk_0 f}{r} e^{-jk_0 r} \int_0^{\theta_0} \left[(e_{\theta'} + e_{\phi'}) J_0(v_1)(\cos \theta - 1) \sin \phi \cos \phi - (e_{\theta'} - e_{\phi'}) J_2(v_1) \right.$$

$$\times (\cos \theta + 1) \sin \phi \cos \phi - 2j J_1(v_1) e_{\theta'}$$

$$\left. \times \sin \theta \sin \phi \cos \phi \tan \frac{\theta'}{2} \right] \left(e^{-jv_2} \tan \frac{\theta'}{2} \right) d\theta' \tag{4.111}$$

The three terms contributing to the cross-polarized field consist of a contribution from the feed copolarized pattern (term with J_0 factor) caused by reflector depolarization, a contribution from the feed cross-polarized pattern, and a contribution from the z component of the induced current. Usually the amount of depolarization caused by the reflector is small. Note that the cross-polarized field is zero in the principal planes and is a maximum in the ±45° planes.

The various aperture-field methods give different results for the cross-polarized field. If the aperture magnetic field formulation, i.e., Eq. (4.109), is used, the results obtained are the same as with Eq. (4.111), except that the small term involving $J_1(v_1)$ is not present. When the aperture electric field method, i.e., Eq. (4.108), is used, the term multiplied by $J_0(v_1)$ has the factor $(1 - \cos \theta)$ and is thus reversed in phase. When both the aperture electric and magnetic fields are used the term involving $J_0(v_1)$ is not even present. These differences are difficult to resolve, so in order to avoid this ambiguity the induced-current method will be accepted as the preferred evaluation of the cross-polarized field until better evidence to the contrary is obtained. However, it should be noted that the term $J_0(v_1)(1 - \cos \theta)$ contributes only a very small amount to the cross-polarized field for reflectors $20\lambda_0$ or more in diameter. That this is the case may be seen by comparing this cross-polarized term with the corresponding copolarized term, which has the factor $J_0(v_1)(1 + \cos \theta)/2 \approx J_0(v_1)$ for θ less than 25°. The cross-polarized term is smaller by the factor

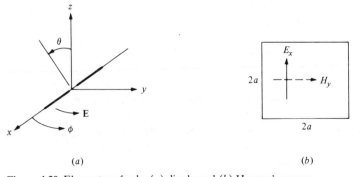

(a)   (b)

Figure 4.30 Elementary feeds: (a) dipole and (b) Huygen's source.

$(1 - \cos \theta)$. For θ less than $10°$ this factor is less than $-36\,\text{dB}$, which means that the cross-polarized field contribution is more than $-36\,\text{dB}$ below the copolarized field. For a reflector $20\lambda_0$ or more in diameter the copolarized field is very small for $\theta > 10°$, so even when $(1 - \cos \theta)$ becomes larger the cross-polarized contribution from this term remains very small relative to the on-axis field.

Significant cross polarization will occur only when $e_{\theta'} \neq e_{\phi'}$. For example, consider the x-directed dipole field shown in Fig. 4.30a. Apart from irrelevant constants the feed pattern is given by

$$\mathbf{E}_f = \frac{e^{-jk_0 r}}{r} (\mathbf{a}_\theta \cos \theta \cos \phi - \mathbf{a}_\phi \sin \phi)$$

$$= \frac{e^{-jk_0 r}}{r} [(\cos \theta \cos^2 \phi + \sin^2 \phi)(\mathbf{a}_\theta \cos \phi$$

$$- \mathbf{a}_\phi \sin \phi)] + \frac{e^{-jk_0 r}}{r} [\tfrac{1}{2} \sin^2 \phi (\cos \theta - 1)$$

$$\times (\mathbf{a}_\theta \sin \phi + \mathbf{a}_\phi \cos \phi)]$$

The second term is the cross-polarized field, and since θ can be as large as the half-angular width of the reflector, the reflector illumination will have a significant cross-polarized component over the outer regions. At $\theta = 45°$ the cross-polarized field is only $15\,\text{dB}$ below the copolarized component. Thus a dipole feed does not give a low cross polarization when used to illuminate a paraboloidal reflector.

A Huygen's source is a small patch of a plane electromagnetic wave, as shown in Fig. 4.30b. If the radiation from this patch is calculated using both electric and magnetic equivalent currents, it is found that

$$E_f = \frac{e^{-jk_0 r}}{r} (1 + \cos \theta) f_x (\mathbf{a}_\theta \cos \phi - \mathbf{a}_\phi \sin \phi)$$

where f_x is the pattern function

$$\frac{\sin k_x a}{k_x a} \frac{\sin k_y a}{k_y a}$$

with $k_x = k_0 \sin \theta \cos \phi$, $k_y = k_0 \sin \theta \sin \phi$. This feed pattern has zero cross polarization.

If the radiation from the Huygen's source is calculated using only the equivalent electric current or only the equivalent magnetic current, then it is found that the feed pattern is proportional to $\mathbf{a}_\theta \cos \phi - \mathbf{a}_\phi \cos \theta \sin \phi$ and $\mathbf{a}_\theta \cos \theta \cos \phi - \mathbf{a}_\phi \sin \phi$, respectively. These patterns have the same level of cross polarization as the dipole feed does, so, depending on the point of view, the Huygen's source can be considered to either have no cross polarization or to have the same cross polarization as a dipole.

Aperture Efficiency

Feeds with radiation patterns of the type described by Eq. (4.101) are an important class of feeds. It is therefore of interest to derive explicit formulas for the aperture efficiency and associated cross polarization, phase error, and illumination efficiency of paraboloidal reflectors illuminated by these feeds.

By using Eq. (4.105) the radiated copolarized field on the z axis is readily found by setting $\theta = 0$; thus

$$\mathbf{E}(r) = \mathbf{a}_y \frac{jk_0 f}{r} e^{-jk_0 r - j2k_0 f} \int_0^{\theta_0} [e_{\theta'}(\theta') + e_{\phi'}(\theta')] \tan\frac{\theta'}{2}\, d\theta'$$

The radiated power per unit solid angle is $\frac{1}{2}Y_0 r^2 |\mathbf{E}|^2$. Let P_a be the total power radiated from the aperture. With uniform illumination the radiated power per unit solid angle on the z axis would be

$$\frac{1}{2}Y_0 r^2 \left(\frac{k_0}{2\pi r}\pi a^2 E_a\right)^2 = \frac{k_0^2 \pi a^2}{4\pi^2} P_a$$

as shown in the previous section. The aperture efficiency η_A is given by

$$\eta_A = \frac{\frac{1}{2}Y_0 r^2 |\mathbf{E}|^2}{k_0^2 \pi a^2 (P_a/4\pi^2)} = \frac{\lambda_0^2 Y_0 r^2 |\mathbf{E}|^2}{2\pi a^2 P_a}$$

The total power radiated from the aperture equals the incident power from the feed that is intercepted by the aperture; thus

$$P_a = \frac{1}{2}Y_0 \int_0^{2\pi}\int_0^{\theta_0} (|e_{\theta'}|^2 \sin^2\phi' + |e_{\phi'}|^2 \cos^2\phi')\sin\theta'\, d\theta'\, d\phi'$$

$$= \frac{\pi Y_0}{2}\int_0^{\theta_0} (|e_{\theta'}|^2 + |e_{\phi'}|^2)\sin\theta'\, d\theta'$$

Hence

$$\eta_A = \frac{4f^2}{a^2} \frac{|\int_0^{\theta_0} (e_{\theta'} + e_{\phi'})\tan(\theta'/2)\, d\theta'|^2}{\int_0^{\theta_0} (|e_{\theta'}|^2 + |e_{\phi'}|^2)\sin\theta'\, d\theta'} \tag{4.112}$$

For a feed with a very low cross polarization $e_{\theta'} \approx e_{\phi'}$ and then

$$\eta_A = \frac{8\pi f^2}{\pi a^2} \frac{|\int_0^{\theta_0} e_{\theta'}\tan(\theta'/2)\, d\theta'|^2}{\int_0^{\theta_0} |e_{\theta'}|^2 \sin\theta'\, d\theta'} \tag{4.113}$$

which agrees with Eq. (4.79) given earlier. The definition used here for the aperture efficiency includes aperture-illumination loss, phase-error loss, and cross-polarization loss, as described in Sec. 4.6. The aperture efficiency η_A can be factored into the product of η_i, η_p, and η_x, as defined by Ludwig and used by Thomas.† However, we will use somewhat different definitions that provide a clearer separation of the various losses discussed in Sec. 4.6.

---

† B. MacA. Thomas, "Theoretical Performance of Prime-Focus Paraboloids Using Hybrid-Mode Feeds," *Proc. IEE*, vol. 118, 1971, pp. 1539–1549.

The gain of the antenna can be expressed in the form given by Eq. (4.77), which we repeat for convenience:

$$G = \frac{4\pi}{\lambda_0^2} \eta_A \eta_s \eta_f \pi a^2 \qquad (4.114)$$

where η_s is the spillover efficiency and η_f is the feed efficiency that accounts for feed losses. For a large-edge taper of order -20 dB, the spillover efficiency is close to unity. The expression (4.112) can be rewritten in the following form:

$$\eta_A = \frac{16\pi f^2}{\pi a^2} \frac{(\int_0^{\theta_0} |e_{\theta'} + e_{\phi'}| \tan(\theta'/2)\, d\theta')^2}{\int_0^{\theta_0} (2|e_{\theta'} + e_{\phi'}|^2 + |e_{\theta'} - e_{\phi'}|^2) \sin\theta'\, d\theta'}$$

$$\times \frac{|\int_0^{\theta_0} (e_{\theta'} + e_{\phi'}) \tan(\theta'/2)\, d\theta'|^2}{(\int_0^{\theta_0} |e_{\theta'} + e_{\phi'}| \tan(\theta'/2)\, d\theta')^2}$$

$$\times \frac{\int_0^{\theta_0} (2|e_{\theta'} + e_{\phi'}|^2 + |e_{\theta'} - e_{\phi'}|^2) \sin\theta'\, d\theta'}{4 \int_0^{\theta_0} (|e_{\theta'}|^2 + |e_{\phi'}|^2) \sin\theta'\, d\theta'} \qquad (4.115)$$

The first factor is the illumination efficiency η_i, while the second and third factors give the phase-error efficiency η_p and cross-polarization efficiency η_x. Note that the copolarized field for the feed is proportional to

$$e_{\theta'} \sin^2\phi' + e_{\phi'} \cos^2\phi' = \frac{e_{\theta'} + e_{\phi'}}{2} + \frac{(e_{\phi'} - e_{\theta'})(\cos 2\phi')}{2}$$

This expression was used to find the total copolarized feed power intercepted by the paraboloid. Phase-error losses occur when the constant-phase surfaces of the feed pattern are not spherical surfaces, when there are surface deviations away from a true paraboloidal surface in the reflector, and when the feed-phase center is displaced from the focal point. These losses are normally quite small and often negligible. Phase errors will, in general, lead to cross-polarization loss. When $e_{\theta'}(\theta') = e_{\phi'}(\theta')$ there is no cross-polarized radiation, and $\eta_x = 1$ even though the phase of this field may vary with the angle θ'. If $|e_{\theta'}| = |e_{\phi'}|$ but the phase of $e_{\theta'}$ is different from that of $e_{\phi'}$ there will be a cross-polarization loss. The expression used by Thomas for η_x gives zero cross-polarization loss whenever $|e_{\theta'}| = |e_{\phi'}|$, which is not generally true. In Eq. (4.115) the last factor, which equals η_x, is the ratio of the total copolarized radiated power to the total radiated power from the feed that is intercepted by the aperture. Since the reflector produces very little depolarization, this is essentially the polarization efficiency of the reflector as well.

The expression for the phase-error efficiency is based on the following considerations. From Eq. (4.110) the on-axis copolarized radiated electric field is given by the integral of $e_{\theta'} + e_{\phi'}$. Maximum radiated electric field strength is obtained when the phase of $e_{\theta'} + e_{\phi'}$ is constant. Thus the phase-error efficiency is chosen as the ratio of the on-axis radiation intensity produced by the field $e_{\theta'} + e_{\phi'}$ to that produced by $|e_{\theta'} + e_{\phi'}|$. Since $\eta_A = \eta_i \eta_p \eta_x$, the expression for the illumination efficiency is determined once η_p and η_x are specified. The illumination efficiency is the ratio of the on-axis radiation intensity produced by the field $|e_{\theta'} + e_{\phi'}|$ to that produced by a uniformly illuminated aperture radiating the same total copolarized power in accord with the definition given in Sec. 4.6.

Let $E_e(\theta)$ and $E_h(\theta)$ be the measured E-plane and H-plane radiation patterns (magnitude and phase). A useful expression for the cross-polarized pattern in the $\phi = \pm 45°$ planes is

$$E_{\text{cross}} = \frac{|E_e(\theta) - E_h(\theta)|}{2} \qquad (4.116)$$

This result follows from the fact that $e_{\theta'}$ gives the E-plane pattern, while $e_{\phi'}$ gives the H-plane pattern. For zero cross polarization both the magnitude and phase of E_e and E_h must be equal.

4.9 FEEDS WITH LOW CROSS POLARIZATION

A very simple feed that has a cross polarization somewhat below -30 dB is a circular waveguide excited in the TE_{11}-dominant mode, provided its diameter is in the range of 0.8 to $1.15\lambda_0$. However, such a feed has a rather broad radiation pattern, with its -10-dB beam width being 140° and dropping to 104° for the larger diameter. Thus this simple feed is useful only for paraboloidal reflectors with an angular aperture of around 115° ($f/2a \approx 0.45$). In order to obtain feeds with higher directivity and yet maintain low cross polarization, it is necessary to use a larger aperture and to excite a mixture of a TE_{11} and a TM_{11} mode in the aperture. A variety of methods exist for accomplishing this objective. Feeds that utilize this principle are called *dual-mode feeds*. Another useful approach in obtaining low cross polarization is to use a conical horn with a corrugated or grooved inner surface. In a structure of this type the dominant mode of propagation is a hybrid mode that consists of a combined TE_{11} and TM_{11} mode that radiates with an inherently low cross polarization. The corrugated horn has a greater bandwidth of operation relative to that of dual-mode feeds.

In this section we will present some theoretical results pertaining to the simple circular waveguide feed, one type of dual-mode feed, and the corrugated horn.

Circular Waveguide Feed with TE₁₁-Mode Excitation

The radiation pattern for a circular waveguide was computed in an approximate manner in Sec. 4.4 using the field of the TE_{11} mode as the aperture field. This calculation is not very accurate because of the small aperture involved. It might be considered acceptable for the copolarized and principal plane patterns, but it is entirely inadequate for giving the cross-polarized pattern. The latter, as noted at the end of the previous section, is critically dependent on the *difference* between the E- and H-plane patterns (both in amplitude as well as phase). Thus a small error in the principal-plane patterns leads to a large error in the cross-polarized pattern.

Fortunately the problem of radiation from a circular waveguide with infinitely thin walls can be found exactly by solving an integral equation of the Wiener-Hopf type.† It is thus possible to evaluate the performance of a circular waveguide radiator excited by an incident TE_{11} mode. The results of such an evaluation are summarized below.

In Fig. 4.31 the principal E- and H-plane normalized patterns are shown for a waveguide with diameter $2a = 0.8\lambda_0$. Figure 4.32 shows the corresponding co- and cross-polarized patterns in the $\phi = 45°$ plane. The cross polarization remains below -30 dB for θ up to 72°. The cross polarization is, to a large extent, caused by the phase difference between the E- and H-plane patterns. The phase of the radiated field is also shown in Fig. 4.31. Figures 4.33–4.36 show similar results for waveguide diameters equal to 0.96 and $1.12\lambda_0$. Again, the cross polarization remains below -30 dB. For a waveguide radius of $0.96\lambda_0$ the -10-dB E- and H-plane patterns are almost identical. However, the relative phase is 8.5°, which results in a cross polarization of

$$\frac{|E_\theta|^2}{4}|e^{-j\theta} - 1| = \frac{1}{40}[(1 - \cos 8.5°)^2 + \sin^2 8.5°]$$

$$= 0.00055 \qquad \text{or} \quad -32.6 \text{ dB}$$

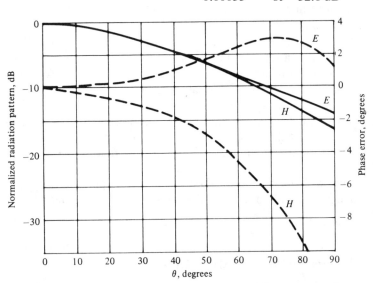

Figure 4.31 Normalized radiation patterns and phase error for TE_{11} mode in a circular waveguide with $2a = 0.8\lambda_0$. E and H refer to E-plane and H-plane patterns.

† L. A. Weinstein, *The Theory of Diffraction and the Factorization Method*, Golem Press, Boulder, Colo., 1969. The computations were carried out by Dr. H. Schilling.

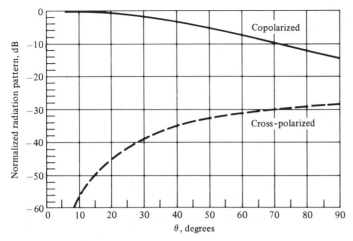

Figure 4.32 Co- and cross-polarized radiation patterns in $\phi = 45°$ plane for TE_{11} mode in a circular waveguide with $2a = 0.8\lambda_0$.

which is quite close to that shown in Fig. 4.34. Figure 4.37 shows the E- and H-plane -10-dB beam widths as a function of $2a/\lambda_0$. For small diameters the E-plane pattern is broader, but for large diameters it is narrower than the H-plane beam width. The crossover occurs for $2a$ equal to $0.96\lambda_0$.

The aperture efficiency, spillover efficiency, and total efficiency that can be obtained with a TE_{11}-mode circular waveguide feed depends on the f/D parameter for the reflector. Typical results are shown in Fig. 4.38 for an optimum circular waveguide with $2a = 0.96\lambda_0$. An overall efficiency of 74

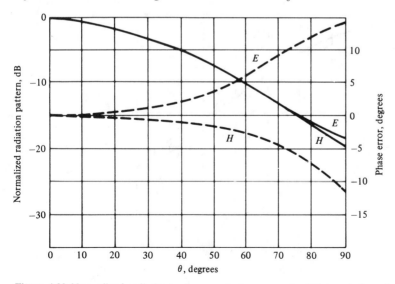

Figure 4.33 Normalized radiation patterns and phase error for TE_{11} mode in a circular waveguide with $2a = 0.96\lambda_0$. E and H refer to E-plane and H-plane patterns.

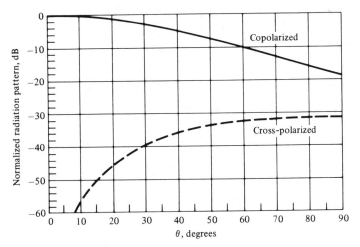

Figure 4.34 Co- and cross-polarized radiation patterns in $\phi = 45°$ plane for TE_{11} mode in a circular waveguide with $2a = 0.96\lambda_0$.

percent is predicted with a reflector having f/D equal to 0.44. The optimum angular aperture is 118°. The feed radiation pattern is -10 dB below its on-axis value at $\theta = 59°$, and the aperture edge illumination is -12.4 dB below its peak value at the center of the reflector. The magnitude of the input reflection coefficient is less than 0.07 for $2a/\lambda_0$ in the range 0.8 to 1.2. Thus the TE_{11}-mode circular waveguide is well matched to free space.

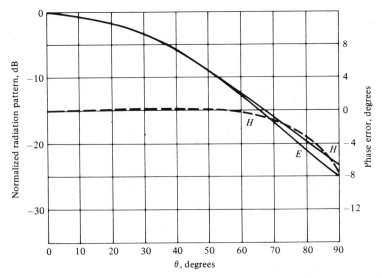

Figure 4.35 Normalized radiation patterns and phase error for TE_{11} mode in a circular waveguide with $2a = 1.12\lambda_0$. E and H refer to E-plane and H-plane patterns.

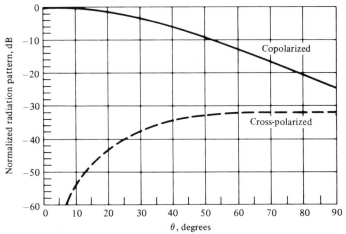

Figure 4.36 Co- and cross-polarized radiation patterns in $\phi = 45°$ plane for TE_{11} mode in a circular waveguide with $2a = 1.12\lambda_0$.

Comparison of exact and approximate radiation patterns. The comparison of the exact results for the radiation pattern of a circular waveguide excited with a TE_{11} mode and the approximate patterns obtained by calculating the radiated field from the tangential electric field in the aperture and those obtained using

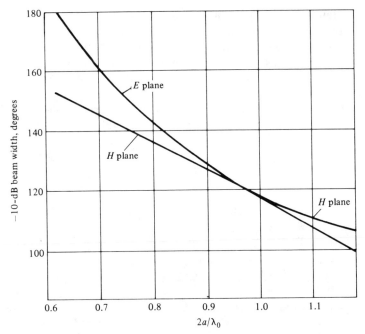

Figure 4.37 E- and H-plane -10-dB beam width as a function of $2a/\lambda_0$ for TE_{11} mode in a circular waveguide.

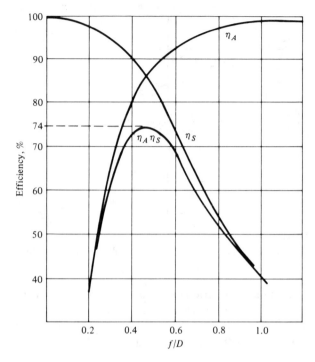

Figure 4.38 Aperture, spillover, and total efficiency of paraboloidal antenna illuminated with a TE$_{11}$ mode in a circular waveguide as a function of f/D. $2a/\lambda_0$ = 0.96.

a combination of the tangential electric and magnetic fields in the aperture are shown in Figs. 4.39 through 4.44 for three different waveguide radii, namely, $2a = 0.8$, 1.28, and $1.6\lambda_0$.† The agreement of the approximate patterns with the exact results is quite good but, as noted earlier, not adequate for determining the cross-polarized radiation patterns. Expressions for the approximate patterns are given below.

When both the aperture electric and magnetic fields are used to compute the radiation field, then from the TE$_{11}$ mode (apart from irrelevant constants) the radiated field is given by

$$E_\theta = q_1(\theta) \sin \phi \qquad (4.117a)$$

$$E_\phi = q_2(\theta) \cos \phi \qquad (4.117b)$$

where $q_1 = \left(\dfrac{k_0}{\beta}\right)^{1/2} \dfrac{a}{(k_c^2 a^2 - 1)^{1/2}} \left(1 + \dfrac{\beta}{k_0} \cos \theta\right) \dfrac{J_1(k_0 a \sin \theta)}{k_0 a \sin \theta}$

$q_2 = \left(\dfrac{k_0}{\beta}\right)^{1/2} \dfrac{a}{(k_c^2 a^2 - 1)^{1/2}} \left(\dfrac{\beta}{k_0} + \cos \theta\right) \dfrac{J_1'(k_0 a \sin \theta)}{1 - (k_0^2/k_c^2) \sin^2 \theta}$

$J_1'(k_c a) = 0 \qquad k_c a = 1.841 \qquad \beta^2 = k_0^2 - k_c^2$

† The approximate patterns were computed by Georg Karawas, while the exact patterns were computed by H. Schilling.

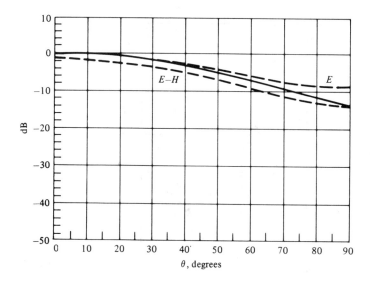

Figure 4.39 Comparison of exact and approximate E-plane radiation patterns for a TE_{11} mode in a circular waveguide. Diameter $2a = 0.8\lambda_0$. Solid curve is exact result. Curve labeled E is based on the aperture electric field only, while curve labeled E-H is based on the aperture electric and magnetic fields.

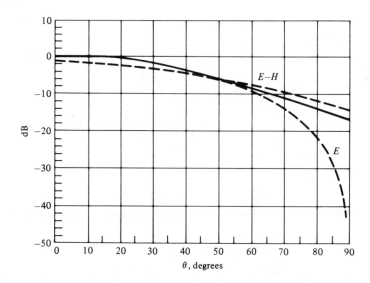

Figure 4.40 Comparison of exact and approximate H-plane radiation patterns for a TE_{11} mode in a circular waveguide. Diameter $2a = 0.8\lambda_0$. Solid curve is exact result. Curve labeled E is based on the aperture electric field only, while curve labeled E-H is based on the aperture electric and magnetic fields.

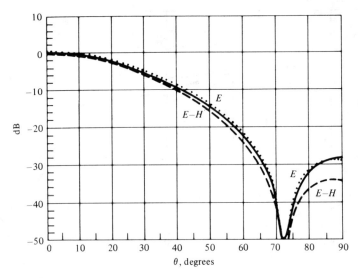

Figure 4.41 Comparison of exact and approximate E-plane radiation patterns for a TE_{11} mode in a circular waveguide. Diameter $2a = 1.28\lambda_0$. Solid curve is exact result. Curve labeled E is based on the aperture electric field, while curve labeled E-H is based on the aperture electric and magnetic fields.

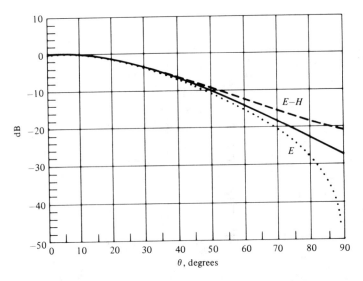

Figure 4.42 Comparison of exact and approximate H-plane radiation patterns for a TE_{11} mode in a circular waveguide. Diameter $2a = 1.28\lambda_0$. Solid curve is exact result. Curve labeled E is based on the aperture electric field, while curve labeled E-H is based on the aperture electric and magnetic fields.

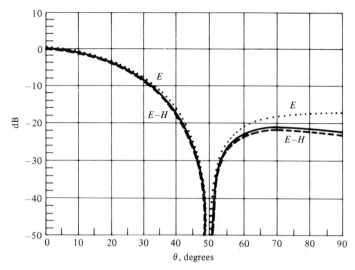

Figure 4.43 Comparison of exact and approximate E-plane radiation patterns for a TE_{11} mode in a circular waveguide. Diameter $2a = 1.6\lambda_0$. Solid curve is exact result. Curve labeled E is based on the aperture electric field, while curve labeled E-H is based on the aperture electric and magnetic fields.

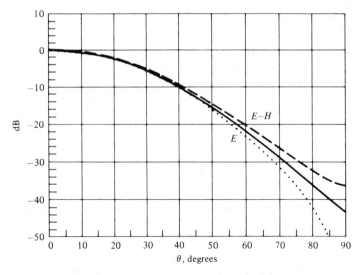

Figure 4.44 Comparison of exact and approximate H-plane radiation patterns for a TE_{11} mode in a circular waveguide. Diameter $2a = 1.6\lambda_0$. Solid curve is exact result. Curve labeled E is based on the aperture electric field, while curve labeled E-H is based on the aperture electric and magnetic fields.

J_1 is the Bessel function of order 1 and the prime denotes the derivative with respect to the argument.

If the patterns are computed using only the electric field in the aperture, then the radiation fields for the TE_{11} mode are

$$E_\theta = p_1(\theta) \sin \phi \qquad (4.118a)$$

$$E_\phi = p_2(\theta) \cos \phi \cos \theta \qquad (4.118b)$$

where $\left(1 + \dfrac{\beta}{k_0} \cos \theta\right) p_1 = 2q_1$

$\left(\dfrac{\beta}{k_0} + \cos \theta\right) p_2 = 2q_2$

The E- and H-plane principal patterns are given by $q_1(\theta)$ and $q_2(\theta)$ for the first case and by $p_1(\theta)$ and $p_2(\theta) \cos \theta$ for the second case. The on-axis field is not the same for the two formulations because of the factor $1 + \beta/k_0$, which does not equal 2. The patterns are all normalized relative to unity for the exact field on-axis.

Dual-Mode Coaxial Waveguide Feed

A dual-mode coaxial waveguide feed is shown in Fig. 4.45. The feed is excited by an incident TE_{11} mode in the input waveguide. The large output waveguide allows both the TE_{11} and TM_{11} modes to propagate. The TM_{11} mode is excited by the internal bifurcation junction. The correct phasing between the TE_{11} and TM_{11} modes is obtained by adjusting the length T of the output waveguide.

In order to obtain very low cross polarization the ratio of the amplitude of the TE_{11} mode to that of the TM_{11} mode, which is incident on the feed aperture, must be carefully controlled. The optimum moding ratio is shown in Fig. 4.46 as a function of outer guide radius b divided by λ_0. The moding ratio is defined with respect to normalized TE_{11}- and TM_{11}-mode functions, the normalization being such that the power carried by the mode equals one-half of the magnitude of its amplitude squared. A moding ratio of -2.5 implies that the incident power in the TE_{11} mode is a factor of $(2.5)^2 = 6.25$ greater than that of the TM_{11} mode. The transverse electric fields for the two modes are given by

$$E_{TE} = C_{TE}\left[\frac{2k_0 Z_0}{\beta_1 \pi (k_1^2 b^2 - 1)}\right]^{1/2} \frac{\mathbf{a}_z \times \nabla_t J_1(k_1 r)}{J_1(k_1 b)} \cos \phi \qquad (4.119)$$

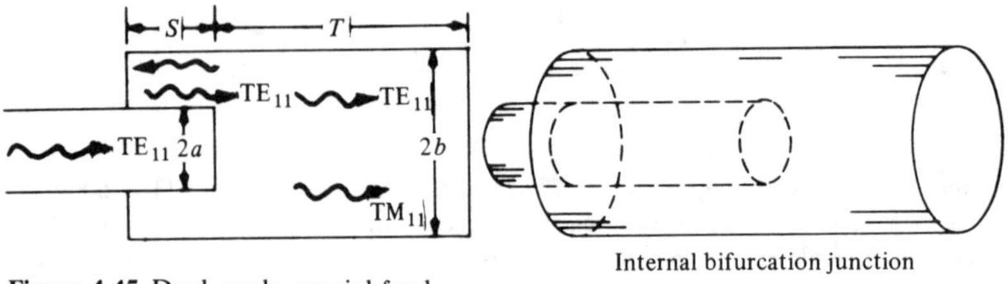

Figure 4.45 Dual-mode coaxial feed.

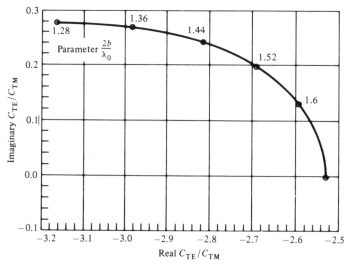

Figure 4.46 Optimum moding ratio C_{TE}/C_{TM} for a dual-mode TE_{11}-TM_{11} coaxial feed as a function of $2b/\lambda_0$.

where $J_1'(k_1 b) = 0$, $\beta_1 = (k_0^2 - k_1^2)^{1/2}$, and J_1 is the Bessel function of order 1, and

$$E_{TM} = C_{TM} \left(\frac{2\gamma_1 Z_0}{\pi k_0} \right)^{1/2} \frac{\nabla_t J_1(l_1 r) \sin \phi}{l_1 b J_1'(l_1 b)} \tag{4.120}$$

where $J_1(l_1 b) = 0$ and $\gamma_1 = (k_0^2 - l_1^2)^{1/2}$. The moding ratio is given by C_{TE}/C_{TM}, which is the ratio of the mode amplitudes.

The reflection coefficient Γ_{11} for the TE_{11} mode is quite small but the reflection coefficient Γ_{22} for the TM_{11} mode and the cross-coupling between the TE_{11} and TM_{11} modes are much larger. These parameters are shown in Fig. 4.47. The strong interaction or coupling between the TE_{11} and TM_{11} modes in the aperture must be taken into account in the optimization of the feed dimensions. The ratio of the total TE_{11}-mode field to that of the total TM_{11}-mode field in the aperture is

$$\frac{(1+\Gamma_{11})C_{TE} + \Gamma_{12}C_{TM}}{(1+\Gamma_{22})C_{TM} + \Gamma_{12}C_{TE}} \tag{4.121}$$

When the feed dimensions are optimized so as to produce the lowest cross polarization, it is found that the cross polarization is no greater than about -58 dB at the design frequency. A typical co- and cross-polarized radiation pattern is shown in Fig. 4.48 for a feed designed to operate at $\lambda_0 = 2.5$ cm (12 GHz). For this feed the optimum parameters are shown in Fig. 4.49. The performance of this feed with respect to cross polarization, phase error, and input reflection coefficient as a function of frequency is shown in Fig. 4.50. The useful bandwidth is around 5 percent, over which the cross polarization does not exceed -30 dB. The narrow bandwidth is caused by the different pro-

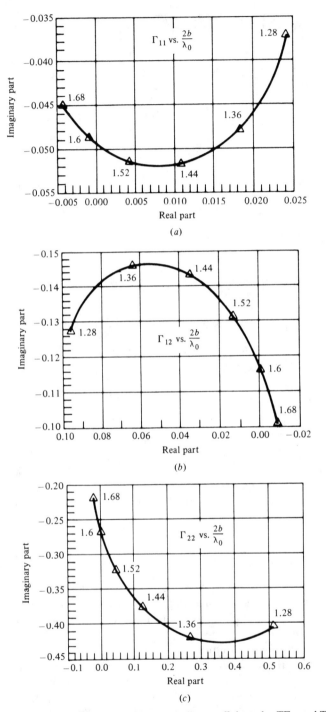

Figure 4.47 Reflection and cross-coupling coefficients for TE$_{11}$ and TM$_{11}$ modes in the aperture of a dual-mode coaxial feed.

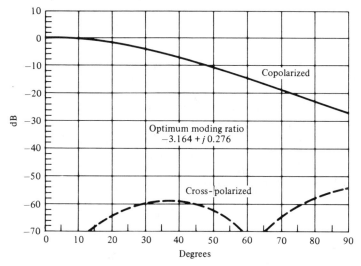

Figure 4.48 Typical co- and cross-polarized radiation patterns in the $\phi = 45°$ plane for an optimized dual-mode coaxial feed. (Optimization is for maximum cross polarization in the range $0 \leq \theta \leq 78°$.) Feed parameters are given in Fig. 4.49 for operation at 12 GHz.

pagation-phase constants of the TE_{11} and TM_{11} modes, which cause the phase difference between these modes to rapidly change from the optimum value as the frequency changes.

The efficiency of a paraboloidal antenna illuminated with a dual-mode coaxial feed can be as high as 75 percent or more. Figure 4.51 shows the aperture efficiency, spillover efficiency, and total efficiency as a function of f/D of the reflector. A number of optimum feeds have been designed and their performance computed. The reader is referred to the literature for a discussion of these.[†]

Dual-mode conical horns operate in a manner similar to that of the feed just described. The dual-mode principle was introduced by Potter.[‡] In Potter's horn the TM_{11} mode is excited by a step at the waveguide-horn throat, as

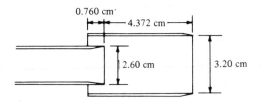

Figure 4.49 Dimensions of an optimum dual-mode feed for operation at 12 GHz. Waveguide walls are tapered to simulate infinitely thin walls.

† H. Schilling, "Dual-Mode Coaxial Feed for Parabolic Antennas," Ph.D. thesis, Case Western Reserve University, Cleveland, Ohio, 1982.

R. E. Collin and H. Schilling, *Dual-Mode Coaxial Feed with Low Cross-Polarization*, to be published.

‡ P. D. Potter, "A New Horn Antenna with Suppressed Sidelobes and Equal Beamwidths," *Microwave Jour.*, vol. 6, 1963, pp. 71–78.

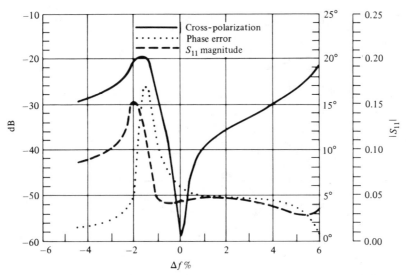

Figure 4.50 Performance of an optimum dual-mode feed shown in Fig. 4.49 as a function of percent change in frequency from the center frequency of 12 GHz. The curves show maximum cross polarization, phase error, and input reflection coefficient.

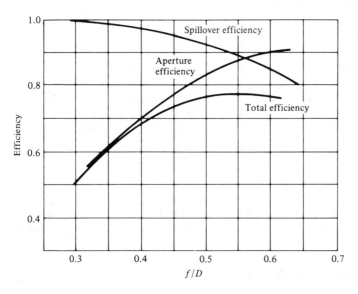

Figure 4.51 Aperture, spillover, and total efficiency of a paraboloidal antenna system illuminated by an optimum dual-mode coaxial feed as a function of f/D for the reflector. Reflector diameter is D, and f is the focal length. Feed diameter $2b = 1.28\lambda_0$.

shown in Fig. 4.52*a*. A variation of the Potter horn is shown in Fig. 4.52*b*† In Satoh's horn the TM_{11} mode is excited by a dielectric insert in the horn. The performance of dual-mode horns is similar to that of the coaxial waveguide feed.

Corrugated Conical Horns

In the previous section it was pointed out that a Huygen's source radiated a field with zero cross polarization under the assumption that the radiated field is found in terms of both equivalent electric and magnetic currents. Rumsey used this property to propose as a basis for no cross polarization that the aperture field in a horn should have the electric and magnetic fields related as in a plane wave.‡

In a normal waveguide the boundary conditions require that the tangential electric field and normal magnetic field components vanish at the perfectly conducting wall. As a consequence, the transverse electric and magnetic field patterns on a transverse cross-sectional plane are not related as in a linearly polarized plane wave, and this is a primary reason why conventional circular waveguides and conical horns radiate fields with a relatively high level of cross polarization. If a conical horn could be constructed such that the boundary conditions for the tangential electric and magnetic fields were the same, the resultant mode pattern would radiate with very little cross polarization. A

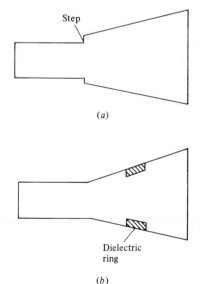

(a)

(b)

Dielectric ring

Figure 4.52 Dual-mode conical horns: (*a*) Potter horn with a step at the input to excite the TM_{11} mode and (*b*) Satoh horn with a dielectric ring insert to excite the TM_{11} mode.

† T. Satoh, "Dielectric-Loaded Horn Antenna," *IEEE Trans.*, vol. AP-20, 1972, pp. 199–201.
‡ V.H. Rumsey, "Horn Antennas with Uniform Power Patterns Around Their Axis," *IEEE Trans.*, vol., AP-14, 1966, pp. 656–658.

corrugated surface with five or more slots per wavelength and $\lambda_0/4$ deep will simulate a surface that requires both the tangential electric and magnetic fields to vanish at the interface. Consider the planar corrugated surface shown in Fig. 4.53. Since the slot spacing is very small, the only mode that can propagate into the grooves is a TEM mode with the electric field normal to the faces of the slot. The magnetic field is parallel with the faces. In the slot the fields are given by

$$E_y = E_0 \sin k_0(d - z) \qquad H_x = jY_0 E_0 \cos k_0(d - z)$$

When the slot depth $d = \lambda_0/4$, it is seen that in the slot $H_x = 0$ at the $z = 0$ interface, while $E_y = E_0$. On the metal part of each tooth the electric field along the surface must be zero, but the tangential magnetic field is nonzero. When there are five or more slots per wavelength the corrugated surface can be approximated as a smooth surface having an equivalent anisotropic surface impedance, which requires the electric field parallel to the slots to be zero ($E_x = 0$ for the structure in Fig. 4.53) and requires the ratio of E_y/H_x to be

$$\frac{E_y}{H_x} = -jZ_0 \frac{a}{b} \tan k_0 d \tag{4.122}$$

The average impedance seen by E_y is the sum of a zero impedance for the tooth surface and an impedance $-jZ_0 \tan k_0 d$ for the groove, and this results in the factor a/b.

Figure 4.54 shows a corrugated circular waveguide and a corrugated conical horn with very thin teeth. The propagation in and radiation from these structures have been studied in detail by Clarricoats and Saha as well as by many other authors.[†] Clarricoats and Saha use boundary conditions of the type described above at the inner surface $r = a$ in Fig. 4.54a. It is then found that it is possible to choose a slot depth such that $E_r = Z_0 H_\phi$, $E_\phi = -Z_0 H_r$, which is called the *balanced hybrid condition*. A combination of a TE_{11} mode and a TM_{11} mode, called an HE_{11} *hybrid mode*, with the property given above, can exist in the corrugated waveguide when the condition

$$\frac{dJ_1(k_0 a)}{d(k_0 a)} Y_1(k_0 b) = J_1(k_0 b) \frac{dY_1(k_0 a)}{d(k_0 a)} \tag{4.123}$$

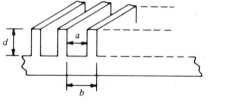

Figure 4.53 A corrugated planar surface.

†P. J. B. Clarricoats, and P. K. Saha, "Propagation and Radiation Behavior of Corrugated Feeds," 2 parts, *Proc. IEE*, vol. 118, Sept. 1971, pp. 1167–1186.

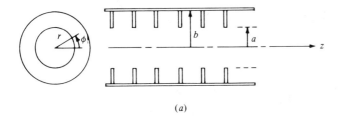

(a)

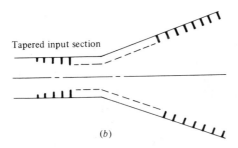

Tapered input section

(b)

Figure 4.54 (a) A corrugated circular waveguide. (b) A corrugated conical horn.

holds. This equation is equivalent to $\cot k_0 d = 0$, which specifies a slot depth equal to $\lambda_0/4$ for a planar corrugated surface. When $k_0 a$ and $k_0 b$ are large Eq. (4.123) can be approximated by $\cos k_0(b - a) = 0$, which is the same as for a planar surface. Under balanced hybrid conditions the transverse fields of the HE_{11} mode in the corrugated waveguide are given by

$$E_r = J_0(k_0 r) \cos \phi$$

$$E_\phi = -J_0(k_0 r) \sin \phi$$

$$H_r = -Y_0 E_\phi$$

$$H_\phi = Y_0 E_r$$

from which we find that $E_x = J_0(k_0 r)$ and $E_y = 0$. This mode pattern satisfies the conditions given by Rumsey and radiates with very little cross polarization.

In a corrugated conical horn with a small flare angle the aperture field is approximately that of the HE_{11} mode in a circular waveguide, apart from a small phase error due to the spherical phase front. The radiation patterns have been computed by Clarricoats and Saha using a combination of both the tangential electric and magnetic fields in the aperture. It was found that the principal plane patterns agreed closely with measured patterns. The approximate theory predicts zero cross-polarized radiation. In practice there is some cross-polarized radiation, but this is typically below -30 dB over a 1.5 to 1 bandwidth or more.† The patterns have a high degree of circular symmetry.

† P. J. Wood, *Reflector Antenna Analysis and Design*, Peter Peregrinus, Ltd., London, 1980.

A corrugated horn used as a prime focus feed can give an aperture efficiency as high as 84 percent. The main disadvantage of a corrugated horn is the rather high manufacturing cost and its bulky structure.

4.10 OFFSET PARABOLOIDAL REFLECTORS

In practice the circularly symmetric paraboloidal reflector illuminated by a feed at the focal point does not have as low a cross polarization or side-lobe radiation as theory predicts because of scattering from the feed and the feed supporting rods. The deterioration in the ideal performance becomes particularly noticeable in systems designed for side lobes and cross polarization 30 dB or more below the on-axis field. One solution for overcoming the obstruction and resultant scatter by the feed and its supporting structure is to use an offset paraboloidal section as shown in Fig. 4.55. A circular section of a paraboloidal reflector may be cut out such that the focal point lies outside the main beam of the reflector. Although this provides for removal of most, if not all, of the feed and its support from the main-beam region of the reflector, a penalty in the form of increased cross-polarized radiation occurs. The offset reflector and feed system no longer have circular symmetry. As a consequence, even if the feed radiates with zero cross polarization, the reflector itself will cause depolarization to occur. Cross polarization lobes as large as -20 to -25 dB are typical in offset reflector systems having only a modest amount of offset. The determination of the aperture field and the radiation from an offset reflector antenna system are described below.

Figure 4.56 shows an offset section of a paraboloidal reflector. Its projected aperture on the focal plane will be referred to as the *aperture surface S_a*. A feed with a rotationally symmetric pattern is assumed to be placed at the focal point

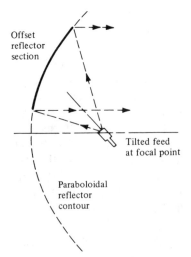

Offset
reflector
section

Tilted feed
at focal point

Paraboloidal
reflector
contour

Figure 4.55 An offset paraboloidal reflector section that avoids aperture blockage by the feed.

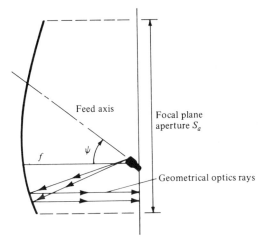

Figure 4.56 Offset paraboloidal reflector and feed orientation.

and to have its axis inclined at an angle ψ relative to the axis of the reflector. The focal-plane aperture electric field will be computed using geometrical optics. The radiation pattern may then be computed from the electric field on the focal-plane aperture. The field on the focal plane is of constant phase if we assume that the feed produces a field with spherical phase fronts. (In practice some deviation from spherical phase fronts usually occurs, but this is normally small.)

In the derivation of the focal-plane aperture field three coordinate systems are used. These are shown in Fig. 4.57a. The $x_0 y_0 z_0$ system has the feed axis as the polar axis, and θ_0, ϕ_0 are the spherical coordinate angles with respect to this system. The wuv system has the reflector axis as the polar axis, and the corresponding spherical coordinate angles are θ', ϕ'. The xyz system is the one used for computing the radiation field, and θ, ϕ are the spherical coordinate angles in this system. Note that $y = -u$, $z = -v$, $w = x_0 = x$; that is, the x axis is common to all systems. The following direction cosines between unit vectors in the wuv and $x_0 y_0 z_0$ system are needed:

$$\mathbf{a}_u \cdot \mathbf{a}_{y_0} = \cos \psi = \mathbf{a}_v \cdot \mathbf{a}_{z_0} \tag{4.124a}$$

$$\mathbf{a}_u \cdot \mathbf{a}_{z_0} = -\mathbf{a}_v \cdot \mathbf{a}_{y_0} = \sin \psi \tag{4.124b}$$

The surface of the reflector is described by any one of the following equations:

$$r = \frac{2f}{1 + \cos \theta'} = \frac{2f}{1 + \cos \psi \cos \theta_0 - \sin \psi \sin \theta_0 \sin \phi_0} \tag{4.125a}$$

$$v = f - \frac{u^2 + w^2}{4f} = \frac{4f^2 - \rho^2}{4f} \tag{4.125b}$$

$$r = 2f - v = \frac{4f^2 + \rho^2}{4f} \tag{4.125c}$$

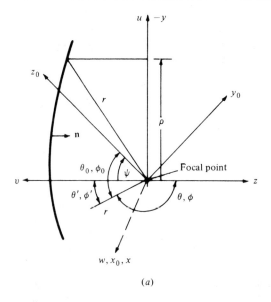

(a)

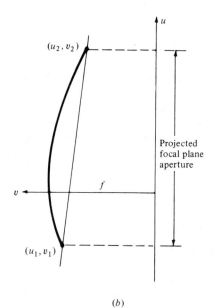

(b)

Figure 4.57 (a) Coordinate systems used in the analysis. (b) Focal-plane aperture.

Note that $\mathbf{a}_r \cdot \mathbf{a}_v = \cos \theta'$, and when $\mathbf{a}_r$ is expressed as components along x_0, y_0, z_0, that is,

$$\mathbf{a}_r = \mathbf{a}_{x_0} \sin \theta_0 \cos \phi_0 + \mathbf{a}_{y_0} \sin \theta_0 \sin \phi_0 + \mathbf{a}_{z_0} \cos \theta_0$$

the second equation in (4.125a) is obtained. Equation (4.125c) follows from (4.125a) by putting $r \cos \theta' = v$. Equation (4.125b) is obtained by squaring both sides of the equation $r = 2f - v$ and cancelling the v^2 term on both sides. Note that $r^2 = w^2 + u^2 + v^2$.

If the paraboloid is cut by a plane, as shown in Fig. 4.57b, the projected focal-plane aperture is a circle. The equation for the projected focal-plane aperture contour is

$$(u - u_0)^2 + w^2 = a^2$$

where $u_0 = \dfrac{u_1 + u_2}{2}$

$a^2 = \left(\dfrac{u_2 - u_1}{2}\right)^2$

If the feed is made from coaxial circular waveguides excited by TE_{1m} and TM_{1m} modes, it will have a radiation pattern of the form

$$\mathbf{E}_f = \frac{e^{-jk_0 r}}{r}[\mathbf{a}_{\theta_0} e_1(\theta_0) \sin \phi_0 + \mathbf{a}_{\phi_0} e_2(\theta_0) \cos \phi_0]$$

For a circularly symmetric pattern with no cross polarization $e_1(\theta_0) = e_2(\theta_0) = e(\theta_0)$. We will assume that $e_1 = e_2 = e(\theta_0)$.

The above feed pattern will be expressed as components in the wuv system. By using ray methods and the law of reflection, we can find the focal-plane aperture field. The reflected field at the reflector surface is given by Eq. (4.56); that is,

$$\mathbf{E}_r = -\mathbf{E}_f + 2(\mathbf{n} \cdot \mathbf{E}_f)\mathbf{n}$$

where $\mathbf{n}$ is the unit normal to the reflector surface.

The feed pattern is first expressed as components along x_0, y_0, z_0. These components are then projected onto the wuv axis using the direction cosines given by Eq. (4.124). By this means we find that

$$\mathbf{E}_f = \frac{e^{-jk_0 r}}{r} e(\theta_0)\{-\mathbf{a}_w[\cos \phi_0 \sin \phi_0(1 - \cos \theta_0)]$$

$$+ \mathbf{a}_u[-\sin \psi \sin \theta_0 \sin \phi_0 + \cos \psi \cos \theta_0$$

$$+ \cos \psi \cos^2 \phi_0(1 - \cos \theta_0)] - \mathbf{a}_v[\cos \psi \sin \theta_0$$

$$\times \sin \phi_0 + \sin \psi \cos \theta_0 + \sin \psi \cos^2 \phi_0(1 - \cos \theta_0)]\} \quad (4.126)$$

The next step is to express this as a function of w, u, and v. If we use the expression for $\mathbf{r}$ given after Eq. (4.125c), then we find that

$$\mathbf{r} \cdot \mathbf{a}_{x_0} = \mathbf{r} \cdot \mathbf{a}_w = w = r \sin \theta_0 \cos \phi_0 \quad (4.127a)$$

$$\mathbf{r} \cdot \mathbf{a}_{z_0} = \mathbf{r} \cdot (\mathbf{a}_v \cos \psi + \mathbf{a}_u \sin \psi) = r \cos \theta_0$$

$$= u \sin \psi + v \cos \psi \quad (4.127b)$$

$$\mathbf{r} \cdot \mathbf{a}_{y_0} = r \sin \theta_0 \sin \phi_0 = u \cos \psi - v \sin \psi \quad (4.127c)$$

The product of Eq. (4.127a) with (4.127c) gives

$$\sin \phi_0 \cos \phi_0 (1 - \cos \theta_0) = \frac{wu \cos \psi - wv \sin \psi}{r^2(1 + \cos \theta_0)} \tag{4.128a}$$

The square of Eq. (4.127a) gives

$$\cos^2 \phi_0 (1 - \cos \theta_0) = \frac{w^2}{r^2(1 + \cos \theta_0)} \tag{4.128b}$$

From Eq. (4.127b) we have

$$1 + \cos \theta_0 = 1 + \frac{u}{r} \sin \psi + \frac{v}{r} \cos \psi \tag{4.128c}$$

From Eq. (4.125b) we have $4fv + u^2 + w^2 - 4f^2 = 0$. The gradient of this is along $-\mathbf{n}$. By normalizing the gradient to unit length we find that the normal $\mathbf{n}$ is given by

$$\mathbf{n} = -\frac{w\mathbf{a}_w + u\mathbf{a}_u + 2f\mathbf{a}_v}{(4f^2 + \rho^2)^{1/2}} \tag{4.129}$$

The focal-plane aperture field may now be evaluated by using Eqs. (4.56), (4.126), and (4.129) and the relations given in (4.127) and (4.128). A considerable amount of algebra is involved to obtain the final expressions. In the simplification procedure the following relations are used:

$$v = f - \frac{\rho^2}{4f} \qquad r = 2f - v \qquad 4fr = 4f^2 + \rho^2$$

$$r + v \cos \psi + u \sin \psi = \frac{4f^2 + \rho^2 + 4fu \sin \psi + (4f^2 - \rho^2) \cos \psi}{4f}$$

It is found that

$$E_{ax} = E_{aw}$$
$$= \frac{4f e^{-j2k_0 f} e(\theta_0)}{(4f^2 + \rho^2)[4f^2 + \rho^2 - 4fy \sin \psi + (4f^2 - \rho^2) \cos \psi]}$$
$$\times [2xy(1 - \cos \psi) - 4fx \sin \psi] \tag{4.130a}$$

$$E_{ay} = -E_{au}$$
$$= \frac{4f e^{-j2k_0 f} e(\theta_0)}{(4f^2 + \rho^2)[4f^2 + \rho^2 - 4fy \sin \psi + (4f^2 - \rho^2) \cos \psi]}$$
$$\times [(4f^2 + \rho^2 - 2x^2) + (4f^2 - \rho^2 + 2x^2) \cos \psi - 4fy \sin \psi] \tag{4.130b}$$

$$E_{az} = 0 \tag{4.130c}$$

where $\rho^2 = x^2 + y^2$

$$\theta_0 = \cos^{-1}\left(\frac{4f^2 - \rho^2}{4f^2 + \rho^2} \cos \psi - \frac{4fy}{4f^2 + \rho^2} \sin \psi\right) \tag{4.131}$$

Note that the denominator in Eq. (4.130a) and (4.130b) can also be expressed as $(4f^2 + \rho^2)^2(1 + \cos\theta_0)$. The aperture-field component E_{ax} is a cross-polarized field, which is an odd function of x and vanishes when $\psi = 0$. This field component is quite small when ψ is small. The presence of this cross-polarized field reduces the aperture efficiency (cross-polarization loss).

If the feed is rotated by 90° so that it is polarized along x_0, then the feed pattern is

$$\mathbf{E}_f = \frac{e^{-jk_0r}}{r}\, e(\theta_0)(\mathbf{a}_{\theta_0}\cos\phi_0 - \mathbf{a}_{\phi_0}\sin\phi_0) \tag{4.132}$$

For this case the focal-plane aperture field is found to be

$$E_{ax} = \frac{-4f\, e^{-j2k_0f}e(\theta_0)}{(4f^2 + \rho^2)[4f^2 + \rho^2 - 4fy\sin\psi + (4f^2 - \rho^2)\cos\psi]}$$

$$\times [(4f^2 + \rho^2 - 2x^2) + (4f^2 - \rho^2 + 2x^2)\cos\psi - 4fy\sin\psi] \tag{4.133a}$$

$$E_{ay} = \frac{4f\, e^{-j2k_0f}e(\theta_0)}{(4f^2 + \rho^2)[4f^2 + \rho^2 - 4fy\sin\psi + (4f^2 - \rho^2)\cos\psi]}$$

$$\times [2xy(1 - \cos\psi) - 4fx\sin\psi] \tag{4.133b}$$

$$E_{az} = 0 \tag{4.133c}$$

Apart from the change in polarization, the cross-polarized aperture field is the same; i.e., Eqs. (4.130a) and (4.133b) are equal. Likewise, the copolarized aperture-field distribution is the same except for a 90° rotation; i.e., Eqs. (4.130b) and (4.133a) are equal. It therefore follows that the E- and H-plane patterns are interchanged upon rotation of the feed by 90°. However, the pattern in a given plane, say, the xz plane, does not change. Only the polarization of the field changes. This is true independent of the shape of the projected focal-plane aperture and is due to the rotational symmetry assumed for the feed pattern.

In general the feed pattern for coaxial feeds does not have rotational symmetry. A nonsymmetric feed pattern may be expressed in the form

$$\mathbf{E}_f = \frac{e^{-jk_0r}}{r}\, e_1(\theta_0)(\mathbf{a}_{\theta_0}\sin\phi_0 + \mathbf{a}_{\phi_0}\cos\phi_0) + \frac{e^{-jk_0r}}{r}\, [e_2(\theta_0) - e_1(\theta_0)](\mathbf{a}_{\phi_0}\cos\phi_0) \tag{4.134}$$

The aperture field produced by $e_1(\theta_0)$ is given by Eq. (4.130). The asymmetrical part contributes an additional aperture field given by $\mathbf{E}'_f$ where

$$E'_f = \frac{4f\, e^{-j2k_0f}[e_2(\theta_0) - e_1(\theta_0)]}{(4f^2 + \rho^2)[4f^2 + \rho^2 - 4fy\sin\psi + (4f^2 - \rho^2)\cos\psi]}$$

$$\times \frac{\mathbf{a}_x[-4fxy\cos\psi - x(4f^2 - \rho^2 + 2x^2)\sin\psi] + \mathbf{a}_y[4fx^2\cos\psi - 2x^2y\sin\psi]}{[4f^2 + \rho^2 + 4fy\sin\psi - (4f^2 - \rho^2)\cos\psi]/4f} \tag{4.135}$$

Radiation Field

The far-zone radiation field, computed from the aperture electric field, is given by Eq. (4.39) and is

$$\mathbf{E} = \frac{jk_0}{2\pi r} e^{-jk_0 r}[\mathbf{a}_\theta(f_x \cos \phi + f_y \sin \phi) + \mathbf{a}_\phi(f_y \cos \phi - f_x \sin \phi) \cos \theta]$$

(4.136)

where the following Fourier transforms are used:

$$f_x(k_x, k_y) = \int_{S_a} E_{ax}(x, y) \, e^{jk_x x + jk_y y} \, dx \, dy$$

$$f_y(k_x, k_y) = \int_{S_a} E_{ay}(x, y) \, e^{jk_x x + jk_y y} \, dx \, dy$$

and $k_x = k_0 \sin \theta \cos \phi$ $k_y = k_0 \sin \theta \sin \phi$

For a y-polarized aperture field the copolarized field is the component along the unit vector $\mathbf{a}_1 = \mathbf{a}_\theta \sin \phi + \mathbf{a}_\phi \cos \phi$. Thus we find

$$E_{\text{COPOL}} = \frac{jk_0 e^{-jk_0 r}}{2\pi r} \left\{ f_y[1 + (\cos \theta - 1) \cos^2 \phi] - f_x(\cos \theta - 1) \frac{\sin 2\phi}{2} \right\}$$

(4.137a)

The cross-polarized field is the component along the unit vector $\mathbf{a}_2 = \mathbf{a}_\theta \cos \phi - \mathbf{a}_\phi \sin \phi$ and is given by

$$E_{\text{CRPOL}} = \frac{jk_0 e^{-jk_0 r}}{2\pi r} \left\{ f_x[1 + (\cos \theta - 1) \sin^2 \phi] + f_y(1 - \cos \theta) \frac{\sin 2\phi}{2} \right\}$$

(4.137b)

The cross-polarized field is generally largest in the $\phi = \pm 45°$ planes but may be large in the $\phi = 0°$ and $90°$ planes also if the cross-polarized aperture field is large.

The aperture efficiency may be found by using Eq. (4.76). The gain of the antenna is given by 4π times the power flux in the desired polarization in the bore-sight direction after dividing by the total power radiated by the feed; thus

$$G = \frac{(4\pi/\lambda_0^2) \int_{S_a} |E_{ay}|^2 \, ds}{\int_0^\pi \int_0^{2\pi} |e(\theta_0)|^2 \sin \theta_0 \, d\phi_0 \, d\theta_0}$$

(4.138)

Numerical Evaluation of the Radiated Field

The integrals in Eq. (4.136) that give the radiated field are best done for each separate pattern cut that is desired. For example, consider the H-plane pattern due to E_{ay}. The integral to be evaluated is

$$\iint\limits_{S_a} E_{ay}(x, y) \, e^{-jk_x x} \, dx \, dy$$

This integral must be evaluated for a number of different values of $k_x = k_0 \sin \theta$. The procedure to use is to divide the aperture into strips parallel and perpendicular to x. The integrals

$$\int E_{ay}(x_i, y) \, dy$$

for each strip along y are evaluated using a numerical integration algorithm such as Simpson's rule. This data is stored and the remaining one-dimensional integral over x is then carried out for each desired value of k_x. A similar procedure may be used for other pattern cuts by using strips parallel and perpendicular to the plane of the pattern cut desired.

Copolarized and cross-polarized patterns were computed using a computer code developed at Ohio State University.† This code requires the projected focal-plane aperture to be a circle and corresponds to what is obtained by choosing a section of a paraboloid cut by a plane inclined to the axis.

The following data was used:

Projected aperture diameter = 1.2 m

Feed tilt angle $\psi = 26.6°$

Focal length $f = 48.77$ cm

Frequency = 12 GHz

The feed was chosen as a circular waveguide excited with the TE_{11} mode. The waveguide diameter was chosen to be λ_0 such that its radiation pattern could be assumed to be circularly symmetric (see Fig. 4.37). The feed pattern was assumed to be given by Eq. (4.117a), apart from irrelevant constants; that is,

$$e(\theta_0) = (1 + 0.81 \cos \theta_0) \frac{J_1(\pi \sin \theta_0)}{\sin \theta_0}$$

The feed pattern is polarized along the y axis. The illumination level of this feed is down by -12 dB at $\theta_0 = 60°$ relative to the on-axis field.

The E-plane pattern is shown in Fig. 4.58. Note that the side-lobe level is below -30 dB. The cross-polarized radiation in this plane is negligible. The H-plane pattern, the copolarized $45°$ plane pattern, and the corresponding cross-polarized patterns in these planes are shown in Figs. 4.59 and 4.60. The

---

† S. H. Lee, and R. C. Rudduck, *Numerical Electromagnetic Code (NEC)—Reflector Antenna Code—Part II: Code Manual*, Ohio State University, Electro-Science Laboratory Report 784508-16, Columbus, Sept. 1979. The patterns were computed by Georg Karawas.

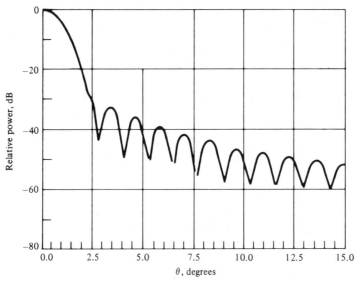

Figure 4.58 E-plane radiation pattern for an offset paraboloidal reflector.

side-lobe level remains below -30 dB, but the cross polarization shows a peak of about -25 dB in the $\phi = 45°$ plane and -22 dB in the $\phi = 0$ plane. The cross-polarization peak occurs about $1.5°$ away from the axis and hence is within the main lobe region.

The computed gain of the antenna system is 42.17 dB, which corresponds to an overall efficiency $\eta_A \eta_s$ equal to 72.5 percent, which is consistent with the

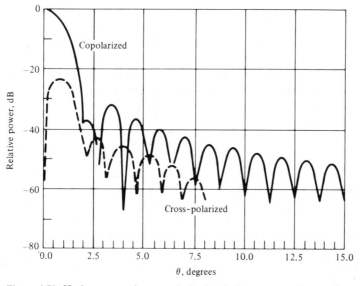

Figure 4.59 H-plane co- and cross-polarized radiation patterns for an offset paraboloidal reflector.

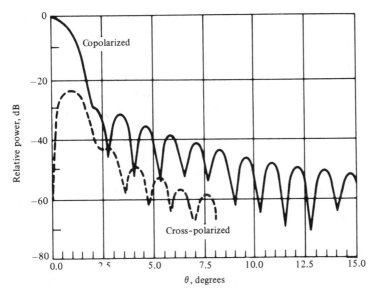

Figure 4.60 Co- and cross-polarized radiation patterns in $\phi = 45°$ plane for an offset paraboloidal reflector.

theoretical value shown in Fig. 4.38 (note that the efficiencies shown in Fig. 4.38 are for the case of $\psi = 0$, that is, with no offset). This example shows that the use of an offset reflector does not cause the gain or side-lobe level to deteriorate but does result in a much higher level of cross polarization.

4.11 DUAL-REFLECTOR ANTENNA SYSTEMS

The paraboloidal antenna with a feed at the focus does not allow very much control over the power distribution over the aperture surface except for what can be accomplished by changing the focal length. The introduction of a second reflecting surface, such as in the cassegrain system shown in Sec. 4.6, allows for more control over the aperture distribution because of the extra degree of freedom that a second reflecting surface gives. This additional control over the aperture field distribution is obtained by shaping both the subreflector and the main reflector so as to change the power distribution on the main reflector aperture but yet maintain the required phase distribution. A single reflector does not allow both the power and phase distribution to be varied independently.

Reflectors made by rotating an ellipse or hyperbola about their respective axes to form ellipsoids or hyperboloids are useful as subreflectors because these conic sections have two focal points. The feed may be placed at one focal point, and the second focal point can be made to coincide with the focal point of the main reflector, which is the paraboloid. These classical subreflectors have the effect of changing the effective focal length of the main reflector. An analysis demonstrating this effect is given below. Although these classical subreflectors do not provide much control over the aperture distribution, they are a useful initial design, which, through a small amount of reshaping, can be optimized.

In order to appreciate the usefulness of the conic sections we briefly review the geometrical properties of the ellipse, hyperbola, and parabola below.

Figure 4.61 shows an ellipse with major and minor semiaxes a and b. The two focal points are located at $x = \pm ae$, where the eccentricity e is given by $e = (1 - b^2/a^2)^{1/2}$, $b < a$. The ellipse has the property that the path length from one focus to the surface and on to the next focus is a constant; that is, $\overline{AP} + \overline{PB} = 2a$. All of the rays from A that are reflected from the surface will come to a focus at B. It may be shown that for these rays Snell's law of reflection is satisfied at the surface. With respect to the xy coordinate system the equation of the ellipse is

$$\frac{x^2}{a^2} + \frac{y^2}{b^2} = 1 \qquad (4.139)$$

For an ellipsoid obtained by rotating the ellipse about the x axis, y^2 is replaced by $y^2 + z^2$. A more useful equation for the ellipse is obtained by choosing the origin at one of the foci. Let r be the distance from one of the focal points to an arbitrary point on the surface, and let θ be the angle between r and the x axis, as shown in Fig. 4.61. The equation describing the ellipse then becomes

$$r = \frac{a(1 - e^2)}{1 \pm e \cos \theta} \qquad (4.140)$$

where the minus sign applies when the origin is at A and the plus sign applies when the origin is at B.

The hyperbola is shown in Fig. 4.62. It has two focal points located at $x = \pm ae$, where now the eccentricity is given by $e = (1 + b^2/a^2)^{1/2}$ and is greater than unity. The hyperbola has the property that the difference in path length from the focus at $-ae$ to a point on the surface and that from the focus at ae to

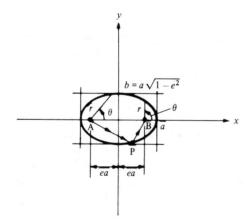

Figure 4.61 The ellipse and its geometrical parameters.

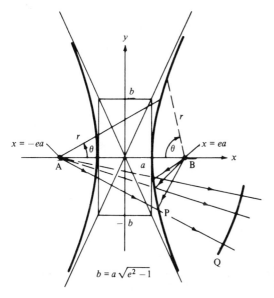

Figure 4.62 The hyperbola and its geometrical parameters.

the same surface point is a constant; that is, $\overline{AP} - \overline{PB} = 2a$. We can readily show that rays emanating from B and reflected from the surface form a bundle with a spherical wave front and appear to come from the focal point at A. All path lengths $\overline{AQ}$ are equal since Q lies on a circle with A as its center. But $\overline{AQ} = \overline{AP} + \overline{PQ} = \overline{BP} + 2a + \overline{PQ}$, so all ray paths $\overline{BP} + \overline{PQ}$ are equal. Snell's law of reflection will be satisfied at the surface for the system of rays as described. The hyperbola is described by the equation

$$\frac{x^2}{a^2} - \frac{y^2}{b^2} = 1 \tag{4.141}$$

It is also described by the equation (the branch for $x > 0$)

$$r = \frac{a(e^2 - 1)}{e \cos \theta \pm 1} \tag{4.142}$$

where r is the distance from one of the focal points and θ is the angle between r and the x axis, as shown in Fig. 4.62. The minus sign applies when the origin is at A, and the plus sign applies when the origin is at B.

Figure 4.63 shows the parabola, which has the property that the sum of the path lengths from the plane a distance f to the left of the vertex and from the focus to a point on the surface is a constant; that is, $\overline{QP} + \overline{PO} = 2f$. The equations describing the parabola are

$$x = \frac{y^2}{4f} \tag{4.143a}$$

or

$$r = \frac{2f}{1 + \cos \theta} \tag{4.143b}$$

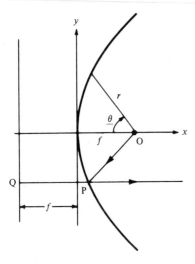

Figure 4.63 The parabola and its geometrical parameters.

All rays from O that are reflected from the surface appear as parallel rays coming from the plane at $x = -f$.

Figure 4.64a to d shows the four possible ways in which ellipsoidal or hyperboloidal subreflectors may be used in connection with a paraboloidal reflector to form a dual-reflector antenna system. When the incident system of parallel rays is brought to a focus by the paraboloidal reflector and then allowed to continue on and be reflected by the subreflector and refocused at the feed, the system is called a *gregorian dual-reflector system*. The ellipsoidal subreflector must be used for this case, since both focal points must be accessible to the rays. One of the focal points of the ellipsoid must coincide with that of the paraboloid, as shown in Fig. 4.64a and b.

In the *cassegrain dual-reflector systems* shown in Fig. 4.64c and d the rays from the paraboloid are reflected before coming to a focus. The subreflector focuses the rays to the accessible focal point at which the feed is located. The second focal point coincides with the focal point of the paraboloid. The hyperboloidal subreflector may have either its convex side (Fig. 4.64c) or its concave side (Fig. 4.64d) facing the paraboloidal reflector. The effect of the subreflector on the power distribution over the aperture is readily determined by ray optics and using the principle of power conservation in a flux tube. In order to illustrate the procedure we will consider the cassegrain system shown in Fig. 4.65.

Let a feed with a circularly symmetric radiation pattern (gain function) $g(\theta)$ be located at the hyperboloid focal point A. The power in a flux tube with solid angle $\sin \theta \, d\theta \, d\phi$ is $g(\theta) \sin \theta \, d\theta \, d\phi$. The reflected flux tube has rays that appear to come from the second focal point at B. If the gain function for the reflected rays is called $g_e(\theta_1)$, power conservation requires that

$$g(\theta) \sin \theta \, d\theta \, d\phi = g_e(\theta_1) \sin \theta_1 \, d\theta_1 \, d\phi$$

This same power appears in the ring of radius y and width dy. Thus the power

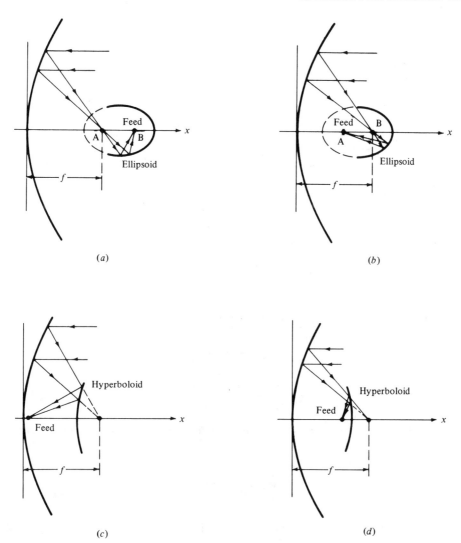

Figure 4.64 Dual-reflector antenna systems: (*a*) and (*b*) gregorian systems using ellipsoidal subreflectors; (*c*) and (*d*) cassegrain systems using hyperboloid subreflectors.

density $P(y)$ on the aperture surface of the paraboloid satisfies the relation

$$P(y)y\, dy\, d\phi = g(\theta) \sin \theta\, d\theta\, d\phi = g_e(\theta_1) \sin \theta_1\, d\theta_1\, d\phi$$

From this expression we find that

$$g_e(\theta_1) = g(\theta) \frac{\sin \theta}{\sin \theta_1} \frac{d\theta}{d\theta_1}$$

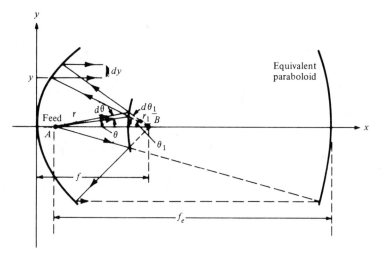

Figure 4.65 Cassegrain dual-reflector antenna system showing the equivalent paraboloid.

From Eq. (4.73) in Sec. 4.6 we also have the relationship

$$P(y) = \frac{1}{y}\frac{d\theta_1}{dy} g_e(\theta_1) = g(\theta)\frac{\sin\theta}{\sin\theta_1}\frac{d\theta}{d\theta_1}\frac{1}{y}\frac{d\theta_1}{dy}$$

$$= g(\theta)\frac{\sin\theta}{\sin\theta_1}\frac{d\theta}{d\theta_1}\frac{(1+\cos\theta_1)^2}{4f^2} \tag{4.144}$$

In order to evaluate $d\theta/d\theta_1$ we use the property $r - r_1 = 2a$ for the hyperbola; that is,

$$\frac{a(e^2-1)}{e\cos\theta - 1} - \frac{a(e^2-1)}{e\cos\theta_1 + 1} = 2a$$

When this equation is differentiated we obtain

$$\frac{\sin\theta\, d\theta}{(e\cos\theta - 1)^2} = \frac{\sin\theta_1\, d\theta_1}{(e\cos\theta_1 + 1)^2} \tag{4.145}$$

The above equation may also be solved to give

$$\cos\theta = \frac{(e^2+1)\cos\theta_1 + 2e}{e^2 + 1 + 2e\cos\theta_1} \tag{4.146a}$$

$$\cos\theta_1 = \frac{-(e^2+1)\cos\theta + 2e}{2e\cos\theta - (e^2+1)} \tag{4.146b}$$

When these relations are used we find that $P(y)$ can be expressed in the following forms:

$$P(y) = g(\theta)\left(\frac{e^2 - 1}{2f}\right)^2 \left(\frac{1 + \cos\theta_1}{2e\cos\theta_1 + e^2 + 1}\right)^2$$

$$= g(\theta)\left(\frac{e - 1}{e + 1}\right)^2 \left(\frac{1 + \cos\theta}{2f}\right)^2 \tag{4.147}$$

The last form shows that $P(y)$ has the same form as Eq. (4.73) for a prime-focus-fed paraboloidal reflector having an effective focal length f_e given by

$$f_e = \frac{e + 1}{e - 1} f \tag{4.148}$$

which can be much longer than f. If $e = 3$ then $f_e = 2f$, while $e = 2$ makes $f_e = 3f$. The equivalent paraboloid is also shown in Fig. 4.65. A paraboloidal reflector with a long focal length has less taper in the aperture-field distribution and also has a better scanning performance (less loss in gain as the feed is moved away from the axis to scan the beam off-axis). This is the main advantage in using the cassegrain system in many applications, since it allows the overall antenna system to be more compact for the same level of performance.

For the concave hyperboloid reflector shown in Fig. 4.64d the analysis shows that

$$P(y) = g(\theta)\left(\frac{e + 1}{e - 1}\right)^2 \left(\frac{1 + \cos\theta}{2f}\right)^2 \tag{4.149}$$

In this case the equivalent paraboloid has a focal length f_e given by

$$f_e = \left(\frac{e - 1}{e + 1}\right) f \tag{4.150}$$

which corresponds to a value less than f. Since the effective focal length is reduced, the aperture-field taper is increased, and for this reason the concave reflector is not commonly used. In Eqs. (4.147) and (4.149) y is given by

$$y = \frac{2f_e \sin\theta}{1 + \cos\theta} = \frac{2f \sin\theta_1}{1 + \cos\theta_1} \tag{4.151}$$

An analysis similar to that carried out above shows that the dual-reflector system using the ellipsoidal reflector in Fig. 4.64a is equivalent to a single paraboloid with an effective focal length $f_e = (1 - e)f/(1 + e)$ which is less than f. The focal length f_e of the paraboloidal reflector that is equivalent to the dual-reflector system shown in Fig. 4.64b is $f_e = (1 + e)f/(1 - e)$, which is longer than f.

Shaped Dual-Reflector Systems

The hyperboloid and ellipsoidal dual-reflector systems may be arranged so as to avoid blocking the main reflector. A typical dual-reflector offset system is shown in Fig. 4.66. In addition, a modest amount of reshaping of the subreflector and the main reflector can be carried out in order to give a more uniform aperture-field distribution and hence higher efficiency. Considerable progress has been made in the development of synthesis methods for shaped dual-reflector systems, and the reader is referred to the literature for a discussion of these synthesis techniques.† It is found that the aperture power distribution may be controlled almost entirely by reshaping the subreflector. The main reflector may subsequently be reshaped to correct the phase distribution without changing the aperture-field amplitude distribution very much. The reason for this behavior is that a small displacement Δl of a portion of the subreflector surface represents a much greater change in shape than a similar displacement of the surface of the much larger main reflector. The correction for phase or path length changes involves similar displacements of both surfaces and hence allows shaping of the subreflector to be used primarily for amplitude control of the aperture field.

The use of ray optics to design dual-reflector systems is subject to some error, since it is not an exact theory. In the design of an antenna system it is desirable to recalculate the field reflected from the subreflector using the physical optics currents on the subreflector. This calculation will then account

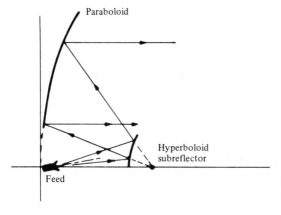

Figure 4.66 An offset cassegrain dual-reflector antenna system.

† V. Galindo, "Design of Dual Reflector Antennas with Arbitrary Phase and Amplitude Distributions," *IEEE Trans.*, vol. AP-12, July 1964, pp. 403–408.

V. Galindo-Israel, R. Mittra, and A. G. Cha, "Aperture Amplitude and Phase Control of Offset Dual Reflectors," *IEEE Trans.*, vol. AP-27, March 1979, pp. 154–164.

J. J. Lee, L. I. Parad, and R. S. Chu, "A Shaped Offset-Fed Dual-Reflector Antenna," *IEEE Trans.*, vol. AP-27, March 1979, pp. 165–171.

J. J. Lee, and R. S. Chu, "Shaping Techniques for Offset Fed Dual Reflector Antennas," in J. A. Kong (ed.), *Research Topics in Electromagnetic Theory*, John Wiley & Sons, Inc., New York, 1981.

for the diffraction effects associated with the subreflector and may subsequently require some redesign of the system.

For a rotationally symmetric dual-reflector system, the design goal is to obtain a specified gain function $g_e(\theta_1)$ from a chosen feed with gain function $g(\theta)$. If we begin with an initial cassegrain system, for example, then the desired aperture power distribution $P(y)$ determines $g_e(\theta_1)$ from the relation

$$P(y) = g_e(\theta_1)\frac{(1 + \cos\,\theta_1)^2}{4f^2}$$

When $g_e(\theta_1)$ has been specified, then the subreflector must be shaped so that

$$g_e(\theta_1)\sin\,\theta_1\,d\theta_1 = g(\theta)\sin\,\theta\,d\theta$$

where θ_1 is determined by Snell's law, the angle of incidence, and the direction of the local normal to the surface. The equations can be formulated and solved on a computer. For rotationally symmetric coaxial dual-reflector systems, an exact ray-optics solution yielding a desired aperture-field amplitude and phase distribution can be found.† In general, for offset systems only approximate but very good solutions can be found.

The available knowledge about and design guidelines for shaped dual-reflector systems is limited at the present time. This is particularly true regarding designs that would be useful in wide-angle scanning or multibeam systems, which are often called for in antennas intended for satellite communications.

4.12 RADIATION FROM SLOTS

A narrow slot, one-half wavelength long and cut in a conducting sheet of metal, is the dual of a half-wave dipole antenna. The slot may be excited from a coaxial line, as shown in Fig. 4.67. The electric field extends across the narrow dimension of the slot and has a standing wave pattern along the slot; that is, $E = E_g \sin k_0(l - |z|)$ for the slot in the figure.

The radiation properties of a slot may be conveniently determined from fictitious magnetic currents $\mathbf{J}_m$, as discussed earlier. If we had a sheet of magnetic current of density $\mathbf{J}_{ms}$, then from

$$\int_S \nabla\times\mathbf{E}\cdot d\mathbf{S} = \oint_C \mathbf{E}\cdot d\mathbf{l} = \int_S -j\omega\mathbf{B}\cdot d\mathbf{S} - \int_S \mathbf{J}_{ms}\cdot d\mathbf{S}$$

we would be led to the boundary condition (see Fig. 4.68)

$$\mathbf{n}\times\mathbf{E}_1 - \mathbf{n}\times\mathbf{E}_2 = -\mathbf{J}_{ms} \tag{4.152}$$

analogous to $\mathbf{n}\times\mathbf{H}_1 - \mathbf{n}\times\mathbf{H}_2 = \mathbf{J}_{es}$, which holds for an electric current sheet.

† Galindo, op. cit.

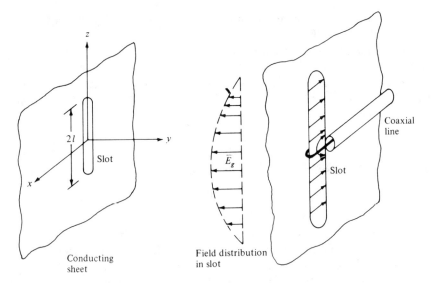

Figure 4.67 The slot antenna.

Based on the above concept we may view the slot antennas as being excited by a magnetic current sheet of strength $2E_g \sin k_0(l - |z|)$ and in the z direction. Figure 4.69 gives a comparison of the slot with a half-wave dipole made from a conducting strip the same shape as the slot. Note that the analogy is not quite the same. The postulated magnetic current sheet will establish the correct electric field over the slot aperture on one side only. On the other side of the sheet the electric field is the negative of what we actually have in the slot. However, we may calculate the correct radiated field on one side of the conducting sheet using the postulated magnetic current as a source. On the other side the radiated field is readily constructed from symmetry considerations.

The basic equations to be solved are those given in Sec. 4.2 and are repeated here for convenience.

$$(\nabla^2 + k_0^2)\mathbf{A}_m = -\epsilon_0 \mathbf{J}_{ms} \tag{4.153a}$$

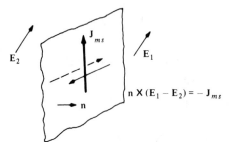

Figure 4.68 Boundary conditions at a magnetic current sheet.

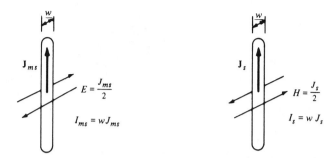

Figure 4.69 Comparison of fields for a slot and a dipole.

$$\mathbf{H} = -j\omega\mathbf{A}_m + \frac{\nabla\nabla\cdot\mathbf{A}_m}{j\omega\mu_0\epsilon_0} \tag{4.153b}$$

$$\mathbf{E} = -\frac{1}{\epsilon_0}\nabla\times\mathbf{A}_m \tag{4.153c}$$

$$\mathbf{A}_m(\mathbf{r}) = \frac{\epsilon_0}{4\pi}\left[\int_S e^{jk_0\mathbf{a}_r\cdot\mathbf{r}'}\mathbf{J}_{ms}(\mathbf{r}')\,dS'\right]\frac{e^{-jk_0r}}{r} \tag{4.153d}$$

If we now consider a half-wave slot dipole with $I_m = I_{mo}\sin k_0(l-|z|)$, we see by direct analogy with Eqs. (2.27), (2.28), (4.153b), and (4.153c) that, corresponding to Eqs. (2.53) and (2.54),

$$\mathbf{H} = \frac{\epsilon_0}{\mu_0}\,j\,\frac{I_{mo}Z_0}{2\pi r}\,e^{-jk_0r}\,\frac{\cos(\pi/2\cos\theta)}{\sin\theta}\,\mathbf{a}_\theta$$

$$= j\,\frac{I_{mo}Y_0}{2\pi r}\,e^{-jk_0r}\,\frac{\cos(\pi/2\cos\theta)}{\sin\theta}\,\mathbf{a}_\theta \tag{4.154a}$$

$$\mathbf{E} = -Z_0\mathbf{a}_r\times\mathbf{H} = -j\,\frac{I_{mo}}{2\pi r}\,e^{-jk_0r}\,\frac{\cos(\pi/2\cos\theta)}{\sin\theta}\,\mathbf{a}_\phi \tag{4.154b}$$

for the field radiated on one side of the conducting sheet containing the slot. Note the dual nature of the radiated field, i.e., the interchange of the role of **E** and **H**. The field given by Eq. (4.154) is that radiated by a magnetic current distribution and is valid for all of space. The field radiated by the slot is given by Eq. (4.154) in the half space $y > 0$ and by the negative of Eq. (4.154) in the half space $y < 0$. The solution for $y < 0$ is simply the image of that for $y > 0$, as illustrated in Fig. 4.70. If we view the slot radiator as a boundary-value problem, then we require the field in $y > 0$ to satisfy the boundary conditions

$$\mathbf{n}\times\mathbf{E} = -\frac{\mathbf{J}_{ms}}{2} = \mathbf{n}\times\mathbf{a}_xE_g\sin k_0(l-|z|)$$

in the slot at $y = 0$ and $\mathbf{n}\times\mathbf{E} = 0$ on the conducting sheet at $y = 0$. But these conditions are satisfied by the field radiated by the strip of magnetic current,

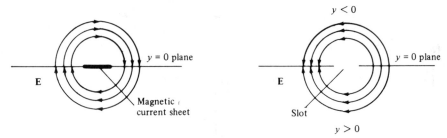

Figure 4.70 Comparison of fields from a magnetic current sheet and a slot radiator.

since this source will produce a field having a zero x and z component on the symmetry plane $y = 0$ outside the source region and reducing to $\pm \mathbf{a}_x E_g \sin k_0(l - |z|)$ on the $y > 0$ and $y < 0$ sides of the current sheet, respectively.

The radiation pattern and directivity of the slot antenna are the same as those for the dipole antenna. We can also find the total radiated power by direct analogy. For the dipole antenna the radiated power is given by

$$P_r = \int_0^{2\pi} \int_0^{\pi} \frac{|\mathbf{E}|^2}{2Z_0} r^2 \sin \theta \, d\theta \, d\phi = \int_0^{2\pi} \int_0^{\pi} \frac{|\mathbf{H}|^2}{2Y_0} r^2 \sin \theta \, d\theta \, d\phi$$

Since the field is independent of ϕ the ϕ integration gives a factor of 2π. For the dipole the result is given by Eq. (2.57), which we now express in the form

$$P_r = I_0^2 Z_0 \zeta \tag{4.155}$$

where $\zeta = 36.56/Z_0$. For the slot we get, by using Eq. (4.154a) for $\mathbf{H}$, the result

$$P_r = I_{mo}^2 Y_0 \zeta \tag{4.156}$$

For the slot we can define a voltage $V_g = w E_g$ at the feed point where w is the width of the slot. We then define the slot radiation conductance G_0 by setting $\frac{1}{2} V_g^2 G_0$ equal to P_r; thus

$$G_0 = \frac{2P_r}{V_g^2} = \frac{2I_{mo}^2 Y_0 \zeta}{V_g^2} = \frac{8 V_g^2 Y_0 \zeta}{V_g^2} = 8 Y_0 \zeta \tag{4.157}$$

since $I_{mo} = 2 E_g w$. Now for the dipole, $\frac{1}{2} I_0^2 R_a = I_0^2 Z_0 \zeta$, or $R_a = 2Z_0 \zeta$, and hence $G_0/R_a = 8 Y_0 \zeta / 2 Z_0 \zeta = 4 Y_0^2$. If we call the dipole radiation resistance R_d and the slot radiation resistance R_s, then

$$\frac{R_a}{G_0} = R_d R_s = \frac{Z_0^2}{4} \tag{4.158}$$

A narrow slot is resonant when its length is a few percent less than $\lambda_0/2$. For a resonant slot the radiation resistance will be

$$R_s = \frac{Z_0^2}{4R_d} = \frac{377^2}{4 \times 73} = 487 \ \Omega$$

which is quite large and results in some practical difficulties in feeding the slot by a coaxial transmission line unless some form of matching network is used.

Single-slot radiators are used as aircraft antennas where the slot is made a part of the aircraft structure itself, such as a tail fin. Quite often a quarter-wave slot, analogous to a monopole antenna, is used instead of a half-wave long slot. Arrays of slots are also frequently used, and these are constructed by cutting the slots in the wall of a waveguide. The general characteristics of a rectangular waveguide slot array are presented in the next section.

4.13 RECTANGULAR WAVEGUIDE SLOT ARRAYS

Figure 4.71 shows a rectangular waveguide of width a and height b. For the dominant TE_{10} mode the field in the waveguide is

$$E_y = E_0 \sin \frac{\pi x}{a} e^{-j\beta z} \tag{4.159a}$$

$$H_x = -E_0 Y_w \sin \frac{\pi x}{a} e^{-j\beta z} \tag{4.159b}$$

$$H_z = jE_0 \frac{\pi Y_0}{k_0 a} \cos \frac{\pi x}{a} e^{-j\beta z} \tag{4.159c}$$

where the propagation constant β is given by

$$\beta = \left[k_0^2 - \left(\frac{\pi}{a} \right)^2 \right]^{1/2} \tag{4.160}$$

and the mode wave admittance $Y_w = Y_0 \beta / k_0$. The wavelength in the guide is given by

$$\lambda_g = \frac{2\pi}{\beta} = \frac{\lambda_0}{(1 - \lambda_0^2 / 4a^2)^{1/2}} \tag{4.161}$$

and is greater than the free-space wavelength λ_0.

The surface current on the upper broad wall of the waveguide is

$$\mathbf{J}_s = -\mathbf{a}_y \times \mathbf{H} = \left(-jE_0 \frac{\pi Y_0}{k_0 a} \mathbf{a}_x \cos \frac{\pi x}{a} - E_0 Y_w \sin \frac{\pi x}{a} \mathbf{a}_z \right) e^{-j\beta z}$$

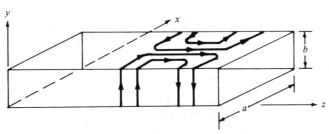

Figure 4.71 A rectangular waveguide and the surface current for the TE_{10} mode.

Along the sidewalls the current is along the y direction. The current flow lines are illustrated in Fig. 4.71.

A narrow slot cut in a waveguide wall in a position parallel to the current will not be excited. However, a slot that is positioned so as to intercept the current will be excited. Thus a longitudinal slot offset from the waveguide centerline, as in Fig. 4.72a, will be excited and will radiate. Likewise, the inclined broad-wall slot and sidewall slot shown in Fig. 4.72b will radiate. The excitation level of the slot can be controlled by the amount of offset x_1 for the slot in Fig. 4.72a and by the inclination angle for the slots in Fig. 4.72b. This feature makes it possible to design slot arrays in waveguides with a specified amplitude variation along the array; i.e., arrays such as the Chebyshev array discussed in Chap. 3 can be designed.

For a resonant longitudinal slot offset by an amount x_1, the conductance of the slot, as seen from the waveguide and normalized with respect to the mode admittance of the TE_{10} mode, is given by†

$$g = 2.09 \frac{\lambda_g}{\lambda_0} \frac{a}{b} \cos^2 \frac{\pi\lambda_0}{2\lambda_g} \sin^2 \frac{\pi x_1}{a} \tag{4.162}$$

The equivalent circuit of the waveguide and slot is a conductance g connected as a shunt element across a transmission line with unit characteristic impedance and having a propagation phase constant β.

There are two basic types of waveguide arrays, the resonant array and the nonresonant array. These two types of arrays will be discussed separately since their design is quite different.

Resonant Arrays

The resonant array is a broadside array with slots spaced $\lambda_g/2$ apart and with alternate slots offset on opposite sides of the centerline, as shown in Fig. 4.73a. By offsetting every other slot on opposite sides of the centerline, an additional phase of π is introduced, which, along with the π radians phase change due to

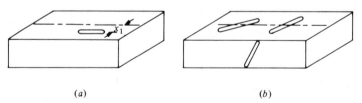

(a)   (b)

Figure 4.72 Waveguide slots: (a) offset broad-wall slot and (b) inclined broad-wall and sidewall slots.

† The derivation of this expression as well as that of the other slot arrangements along with a treatment of slot arrays may be found in R. E. Collin, and F. J. Zucker (ed.), *Antenna Theory, Part I*, McGraw-Hill Book Co., New York, 1969, Chap. 14.

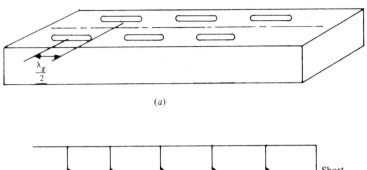

(a)

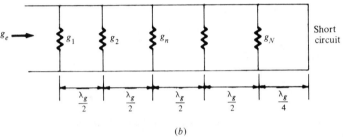

(b)

Figure 4.73 (a) Longitudinal slot resonant array. (b) Equivalent transmission-line circuit.

the $\lambda_g/2$ spacing, results in all slots being excited in phase. The equivalent circuit of the array consists of the N conductances connected across a transmission line with spacing $\lambda_g/2$, as shown in Fig. 4.73b. A short circuit placed $\lambda_g/4$ beyond the last slot presents an open circuit in shunt with the last slot. Since all slots are spaced $\lambda_g/2$ apart, the equivalent input conductance to the array is simply the sum of all the individual slot conductances g_n; thus

$$g_e = \sum_{n=1}^{N} g_n \qquad (4.163)$$

If V is the equivalent voltage acting across the equivalent circuit, the power radiated by slot n will be $\frac{1}{2}V^2 g_n$. Thus the relative excitation level of the nth slot is proportional to $g_n^{1/2}$ and may be controlled by the offset parameter x_1 for this slot. In order to radiate all of the available input power, the total equivalent array conductance g_e should equal unity. Thus if we choose

$$g_n = Ka_n^2 \qquad (4.164)$$

we will require that $g_e = 1$ so that

$$K \sum_{n=1}^{N} a_n^2 = 1 \qquad (4.165)$$

which will determine the constant K once the relative slot excitation amplitudes a_n have been specified. In order to illustrate the design procedure we will consider the design of a five-element array with relative excitation levels of 1, 2, 3, 2, 1, that is, a triangular amplitude distribution along the array.

With the above choice for the a_n, the constant K equals $(1+4+9+4+$

$1)^{-1} = 0.0526$ and the required slot conductances are

$$g_1 = g_5 = 0.0526$$

$$g_2 = g_4 = 4 \times 0.0526 = 0.21$$

$$g_3 = 9 \times 0.0526 = 0.473$$

For a WR-90 waveguide operating at 10 GHz the following parameter values apply:

$$a = 0.9 \text{ in} \qquad b = 0.4 \text{ in}$$

$$\lambda_0 = 3 \text{ cm} \qquad \lambda_g = 3.975 \text{ cm}$$

By using Eq. (4.162) the required slot offsets may be found and are given by

$$\sin \frac{\pi x_1}{a} = 1.066\sqrt{g_n} \qquad \text{or } 0.071, 0.146, \text{ and } 0.236 \text{ in}$$

respectively, for slots 1 and 5, 2 and 4, and 3. The required slot spacing is $\lambda_g/2$, or 0.782 in.

In practice if an array with a required side-lobe level is to be achieved the design is carried out for a somewhat lower side-lobe level in order to compensate for the effect of tolerances required in the construction of the array. Thus, for example, to realize a Chebyshev array with side lobes 30 dB below the main lobe, the array might be designed for side lobes 35 dB below the main lobe. For side lobes no more than 20 dB down from the main lobe overdesign would not normally be required.

The frequency band of operation for the resonant array is only a few percent because correct phasing of the slots requires a $\lambda_g/2$ spacing. The reflection from each slot and the short circuit combine in such a way as to cancel at the input of the array at only one frequency. Hence the array has an overall frequency-dependent input impedance typical of that for a resonant structure, and this accounts for the name *resonant array*.

Nonresonant Arrays

In the nonresonant array the slot spacing differs from $\lambda_g/2$, and the waveguide is terminated in a matched load at the end. The slot spacing d can be chosen so as to produce a main lobe at almost any arbitrary angle ψ relative to the normal of the array but in the plane containing the array axis, as shown in Fig. 4.74a. The equivalent circuit for the array is shown in Fig. 4.74b. We have assumed that the slots are resonant with a pure conductive input admittance and that the mutual admittance between slots is negligible.

If alternate slots are offset on opposite sides of the centerline and x_n is the offset for the nth slot, then the array factor will be

$$F = \sum_{n=1}^{N} a_n e^{jk_0(x_n \mathbf{a}_x \cdot \mathbf{a}_r + nd\mathbf{a}_z \cdot \mathbf{a}_r) - j\beta nd + jn\pi} \tag{4.166}$$

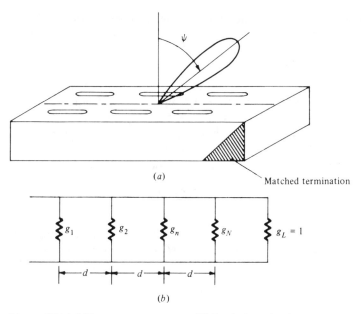

(a)

Matched termination

(b)

Figure 4.74 (a) The nonresonant array. (b) Equivalent circuit.

In this expression the factor $e^{-j\beta nd}$ represents the phase of the propagating mode in the waveguide at the position of the nth slot and will be the phase angle of the field that excites the nth slot. The factor $e^{jn\pi}$ accounts for the phase reversal that occurs when alternate slots are offset on opposite sides of the centerline. The remaining factor accounts for the difference in the propagation path length from each slot. We have also assumed that there is negligible reflection from each slot so that there is no wave propagating in the $-z$ direction in the waveguide. In the plane of the array where $\phi = \pi/2$ we have $\mathbf{a}_x \cdot \mathbf{a}_r = 0$ and $\mathbf{a}_z \cdot \mathbf{a}_r = \cos\theta = \sin\psi$, and the array factor becomes

$$F = \sum_{n=1}^{N} a_n e^{j(k_0 \sin\psi - \beta)nd + jn\pi} \tag{4.167}$$

In order to obtain an in-phase addition in the direction ψ we require

$$(k_0 \sin\psi - \beta)d + \pi = 2m\pi \qquad m = 0, \pm1, \pm2, \ldots$$

which gives

$$d = \frac{(2m-1)\pi}{k_0 \sin\psi - \beta} = \frac{(2m-1)\lambda_0\lambda_g}{2(\lambda_g \sin\psi - \lambda_0)} \tag{4.168}$$

If we choose $m = 0$ then Eq. (4.168) gives

$$\sin\psi = \frac{\lambda_0}{\lambda_g} - \frac{\lambda_0}{2d} \tag{4.169}$$

It is necessary that $-1 < \sin \psi < 1$, which imposes on d the restriction

$$\frac{\lambda_0 \lambda_g}{2(\lambda_0 + \lambda_g)} < d < \frac{\lambda_0 \lambda_g}{2(\lambda_g - \lambda_0)}$$

For $m = -1$ the value of d is similarly found to be greater than $3\lambda_0 \lambda_g / 2(\lambda_g + \lambda_0)$ while for $m = 1$ we must have $d > \lambda_0 \lambda_g / 2(\lambda_g - \lambda_0)$. In the useful frequency range of the waveguide, $1.25\lambda_0 < \lambda_g < 2\lambda_0$, so we find that $1.5/(\lambda_g + \lambda_0) < 0.5/(\lambda_g - \lambda_0)$. Thus $m = -1$ allows a smaller value of d than the $m = 1$ case does. In order to have only one main lobe there should be only one solution for ψ in Eq. (4.168) for different values of m. This will be the case provided

$$\frac{\lambda_0 \lambda_g}{2(\lambda_g + \lambda_0)} < d < \frac{3\lambda_0 \lambda_g}{2(\lambda_g + \lambda_0)} \tag{4.170}$$

which corresponds to choosing $m = 0$ and d less than the $m = -1$ case requires. With this restriction on d we find from Eq. (4.169) that the range of allowed angles for the main lobe is

$$-\frac{\pi}{2} < \psi < \sin^{-1} \frac{2\lambda_0 - \lambda_g}{3\lambda_g} \tag{4.171}$$

which covers the complete backward radiation region and up to 11.5° in the forward direction for $\lambda_g = 1.25\lambda_0$.

It is also possible to place all the slots on one side of the centerline only, and in this case it is found that

$$\frac{\lambda_0 \lambda_g}{\lambda_0 + \lambda_g} < d < \frac{2\lambda_0 \lambda_g}{\lambda_0 + \lambda_g} \tag{4.172}$$

and

$$-\frac{\pi}{2} < \psi < \sin^{-1} \frac{2\lambda_0 - \lambda_g}{\lambda_g} \tag{4.173}$$

The maximum angle in the forward direction is now 37° for $\lambda_g = 1.25\lambda_0$. When the above conditions are adhered to only one main lobe will occur in physical space.

For the nonresonant array a simplified design procedure may be used, provided the array consists of many slots (10 or more) and is designed for a beam angle not along the normal to the array. In this case each slot radiates very little of the total power and hence represents a small discontinuity in the waveguide and produces only a small reflection of the incident wave. Furthermore, the slots are not spaced by $\lambda_g/2$ so the reflections from the different slots do not add up in phase and the total reflection coefficient at the input to the array will also be small. An exception occurs when $d = \lambda_g/2$, which is the required spacing for a beam angle coinciding with the normal to the array, since in this case the individual slot reflections will add in phase at the input (resonant condition).

If the relative excitation level of the nth slot is a_n, the power P_n radiated by this slot will be proportional to a_n^2. Thus when we specify the required amplitude distribution a_n to yield the desired beam width and side-lobe level we will know the P_n to within a constant of proportionality. Let r be the fraction of the incident power to be dissipated in the matched load. The power incident at slot N will then be $r + P_N$ for unit input power to the array. The equivalent voltage across the transmission line of unit characteristic impedance at this point is V_N and is such that $\frac{1}{2}|V_N|^2 = r + P_N$, since reflections are being neglected. The power radiated by the Nth slot with conductance g_N is thus given by $\frac{1}{2}|V_N|^2 g_N$ and must equal P_N; hence

$$g_N = \frac{2P_N}{|V_N|^2} = \frac{P_N}{r + P_N} \tag{4.174}$$

The power incident at slot $N - 1$ is $r + P_N + P_{N-1}$ and must equal $\frac{1}{2}|V_{N-1}|^2$. The radiated power P_{N-1} equals $\frac{1}{2}|V_{N-1}|^2 g_{N-1}$, and hence

$$g_{N-1} = \frac{2P_{N-1}}{|V_{N-1}|^2} = \frac{P_{N-1}}{r + P_N + P_{N-1}} \tag{4.175}$$

By continuing this analysis it is readily found that

$$g_n = \frac{P_n}{r + \sum_{i=n}^{N} P_i} = \frac{P_n}{1 - \sum_{i=1}^{n-1} P_i} \tag{4.176}$$

since r plus the sum of all radiated powers must add up to unity. When the g_n have been found the slot offsets can be determined from Eq. (4.162). The design procedure is illustrated in the following example.

Example 4.1 Ten-element array with a beam angle of $-30°$ A 10-element array having a beam at $30°$ to the array normal in the backward direction will be designed. The amplitude distribution over the array will be chosen as a triangular distribution superimposed on a constant lower level; thus

$$a_1 = a_{10} = 1 + 2 \qquad a_2 = a_9 = 2 + 2$$
$$a_3 = a_8 = 3 + 2 \qquad a_4 = a_7 = 4 + 2$$
$$a_5 = a_6 = 5 + 2$$

The required P_n are then proportional to 9, 16, 25, 36, and 49. We will let 25 percent of the power be dissipated in the matched load, so $r = 0.25$. Then, since

$$r + \sum_{n=1}^{10} P_n = 1$$

we must normalize the values given above such that $2K(9 + 16 + 25 + 36 + 49) = 1 - r = 0.75$, which gives $K = 2.777 \times 10^{-3}$. The required P_n are found to be

$$P_1 = P_{10} = 9K = 0.025 \qquad P_2 = P_9 = 0.0444$$

$$P_3 = P_8 = 0.0694 \qquad P_4 = P_7 = 0.10$$

$$P_5 = P_6 = 0.136$$

By using Eq. (4.176) we find that the g_n are

$$g_1 = 0.025 \qquad g_2 = 0.0455 \qquad g_3 = 0.075 \qquad g_4 = 0.116$$

$$g_5 = 0.179 \qquad g_6 = 0.218 \qquad g_7 = 0.204 \qquad g_8 = 0.178$$

$$g_9 = 0.139 \qquad g_{10} = 0.091$$

For this array the maximum g_n is 0.218, so a smaller fraction of dissipated power could have been used without getting excessively large values for the g_n. A value of $r = 0.15$ would be acceptable and would have given the following values for the g_n: 0.028, 0.052, 0.085, 0.134, 0.212, 0.268, 0.269, 0.256, 0.22, and 0.159.

The slot spacing may be found from Eq. (4.168). If we assume $\lambda_0 = 3$ cm, $\lambda_g = 3.975$ cm, as in the resonant array example, then (note that $m = 0$)

$$d = \frac{\lambda_0 \lambda_g}{2(\lambda_0 - \lambda_g \sin \psi)} = 0.398\lambda_0 = 1.19 \text{ cm}$$

The slot offsets may be found using Eq. (4.162) but will not be computed. ■

If we had designed a broadside array with 10 elements by the above method, the input conductance to the array would be ($d = \lambda_g/2$ in this case)

$$g_{in} = 1 + \sum_{n=1}^{10} g_n = 2.27$$

which is considerably larger than unity. This discrepancy is due to the neglect of reflections from each slot in the derivation of the design formula, Eq. (4.176). Such reflections cannot be neglected when the slot spacing equals $\lambda_g/2$. For $d \neq \lambda_g/2$ the neglect of reflections is not as serious because of cancellation effects, so that in practice the use of Eq. (4.176) gives acceptable results when a large number of slots are used. It is, of course, possible to take reflections into account as well as losses in the waveguide, but the design procedure is then more complex.† It has been found that for arrays with many slots and only a modest requirement on the side-lobe level (30 dB or less below the main lobe) the above simple design procedure is acceptable.‡ However, for high-performance arrays with side lobes 40 dB or more below the main lobe it is necessary to take into account the mutual admittance between slots as well as reflections in the waveguide. When this is done and the slot dimensions are

† Ibid.
‡ A. Dion, "Nonresonant Slotted Arrays," *IRE Trans.*, vol. AP-6, Oct. 1958, pp. 360–365.

carefully controlled in the manufacture of the array, the theoretical performance can be obtained. When the interaction between slots is taken into account it is generally necessary to use nonresonant slots so as to obtain the correct phasing by means of appropriate choices for the slot susceptances.†

4.14 MICROSTRIP ANTENNAS

The widespread use of printed circuits led to the idea of constructing radiating elements and interconnecting transmission lines using the same technology. Antennas made from patches of conducting material on a dielectric substrate above a ground plane are referred to as *microstrip antennas*. The patch is typically of rectangular or circular shape with dimensions of order one-half wavelength. Other shapes such as diamond, triangle, ring, etc., may also be used. Some typical microstrip antenna configurations are shown in Fig. 4.75.

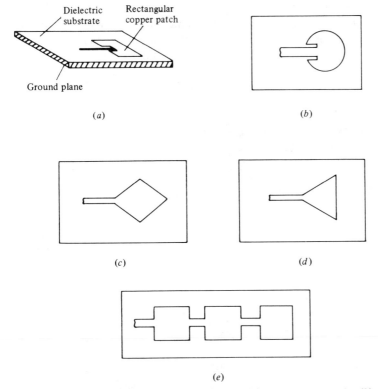

Figure **4.75** Microstrip antenna configurations: (*a*) rectangular patch; (*b*) circular patch; (*c*) diamond-shaped patch giving circular polarization; (*d*) triangular patch; and (*e*) three-element array.

† R. S. Elliott, *Antenna Theory and Design*, Prentice-Hall, Inc., Englewood Cliffs, N.J. 1981.

The antenna may be fed with a microstrip transmission line or a coaxial line, as shown in Fig. 4.76. The feed point is positioned away from the edge by an amount that will give a good impedance match.

The main advantage of microstrip antennas is their ease of construction and relatively low cost. Other advantages are the compact low-profile configuration and the possibility of wrapping the antenna around a cylinder or aircraft fuselage by printing the elements on a flexible substrate material.

In many ways the small patch and ground plane behave like a lossy cavity resonator, with the predominant loss being radiation loss from leakage at the open boundary. Since the height of the patch above the ground plane is very small, the radiated power is also quite small and the resonator exhibits a relatively high Q of order 25 to 100. Thus the bandwidth of the antenna is small, usually only a few percent, and this is one disadvantage of this type of antenna. Other disadvantages are low power-handling capability, poor end-fire radiation characteristics, and limited gain.

Microstrip antennas have found application in telemetry, satellite communications, and various military radar systems operating in the 1- to 10-GHz frequency band. Integrating the microstrip antenna with a solid-state receiving or transmitting module opens up the possibility of building large antenna-array systems, with each element being an active, individually controlled element.

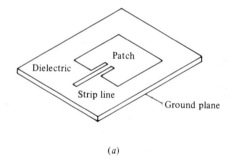

(a)

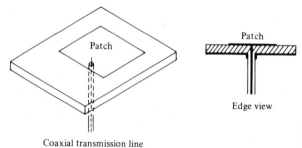

(b)

Figure 4.76 Two methods of feeding a microstrip antenna: (a) strip line feed, (b) coaxial line feed.

Various forms of low-cost signal-processing antennas are thus made possible.

A considerable amount of theoretical analysis of microstrip antennas has been carried out in recent years.[†] In this section we will only consider the more elementary features of a microstrip antenna in order to illustrate the basic properties and the mechanism of radiation. Various analytical approaches have been used by different authors. These include transmission-line models, cavity models, and full modal expansion techniques. It has been found that a simplified transmission line model or cavity model can give useful engineering design information and predict the performance quite accurately. The transmission-line model is limited to rectangular or square patches, while the cavity model can be applied to other shapes as well. For this reason we will present the main features of the cavity model following the work of Carver.[‡]

Consider the rectangular patch shown in Fig. 4.77. The patch is of length a, width b, and is at a height h above the ground plane. The dielectric substrate has a permittivity ϵ. Initially we will assume that the boundaries at $x = 0$, a and $y = 0$, b act as ideal open circuits. The boundary conditions to be applied at these boundaries are zero tangential magnetic fields along $x = 0$, a and $y = 0$, b. The modes of interest are the transverse magnetic modes (TM), which have $H_z = 0$ but a nonzero value of E_z. We can assume that the fields have no dependence on z since h is very small. Suitable solutions for E_z are of the form

$$E_z = C_{nm} \cos \frac{n\pi x}{a} \cos \frac{m\pi y}{b} \qquad (4.177)$$

where n and m are integers and C_{nm} is an amplitude constant. The above equation describes the z-directed electric field for the TM_{nm} mode. A general field can be constructed by means of a summation of these modes over all values of n and m.

The electric field has zero divergence, and since E_z is not a function of z

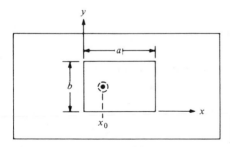

Figure 4.77 A rectangular-patch microstrip antenna.

[†] A good description of microstrip antennas may be found in I. J. Bahl and P. Bhartia, *Microstrip Antennas*, Artech House, Inc., Dedham, Mass., 1980.

[‡] K. R. Carver, "Practical Analytical Techniques for the Microstrip Antenna," *Proc. Workshop on Printed Circuit Antennas*, New Mexico State University, Las Cruces, Oct. 1979, pp. 7.1–7.20.

we have

$$\frac{\partial E_x}{\partial x} + \frac{\partial E_y}{\partial y} = 0$$

This equation does not relate E_x or E_y to E_z. The magnetic field is given by

$$-j\omega\mu_0 \mathbf{H} = \nabla \times \mathbf{E} = \mathbf{a}_x \left(\frac{\partial E_z}{\partial y} - \frac{\partial E_y}{\partial z} \right) + \mathbf{a}_y \left(\frac{\partial E_x}{\partial z} - \frac{\partial E_z}{\partial x} \right)$$

$$= \mathbf{a}_x \frac{\partial E_z}{\partial y} - \mathbf{a}_y \frac{\partial E_z}{\partial x}$$

Since $\mathbf{H}$ depends only on E_z, which is not related to E_x or E_y, we conclude that $E_x = E_y = 0$ is a valid solution for the TM_{nm} modes. We now find that for the nmth mode

$$\mathbf{H}_{nm} = -\frac{j}{k_0 Z_0} C_{nm} \left(\frac{m\pi}{b} \cos \frac{n\pi x}{a} \sin \frac{m\pi y}{b} \mathbf{a}_x + \frac{n\pi}{a} \sin \frac{n\pi x}{a} \cos \frac{m\pi y}{b} \mathbf{a}_y \right)$$

$$(4.178)$$

where we have replaced $\omega\mu_0$ by $\omega(\mu_0\epsilon_0)^{1/2}(\mu_0/\epsilon_0)^{1/2} = k_0 Z_0$. Note that the choice of modal functions is such that $\mathbf{H}_{nm}$ has zero tangential components on the boundaries, as required by the assumption of ideal open-circuit conditions.

We will now assume that the cavity is driven from a coaxial line located at $y = b/2$ and $x = x_0$. We will let the total current in the probe be I_0. When the probe has a radius r_0 the current density on the probe surface is $I_0/2\pi r_0$. The equation satisfied by the electric field excited by a current $\mathbf{J}(\mathbf{r}')$ is

$$\nabla \times \nabla \times \mathbf{E} - k^2 \mathbf{E} = -j\omega\mu_0 \mathbf{J}$$

where $k^2 = \omega^2 \mu_0 \epsilon$. But $\nabla \times \nabla \times \mathbf{E} = \nabla\nabla \cdot \mathbf{E} - \nabla^2 \mathbf{E}$ and $\nabla \cdot \mathbf{E} = 0$, so we have

$$\nabla^2 E_z + k^2 E_z = j\omega\mu_0 J_z \qquad (4.179)$$

In order to solve this equation we let

$$E_z = \sum_{n=0}^{\infty} \sum_{m=0}^{\infty} C_{nm} \cos \frac{n\pi x}{a} \cos \frac{m\pi y}{b}$$

When we substitute into Eq. (4.179) and take note of the fact that there is no variation with z we obtain

$$\sum_{n=0}^{\infty} \sum_{m=0}^{\infty} C_{nm} (k^2 - k_{nm}^2) \cos \frac{n\pi x}{a} \cos \frac{m\pi y}{b} = jk_0 Z_0 J_z \qquad (4.180)$$

where $k_{nm}^2 = (n\pi/a)^2 + (m\pi/b)^2$. The above equation can be viewed as a Fourier series expansion of the current J_z. We can solve for the C_{nm} using Fourier series analysis. We find that

$$C_{nm} = \frac{\epsilon_{0n}\epsilon_{0m}}{ab} \int_0^b \int_0^a \frac{jk_0 Z_0 J_z(x, y) \cos(n\pi x/a) \cos(m\pi y/b)}{k^2 - k_{nm}^2} dx \, dy \qquad (4.181)$$

where

$$\epsilon_{0n} = \begin{cases} 1 & n = 0 \\ 2 & n > 0 \end{cases}$$

From this solution we see that the patch behaves like a cavity, with k_{nm} being the resonant wave number of the nmth mode. Only that mode for which $k \approx k_{nm}$ is excited with a large amplitude. Since all losses were neglected, C_{nm} becomes infinite if $k = k_{nm}$, which is typical of the response function for an ideal loss-free resonator. When dielectric losses are included, that is, $k^2 = \omega^2 \mu_0 (\epsilon' - j\epsilon'')$ and copper losses are taken into account, the effect is to replace the loss-free resonant frequency ω_{nm} of the nmth mode by a complex resonant frequency. We can express $k^2 - k_{nm}^2$ in the form

$$\mu_0 \epsilon \left[\omega^2 - \frac{k_{nm}^2}{\mu_0(\epsilon' - j\epsilon'')} \right] = \mu_0 \epsilon \left[\omega^2 - \frac{k_{nm}^2}{\mu_0 \epsilon'} \left(1 - \frac{j\epsilon''}{\epsilon'} \right)^{-1} \right]$$

The complex resonant radian frequency ω'_{nm} is given by

$$\omega'_{nm} = \frac{k_{nm}}{\sqrt{\mu_0 \epsilon'}} \left(1 - j\frac{\epsilon''}{\epsilon'} \right)^{-1/2} \approx \frac{k_{nm}}{\sqrt{\mu_0 \epsilon'}} \left(1 + j\frac{\epsilon''}{2\epsilon'} \right) \qquad (4.182)$$

since normally $\epsilon'' \ll \epsilon'$. The quality factor of the resonator due to dielectric loss is Q_d where

$$Q_d = \frac{\epsilon'}{\epsilon''} \qquad (4.183)$$

If we let $\omega_{nm} = k_{nm}/\sqrt{\mu_0 \epsilon'}$ then

$$\omega'_{nm} = \omega_{nm} \left(1 + \frac{j}{2Q_d} \right) \qquad (4.184)$$

There will also be losses in the metal patch and ground plane due to the finite conductivity. These losses may be found by means of the methods described in Sec. 2.1 and are given by

$$P_l = 2 \frac{1}{\sigma \delta_s} \int_0^b \int_0^a \tfrac{1}{2} |\mathbf{H}_{\tan}|^2 \, dx \, dy$$

$$= \frac{|C_{nm}|^2}{\sigma \delta_s (k_0 Z_0)^2} \frac{ab}{\epsilon_{0n} \epsilon_{0m}} k_{nm}^2$$

for the TM_{nm} mode. The total stored energy W at the resonant frequency is $W_e + W_m = 2W_e$, since the stored electric energy W_e equals the stored magnetic energy W_m at resonance. Hence for the nmth mode

$$W = 2 \frac{\epsilon'}{4} h \int_0^b \int_0^a |C_{nm}|^2 \cos^2 \frac{n\pi x}{a} \cos^2 \frac{m\pi y}{b} \, dx \, dy$$

$$= \frac{\epsilon'}{2} h \frac{|C_{nm}|^2 ab}{\epsilon_{0n} \epsilon_{0m}}$$

The quality factor due to conductor loss for the nmth mode is given by

$$Q = \omega \frac{W}{P_l} = \frac{\omega \epsilon' h \sigma \delta_s (k_0 Z_0)^2}{2k_{nm}^2}$$

The total cavity Q, which we will call Q_{nm}, for the nmth mode is

$$Q_{nm} = \left(\frac{1}{Q} + \frac{1}{Q_d}\right)^{-1} = \left[\frac{\epsilon''}{\epsilon'} + \frac{2k_{nm}^2}{\omega \epsilon'(k_0 Z_0)^2 h \sigma \delta_s}\right]^{-1} \tag{4.185}$$

In this equation σ is the conductivity of the metal in siemens per meter and δ_s is the skin depth. In place of Eq. (4.184) the complex resonant frequency is given by

$$\omega'_{nm} = \omega_{nm}\left(1 + \frac{j}{2Q_{nm}}\right) \tag{4.186}$$

when the losses due to the finite conductivity are included.†

For the microstrip antenna the desired mode is the TM_{10} mode. If we choose $k \approx k_{10}$ this mode is excited with a large amplitude. In Eq. (4.181) $\cos \pi x/a$ is nearly equal to $\cos \pi x_0 a$ over the region occupied by the current $J_z(x, y)$ which lies on the surface of the probe. Thus we can readily evaluate Eq. (4.181) for C_{10} to obtain

$$C_{10} = \frac{2jk_0 Z_0 I_0 \cos(\pi x_0/a)}{ab(k^2 - k_{10}^2)} \tag{4.187}$$

When $\omega = \omega_{10}$ the value of C_{10} is given by

$$C_{10} = -\frac{2k_0 Z_0 Q_{10}\epsilon' I_0 \cos(\pi x_0/a)}{k_{10}^2 ab\epsilon} \tag{4.188}$$

The amplitude remains finite at the resonant frequency but will be large whenever the quality factor Q_{10} is large.

From the definition of Q_{10} we have

$$P_T = \frac{2\omega W_e}{Q_{10}}$$

for the total dissipated power. We can define an input resistance, as seen from the coaxial line, by the relationship $\frac{1}{2}|I_0|^2 R_{in} = P_T$. Hence at resonance we find that

$$R_{in} = \frac{4\omega W_e}{Q_{10}|I_0|^2} = \frac{2\omega \epsilon' h[k_0 Z_0 \epsilon' \cos(\pi x_0/a)]^2 Q_{10}}{k_{10}^4 ab|\epsilon|^2} \tag{4.189}$$

Note that R_{in} can be changed by changing the probe position x_0, since it

---

† For a more complete discussion of lossy cavities see R. E. Collin, *Foundations for Microwave Engineering*, McGraw-Hill Book Company, New York, 1965, Chap. 7.

depends on $\cos^2(\pi x_0/a)$. By choosing x_0 appropriately the cavity can be matched to the input coaxial line.

The above analysis is, of course, only applicable to a cavity with ideal open-circuit boundary conditions. In reality, power is lost from the cavity by radiation, and there is additional energy storage in the fringing fields that exist beyond the boundaries of the cavity. There may also be power lost due to the excitation of propagating surface wave modes along the dielectric substrate. The surface-wave loss is very small, provided the dielectric thickness is small, say, $h < 0.1\lambda_0/\sqrt{\kappa}$, where κ is the dielectric constant ϵ'/ϵ_0 of the substrate material. The effect of radiation loss and energy storage outside the cavity can be accounted for by modeling the cavity walls as walls having a finite complex admittance instead of zero admittance. The boundary conditions then become

$$\mathbf{H} = Y_w \mathbf{n} \times \mathbf{E}$$

where $\mathbf{n}$ is a unit outward normal at each sidewall and Y_w is the wall admittance in siemens. The wall admittance Y_w will, in general, have a different value on the walls along x than on those along y.

We will use the above boundary conditions to obtain a solution for the perturbed TM_{10} mode. It will be convenient to choose the origin at the center of the rectangular patch, as shown in Fig. 4.78. For the TM_{10} mode the fields are given by

$$E_z = C_{10} \sin k_x x \cos k_y y \qquad (4.190a)$$

$$jk_0 Z_0 \mathbf{H} = -\nabla \times \mathbf{E} = \mathbf{a}_z \times \nabla E_z$$

$$= \mathbf{a}_x C_{10} k_y \sin k_x x \sin k_y y + \mathbf{a}_y C_{10} k_x \cos k_x x \cos k_y y \qquad (4.190b)$$

where $k_x \approx \pi/a$ and $k_y \approx 0$ for the perturbed mode. The boundary condition $H_y = -Y_{wx} E_z$ at $x = a/2$ gives

$$\tan k_x \frac{a}{2} = -\frac{k_x}{\alpha_x} \qquad (4.191a)$$

where $\alpha_x = jk_0 Z_0 Y_{wx}$. At $y = b/2$ the boundary condition is $H_x = Y_{wy} E_z$, which becomes

$$\cot k_y \frac{b}{2} = \frac{k_y}{\alpha_y} \qquad (4.191b)$$

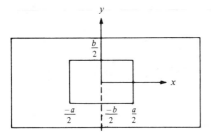

Figure 4.78 Coordinate system for analysis of a microstrip antenna.

where $\alpha_y = jk_0Z_0Y_{wy}$. The equations for k_x and k_y can be expressed in an alternative form by using the expansion $\tan 2\theta = 2\tan\theta/(1 - \tan^2\theta)$. It is readily found that Eq. (4.191) becomes

$$\tan k_x a = \frac{2\alpha_x k_x}{k_x^2 - \alpha_x^2} \qquad (4.192a)$$

$$\tan k_y b = \frac{2\alpha_y k_y}{k_y^2 - \alpha_y^2} \qquad (4.192b)$$

The last equation suggests that $k_y = 0$ is a solution. However, from an examination of Eq. (4.191b) we see that this is not a valid solution.†
Carver gives the following expressions for α_x and α_y:

$$\alpha_x = jk_0Z_0Y'_{wx}F_x \qquad (4.193a)$$

$$\alpha_y = jk_0Z_0Y'_{wy}F_y \qquad (4.193b)$$

where $Y'_{wx} = 0.00836\dfrac{h}{\lambda_0} + j0.01668\dfrac{\Delta l}{\lambda_0}\kappa_e$

$$\Delta l = 0.412h\frac{\kappa_e + 0.3}{\kappa_e - 0.258}\frac{0.262 + b/h}{0.813 + b/h}$$

$$\kappa_e = \frac{\kappa + 1}{2} + \frac{\kappa - 1}{2}\left(1 + \frac{10h}{b}\right)^{-1/2}$$

$$F_x = 0.7747 - 0.5977\left(1 - \frac{b}{a}\right) - 0.1638\left(1 - \frac{b}{a}\right)^2$$

An expression for Y'_{wy} is apparently not available. However, along the $y = \pm b/2$ walls E_z has an odd variation with x, so very little radiation takes place from these walls. Thus it is a good approximation to simply choose $k_y = 0$, which corresponds to ideal open-circuit conditions along these walls. This corresponds to setting $\alpha_y = 0$ in Eq. (4.192b).

The transcendental equation (4.192a) must be solved for k_x. Since k_x is close to π/a we can approximate the equation by

$$\tan k_x a = \frac{2\alpha_x(\pi/a)}{(\pi/a)^2 - \alpha_x^2}$$

which can be readily solved by now letting $k_x a = \pi - \delta$ and using $\tan(\pi - \delta) = -\tan\delta \approx -\delta$. By this means we obtain

$$k_x = \frac{\pi}{a} + \frac{2\alpha_x\pi}{\pi^2 - (\alpha_x a)^2} \qquad (4.194)$$

---

† See Carver, op. cit. In his original paper, Carver assumed that $k_y = 0$ was an acceptable solution. This is a valid solution only when $Y_{wy} = 0$ so that $\alpha_y = 0$.

If greater accuracy is desired, then the procedure can be repeated using the above value for k_x on the right-hand side of Eq. (4.192a)

Let $k_x = k'_x + jk''_x$, and then the quality factor Q_r due to radiation loss is given by

$$Q_r = \frac{k'_x}{2k''_x} \tag{4.195}$$

The total Q_T for the cavity is

$$Q_T = \left(\frac{1}{Q_{10}} + \frac{1}{Q_r} \right)^{-1} \tag{4.196}$$

The resonant frequency is given by

$$\omega'_{10} = \frac{k'_x}{\sqrt{\mu_0 \kappa \epsilon_0}} \left(1 + \frac{j}{2Q_T} \right) \tag{4.197}$$

The input resistance seen by the probe may be found from Eq. (4.189) by replacing Q_{10} by Q_T. An expression for the input impedance Z_a may be obtained from an application of Eq. (2.61), which gives

$$Z_a = \frac{P_T + 2j\omega(W_m - W_e)}{\frac{1}{2}I_0 I_0^*}$$

where P_T now includes the radiated power as well as the dielectric and metal losses. The complex power radiated by the probe is given by

$$P_T + 2j\omega(W_m - W_e) = \frac{1}{2} \int_S \mathbf{E} \times \mathbf{H}^* \cdot \mathbf{n} \, dS$$

where the integration is over the surface of the probe. Since $\mathbf{E} \times \mathbf{H}^* \cdot \mathbf{n} = \mathbf{E} \cdot \mathbf{H}^* \times \mathbf{n} = -\mathbf{E} \cdot \mathbf{n} \times \mathbf{H}^* = -E_z J_z^*$ and $J_z = I_0/2\pi r_0$, where r_0 is the radius of the probe, we readily find that the contribution of the TM_{10} mode to Z_a is given by [see (Eqs. (4.177) and (4.187)]

$$-\frac{2jk_0 Z_0 h I_0 I_0^* \cos^2(\pi x_0/a)}{ab I_0 I_0^* \mu_0 \epsilon_0 \kappa (\omega^2 - \omega'^2_{10})} = -\frac{2j Z_0 h \cos^2(\pi x_0/a)}{\kappa k_0 ab} \frac{\omega^2}{\omega^2 - \omega_{10}^2 (1 + j/2Q_T)^2}$$

The result follows from approximating the integral by $-\frac{1}{2}E_z(x_0)h I_0^*$. All of the nonresonant modes combine to give the inductive self-reactance of the probe. An approximate expression for the self-reactance is

$$j\omega L = \frac{j\omega h \mu_0}{2\pi} \ln \sqrt{\frac{ab}{\pi r_0^2}} \tag{4.198}$$

This expression is obtained by considering the probe as the inner conductor of a short section of coaxial transmission line, with inner radius r_0 and an outer radius R_0 chosen such that the patch area ab equals πR_0^2. When we combine the above expressions we obtain

$$Z_a = \frac{j\omega\mu_0 h}{2\pi}\ln\sqrt{\frac{ab}{\pi r_0^2}} - \frac{2jZ_0 h\,\cos^2(\pi x_0/a)}{\kappa k_0 ab}\frac{\omega^2}{\omega^2 - \omega_{10}^2(1 + j/2Q_T)^2} \quad (4.199)$$

for the input impedance of the microstrip antenna driven from a coaxial line located at $x = x_0$, $y = b/2$. Carver uses $j(Z_0/\sqrt{\kappa})\tan k_0 h \approx j\omega\mu_0 h/\sqrt{\kappa}$ for the self-reactance. This expression does not depend on the probe radius and consequently would not be expected to be very accurate. The self-reactance should vary like $\ln r_0$, so the equivalent coaxial-line model is expected to give a better estimate.

Radiation from Microstrip Antennas

When the substrate thickness h is very small, then the dielectric layer has only a minor effect on the radiation pattern. If we neglect its effect and use the expression given for E_z under ideal open-circuit boundary conditions, then the equivalent magnetic current in the aperture or sidewalls is given by

$$\mathbf{J}_{ms} = -\mathbf{n}\times\mathbf{E} = \mathbf{a}_z\times\mathbf{n}E_z$$

The equivalent electric current is zero because $\mathbf{n}\times\mathbf{H} = 0$ on the sidewalls. Since h is small we can assume that the total magnetic current $h\mathbf{J}_{ms}$ is concentrated as a line source just above the ground plane. By using image theory we can remove the ground plane and double the source strength. With reference to Fig. 4.79 we then find that, with $E_z = C_{10}\cos(\pi x/a)$, the equivalent free-space radiating magnetic-current line sources are

$$I_m = \begin{cases} -2hC_{10} & \text{along } x = 0, a \\ 2hC_{10}\cos\dfrac{\pi x}{a} & \text{along } y = 0 \\ -2hC_{10}\cos\dfrac{\pi x}{a} & \text{along } y = b \end{cases}$$

The two line sources along $y = 0$, b are oppositely directed and vary according to $\cos(\pi x/a)$ and hence produce no radiation in the z direction and relatively little radiation in other directions. The field from the line sources along $x = 0$, a add up in phase in the broadside direction. These two line sources give

$$A_{my} = -\frac{\epsilon_0}{4\pi r}e^{-jk_0 r}(1 + e^{jk_0 a\sin\psi\sin\phi})2hC_{10}\int_0^b e^{jk_0 y\cos\psi}\,dy$$

$$= \frac{-2hC_{10}\epsilon_0}{4\pi r}e^{-jk_0 r}(1 + e^{jk_0 a\sin\psi\sin\phi})\frac{e^{jk_0 b\cos\psi} - 1}{jk_0\cos\psi}$$

Note that we have chosen y as the polar axis, ψ as the polar angle, and ϕ as

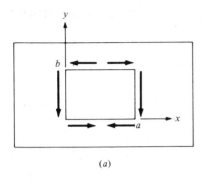

(a)

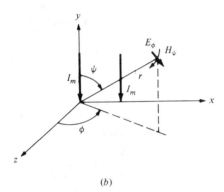

(b)

Figure 4.79 (a) Microstrip antenna. (b) Equivalent free-space magnetic-line sources for finding the radiated field.

the azimuth angle in the zx plane, as shown in Fig. 4.79. The factor in parentheses before the integral is the array factor and accounts for the second line source. The expression for A_{my} can be simplified and expressed in the form

$$A_{my} = -\frac{bhC_{10}\epsilon_0}{\pi r} e^{-jk_0 r + jk_0(a/2)\sin\psi\sin\phi + jk_0(b/2)\cos\psi}$$

$$\times \cos\left(k_0\frac{a}{2}\sin\psi\sin\phi\right)\frac{\sin[k_0(b/2)\cos\psi]}{(k_0 b/2)\cos\psi} \qquad (4.200)$$

In the radiation zone the fields are given by

$$H_\psi = j\omega\sin\psi A_{my} \qquad (4.201a)$$

$$E_\phi = -j\omega Z_0\sin\psi A_{my} \qquad (4.201b)$$

Since a and b are both typically around $\lambda_0/2$ in length, the pattern is broad and without side lobes in visible space.

APPENDIX: ASYMPTOTIC EVALUATION OF THE APERTURE RADIATION FIELD

The integral to be evaluated for large values of r is

$$\mathbf{E}(\mathbf{r}) = \frac{1}{4\pi^2} \int\int_{-\infty}^{\infty} \mathbf{f}(k_x, k_y) e^{-j\mathbf{k}\cdot\mathbf{r}} \, dk_x \, dk_y \qquad (A.1)$$

The technique that will be used is Rayleigh's method of stationary phase. The rationale underlying this method is as follows: We note that when r is very large $e^{-j\mathbf{k}\cdot\mathbf{r}}$ is a very rapidly oscillating function. Thus the contributions to the integral from various points in the $k_x k_y$ plane tend to cancel because there is a lack of in-phase addition from the various regions. An exception is a point where $\mathbf{k} \cdot \mathbf{r}$, which is a function of k_x and k_y, to first order does not vary with small changes in k_x, k_y. Such a point is called a *stationary phase point* and is characterized by the vanishing of the first derivatives of $\mathbf{k} \cdot \mathbf{r}$ with respect to k_x and k_y; that is,

$$\frac{\partial(\mathbf{k}\cdot\mathbf{r})}{\partial k_x} = 0 \qquad \frac{\partial(\mathbf{k}\cdot\mathbf{r})}{\partial k_y} = 0 \qquad (A.2)$$

At a stationary phase point the phase of $e^{-j\mathbf{k}\cdot\mathbf{r}}$ does not vary rapidly, and a nonzero contribution to the integral would be obtained from this region of the $k_x k_y$ plane. In the small region surrounding the stationary phase point, which we denote by $k_x = k_1$, $k_y = k_2$, the slowly varying function $\mathbf{f}(k_x, k_y)$ is put equal to its value at the stationary phase point. The integral that remains then only involves the function $e^{-j\mathbf{k}\cdot\mathbf{r}}$ and can be evaluated.

In order to facilitate the evaluation we express $\mathbf{k} \cdot \mathbf{r} = k_x x + k_y y + k_z z$ in spherical coordinates by using $x = r \sin\theta \cos\phi$, $y = r \sin\theta \sin\phi$, $z = r \cos\theta$; thus

$$\mathbf{k} \cdot \mathbf{r} = r(k_x \sin\theta \cos\phi + k_y \sin\theta \sin\phi + \sqrt{k_0^2 - k_x^2 - k_y^2}\cos\theta)$$

The stationary phase point is the point where

$$\frac{\partial \mathbf{k}\cdot\mathbf{r}}{\partial k_x} = 0 \qquad \frac{\partial \mathbf{k}\cdot\mathbf{r}}{\partial k_y} = 0$$

that is, where

$$k_x = k_1 = k_0 \sin\theta \cos\phi \qquad (A.3a)$$

$$k_y = k_2 = k_0 \sin\theta \sin\phi \qquad (A.3b)$$

A Taylor series expansion of $\mathbf{k} \cdot \mathbf{r}$ in vicinity of k_1, k_2 gives

$$\mathbf{k} \cdot \mathbf{r} = k_0 r + \frac{1}{2}\frac{\partial^2 \mathbf{k}\cdot\mathbf{r}}{\partial k_x^2}(k_x - k_1)^2 + \frac{1}{2}\frac{\partial^2 \mathbf{k}\cdot\mathbf{r}}{\partial k_y^2}(k_y - k_2)^2$$

$$+ \frac{\partial^2 \mathbf{k}\cdot\mathbf{r}}{\partial k_x \partial k_y}(k_x - k_1)(k_y - k_2) = k_0 r - (Au^2 + Bv^2 + Cuv)$$

$$(A.4)$$

where $u = k_x - k_1$, $v = k_y - k_2$, and A, B, and C are constants defined by this equation.

The asymptotic solution for $\mathbf{E(r)}$ is thus

$$\mathbf{E(r)} \sim \frac{e^{-jk_0r}}{4\pi^2} \mathbf{f}(k_0 \sin\theta \cos\phi, \ k_0 \sin\theta \sin\phi) \iint_{\Delta s} e^{j(Au^2 + Bv^2 + Cuv)} \, du \, dv \qquad \text{(A.5)}$$

where we have put $\mathbf{f}$ equal to its value at the stationary phase point and Δs is a small region centered on the stationary phase point which is at $u = v = 0$ in the uv plane. We now use the stationary phase argument again to note that $e^{j(Au^2 + Bv^2 + Cuv)}$ will oscillate very rapidly when u and v are not zero, since the constants A, B, and C are proportional to r and hence very large for large values of r. Thus the integral can be extended to cover the whole uv plane, since in the limit as r becomes infinite the contributions from u and v outside of Δs will cancel from phase interference. Hence we need to evaluate the following expression:

$$\iint_{-\infty}^{\infty} e^{j(Au^2 + Bv^2 + Cuv)} \, du \, dv \qquad \text{(A.6)}$$

We now write

$$Au^2 + Bv^2 + Cuv = \left(\sqrt{A}u + \frac{Cv}{2\sqrt{A}}\right)^2 - \frac{C^2v^2}{4A} + Bv^2$$

and put $\sqrt{A}u + (Cv/2\sqrt{A}) = w$ to get for the integral the result

$$I = \iint_{-\infty}^{\infty} e^{jw^2} \, e^{j(4AB - C^2)v^2/4A} \, \frac{dw}{\sqrt{A}} \, dv$$

Next we use the known result

$$\int_{-\infty}^{\infty} e^{j\gamma(x - x_0)^2} \, dx = \sqrt{\frac{\pi}{\gamma}} \, e^{j\pi/4} \qquad \text{(A.7)}$$

to evaluate the integrals over w and v. We then obtain

$$I = \frac{j2\pi}{\sqrt{4AB - C^2}} = 2\pi j \, \frac{k_0}{r} \cos\theta$$

upon using

$$A = \frac{r}{2}\left(\frac{1}{k_0} + \frac{k_1^2}{k_0^3 \cos^2\theta}\right)$$

$$B = \frac{r}{2}\left(\frac{1}{k_0} + \frac{k_2^2}{k_0^3 \cos^2\theta}\right)$$

$$C = \frac{k_1 k_2 r}{k_0^3 \cos^2\theta}$$

Our final result is

$$E(r) \sim \frac{jk_0 \cos\theta}{2\pi r} e^{-jk_0 r} \mathbf{f}(k_0 \sin\theta \cos\phi, \ k_0 \sin\theta \sin\phi) \tag{A.8}$$

with

$$\mathbf{f}_t(k_x, k_y) = \iint_{S_a} \mathbf{E}_a(x, y) \, e^{jk_x x + jk_y y} \, dx \, dy \tag{A.9}$$

PROBLEMS

4.1 On a rectangular aperture as shown in Fig. 4.2a the aperture field is given by

$$\mathbf{E}_a = E_0 \mathbf{a}_x \cos^2 \frac{\pi x}{2a} \qquad |x| \le a \qquad |y| \le b$$

Find the radiated field. Find the beam width in the xz or $\phi = 0$ plane. Find the amplitude of the first side lobe in this plane. Sketch the radiation pattern as a function of u. (See hint in Prob. 4.2.)

4.2 For an aperture field of the form

$$\mathbf{E}_a = E_0 \mathbf{a}_x (1 + C \cos lx) \qquad |x| \le a \qquad |y| \le b$$

on a rectangular aperture find the radiated field and show that the effect on the pattern as a function of u is to superimpose on the uniform aperture-field pattern two similar patterns of relative amplitude $C/2$ and positioned at $u = \pm u_0 = \pm la$. *Hint*: Express $\cos lx$ as $\frac{1}{2}(e^{-jlx} + e^{jlx})$ and compare it with Eqs. (4.23) and (4.24).

4.3 Determine the effect that a small quadratic phase error has on the radiation pattern from a rectangular aperture. Assume that

$$\mathbf{E}_a = E_0 \mathbf{a}_x e^{-j\alpha x^2} \qquad |x| \le a \qquad |y| \le b$$

and with $\alpha a^2 \ll 1$. Sketch the E-plane pattern when $\alpha a^2 = \pi/4$ and compare this with the pattern for the case $\alpha = 0$. *Hint*: $e^{-j\alpha x^2} \approx 1 - j\alpha x^2$. Now make note of the following operational properties of the Fourier transform [see Eq. (4.5)]:

$$\mathscr{F}_{k_x}^{-1} W(k_x) = w(x)$$

$$\mathscr{F}_{k_x}^{-1} \frac{dW(k_x)}{dk_x} = jxw(x)$$

so

$$\mathscr{F}_{k_x}^{-1} \frac{d^2 W(k_x)}{dk_x^2} = -x^2 w(x)$$

$$\mathscr{F}_x x^2 w(x) = -\frac{d^2 W(k_x)}{dk_x^2}$$

4.4 What is the required phase variation for the aperture field in the rectangular aperture of Fig. 4.2a to produce a radiation lobe maximum at $\theta = \pi/4$ in the xz plane? What is the total phase variation across the aperture from $x = -a$ to $x = a$? Show that this phase variation just compensates for the difference in the path length from the two sides of the aperture to the far-zone point of observation.

4.5 Sources at $z = -\infty$ radiate a plane wave $\mathbf{E} = E_0 \mathbf{a}_x e^{-jk_0z}$, $\mathbf{H} = H_0 \mathbf{a}_y e^{-jk_0z}$, $H_0 = E_0 Y_0$. The plane wave in $z \geq 0$ can be reproduced by radiation from secondary sources consisting of current sheets $\mathbf{J} = \mathbf{a}_z \times \mathbf{H}$, $\mathbf{J}_m = -\mathbf{a}_z \times \mathbf{E}$ on the $z = 0$ plane. Consider radiation from the current sheet $\mathbf{J} = \mathbf{a}_z \times \mathbf{H} = -\mathbf{a}_x H_0$. By symmetry this current sheet radiates a magnetic field $\mathbf{H}^+ = H_1 \mathbf{a}_y e^{-jk_0z}$, $z > 0$ and $\mathbf{H}^- = -H_1 \mathbf{a}_y e^{jk_0z}$, $z < 0$ and since $\mathbf{H}^+ - \mathbf{H}^- = \mathbf{J} = 2H_1$ we have $H_1 = J/2$. From $\nabla \times \mathbf{H} = j\omega\epsilon_0\mathbf{E}$ one finds that $\mathbf{E}^+ = Z_0 H_1 \mathbf{a}_x e^{-jk_0z}$, $z > 0$ and $\mathbf{E}^- = Z_0 H_1 \mathbf{a}_x e^{jk_0z}$, $z < 0$. By a similar procedure find the fields $\mathbf{H}_m^{\pm}$, $\mathbf{E}_m^{\pm}$ radiated by the magnetic current sheet and thus show that the secondary sources reproduce the original field $\mathbf{E}$, $\mathbf{H}$ in $z > 0$ and give a zero total field in $z < 0$. For a magnetic current sheet $\mathbf{a}_z \times (\mathbf{E}_m^+ - \mathbf{E}_m^-) = -\mathbf{J}_m$ and $\mathbf{a}_z \times \mathbf{H}_m^+ = \mathbf{a}_z \times \mathbf{H}_m^-$ at $z = 0$; that is, tangential $\mathbf{E}$ is discontinuous and tangential $\mathbf{H}$ is continuous across the magnetic current sheet (see Fig. P4.5).

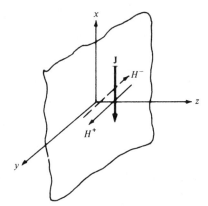

Figure P4.5

4.6 Derive an expression for the radiated electric field of a TE_{10} mode in a rectangular waveguide by using both the tangential electric and magnetic fields in the aperture. The aperture fields are given by Eq. (4.41). Compare the results with those given in the text, which are based on the tangential electric field in the aperture. Show that the directivity differs from that given by Eq. (4.45) by the factor $(k_0 + \beta)^2/4k_0^2$.

4.7 Assume that the field in the H-plane horn is a cylindrical wave, as shown in Fig. 4.8. Show that the phase of the field in the aperture is described by the function $e^{-jk_0[(R_1^2+x^2)^{1/2}-R_1]}$. When $a' \ll 2R_1$ the binomial expansion may be used to give $e^{-jk_0x^2/2R_1}$. The results of Prob. 4.3 may now be applied.

4.8 The electric field in a rectangular aperture is given by the following finite Fourier series:

$$E_y = E_0 \sum_{n=-N}^{N} C_n e^{-j2n\pi x/a}$$

$$-\frac{a}{2} \leq x \leq \frac{a}{2} \qquad -\frac{b}{2} \leq y \leq \frac{b}{2}$$

Show that the radiation pattern in the $\phi = 0$ plane is proportional to

$$f_y(u) = a \sum_{n=-N}^{N} C_n \frac{\sin(u - n\pi)}{u - n\pi}$$

where $u = k_0(a/2) \sin \theta$. Each term in the series represents a displaced uniform aperture-field pattern. If $u = m\pi$, every term in the series is zero except the term $n = m$. Show that $C_m = a^{-1} f_y(m\pi)$. If the desired pattern is specified by its values at the $(2N + 1)$ points $u = m\pi$, $m = 0, \pm 1, \pm 2, \ldots, \pm N$, that is, $\sin \theta_m = m\lambda_0/a$, then this pattern is obtained from the aperture field with the Fourier coefficients determined as above. This aperture-field synthesis method is called the *Woodward synthesis method.*

4.9 If the number of elements in a broadside Chebyshev array is increased to an infinite number, the resultant pattern becomes $f_y(u) = \cosh(R^2 - u^2)^{1/2}$ where $\cosh R$ is the main lobe to side-lobe amplitude ratio and u is given in Prob. 4.8. Plot this pattern as a function of u. Note that all the side lobes have the same peak value. This is the pattern of the ideal Taylor line source, but it cannot be realized because it requires an aperture field that is infinite at the edges $x = \pm a/2$. (See T. T. Taylor, "Design of Line Source Antennas for Narrow Beamwidth and Low Side Lobes," *IRE Trans.*, vol. AP-3, Jan. 1955, pp. 16–28.) *Hint*: Note that $\cosh j\omega = \cos \omega$.

4.10 Show that the zeros in the pattern function given in Prob. 4.9 occur at $u_n = \pm[R^2 + (2n - 1)^2\pi^2/4^2]^{1/2}$, $n = 1, 2, 3, 4, \ldots$. An approximation to the ideal Taylor line source pattern is obtained by replacing all of the zeros in the pattern function given in Prob. 4.9 for $n \geq \bar{n}$ by those associated with a uniform aperture-field pattern $(\sin u)/u$. This approximate ideal pattern is given by

$$f_y(u) = \cosh R \, \frac{\sin u}{u} \left[\prod_{n=1}^{\bar{n}-1} \frac{1 - (u/u_n)^2}{1 - (u/n\pi)^2} \right]^{-1}$$

Using the results of Prob. 4.8 to show that the Fourier coefficients for the required aperture field are given by

$$aC_m = -\tfrac{1}{2} \cosh R \cos m\pi \prod_{n=1}^{\bar{n}-1} 1 - \left(\frac{m\pi}{u_n}\right)^2 \prod_{\substack{n=1 \\ n \neq m}}^{\bar{n}-1} \left(1 - \frac{m^2}{n^2}\right)$$

Hint: Use l'Hospital's rule to evaluate the term

$$\lim_{u \to m\pi} \frac{\sin u}{1 - (u/m\pi)^2}$$

4.11 For a uniform aperture field in a square aperture $|x| \leq a$, $|y| \leq a$, show that the side lobes in the $\phi = \pm 45°$ planes are much smaller than in the principal planes. What is the relative value of the first side lobe in decibels in the $\phi = 0°$ plane and in the $\phi = 45°$ plane?

4.12 Find expressions for the E- and H-plane patterns for the TE_{11} mode in a circular waveguide by using both the tangential electric and magnetic fields in the aperture. The electric field is given by Eq. (4.46). The tangential magnetic field is given by $H_y = Y_w E_x$, $H_x = -Y_w E_y$, where the mode admittance $Y_w = \beta Y_0/k_0$ and $\beta = [k_0^2 - (1.84/a)^2]^{1/2}$ is the propagation constant. *Hint*: see Eq. (4.37) and compare the Fourier transforms for g_x and f_y and g_y and f_x.

4.13 A rectangular waveguide of dimensions $a = 0.9$ in and $b = 0.4$ in is flared in both the E and H planes to form a pyramidal horn. Design an optimum-gain horn to give a directivity of 15 dB. What are the aperture dimensions a' and b' and the axial length of the horn? $\lambda_0 = 3$ cm.

4.14 A plane wave with electric field

$$\mathbf{E}_i = E_0 \mathbf{a}_z \, e^{-jk_0(x \cos \theta_i + y \sin \theta_i)}$$

is incident on an air-dielectric interface. The reflected and transmitted fields are

$$\mathbf{E}_r = \Gamma E_0 \mathbf{a}_z \, e^{-jk_0(-x \cos \theta_i + y \sin \theta_i)}$$

$$\mathbf{E}_t = T E_0 \mathbf{a}_z \, e^{-jk(x \cos \theta_r + y \sin \theta_r)}$$

as shown in Fig. P4.14. Find the magnetic field for each wave. By matching the tangential field components at the boundary obtain expressions for the reflection coefficient Γ and transmission coefficient T. Note that $k = \sqrt{\kappa} \, k_0$ and that the fields must have the same propagation-phase constant along y in order to satisfy the boundary conditions for all y. This condition will lead to Snell's law of refraction. State this law.

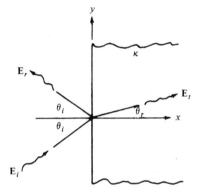

Figure P4.14

4.15 Figure P4.15 shows a stepped microwave lens. Show that the surface of the Kth zone is given by

$$r = \frac{(n-1)f - (K-1)\lambda_0}{n \cos \theta - 1}$$

Hint: At each step the ray path length is reduced by the equivalent of a 360° change in phase delay.

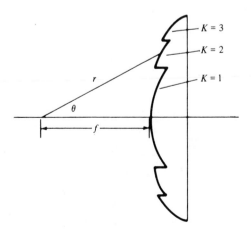

Figure P4.15

4.16 The effect of feed blockage on the pattern of a paraboloidal reflector may be evaluated approximately by assuming that the part of the aperture that corresponds to the area of the feed horn projected onto the aperture surface does not contribute to the radiation field, as shown in Fig. P4.16. Consider a uniformly illuminated circular aperture of radius a. The projection of the feed-horn area onto the aperture plane is a circle of radius $r_0 = a/10$. The radiation field is then the field of a uniform aperture of radius a minus the field from an aperture of radius r_0. Find the resultant radiated field and determine the effect that blockage of the aperture by the feed has on the maximum on-axis gain and the amplitude of the first side lobe.

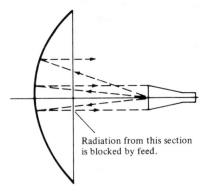

Radiation from this section is blocked by feed.

Figure P4.16

4.17 Find the equation for the subreflector in the cassegrain feed system shown in Fig. P4.17. Note that all ray paths OP + PR + RS are equal, as are the paths QP + PR + RS. Thus OP − QP must be equal to a constant $f - 2d$ where d is shown in the figure. If the subreflector radius b is given then $d = b \cot \psi/2$ where ψ is the angular aperture of the paraboloid.

$$Answer: \ r = \frac{2(f-d)d}{f(\cos\theta - 1) + 2d}$$

where f is the paraboloid focal length.

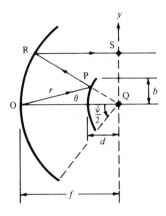

Figure P4.17

4.18 In a cassegrain antenna system the feed has an axially uniform power radiation pattern $P_f(\theta)$. With reference to Fig. P4.17 derive an expression for the power distribution $P(y)$ on the aperture focal plane. *Hint*: Consider a ray bundle originating at 0 and use power conservation in a ray tube.

4.19 Consider two real scalar functions $E_0(x, y)$ and $E_1(x, y)$. The Schwartz inequality states that

$$\left| \int_S E_0 E_1 \, dx \, dy \right|^2 \le \int_S E_0^2 \, dx \, dy \int_S E_1^2 \, dx \, dy$$

where S is a given surface in the xy plane. Use this theorem to prove that for all constant-phase, linearly polarized aperture fields the uniform aperture field gives the largest aperture directivity. *Hint*: The aperture directivity equals $(4\pi/\lambda_0^2)\eta_A S$ where S is the aperture area. Use Eq. (4.76) for η_A, let E_0 be a constant and E_1 be an arbitrary aperture field and show that $\eta_A \le 1$, with the equality holding only if E_1 is a constant.

4.20 A paraboloidal antenna with $f/2a = 0.4$ has a prime-focus feed with a gain function $g(\theta) = 10 \cos^4 \theta$. Find the required diameter of the reflector in order to obtain an antenna gain of 40 dB at 10 GHz. The feed has negligible loss. Find the efficiency $\eta_s \eta_A$.

4.21 A feed with a gain function $14 \cos^6 \theta$ is to be used with a paraboloidal reflector in an optimum design. The required gain is 50 dB at 12 GHz. Find the required diameter and focal length of the reflector.

4.22 A paraboloidal reflector is illuminated by a half-wave dipole antenna located at the focus. The radiation pattern of the dipole is given by

$$\mathbf{E} = \frac{jI_0 Z_0}{2\pi r} e^{-jk_0 r} \frac{\cos(\pi/2 \cos \psi)}{\sin \psi} \mathbf{a}_\psi$$

Find the electric field on the aperture plane that passes through the focal point. ψ is the polar angle with respect to the dipole axis (x axis). With respect to the coordinate system shown in Fig. 4.18, $\cos \psi = \sin \theta \cos \phi$, $\sin \psi = (1 - \cos^2 \psi)^{1/2}$, $\mathbf{a}_\psi = (\mathbf{a}_\theta \cos \theta \cos \phi - \mathbf{a}_\phi \sin \phi)/\sin \psi$.

4.23 Derive Eq. (4.95) by using the far-field expression for $\mathbf{E}$ and integrating the Poynting vector over a large hemisphere (0 to 2π in ϕ, 0 to $\pi/2$ in θ). Note that $dk_x \, dk_y = k_0^2 \cos \theta \sin \theta \, d\theta \, d\phi$.

4.24 With reference to Eq. (4.115) show that when $e_{\phi'} = je_{\theta'}$ the phase-error efficiency $\eta_p = 1$ but the cross-polarization efficiency $\eta_x = 0.75$, provided $e_{\theta'}$ is real. Find η_p and η_x also for the case when $e_{\phi'} = ce_{\theta'}$ where $e_{\theta'}$ is real and c is a given complex number.

Answer: $\eta_x = \frac{3}{4} + \dfrac{\text{Re } c}{2(1 + |c|^2)}$

4.25 When $e_{\theta'}$ and $e_{\phi'}$ have zero phase show that the magnitude of the aperture field given by Eq. (4.107) is proportional to $(e_{\theta'}^2 \sin^2 \phi' + e_{\phi'}^2 \cos^2 \phi')^{1/2}$ and thus is proportional to the magnitude of the feed pattern given by Eq. (4.101). For this case the square of the aperture field is clearly proportional to the aperture power density $P(\rho, \phi)$ and hence to $g(\theta, \phi)$, as given by Eq. (4.72).

4.26 A paraboloidal antenna is illuminated by a circular waveguide feed excited with a TE_{11} mode. The guide radius is chosen equal to $0.48\lambda_0$ in order to achieve low cross polarization. The aperture field is required to be down by -10 dB at the edge. Determine the reflector diameter, focal length, and guide radius for an antenna system having a gain of 42 dB at 12 GHz. Neglect losses due to aperture blocking and feed losses.

4.27 Derive Eq. (4.126).

4.28 Derive Eq. (4.130).

4.29 Derive Eq. (4.147).

4.30 Find the conductances g_n in a five-element resonant Chebyshev slot array that will have side lobes 25 dB below the main lobe. Determine the slot offsets and spacing when a WR-90 rectangular waveguide is used at a frequency $f = 10$ GHz. For a WR-90 guide $a = 0.9$ in, $b = 0.4$ in. Note that since $d > \lambda_0/2$ Eq. (3.84) must be used for the design. Plot the pattern as a function of u and comment on the effect of nonoptimum spacing.

4.31 Find the required slot conductances for a 10-element array with uniform excitation. Assume $r = 0.15$. If this leads to values of g_n greater than 0.5, repeat the design using a larger value for r, say, 0.25.

4.32 A microstrip antenna is made from a rectangular patch with $a = 2$ cm, $b = 2.5$ cm, and $h = 0.2$ cm. The substrate has a permittivity $\epsilon = (2.5 - j0.002)\epsilon_0$. The patch and ground plane are made from copper with a conductivity $\sigma = 5.8 \times 10^7$ S/m.

    (*a*) Find the resonant frequency of the cavity by using Eq. (4.182) for the TM_{10} mode.

    (*b*) Find Q_d and Q_{10} for the cavity by using Eqs. (4.183) and (4.185).

    (*c*) Evaluate R_{in} by using Eq. (4.189) and $x_0 = a/4$.

4.33 For the antenna described in Prob. 4.32 find k_x and Q_r by using Eqs. (4.194) and (4.195). Compare Q_r with Q_{10}. The antenna efficiency is given by $\eta = Q_{10}/(Q_{10} + Q_r)$. Evaluate η. Also compute R_{in} at the resonant frequency as found from Eq. (4.197). Compare ω_{10} found in part (a) of Prob. 4.32 with that found from Eq. (4.197).

4.34 Carry out the steps needed to derive Eq. (4.199).

FIVE

RECEIVING ANTENNAS

Electromagnetic radiation from a transmitting antenna when received by another antenna results in a signal voltage at the output terminals of the latter. In most situations the general reciprocity principles of conventional network theory apply, so that the properties of an antenna used for receiving electromagnetic waves are very closely related to the corresponding properties of the antenna when it is used to radiate electromagnetic waves. Thus an antenna that exhibits a gain G in a given direction when radiating will exhibit the same gain when receiving electromagnetic radiation from the same direction, provided the incident wave has the right polarization.

It is convenient to characterize an antenna used for receiving purposes by an effective receiving area A_e such that the received power will equal the incident power per unit area multiplied by the effective area A_e. When this is done it is found that under matched polarization and impedance conditions the effective area A_e is related to the gain G as follows:

$$A_e = \frac{\lambda_0^2}{4\pi} G$$

This relationship applies to all antennas, even to a small dipole antenna for which it is not easy to visualize any particular area that might be considered to be related to A_e. For aperture-type antennas A_e is directly proportional to the aperture area but is generally smaller in value because of less than 100 percent aperture efficiency, a condition brought about by nonuniform illumination of the aperture.

The polarization properties of an antenna may be accounted for by using a complex effective length parameter **h** to describe the receiving properties of an antenna. If $\mathbf{E}_i$ is the incident electric field then **h** is defined in such a way that the received open-circuit voltage is given by

$$V_{oc} = \mathbf{h} \cdot \mathbf{E}_i$$

For dipole antennas **h** is proportional to the length of the antenna, although generally less because of the nonuniform current distribution on the antenna. The two characteristic parameters A_e and **h** are, of course, related to each other.

The first part of this chapter will develop the reciprocity principle for antennas and provide a derivation of the expressions for the effective receiving area and effective length. As part of this discussion the polarization properties of electromagnetic radiation will be examined.

In the application of a receiving antenna, noise must be taken into account since it determines the minimum useful signal that must be received. The effect of atmospheric noise and galactic noise, in particular, is a serious limiting factor at the lower frequencies. This noise is usually expressed in terms of an equivalent antenna-noise temperature. An interesting aspect of atmospheric noise at frequencies below 30 MHz is that it is often so large that no improvement in signal-to-noise ratio is obtained by using a highly efficient antenna. For this reason simple "loop stick" or ferrite-rod antennas will often suffice for receiving purposes, even though these antennas would be entirely inadequate for transmitting purposes. The theory of noise in antenna systems and its characterization are important aspects of a communication system and are therefore treated in detail here.

With the theory developed in this chapter, it is possible to evaluate satellite communication links, radar systems, and other line-of-sight communication systems, and several such examples are included for illustrative purposes.

5.1 RECIPROCITY THEOREM AND EFFECTIVE AREA FOR ANTENNAS

In order to establish the receiving properties of an antenna and to relate these to the properties of the antenna when it is used for transmitting it is necessary to first develop the reciprocity theorem known as the *Lorentz reciprocity theorem*. This is carried out in this section.

Let $\mathbf{E}_1$, $\mathbf{H}_1$, $\mathbf{J}_1$ and $\mathbf{E}_2$, $\mathbf{H}_2$, $\mathbf{J}_2$ be two sets of solutions to Maxwell's equations for which

$$\nabla \times \mathbf{E}_1 = -j\omega\mu_0\mathbf{H}_1$$

$$\nabla \times \mathbf{H}_1 = j\omega\epsilon_0\mathbf{E}_1 + \mathbf{J}_1$$

$$\nabla \times \mathbf{E}_2 = -j\omega\mu_0\mathbf{H}_2$$

$$\nabla \times \mathbf{H}_2 = j\omega\epsilon_0\mathbf{E}_2 + \mathbf{J}_2$$

Consider $\nabla \cdot (\mathbf{E}_1 \times \mathbf{H}_2 - \mathbf{E}_2 \times \mathbf{H}_1)$, which may be expanded to give

$$\nabla \times \mathbf{E}_1 \cdot \mathbf{H}_2 - \mathbf{E}_1 \cdot \nabla \times \mathbf{H}_2 - \nabla \times \mathbf{E}_2 \cdot \mathbf{H}_1 + \mathbf{E}_2 \cdot \nabla \times \mathbf{H}_1$$

The curl terms may be eliminated by using Maxwell's equations, and when this is done we obtain

$$\nabla \cdot (\mathbf{E}_1 \times \mathbf{H}_2 - \mathbf{E}_2 \times \mathbf{H}_1) = \mathbf{J}_1 \cdot \mathbf{E}_2 - \mathbf{J}_2 \cdot \mathbf{E}_1$$

since all other terms cancel. When we integrate over a volume V and use the divergence theorem we find that

$$\oint_S (\mathbf{E}_1 \times \mathbf{H}_2 - \mathbf{E}_2 \times \mathbf{H}_1) \cdot \mathbf{n} \, dS = \int_V (\mathbf{J}_1 \cdot \mathbf{E}_2 - \mathbf{J}_2 \cdot \mathbf{E}_1) \, dV \qquad (5.1)$$

which is our desired reciprocity theorem. We will use this result to find the power received by an antenna.

Consider the antenna shown in Fig. 5.1a and which, for convenience, we assume is connected to a signal generator by a coaxial transmission line. We assume that the antenna is perfectly conducting so that $\mathbf{n} \times \mathbf{E} = 0$ on the surface surrounding the antenna except on the reference plane in the coaxial line. The antenna is first considered as a transmitting antenna, and the field produced by the source is $\mathbf{E}_1$, $\mathbf{H}_1$. A reflector may also be assumed to be present. In this case the surface S_1 shown in Fig. 5.1a also encloses the reflector. The reflector is assumed to be perfectly conducting so that $\mathbf{n} \times \mathbf{E} = 0$ on its surface.

When the same antenna is used for receiving we can establish an open-circuit load condition at the reference plane by placing a short circuit $\lambda_0/4$ away, as shown in Fig. 5.1b. This makes the impedance looking towards the short circuit from the reference plane infinite (open-circuit condition). A current element $I_0 \Delta l$ located at a distance r from the antenna provides the source for the incident field $\mathbf{E}_2$, $\mathbf{H}_2$. This incident field is assumed to include the scattered field from the receiving antenna and reflector such that $\mathbf{n} \times \mathbf{E}_2 = 0$ on the conducting surfaces.

Under transmitting conditions the field in the coaxial transmission line, at the reference plane, will be

$$\mathbf{E}_1 = \frac{V \mathbf{a}_\rho}{\rho \ln(b/a)} \qquad \mathbf{H}_1 = \frac{Y_{in} V \mathbf{a}_\phi}{2\pi\rho}$$

where V is the voltage; Y_{in} is the admittance looking towards the antenna; ρ, ϕ are coordinates in the coaxial line cross section; and a, b are the inner and outer radii of the coaxial line conductors. Under open-circuit receiving conditions there will be a current node at the reference plane and a voltage maximum equal to the open-circuit received voltage V_{oc}. The field on the reference plane is thus

$$\mathbf{E}_2 = \frac{V_{oc} \mathbf{a}_\rho}{\rho \ln(b/a)} \qquad \mathbf{H}_2 = 0$$

In order to apply Eq. (5.1) we choose for S the surface S_1 around the

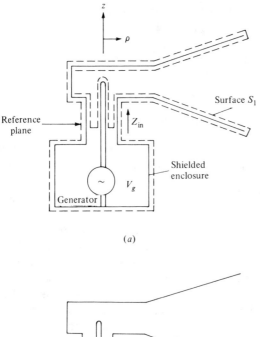

(a)

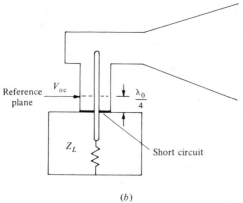

(b)

Figure 5.1 (a) Transmitting antenna.
(b) Receiving antenna.

antenna (and reflector, if present) and the surface S_∞ of a sphere of infinite radius. At infinity the fields $\mathbf{E}_1$, $\mathbf{H}_1$, and $\mathbf{E}_2$, $\mathbf{H}_2$ are spherical TEM waves for which $\mathbf{H}_1 = Y_0 \mathbf{a}_r \times \mathbf{E}_1$ and $\mathbf{H}_2 = Y_0 \mathbf{a}_r \times \mathbf{E}_2$. Hence on S_∞ we have

$$\mathbf{E}_1 \times \mathbf{H}_2 \cdot \mathbf{a}_r - \mathbf{E}_2 \times \mathbf{H}_1 \cdot \mathbf{a}_r = \mathbf{a}_r \times \mathbf{E}_1 \cdot \mathbf{H}_2 - \mathbf{a}_r \times \mathbf{E}_2 \cdot \mathbf{H}_1$$

$$= Z_0 \mathbf{H}_1 \cdot \mathbf{H}_2 - Z_0 \mathbf{H}_2 \cdot \mathbf{H}_1 = 0$$

so we get zero contribution from the integral over S_∞. From the integral over S_1 we only get a contribution from the reference plane in the coaxial feed line since $\mathbf{n} \times \mathbf{E}_1 = \mathbf{n} \times \mathbf{E}_2 = 0$ on the conductors.† For transmitting conditions we have $\mathbf{J}_1 = 0$, while $\mathbf{J}_2$ is the current density associated with the current element

---

† Lossy conductors can be treated by using the boundary condition $\mathbf{E}_i = Z_s \mathbf{n} \times \mathbf{H}_i$, $i = 1, 2$, as shown in Sec. 2.1. It is readily shown that $\mathbf{n} \times \mathbf{E}_1 \cdot \mathbf{H}_2 = \mathbf{n} \times \mathbf{E}_2 \cdot \mathbf{H}_1$ on the boundary of the lossy conductors, so again there is no contribution from this part of S_1.

$I_0 \Delta l$ when the antenna is used for receiving. Thus we readily find that Eq. (5.1) gives

$$\int_a^b \int_0^{2\pi} \left[-\frac{V_{oc}}{\rho \ln(b/a)} \mathbf{a}_\rho \times \frac{VY_{in}}{2\pi\rho} \mathbf{a}_\phi \right] \cdot (-\mathbf{a}_z \rho \, d\phi \, d\rho)$$

$$= \frac{V_{oc} VY_{in}}{\ln(b/a)} \int_a^b \frac{d\rho}{\rho} = VV_{oc} Y_{in} = -\int_V \mathbf{J}_2 \cdot \mathbf{E}_1 \, dV \tag{5.2}$$

Let us assume that the antenna radiates a linearly polarized field and let us choose $I_0 \Delta l$ oriented parallel to $\mathbf{E}_1$. Then Eq. (5.2) yields

$$V_{oc} = -\frac{I_0 \Delta l \, E_1(\mathbf{r})}{VY_{in}} \tag{5.3}$$

We may choose I_0 to be real, so

$$|V_{oc}| = I_0 \Delta l \left| \frac{E_1(\mathbf{r})}{VY_{in}} \right| = I_0 \Delta l \left| \frac{E_1(\mathbf{r})}{I_{in}} \right| \tag{5.4}$$

We will let the generator impedance Z_g be equal to the characteristic impedance Z_c of the coaxial line so that this part of the system is impedance-matched, as in Fig. 5.2a. Under transmitting conditions we then have $|V| = |Z_{in}/(Z_{in} + Z_c)| \, |V_g|$ and the power delivered to the antenna will be

$$\tfrac{1}{2} \operatorname{Re} VI_{in}^* = \tfrac{1}{2} \operatorname{Re} \frac{VV^*}{Z_{in}^*} = \frac{|V|^2}{2} \operatorname{Re} \frac{Z_{in}}{Z_{in}Z_{in}^*} = \frac{|V|^2}{2} \operatorname{Re} Y_{in}^* = \frac{|V_g|^2}{2} \frac{\operatorname{Re} Z_{in}}{|Z_{in} + Z_c|^2}$$

If the input power were uniformly radiated it would produce a power density

$$\frac{|V|^2 \operatorname{Re} Z_{in}}{2|Z_{in}|^2 4\pi r^2} \text{ W/m}^2$$

By definition of the gain $G(\theta, \phi)$ of the antenna, the actual power density produced in the direction θ, ϕ will be (we are putting $\operatorname{Re} Z_{in}/|Z_{in}|^2 = \operatorname{Re} Y_{in}^*$)

$$\frac{|V|^2 \operatorname{Re} Y_{in}^*}{8\pi r^2} G(\theta, \phi) = \frac{Y_0}{2} |E_1(\mathbf{r})|^2 \tag{5.5}$$

since the power density in a radiated spherical TEM wave is $\tfrac{1}{2} Y_0 |E_1(\mathbf{r})|^2$. When

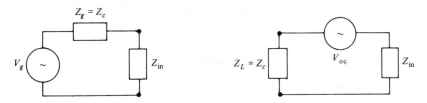

Figure 5.2 Equivalent circuits: (a) transmitting antenna and (b) receiving antenna.

we solve for $|\mathbf{E}_1|$ we obtain

$$|\mathbf{E}_1(\mathbf{r})| = \frac{|V|\sqrt{G \, \mathrm{Re} \, Y_{\mathrm{in}}^*}}{\sqrt{4\pi Y_0}\, r}$$

which may be used in Eq. (5.4) to give

$$|V_{\mathrm{oc}}| = \frac{I_0 \, \Delta l \sqrt{G \, \mathrm{Re} \, Y_{\mathrm{in}}^*}}{\sqrt{4\pi Y_0}\,|Y_{\mathrm{in}}|\,r} \tag{5.6}$$

Note that we have now assumed the current element $I_0 \, \Delta l$ to be located in the radiation zone (far zone) of the antenna so that Eq. (5.5) giving $|\mathbf{E}_1|$ will be valid.†

If we choose a load $Z_L = Z_c$, as in Fig. 5.2b, the received power will be (we use Thevenin's theorem)

$$P_{\mathrm{rec}} = \tfrac{1}{2}\,\mathrm{Re}\left|\frac{V_{\mathrm{oc}}}{Z_c + Z_{\mathrm{in}}}\right|^2 Z_c = \tfrac{1}{2}\frac{|V_{\mathrm{oc}}|^2 Z_c}{|Z_c + Z_{\mathrm{in}}|^2}$$

When we use Eq. (5.6) for V_{oc} in this expression we obtain

$$P_{\mathrm{rec}} = \frac{(I_0 \, \Delta l)^2 G(\theta, \phi) Z_c |Z_{\mathrm{in}}|^2 \, \mathrm{Re} \, Y_{\mathrm{in}}^*}{8\pi r^2 Y_0 |Z_c + Z_{\mathrm{in}}|^2}$$

$$= \frac{(I_0 \, \Delta l)^2 G(\theta, \phi) Z_c \, \mathrm{Re} \, Z_{\mathrm{in}}}{8\pi r^2 Y_0 |Z_c + Z_{\mathrm{in}}|^2} \tag{5.7}$$

The received power is dependent only on the field incident on the antenna and not on the source of that field. Consider therefore the case when the antenna is matched to the feed line, that is, $Z_{\mathrm{in}} = Z_c$, in which case Eq. (5.7) becomes

$$P_{\mathrm{rec}} = \frac{Z_0 (I_0 \, \Delta l)^2 G(\theta, \phi)}{32\pi r^2} \tag{5.8}$$

Now $Z_0 (I_0 \, \Delta l)^2 k_0^2 / (32\pi^2 r^2)$ is the free-space incident power density from the current element if we orient $I_0 \, \Delta l$ perpendicular to the radius vector $\mathbf{r}$ so that $\sin \theta_2 = 1$ (as in Fig. 5.3). Hence we can express Eq. (5.8) in the form

$$P_{\mathrm{rec}} = A_e P_{\mathrm{inc}} = \frac{\pi G(\theta, \phi)}{k_0^2} P_{\mathrm{inc}} = \frac{\lambda_0^2}{4\pi} G(\theta, \phi) P_{\mathrm{inc}} \tag{5.9}$$

The presence of the reflector manifests itself in the gain function $G(\theta, \phi)$, since the reflector is a part of the total antenna system if it is present. This fundamental result states that an antenna, *under matched impedance and polarization conditions,* has an effective receiving cross section or area A_e given

---

† When $I_0 \, \Delta l$ is located in the near zone we must use Eq. (5.3) to find V_{oc}, and $\mathbf{E}_1(\mathbf{r})$ is then the near-zone field radiated by the antenna.

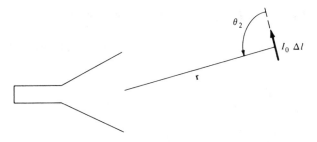

Figure 5.3 Orientation of current element for maximum received power.

by

$$A_e = \frac{\lambda_0^2}{4\pi} G(\theta, \phi) \tag{5.10}$$

When $Z_{in} \neq Z_c$ we have, from Eq. (5.7)

$$P_{rec} = \frac{\lambda_0^2}{4\pi} G(\theta, \phi) P_{inc} \left(\frac{4Z_c \operatorname{Re} Z_{in}}{|Z_c + Z_{in}|^2} \right)$$

where the term in parentheses reduces to 1 when $Z_{in} = Z_c$. For the mismatched antenna the reflection coefficient Γ is given by $\Gamma = (Z_{in} - Z_c)/(Z_{in} + Z_c)$, and $1 - |\Gamma|^2 = 1 - \Gamma\Gamma^*$ equals

$$1 - \frac{(Z_{in} - Z_c)(Z_{in}^* - Z_c)}{|Z_{in} + Z_c|^2} = \frac{(Z_{in} + Z_c)(Z_{in}^* + Z_c) - (Z_{in} - Z_c)(Z_{in}^* - Z_c)}{|Z_{in} + Z_c|^2}$$

$$= \frac{2Z_c(Z_{in} + Z_{in}^*)}{|Z_{in} + Z_c|^2} = \frac{4Z_c \operatorname{Re} Z_{in}}{|Z_{in} + Z_c|^2}$$

Thus

$$\frac{4Z_c \operatorname{Re} Z_{in}}{|Z_{in} + Z_c|^2} = 1 - |\Gamma|^2 \tag{5.11}$$

Hence under unmatched conditions we have

$$P_{rec} = \frac{\lambda_0^2}{4\pi} (1 - |\Gamma|^2) G(\theta, \phi) P_{inc}$$

$$= (1 - |\Gamma|^2) A_e P_{inc} \tag{5.12}$$

where $|\Gamma|^2$ is the power reflection coefficient for the unmatched antenna.

In deriving the above results we assumed that the antenna radiated a linearly polarized field so that we could orient the current element $I_0 \Delta l$ along E_1. This corresponds to matched polarization conditions. In general, if the incoming radiation is not properly polarized, the received power will be less than that given by Eq. (5.9) or Eq. (5.12). We examine this aspect of the problem in the next section.

5.2 POLARIZATION MISMATCH FOR ANTENNAS

In general, in a given direction, an antenna will radiate an electric field with an E_θ and an E_ϕ component that are not in phase. Thus let the far-zone radiated field be

$$E_\theta = E_0 \frac{e^{-jk_0 r}}{4\pi r} \qquad E_\phi = \tau\, e^{j\beta} E_0 \frac{e^{-jk_0 r}}{4\pi r}$$

in a given direction, where τ and β are real. Thus $E_\phi = \tau\, e^{j\beta} E_\theta$. In the time domain the fields are

$$E_\theta = \frac{E_0}{4\pi r} \cos(\omega t - k_0 r)$$

$$E_\phi = \frac{\tau E_0}{4\pi r} \cos(\omega t + \beta - k_0 r)$$

if we assume that E_0 is real. Let $k_0 r - \omega t = \alpha$, then

$$E_\theta = \frac{E_0}{4\pi r} \cos \alpha$$

and
$$E_\phi = \frac{\tau E_0}{4\pi r} (\cos \alpha \cos \beta + \sin \alpha \sin \beta)$$

To find the resultant total-field magnitude we eliminate the time as follows:

$$\frac{4\pi r E_\theta}{E_0} = \cos \alpha$$

$$1 - \left(\frac{4\pi r E_\theta}{E_0} \right)^2 = \sin^2 \alpha$$

From the expression for E_ϕ we can write

$$\left(\frac{4\pi r E_\phi}{\tau E_0} - \cos \beta\, \frac{4\pi r E_\theta}{E_0} \right)^2 = \sin^2 \beta \left[1 - \left(\frac{4\pi r E_\theta}{E_0} \right)^2 \right]$$

which can also be expressed as

$$\left(\frac{4\pi r E_\phi}{\tau E_0} \right)^2 + \left(\frac{4\pi r E_\theta}{E_0} \right)^2 - 2 \cos \beta\, \frac{(4\pi r)^2 E_\theta E_\phi}{\tau E_0^2} = \sin^2 \beta$$

or
$$\left(\frac{E_\phi}{\tau} \right)^2 + E_\theta^2 - \frac{2 \cos \beta}{\tau} E_\theta E_\phi = \frac{E_0^2 \sin^2 \beta}{(4\pi r)^2} \qquad (5.13)$$

This is the equation of an ellipse. At a given point in space the resultant field vector traces out an ellipse, once per period in time. If the direction of rotation is clockwise, looking in the direction of propagation, the field is said to be *positive* or *right-elliptical polarized*. If the direction of rotation is counter-clockwise the field is *negative* or *left-elliptical polarized*. If $\tau = 1$ and $\beta = \pm\pi/2$

then Eq. (5.13) reduces to

$$E_\phi^2 + E_\theta^2 = \frac{E_0^2}{(4\pi r)^2} \qquad (5.14)$$

which is the equation of a circle. For this case the field is circularly polarized, as is illustrated in Fig. 5.4.

It is convenient to express the far-zone field radiated by an antenna relative to that which a unit current element would radiate. Thus let the radiated field be

$$\mathbf{E} = \frac{jZ_0 k_0 I_{\text{in}}}{4\pi r} \mathbf{h} \, e^{-jk_0 r} \qquad (5.15)$$

where I_{in} is the input current to the antenna and equals VY_{in}, while $\mathbf{h} = h_\theta \mathbf{a}_\theta + h_\phi \mathbf{a}_\phi$ is a complex vector called the *effective complex length of the antenna*. [Compare Eq. (5.15) with

$$E_\theta = \frac{jZ_0 k_0 \, e^{-jk_0 r}}{4\pi r} (I_0 \, \Delta l) \sin \theta$$

for the field from a current element.] Note that $\mathbf{h}$ is a function of direction specified by the angles θ and ϕ.

In general, the field incident on an antenna is also elliptically polarized. In order to utilize Eq. (5.2) for the received open-circuit voltage it is convenient to think of the incident field as being produced by two current elements $I_\theta \, \Delta l \mathbf{a}_\theta$ and $I_\phi \, \Delta l \mathbf{a}_\phi$, as shown in Fig. 5.5. The field that current elements $I_\theta \, \Delta l$ and $I_\phi \, \Delta l$ produce at the receiving antenna is

$$E_\theta = \frac{-jk_0 Z_0 I_\theta \, \Delta l}{4\pi r} e^{-jk_0 r} \qquad E_\phi = \frac{-jk_0 Z_0 I_\phi \, \Delta l}{4\pi r} e^{-jk_0 r}$$

(The negative sign is due to the current orientations.) To reproduce the

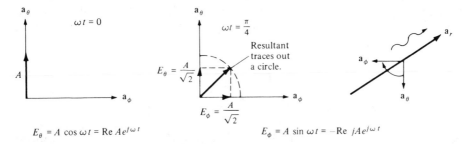

Figure 5.4 Positive or right-circular polarized field. Rotation is from $\mathbf{a}_\theta$ into $\mathbf{a}_\phi$. If $E_\theta = \text{Re } A e^{j\omega t}$ and $E_\phi = \text{Re } jA e^{j\omega t}$ the field is left- or negative-circular polarized.

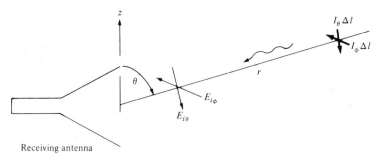

Figure 5.5 Arbitrary incident field produced by two current elements.

incident field we must choose

$$I_\theta \, \Delta l = \frac{-4\pi r \, e^{jk_0 r}}{jk_0 Z_0} E_{i\theta} \tag{5.16a}$$

$$I_\phi \, \Delta l = \frac{-4\pi r \, e^{jk_0 r}}{jk_0 Z_0} E_{i\phi} \tag{5.16b}$$

where $E_{i\theta}$ and $E_{i\phi}$ are the actual incident fields.

We now apply Eq. (5.2) and use Eqs. (5.15) and (5.16) to obtain

$$V_{oc} V Y_{in} = V_{oc} I_{in} = -\int_V \mathbf{J}_2 \cdot \mathbf{E}_1 \, dV$$

$$= -\frac{jZ_0 k_0 I_{in}}{4\pi r} e^{-jk_0 r} \mathbf{h} \cdot (I_\theta \, \Delta l \mathbf{a}_\theta + I_\phi \, \Delta l \mathbf{a}_\phi)$$

$$= I_{in} \mathbf{h} \cdot \mathbf{E}_i$$

Hence

$$V_{oc} = \mathbf{h} \cdot \mathbf{E}_i \tag{5.17}$$

This equation further illuminates why $\mathbf{h}$ is called the effective length of the antenna, since it shows that V_{oc} can be thought of as the voltage induced in a wire of length h when $\mathbf{h}$ and $\mathbf{E}_i$ are linearly polarized. The maximum value that $\mathbf{h} \cdot \mathbf{E}_i$ can have is $|\mathbf{h}||\mathbf{E}_i|$, and this occurs when $\mathbf{h}$ equals a real constant times the complex conjugate of $\mathbf{E}_i$. To the extent that $|\mathbf{h} \cdot \mathbf{E}_i| < |\mathbf{h}||\mathbf{E}_i|$ the antenna polarization is mismatched to that of the incident field. The polarization-mismatch factor p is defined as follows:

$$p = \frac{|\mathbf{h} \cdot \mathbf{E}_i|^2}{|\mathbf{h}|^2|\mathbf{E}_i|^2} \tag{5.18}$$

Thus the received power in general is given by

$$P_{rec} = (1 - |\Gamma|^2) p \frac{\lambda_0^2}{4\pi} G(\theta, \phi) P_{inc} \tag{5.19}$$

and is reduced by the factor p when the polarizations are not matched. The following example will illustrate the application of Eq. (5.18).

Example 5.1 Circular polarized antenna and incident field Let $\mathbf{h} = h_0(\mathbf{a}_\theta - j\mathbf{a}_\phi)$, which corresponds to a right-circular polarized antenna. Let the incident field be $\mathbf{E}_i = E_0(\mathbf{a}_\theta - j\mathbf{a}_\phi)$. The electric vector of the incident field rotates from $\mathbf{a}_\theta$ into $\mathbf{a}_\phi$, but because it corresponds to a wave propagating toward the antenna it represents a left-circular polarized field. From Eq. (5.18) we obtain

$$p = \frac{(h_0 E_0)^2[(\mathbf{a}_\theta - j\mathbf{a}_\phi) \cdot (\mathbf{a}_\theta - j\mathbf{a}_\phi)]^2}{4h_0^2 E_0^2} = 0$$

Thus a right-circular polarized antenna *will not* receive a left-circular polarized wave.

If $\mathbf{E}_i = E_0(\mathbf{a}_\theta + j\mathbf{a}_\phi)$ (right-circular polarized wave) then $\mathbf{E}_i = (E_0/h_0)\mathbf{h}^*$ and

$$p = \frac{(h_0 E_0)^2[(\mathbf{a}_\theta - j\mathbf{a}_\phi) \cdot (\mathbf{a}_\theta + j\mathbf{a}_\phi)]^2}{4h_0^2 E_0^2} = 1$$

This corresponds to perfectly matched polarization.

If $\mathbf{E}_i = E_0\mathbf{a}_\theta$ (linearly polarized incident field) then

$$p = \frac{(h_0 E_0)^2[(\mathbf{a}_\theta - j\mathbf{a}_\phi) \cdot \mathbf{a}_\theta]^2}{2h_0^2 E_0^2} = \tfrac{1}{2}$$

so a 3-dB loss occurs in receiving linear polarization with a circular polarized antenna. ∎

5.3 FRIIS TRANSMISSION FORMULA

For line-of-sight free-space propagation conditions it is relatively easy to derive an expression for the received signal in a communication link. With reference to Fig. 5.6 let the transmitting antenna have a gain $G_t(\theta_t, \phi_t)$ in the direction of the receiving antenna; i.e., the position angles of the receiving antenna relative to the transmitting antenna are θ_t, ϕ_t. The available input power to the transmitting antenna is P_{in}, and Γ_t is the reflection coefficient in the feed line.

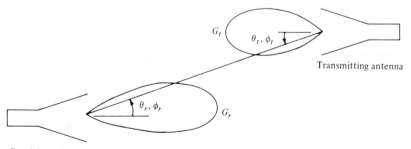

Receiving antenna

Figure 5.6 A transmitting and receiving system.

The total radiated power is thus $(1 - |\Gamma_t|^2)P_{in}$. In the direction of the receiving antenna a distance r away the power density per unit area will be $P_{inc} = (1 - |\Gamma_t|^2)P_{in}G_t(\theta_t, \phi_t)/4\pi r^2$. By using Eq. (5.12) we find that the received signal power is given by

$$P_{rec} = (1 - |\Gamma_r|^2)\frac{\lambda_0^2}{4\pi} G_r(\theta_r, \phi_r)(1 - |\Gamma_t|^2)\frac{P_{in}}{4\pi r^2} G_t(\theta_t, \phi_t) \qquad (5.20)$$

where Γ_r is the input reflection coefficient for the receiving antenna and $G_r(\theta_r, \phi_r)$ is the gain of the receiving antenna in the direction of the transmitting antenna. This formula is called the *Friis transmission formula*, and in the form given it assumes that the polarization of the incident field is matched to the polarization of the receiving antenna.†

If there is a polarization mismatch then the received signal is given by multiplying Eq. (5.20) by the polarization mismatch factor p given by Eq. (5.18); thus in general

$$P_{rec} = p(1 - |\Gamma_r|^2)(1 - |\Gamma_t|^2)\frac{P_{in}\lambda_0^2}{16\pi^2 r^2} G_r(\theta_r, \phi_r)G_t(\theta_t, \phi_t) \qquad (5.21)$$

In this latter case it is necessary to be able to determine the incident electric field $\mathbf{E}_i$ and the effective length $\mathbf{h}$ of the receiving antenna, or at least complex numbers proportional to these quantities so that the polarization mismatch p can be computed. The application of the above formulas will be illustrated in the following examples.

Example 5.2 Receiving properties of a half-wave dipole antenna Figure 5.7 illustrates a linearly polarized field $\mathbf{E}_i = -E_0\mathbf{a}_\theta$ incident on a half-wave dipole antenna where E_0 is the field strength in volts per meter at the dipole antenna. If we assume that the dipole antenna is connected to a matched load its effective receiving area is

$$A_e = \frac{\lambda_0^2}{4\pi} 1.64\left[\frac{\cos(\pi/2 \cos \theta_i)}{\sin \theta_i}\right]^2 \qquad (5.22)$$

where the gain function for the dipole antenna in the direction θ_i of the

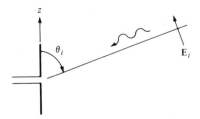

Figure 5.7 A plane wave incident on a dipole antenna.

† H. T. Friis, "A Note on a Simple Transmission Formula," *Proc. IRE.*, vol. 34, May 1946, pp. 254–256.

incident wave is

$$G(\theta_i) = 1.64 \left[\frac{\cos(\pi/2 \cos \theta_i)}{\sin \theta_i} \right]^2$$

The incident power per unit area is $|E_i|^2/2Z_0$, and hence the received power is

$$P_{rec} = A_e P_{inc} = 1.64 \left[\frac{\cos(\pi/2 \cos \theta_i)}{\sin \theta_i} \right]^2 \frac{\lambda_0^2 |E_0|^2}{8\pi Z_0} \tag{5.23}$$

The incident field has been assumed to be oriented in the same direction as the field would be when the dipole is radiating in the direction θ_i.

If the dipole antenna is used to transmit a field, then with an input current I_0 the radiated field would be [see Eq. (2.53)]

$$E_\theta = \frac{jk_0 I_0 Z_0}{4\pi r} e^{-jk_0 r} \frac{2\cos(\pi/2 \cos \theta)}{k_0 \sin \theta}$$

from which we see that the effective length of the half-wave dipole antenna is

$$\mathbf{h} = \frac{\lambda_0}{\pi} \frac{\cos(\pi/2 \cos \theta)}{\sin \theta} \mathbf{a}_\theta \tag{5.24}$$

The maximum effective length is λ_0/π, which is smaller than $\lambda_0/2$, and this is due to the fact that the current on the dipole is sinusoidal when it is radiating. If the current were uniform it would be found, as in Prob. 5.2, that the maximum effective length would be equal to the dipole length $\lambda_0/2$. The sinusoidal current distribution results in an inefficient use of the available antenna length.

We may use Eq. (5.17) to find the received open-circuit voltage, which is

$$V_{oc} = \mathbf{h} \cdot \mathbf{E}_i = -\frac{\lambda_0 E_0}{\pi} \frac{\cos(\pi/2 \cos \theta_i)}{\sin \theta_i}$$

If the dipole is terminated in a matched load $R_L = R_a = 73\,\Omega$, then from the equivalent circuit shown in Fig. 5.2b the received power will be

$$P_{rec} = \frac{1}{2} \left| \frac{V_{oc}}{R_L + R_a} \right|^2 R_L = \frac{|V_{oc}|^2}{8R_a} = \frac{\lambda_0^2 |E_0|^2}{8\pi^2 R_a} \left[\frac{\cos(\pi/2 \cos \theta_i)}{\sin \theta_i} \right]^2 \tag{5.25}$$

The result should, of course, agree with that given by Eq. (5.23). This will be the case, provided

$$\frac{1.64}{Z_0} = \frac{1}{\pi R_a}$$

or

$$R_a = \frac{Z_0}{1.64\pi} = \frac{120\pi}{1.64\pi} = \frac{120}{1.64} = 73$$

which is correct. Note that the maximum gain of the dipole antenna is defined by

$$G = 4\pi \frac{|I_0|^2(Z_0/8\pi^2)}{|I_0|^2(R_a/2)} = \frac{Z_0}{R_a} \tag{5.26}$$

where $|I_0|^2(R_a/2)$ is the input power. Thus $1.64R_a = Z_0$, as was found above. ∎

Example 5.3 Radar system The term *radar* is coined from the phrase radio detection and ranging. A radar is used to measure the range or distance to some object or target, such as an aircraft, that is located in the radiated beam of the transmitting antenna, as shown in Fig. 5.8. The transmitter sends a short pulse of sinusoidally time-varying energy. Some of this energy is reflected back towards the radar unit by the target and is received by the same antenna as is used for transmitting (a special TR or transmit-receive switch couples the antenna alternately between the transmitter and receiver). The elapsed time between the transmitted pulse and the received pulse is $2r/c$, where r is the range and c is the speed of light. By measuring this elapsed time the range r is determined.

The power incident on the target is given by

$$P_{inc} = (1 - |\Gamma_t|^2)P_{in} \frac{G(\theta, \phi)}{4\pi r^2}$$

The ability of the target to reflect energy back to the radar is described in terms of the target's radar cross section σ. The cross section σ is defined as that equivalent area which when multiplied by the incident power per unit area and which if it then scatters this power isotropically in all directions will produce the same incident returned power at the radar as the target actually does. Thus the equivalent power that is scattered isotropically is σP_{inc}, and the resultant incident power at the radar will be $P'_{inc} = \sigma P_{inc}/4\pi r^2$. The received power is thus given by

$$P_{rec} = (1 - |\Gamma_r|^2)A_e P'_{inc}$$

$$= (1 - |\Gamma_r|^2)(1 - |\Gamma_t|^2)P_{in} \frac{\lambda_0^2 \sigma G^2(\theta, \phi)}{(4\pi)^3 r^4} \tag{5.27}$$

where Γ_r and Γ_t are the reflection coefficients in the antenna feed line

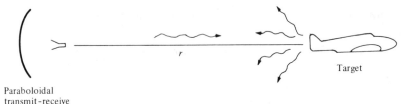

Paraboloidal
transmit-receive
antenna

r

Target

Figure 5.8 A radar system.

under receiving and transmitting conditions, respectively, and θ, ϕ give the target's position relative to the antenna bore sight. The above equation is called the *radar equation*. Note that because of the two-way transmission the received power decreases as the inverse fourth power of the distance. Hence there will be a decrease in received signal power by 12 dB for every doubling of the range.

The frequency of the returned signal from a moving target is different from the transmitted frequency (Doppler effect), and this change in frequency may be used to measure the velocity of the target in the radial direction. If f is the transmitted frequency and v is the velocity of the target in the radial direction, the received frequency is given by

$$f_r = f\left(1 \mp \frac{2v}{c}\right) \tag{5.28}$$

where the negative sign applies to a receding target and the positive sign applies to an approaching target. This is the principle on which police traffic-control radar operates. ∎

Example 5.4 Receiving properties of a small loop antenna Figure 5.9a shows a small loop antenna consisting of N turns wound into a circular coil of radius $a \ll \lambda_0$. The loss resistance of the coil is R_c, its radiation resistance R_a is given by Eq. (2.46), and L is the inductance of the loop. The usual way of using a loop antenna is as part of the tuned input circuit to the receiver. Thus we assume that the loop is tuned to resonance by a capacitor C and that a load R_L equal to the input impedance at resonance is connected in parallel with C, as in Fig. 5.9b. The input impedance of the tuned loop is

$$Z_{\text{in}} = \frac{(R + j\omega L)/j\omega C}{R + j\omega L - (j/\omega C)} = \frac{(R + j\omega L)/j\omega C}{R + j\omega L(1 - \omega_0^2/\omega^2)} \tag{5.29}$$

where $R = R_c + R_a$, $\omega_0^2 = 1/LC$. The unloaded Q, or quality factor, of the

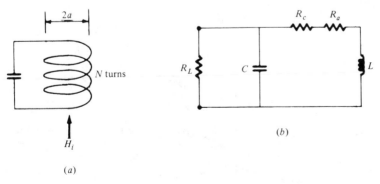

N turns

H_i

(a)

(b)

Figure 5.9 A tuned loop antenna.

loop antenna is $R/\omega L = Q$. For ω close to the resonant frequency ω_0, we can replace $1 - \omega_0^2/\omega^2 = (\omega^2 - \omega_0^2)/\omega^2$ by $2\omega_0(\omega - \omega_0)/\omega_0^2 = 2\,\Delta\omega/\omega_0$. In all other terms in Z_{in} we also replace ω by ω_0; thus

$$Z_{in} \approx \frac{1 + jQ}{j\omega_0 C[1 + (j2Q\,\Delta\omega/\omega_0)]}$$

$$\approx \frac{Q^2 R}{1 + (2jQ\,\Delta\omega/\omega_0)} \tag{5.30}$$

since for a small loop the Q is normally quite large and we have replaced $\omega_0 C$ by $R/\omega_0 LR = 1/QR$. At resonance the input impedance is essentially equal to $Q^2 R$ and R_L is chosen equal to this value for maximum power transfer. If we use the exact expression (5.29), then Z_{in} is a pure resistance equal to $Q^2 R$ but at the frequency

$$\omega = \omega_r = \omega_0\left(1 - \frac{1}{Q^2}\right)^{1/2} \tag{5.31}$$

Since Q is normally quite large $\omega_r \approx \omega_0$.

We will assume that the incident magnetic field $\mathbf{H}_i$ is along the axis of the loop antenna. The open-circuit induced voltage is then given by

$$V_{oc} = -j\omega\mu_0 H_i N\pi a^2$$

When we use Thevenin's theorem we then find that the power delivered to R_L at resonance is (see Prob. 5.3)

$$P_{rec} = \frac{Q^2|V_{oc}|^2}{8R_L} = \frac{Q^2 k_0^2 Z_0^2 N^2 (\pi a^2)^2 |\mathbf{H}_i|^2}{8R_L} \tag{5.32}$$

This result has been derived without using either the effective area A_e or effective length $\mathbf{h}$ for the loop antenna. We will now show that using these other parameters will lead to the same result.

When the loop antenna is used for transmitting, its efficiency is R_a/R because of coil losses. The maximum directivity is 1.5, so the maximum gain of the loop antenna is

$$G = \frac{1.5 R_a}{R} \tag{5.33}$$

and the effective receiving area will be

$$A_e = \frac{\lambda_0^2}{4\pi} G = 1.5 \frac{R_a \lambda_0^2}{4\pi R}$$

The incident power per unit area is $\frac{1}{2} Z_0 |\mathbf{H}_i|^2$ so the received power with a matched load is given by

$$P_{rec} = \frac{1.5 R_a}{2R} \frac{\lambda_0^2}{4\pi} Z_0 |\mathbf{H}_i|^2 \tag{5.34}$$

The radiation resistance R_a is given by

$$R_a = 20(k_0^2 N\pi a^2)^2$$

When we use this in Eq. (5.34) and note that $R = R_L/Q^2$ and $Z_0 = 120\pi$ we find that Eq. (5.34) is identical with Eq. (5.32).

The radiated electric field from a loop antenna with input current I_0 is [see Eq. (2.44)]

$$E_\phi = \frac{jk_0 I_0 Z_0}{4\pi r} e^{-jk_0 r}(-jk_0 N\pi a^2 \sin\theta)$$

from which we find

$$\mathbf{h} = -jk_0 N\pi a^2 \sin\theta \mathbf{a}_\phi = -j\omega\mu_0 Y_0 N\pi a^2 \sin\theta \mathbf{a}_\phi$$

If $\mathbf{H}_i = H_i \mathbf{a}_\theta$ then $\mathbf{E}_i = Z_0 H_i \mathbf{a}_\phi$, and the open-circuit voltage induced in the loop antenna will be

$$V_{oc} = \mathbf{h} \cdot \mathbf{E}_i = -j\omega\mu_0 H_i N\pi a^2$$

which is the same as that found earlier from the time rate of change of magnetic flux through the loop. Consequently the received power will then be given by Eq. (5.32), as found earlier. ∎

Example 5.5 Ferrite-core loop antenna The losses in a small loop antenna can be decreased by winding the coil on a ferrite core, which in practice is usually a long cylindrical rod, as shown in Fig. 5.10a. The cylindrical rod is essentially equivalent to the ellipsoid shown in Fig. 5.10b. For a loop antenna that is small compared with a wavelength, the incident magnetic field may be considered uniform over the extent of the ferrite core. For an ellipsoid with the applied magnetic field along the long axis the magnetic flux in the core is uniform and axially directed. If the permeability of the ferrite is μ the flux density is less than μH_i because of demagnetization effects. The ferrite core may be characterized by an effective relative permeability μ_e, which is given by

$$\mu_e = \frac{\mu_r}{1 + D(\mu_r - 1)} \tag{5.35}$$

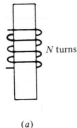

(a)

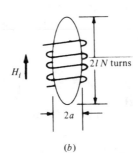

(b)

Figure 5.10 Ferrite-core loop antennas.

where $\mu_r = \mu/\mu_0$ is the relative intrinsic permeability of the ferrite and D is the demagnetization factor. For an ellipsoid with $l \gg a$ the demagnetization factor is given by

$$D = \frac{a^2}{l^2}\left(\ln\frac{2l}{a} - 1\right) \tag{5.36}$$

while for a sphere $D = 1/3$. Normally μ_r is large so that $\mu_e \approx D^{-1}$. Thus for a sphere the flux density is increased only by a factor of 3 over that in a similar air-core loop. For an ellipsoid with $l/a = 10$ we get $D = 0.02$, so $\mu_e \approx 50$.

If a ferrite-core loop antenna is used, the induced open-circuit voltage will be

$$V_{oc} = -j\omega\mu_e\mu_0 N\pi a^2 H_i \tag{5.37}$$

In practice the loop inductance is usually specified, and since the inductance is proportional to $\mu_e N^2$ we see that fewer turns would be used compared with an air-core loop antenna. For the same inductance the number of turns would be reduced by a factor $\mu_e^{-1/2}$, and hence V_{oc} is only increased by a factor of $\mu_e^{1/2}$ over that for an air-core loop. However, with fewer turns, the coil losses will be smaller and a higher Q and efficiency will result. There will also be some loss due to losses in the ferrite core, but these are usually small compared with the coil losses.

In practice the main advantage gained from using a ferrite core is a more compact or smaller loop antenna having an efficiency as good as that of a larger-diameter air-core loop. The inductance of a coil is proportional to its linear dimensions, so if we keep L fixed then $\mu_e N^2 a$ is a constant. Now V_{oc} is proportional to $\mu_e N a^2$ and hence proportional to $\mu_e^{1/2}a^{3/2}L^{1/2}$ so that increasing μ_e and a leads to improved performance. If $\mu_e = 50$ then the equivalent air-core loop antenna has a diameter about 3.7 times greater than an equivalent ferrite-core loop antenna.

If a ferrite-core loop antenna is used for transmitting, its radiation resistance is increased by a factor of μ_e^2, since, as Eq. (5.37) shows, the effective length is increased by μ_e, and hence the radiated field is also increased by this factor. Thus the radiated power is proportional to μ_e^2. ∎

Example 5.6 Satellite communication system The parameters that describe a typical synchronous orbit satellite communication system, as shown in Fig. 5.11, are listed below.

Ground station:

Antenna gain = 54 dB
Feed-line loss = 2 dB
Transmitter power = 1250 W, or 30.97 dBW (decibels above 1 W)
Range = 23,074 mi, or 37,132 km
Frequency = 14 GHz; $\lambda_0 = 2.14$ cm

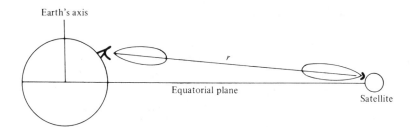

Figure 5.11 A satellite communication system.

Satellite:

> Antenna gain = 36 dB
> Transmitter power = 200 W, or 23.01 dBW
> Frequency = 12 GHz; λ_0 = 2.5 cm

In systems calculations it is convenient to express all factors involved in the fundamental equation (5.21) in decibels and then add these together to get P_{rec} expressed in decibels relative to 1 watt (dBW) or relative to 1 milliwatt (dBM). The product of antenna gain and transmitter power is the *effective isotropic radiated power EIRP*. For the up link this equals (54 + 30.97) dBW = 84.97 dBW. The factor $\lambda_0^2/(4\pi r)^2$ is called the *free-space propagation loss*. It is given by

$$20 \log\left(\frac{0.0214}{4\pi \times 37.13 \times 10^6}\right) = -206.8 \text{ dB}$$

The received power in dBW is the sum of the following factors expressed in decibels: EIRP, propagation loss, feed-line loss, receiving-antenna gain, plus any other losses such as polarization mismatch and antenna pointing error, if applicable. For the present example

$$P_{rec} \text{ in dBW} = 84.97 - 2 - 206.8 + 36 = -87.8 \text{ dBW}$$

and hence $P_{rec} = 1.6 \times 10^{-9}$ W.

For the down link the same parameters apply, except that the EIRP equals 59.01 dBW, and since $\lambda_0 = 2.5$ cm the free-space propagation loss is -205.4 dB. Hence at the ground station

$$P_{rec} \text{ in dBW} = 59.01 - 2 - 205.4 + 54 = -94.4 \text{ dBW}$$

or 3×10^{-10} W.

The above calculations do not have much significance as far as the performance of the system is concerned, since they do not include the effects of bandwidth, noise, and the type of modulation applied to the carrier (AM, FM, digital pulse, etc.). The effects of noise are discussed in the next section. ∎

5.4 NOISE IN COMMUNICATIONS SYSTEMS

In this section we will review some of the basic results pertaining to noise in a communication system. This background will be useful for the discussion of noise in an antenna, which will be treated in the following section. Our starting point will be Nyquist's formula governing thermal noise in a network.

Thermal Noise

The random motion of electrons in a resistor R at an absolute temperature T exhibits a random noise voltage across its terminals. The power spectral density of this noise voltage is given by Planck's distribution law

$$P_n = \frac{4hfR\,\Delta f}{e^{hf/KT} - 1} \tag{5.38}$$

where h is *Planck's constant* and $K = 1.38 \times 10^{-23}$ J/K (joules per kelvin) is *Boltzmann's constant*. For the normal range of temperatures and frequencies below the optical range the parameter hf/KT is very small so that $e^{hf/KT} \approx 1 + (hf/KT)$, and Eq. (5.38) can be approximated by

$$P_n = 4KTR\,\Delta f \tag{5.39}$$

The root-mean-square (RMS) noise voltage appearing across the terminals of a resistor is thus given by

$$V_n = 2\sqrt{KTR\,\Delta f} \tag{5.40}$$

which is *Nyquist's formula*. In Eq. (5.40) Δf is the bandwidth in which the noise is observed, and only positive frequencies are considered. The noise-voltage spectrum given by Eq. (5.39) is independent of frequency and hence is referred to as a *white-noise spectrum*.

Let a resistor R be connected to a one-port network, as shown in Fig. 5.12. We also assume that an ideal narrow-band lossless filter is inserted between R and the network. The resistor R will deliver thermal noise to the network in a narrow band of frequencies Δf centered on f. When the system is in thermodynamic equilibrium the network must deliver an equal amount of noise power to R at the same frequency. This principle, which is known as the *principle of detailed balancing*, enables one to evaluate the thermal noise from any frequency-dependent network. The use of a lossless narrow-band filter is

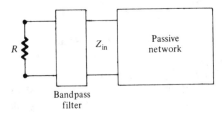

Bandpass
filter

Figure 5.12 A resistor connected to a passive network.

simply a method used to demonstrate that the flow of noise energy from R to the network and from the network to R must balance at each frequency.

If the input impedance to the network is Z_{in}, then the noise power delivered to the network is

$$P = \left|\frac{V_n}{R + Z_{in}}\right|^2 R_{in}$$

where R_{in} is the resistive component of Z_{in}. When we use Eq. (5.40) we obtain

$$P = \frac{4KTR\,\Delta f}{|R + Z_{in}|^2} R_{in} \qquad (5.41)$$

Let V'_n be the thermal noise voltage at the terminals of the network when R is removed. This is the Thevenin equivalent voltage of all internal noise sources. In terms of this voltage the noise power delivered by the network to R is given by

$$P' = \left|\frac{V'_n}{R + Z_{in}}\right|^2 R$$

and must be equal to P. Hence we see that

$$|V'_n|^2 R = |V_n|^2 R_{in}$$

or
$$V'_n = 2\sqrt{KTR_{in}\,\Delta f} \qquad (5.42)$$

which shows that Nyquist's formula applies to any passive network with input resistance R_{in}. The above derivation cannot be applied to an active network since in an active network power is supplied from an external source and thermodynamic equilibrium will not hold.

If $Z_{in} = R$, which is the condition for maximum power transfer, we find that Eq. (5.41) gives

$$P = KT\,\Delta f \qquad (5.43)$$

and hence $KT\,\Delta f$ is the *available noise power* from a resistor under matched conditions.

Noise Figure and Noise Temperature of an Amplifier

Consider an amplifier of effective bandwidth Δf, power gain A, and matched to a source with source resistance R at room temperature $T_0 = 290$ K, as in Fig. 5.13. The amplifier noise figure F is defined, under the above *standard conditions*, by

$$F = \frac{\text{signal-to-noise power ratio at input}}{\text{signal-to-noise power ratio at output}}$$

$$= \frac{P_{si}/KT_0\,\Delta f}{AP_{si}/(AKT_0\,\Delta f + P_{nA})} \qquad (5.44)$$

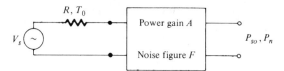

Figure 5.13 A noisy amplifier.

where P_{si} is the input signal power, P_{nA} is the additional noise contributed by the amplifier at the output, and $AKT_0 \Delta f$ is the amplified input thermal noise at the output. The above expression simplifies to

$$F = 1 + \frac{P_{nA}}{AKT_0 \Delta f} \tag{5.45}$$

The noise contributed by the amplifier at the output is

$$P_{nA} = A(F - 1)KT_0 \Delta f \tag{5.46}$$

It is convenient to view this noise as though it were due to the thermal noise in the input resistance R at a temperature $(F - 1)T_0$. This effective temperature is called the *amplifier-noise temperature* and will be denoted by the symbol T_F where

$$T_F = (F - 1)T_0 \tag{5.47}$$

A system is not always operated under the standard conditions used in defining the noise figure F. Thus the noise figure is often best considered as a parameter from which the amplifier noise may be found by means of the relation (5.46). The following example will illustrate this point.

Example 5.7 Noise figure for nonstandard conditions Consider a signal source V_g with source impedance Z_g at a temperature T and connected to an amplifier with power gain A, noise figure F, and input impedance $Z_{in} = R_{in} + jX_{in}$. The noise power delivered to the amplifier is given by Eq. (5.41) and may be expressed in the form

$$P = (KT \Delta f) \frac{4R_g R_{in}}{|Z_g + Z_{in}|^2} = M(KT \Delta f) \tag{5.48}$$

where $M = 4R_g R_{in}/|Z_g + Z_{in}|^2$ is the *impedance mismatch factor*. The amplified output noise will be $AMKT \Delta f$, which, along with the noise contributed by the amplifier, gives a total output noise power of amount

$$P_{no} = AMKT \Delta f + P_{nA} = AKT_0 \Delta f \left[M \frac{T}{T_0} + (F - 1) \right] \tag{5.49}$$

The signal power at the output will be (V_g is the RMS signal voltage)

$$P_{so} = A \left| \frac{V_g}{Z_g + Z_{in}} \right|^2 R_{in} = \frac{|V_g|^2}{4R_g} AM \tag{5.50}$$

where $|V_g|^2/4R_g$ is the *available signal power*.

The input available signal-to-noise ratio is $|V_g|^2/4R_gKT\,\Delta f$ and the output signal-to-noise ratio is given by Eq. (5.50) divided by Eq. (5.49), which is

$$\frac{P_{so}}{P_{no}} = \frac{|V_g|^2}{4R_gKT_0\,\Delta f}\frac{M}{M\dfrac{T}{T_0}+(F-1)} \tag{5.51}$$

If we define a noise figure F' for this system under these nonstandard conditions by means of the same relation (5.44) we find that

$$F' = \left(\frac{T}{T_0}+\frac{F-1}{M}\right)\frac{T_0}{T} \tag{5.52}$$

which shows that the concept of a noise figure is unique only if specified for a set of standard conditions. The same result as given by Eq. (5.51) can be obtained by using the amplifier-noise temperature T_F, since this would simply replace $(F-1)T_0$ by T_F in Eq. (5.49). It should be noted that the excess amplifier noise P_{nA} will be a function of the ambient temperature that the amplifier is operated in. Thus Eqs. (5.46) and (5.47) apply only when the ambient temperature is equal to the standard temperature T_0. If the ambient temperature differs from T_0 it is necessary to specify the amplifier-noise temperature T_F at this new ambient temperature if accurate results for the amplifier excess noise at the output are to be obtained. Fortunately, operating ambient temperatures are close enough to T_0 so that Eqs. (5.46) and (5.47) can be used with little error in most system-noise calculations encountered in practice. At times other factors also enter in, such as the dependence of the noise figure F on the source resistance R_g, as well as flicker noise varying as $1/f$ at low audio frequencies. The systems engineer needs to be aware of such factors that may apply in a particular system. ∎

System-Noise Temperature

It is often convenient to view the amplifier noise at the output as arising from the source resistance R_g by assigning to R_g a higher temperature. The system-noise temperature T_S is the temperature the source resistance would have to be in order to produce the same total output noise, but considering the amplifier now as a noiseless amplifier. We readily see that the noise ouput from R_g at temperature T_S is $MKT_S\,\Delta fA$, and when we equate this to Eq. (5.49) we find that the system-noise temperature is given by

$$T_S = T+\frac{F-1}{M}T_0 = T+\frac{1}{M}T_F \tag{5.53}$$

For an impedance-matched system the system-noise temperature is the sum of the source temperature T and the amplifier-noise temperature T_F.

Thermal Noise from a Lossy Transmission Line

Consider a lossy transmission line of length l connected to a source V_g with impedance $Z_g = R_g + jX_g$ and terminated in a load $Z_L = R_L + jX_L$, as in Fig. 5.14. The voltage waves on the line are $V^+ e^{-\gamma z} + V^- e^{\gamma z}$, where $\gamma = j\beta + \alpha$ is the propagation constant and V^+, V^- are the RMS voltages of the incident and reflected waves. At the load end $z = 0$ and $V^- = \Gamma_L V^+$ where $\Gamma_L = (Z_L - Z_c)/(Z_L + Z_c)$ is the load reflection coefficient. The power delivered to the load is $(1 - |\Gamma_L|^2)|V^+|^2 Y_c$, where Y_c is the characteristic impedance of the line. We assume that the loss per unit length is small enough so that Y_c may be taken as a real quantity. At the input end $z = -l$, the total line voltage equals $Z_{in} V_g/(Z_{in} + Z_g)$; hence

$$V^+(e^{\gamma l} + \Gamma_L e^{-\gamma l}) = \frac{V_g Z_{in}}{Z_{in} + Z_g}$$

and

$$V^+ = \frac{V_g Z_{in} e^{-\gamma l}}{(Z_{in} + Z_g)(1 + \Gamma_L e^{-2\gamma l})}$$

We note that

$$Z_{in} = \frac{Z_c(1 + \Gamma_L e^{-2\gamma l})}{1 - \Gamma_L e^{-2\gamma l}}$$

If we let

$$\Gamma_g = \frac{Z_g - Z_c}{Z_g + Z_c}$$

then

$$Z_g + Z_{in} = Z_g + \frac{Z_c(1 + \Gamma_L e^{-2\gamma l})}{1 - \Gamma_L e^{-2\gamma l}}$$

$$= \frac{Z_g + Z_c - \Gamma_L e^{-2\gamma l}(Z_g - Z_c)}{1 - \Gamma_L e^{-2\gamma l}}$$

$$= \frac{(Z_g + Z_c)(1 - \Gamma_L \Gamma_g e^{-2\gamma l})}{1 - \Gamma_L e^{-2\gamma l}}$$

With the aid of these expressions we find that

$$\frac{Z_{in}}{(Z_{in} + Z_g)(1 + \Gamma_L e^{-2\gamma l})} = \frac{Z_c}{Z_g + Z_c} \frac{1}{1 - \Gamma_L \Gamma_g e^{-2\gamma l}}$$

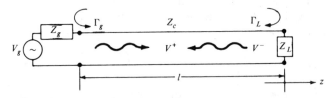

Figure 5.14 A lossy transmission line.

and thus the power delivered to R_L is

$$P_L = \frac{|V_g|^2}{4R_g} \frac{4R_g Z_c}{|Z_g + Z_c|^2} (1 - |\Gamma_L|^2) \frac{e^{-2\alpha l}}{|1 - \Gamma_L \Gamma_g e^{-2\gamma l}|^2} \tag{5.54}$$

We will define the input and output mismatch factors M_1 and M_2 to be the *mismatch when the opposite end of the line is terminated in a matched load.* Thus we choose [see derivation of Eq. (5.11)]

$$M_1 = \frac{4R_g Z_c}{|Z_g + Z_c|^2} = 1 - |\Gamma_g|^2 \tag{5.55a}$$

$$M_2 = 1 - |\Gamma_L|^2 = \frac{4R_L Z_c}{|Z_L + Z_c|^2} \tag{5.55b}$$

The term $|V_g|^2/4R_g$ is the available power from the source, and the loss introduced by the transmission line is

$$L = |1 - \Gamma_L \Gamma_g e^{-2\gamma l}|^2 e^{2\alpha l} \tag{5.56}$$

For $L > 10$ this can be approximated by $L = e^{2\alpha l}$ with negligible error. In terms of these parameters

$$P_L = \frac{|V_g|^2}{4R_g} \frac{M_1 M_2}{L} \tag{5.57}$$

For the thermal noise in R_g the available noise power is $KT \Delta f$, since $V_n^2 = 4KT \Delta f R_g$. Thus the thermal noise delivered to R_L from R_g is

$$P_{Ln} = KT \Delta f \frac{M_1 M_2}{L} \tag{5.58}$$

There will also be thermal noise from the transmission line delivered to R_L. To find this noise we make use of the fact that the thermal noise delivered by R_L to R_g and the lossy line must equal P_{Ln} plus the thermal noise delivered by the line to R_L under thermodynamic equilibrium conditions. The noise power that R_L delivered to R_g is given by an expression like Eq. (5.58), since that equation is symmetrical in terms of input and output quantities. The total noise power delivered by R_L to the system is given by

$$P_t = \frac{4KT \Delta f R_L}{|Z'_{in} + Z_L|^2} \text{Re } Z'_{in}$$

where Z'_{in} is the input impedance at the load end looking towards Z_g. Now

$$Z'_{in} + Z_L = \frac{(Z_L + Z_c)(1 - \Gamma_L \Gamma_g e^{-2\gamma l})}{1 - \Gamma_g e^{-2\gamma l}}$$

$$\text{Re } Z'_{in} = \tfrac{1}{2}(Z'_{in} + Z'^*_{in}) = Z_c \frac{1 - |\Gamma_g|^2 e^{-4\alpha l}}{|1 - \Gamma_g e^{-2\gamma l}|^2}$$

and hence

$$P_t = KT \, \Delta f \frac{4R_L Z_c}{|Z_L + Z_c|^2} \frac{1 - |\Gamma_g|^2 \, e^{-4\alpha l}}{|1 - \Gamma_L \Gamma_g \, e^{-2\gamma l}|^2}$$

$$= KT \, \Delta f \frac{M_2}{L} e^{2\alpha l}(1 - |\Gamma_g|^2 \, e^{-4\alpha l}) \tag{5.59}$$

Thus the thermal noise from losses in the transmission line that is delivered to R_L is

$$P_n = P_t - P_{Ln} = KT \, \Delta f \frac{M_2}{L} (e^{2\alpha l} - |\Gamma_g|^2 \, e^{-2\alpha l} - M_1) \tag{5.60}$$

In the special case $M_1 = M_2 = 1$, that is, $Z_g = Z_L = Z_c$, we obtain

$$P_n = \frac{KT \, \Delta f}{L}(L - 1) \tag{5.61}$$

since $L = e^{2\alpha l}$ in this case. If we compare this expression with Eq. (5.46) we see that under matched conditions and with $T = T_0$ the lossy line is similar to an amplifier, with power gain $1/L$ and noise figure F given by

$$F = L \tag{5.62}$$

The simple relationship holds only under the special conditions given above. In general, the appropriate formulas to use to find the total output noise $P_n + P_{Ln}$ are Eqs. (5.58) and (5.60) and Eq. (5.56) for the loss factor. With these formulas the temperature of the input resistance R_g does not have to be the same as the temperature of the transmission line, and matched terminations are not required.

Noise in Cascaded Systems

Figure 5.15 shows N amplifier stages connected in cascade. The power gain of stage n is A_n, its noise figure is F_n, and the mismatch at the input of stage n is M_n. The noise at the output from the source resistor R_g at temperature T is

$$KT \, \Delta f \, M_1 A_1 M_2 A_2 \cdots M_N A_N$$

The noise from the first amplifier will be

$$(F_1 - 1)KT_0 \, \Delta f \, A_1 M_2 A_2 \cdots M_N A_N$$

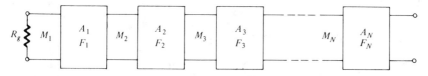

Figure 5.15 A cascade connection of N amplifiers.

at the output. From the ith amplifier the output noise will be

$$(F_i - 1)KT_0 \, \Delta f \, A_i M_{i+1} A_{i+1} \cdots M_N A_n$$

The total output noise is the sum of all of these individual contributions and is

$$P_{no} = KT_0 \, \Delta f \left[\frac{T}{T_0} \prod_{n=1}^{N} M_n A_n + (F_1 - 1)A_1 \prod_{n=2}^{N} M_n A_n \right.$$
$$\left. + (F_2 - 1)A_2 \prod_{n=3}^{N} M_n A_n + \cdots (F_N - 1) A_N \right] \qquad (5.63)$$

where $\Pi_{n=i}^{N}$ stands for the product of all factors from $n = i$ to $n = N$. If all $M_n = 1$ and $T = T_0$ then the overall noise figure of the cascaded system is given by

$$\frac{P_{no}}{KT_0 \, \Delta f \, \Pi_{n=1}^{N} A_n}$$

or
$$F = F_1 + \frac{F_2 - 1}{A_1} + \frac{F_3 - 1}{A_1 A_2} + \cdots \frac{F_N - 1}{A} A_N \qquad (5.64)$$

where A is the total gain. This expression shows that the noise figure is determined primarily by the input stage, since the noise from the other stages is less because of less overall amplification of their contributions to the output noise. It should be noted that Eq. (5.64) applies *only to a system that is impedance-matched throughout.*

5.5 ANTENNA-NOISE TEMPERATURE

An antenna will receive noise signals from bodies in space such as the sun and radio stars that emit electromagnetic radiation. These high-temperature objects radiate like black bodies and produce a white-noise spectrum at frequencies in the microwave range and below. An antenna will also receive noise radiation from any absorbing body. A body that absorbs electromagnetic radiation acts like a resistor and hence also radiates. The noise that an antenna receives can be accounted for by assigning an effective temperature T_A, called the *antenna-noise temperature*, to the radiation resistance of an antenna. The antenna-noise temperature is a function of frequency and direction in the sky that the antenna is pointed. There is considerable variation in the amount of noise that an antenna receives with time of day, month, year, and location. Thus for system evaluation, average values or typical values for T_A are used.

Consider a resistor R at temperature T connected at the input terminals of an antenna, as shown in Fig. 5.16. The resistor R has a value equal to the characteristic impedance Z_c of the feed line. The noise power from R that is delivered to the antenna will be $(1 - |\Gamma|^2)KT \, \Delta f$, where Γ is the input reflection coefficient. The noise power radiated into an element of solid angle $d\Omega$ in the

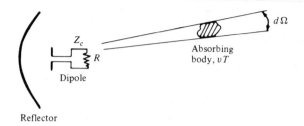

Dipole

Reflector

Figure 5.16 A resistor R connected to antenna input.

direction θ, ϕ is

$$(1 - |\Gamma|^2)KT\,\Delta f\,\frac{G(\theta, \phi)}{4\pi}\,d\Omega$$

If a fraction $\nu(\theta, \phi)$ of this power is absorbed by bodies with a temperature $T(\theta, \phi)$ and located within the cone $d\Omega$, then these bodies must return an equal amount of power to R for thermodynamic equilibrium to exist; that is, we imagine that the only bodies present in all space are the resistor R and the bodies within $d\Omega$ and that these are in equilibrium. Thus the noise power delivered to the resistor R from the bodies within $d\Omega$ must be

$$(1 - |\Gamma|^2)K\,\Delta f\,\frac{G(\theta, \phi)}{4\pi}\,\nu(\theta, \phi)T(\theta, \phi)\,d\Omega$$

This must be the noise power delivered to R even if R is not at the temperature $T(\theta, \phi)$, since we do not require thermodynamic equilibrium to exist in a real system and the reception of power by R is not dependent on how much power is radiated away from R. Hence from all absorbing bodies in space the total received noise power will be

$$P_n' = (1 - |\Gamma|^2)K\,\Delta f\,\frac{1}{4\pi}\int_0^\pi\int_0^{2\pi} G(\theta, \phi)\nu(\theta, \phi)T(\theta, \phi)\sin\theta\,d\phi\,d\theta \quad (5.65)$$

If the antenna input impedance is $Z_{\text{in}} = R_{\text{in}} + jX_{\text{in}}$ and R_{in} (mostly radiation resistance) is assigned a temperature T_A, then R_{in} will deliver a noise power

$$\frac{4KT_A\,\Delta f\,R_{\text{in}}R}{|R + R_{\text{in}} + jX_{\text{in}}|^2}$$

to R. This also equals $(1 - |\Gamma|^2)KT_A\,\Delta f$, and in order to be equal to the actual noise delivered to R we see that we must choose T_A, the antenna-noise temperature, to be

$$T_A = \frac{1}{4\pi}\int_0^\pi\int_0^{2\pi} G(\theta, \phi)\nu(\theta, \phi)T(\theta, \phi)\sin\theta\,d\phi\,d\theta \quad (5.66)$$

The derivation of Eqs. (5.65) and (5.66) is based on the assumption that all bodies located within an element of solid angle $d\Omega$ in the direction specified by the angles θ and ϕ have the same temperature $T(\theta, \phi)$. In general this is not the case, since the medium may have an absorption coefficient and temperature that are functions of the radial distance r from the antenna where the medium is located. Let $\alpha(\theta, \phi, r)$ be the attenuation coefficient at the point θ, ϕ, r. The fraction of the input power at $r = 0$ that is present at r is given by

$$\exp - \int_0^r \alpha(\theta, \phi, r') \, dr'$$

The absorption that takes place in an interval dr is $\alpha \, dr$, so the fraction of the input power absorbed in the interval dr centered on r is

$$\alpha(\theta, \phi, r) \, dr \exp - \int_0^r \alpha(\theta, \phi, r') \, dr'$$

If the local temperature is $T(\theta, \phi, r)$, then in place of $\nu(\theta, \phi)T(\theta, \phi)$ we have

$$\nu_e(\theta, \phi)T_e(\theta, \phi) = \int_0^\infty T(\theta, \phi, r)\alpha(\theta, \phi, r) \exp - \int_0^r \alpha(\theta, \phi, r') \, dr' \, dr$$

where $T_e(\theta, \phi)$ is the effective temperature in the direction θ, ϕ and ν_e is an effective overall absorption coefficient given by

$$\nu_e(\theta, \phi) = \int_0^\infty \alpha(\theta, \phi, r) \exp - \int_0^r \alpha(\theta, \phi, r') \, dr' \, dr$$

The integration over r should, in principle, not be extended all the way to $r = 0$, since our formulation is based on the far-zone expressions for gain. In practice the error is usually small by integrating all the way from 0 to ∞. As an example, consider a cloud layer extending from r_1 to r_2 with a temperature T_1, and let the medium beyond this cloud layer have a temperature T_2. Let ν_1 be the fraction of the radiated power absorbed by the cloud layer; then

$$\nu_e T_e = \nu_1 T_1 + (1 - \nu_1)T_2 \qquad \nu_1 = 1 - e^{-\alpha(r_2 - r_1)}$$

In addition to noise from thermal radiation an antenna picks up noise from lightning discharges, human-induced noise of electrical origin, and other active sources of a nonthermal character. The received noise power from these other sources can be included by increasing the antenna-noise temperature by an appropriate amount. The antenna-noise temperature provides a convenient way to account for the noise picked up by an antenna by viewing this noise as arising from thermal noise in R_{in} when R_{in} is at the temperature T_A.

At the higher frequencies—for example, at microwave frequencies—the noise power received from outer space is often quite small. If the antenna is connected to a receiver by means of a lossy transmission line, as in Fig. 5.17, the thermal noise from this lossy transmission line may be significant. We will let $R + jX$ be the impedance terminating the transmission line. The noise power P_n'' delivered to R from the lossy transmission line is given by Eq. (5.60) and is

$$P_n'' = KT \, \Delta f \, (1 - |\Gamma_g|^2)\frac{1}{L}\left(e^{2\alpha l} - |\Gamma|^2 \, e^{-2\alpha l} - M_1\right) \tag{5.67}$$

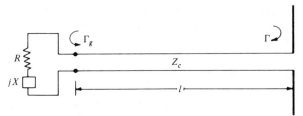

Figure 5.17 A resistor R connected to an antenna by a lossy transmission line.

where L is given by Eq. (5.56). Note that the input and output ends are interchanged so that Γ_g in Eq. (5.60) becomes Γ, $M_1 = 1 - |\Gamma|^2$, and Γ_L in Eq. (5.55b) is replaced by $\Gamma_g = (R + jX - Z_c)/(R + jX + Z_c)$. The total noise delivered to R may be viewed as the sum of the noise P_n'' from the lossy line plus the noise from the antenna input resistance R_{in} at temperature T_A modified by the attenuation of the lossy line and the mismatch factors at each end. The noise power from R_{in} delivered to R is given by Eq. (5.58), and hence the total noise power delivered to R is

$$P_n = P_n'' + (1 - |\Gamma|^2)(1 - |\Gamma_g|^2)\frac{KT_A\,\Delta f}{L}$$

$$= (1 - |\Gamma|^2)(1 - |\Gamma_g|^2)\frac{K\,\Delta f}{L}\left(T_A + T\frac{e^{2\alpha l} - |\Gamma|^2\,e^{-2\alpha l}}{1 - |\Gamma|^2} - T\right) \quad (5.68)$$

For most systems the term $\Gamma\Gamma_g\,e^{-2\gamma l}$ in the expression for L can be neglected and likewise for the term $|\Gamma|^2\,e^{-2\alpha l}$ in the expression (5.68). Then, since $L = e^{2\alpha l}$ in this instance, we obtain

$$P_n = (1 - |\Gamma_g|^2)K\,\Delta f\left[\frac{(1 - |\Gamma|^2)(T_A - T)}{L} + T\right] \quad (5.69)$$

in place of Eq. (5.68). Furthermore, if the reflection coefficient Γ at the antenna input is zero then

$$P_n = (1 - |\Gamma_g|^2)K\,\Delta f\frac{T_A + (L - 1)T}{L} \quad (5.70)$$

This expression shows that the lossy transmission line reduces the effects of the antenna noise, since T_A is divided by the loss L. But at the same time the transmission line contributes thermal noise proportional to its temperature multiplied by $(L - 1)/L$. We can define an equivalent antenna temperature T_A' that includes the transmission line contribution. The transmission-line noise power can be accounted for by raising the temperature of the antenna input resistance to T_A'. The transmission line thus adds an additional noise temperature $T_A' - T_A$ that may be found by replacing T by $T_L = T_A' - T_A$ in Eq. (5.58) and equating this to Eq. (5.60). Hence it is found that

$$T_A' = T_A + T\frac{L - 1 + |\Gamma|^2}{1 - |\Gamma|^2} \quad (5.71a)$$

which for $\Gamma = 0$ becomes

$$T'_A = T_A + (L - 1)T \tag{5.71b}$$

Note that in Eq. (5.71a) the term $-|\Gamma|^2 e^{-2\alpha l}$ has not been included, since it is usually very small.

In principle one can consider the lossy transmission line as being part of the antenna system. If the input reflection coefficient to this system is Γ_{in}, then a fraction $1 - |\Gamma_{in}|^2$ of the available power from a source with internal impedance equal to Z_c is delivered to the antenna system. If ν_0 is the fraction of this power that is lost in the feed line, then the antenna radiates $(1 - \nu_0)$ of the input power. Thus the effective antenna gain becomes $(1 - \nu_0)G = G_e$. The thermodynamic equilibrium equation (5.65) would now become

$$P'_n = (1 - |\Gamma_{in}|^2)K \,\Delta f \left[\nu_0 T + \frac{1}{4\pi} \int_0^{\pi} \int_0^{2\pi} G_e(\theta, \phi)\nu(\theta, \phi)T(\theta, \phi)\sin\theta \, d\phi \, d\theta \right]$$

$$= (1 - |\Gamma_{in}|^2)K \,\Delta f \left[\nu_0 T + (1 - \nu_0)T_A \right] \tag{5.72}$$

which demonstrates, in a simpler way, the feed-line contribution to the received thermal noise. Although Eq. (5.72) has an apparent simplicity compared with Eqs. (5.68) and (5.69) the evaluation of ν_0, the fraction of the input power dissipated in the lossy feed line, and the effect of a source impedance different from Z_c would lead us back to the earlier equations. In the particular case $\Gamma = 0$, we have $\Gamma_{in} = 0$ and $\nu_0 = 1 - 1/L = (L - 1)/L$, and the effective antenna temperature at the input to the antenna system becomes $T_{Ae} = \nu_0 T + (1 - \nu_0)T_A = [T_A + (L - 1)T]/L$. This differs from that given by Eq. (5.71b) by the factor $1/L$, since T'_A is referred to the antenna terminals and T_{Ae} is referred to the transmission-line input, which is regarded as the input to the combined antenna system.

Equation (5.65) or (5.72) clearly shows that when electromagnetic radiation is absorbed by atmospheric molecules or water vapor, then these atmospheric constituents act as thermal radiators and will produce thermal noise at the antenna terminals. This principle is often used at microwave frequencies, as well as at infrared frequencies, to produce thermal maps of the earth's surface, buildings, etc. These maps measure the relative absorption and temperature of the bodies viewed by the antenna. The overall system used to carry out such measurements is called a *radiometer*. Radiometer measurements may also be used to determine the total attenuation through the atmosphere by pointing the antenna towards the zenith and measuring the received thermal noise. For this measurement it is important that other possible sources of thermal radiation be negligible or known and that the temperature profile through the atmosphere also be known.

A number of people have carried out measurements to determine the antenna noise temperature at different frequencies. Figure 5.18 shows the contribution of atmospheric noise to T_A at frequencies below 100 MHz, while Fig. 5.19 gives some results for T_A at microwave frequencies. Note in particular

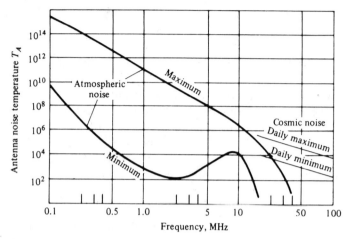

Figure 5.18 Antenna-noise temperature.

that T_A is very large at frequencies below 1 MHz, and this is attributed in part to electrical discharges, such as lightning, that generally occur at almost all times somewhere in the atmosphere. In Fig. 5.19, the variation in T_A with elevation angle is due to the increased path length, hence greater absorption, through the atmosphere at low elevation angles. At a frequency of a few Gigahertz, the antenna temperature due to cosmic noise and atmospheric attenuation may be as low as 10 K. Thus it is important to avoid feed-line losses and antenna side lobes directed towards the warm ground in order to keep the total effective antenna-noise temperature small.

The equivalent noise temperature of the quiet sun is given by†

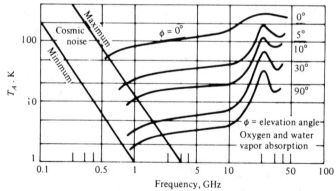

Figure 5.19 Microwave antenna-noise temperature.

† D. C. Hogg and W. W. Mumford, "The Effective Noise Temperature of the Sky," *Microwave Jour.*, vol. 3, March 1960.

W. L. Flock and E. K. Smith, "Natural Radio Noise—A Mini-Review," *IEEE Trans.*, vol. AP-32, July 1984, pp. 762–767.

$$T_{\text{sun}} = T_0 \frac{675}{f \text{ GHz}} \tag{5.73}$$

The average temperature due to cosmic noise is given with acceptable accuracy by

$$T_{\text{cosmic}} = T_0 \lambda_0^2 \tag{5.74}$$

where λ_0 is in meters and $T_0 = 290$ K.

5.6 NOISE EVALUATION OF COMMUNICATION SYSTEMS

In this section we will illustrate the application of the various formulas derived earlier for received signal power and noise power in typical communication links. Three examples will be covered that are representative of typical practical communication systems.

Example 5.8 AM broadcast receiving system As a first example consider a 1-MHz broadcast system. For a receiving antenna we will use a small loop antenna consisting of the coil in the tuned input circuit of the receiver, as shown in Fig. 5.20. The receiving cross section under matched conditions is

$$A_e = \frac{\lambda_0^2}{4\pi} G$$

so we must evaluate the gain G. Let the coil have an ohmic resistance R_c and radiation resistance R_a. As a transmitting antenna with input RMS voltage V_g, its input power under matched conditions will be $P_{\text{in}} = V_g^2/4(R_c + R_a)$, of which a fraction $\eta = R_a/(R_c + R_a)$ is dissipated in R_a, that is, radiated. The radiation pattern of a small coil is the same as that for a current element $I_0 \Delta l$, so the maximum directivity D is 1.5. Hence the gain is 1.5 $\eta = G$, as found earlier in Sec. 5.3 and given by Eq. (5.33).

When used as a receiving antenna, its received power under matched conditions will be

$$P_{\text{rec}} = \frac{\lambda_0^2}{4\pi} GP_{\text{inc}} = \frac{\lambda_0^2}{4\pi} 1.5\eta P_{\text{inc}} \tag{5.75}$$

In order to find the equivalent input noise we choose R_c to be at the ambient temperature $T_0 = 290$ K and take R_a to be at the antenna-noise

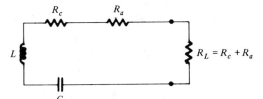

Figure 5.20 Equivalent circuit of a loop antenna used for reception of a radio signal.

temperature T_A. If the receiver has a noise figure F, then the equivalent additional input noise is obtained by raising the temperature of $R_c + R_a$ by $(F-1)T_0$, the receiver-noise temperature. Since noise powers from uncorrelated sources add, the total noise power that will be delivered to the load $R_L = R_c + R_a$ is the sum of each contribution; so

$$P_n = \frac{K\,\Delta f\,[R_c T_0 + R_a T_A + (F-1)T_0(R_c + R_a)]}{R_c + R_a}$$

$$= K\,\Delta f\,[(1-\eta)FT_0 + \eta T_A + \eta(F-1)T_0] \tag{5.76}$$

where we have used $4K\,\Delta f\,RT$ for the mean-square noise voltage from each source, summed these, and divided by $4(R_a + R_c)$ to get the noise power in R_L. Note that $1 - \eta = R_c/(R_c + R_a)$, $\eta = R_a/(R_c + R_a)$. At broadcast frequencies T_A is of order 10^8, so for a small loop antenna for which the efficiency is very small, the term ηT_A may not necessarily dominate over the thermal noise contribution. For example, for a coil with $N = 100$, $A = 2\,\text{cm}^2 = 2 \times 10^{-4}\,\text{m}^2$, and $\lambda_0 = 300\,\text{m}$ we get

$$R_a = \frac{16\pi^4 \times 120\pi \times 10^4 \times 4 \times 10^{-8}}{6\pi \times (9 \times 10^4)^2} = 1.54 \times 10^{-9}\,\Omega$$

If $L = 200\mu h$ and $Q = 100$, then $R_c = \omega L/Q = 2\pi \times 200/100 = 4\pi\,\Omega$ at $1\,\text{MHz}$. Thus $\eta = 1.22 \times 10^{-10}$. The extremely small efficiency of a small loop antenna means that the receiver performance is limited by thermal noise, not by antenna noise. This is why no unusual noise levels are present in small portable broadcast receivers when they are tuned between stations.

The signal-to-noise ratio at the receiver will be

$$\frac{P_{\text{rec}}}{P_n} = \frac{1.5\eta P_{\text{inc}}(\lambda_0^2/4\pi)}{K\,\Delta f\,[(1-\eta)FT_0 + \eta T_A + \eta(F-1)T_0]} \tag{5.77}$$

This equation gives the signal-to-noise ratio at the receiver output because we have referred the total noise to the input and compared it with the signal power at the input, which is fully equivalent to evaluating the signal-to-noise ratio at the output. The signal-to-noise ratio continues to improve until the efficiency η is such that $\eta T_A \gtrsim (1-\eta)FT_0$, at which point a further increase in η increases both P_{rec} and P_n by about the same amount. For $F = 4$ and $T_0 = 290\,\text{K}$ this occurs for $\eta \approx 1160/T_A \approx 10^{-5}$ or so in the broadcast band. Thus a low-efficiency loop antenna is acceptable as a receiving antenna at these frequencies.

For the loop antenna in our example the thermal noise is the limiting factor. For $F = 4$ and a signal-to-noise ratio of 10 we will require

$$P_{\text{rec}} = 1.5\eta P_{\text{inc}}\frac{\lambda_0^2}{4\pi} = 10K\,\Delta f\,(1-\eta)FT_0 \simeq 10K\,\Delta f\,FT_0$$

$$= 10 \times 1.38 \times 10^{-23} \times 10^4 \times 4 \times 290$$

$$= 1.6 \times 10^{-15}\,\text{W}$$

where we have assumed that $\Delta f = 10\,\text{kHz}$. Hence the required P_{inc} is

$$P_{\text{inc}} = \frac{4 \times 1.38 \times 2.9 \times 4\pi \times 10^{-16}}{9 \times 10^4 \times 1.5 \times 1.22 \times 10^{-10}} = 1.22 \times 10^{-9}\,\text{W/m}^2$$

or an RMS field strength of $6.7 \times 10^{-4}\,\text{V/m}$. For a signal of high quality the signal-to-noise ratio should be about 30 dB, which requires a field strength of 6.7 mV/m.

In this example an extra complication arises because the antenna resistance is the sum of an ohmic resistance R_c at temperature T_0 and a radiation resistance R_a at temperature T_A. The sum of the two noise voltages squared is $4K\,\Delta f\,(R_c T_0 + R_a T_A)$. This is equivalent to an effective noise temperature T_1 for both resistors, where $T_1(R_c + R_a) = R_c T_0 + R_a T_A$, or

$$T_1 = \frac{R_c}{R_c + R_a}\,T_0 + \frac{R_a}{R_c + R_a}\,T_A \tag{5.78}$$

As may be seen, this is the temperature weightings that occur in Eq. (5.76). By using this effective temperature, Eq. (5.76) may be written as

$$P_n = K\,\Delta f\,[T_1 + (F-1)T_0]$$

which is in accord with Eq. (5.49) when the mismatch factor $M = 1$ and the power gain A is set to unity to obtain the amplifier equivalent input noise power. ∎

Example 5.9 Microwave receiving system A microwave line-of-sight communication link utilizes a receiving terminal with an antenna having a gain of 40 dB, a superheterodyne receiver having a mixer with a 6-dB conversion loss and a noise figure of 10 dB, and an intermediate-frequency (IF) amplifier with a noise figure of 4 dB and a bandwidth of 10 MHz. The transmitting antenna has a gain of 40 dB also. The receiving antenna is connected to the receiver with a transmission line having a total attenuation of 10 dB. The system is impedance-matched throughout. We wish to determine the required transmitter power to give a signal-to-noise ratio of 30 dB at the IF amplifier output when the distance separating the two terminals is 30 km. The frequency of operation is 6 GHz ($\lambda_0 = 5$ cm). The antenna noise temperature is 100 K.

The noise power delivered to the mixer input from the antenna and lossy transmission line is given by Eq. (5.70), with $\Gamma_g = 0$. In decibel measure $K\,\Delta f = 1.38 \times 10^{-23} \times 10^7$ has a value of -158.6 dB, and $T_A + (L-1)T_0 = 2710$ has a value of 34.33 dB. Hence P_n in decibels is given by $-158.6 + 34.33 - 10 = -134.27$ dBW at the mixer input. The mixer, which has a conversion loss L_c in converting the RF power to IF power at the intermediate frequency, may be viewed as equivalent to an amplifier with the same noise figure F_M but having a gain $1/L_c$ (less than unity). Thus the IF amplifier noise $KT_0\,\Delta f\,(F_{\text{IF}} - 1)A$ plus the mixer noise $KT_0\,\Delta f\,(F_M -$

$1)/L_c$ when referred to the mixer input is [see Eq. (5.64)]

$$KT_0 \, \Delta f \, [(F_M - 1) + (F_{IF} - 1)L_c] = KT_0 \, \Delta f \, (F - 1)$$

where $F = F_M + (F_{IF} - 1)L_c$ is the noise figure of the mixer and IF amplifier combined. Now $F_M = 10$, $F_{IF} = 2.5$, so $F_M - 1 + L_c(F_{IF} - 1) = 9 + 4 \times 1.5 = 15$, or 11.76 dB. Thus in decibel-watt measure the mixer and IF amplifier noise at the mixer input is $-158.6 + 24.62 + 11.76 = -122.22$ dBW. In order to find the total noise at the mixer input we must convert back to noise power in watts and then add the antenna, transmission line, mixer, and IF amplifier noise powers. We thus find that the total noise at the mixer input is 6.37×10^{-13} W.

From Eq. (5.20) we find that the received power at the input of the transmission line is

$$\frac{25 \times 10^{-4}}{(4\pi)^2} \frac{10^8}{9 \times 10^8} P_{in} = 1.76 \times 10^{-6} P_{in}$$

At the mixer input the signal power will be $1.76 \times 10^{-7} P_{in}$. In order to have a 30-dB signal-to-noise ratio we require a transmitter power P_{in} equal to

$$P_{in} = \frac{6.37 \times 10^{-13} \times 10^3}{1.76 \times 10^{-7}} = 3.62 \times 10^{-3} \text{ W}$$

This problem can also be solved by finding the system noise temperature T_S, which is the equivalent temperature of the antenna input resistance that will account for all of the noise. The IF amplifier noise referred to the antenna terminals will be $KT_0 \, \Delta f \, (F_{IF} - 1)L_c L$, and the mixer noise referred to the antenna terminals will be $(F_M - 1)LKT_0 \, \Delta f$. The transmission-line thermal noise referred to the antenna terminals is obtained by equating (5.60) with $T = T_0$ to Eq. (5.58) to find the required input available noise power $KT \, \Delta f$ that will give the same output noise power, as was done to obtain Eq. (5.71). Thus because of the transmission-line losses the input temperature is raised by an amount T_L given by

$$T_L = \frac{T_0}{M_1} (e^{2\alpha l} - |\Gamma|^2 \, e^{-2\alpha l} - M_1) \tag{5.79}$$

which for the present system reduces to [see Eq. (5.71b)]

$$T_L = T_0(L - 1) = T_0(F_L - 1)$$

where $F_L = L$ is the noise figure for the matched lossy line as given by Eq. (5.62). The system-noise temperature T_S is hence given by

$$T_S = T_A + (F_M - 1)LT_0 + (F_{IF} - 1)LL_cT_0 + (L - 1)T_0$$

$$= 46210 \text{ K}$$

The available noise power in a bandwidth $\Delta f = 10^7$ Hz is $KT_S \, \Delta f = 6.37 \times 10^{-12}$ W. The required received signal power is 6.37×10^{-9} W in order to give a 30-dB signal-to-noise ratio. When we equate this to $1.76 \times 10^{-6} P_{in}$

we find, as before, that $P_{in} = 3.62 \times 10^{-3}$ W. The small transmitter input power required is due to the high antenna gains in this system. ∎

Example 5.10 Radar system A radar system is characterized by the following parameters:

> Antenna gain = 30 dB
> Peak transmitter pulse power = 200 kW
> Frequency = 10 GHz
> Pulse length = 1 μs
> Receiver mixer = 10-dB conversion loss and 3-dB noise figure
> IF amplifier-noise figure = 6 dB
> Antenna-noise temperature = 200 K

The objective is to find the maximum range r that will result in a signal-to-noise ratio of 10 dB for a target with a 5-m^2 radar cross section.

As a first step we will find the equivalent system noise temperature. The receiver bandwidth can be taken as the reciprocal of the pulse length; thus $\Delta f = 10^6$ Hz. As in the previous example, the IF amplifier and mixer noise referred to the mixer input is

$$KT_0\,\Delta f\,[(F_M - 1) + L_c(F_{IF} - 1)] = KT_0\,\Delta f\,[1 + 10(4 - 1)]$$

$$= 31KT_0\,\Delta f$$

Thus the system noise temperature is $T_S = (200 + 31T_0) = 9190$ K. The total input noise power is thus $KT_S\,\Delta f = 1.27 \times 10^{-13}$ W.

The receiver power is given by Eq. (5.27) and is

$$P_{rec} = \frac{P_{in}\lambda_0^2\sigma G^2}{(4\pi)^3 r^4} = \frac{2 \times 10^5 \times 9 \times 10^{-4} \times 5 \times 10^6}{(4\pi)^3 r^4}$$

$$= \frac{4.53 \times 10^5}{r^4}$$

We now equate P_{rec} to the noise power multiplied by the specified signal-to-noise ratio; thus we find that

$$r^4 = \frac{4.53 \times 10^5}{1.27 \times 10^{-12}} = 3.57 \times 10^{17}$$

and hence the maximum range $r = 2.44 \times 10^4$ m, or 15.2 mi. The dependence of the received signal on the inverse fourth power of distance makes the power requirements of a radar system much greater than those of a communication link operated over the same range. ∎

5.7 ANTENNA INTERACTION WITH A SCATTERER

A receiving antenna is often used in the presence of scatterers such as raindrops or other obstructions like buildings and trees. It is therefore of interest to develop some basic relationships for the received open-circuit voltage in the presence of a scattering obstacle.

In Fig. 5.21 a receiving antenna, which for illustrative purposes is chosen as a horn, is shown in the presence of a scatterer. The scatterer is contained in a volume V_i bounded by a surface S_i and has electrical parameters ϵ and μ.

If we include equivalent magnetic currents $\mathbf{J}_m$ in Maxwell's equation, that is, $\nabla \times \mathbf{E} = -(\partial \mathbf{B}/\partial t) - \mathbf{J}_m = -j\omega\mu\mathbf{H} - \mathbf{J}_m$, then the reciprocity theorem states that

$$\oint_S (\mathbf{E}_1 \times \mathbf{H}_2 - \mathbf{E}_2 \times \mathbf{H}_1) \cdot \mathbf{n} \, dS = \int_V (\mathbf{E}_2 \cdot \mathbf{J}_1 - \mathbf{E}_1 \cdot \mathbf{J}_2 - \mathbf{H}_2 \cdot \mathbf{J}_{m1} + \mathbf{H}_1 \cdot \mathbf{J}_{m2}) \, dV$$

(5.80)

The derivation of this equation is the same as that of Eq. (5.1), with the inclusion of magnetic currents. We now let $\mathbf{E}_1$, $\mathbf{H}_1$ be the field radiated by the antenna with input current I_{in} and *in the absence of the scatterer*. The field $\mathbf{E}_2$, $\mathbf{H}_2$ is chosen as the field scattered by the scatterer when illuminated by $\mathbf{E}_1$, $\mathbf{H}_1$ but with open-circuit conditions at the antenna input terminals. [This field is a valid solution of Maxwell's equations and hence may be used in the reciprocity theorem given by Eq. (5.80).] The surface S is chosen as the surface of the perfectly conducting antenna, the terminal plane, the surface S_i surrounding the scatterer, plus the surface of a sphere of infinite radius, as shown in Fig. 5.21. On the antenna surface $\mathbf{n} \times \mathbf{E}_1 = \mathbf{n} \times \mathbf{E}_2 = 0$, so this surface, as well as the surface at infinity, does not give a contribution. On the terminal plane the surface integral gives $V_{oc}I_{in}$, as in Eq. (5.2). Thus, since no sources are enclosed, Eq. (5.80) gives

$$V_{oc} = -\oint_{S_i} (\mathbf{E}_R \times \mathbf{H}_2 - \mathbf{E}_2 \times \mathbf{H}_R) \cdot \mathbf{n} \, dS$$

(5.81)

where $\mathbf{E}_1 = I_{in}\mathbf{E}_R$, $\mathbf{H}_1 = I_{in}\mathbf{H}_R$ and V_i has been excluded from the volume enclosed by S.

If the scatterer were a perfectly conducting obstacle, then $\mathbf{n} \times \mathbf{E}_2 = -\mathbf{n} \times I_{in}\mathbf{E}_R$ on S_i, and the induced surface current is $\mathbf{J}_s = -\mathbf{n} \times (I_{in}\mathbf{H}_R + \mathbf{H}_2)$ on S_i. Hence Eq.

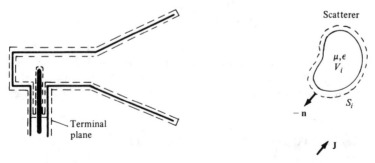

Figure 5.21 A receiving horn antenna in the presence of a scatterer.

(5.81) can be rewritten in the form

$$V_{oc}I_{in} = -\oint_{S_i} [I_{in}\mathbf{E}_R \cdot (I_{in}\mathbf{H}_R + \mathbf{H}_2) \times \mathbf{n}] \, dS$$

$$= -\oint_{S_i} I_{in}\mathbf{E}_R \cdot \mathbf{J}_s \, dS \qquad (5.82)$$

when $\mathbf{n} \times \mathbf{E}_2$ is expressed in terms of $\mathbf{n} \times \mathbf{E}_R$. This result is similar to that given by Eq. (5.2).

In general Eq. (5.81) can be rewritten in the form

$$V_{oc} = -\oint_{S_i} [\mathbf{E}_R \times (I_{in}\mathbf{H}_R + \mathbf{H}_2) - (\mathbf{E}_2 + I_{in}\mathbf{E}_R) \times \mathbf{H}_R] \cdot \mathbf{n} \, dS$$

by adding and subtracting the term $I_{in}\mathbf{E}_R \times \mathbf{H}_R$. By using the divergence theorem and Maxwell's equations we obtain (note that $I_{in}\mathbf{E}_R + \mathbf{E}_2$, $I_{in}\mathbf{H}_R + \mathbf{H}_2$ is the total field inside the scatterer volume V_i)

$$V_{oc} = \int_{V_i} \nabla \cdot [\mathbf{E}_R \times (I_{in}\mathbf{H}_R + \mathbf{H}_2) - (\mathbf{E}_2 + I_{in}\mathbf{E}_R) \times \mathbf{H}_R] \, dV$$

$$= \int_{V_i} [(\nabla \times \mathbf{E}_R) \cdot (I_{in}\mathbf{H}_R + \mathbf{H}_2) - \mathbf{E}_R \cdot \nabla \times (I_{in}\mathbf{H}_R + \mathbf{H}_2)$$

$$- \nabla \times (\mathbf{E}_2 + I_{in}\mathbf{E}_R) \cdot \mathbf{H}_R + \nabla \times \mathbf{H}_R \cdot (\mathbf{E}_2 + I_{in}\mathbf{E}_R)] \, dV$$

$$= \int_{V_i} [-j\omega\mu_0\mathbf{H}_R \cdot (I_{in}\mathbf{H}_R + \mathbf{H}_2) - j\omega\epsilon(I_{in}\mathbf{E}_R + \mathbf{E}_2)$$

$$\cdot \mathbf{E}_R + j\omega\mu(\mathbf{H}_2 + I_{in}\mathbf{H}_R) \cdot \mathbf{H}_R + j\omega\epsilon_0\mathbf{E}_R$$

$$\cdot (\mathbf{E}_2 + I_{in}\mathbf{E}_R)] \, dV$$

$$= \int_{V_i} \{-\mathbf{E}_R \cdot [j\omega(\epsilon - \epsilon_0)(I_{in}\mathbf{E}_R + \mathbf{E}_2)] + \mathbf{H}_R$$

$$\cdot [j\omega(\mu - \mu_0)(I_{in}\mathbf{H}_R + \mathbf{H}_2)]\} \, dV$$

The polarization current densities are $\mathbf{J}_p = j\omega(\epsilon - \epsilon_0)(I_{in}\mathbf{E}_R + \mathbf{E}_2)$ and $\mathbf{J}_m = j\omega(\mu - \mu_0)(I_{in}\mathbf{H}_R + \mathbf{H}_2)$, so upon introducing these we find that

$$V_{oc} = \int_{V_i} (-\mathbf{E}_R \cdot \mathbf{J}_p + \mathbf{H}_R \cdot \mathbf{J}_m) \, dV \qquad (5.83)$$

in accordance with Eq. (5.80). Note that $\nabla \times \mathbf{E} = -j\omega\mu\mathbf{H} = -j\omega\mu_0\mathbf{H} - j\omega(\mu - \mu_0)\mathbf{H}$. Thus we can identify $\mathbf{J}_m$ with $j\omega(\mu - \mu_0)\mathbf{H}$.

We can also express the second term in Eq. (5.83) in terms of equivalent amperian (electric) magnetization currents. We have

$$\int_{V_i} j\omega \mathbf{H}_R \cdot (\mu - \mu_0)(I_{in}\mathbf{H}_R + \mathbf{H}_2)\, dV = \int_{V_i} j\omega\mu_0 \mathbf{H}_R \frac{\mu - \mu_0}{\mu_0} \cdot (I_{in}\mathbf{H}_R + \mathbf{H}_2)\, dV$$

$$= \int_{V_i} j\omega\mu_0 \mathbf{H}_R \cdot \mathbf{M}\, dV$$

where from $\mathbf{B} = \mu\mathbf{H} = \mu_0(\mathbf{H} + \mathbf{M})$ we obtained $\mathbf{M} = [(\mu - \mu_0)/\mu_0]\mathbf{H}$. Replacing $j\omega\mu_0\mathbf{H}_R$ by $-\nabla \times \mathbf{E}_R$ gives

$$-\int_{V_i} (\nabla \times \mathbf{E}_R) \cdot \mathbf{M}\, dV = -\int_{V_i} [\nabla \cdot (\mathbf{E}_R \times \mathbf{M}) + \mathbf{E}_R \cdot \nabla \times \mathbf{M}]\, dV$$

$$= \int_{V_i} -\mathbf{E}_R \cdot \nabla \times \mathbf{M}\, dV + \oint_{S_i} \mathbf{E}_R \cdot (\mathbf{M} \times \mathbf{n})\, dS$$

The equivalent amperian volume currents are given by $\mathbf{J}_a = \nabla \times \mathbf{M}$ and the amperian surface currents by $\mathbf{J}_{as} = \mathbf{n} \times \mathbf{M}$. Hence in place of Eq. (5.83) we can write

$$V_{oc} = -\int_{V_i} \mathbf{E}_R \cdot (\mathbf{J}_p + \mathbf{J}_a)\, dV - \oint_{S_i} \mathbf{E}_R \cdot \mathbf{J}_{as}\, dS \qquad (5.84)$$

This expression gives the open-circuit received voltage in terms of the interaction of the electric field radiated by the antenna, with the total current induced in the scatterer by that field.

If the scatterer is a small sphere with radius $a \ll \lambda_0$ then $\mathbf{E}_R$, $\mathbf{H}_R$ are uniform over the sphere, with the center at r. We may use static-field theory to find the total dipole moments and thus (see Prob. 2.7)

$$\int_{V_i} \mathbf{J}_p\, dV = j\omega 4\pi a^3 \epsilon_0 \frac{\epsilon - \epsilon_0}{\epsilon + 2\epsilon_0} I_{in}\mathbf{E}_R(\mathbf{r})$$

$$\int_{V_i} \mathbf{J}_m\, dV = j\omega 4\pi a^3 \mu_0 \frac{\mu - \mu_0}{\mu + 2\mu_0} I_{in}\mathbf{H}_R(\mathbf{r})$$

Hence

$$V_{oc} = -j\omega\epsilon_0 4\pi a^3 \frac{\epsilon - \epsilon_0}{\epsilon + 2\epsilon_0} I_{in}|\mathbf{E}_R(\mathbf{r})|^2 + j\omega\mu_0 4\pi a^3 \frac{\mu - \mu_0}{\mu + 2\mu_0} I_{in}|\mathbf{H}_R(\mathbf{r})|^2 \qquad (5.85)$$

which gives the radar backscattering from the sphere. The case of a perfectly conducting sphere is obtained by setting $\epsilon = \infty$, $\mu = 0$.

Scatterer Excited by an External Field

Let $\mathbf{E}_2$, $\mathbf{H}_2$ be the field $\mathbf{E}$, $\mathbf{H}$ from an external source $\mathbf{J}$ in the presence of the scatterer and the antenna under open-circuit conditions. In particular, $\mathbf{E}$, $\mathbf{H}$ is the total field in V_i. We now find that

$$V_{oc} = \int_{V_i} [-\mathbf{E}_R \cdot j\omega(\epsilon - \epsilon_0)\mathbf{E} + \mathbf{H}_R \cdot j\omega(\mu - \mu_0)\mathbf{H}] \, dV - \int_V \mathbf{E}_R \cdot \mathbf{J} \, dV \quad (5.86)$$

in place of Eq. (5.83), upon putting $\mathbf{J}_p = j\omega(\epsilon - \epsilon_0)\mathbf{E}$ and $\mathbf{J}_m = j\omega(\mu - \mu_0)\mathbf{H}$.

We can express $\mathbf{E}$, $\mathbf{H}$ as a field $\mathbf{E}_i$, $\mathbf{H}_i$ produced by $\mathbf{J}$ in the absence of the scatterer, plus a scattered field $\mathbf{E}_s$, $\mathbf{H}_s$. For a small dielectric sphere we then have

$$j\omega \int_{V_i} \mathbf{J}_p \, dV = j\omega\epsilon_0 \mathbf{E}_i(\mathbf{r}) 4\pi a^3 \frac{\epsilon - \epsilon_0}{\epsilon + 2\epsilon_0}$$

and

$$V_{oc} = -\int_V \mathbf{E}_R \cdot \mathbf{J} \, dV - j\omega\epsilon_0 4\pi a^3 \frac{\epsilon - \epsilon_0}{\epsilon + 2\epsilon_0} \mathbf{E}_R(\mathbf{r}) \cdot \mathbf{E}_i(\mathbf{r}) \quad (5.87)$$

in place of Eq. (5.85). The first term is the direct contribution from the external source $\mathbf{J}$, and the second term is caused by scattering from the obstacle.

The above results are readily extended to the case of many scatterers. The significant feature is that $\mathbf{E}_R$, $\mathbf{H}_R$ is still the field radiated by the antenna in the absence of the scatterers. The general result is Eq. (5.86) summed over all scatterers, and $\mathbf{E}$, $\mathbf{H}$ is the field from $\mathbf{J}$ plus the sum of all scattered fields. If multiple scattering between obstacles is negligible, then the expression for V_{oc} is the sum of Eq. (5.86) over all scatterers [or Eq. (5.87) if we assume that all obstacles are small dielectric spheres]. When the scatterers are randomly positioned so that the phase of $\mathbf{E}_R(\mathbf{r}_i) \cdot \mathbf{E}_i(\mathbf{r}_i)$ can be considered uniformly distributed over 2π radians the received power is the sum of that from each scatterer. In the next chapter these results will be applied to the problem of scattering by raindrops.

PROBLEMS

5.1 In the derivation of the Lorentz reciprocity theorem show that if the antenna conductors are lossy and if the boundary condition $\mathbf{n} \times \mathbf{E} = Z_s \mathbf{n} \times (\mathbf{n} \times \mathbf{H})$ is used, $\mathbf{n} \times \mathbf{E}_1 \cdot \mathbf{H}_2 - \mathbf{n} \times \mathbf{E}_2 \cdot \mathbf{H}_1 = 0$ and the surface integral over the conductors will vanish.

5.2 Assume that the current on a half-wave dipole antenna is a constant I_0 and find the radiated field. Express this in the form given in Eq. (5.15) and show that the maximum effective length $|\mathbf{h}|$ equals $\lambda_0/2$.

5.3 For the loop antenna discussed in Example 5.4 in Sec. 5.3, show that at resonance the Thevenin equivalent voltage is

$$V_{TH} = \frac{V_{oc}}{\dfrac{R^2C}{L} + jRC\sqrt{1 - Q^{-2}}\omega_0}$$

and the Thevenin impedance is Q^2R where $Q = \omega_0 L/R$ and the resonant frequency is given exactly by Eq. (5.31). Show that at the exact resonant frequency $|V_{TH}|^2 = Q^2|V_{oc}|^2$. Note that $R^2 C/L = 1/Q^2$.

5.4 Show in detail that Eqs. (5.32) and (5.34) are equivalent.

5.5 For the parallel-tuned circuit shown in Fig. 5.9b but with R_L removed, show that the impedance across C becomes a pure resistance $Q^2R = (\omega_0 L)^2/R = L/RC$ at the frequency given by Eq. (5.31).

5.6 The incident field on the half-wave dipole antenna shown in Fig. 5.7 is $E_0 \mathbf{a}_\theta$, with $E_0 = 5 \ \mu\text{V/m}$. The direction of incidence is $\theta_i = 60°$. Find the open-circuit voltage at the dipole terminals when $\lambda_0 = 10$ m.

5.7 A field $E_0(\mathbf{a}_\theta + j\mathbf{a}_\phi)$ is incident on the half-wave dipole antenna in Fig. 5.7 at $\theta_i = 90°$. The dipole is connected to a load $R_L = 50 \ \Omega$ by a transmission line with $Z_c = 73 \ \Omega$ and located $\lambda_0/2$ from the dipole terminals. The dipole input impedance is $73 \ \Omega$. Draw the equivalent Thevenin circuit for this system and find the power delivered to R_L when $E_0 = 10 \ \mu\text{V/m}$ and $\lambda_0 = 10$ m.

5.8 In the derivation of Eq. (5.59) the relationship

$$\text{Re } Z'_{\text{in}} = Z_c \frac{1 - |\Gamma_g|^2 \, e^{-4\alpha l}}{|1 - \Gamma_g \, e^{-2\gamma l}|^2}$$

was used. Derive this relationship by expressing Z'_{in} in terms of Γ_g.

5.9 A quarter-wave monopole antenna has $Z_{\text{in}} = R_a + R + jX$ where $R_a = 36 \ \Omega$, $R = 5 \ \Omega$, $jX = j10$. This antenna is connected to a receiver with input impedance of $50 \ \Omega$ and noise figure $F = 5$, as in Fig. P5.9. The antenna has a directivity of 3.2 and $\lambda_0 = 10$ m. The antenna-noise temperature is 10^6 K and R is at 290 K. The effective receiver bandwidth is 10 kHz. Find the required incident power per meter squared and the incident electric field in volts per meter to give an output signal-to-noise ratio of 10 dB. What is the effective receiver-noise temperature and the system-noise temperature? R_a is the antenna radiation resistance, R is the antenna ohmic resistance. What is the efficiency η and gain G for this antenna?

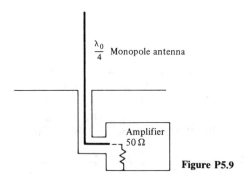

$\dfrac{\lambda_0}{4}$ Monopole antenna

Amplifier
$50 \ \Omega$

Figure P5.9

5.10 A microwave receiver shown in Fig. P5.10 uses a paraboloidal reflector antenna with a gain of 30 dB. The 50 ft of waveguide connecting the antenna and mixer produces a total loss of 3 dB. The mixer has a conversion loss of 3 dB and a noise figure of 4 dB. The IF amplifier has a noise figure of 6 dB and a bandwidth of 1 MHz. The antenna-noise temperature is 20 K and the waveguide is at 290 K. Find the required incident signal power per unit area to give an output signal-to-noise ratio of 10 dB at the IF amplifier output. $\lambda_0 = 3$ cm. Find the overall system-noise temperature. The system is impedance-matched.

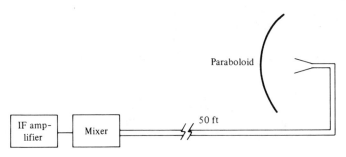

Figure P5.10

5.11 A radar system as shown in Fig. P5.11 has a system-noise temperature of 1000 K and a bandwidth of 2 MHz. The system uses an antenna with a 40-dB gain and has peak transmitter power of 10^5 W. If the target has a radar cross section $\sigma = 2$ m², find the maximum range R that will yield a signal-to-noise ratio of 12 dB at the receiver. The wavelength $\lambda_0 = 10$ cm.

Figure P5.11

5.12 In the microwave relay link shown in Fig. P5.12 the range $R = 50$ km. The receiver-system-noise temperature is 1000 K. The bandwidth of the system is 10^8 Hz and $\lambda_0 = 3$ cm. The antenna gains for transmitter and receiver are 40 dB. Find the required transmitter power to yield a signal-to-noise ratio of 40 dB. Assume impedance and polarization are optimally matched.

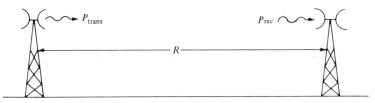

Figure P5.12

5.13 An antenna with a gain of 40 dB is connected to a preamplifier (impedance-matched) with a gain of 30 dB and a noise figure of 6 dB. The preamplifier output is connected to a receiver having a noise figure of 10 dB by means of a transmission line having a length of 20 m and an attenuation of 0.5-dB/m. The preamplifier output impedance is 60 Ω, the receiver input impedance is 75 Ω, and the transmission-line characteristic impedance is 50 Ω. The antenna-noise temperature is 50 K, the system bandwidth is 10 MHz, and β for the transmission line is 20π rad/m. The wavelength of operation is 10 cm. Find the following parameters for the system: the attenuation α for the transmission line; the mismatch factors M_1, M_2; the line loss L; and the system-noise temperature T_S. What is the required incident power per unit area in order to give a signal-to-noise ratio of 30 dB at the receiver output?

5.14 For the satellite communication system discussed as Example 5.6 in Sec. 5.3 the following additional system parameters apply:

> Bandwidth = 10 MHz
> Satellite-receiver system-noise temperature = 1100 K
> Ground-station antenna-noise temperature = 100 K
> Feed-line temperature = 300 K
> Receiver-noise temperature T_F = 400 K

Find the signal-to-noise ratio at the satellite and at the ground station.

5.15 Find the radar cross section σ for a small dielectric sphere with the following parameters: $\epsilon = 2.5\epsilon_0$, radius $a = 1$ cm. Compare your result for σ with the cross-sectional area πa^2. $\lambda_0 = 10$ cm. See Prob. 2.7.

5.16 A police traffic-control radar has the following parameters:

> Transmitter input power to antenna = 100 mW
> Antenna size = 20-cm-diameter parabolic reflector with an overall
>   antenna efficiency of 0.6
> Frequency = 10.55 GHz
> Receiver antenna same as used for transmitting
> System-noise temperature = 1000 K
> Bandwidth = 1 kHz
> Minimum signal-to-noise ratio for reliable detection = 10 dB

(a) Compute the antenna gain.
(b) Find the maximum range at which a small car with a radar cross section of 0.2 m² can be detected.

5.17 A motorist uses a small microwave receiver to detect the presence of police radar. The receiver uses an antenna with a gain of 15 dB and has a minimum detectable signal sensitivity of −60 dBM (10^{-6} mW). At what range can the police radar be detected, assuming that this radar has the parameters given in Prob. 5.16? A sensitivity of −60 dBM can be achieved with a diode detector. If a superheterodyne receiver is used with a bandwidth of 10 kHz and a system-noise temperature of 5000 K, what is the maximum range at which the police radar will produce a signal with a signal-to-noise ratio of 4? What factor gives the motorist an advantage over the police officer?

TWO

PROPAGATION

SIX

RADIO-WAVE PROPAGATION

In the previous chapter a number of examples involving the determination of the received signal power in a communication link were given. These all involved systems for which the propagation of the electromagnetic energy between the transmitting and receiving antennas took place under free-space conditions. Free-space propagation does essentially occur for some communication links under ideal conditions—a satellite-to-ground-station link is a typical example. However, for most communication links the signal propagation is modified by the presence of the earth, the atmosphere, the ionosphere, and atmospheric hydrometeors such as raindrops, snow, and hail. The influence that the natural environment has on the propagation of radio waves is highly dependent on the frequency used, the directionality of the antennas involved, and the proximity of the antennas to the ground. The physical nature of the intervening path also may have a significant effect, since propagation over water is different from propagation over land, over heavily vegetated areas, or over urbanized areas where tall buildings produce a variety of scattering and diffraction effects.

The evaluation of a proposed communication link must be carried out with due attention paid to propagation effects. In many cases where propagation is strongly affected by the refractive index variations of the atmosphere or ionosphere, or by prevailing rain rates, the evaluation should be carried out in a statistical sense. The goal would be to ensure that sufficient signal-to-noise margin is available so that under adverse propagation conditions outages will occur for only small intervals of time. The type of communication service involved generally dictates the tolerable probability of an outage occurring.

We can generally predict the performance of a communication link on the basis of assumed typical characteristics for the propagation path. It is convenient to break the discussion of propagation effects into those categories that represent the most significant phenomena that influence radio-wave propagation in four broad frequency intervals. The first is extremely low or very low frequency propagation involving frequencies below a few kilohertz. In this frequency range the wavelength λ_0 is greater than 10^5 m. The antennas used are very large and are of necessity close to the ground, or buried in the ground. The radio wave is reflected from the ionosphere, and a form of earth-ionosphere waveguide exists that may be thought of as providing a guiding path for the waves as they propagate around the earth. This waveguide model is particularly useful for frequencies below 1 kHz. Extremely low frequencies are useful in communicating with submerged submarines. The higher frequencies are attenuated very rapidly by the high conductivity of seawater.

The second range of frequencies is from 1 kHz up to a few megahertz. In this frequency range the propagation is strongly influenced by the presence of the ground. Local communication over distances of a few hundred miles is by means of the surface wave. Standard AM broadcasting occurs in this frequency range.

The third frequency range is from a few megahertz up to 30 to 40 MHz. In this band, which includes international shortwave broadcasting, the radio wave is reflected from the ionosphere to provide communication over long skip distances that may be thousands of miles in length. Over the propagation path, free-space propagation conditions are approached, but the variability of the electron concentration with time of day, yearly variations, etc., produces a considerable amount of fading as well as periods of time when only certain frequencies are usable.

The fourth category involves frequencies above 50 MHz. In this case the antennas are relatively small and may be placed at heights of many wavelengths above the ground. The main propagation effects are those associated with interference between the signals propagated along the direct line-of-sight path and those reflected from the ground. At very high frequencies, several gigahertz and up, attenuation and scatter by rain and atmospheric gases, predominantly water vapor, must also be considered. Scattering and diffraction of radio waves by hills, buildings, trees, etc., is also much more pronounced at the higher frequencies.

The propagation phenomena of importance at frequencies above 50 MHz are predominantly those associated with interference effects from ground reflections. These interference effects are relatively easy to analyze and are therefore discussed first. After high-frequency interference effects have been discussed, surface-wave propagation of radio waves in the frequency range of a few kilohertz up to a few megahertz will be described. The sections that follow will treat shortwave propagation involving ionospheric reflection, attenuation and scattering of microwaves by rain and other atmospheric constituents, tropospheric scatter propagation, the earth-ionosphere waveguide model for extremely low frequency propagation, propagation into seawater, and the phenomena of ducting.

6.1 ANTENNAS LOCATED OVER A FLAT EARTH

The general features of the interference phenomena associated with antennas placed over the earth can be determined by studying the effects associated with antennas located above a flat earth. Figure 6.1 shows a transmitting antenna at height h_1 and a receiving antenna at height h_2, with separation d. The figure also shows the direct ray and indirect or reflected ray that reach the receiving antenna. When the two path lengths R_1 and R_2 differ by an appropriate amount there may be either constructive or destructive interference at the receiving antenna.

With reference to Fig. 6.1, the field that reaches the receiving antenna directly will produce a voltage proportional to

$$f_1(\theta_1)f_2(\theta_1')\frac{e^{-jk_0R_1}}{4\pi R_1}$$

where f_1 and f_2 are the *radiation field strength patterns* of the two antennas. The voltage produced by the indirect wave is proportional to

$$f_1(\theta_2)f_2(\theta_2')\rho\, e^{j\phi}\frac{e^{-jk_0R_2}}{4\pi R_2}$$

where $\rho\, e^{j\phi}$ is the reflection coefficient at the ground. In the usual situation h_1 and h_2 are very small compared with the separation d, so the angles θ_1, θ_2, θ_1', θ_2' are very small, and the antenna radiation patterns can be assumed constant over the range of angles involved. An exception would be the case when highly

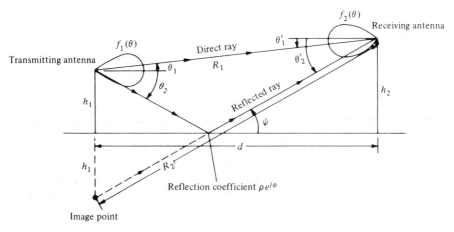

Figure 6.1 Illustration of direct and reflected rays.

directive antennas are used and h_2 is large, such as occurs if the transmitting antenna is located on the ground and the receiving antenna is located aboard a high-flying aircraft. In this case very little power might be radiated toward the ground; that is $f_1(\theta_2) \ll f_1(\theta_1)$. The total received voltage will be proportional to (we use $R_2 \approx R_1$ in the denominator)

$$\left| f_1(\theta_1) f_2(\theta_1') \frac{e^{-jk_0R_1}}{4\pi R_1} \left[1 + \rho e^{j\phi} \frac{f_1(\theta_2) f_2(\theta_2')}{f_1(\theta_1) f_2(\theta_1')} e^{-jk_0(R_2-R_1)} \right] \right| = \left| f_1(\theta_1) f_2(\theta_1') \frac{e^{-jk_0R_1}}{4\pi R_1} \right| F$$

(6.1)

The factor F, called the *path-gain factor*, shows how the field at the receiving antenna differs from the value it would have under free-space propagation conditions. When it can be assumed that $f_1(\theta_2) \approx f_1(\theta_1)$ and $f_2(\theta_2') \approx f_2(\theta_1')$, then F can be expressed as

$$F = |1 + \rho e^{j\phi - jk_0(R_2 - R_1)}|$$

(6.2)

The path-gain factor is the array factor associated with the antenna at height h_1 and its image below the surface, with the relative excitation of the image antenna being $\rho e^{j\phi}$.

With reference to Fig. 6.1, it can be seen that $R_1 = [d^2 + (h_2 - h_1)^2]^{1/2}$ and $R_2 = [d^2 + (h_1 + h_2)^2]^{1/2}$. When h_1 and h_2 are very small compared with d, a binomial expansion gives

$$R_1 \approx d + \frac{1}{2}\frac{(h_2 - h_1)^2}{d} \qquad R_2 \approx d + \frac{1}{2}\frac{(h_2 + h_1)^2}{d}$$

from which we obtain

$$R_2 - R_1 = \frac{2h_1 h_2}{d}$$

If $\rho e^{j\phi}$ were equal to -1 then

$$F = |1 - e^{-jk_02h_1h_2/d}| = 2\left|\sin\frac{k_0 h_1 h_2}{d}\right|$$

(6.3)

This shows that interference effects can lead to a doubling of the field strength relative to its value under free-space conditions. With reference to Fig. 6.2 we let ψ_0 be the elevation angle given by $\tan\psi_0 = h_2/d$ so that Eq. (6.3) can be written as

$$F = 2|\sin(k_0 h_1 \tan \psi_0)|$$

(6.4)

The relationship expressed by Eq. (6.4) is usually plotted in the form of a coverage diagram showing the variation of F with h_2 and d, that is, with ψ_0, for given values of h_1 and λ_0 expressed as a ratio h_1/λ_0. Note that F is a maximum when

$$\tan \psi_0 = \frac{1}{k_0 h_1}\left(\frac{\pi}{2} + n\pi\right) = \frac{\lambda_0}{h_1}\left(\frac{1}{4} + \frac{n}{2}\right) \qquad n = 0, 1, 2, \ldots$$

(6.5a)

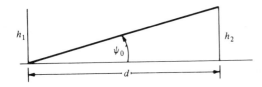

Figure 6.2 Elevation angle ψ_0.

and is a minimum when

$$\tan \psi_0 = \frac{\lambda_0}{h_1} \frac{n}{2} \qquad n = 0, 1, 2, \ldots \tag{6.5b}$$

A coverage diagram is a plot of the relative field strength as a function of direction in space from the transmitting antenna. It is analogous to the field-strength radiation pattern of an antenna. In any coverage diagram the fixed parameters are the height h_1 of the transmitting antenna and the wavelength λ_0. The distance d to the location of the receiving antenna and the height h_2 of the receiving antenna are variable parameters, and each pair of values h_2, d determines a point in space. The coverage diagram is a plot of the curves $F/r =$ constant in the $h_2 d$ plane. In most situations the direct line-of-sight distance r between antennas is very nearly equal to the horizontal distance d. The various curves of F/r that are plotted are usually chosen to represent the same signal level that would be obtained at a distance of a multiple or a fractional multiple of a convenient free-space reference range r_f; for example, $F/r = m/r_f$ or $F = mr/r_f \approx md/r_f$, with $m = 1, \sqrt{2}, 2, \ldots$ or $1/\sqrt{2}$, $1/2, \ldots$. The difference in signal level between successive curves is then 3 dB. By using Eq. (6.3) we find that the constant signal level curves are given by (we assume that $r \approx d$ and $r_f \approx d_f$)

$$F = 2 \left| \sin \frac{k_0 h_1 h_2}{d} \right| = m \frac{d}{d_f} \tag{6.6a}$$

when the reflection coefficient equals -1. For the flat-earth case it is more convenient to use Eq. (6.4) or (6.5) which gives

$$2|\sin k_0 h_1 \tan \psi_0| \approx 2|\sin k_0 h_1 \psi_0| = m \frac{d}{d_f} \tag{6.6b}$$

In this equation d can be treated as the radial coordinate and ψ_0 as the angle coordinate in a polar-coordinate reference frame. However, note that since the vertical scale representing h_2 is usually expanded relative to that for d, the angle ψ_0 appears much larger than it actually is.

Whenever $h_1 \gg \lambda_0$ and n is small, $\tan \psi_0 \approx \psi_0$ and the above relations show that the lobe structure is very fine; i.e., the angular separation between lobes is very small. For example, if $h_1 = 100\lambda_0$, then the lobes are separated by $\lambda_0/2h_1 = 1/200$ rad, or by approximately 0.3°. Figure 6.3 shows a typical coverage diagram. If r_f is the free-space range for a given received signal strength, then with interference taken into account the maximum range is $2r_f$, which corresponds to a horizontal distance $d = 2r_f \cos \psi_0$. For small values of ψ_0

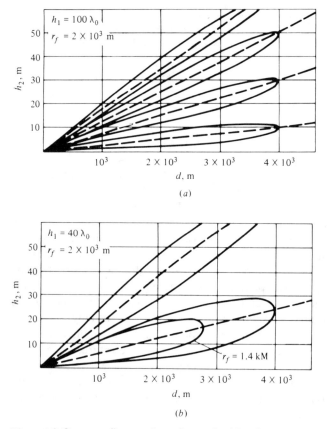

Figure 6.3 Coverage diagrams for a flat earth with reflection coefficient equal to -1.

we have $d \approx 2r_f$. The curves corresponding to $d = 2r_f \cos \psi_0$ appear as vertical lines in Fig. 6.3 because of the greatly expanded vertical scale. The coverage diagrams shown in Fig. 6.3 are plotted for a free-space propagation distance of 2 km. Any pair of values of h_2 and d that lies on the curve describing a lobe represents a point in space where the received signal strength is the same as it would be at a distance of 2 km under free-space propagation conditions. The smaller lobe shown in Fig. 6.3b represents a constant signal level 3 dB greater than that of the larger lobe and comes from using $m = \sqrt{2}$ in Eq. (6.6b).

When the coverage diagram has been plotted it is a simple matter to determine the field strength at the receiving antenna relative to the free-space value. For example, if the receiving antenna height is 10 m, Fig. 6.3b shows that the received signal strength at a distance of 3.2 km is the same as that at 2 km under free-space conditions. The same figure shows that by raising the antenna height to 25 m at a distance of 4 km a maximum signal level will be received. This signal level will be the same as that at 2 km with free-space propagation.

When the angle ψ_0 is considerably below the first lobe maximum, Eq. (6.4) can be approximated by $2k_0h_1\psi_0$, so

$$F = 2k_0h_1\psi_0 = \frac{2k_0h_1h_2}{d} \qquad (6.7)$$

which makes the received signal voltage vary as the inverse square of the distance, thus reducing the maximum useful range quite severely.

The coverage diagrams shown in Fig. 6.3 are based on taking $\rho = 1$, $\phi = \pi$. In practice this is a good approximation for the reflection coefficient for both horizontal and vertical polarization when the grazing angle ψ is small, say, $1°$ or less. When ψ is larger than $1°$, $\rho e^{j\phi}$ may depart appreciably from -1 for vertical polarization but may still be approximated by -1 for horizontal polarization for values of ψ up to $10°$ or more.

The reflection coefficient $\rho e^{j\phi}$ is given by the Fresnel expressions for the reflection coefficients for a plane TEM wave polarized with the electric field in the plane of incidence (vertical polarization) and for a wave polarized with the electric field perpendicular to the plane of incidence (horizontal polarization). The Fresnel reflection coefficients depend on the ground conductivity, permittivity, frequency, and angle of incidence. If the ground conductivity is σ, the permittivity ϵ is $\kappa\epsilon_0$, and ψ is the grazing angle of incidence, then

$$\rho\, e^{j\phi} = \frac{(\kappa - j\chi)\sin\psi - \sqrt{(\kappa - j\chi) - \cos^2\psi}}{(\kappa - j\chi)\sin\psi + \sqrt{(\kappa - j\chi) - \cos^2\psi}} \qquad \text{vertical polarization} \qquad (6.8a)$$

$$\rho\, e^{j\phi} = \frac{\sin\psi - \sqrt{(\kappa - j\chi) - \cos^2\psi}}{\sin\psi + \sqrt{(\kappa - j\chi) - \cos^2\psi}} \qquad \text{horizontal polarization} \qquad (6.8b)$$

where $\chi = \sigma/\omega\epsilon_0$. Typical values for the dielectric constant κ are around 15, while the conductivity σ may range from 10^{-3} to 3×10^{-2} S/m, with 10^{-2} S/m being a typical value for flat prairie land. The conductivity of mountainous regions is much lower. In general, κ is smaller, around 6 or 7, for soil with poor conductivity and will increase up to about 30 for soil with a high conductivity.

Figure 6.4 shows the behavior of ρ and ϕ as a function of the grazing angle ψ. Of particular significance is the Brewster angle effect for vertical polarization, which causes ρ to go through a minimum for values of ψ below about $15°$. As ρ moves through the minimum with decreasing values of ψ, the phase angle ϕ undergoes a rapid change from near $0°$ to $180°$. This effect makes $\rho e^{j\phi}$ nearly equal to -1 for both vertical and horizontal polarizations when the grazing angle ψ approaches zero. For a perfectly conducting surface $\rho e^{j\phi}$ would equal $+1$ for vertical polarization. As the frequency ω increases, the effect of a finite ground conductivity decreases, since the parameter $\chi = \sigma/\omega\epsilon_0$ decreases. Thus for frequencies above 50 MHz, the ground behaves very nearly like a dielectric medium, since the displacement current $j\omega\epsilon\mathbf{E}$ is then much larger than the conduction current $\sigma\mathbf{E}$. If the point of reflection occurs over water, particularly seawater, the reflection coefficient can be approximated by -1 for horizontal

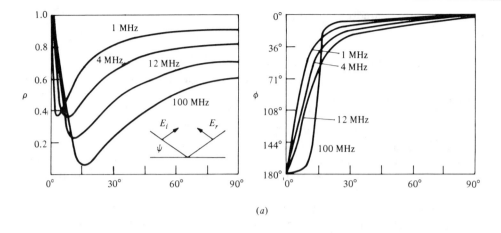

(a)

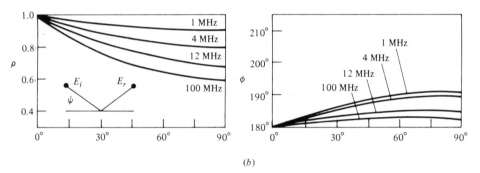

(b)

Figure 6.4 Typical reflection coefficients for the ground as a function of grazing angle ψ. $\kappa = 15$, $\sigma = 10^{-2}$ S/m. (a) Vertical polarization and (b) horizontal polarization.

polarization but may differ significantly from -1 for vertical polarization, as reference to Fig. 6.5 shows. In the case of a rough sea the reflection coefficient could be quite small for either polarization.

Whenever the point of reflection occurs over a rough surface the field is scattered in a more diffuse manner, and the specular reflected component, and hence ρ, is reduced in value. A measure of the height of the surface irregularities that constitute a "rough surface" may be obtained by considering the effective wavelength of the incident wave in the direction perpendicular to the surface. If z is the coordinate perpendicular to the surface and x is the coordinate along the surface, the incident wave will have a propagation factor $e^{jk_0 z \sin \psi - jk_0 x \cos \psi}$. Thus in the vertical direction the effective wavelength λ_v is given by

$$\lambda_v = \frac{2\pi}{k_0 \sin \psi} = \frac{\lambda_0}{\sin \psi} \tag{6.9}$$

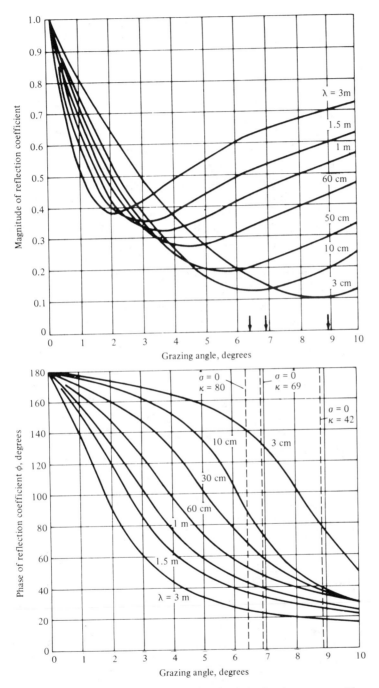

Figure 6.5 Reflection coefficient for vertical polarization for seawater. The marked angles are the Brewster angles when the conductivity is zero. (*From D. E. Kerr, Propagation of Short Radio Waves, McGraw-Hill Book Company, New York, 1951.*)

When the grazing angle of incidence is small, λ_v will be large compared with λ_0, often by a factor of 10 to 100. If the point of reflection is raised by an amount $\lambda_v/10$ the change in phase of the reflected wave reaching the receiving antenna will be $(2k_0 \sin \psi)\lambda_v/10 = 0.4\pi$. This may be regarded as being the boundary between what can be considered to be a rough surface and a smooth surface.[†] With this criterion the surface of generally flat land can be considered "smooth" whenever the surface irregularities have an average height variation of $\lambda_0/10 \sin \psi$. For example, with $\lambda_0 = 1$ m and $\psi = 1°$, we find that height variations of up to 6 m can still be regarded as a smooth surface. At the longer wavelengths most surfaces appear to be smooth, but at microwave frequencies most surfaces would be rough and the reflection coefficient would be smaller than that given by the Fresnel formulas.

A complication that has not been included in the flat-earth interference formulas is the effect of the decrease in the index of refraction of the atmosphere with height above the surface.[‡] At greater heights the less dense atmosphere results in a smaller index of refraction. This has the effect of causing the ray that leaves the antenna at a finite angle relative to the ground to curve or bend in a downward direction in accordance with Snell's law of refraction. The phenomenon of ray curvature may be readily understood by dividing the atmosphere into layers, with discrete values for the index of refraction in each layer, as shown in Fig. 6.6. For this staircase approximation to the continuous variation in the index of refraction, Snell's law gives

$$n_1 \sin \theta_1 = n_2 \sin \theta_2 = \cdots n_n \sin \theta_n = \cdots$$

Thus since each successive value of n_n is smaller than the preceding value, the angles θ_n must increase and the ray curves in the downward direction. For propagation over a spherical earth this ray curvature extends the radio horizon beyond the geometrical horizon.

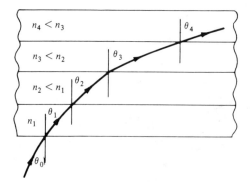

Figure 6.6 Illustration of ray curvature.

[†] The Rayleigh criterion allows for an obstruction with a height of $\lambda_v/8$ leading to a maximum phase change of 0.5π.

[‡] The decrease in the refractive index with height is not always monotonic. Inversion layers leading to a phenomenon known as *ducting* can occur. Such effects are discussed in Sec. 6.12.

The effect of ray curvature can be taken into account in a simple way for propagation over a spherical earth by replacing the earth with an earth having a larger radius and considering the rays to propagate along straight lines, provided the index of refraction decreases linearly with height. By means of this artifice the height of any point on the ray above the surface of the earth remains the same. For propagation studies a standard index-of-refraction profile is commonly chosen such that it is equivalent to increasing the radius of the earth by a factor of 4/3. Thus the effective earth's radius a_e is chosen to be 5280 mi (8497 km). With reference to Fig. 6.7, it is seen that $(h_1 + a_e)^2 = R^2 + a_e^2$, so $R^2 = 2h_1 a_e + h_1^2 \approx 2h_1 a_e$. Since the antenna height h_1 is small compared with the distance to the horizon, the slant distance R is nearly equal to the horizontal distance d_T to the horizon. Thus the distance to the horizon is given by $d_T = (2h_1 a_e)^{1/2}$, and if d_T is expressed in miles and h_1 in feet we have

$$d_T \text{ mi} = \sqrt{2h_1 \text{ ft}} \tag{6.10}$$

The maximum line-of-sight distance in miles between two antennas at heights h_1 and h_2 ft above a spherical earth with standard refraction conditions is then readily seen to be given by

$$d_M = \sqrt{2h_1} + \sqrt{2h_2} \text{ mi} \tag{6.11}$$

The flat-earth interference formulas are generally not valid for distances approaching the maximum horizontal line-of-sight range. The exact distance over which the flat-earth formulas can be used depends on a number of factors, including wavelength. It is difficult to establish the range of validity without direct comparison with the interference effects based on using a spherical earth model. The evaluation of interference effects over a spherical earth is considerably more complex than that for a flat earth and is discussed in the next section.

6.2 ANTENNAS LOCATED OVER A SPHERICAL EARTH

For antennas located over a spherical earth, with an effective radius a_e to account for standard refraction, it is quite tedious to derive the appropriate formulas for the interference effects. The complications that arise are due to a

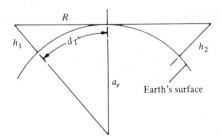

Figure 6.7 Illustration of horizontal range.

number of factors, including the difficulty of expressing the path-length difference between the direct ray and reflected ray in terms of the antenna heights h_1 and h_2 and horizontal distance d shown in Fig. 6.8. In addition, the grazing angle ψ relative to the tangent plane at the point of reflection must be determined in order to evaluate the reflection coefficient. Also for reflection from a spherical surface the rays in the reflected flux tube have a greater divergence than the rays in the incident flux tube, as pointed out in Sec. 4.5 and illustrated in Fig. 6.9. This increase in the divergence of the rays in a flux tube weakens the reflected field at the receiving antenna such that the appropriate expression for the path-gain factor F becomes

$$F = |1 + D\rho\, e^{j\phi - jk_0 \Delta R}|$$
$$= \{[1 + D\rho \cos(\phi - k_0 \Delta R)]^2 + [D\rho \sin(\phi - k_0 \Delta R)]^2\}^{1/2}$$
$$= \left[(1 + D\rho)^2 - 4D\rho \sin^2 \frac{\phi - k_0 \Delta R}{2}\right]^{1/2} \tag{6.12}$$

where D is the ray-amplitude divergence factor and ΔR is the path-length difference. [The divergence factor used here is the square root of that given by Eq. (4.59).]

An examination of Fig. 6.8 suggests that the relationships between the geometrical parameters describing the propagation paths would be relatively simple. This, unfortunately, is not the case. The known parameters are the two antenna heights h_1 and h_2 and the total range d. The point of reflection, which determines d_1, d_2, the grazing angle ψ, and the divergence factor D, is governed by a cubic equation. The evaluation of the path-gain factor governing the interference region for a spherical earth has been systematized by the introduction of a set of parameters K and J that are functions of known parameters S and T related to the antenna heights and total range d. The relevant equations are given below without derivation and include formulas for the

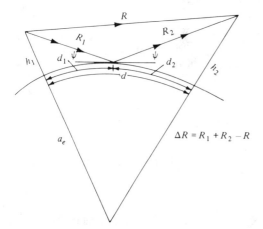

$$\Delta R = R_1 + R_2 - R$$

Figure 6.8 Reflection from a spherical earth.

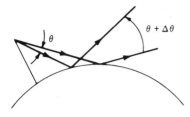

Figure 6.9 Illustration of ray divergence upon reflection from a spherical surface.

path-length difference $\Delta R = R_1 + R_2 - R$ and the divergence factor D.†

$$\Delta R = \frac{2h_1 h_2}{d} J(S, T) \tag{6.13}$$

$$\tan \psi = \frac{h_1 + h_2}{d} K(S, T) \tag{6.14}$$

$$D = \left[1 + \frac{4S_1 S_2^2 T}{S(1 - S_2^2)(1 + T)} \right]^{-1/2} \tag{6.15}$$

where $S_1 = \dfrac{d_1}{\sqrt{2a_e h_1}}$

$S_2 = \dfrac{d_2}{\sqrt{2a_e h_2}}$

$S = \dfrac{d}{\sqrt{2a_e h_1} + \sqrt{2a_e h_2}} = \dfrac{S_1 T + S_2}{1 + T}$

$T = \sqrt{h_1/h_2} \leq 1$

$J(S, T) = (1 - S_1^2)(1 - S_2^2)$

$K(S, T) = \dfrac{(1 - S_2^2) + T^2(1 - S_1^2)}{1 + T^2}$

and d_1, d_2, d, and ψ are given in Fig. 6.8. Note that T must be chosen less than unity, so h_1 is taken as the height of the lowest antenna. The above formulas show that ΔR and D are functions of S_1 and S_2 and hence are functions of S and T only, since S_1 and S_2 are determined by given values of S and T. The range d_1, which determines $d_2 = d - d_1$ and S_1, S_2, may be found by solving the equations given below:

$$d_1 = \frac{d}{2} + p \cos\left(\frac{\Phi + \pi}{3}\right) \tag{6.16a}$$

† D. E. Kerr, *Propagation of Short Radio Waves*, McGraw-Hill Book Company, New York, 1951, Sec. 2.13. Note that we have interchanged h_1, h_2 and S_1, S_2.

where
$$p = \frac{2}{\sqrt{3}} \left[a_e(h_1 + h_2) + \frac{d^2}{4} \right]^{1/2} \tag{6.16b}$$

$$\Phi = \cos^{-1} \frac{2a_e(h_1 - h_2)d}{p^3} \qquad h_1 \le h_2 \tag{6.16c}$$

The phase angle of the reflected wave relative to that of the direct wave due to the path-length difference ΔR only is given by

$$k_0 \Delta R = \frac{2k_0 h_1 h_2}{d} (1 - S_1^2)(1 - S_2^2)$$

$$= \frac{4\pi h_1^{3/2}}{\sqrt{2a_e} \lambda_0} \frac{h_2/h_1}{d/d_T} (1 - S_1^2)(1 - S_2^2) = \nu \zeta \pi \tag{6.17a}$$

where
$$\nu = \frac{4h_1^{3/2}}{\sqrt{2a_e}\lambda_0} = \frac{h_1^{3/2}}{1030\lambda_0} \tag{6.17b}$$

when h_1 and λ_0 are in meters, and

$$\zeta = \frac{h_2/h_1}{d/d_T} (1 - S_1^2)(1 - S_2^2) \tag{6.17c}$$

with $d_T = \sqrt{2a_e h_1}$. The parameter ζ depends only on S and T.

Coverage Diagrams

Coverage diagrams for a spherical earth are usually plotted on a chart where the constant-height contours above the earth's surface are shown as parabolic curves whose derivation is described below. With reference to Fig. 6.10 a curve of constant height h_2 above the earth's surface is given by

$$(y + a_e)^2 + x^2 = (a_e + h_2)^2$$

or
$$y^2 + 2a_e y + a_e^2 + x^2 = a_e^2 + 2a_e h_2 + h_2^2$$

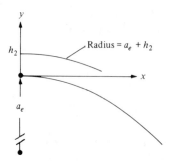

Figure 6.10 Illustration for constant-height curves.

Since $y \ll a_e$ and $h_2 \ll a_e$ this equation simplifies to

$$y = h_2 - \frac{x^2}{2a_e} \qquad (6.18a)$$

which describes a parabola. When we divide by h_1 we obtain

$$\frac{y}{h_1} = \frac{h_2}{h_1} - \frac{x^2}{2a_e h_1} = \frac{h_2}{h_1} - \frac{x^2}{d_T^2} \qquad (6.18b)$$

or

$$\hat{y} = \frac{h_2}{h_1} - \hat{x}^2 \qquad (6.18c)$$

where $\hat{y} = y/h_1$ and $\hat{x} = x/d_T$ are normalized variables. If the scale length along y is increased relative to that for x only the shape of these parabolic curves changes.

It is convenient to plot curves of constant values for the divergence factor D and path-length phase-difference parameter ζ on a curvilinear grid, in which the horizontal coordinate is d/d_T and the vertical coordinate is h_2/h_1. Such plots are given in Figs. 6.11 and 6.12. Each parabolic curve is a plot of $y/h_1 = \hat{y}$ as a function of $\hat{x} = x/d_T$, with $x = d$, for a given choice of h_2/h_1. For example, for $h_2/h_1 = 4$ we have $y/h_1 = 4 - (d/d_T)^2$ which gives $y/h_1 = 4$ at $d = 0$. The curves

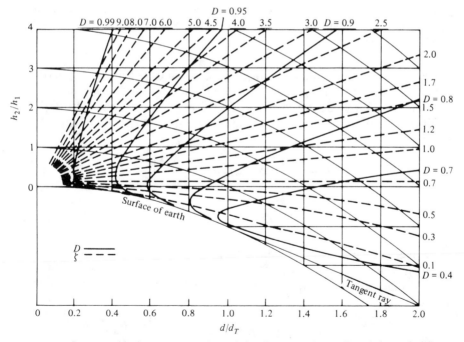

Figure 6.11 Contours showing constant values of the divergence factor D and the path-difference phase variable ζ for h_2/h_1 up to 4. [*From C. R. Burrows and S. S. Attwood (eds.), Radio Wave Propagation, Academic Press, New York, 1949.*]

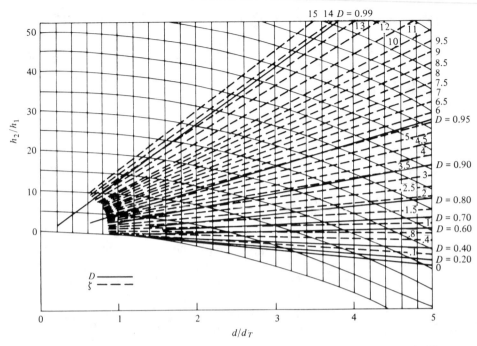

Figure 6.12 Contours showing constant values of the divergence factor D and the path-difference phase variable ζ for h_2/h_1 up to 50. [*From C. R. Burrows and S. S. Attwood (eds.), Radio Wave Propagation, Academic Press, New York, 1949.*]

are labeled by the parameter h_2/h_1. Since D and ζ can be expressed as functions of S and T, they are functions of h_2/h_1 and d/d_T only and can be plotted as constant-value curves on the h_2/h_1 versus d/d_T curvilinear grid.

If the reflection coefficient is assumed to be equal to -1, then the path-gain factor becomes

$$F = \left[(1+D)^2 - 4D \cos^2 \frac{k_0 \Delta R}{2} \right]^{1/2}$$

$$= \left[(1+D)^2 - 4D \cos^2 \left(\frac{\pi}{2} \nu \zeta \right) \right]^{1/2} \tag{6.19}$$

For a spherical earth it is convenient to use the normalized coordinates h_2/h_1 and d/d_T, where $d_T = \sqrt{2a_e h_1}$. The free-space reference range for a given coverage diagram is usually chosen as a suitable multiple of the horizontal range d_T. Hence a coverage diagram is a plot of

$$F = \left[(1+D)^2 - 4D \cos^2 \left(\frac{\pi}{2} \nu \zeta \right) \right]^{1/2} = m \frac{d}{d_T}$$

The following example shows how a coverage diagram may be constructed.

Example 6.1 Construction of a coverage diagram In this example we will illustrate the procedure for constructing a coverage diagram like those shown in Figs. 6.15 through 6.22. Consider the case where $h_1 = 45.7$ m and $\lambda_0 = 3$ m corresponding to a frequency of 100 MHz. This situation could represent an FM antenna installation. The parameter ν as given by Eq. (6.17b) has the value

$$\nu = \frac{45.7^{3/2}}{3090} = 0.1$$

For a reflection coefficient of -1 the lobe maxima occur when $\nu\zeta = 1, 3, 5, \ldots$, and the nulls occur when $\nu\zeta = 2, 4, 6, \ldots$. The corresponding values of ζ are $10, 30, 50, \ldots$ and $20, 40, 60, \ldots$.

The first step is to prepare a blank chart with the constant h_2/h_1 contours as a function of d/d_T. These contours are given by Eq. (6.18b) or (6.18c) and are parabolic curves. Note that in Eq. (6.18b) y and x are not normalized with respect to h_1 and d_T, respectively, but in Eq. (6.18c) they are. On this chart the tangent ray starting at $d/d_T = 1$ and intersecting the $h_2/h_1 = 1$ contour at $d/d_T = 2$ may be drawn as shown in Fig. 6.14. The equation for the tangent ray, which is a straight line, is $y = h_1 - 2(x/d_T)h_1$. This line intersects the h_2/h_1 curve at $d/d_T = 1 + \sqrt{h_2/h_1}$. It intersects the $h_2/h_1 = 4$ contour at $d/d_T = 3$.

The path-gain factor is

$$F = \left[(1 + D)^2 - 4D \cos^2 \frac{\pi\nu\zeta}{2} \right]^{1/2}$$

and is a function of h_2/h_1 and d/d_T, since D and ζ depend on these parameters. If we choose a lobe corresponding to a free-space range of $2d_T$, then the maximum value $\hat{x} = d/d_T$ can achieve will be 4 when $D = 1$, and we are located in a lobe maximum. In general, for other values of D and ζ we have

$$\hat{x} = \frac{d}{d_T} = 2F$$

while for a free-space range of $\sqrt{2}d_T$ and d_T, $\hat{x} = \sqrt{2}F$ and $\hat{x} = F$, respectively. For given values of h_2/h_1 and d/d_T we find ζ and D from Figs. 6.11 and 6.12 (for values covered by these charts) and thus compute F as a function of d/d_T for various values of h_2/h_1 as shown in Fig. 6.13. We must also satisfy the relationship

$$F = m \frac{d}{d_T} = \frac{d/d_T}{r_f/d_T}$$

which is a series of straight lines with slope $d_T/r_f = m$ where r_f/d_T is the chosen free-space range parameter. The intersection of these straight lines with the other curves of F as a function of d/d_T gives those values of d/d_T

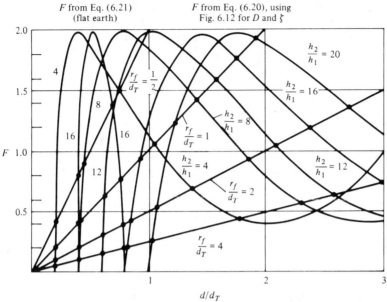

$$\frac{F \text{ from Eq. (6.21)}}{\text{(flat earth)}} \qquad \frac{F \text{ from Eq. (6.20), using}}{\text{Fig. 6.12 for } D \text{ and } \zeta}$$

Figure 6.13 Data for constructing a coverage diagram for $\nu = 0.1$.

that satisfy the equation

$$\frac{d}{d_T} = \frac{r_f}{d_T} F\left(\frac{d}{d_T}, \frac{h_2}{h_1}\right) = \frac{F}{m} \qquad (6.20)$$

For values of ζ greater than those given in Figs. 6.11 and 6.12 the flat-earth formulas apply, so $k_0 \Delta R = 2k_0 h_1 h_2/d = \nu\pi(h_2/h_1)/(d/d_T)$ and hence $\zeta = (h_2/h_1)/(d/d_T)$. In this range $D = 1$ and the path-gain factor simplifies to

$$F = 2\left|\sin\frac{\pi}{2}\nu\zeta\right| = 2\left|\sin\left(\frac{\pi}{2}\nu\frac{h_2/h_1}{d/d_T}\right)\right| \qquad (6.21)$$

The various lobes may now be drawn on the blank chart prepared earlier and showing the constant h_2/h_1 contours as a function of d/d_T. The resultant coverage diagram is shown in Fig. 6.14. ∎

Precaution must be exercised when constructing coverage diagrams, for the interference formulas giving the path-gain factor F become inaccurate as the region close to the tangent ray is approached. This region is characterized by a path-length-difference phase factor $\nu\pi\zeta$ less than $\pi/2$ and small values for the divergence factor D. As the tangent ray is approached, the divergence factor D approaches zero, and the path-gain factor F then begins to increase and becomes equal to unity, i.e., the same as for free space at the position of the tangent ray. This is not what really occurs, since in actual fact the field strength

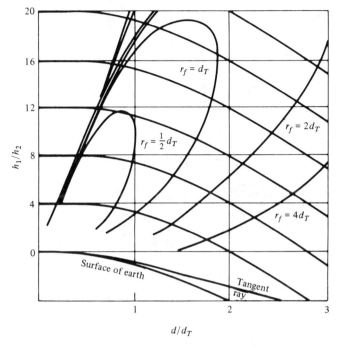

Figure 6.14 Coverage diagram for $\nu = 0.1$ based on data in Fig. 6.13.

decreases rapidly as the tangent ray is approached and beyond this point. The field in this region is governed by diffraction effects, which are discussed in the next section.

With reference to Fig. 6.13, it is seen that one of the plotted curves of F versus d/d_T increases for values of d/d_T greater than about 2. The reason for this is because D in this range is becoming small, and at the same time $\nu\pi\zeta$ is also very small. Hence the points of intersection of the straight lines with this curve of F for $h_2/h_1 = 4$ in the region of d/d_T greater than 2 do not give an accurate expression for the relative field strength and are therefore not included in the coverage diagram shown in Fig. 6.14. It is this same effect that does not permit the extension of the bottom lobes shown in Figs. 6.12 through 6.22 beyond the regions shown, since F would begin to increase because of the decreasing value of D as the tangent ray is approached.

A number of different coverage diagrams are shown in Figs. 6.15 through 6.22 for different values of ν. The reflection coefficient equals -1, and an equivalent earth radius equal to $4a/3$ is assumed. The path-gain factor F is plotted as a function of h_2/h_1 and d/d_T in these figures for various values of the parameter ν. These curves are obtained by using the data in Figs. 6.11 and 6.12 to obtain D and ζ for given values of h_2/h_1 and d/d_T. The numbers on the curves give the corresponding free-space range for the same signal level as obtained taking interference into account. For example, a curve labeled 4

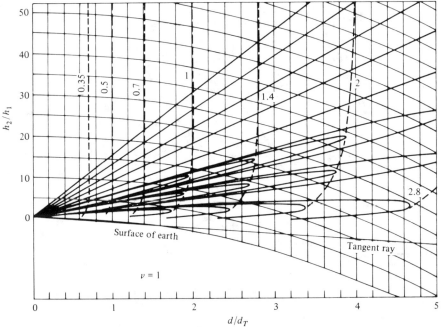

Figure 6.15 Coverage diagram for $\nu = 1$. [*From C. R. Burrows and S. S. Attwood (eds.), Radio Wave Propagation, Academic Press, New York, 1949.*]

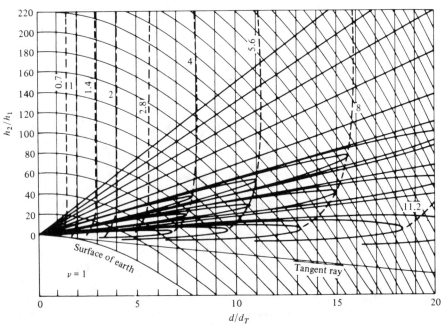

Figure 6.16 Coverage diagram for $\nu = 1$. [*From C. R. Burrows and S. S. Attwood (eds.), Radio Wave Propagation, Academic Press, New York, 1949.*]

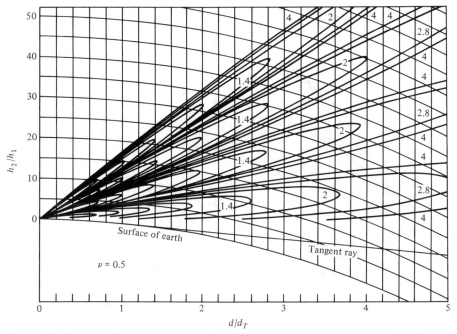

Figure 6.17 Coverage diagram for $\nu = 0.5$. [*From C. R. Burrows and S. S. Attwood (eds.), Radio Wave Propagation, Academic Press, New York, 1949.*]

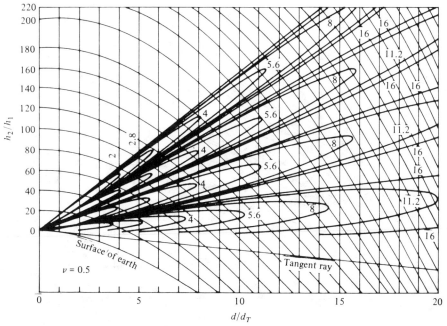

Figure 6.18 Coverage diagram for $\nu = 0.5$. [*From C. R. Burrows and S. S. Attwood (eds.), Radio Wave Propagation, Academic Press, New York, 1949.*]

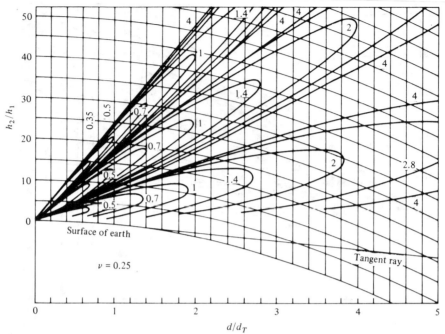

Figure 6.19 Coverage diagram for $\nu = 0.25$. [*From C. R. Burrows and S. S. Attwood (eds.), Radio Wave Propagation, Academic Press, New York, 1949.*]

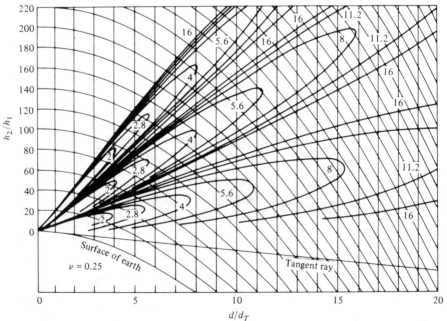

Figure 6.20 Coverage diagram for $\nu = 0.25$. [*From C. R. Burrows and S. S. Attwood (eds.), Radio Wave Propagation, Academic Press, New York, 1949.*]

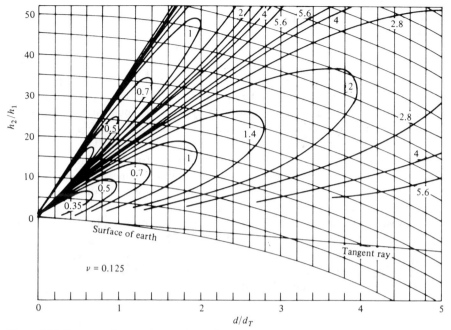

Figure 6.21 Coverage diagram for $\nu = 0.125$. [*From C. R. Burrows and S. S. Attwood (eds.), Radio Wave Propagation, Academic Press, New York, 1949.*]

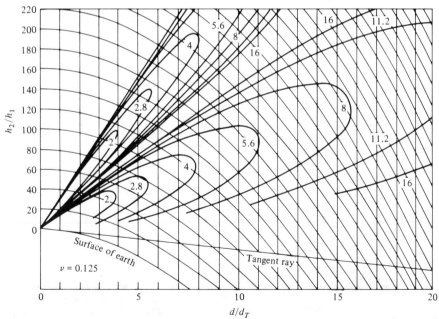

Figure 6.22 Coverage diagram for $\nu = 0.125$. [*From C. R. Burrows and S. S. Attwood (eds.), Radio Wave Propagation, Academic Press, New York, 1949.*]

corresponds to a free-space range of $r_f = 4d_T$. There is a 3-dB change in signal level between adjacent curves for one-way transmission.

When the reflection coefficient differs significantly from -1, then a coverage diagram describing the path gain factor F for that particular case must be constructed, since the generalized coverage diagrams shown in Figs. 6.15 through 6.22 no longer apply. The parameters D and ζ may still be found from Figs. 6.11 and 6.12, but now the grazing angle ψ must also be found in order to determine the reflection coefficient. For this purpose Fig. 6.23 giving the function $K(S, T)$ can be used to determine ψ by means of Eq. (6.14).

The formulas for evaluating interference effects for a spherical earth are much more involved than the relatively simple formulas that apply to a flat-earth model. It is therefore of interest to determine the conditions under which the flat-earth formulas will hold with acceptable accuracy.

The most critical parameter determining the interference phenomena is the phase associated with the path-length difference ΔR. For a flat earth this phase angle is given by $2k_0h_1h_2/d$ [see Eq. (6.3)], while for a spherical earth it is given by Eq. (6.17a) in the form $\pi\nu\zeta$. If we require that the flat-earth formula be accurate to within 0.1π, then we need

$$\frac{2k_0h_1h_2}{d} - \pi\nu\zeta \le 0.1\pi$$

By introducing the parameter ν into the flat-earth formula this expression can be written in the form

$$\nu\pi\left(\frac{h_2/h_1}{d/d_T} - \zeta\right) \le 0.1\pi$$

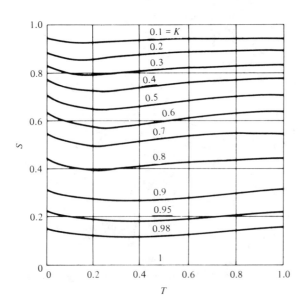

Figure 6.23 Constant K contours as a function of S and T (*Data from D. E. Kerr, Propagation of Short Radio Waves, McGraw-Hill Book Company, New York, 1951.*)

or equivalently

$$\frac{\nu\pi\hat{y}}{\hat{x}}\left[1-\left(1-\frac{d_1^2}{2a_eh_1}\right)\left(1-\frac{d_2^2}{2a_eh_2}\right)\right]\leq 0.1\pi \tag{6.22}$$

where $\hat{y}=h_2/h_1$ and $\hat{x}=d/d_T$, and Eq. (6.17c) is used to replace ζ. Since the above expression marks the boundary at which the flat-earth formulas will be valid, we will use the flat-earth relationship $h_2/h_1=d_2/d_1$ along with $d=d_1+d_2$ to simplify this expression. We can replace d_2 by $\hat{y}d_1$ and use $d=(1+\hat{y})d_1$ or $d_1=d/(1+\hat{y})$ to obtain

$$\left(1-\frac{d_1^2}{2a_eh_1}\right)\left(1-\frac{d_2^2}{2a_eh_2}\right)=\left[1-\left(\frac{\hat{x}}{1+\hat{y}}\right)^2\right]\left[1-\hat{y}\left(\frac{\hat{x}}{1+\hat{y}}\right)^2\right]$$

since $d_T^2=2a_eh_1$. In terms of the variables $\hat{x}$ and $\hat{y}$ Eq. (6.22) becomes

$$\hat{y}^2\hat{x}^3-\hat{y}(1+\hat{y})^3\hat{x}+\frac{0.1}{\nu}(1+\hat{y})^4\geq 0 \tag{6.23}$$

The regions in which this condition is satisfied are to the left of the $\nu=$ constant curves shown in Figs. 6.24 and 6.25.

In addition to keeping the phase error less than 0.1π we also require that the divergence factor D for a spherical earth should be close to unity, since this factor reduces the strength of the reflected field and is not present in the flat-earth model. In Figs. 6.24 and 6.25 the curves corresponding to $D=0.9$ and

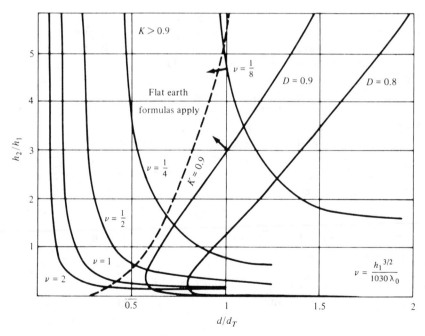

Figure 6.24 Illustration of region in which the flat-earth interference formulas are valid.

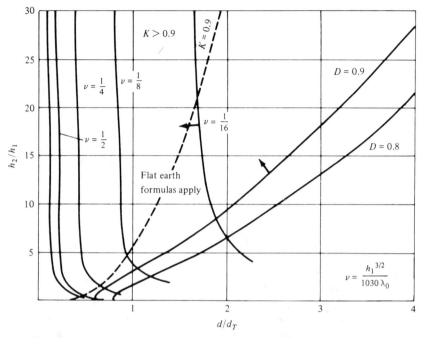

Figure 6.25 Illustration of region in which the flat-earth interference formulas are valid.

0.8 are shown. For reasonable accuracy we should require $D \geq 0.9$, and hence the region in which the flat-earth formulas can be applied with fair accuracy is above the $D = 0.9$ curve and to the left of a given $\nu =$ constant curve. For an expanded range of applications one could permit D to become as small as 0.8, but the resultant accuracy is then poorer.

The last parameter of interest is the grazing angle ψ, since when ψ is not small it is generally not possible to replace the reflection coefficient by -1. According to Eq. (6.14) $\tan \psi = (h_1 + h_2)K(S, T)/d$, which would be the same as for a flat earth if $K(S, T)$ is equal to unity. If we require an error not exceeding 10 percent for $\tan \psi$, then $K \geq 0.9$. The parameter K is relatively independent of the height ratio h_2/h_1 and will be greater than 0.9, provided $S \leq 0.3$.† The latter condition can be stated in the form

$$\hat{x} \leq 0.3(1 + \hat{y}^{1/2}) \tag{6.24}$$

upon substituting $\hat{x}$ and $\hat{y}$ into the expression for S given after Eq. (6.15). These curves are also shown in Figs. 6.24 and 6.25 and place a further restriction on the range of validity of the flat-earth formulas whenever it is necessary to evaluate the reflection coefficient from a knowledge of the grazing angle because ψ is too large to allow using -1 for the reflection coefficient.

---

† This is deduced from the chart of K versus S and T given in Kerr.

Figures 6.24 and 6.25 show that the flat-earth formulas apply for distances d that are generally considerably less than the total horizontal line-of-sight range $\sqrt{2a_eh_1} + \sqrt{2a_eh_2} = d_T(1 + \sqrt{\hat{y}})$, that is, for values of $\hat{x}$ considerably less than $1 + \sqrt{\hat{y}}$. The requirement that $K \geq 0.9$ restricts the maximum range to 0.3 of the total horizontal range. However, when ψ is small so that the reflection coefficient can be approximated by -1, then it is not necessary to know the grazing angle, and somewhat larger distances are allowed, particularly at the lower frequencies where the parameter ν is small. However, at the lower frequencies λ_0 is large and the antenna terminal heights are relatively small so $h_2/h_1 = \hat{y}$ would normally not be large; as Fig. 6.24 shows, the maximum distance over which the flat-earth formulas would apply is less than $\hat{x} = 1$ or d_T, which is the distance to the horizon from the antenna at height h_1, that is, $d < d_T = \sqrt{2a_eh_1}$.

Applications of Coverage Diagrams and Interference Formulas

The following examples will illustrate the use of the interference formulas and the coverage diagrams given in Figs. 6.15 through 6.22.

Example 6.2 Radar system A radar has its antenna at a height $h_1 = 15$ m above the ground. It is tracking an approaching aircraft flying at a height $h_2 = 300$ m. The wavelength $\lambda_0 = 10$ cm. The radar uses horizontal polarization so that the reflection coefficient will be assumed to be equal to -1. The objective is to determine at what range the aircraft can be detected when the free-space maximum-range capability of the radar is 40 km.

This problem is best solved by constructing a plot of relative received signal as a function of d/d_T as the aircraft flies towards the radar at a constant height h_2. From Eq. (6.17b) the parameter ν equals $h_1^{3/2}/1030\lambda_0 = 0.564$. A coverage diagram for $\nu = 0.564$ is not available, but the diagram given in Fig. 6.17 for $\nu = 0.5$ will be nearly correct and will therefore be used to illustrate the procedure. If we changed h_1 to 13.85 m we would get $\nu = 0.5$. The horizontal range d_T, assuming standard refraction, is $d_T = \sqrt{2a_eh_1} = 4122\sqrt{h_1} = 15.96$ km. The free-space maximum range is thus $40/15.96 = 2.5d_T$. In a radar the power incident on the target is modified by the square of the path gain factor, i.e., by F^2 relative to its value under free-space conditions. The power scattered by the target back to the radar is also modified by this same factor. Hence the received power is modified by the factor F^4 from its value under free-space conditions. Thus the signal level corresponding to adjacent lobes shown in the coverage diagram in Fig. 6.17 differs by 6 dB for the purpose of evaluating the performance of a radar system; for example, received power varies as r^{-4}, so an increase in r by a factor of $\sqrt{2}$ corresponds to a signal-level change of 6 dB.

We will let the lobe labeled 2 correspond to a received reference signal level S_0. With reference to Fig. 6.17, if we move along the constant-height contour $h_2/h_1 = 300/15 = 20$ we intersect the lowest lobe labeled 2.8 at a maximum range $d = 4.15d_T$. At this point the received signal will be 6 dB smaller than the reference level S_0. At $d = 4.35d_T$ we intersect the lobe labeled 4, which gives a signal level 12 dB below S_0. At $d = 3.6d_T$ we almost touch the lobe labeled 2 corresponding to a signal level S_0. As the target moves in, the lobes labeled 2.8 and 4 are intersected at $d = 3.3$ and $3.2d_T$, with corresponding signal levels 6 and 12 dB below S_0. The signal level then drops rapidly as the target moves through the interference null. At $d = 2.85, 2.8, 2.7$, and $2.55d_T$ the signal level goes from 12 dB below S_0 to 6 dB below S_0, to S_0, and to 6 dB above S_0, respectively, as the target moves through the second interference lobe. A maximum signal level occurs at $2.45d_T$, and by using linear interpolation between the 1.4 and 1 lobes this signal level is found to be about 8 dB above S_0. By continuing to move in along the constant-height contour, the signal variation as a function of d/d_T can be determined as the target passes through the various lobes. In Fig. 6.26 we show the relative signal level as a function of d/d_T.

The maximum free-space range of the radar is $2.5d_T$. Since S_0 corresponds to the signal level received with a maximum free-space range of $2d_T$ we see that the minimum detectable signal S_m will be $(2/2.5)^4 S_0 = 0.415 S_0$, or 3.88 dB below S_0 because of the r^{-4} dependence. In Fig. 6.26 a horizontal line is drawn at a signal level corresponding to 3.88 dB below the chosen reference level S_0. Whenever the target is located at a distance d such that the received signal is above this level it will be detected. Note that there are many blind spots and that as the target comes closer to the radar the signal level varies more rapidly and reaches higher peak values.

When the target reaches a distance such that the grazing angle ψ is several degrees, then the finite beam width of the radar antenna (which might be less than 5°) will prevent any significant radiation from striking

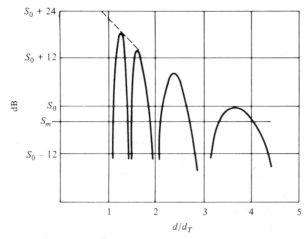

Figure 6.26 Relative signal strength as a function of d/d_T.

the ground. When this occurs the ground interference effects vanish, and the signal level will increase monotonically and proportional to d^{-4}, the same as for free-space conditions.

If we use the flat-earth formula then

$$\tan \psi = \frac{h_1 + h_2}{d}$$

We will assume that the radar antenna is always pointed at the target and that the antenna gain is reduced by 10 dB at an angle of 6° off axis. Furthermore we will assume that when the ray incident on the ground is reduced by an amplitude factor of $\sqrt{10}$ we can consider interference effects to be negligible. With reference to Fig. 6.27 we see that this occurs when $\psi + \psi_1 = 6°$; thus

$$\tan(\psi + \psi_1) = \frac{\tan \psi + \tan \psi_1}{1 - \tan \psi \tan \psi_1} = \frac{2h_2 d}{d^2 - (h_2^2 - h_1^2)} = \tan 6°$$

upon using $d \tan \psi_1 = h_2 - h_1$ and $d \tan \psi = h_2 + h_1$. The above equation may be solved for d to give $d = 5.72$ km $= 0.36 \, d_T$. Thus the target must get quite close to the radar before the ground interference effects become negligible. ∎

Example 6.3 FM communication link An FM transmitter has its antenna at a height h_2 equal to 80 m. The antenna gain is 5, and the transmitter power is 500 W. The receiving antenna is at a height h_1 equal to 10 m. The frequency of operation is 100 MHz. For this system $\nu = 0.01$ and $d_T = 4122\sqrt{10} = 13.03$ km, or $\sqrt{2 \times 32.8} = 8.1$ mi. We wish to find the field strength in volts per meter at a distance of 8.1 mi from the transmitter. If we refer to Fig. 6.25 we see that the flat earth formula (6.21) can be used. The path gain factor equals 0.25 so the power density is given by

$$\frac{1}{2Z_0}|\mathbf{E}|^2 = \frac{P_t G}{4\pi(4d_T)^2}$$

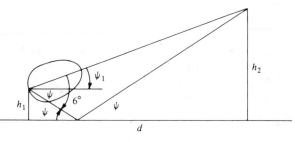

Figure 6.27 Illustration of effect of antenna pattern on the field incident on the ground.

Hence

$$|\mathbf{E}| = \left(\frac{Z_0 P_t G}{32\pi d_T^2}\right)^{1/2} = \left(\frac{120 \times 500 \times 5}{32 \times 1.3^2 \times 10^8}\right)^{1/2} = 7.4 \text{ mV/m}$$

At the receiving site the value of the path-gain factor is $d_T/4d_T = 0.25$. ∎

Example 6.4 Microwave communication link In a microwave communication link the antennas are mounted on towers at a height of 35 m above the ground. The wavelength of operation is 10 cm. It is required to find the maximum distance d that can be used so that the signal level is not reduced below its free-space value. Thus a path-gain factor F equal to 1 is required. The parameter ν is equal to $h_1^{3/2}/1030\lambda_0 = 2.01$. If we use the flat-earth interference formula [Eq. (6.3)] we have

$$F = 2\left|\sin\left(\frac{\pi}{2}\nu\frac{h_2/h_1}{d/d_T}\right)\right| = 2\left|\sin\pi\frac{d_T}{d}\right| = 1$$

and hence $d = 6d_T$ in order to make $F = 1$. But since $h_2 = h_1$ the maximum line-of-sight range is $2d_T$; quite clearly the flat-earth interference formula is not applicable.

A coverage diagram for $\nu = 2$ has not been included in this text. Thus we must use the formulas (6.14) to (6.17). Since $h_2 = h_1$, the parameters S_1 and S_2 are equal and $T = 1$, $S = d/2d_T = S_1$. Hence the divergence factor D equals

$$D = \left[1 + \frac{d^2/2}{d_T^2(1 - d^2/4d_T^2)}\right]^{-1/2} = \frac{(1 - d^2/4d_T^2)^{1/2}}{(1 + d^2/4d_T^2)^{1/2}}$$

and

$$\zeta = \frac{h_2/h_1}{d/d_T}\left(1 - \frac{d^2}{4d_T^2}\right)^2$$

When we equate the path-gain factor given by Eq. (6.19) to unity we obtain

$$\cos^2\frac{\pi\nu\zeta}{2} = \frac{D+2}{4}$$

This equation can be solved numerically, and it yields $d = 1.39d_T$, $D = 0.59$, and $\zeta = 0.19$. Thus the maximum range is $4122 \times 1.39\sqrt{35} = 33.88$ km. ∎

Example 6.5 Microwave link with unequal tower heights This example is the same as the previous one, with the exception that $h_2 = 50$ m. The path-gain factor F at a distance $d = 50$ km is to be determined. Since $h_1 \neq h_2$ we must find d_1 using Eq. (6.16). From Eq. (6.16b) we obtain

$$p = \frac{2}{\sqrt{3}}\left[8497(0.085) + \frac{50^2}{4}\right]^{1/2} = 42.38 \text{ km}$$

By using Eq. (6.16c) we find that

$$\Phi = \cos^{-1}\left(\frac{-.030 \times 50 \times 8497}{42.38^3}\right) = 1.739$$

We now use Eq. (6.16a) to get

$$d_1 = 25 + 42.38 \cos \frac{1.739 + \pi}{3} = 22.625 \text{ km}$$

Hence $d_2 = 50 - d_1 = 27.375$ km. The parameters S_1, S_2, and T given after Eq. (6.15) are $S_1 = 0.9277$, $S_2 = 0.9391$, and $T = 0.8367$, while $J = 0.01646$ and $K = 0.1269$. From Eq. (6.14) $\tan \psi = 2.16 \times 10^{-4}$. In this example ψ is so small that we can assume the reflection coefficient to be equal to -1. From Eq. (6.15) we obtain $D = 0.262$, while Eq. (6.17c) gives $\zeta = 0.01147$. We can now compute F from Eq. (6.19); thus

$$F = \left[1.262^2 - 4 \times 0.262 \cos^2\left(\frac{\pi}{2} \times 2.01 \times 0.01147\right)\right]^{1/2}$$

$$= 0.739 .$$

The received signal voltage will be 0.739 of what it would have been with free-space propagation conditions. ∎

6.3 THE FIELD IN THE DIFFRACTION ZONE

According to geometrical optics the field strength below the line of sight or tangent ray is zero. However, because of diffraction effects the radiated field penetrates into the shadow zone below the tangent ray. Although the field strength decreases rapidly as the point of observation moves deeper into the shadow zone, the field is still finite and often of sufficient strength to produce a useful signal. The field strength is also influenced by diffraction effects in the region above but close to the tangent ray.

There is no simple method of calculating the field strength in the near vicinity of the tangent ray. However, once the point of observation is sufficiently far into the shadow (diffraction) zone, a simple expression exists for finding the path-gain factor F. In the intermediate zone the path-gain factor can be determined with acceptable accuracy by drawing a smooth curve connecting the values of F in the interference region to those values determined for points well into the shadow zone. Thus one should find the values of d/d_T that correspond to the first maximum where $\pi v \zeta/2 = \pi/2$ and $F = 1 + D$ and the point where $\pi v \zeta/2 = \pi/4$ and $F = (1 + D)^{1/2}$ and join these by a smooth curve to several values of F determined for values of d/d_T in the diffraction zone.

In the diffraction zone F is given by†

$$F = V_1(X)U_1(Z_1)U_1(Z_2) \tag{6.25}$$

† Ibid.

where the main attenuation function $V_1(X)$ is given by

$$V_1(X) = 2\sqrt{\pi X}\ e^{-2.02X} \tag{6.26}$$

and X is the distance measured in natural units of length L and Z_1 and Z_2 are the antenna heights measured in natural units of height H. These natural units are given by

$$L = 2\left(\frac{a_e^2}{4k_0}\right)^{1/3} = 28.41\lambda_0^{1/3}\ \text{km} \tag{6.27a}$$

$$H = \left(\frac{a_e}{2k_0^2}\right)^{1/3} = 47.55\lambda_0^{2/3}\ \text{m} \tag{6.27b}$$

where λ_0 is measured in meters. In natural units $X = d/L$ and $Z_{1,2} = h_{1,2}/H$. The attenuation function V_1 is shown in Fig. 6.28, while the height-gain function $U_1(Z)$ is shown in Fig. 6.29.

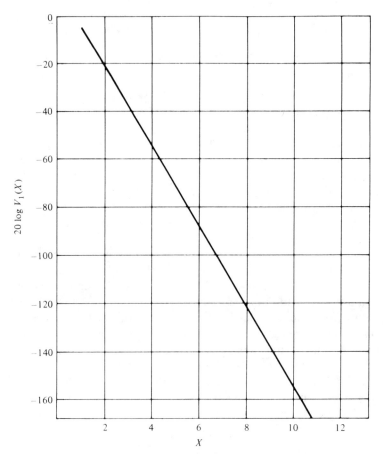

Figure 6.28 The attenuation function $V_1(X)$.

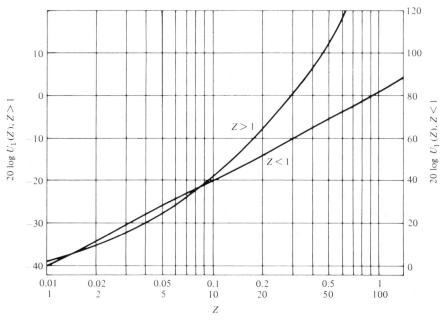

Figure 6.29 The height-gain function $U_1(Z)$.

Example 6.6 Path-gain factor for a microwave link In order to illustrate the use of Eq. (6.25) we will construct a plot of F versus d/d_T for the microwave link discussed in Example 6.4 in the previous section. For this system $h_1 = h_2 = 35$ m, $\lambda_0 = 10$ cm, $d_T = 24.39$ km, and $\nu = 2$. The path-gain factor F has its first maximum when $\nu\zeta = 2\zeta = 1$, or $\zeta = 0.5$. From Fig. 6.11 we find that this occurs when $d = 1.06d_T$ and the corresponding value of D is 0.75, so $F = 1 + D = 1.75$, or 4.86 dB. At the point of quadrature $\nu\zeta = 0.5$, so $\zeta = 0.25$. This point occurs at $d = 1.3d_T$ and $D = 0.58$ and $F = (1 + D)^{1/2} = 1.26$, or 1.97 dB. For the points in the diffraction zone we will choose $d = 2.5, 3,$ and $3.5d_T$. The corresponding values of X are

$$X_1 = \frac{2.5 \times 24.39}{28.41 \times (0.1)^{1/3}} = 4.62 \qquad X_2 = 5.55 \qquad X_3 = 6.47$$

From Fig. 6.28 we find that the attenuation function V_1 equals -64, -80, and -96 dB, respectively. The parameters Z_1 and Z_2 are given by

$$Z_1 = Z_2 = \frac{35}{47.55 \times (0.1)^{2/3}} = 3.42$$

and the height-gain function (from Fig. 6.29) $U_1(Z_1) = 17$ dB. Hence in the diffraction zone at the given values of d/d_T the values of $20 \log F$ are -30, -46, and -62 dB. The path-gain factor is shown in Fig. 6.30.

If P_t is the transmitted power, G is the antenna gain, and d is the distance to the receiver, then the incident power per unit area at the receiving terminal will be

$$P_{inc} = \frac{P_t G}{4\pi d^2} F^2 = \frac{P_t G}{4\pi d_T^2} \frac{F^2}{(d/d_T)^2}$$

This expression is best evaluated by making a plot of $F^2/(d/d_T)^2$ or of $20 \log F - 20 \log d/d_T$. The latter is simply a reduction of the value of $20 \log F$ by 6 dB for every doubling of d beyond the point $d/d_T = 1$ and is shown as the broken curve in Fig. 6.30.

In general, for receiving points located below or near the tangent plane the path-gain factor should be plotted as a function of d/d_T. The required curve is obtained by joining the curve in the interference region to that which applies well into the diffraction zone. The error made in this extrapolation from the two regions towards the tangent ray is generally small. ■

6.4 MIDPATH-OBSTACLE DIFFRACTION LOSS

It is not always possible to install a communication link so that there are no obstructions such as hills or large buildings that block part of the field from the transmitting antenna, impeding its arrival at the receiving terminal. Fig. 6.31a shows a ridge or hill that partially blocks the propagation path. The effect of the hill can be modeled as a thin plane or knife-edge having the same clearance

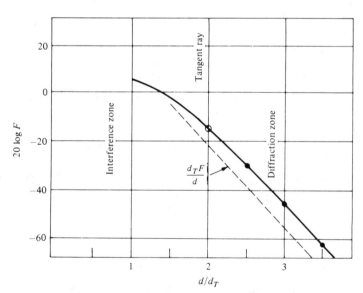

Figure 6.30 Path-gain factor F in decibels for $h_1 = h_2 = 35$ m, $\lambda_0 = 10$ cm. Note that $F = 1$ at $d = 1.36 d_T$, as in Example 6.4.

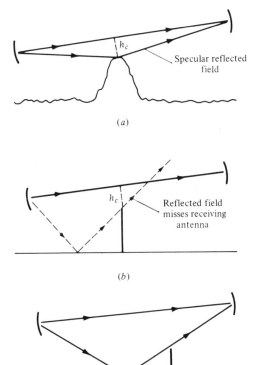

(a)

(b)

(c)

Figure 6.31 (a) A hill obstructing the propagation path. (b) Knife-edge model for an obstruction blocking a reflected ray. (c) Knife-edge model for an obstruction not blocking the reflected ray.

distance h_c from the line-of-sight path, provided there is no specular reflection from the top of the hill; that is, the reflected ray shown in Fig. 6.31a is absent. The knife-edge model is shown in Fig. 6.31b. We will show that when the clearance height h_c is zero there will be a 6-dB diffraction loss relative to free-space propagation, provided a specularly reflected field behind the screen cannot reach the receiving terminal, as shown in Fig. 6.31b. If the obstruction is such that a reflected field is also diffracted by the knife-edge, as shown in Fig. 6.31c, then the computation of the diffraction loss is more complex. In the discussion below we assume that there is no significant contribution to the received field from specular reflection. This is equivalent to saying that the received field is modified from its free-space value by the diffraction effect of a knife-edge. Thus the appropriate diffraction problem to analyze is that shown in Fig. 6.32. In terms of the path parameters, the height of point P shown in Fig. 6.32a is $h_1 + (h_2 - h_1)d_1/d = (d_2h_1 + d_1h_2)/d$. Hence it is readily seen that the clearance height is given by

$$h_c = \left(\frac{d_2h_1 + d_1h_2}{d} - h\right)\cos\theta_c \qquad (6.28)$$

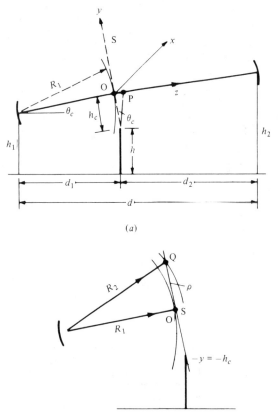

(a)

(b)

Figure 6.32 Knife-edge diffraction model showing propagation-path parameters.

where h is the height of the obstruction. In many practical cases $\cos \theta_c$ can be replaced by unity, since θ_c is very small.

The following procedure will be used to determine the diffraction loss: The field incident on the surface S shown in Fig. 6.32 will be approximated by an expression corresponding to a gaussian-shaped beam. The free-space field at the receiving site will be expressed as a field radiated from the effective aperture surface S and compared with that in the absence of the knife-edge. The ratio of these two fields gives the diffraction loss. Since it is the ratio that is being determined, the result is not critically dependent on the expression chosen to represent the field incident on the surface S.

The incident field on S is a spherical wave with a propagation factor $e^{-jk_0 R_1}$ at the point O. At the point Q, a distance ρ from O, the corresponding factor is $e^{-jk_0 R_2}$ where $R_2 = (R_1^2 + \rho^2)^{1/2}$. Since $R_1 \gg \rho$ we have

$$R_2 \approx R_1 + \frac{\rho^2}{2R_1}$$

Hence on the surface S, the propagation factor that determines the phase of the incident field is $e^{-jk_0R_1 - jk_0\rho^2/2R_1}$. The incident field is a beam of finite width inversely proportional to the diameter of the transmitting antenna. We will use a gaussian function $e^{-\rho^2/\alpha^2}$ to describe the amplitude decay of the incident field as the point of observation moves away from the bore-sight direction. Thus the electric field on the surface S is chosen to be

$$\mathbf{E}_i = \mathbf{a}_y \frac{E_0}{R_1} e^{-jk_0R_1 - j(k_0\rho^2/2R_1) - \rho^2/\alpha^2} \tag{6.29}$$

where E_0 is an amplitude constant and we have assumed that the incident field is polarized along y. The xyz coordinate system is shown in Fig. 6.32a and has its origin at O. The radial distance ρ is equal to $(x^2 + y^2)^{1/2}$.

The field incident on the receiving antenna can be found by considering the surface S as an aperture surface and using Eq. (4.12) to find the resultant radiated field. The radiated field is given by

$$\mathbf{E(r)} = \frac{1}{4\pi^2} \int\int_{-\infty}^{\infty} \mathbf{f}(k_x, k_y)\, e^{-j\mathbf{k}_t \cdot \mathbf{r} - jk_z z}\, dk_x\, dk_y \tag{6.30}$$

where $\mathbf{f} = \mathbf{a}_y f_y + \mathbf{a}_z f_z$ and f_y is the Fourier transform of E_i; that is,

$$f_y = \int\int_S E_i(x, y)\, e^{jk_x x + jk_y y}\, dx\, dy \tag{6.31}$$

At the receiving antenna $\mathbf{r}$ is very nearly equal to $\mathbf{a}_z z$, so only those waves in the plane wave spectrum with $\mathbf{k}_t$ close to zero will be incident on the antenna. Thus in Eq. (6.30) we can approximate k_z as follows:

$$k_z = (k_0^2 - k_t^2)^{1/2} \approx k_0 - \frac{k_t^2}{2k_0}$$

Since the field is also predominantly a spherical wave f_z is very small. Hence the incident field on the receiving antenna can be expressed as

$$\mathbf{E(r)} = \frac{\mathbf{a}_y}{4\pi^2} e^{-jk_0 z} \int\int_{-\infty}^{\infty} f_y(k_x, k_y)\, e^{-jk_x x - jk_y y + jk_t^2 z/2k_0}\, dk_x\, dk_y$$

where $k_t^2 = k_x^2 + k_y^2$. When we substitute for f_y from Eq. (6.31) and use Eq. (6.29) we obtain

$$\mathbf{E(r)} = \frac{\mathbf{a}_y E_0}{4\pi^2 R_1} e^{-jk_0(z + R_1)} \int\int_{-\infty}^{\infty} \int_{-\infty}^{\infty} \int_{-h_c}^{\infty} e^{-jk_0(x_1^2 + y_1^2)/2R_1}$$

$$\times\, e^{-(x_1^2 + y_1^2)/\alpha^2 + jk_x(x_1 - x) + jk_y(y_1 - y) + jk_t^2 z/2k_0}\, dy_1\, dx_1\, dk_x\, dk_y \tag{6.32}$$

where the aperture coordinates have been labeled with a subscript 1. The integral over y_1 extends from $-h_c$ to infinity because of the shadowing effect of the knife-edge screen. If the screen were not present, the integral would extend from minus to plus infinity. On axis at the receiving antenna $x = y = 0$.

The integrals over k_x, k_y, and x_1 can be carried out, using the result

$$\int_{-\infty}^{\infty} e^{-au^2+2bu}\, du = \sqrt{\frac{\pi}{a}}\, e^{b^2/a}$$

After doing the integrals over k_x and k_y we obtain (we have put $x = y = 0$)

$$\mathbf{E}(\mathbf{r}) = \frac{jk_0 E_0 \mathbf{a}_y}{2\pi z R_1}\, e^{-jk_0(z+R_1)} \int_{-h_c}^{\infty} \int_{-\infty}^{\infty} e^{-a(x_1^2+y_1^2)}\, dx_1\, dy_1$$

where

$$a = jk_0\left(\frac{1}{2z} + \frac{1}{2R_1}\right) + \frac{1}{\alpha^2}$$

The integral over x_1 is now performed to give

$$\mathbf{E}(\mathbf{r}) = \frac{jk_0 E_0 \mathbf{a}_y}{2\pi z R_1}\, e^{-jk_0(z+R_1)} \sqrt{\frac{\pi}{a}} \int_{-h_c}^{\infty} e^{-ay_1^2}\, dy_1 \tag{6.33}$$

The ratio of the integrals over y_1 in the presence of the screen to that when the screen is absent will give the diffraction loss. Hence the path-gain factor due to diffraction is

$$F_d = \sqrt{\frac{a}{\pi}}\left| \int_{-h_c}^{\infty} e^{-ay_1^2}\, dy_1 \right| \tag{6.34}$$

where the integral from minus to plus infinity was replaced by $(\pi/a)^{1/2}$. When $h_c = 0$ the integral equals $0.5(\pi/a)^{1/2}$, since it is an even function of y_1. Thus when the clearance height is zero, one-half of the incident radiation is blocked, which results in a 6-dB loss.

If we let $ay_1^2 = j\pi u^2/2$, then $dy_1 = (j\pi/2a)^{1/2}\, du$ and

$$F_d = \frac{\sqrt{2}}{2}\left| \int_{-H_c}^{\infty} e^{-j\pi u^2/2}\, du \right| \tag{6.35a}$$

where

$$H_c = \sqrt{\frac{2a}{j\pi}}\, h_c = \left[\frac{2(R_1+z)}{\lambda_0 R_1 z} - \frac{2j}{\pi \alpha^2}\right]^{1/2} h_c \approx \left(\frac{2d}{\lambda_0 d_1 d_2} - \frac{2j}{\pi \alpha^2}\right)^{1/2} h_c \tag{6.35b}$$

The integral giving the diffraction loss is a Fresnel integral. For the case of a transmitting antenna with modest gain such that the effective beam radius α can be assumed to be very large, H_c is real and given by $(2d/\lambda_0 d_1 d_2)^{1/2} h_c$. For this case F_d in decibels, that is, $20 \log F_d$, is shown in Fig. 6.33. The diffraction loss is negligible whenever the parameter H_c is greater than 0.8.

If the antenna beam width between points where the field strength has dropped by e^{-1} from its on-axis value is θ_A, then $\alpha \approx d_1 \tan \theta_A$. In order that

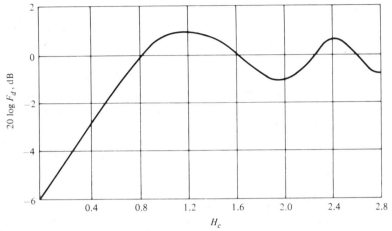

Figure 6.33 The path-gain factor F_d caused by knife-edge diffraction loss expressed in decibels as a function of the normalized clearance parameter H_c.

$1/\alpha^2$ be very small relative to $2d/\lambda_0 d_1 d_2$ we require that

$$d_1^2 \tan^2 \theta_A \gg \frac{\lambda_0 d_1 d_2}{2d}$$

or

$$\frac{d_2}{d_1} \frac{\lambda_0}{2d} \ll \tan^2 \theta_A \qquad (6.36)$$

For most communication links the path length d is so large relative to the wavelength that the above condition is satisfied and F_d can be determined from Fig. 6.33.

For an obstruction such as a hill, the clearance height h_c should be chosen to provide some margin of safety against fading introduced by subrefraction. Under standard atmospheric conditions the clearance height can be determined by plotting the path profile above an earth with effective radius equal to 4/3 the actual radius. However, under some conditions the refractive index can increase with height, and the rays will then curve upward and thereby reduce the effective clearance. Typically it is necessary to ensure that H_c is equal to about 0.8 for refractive conditions corresponding to an effective earth radius equal to 0.7 of the actual radius.† The path profile should be drawn above an earth with this effective radius to ensure that there is adequate path clearance such that the probability of fading due to diffraction loss will be negligible.

6.5 SURFACE-WAVE PROPAGATION

In the previous four sections interference effects between the direct and reflected field were analyzed. This field is often referred to as the *ground wave*

† M. P. M. Hall, *Effects of the Troposphere on Radio Communication*, Peter Peregrinus, London, 1979, Sec. 4.2.

to distinguish it from a wave reflected from the ionosphere and called the *sky wave*. It is also called the *space wave* to distinguish it from the *surface wave*. When the antennas are located close to or on the ground the space wave vanishes because the reflected field cancels the direct wave. For this situation the field at the receiving antenna is due to a surface-wave field. Propagation by means of the surface wave is the primary mode of propagation in the frequency range from a few kilohertz up to several megahertz. The attenuation in signal power is nearly proportional to the inverse of the fourth power of the distance separating the receiving and transmitting antennas. In this regime the antennas are usually large towers, the transmitter power may range from 10 kW upwards to 1 MW, and useful propagation distances of several hundred miles are achieved.

In this section we will outline the analytical solution for the radiation from an elementary vertical dipole above a flat lossy earth. From this solution the space-wave and surface-wave contributions can be identified. The surface-wave attenuation function will be presented in graphical form. Examples of communication link evaluations will be given to illustrate typical power levels, propagation distances, and signal levels involved.

The fundamental problem of radiation from a short current filament oriented in the vertical direction and located above a flat lossy earth was solved by Sommerfeld in 1909. Later work by Sommerfeld in 1926, plus that of many other investigators, led eventually to extensive numerical evaluation of the theoretical formulas by Norton in 1936 and 1937.†

Figure 6.34 shows a z-directed current element of unit strength located at a height h above the surface of the earth. The earth is characterized by a complex dielectric constant

$$\kappa = \kappa' - j\kappa'' = \kappa' - j\frac{\sigma}{\omega\epsilon_0} \qquad (6.37)$$

where σ is the conductivity. The current density can be represented by the product of three delta functions, since it is viewed as a localized point source;

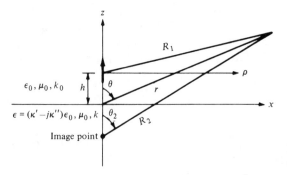

Figure 6.34 A unit vertical current element above a lossy flat earth.

† K. A. Norton, "The Propagation of Radio Waves over the Surface of the Earth and in the Upper Atmosphere," *Proc. IRE*, vol. 24, 1936, pp. 1367–1387, and vol. 25, 1937, pp. 1203–1236.

thus

$$\mathbf{J} = \mathbf{a}_z \delta(x)\delta(y)\delta(z-h) \tag{6.38}$$

The air-earth interface is located at $z=0$. The vector potential has a z component only and satisfies the equation

$$\nabla^2 \psi + k_0^2 \psi = -\mu_0 J = -\mu_0 \delta(x)\delta(y)\delta(z-h) \qquad z>0 \tag{6.39a}$$

$$\nabla^2 \psi_3 + \kappa k_0^2 \psi_3 = 0 \qquad z<0 \tag{6.39b}$$

where $A_z = \psi$ in air and $A_z = \psi_3$ in the earth. The wave number $\kappa^{1/2}k_0$ will be denoted by k. We will construct a formal solution of Eq. (6.39) by using Fourier transforms with respect to x and y.

Let the transforms of ψ and ψ_3 be $\hat{\psi}(\beta_x, \beta_y, z)$ and $\hat{\psi}_3(\beta_x, \beta_y, z)$ where

$$\hat{\psi}(\beta_x, \beta_y, z) = \int\int_{-\infty}^{\infty} \psi(x, y, z)\, e^{j\beta_x x + j\beta_y y}\, dx\, dy \tag{6.40a}$$

$$\hat{\psi}_3(\beta_x, \beta_y, z) = \int\int_{-\infty}^{\infty} \psi_3(x, y, z)\, e^{j\beta_x x + j\beta_y y}\, dx\, dy \tag{6.40b}$$

The Fourier transform of Eq. (6.39) gives $(\beta^2 = \beta_x^2 + \beta_y^2)$

$$\left(\frac{\partial^2}{\partial z^2} + k_0^2 - \beta^2\right)\hat{\psi}(\beta_x, \beta_y, z) = -\frac{\mu_0}{4\pi^2}\,\delta(z-h) \qquad z\geq 0 \tag{6.41a}$$

$$\left(\frac{\partial^2}{\partial z^2} + k^2 - \beta^2\right)\hat{\psi}_3(\beta_x, \beta_y, z) = 0 \qquad z\leq 0 \tag{6.41b}$$

Continuity of the tangential electric and magnetic fields at $z=0$ requires that $\hat{\psi}(z+) = \hat{\psi}_3(z-)$ and

$$\frac{1}{\kappa}\frac{\partial \hat{\psi}_3}{\partial z}\bigg|_{z-} = \frac{\partial\hat{\psi}}{\partial z}\bigg|_{z+}$$

We may choose

$$\hat{\psi} = \hat{\psi}_1 = A\, e^{-\gamma_0(z-h)} \qquad z\geq h$$

$$\hat{\psi} = \hat{\psi}_2 = \frac{A(e^{\gamma_0 z} - \Gamma_v e^{-\gamma_0 z})}{e^{\gamma_0 h}(1 - \Gamma_v e^{-2\gamma_0 h})} \qquad 0\leq z\leq h$$

where $\gamma_0^2 = (\beta^2 - k_0^2)$. This solution is the sum of a downward and upward propagating wave, with constants A and Γ_v chosen so that $\hat{\psi}_1 = \hat{\psi}_2$ at $z=h$. Γ_v can be interpreted as a reflection coefficient. For $z\leq 0$ we let $A_z = \hat{\psi}_3$ and choose $\hat{\psi}_3$ so that it equals $\hat{\psi}_2$ at $z=0$ and is a downward propagating wave;

thus

$$\hat{\psi}_3 = \frac{A(1 - \Gamma_v)\, e^{\gamma z}}{e^{\gamma_0 h}(1 - \Gamma_v e^{-2\gamma_0 h})}$$

where $\gamma^2 = \beta^2 - k^2$. At $z = 0$ the boundary condition $\kappa^{-1}\partial\hat{\psi}_3/\partial z = \partial\hat{\psi}_2/\partial z$ must hold. At $z = h$ the step change in the derivative is given by

$$\frac{\partial\hat{\psi}}{\partial z}\bigg|_{h-}^{h+} = -\frac{\mu_0}{4\pi^2}$$

These two conditions determine A and Γ_v. It is found that

$$\Gamma_v = \frac{\gamma - \kappa\gamma_0}{\gamma + \kappa\gamma_0} \tag{6.42}$$

$$A = \frac{\mu_0}{4\pi^2\gamma_0[1 + (1 + \Gamma_v e^{-2\gamma_0 h})/(1 - \Gamma_v e^{-2\gamma_0 h})]}$$

For $z \geq h$ we now get

$$\psi = \psi_1 = \frac{\mu_0}{8\pi^2}\int\!\!\int_{-\infty}^{\infty} \frac{1}{\gamma_0}\left(1 - e^{-2\gamma_0 h}\frac{\gamma - \kappa\gamma_0}{\gamma + \kappa\gamma_0}\right) e^{-j\beta_x x - j\beta_y y - \gamma_0(z-h)}\, d\beta_x\, d\beta_y \tag{6.43}$$

This represents the solution as a spectrum of plane waves radiated directly from the source plus plane waves reflected from the interface and appearing to come from the image point at $z = -h$. Γ_v is the Fresnel reflection coefficient.

To transform to cylindrical coordinates let $\beta_x = w \cos\phi'$, $\beta_y = w \sin\phi'$, $x = \rho \cos\phi$, and $y = \rho \sin\phi$. We then obtain

$$\psi_1 = \frac{\mu_0}{8\pi^2}\int_0^{2\pi}\!\!\int_0^{\infty} \frac{1}{\gamma_0}\left(1 - e^{-2\gamma_0 h}\frac{\gamma - \kappa\gamma_0}{\gamma + \kappa\gamma_0}\right) e^{-jw\rho\cos(\phi'-\phi) - \gamma_0(z-h)}w\, dw\, d\phi' \tag{6.44}$$

where now $\gamma_0 = j\sqrt{k_0^2 - w^2}$ and $\gamma = j\sqrt{k^2 - w^2}$. Using the result

$$\int_0^{2\pi} e^{-jw\rho\cos(\phi'-\phi)}\, d\phi' = 2\pi J_0(w\rho)$$

where J_0 is the zero-order Bessel function, we obtain Sommerfeld's classical result:

$$\psi_1 = \frac{\mu_0}{4\pi}\int_0^{\infty} \frac{1}{\gamma_0}(1 - \Gamma_v e^{-2\gamma_0 h})J_0(w\rho)\, e^{-\gamma_0(z-h)}w\, dw$$

For $\Gamma_v = 0$ we must obtain the well-known result:

$$\psi_1 = \frac{\mu_0}{4\pi}\frac{e^{-jk_0\sqrt{\rho^2 + (z-h)^2}}}{\sqrt{\rho^2 + (z-h)^2}}$$

from a current element in free space. Therefore we see that

$$\int_0^\infty \frac{wJ_0(w\rho)}{j\sqrt{k_0^2 - w^2}} e^{-j\sqrt{k_0^2 - w^2}(z-h)} \, dw = \frac{e^{-jk_0R_1}}{R_1}$$

where $R_1^2 = \rho^2 + (z - h)^2$. We are now able to express ψ_1 in the form

$$\psi_1 = \frac{\mu_0}{4\pi}\left[\frac{e^{-jk_0R_1}}{R_1} - \frac{e^{-jk_0R_2}}{R_2} + 2\kappa\int_0^\infty \frac{e^{-j\gamma_0(z+h)}J_0(w\rho)}{\gamma + \kappa\gamma_0} w\,dw\right] \tag{6.45}$$

where $R_2^2 = \rho^2 + (z + h)^2$. For infinite conductivity κ becomes infinite and the integral gives twice the term in R_2 above to yield

$$\psi_1 = \frac{\mu_0}{4\pi}\left(\frac{e^{-jk_0R}}{R_1} + \frac{e^{-jk_0R_2}}{R_2}\right) \qquad \kappa \to \infty \tag{6.46}$$

which is the expected solution for a current element above a perfectly conducting plane.

To examine the problem further, note that $J_0(w\rho) = \frac{1}{2}[H_0^2(w\rho) + H_0^1(w\rho)]$, where H_0^1 and H_0^2 are the Hankel functions of the first and second kind. In the part of the integral involving H_0^1 we can put $w = -Z$ to get

$$\int_0^{-\infty} \frac{e^{-\gamma_0(z+h)}H_0^1(-Z\rho)(-Z)(-dZ)}{\gamma + \kappa\gamma_0}$$

and since γ, γ_0 are even functions of Z and $H_0^1(-Z\rho) = -H_0^2(Z\rho)$, we obtain

$$\int_{-\infty}^0 \frac{e^{-\gamma_0(z+h)}H_0^2(Z\rho)Z}{\gamma + \kappa\gamma_0}\,dZ$$

Using this result enables us to express ψ_1 as

$$\psi_1 = \frac{\mu_0}{4\pi}\left(\frac{e^{-jk_0R_1}}{R_1} - \frac{e^{-jk_0R_2}}{R_2} + 2\kappa I\right) \tag{6.47}$$

where

$$I = \int_{-\infty}^\infty \frac{wH_0^2(w\rho)\,e^{-\gamma_0(z+h)}}{2(\gamma + \kappa\gamma_0)}\,dw \tag{6.48}$$

Note that there is a pole when $\gamma + \kappa\gamma_0 = 0$, which is the Zenneck surface-wave pole. This pole occurs for $w = w_0 = k_0\sqrt{\kappa/(\kappa + 1)}$. There has been considerable controversy in the past regarding whether the Zenneck surface wave is excited.[†] In principle the contour of integration, which is the real axis in the w plane, can be deformed so that it encircles the pole. If this is done the residue at the pole gives the following discrete-mode solution:

$$\psi_s = \frac{\pi k}{\kappa^2 - 1}\sqrt{\frac{\kappa}{\kappa + 1}}\,H_0^2\left(\frac{k\rho}{\sqrt{\kappa + 1}}\right)e^{-jk_0(z+h)/\sqrt{\kappa+1}} \tag{6.49}$$

† I. Kahan and G. E. Eckart, "On the Existence of a Surface Wave in Dipole Radiation over a Plane Earth," *Proc. IRE*, vol. 38, July 1950, pp. 807–812.

which is called the *Zenneck surface wave*. When the horizontal radial distance ρ is large and $z = 0$, we find, by using the asymptotic expression for the Hankel function, that

$$\psi_s \sim C \frac{e^{-jk\rho/\sqrt{\kappa+1}}}{\sqrt{\rho}} \tag{6.50}$$

where C is a suitable constant. This field solution decays with distance like $\rho^{-1/2}$ instead of the usual ρ^{-1} for free-space propagation. The surface wave is guided by the interface, and its field is confined to the region close to the surface; this is why it decays like a cylindrical wave and not a spherical wave.

However, the residue term is not the dominant contribution from the integral in Eq. (6.48). When the integral is evaluated asymptotically for large ρ it turns out that the surface-wave term is cancelled and what is left over is a much more rapidly attenuating surface field, which is sometimes called the *Norton surface wave*. This field is not a true surface wave but nevertheless is generally referred to as the surface-wave field.

An examination of the solution given by Eqs. (6.47) and (6.48) shows that the space wave, which consists of the directly radiated free-space field plus the specularly reflected field, vanishes at the surface $z = 0$, where $R_1 = R_2$. The remaining field, that is, the vector potential A_z, is given by $2\kappa\mu_0 I/4\pi$, where the integral I is that in Eq. (6.48). The approximate expression for the z component of electric field E_z at the surface is ($R_1 = R_2 = R = d$)

$$E_z = -j\omega A_z = \frac{jk_0 Z_0}{4\pi R} e^{-jk_0 R} \frac{2(\kappa - 1)}{\kappa} A_s \tag{6.51}$$

where the surface-wave attenuation factor A_s is given by

$$A_s = 1 - j\sqrt{\pi\Omega}\, e^{-\Omega}\, \text{erfc}(j\sqrt{\Omega}) \tag{6.52a}$$

$$\Omega = -jk_0 \frac{R}{2\kappa^2}(\kappa - 1) \tag{6.52b}$$

and erfc $j\sqrt{\Omega}$ is the complement of the error function and is expressed by the following integral:

$$\text{erfc}\, j\sqrt{\Omega} = \frac{2}{\sqrt{\Omega}} \int_{j\sqrt{\Omega}}^{\infty} e^{-u^2}\, du \tag{6.52c}$$

The field strength differs from its free-space value by the factor $2(\kappa - 1)A_s/\kappa \approx 2A_s$, since the effective dielectric constant is typically greater than 10.

In general A_s decreases rapidly for increasing values of Ω beyond a certain minimum value. As R approaches zero, A_s approaches a value of unity and remains close to unity until R exceeds a few wavelengths.

The parameter Ω is usually expressed in the form

$$\Omega = -jk_0 d \frac{\kappa - 1}{2\kappa^2} = p\, e^{-jb} \tag{6.53}$$

where $p = |\Omega|$ is called the *numerical distance*. In Eq. (6.53) we have replaced R by the horizontal distance d. Since κ is quite large for most soils,

$$p \approx \frac{k_0 d}{2|\kappa|} = \frac{k_0 d}{2\sqrt{\kappa'^2 + (\sigma/\omega\epsilon_0)^2}} \tag{6.54a}$$

and

$$b \approx \tan^{-1} \frac{\kappa'\omega\epsilon_0}{\sigma} \tag{6.54b}$$

The term $\sigma/\omega\epsilon_0$ can be expressed as

$$\frac{\sigma}{\omega\epsilon_0} = \frac{1.8 \times 10^4 \sigma}{f_{MHz}} \tag{6.55}$$

For a typical ground σ has a value of 10^{-3} to 10^{-2} S/m, so $\sigma/\omega\epsilon_0$ is of order 18 to $180/f_{MHz}$ where f_{MHz} is the frequency in megahertz. The dielectric constant κ' is usually in the range 10 to 15. With κ' of order 10 to 15 we see that for broadcast frequencies ($f \approx 1$ MHz) and good ground conductivity

$$p \approx \frac{k_0 d\omega\epsilon_0}{2\sigma}$$

which is proportional to d/λ_0^2. Note that p increases rapidly with frequency, and thus for a given value of distance d the numerical distance and hence the attenuation is much greater at higher frequencies. In Fig. 6.35 we show the value of $|A_s|$ as a function of the numerical distance p. When p equals 500 the

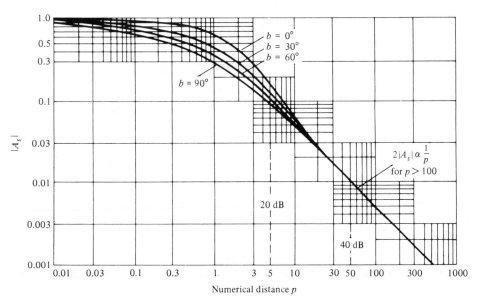

Figure 6.35 The surface-wave attenuation factor $|A_s|$ as a function of the numerical distance for a flat earth.

attenuation is 60 dB. For $p = 50$ the attenuation is 40 dB. This attenuation is in addition to that contributed by the $1/d$ factor in the expression for the surface-wave field. For $b \leq 90°$ the attenuation factor $|A_s|$ can be approximated by

$$|A_s| = \frac{2 + 0.3p}{2 + p + 0.6p^2} - \sqrt{p/2}\, e^{-0.6p} \sin b \qquad (6.56)$$

The surface-wave attenuation given in Fig. 6.35 is based on formulas for a flat earth. The results are accurate for the surface-wave attenuation over a spherical earth out to a distance of the order of $50\,\mathrm{mi}/f_{\mathrm{MHz}}^{1/3}$. Beyond this distance the surface wave over a spherical earth attenuates much more rapidly. Figure 6.36 shows the value of $|A_s|$ for a spherical earth with good conductivity ($\sigma = 10^{-2}\,\mathrm{S/m}$) at four frequencies, namely 0.5, 1, 2, and 5 MHz. Beyond the distance for which the flat-earth formulas hold, the decrease in the field strength is very rapid. For the case of a spherical earth, $|A_s|$ depends on the frequency and conductivity in a complex way, and a single curve as a function of p no longer holds. A procedure for calculating $|A_s|$ over a spherical earth may be found in Terman's book.†

In view of the rapid decrease in signal level for distances greater than $50\,\mathrm{mi}/f_{\mathrm{MHz}}^{1/3}$, the practical range at broadcast frequencies is a few hundred miles, dropping to 10 mi or so at 100 MHz for surface-wave propagation. At broadcast

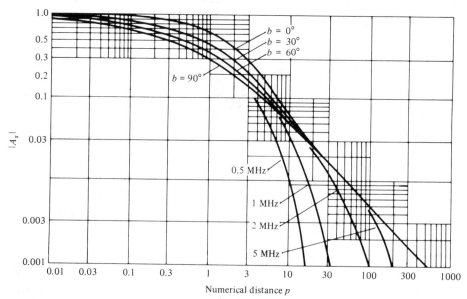

Figure 6.36 The surface-wave attenuation factor over a spherical earth for four different frequencies. $\kappa' = 15$ and $\sigma = 10^{-2}\,\mathrm{S/m}$.

† F. E. Terman, *Radio Engineers Handbook*, McGraw-Hill Book Company, New York, 1943.

frequencies the prevailing noise level in urban areas is so high that a field strength of order 1 to 10 mV/m at the receiving antenna is required for acceptable reception. In rural areas a signal level an order of magnitude less is satisfactory.

For an antenna located very near to the ground the surface-wave field near the ground is essentially $2A_s$ times the field that would be radiated by the antenna in free space. We will use this result to evaluate the range from ground-based antennas at low to medium frequencies.

Example 6.7 AM broadcasting system We will consider a 1-MHz broadcast system. The receiving antenna is a small loop antenna consisting of the coil in the tuned input circuit of the receiver, as shown in Fig. 6.37a. The receiving cross section with matched impedance and polarization conditions are $A_e = \lambda_0^2 G/4\pi$. Let the coil have an ohmic resistance r, and let the radiation resistance be R_a. The efficiency of the loop antenna is

$$\eta = \frac{R_a}{R_a + r} \tag{6.57}$$

The radiation resistance is given by

$$R_a = \frac{k_0^4 Z_0 N^2 A^2}{6\pi} \tag{6.58}$$

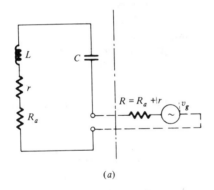

(a)

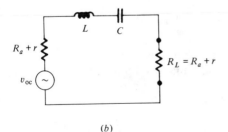

(b)

Figure 6.37 (a) Receiver input tuned circuit. (b) Thevenin equivalent circuit.

where A is the cross-sectional area of the coil and N is the number of turns. The gain is given by $G = 1.5\eta$. Hence the received power is given by

$$P_r = A_e P_{inc} = \frac{k_0^2 Z_0 N^2 A^2}{4(r + R_a)} P_{inc} \tag{6.59}$$

where P_{inc} is the incident power per square meter.

The properties of this antenna, in particular the noise problem, are discussed in Example 5.8. Let r be at the ambient temperature $T_0 = 300$ K and R_a be at the antenna-noise temperature T_A. When the receiver has a noise figure F, then the equivalent additional input noise is obtained by raising the temperature of $r + R_a$ by $(F - 1)T_0$, the receiver-noise temperature. The total noise power that will be delivered to the load $R_L = r + R_a$ is [see Eq. (5.76)]

$$P_n = \frac{K \,\Delta f \,[rT_0 + R_a T_A + T_0(F - 1)(r + R_a)]}{r + R_a}$$

$$= K \,\Delta f \,[(1 - \eta)FT_0 + \eta T_A + \eta T_0(F - 1)] \tag{6.60}$$

The signal-to-noise ratio at the receiver will be

$$\frac{P_r}{P_n} = \frac{\lambda_0^2 1.5\eta P_{inc}}{4\pi K \,\Delta f \,[(1 - \eta)FT_0 + \eta T_A + \eta T_0(F - 1)]} \tag{6.61}$$

For the loop antenna we assume that $N = 200$ and $A = 100\,cm^2$ and then find that $R_a = 1.54 \times 10^{-5}\,\Omega$. We will also assume that $L = 200\,\mu h$ and $Q = 100$, for which $r = 4\pi\,\Omega$ and $\eta = 1.22 \times 10^{-6}$.

For the loop antenna in our example the thermal noise and antenna noise are comparable. For $F = 4$, $T_A = 10^9$ K, and a signal-to-noise ratio of 100, we will require

$$P_{rec} = \frac{\lambda_0^2}{4\pi} 1.5\eta P_{inc} = 100K \,\Delta f \,[(F - \eta)T_0 + \eta T_A]$$

$$\approx 100K \,\Delta f \,(FT_0 + \eta T_A)$$

$$= 10^6 \times 1.38 \times 10^{-23}(4 \times 300 + 1.22 \times 10^3)$$

for $\Delta f = 10$ kHz. Hence the required incident power is

$$P_{inc} = \frac{4\pi \times 1.38 \times 2.42 \times 10^{-14}}{(300)^2 \times 1.5 \times 1.22 \times 10^{-6}} = 2.55 \times 10^{-12}\,W/m^2$$

which corresponds to a field strength of 43.8 μV/m.

If we assume that the transmitting antenna has unity gain, then

$$P_{inc} = \frac{P_{trans}}{4\pi d^2} 4|A_s|^2 \tag{6.62}$$

At 1 MHz and with a good ground conductivity ($\sigma = 10^{-2}$ S/m), the numerical distance p is given by

$$p = \frac{k_0 d \omega \epsilon_0}{2\sigma} = \frac{\pi d}{180 \times 300}$$

so $d = 17,189p$ m, or $10.7p$ mi. From Fig. 6.36 we find that $|A_s|^2 = 10^{-4}$ at $p = 18$, so for a range of 193 mi we require

$$P_{trans} = \frac{4\pi d^2}{4|A_s|^2} P_{inc} = \frac{\pi(1.72 \times 18 \times 10^4)^2}{10^{-4}} \times 2.55 \times 10^{-12}$$

$$= 7679 \text{ W}$$

This is a realistic power level. If we reduce the range by a factor of 2 to 96.5 mi, the power requirements are reduced by a factor of $(.01/.05)^2 \times 0.25 = 0.01$ to 76.8 W because of the large increase in $|A_s|/d$.

Under adverse atmospheric conditions the antenna-noise temperature could be a factor of 10 higher. Also, local noise in an urban area would increase the noise power further, so a transmitter power of order 50 kW might be required for satisfactory broadcasting service under adverse conditions. Power levels of 10 to 100 kW are quite typical for many broadcasting stations. As shown by this example a service range up to 200 mi would be expected. For a range of 278 mi $|A_s|^2$ is smaller by a factor of 10^{-2}, which would require more than a 100-fold increase in transmitter power for only a modest increase in range from 193 to 278 mi. ∎

Example 6.8 Citizen's-band communication link In this example we will evaluate the performance of a citizen's-band system operating at 27 MHz in a rural environment. It is assumed that both the transmitting and receiving antennas are located on cars, so propagation between the two is by means of the surface wave. The following parameters are assumed to hold:

Transmitter power = 5 W

Antenna gain = unity

Receiver-noise figure $F = 4$

Receiver bandwidth = 5 kHz

Ground parameters $\kappa' = 12$

$$\sigma = 5 \times 10^{-3} \text{ S/m}$$

Figure 5.18 shows that an average value for the antenna-noise temperature is 10^4 K.

The numerical distance p is given by

$$p = \frac{\pi d / \lambda_0}{\sqrt{12^2 + (90/27)^2}} = 0.25 \frac{d}{\lambda_0} = 0.0225d$$

for d expressed in meters. At the maximum range $50/f_{MHz}^{1/3} = 50/3 = 16.7$ mi, for which the flat-earth formulas hold $p = 601$. For this large numerical distance $|A_s| = (5/6) \times 10^{-3} = 8.83 \times 10^{-4}$. The received power is given by

$$P_{rec} = \frac{P_t}{4\pi d^2} |2A_s|^2 \frac{\lambda_0^2}{4\pi} = \frac{5 \times (8.33 \times 10^{-4})^2}{4\pi^2 (4 \times 601)^2}$$

$$= 1.52 \times 10^{-14} \text{ W}$$

In the calculation we used $d/\lambda_0 = 4p$. The noise power at the receiver input is given by (we assume that the antenna efficiency is unity)

$$P_n = K \Delta f [T_A + (F - 1)T_0]$$

$$= 1.38 \times 10^{-23} \times 5 \times 10^3 (10^4 + 3 \times 300) = 7.52 \times 10^{-16} \text{ W}$$

This noise level is considerably less than the received signal power, so a range of 16.7 mi is quite realistic. The signal-to-noise ratio at this distance is 20.2. Beyond a range of 16.7 mi the effect of the spherical earth will cause the received signal to attenuate very rapidly. For communication over longer distances it is necessary to use elevated antennas, at least at one terminal. ∎

Surface-Wave Attenuation for Horizontal Polarization

For horizontal polarization the surface-wave attenuation approaches

$$\left| \left[\frac{1}{\kappa - j(\sigma/\omega\epsilon_0)} \right]^2 A_s(p) \right|$$

where the numerical distance p is now given by

$$p = \frac{\pi d}{\lambda_0} \frac{1.8 \times 10^4 \sigma}{f_{MHz} \cos b} \qquad \tan b = \frac{\kappa' - 1}{\sigma/\omega\epsilon_0}$$

Since $\sigma/\omega\epsilon_0$ now occurs in the numerator instead of the denominator of p, the numerical distance p for a given range d is much larger for horizontal polarization than for vertical polarization at low frequencies. Because of this, horizontal polarization is generally not used when communicating by means of the surface wave.

6.6 IONOSPHERIC PROPAGATION

The ionosphere is that region of the atmosphere surrounding the earth that is ionized (primarily by solar radiation). During the day the ionized layers exist between about 90 and 1000 km above the earth's surface. The electron density is of order 10^{10} to 10^{12} electrons per cubic meter. There are primarily three layers in which the electron density peaks up. These are called the D, E, and F layers. During the daytime the F layer splits into two layers called the F_1 and F_2 layers. Figure 6.38 shows typical electron density curves versus height for daytime and nighttime conditions. The D layer vanishes at night.

We will show that these ionized layers will cause radio waves in the frequency range up to 40 MHz to be effectively reflected back to earth. These reflecting layers thus allow communication by radio waves to take place over distances of several thousand miles, as shown in Fig. 6.39. One or more skips may be involved. The electron concentration varies with the time of day, with season, and over periods of several years in accordance with solar activity. The effective dielectric constant, as will be shown, depends on frequency and the electron concentration. Thus for a given electron density there exists a maximum upper useful frequency above which the radio wave penetrates through the ionosphere. The ionosphere propagation path is not a very stable one, so a considerable amount of signal fading occurs. For highly reliable communication links some form of diversity, such as several spaced receiving antennas or several different frequencies used simultaneously, must be employed.

In simple qualitative terms the existence of ionization layers may be explained as follows. At great heights the solar radiation that causes the ionization of the gas molecules is very intense, but there are very few molecules to be ionized, so the electron concentration is small. At somewhat lower heights there will be a much greater concentration of molecules, so a peak in ionization density occurs. At sufficiently low heights most of the ionizing radiation has been absorbed, so the electron concentration again becomes very low. On this basis one expects to have a broad layer of ionized gas and high free-electron density at some height above the earth's surface. Since the atmosphere is composed of several different gases, although predominantly nitrogen and oxygen, and these gases have different ionization and recombination characteristics, several peaks or layers in the electron concentration occur. The E and F layers have a permanent existence, even though the height varies on a daily basis. These two layers are the most important ones for radio communications in the frequency range of 3 to 40 MHz. Above 40 MHz the

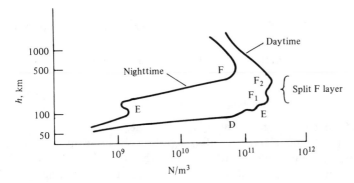

Figure 6.38 Typical variation of electron density versus height.

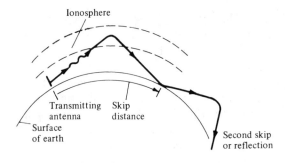

Figure 6.39 Illustration of radio-wave reflection from the ionosphere.

wave will penetrate through the ionosphere. In the D layer the collision frequency is quite high, so even though lower frequency waves (2 MHz or below) can be reflected from this layer the absorption is very high. At higher frequencies collisions have a smaller effect, since ω is then much higher.

Dielectric Constant of Ionized Gas

In an ionized gas only the motion of electrons is important under the action of a high-frequency electric field, since the ions are more than 1800 times heavier. The equation of motion for a single electron of mass m, charge $-e$, with velocity $\mathbf{v}$, and acted upon by an electric field $\mathscr{E}$ is

$$m\frac{d\mathbf{v}}{dt} = -e\mathscr{E} \tag{6.63}$$

For a sinusoidal field we can write

$$j\omega m\,\mathbf{V} = -e\,\mathbf{E} \tag{6.64}$$

For N electrons per unit volume the induced current in the ionized gas will be

$$\mathbf{J} = -eN\mathbf{V} = \frac{Ne^2}{j\omega m}\,\mathbf{E} \tag{6.65}$$

From Maxwell's equation we have

$$\nabla \times \mathbf{H} = j\omega\epsilon_0\mathbf{E} + \mathbf{J} = j\omega\epsilon_0\left(1 - \frac{Ne^2}{\omega^2 m\epsilon_0}\right)\mathbf{E} \tag{6.66}$$

from which we find that the dielectric constant of the ionized gas is

$$\kappa = 1 - \frac{Ne^2}{\omega^2 m\epsilon_0} = 1 - \frac{\omega_p^2}{\omega^2} \tag{6.67}$$

where the plasma frequency ω_p is given by $\omega_p = \sqrt{Ne^2/m\epsilon_0}$.

At the lower altitudes the electrons suffer a relatively large number of collisions with the neutral molecules and ions. For this case Eq. (6.64) for momentum conservation requires a collisional damping force $-\nu m\,\mathbf{v}$ added on the right-hand side. In this term ν is the collision frequency. When the collision term is included it is found that the effective dielectric constant κ is complex and is given by

$$\kappa = 1 - \frac{\omega_p^2}{\omega(\omega - j\nu)} \qquad (6.68)$$

This formula shows that collisions will produce higher absorption of low-frequency waves, for which ω is more nearly comparable in value to the collision frequency ν. Note that for $\omega > \omega_p$ κ is less than unity. When $\omega = \omega_p$ we have $\kappa = 0$ and for $\omega < \omega_p$ we get a negative value for κ. Plane waves propagating in an ionized gas will have a propagation constant $k = \omega\sqrt{\mu_0\kappa\epsilon_0} = \sqrt{\kappa}k_0$. Thus when $\omega < \omega_p$, k will be pure imaginary for $\nu = 0$, indicating that the plane wave will become evanescent and decay exponentially with distance.

Consider first a plane wave incident normally on an ionized layer in which the electron density increases with height, as shown in Fig. 6.40. When the wave reaches the height at which the electron density is sufficient to make $\kappa = 0$, propagation ceases and the wave is reflected back toward the earth.

Consider next the case of oblique incidence, also shown in Fig. 6.40. If N increases with height then κ decreases with height, and the ray is bent downward and will be turned around and returned to earth if a height at which

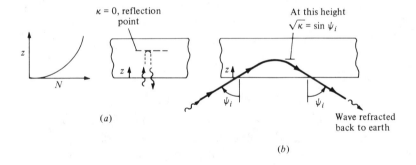

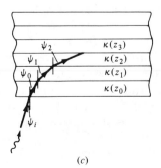

Figure 6.40 (a) Normal incidence of a wave on the ionosphere. (b) Oblique incidence. (c) A layered model used to describe the ionosphere.

$\sqrt{\kappa}$ = sin ψ_i exists. This behavior may be understood by breaking the layer into a number of thin layers with a thickness Δz and with a constant value of $\kappa(z)$ in each layer, as shown in Fig. 6.40c. Snell's law requires that sin ψ_i = $\sqrt{\kappa(z_0)}$ sin ψ_0 = $\sqrt{\kappa(z_1)}$ sin ψ_1 = $\sqrt{\kappa(z_2)}$ sin ψ_2, etc. Thus the ray will follow a path such that the tangent to the ray satisfies the condition $\sqrt{\kappa(z)}$ sin $\psi(z)$ = sin ψ_i. The ray will return to earth if $\psi(z)$ reaches $\pi/2$, which requires that $\sqrt{\kappa(z)}$ = sin ψ_i at this height. Note that for a given value of ψ_i the requirement for the ray to return to earth requires a higher electron density for higher frequencies, since $\kappa = 1 - \omega_p^2/\omega^2$ decreases with ω. Conversely, for a given electron-density maximum the maximum value of ψ_i that will result in the ray returning to earth increases with an increase in ω. Thus there is an upper limit on frequency which will result in the wave being returned to earth. The required relationship between electron density ω or frequency $f = \omega/2\pi$ and the angle of incidence is

$$N_{\text{critical}} = \frac{f^2 \cos^2 \psi_i}{81} \tag{6.69}$$

For example, if $\psi_i = \pi/4$ and $N = 2 \times 10^{10}/\text{m}^3$ then $f_{\text{max}} = (81 \times 4 \times 10^{10})^{1/2} = 18 \times 10^5 = 1.8\,\text{MHz}$. If we increase ψ_i to 60°, then $f_{\text{max}} = 1.8\sqrt{2}\,\text{MHz}$.

When N is given in electrons per cubic meter $\kappa = 1 - (81N/f^2)$. For normal incidence the wave is returned to earth or reflected if N reaches a value that makes $\kappa = 0$. For a given value of N_{max} the frequency that makes $\kappa = 0$ is called the *critical frequency f_c* and is given by

$$f_c = 9\sqrt{N_{\text{max}}} \tag{6.70}$$

From Eq. (6.69) we can write

$$f = 9\sqrt{N_{\text{max}}} \sec \psi_i = f_c \sec \psi_i \tag{6.71}$$

This value of f is called the *maximum usable frequency (MUF)* when sec ψ_i has its maximum value. The maximum usable frequency generally does not exceed 40 MHz. During periods of low solar activity the upper frequency limit is 25 to 30 MHz.

If the incident and returned rays are extrapolated to a vertex they meet at a height h', called the *virtual height* of the ionospheric layer, that is instrumental in returning the wave to earth (see Fig. 6.41). This is the apparent height of reflection. The virtual height of the F_2 layer ranges from 250 to 400 km, while for the F_1 layer the virtual height lies between 200 and 250 km. The F layer at night is at around 300 km in virtual height. The virtual height of the E layer is around 110 km. The virtual heights are important in determining the maximum value of the angle of incidence ψ_i and the maximum skip distance, as shown in Fig. 6.42. For radiation leaving the antenna in the horizontal direction the skip distance d is given by $d = 2 \times \sqrt{2a_e h'}$. The corresponding maximum value of ψ_i is given by

$$\cot \psi_i = \frac{h'}{d/2} = \frac{2h'}{d}$$

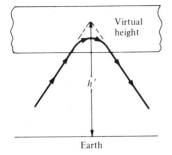

Virtual
height

h'

Earth

Figure 6.41 Illustration of virtual height.

This maximum angle is about 74° and when used in Eq. (6.71) gives

$$MUF = f_{max} = 3.6 f_c \qquad (6.72)$$

An electron concentration of $10^{12}/m^3$ will give $f_c = 9\,MHz$ and $f_{max} = 32.4\,MHz$. If we use $h' = 300\,km$ then d_{max} is approximately 2500 mi for reflection from the F_2 layer. For reflection from the E layer the maximum skip distance is about one-half of this value, or 1250 mi. If the desired range is less than d_{max} then ψ_i is smaller, and a lower frequency must be used in order to satisfy the relationship $f = f_c \sec \psi_i$, which must hold at the point in the ionosphere where the ray is turned around to propagate toward the earth. Figure 6.43 gives typical values of the maximum usable frequency for different ranges. The data is typical for winter conditions at Washington, D.C., during a peak period in solar activity. Note that daytime conditions must occur at the point of reflection, i.e., midway between the transmitter and receiver (1040 mi corresponds to a 1-h time difference) if the path was designed on the basis of daytime conditions in the ionosphere.

In order to determine the parameters of ionospheric propagation paths it is necessary to know the relationship between the skip distance d, the virtual height h', and the angle of incidence ψ_i. With reference to Fig. 6.44, let θ be the angle subtended by one-half of the skip distance; thus

$$\theta = \frac{d}{2a_e} \qquad (6.73)$$

where the effective radius of the earth equals 5280 mi, or 8497 km. The law of sines gives

$$\frac{a_e + h'}{\sin \phi} = \frac{a_e}{\sin \psi_i}$$

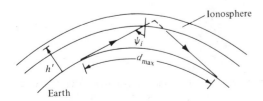

Ionosphere

ψ_i

d_{max}

h'

Earth

Figure 6.42 Illustration of maximum skip distance d_{max}.

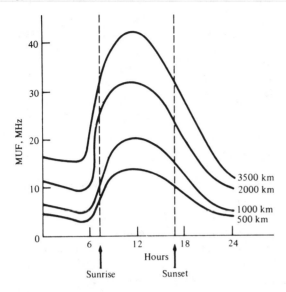

Figure 6.43 Maximum usable frequency (MUF) for wintertime for different skip distances. MUF is lower in the summertime.

where ϕ is the angle shown in Fig. 6.44 and also equals $\pi - \theta - \psi_i$. With this replacement for ϕ we get $\sin \phi = \sin(\pi - \theta - \psi_i) = \sin(\theta + \psi_i)$; hence

$$1 + \frac{h'}{a_e} = \frac{\sin(\theta + \psi_i)}{\sin \psi_i} = \sin \theta \cot \psi_i + \cos \theta$$

We now find that

$$\left(1 + \frac{h'}{a_e} - \cos \theta\right) \csc \theta = \cot \psi_i \qquad (6.74)$$

The transmitted ray leaves at an angle $\phi - \pi/2$ relative to the local horizon where

$$\phi - \frac{\pi}{2} = \frac{\pi}{2} - \theta - \psi_i \qquad (6.75)$$

The application of these relationships will be illustrated in the following example.

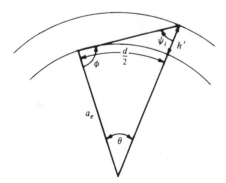

Figure 6.44 Relationships between skip distance, virtual height, and angle of incidence.

Example 6.9 Determination of radiation angle and frequency for a short-wave radio station In this example we assume that a short-wave broadcasting station located in Ohio wants to establish a broadcasting service to central Europe. The great-circle nominal distance is 4200 mi, or 6760 km. For single-skip propagation the reflecting height h' is given by h' ft $= d^2/8 = 4.2^2 \times 10^6 \times 0.125 = 2.2 \times 10^6$ ft, or 670 km, provided the radiation is beamed in the horizontal direction at the transmitting site. The required reflection point lies above the ionosphere, and hence the required service must be based on a double skip, each of length 2100 mi. The required reflection point is now only 167.5 km above the earth. The F_1 and F_2 layers have virtual heights ranging from 200 to 400 km and may be used as the reflecting layers, provided the transmitting beam is directed above the horizon. We will assume a nominal virtual height of 300 km. From Eqs. (6.73) and (6.74) we then find that $\psi_i = 74.44°$ and $\phi - \pi/2 = 4.16°$. The transmitting antenna should have its direction of maximum radiation 4.16° above the local horizon.

Figure 6.38 shows that the electron concentration in the F layer under daytime conditions is $5 \times 10^{11}/\text{m}^3$. The critical frequency f_c is given by Eq. (6.70) and is 6.36 MHz. The maximum usable frequency may be found from Eq. (6.71), which gives $f_{max} = 6.36 \sec 74.44° = 23.71$ MHz. Operation in the international shortwave 16-m band (17.7–17.9 MHz) would be acceptable.

Although this example has illustrated the use of the previously derived formulas, the sample calculations are an oversimplification of the real problem. In practice it is necessary to consider the time of day that service is to be provided, the difference in local time between the two reflecting points, the time of year, and the time within the solar cycle. A great deal of statistical data on electron concentrations and virtual heights is available, so realistic path designs can be carried out. In general, for 24-h service, different frequencies are used at different times of the day. The highest possible frequency should be used so as to minimize the attenuation. However this frequency should be at least 15 percent below the maximum usable frequency because of variations in electron density on a daily basis. ∎

Effect of the Earth's Magnetic Field

In the discussion up to this point the effect of the earth's magnetic field on the motion of the electrons has been neglected. This approximation is reasonably good at frequencies above 10 MHz but is generally not valid at frequencies below 5 MHz. The earth's magnetic field causes the ionospheric medium to become anisotropic, and the effective dielectric constant must be represented by a matrix or dyadic. It is now found that there are two distinct modes of propagation called the *ordinary* and *extraordinary waves*. An incident plane wave entering the ionosphere will split into the above two modes, and when these modes reemerge from the ionosphere they recombine into a single plane wave again. However, the plane of polarization will usually have changed, a phenomenon known as *Faraday rotation*. Faraday rotation is a variable effect and will result in some loss of signal power at the receiving antenna, since a polarization mismatch will occur in most instances.

A free electron with velocity **v** will rotate or move in a circular orbit under the influence of a steady magnetic field $\mathbf{B}_0$. The angular frequency, which is called the *cyclotron frequency*, is given by

$$\omega_c = \frac{eB_0}{m} \tag{6.76}$$

where e is the electron charge and m is the mass of the electron. The earth's magnetic field is around 5×10^{-5} Wb/m, so ω_c is around 8.83×10^6 and the cyclotron frequency f_c is 1.4 MHz.

If we let $\mathbf{B}_0 = B_0\mathbf{a}_z$ be the magnetic field of the earth, then under the action of a high-frequency ac field $\mathbf{E}\,e^{j\omega t}$, $\mathbf{H}\,e^{j\omega t}$ the force acting on an electron is given by

$$\mathbf{F} = -e(\mathbf{E} + \mathbf{V} \times \mathbf{B}_0)$$

Since **H** is of order $Y_0\mathbf{E}$ the force due to **H** is of order (v/c) smaller than that due to the electric field **E** and can be neglected (c is the speed of light). If we also include a collisional damping force, then the equation of motion for the electron becomes

$$(j\omega + \nu)m\mathbf{V} = -e(\mathbf{E} + \mathbf{V} \times \mathbf{B}_0)$$

For N electrons per cubic meter the ac current is

$$\mathbf{J} = -Ne\mathbf{V}$$

By combining the above two equations we find that **J** is determined by the equation

$$(j\omega + \nu)\mathbf{J} + \omega_c\mathbf{J} \times \mathbf{a}_z = \frac{Ne^2}{m}\mathbf{E} = \omega_p^2\epsilon_0\mathbf{E} \tag{6.77}$$

In this equation ω_c was introduced from Eq. (6.76). We can rewrite Eq. (6.77) in matrix form by writing out each vector component explicitly; thus

$$\begin{bmatrix} (j\omega + \nu) & \omega_c & 0 \\ -\omega_c & j\omega + \nu & 0 \\ 0 & 0 & j\omega + \nu \end{bmatrix} \begin{bmatrix} J_x \\ J_y \\ J_z \end{bmatrix} = \epsilon_0\omega_p^2 \begin{bmatrix} E_x \\ E_y \\ E_z \end{bmatrix} \tag{6.78}$$

This equation is readily inverted to give

$$\begin{bmatrix} J_x \\ J_y \\ J_z \end{bmatrix} = \frac{\epsilon_0\omega_p^2}{\omega_c^2 - \omega^2 + \nu^2 + 2j\omega\nu} \begin{bmatrix} j\omega + \nu & -\omega_c & 0 \\ \omega_c & j\omega + \nu & 0 \\ 0 & 0 & j\omega + \nu \end{bmatrix} \begin{bmatrix} E_x \\ E_y \\ E_z \end{bmatrix} \tag{6.79}$$

The presence of a static magnetic field results in a relationship between $\mathbf{J}$ and $\mathbf{E}$ that is not a simple scalar constant. The conductivity is a tensor represented by the matrix in Eq. (6.79). It is convenient to associate a pair of unit vectors with each element of the matrix so as to obtain the following dyadic:

$$\bar{\sigma} = \frac{\epsilon_0 \omega_p^2}{\omega_c^2 - \omega^2 + \nu^2 + 2j\omega\nu} [(j\omega + \nu)\mathbf{a}_x\mathbf{a}_x - \omega_c(\mathbf{a}_x\mathbf{a}_y - \mathbf{a}_y\mathbf{a}_x) + (j\omega + \nu)\mathbf{a}_z\mathbf{a}_z]$$

(6.80)

The equation

$$\mathbf{J} = \bar{\sigma} \cdot \mathbf{E}$$

(6.81)

where the scalar product between unit vectors on adjacent sides of the dot is taken is the same as the matrix product in Eq. (6.79). From Maxwell's equation

$$\nabla \times \mathbf{H} = j\omega\epsilon_0 \mathbf{E} + \bar{\sigma} \cdot \mathbf{E}$$

$$= j\omega\epsilon_0 \left(\bar{\mathbf{I}} + \frac{\bar{\sigma}}{j\omega\epsilon_0} \right) \cdot \mathbf{E}$$

where $\bar{\mathbf{I}}$ is the unit dyadic $\mathbf{a}_x\mathbf{a}_x + \mathbf{a}_y\mathbf{a}_y + \mathbf{a}_z\mathbf{a}_z$, we see that the tensor dielectric constant for the ionospheric plasma is given by

$$\bar{\kappa} = \bar{\mathbf{I}} + \frac{\bar{\sigma}}{j\omega\epsilon_0}$$

(6.82)

Note that $\bar{\mathbf{I}} \cdot \mathbf{E} = \mathbf{E}$.

The solution for plane waves propagating in a uniform ionosphere can be found using Maxwell's equations and this dielectric constant tensor. For this purpose it is convenient to express $\bar{\kappa}$ in the form

$$\bar{\kappa} = \begin{bmatrix} \kappa_1 & -j\kappa_2 & 0 \\ j\kappa_2 & \kappa_1 & 0 \\ 0 & 0 & \kappa_1 \end{bmatrix}$$

(6.83)

where

$$\kappa_1 = 1 - \frac{\omega_p^2(1 - j\nu/\omega)}{\omega^2 - \omega_c^2 - \nu^2 - 2j\omega\nu}$$

(6.84a)

$$\kappa_2 = \frac{\omega_p^2(\omega_c/\omega)}{\omega^2 - \omega_c^2 - \nu^2 - 2j\omega\nu}$$

(6.84b)

When the collision frequency ν is zero, both κ_1 and κ_2 are real. If the frequency ω is such that $\omega^2 = \omega_c^2 + \nu^2$ both κ_1 and κ_2 will have large imaginary components, which results in high attenuation of a radio wave at frequencies close to the cyclotron frequency (approximately 1.4 MHz).

Plane-wave solutions to Maxwell's equations are of the form

$$\mathbf{E} = \mathbf{E}_0 \, e^{-j\mathbf{k}\cdot\mathbf{r}}$$

(6.85a)

$$\mathbf{H} = \mathbf{H}_0 \, e^{-j\mathbf{k}\cdot\mathbf{r}}$$

(6.85b)

where $\mathbf{E}_0$ and $\mathbf{H}_0$ are constant vectors and $\mathbf{k}$ is the propagation vector. When $\nabla \times \mathbf{E}$ and $\nabla \times \mathbf{H}$ are expanded in rectangular coordinates, it is readily verified that $\nabla \times$ can be replaced by $-j\mathbf{k} \times$. Thus Maxwell's two curl equations give

$$-j\mathbf{k} \times \mathbf{E}_0 = -j\omega\mu_0\mathbf{H}_0$$

$$-j\mathbf{k} \times \mathbf{H}_0 = j\omega\epsilon_0\bar{\mathbf{\kappa}} \cdot \mathbf{E}_0$$

after dropping the common propagation factor. A cross product of the first equation with $\mathbf{k}$ and substitution into the second equation gives

$$\mathbf{k} \times (\mathbf{k} \times \mathbf{E}_0) = -\omega^2\mu_0\epsilon_0\bar{\mathbf{\kappa}} \cdot \mathbf{E}_0 = \mathbf{k}\mathbf{k} \cdot \mathbf{E}_0 - k^2\mathbf{E}_0$$

This equation may be rewritten in the form

$$(k^2\bar{\mathbf{I}} - k_0^2\bar{\mathbf{\kappa}} - \mathbf{k}\mathbf{k}) \cdot \mathbf{E}_0 = 0 \tag{6.86a}$$

or in matrix form as

$$\begin{bmatrix} k^2 - \kappa_1 k_0^2 - k_x^2 & j\kappa_2 k_0^2 - k_x k_y & -k_x k_z \\ -j\kappa_2 k_0^2 - k_y k_x & k^2 - \kappa_1 k_0^2 - k_y^2 & -k_y k_z \\ -k_z k_x & -k_z k_y & k^2 - \kappa_1 k_0^2 - k_z^2 \end{bmatrix} \begin{bmatrix} E_{0x} \\ E_{0y} \\ E_{0z} \end{bmatrix} = 0$$

A nontrivial solution for $\mathbf{E}_0$ will exist only if the determinant of the above system of equations vanishes. By setting the determinant equal to zero, the equation obtained for the propagation constant $\mathbf{k}$ is called the *Appleton-Hartree equation*. We will not consider the solution for the most general case. Instead we will consider three special cases only, which will, however, give some insight into the nature of the solutions.

Case 1: Propagation perpendicular to $\mathbf{B}_0$, $\mathbf{E}_0$ along $\mathbf{B}_0$ Let $\mathbf{k} = k_x\mathbf{a}_x$ and assume $\mathbf{E}_0 = E_0\mathbf{a}_z$. For this case the electron velocity is parallel to $\mathbf{B}_0$, so the force term $-e\mathbf{V} \times \mathbf{B}_0$ is zero and $\mathbf{B}_0$ has no effect. The matrix equation becomes

$$\begin{bmatrix} -\kappa_1 k_0^2 & j\kappa_2 k_0^2 & 0 \\ -j\kappa_2 k_0^2 & k_x^2 - \kappa_1 k_0^2 & 0 \\ 0 & 0 & k_x^2 - \kappa_1 k_0^2 \end{bmatrix} \begin{bmatrix} 0 \\ 0 \\ E_0 \end{bmatrix} = 0$$

The determinant vanishes when $k_x = k = \sqrt{\kappa_1}k_0$, which is the same value as for the case $\mathbf{B}_0 = 0$, as expected. The plane wave is linearly polarized with the electric vector along $\mathbf{B}_0$, as shown in Fig. 6.45a. This solution is called the ordinary wave.

Case 2: Propagation perpendicular to $\mathbf{B}_0$, $\mathbf{E}_0$ perpendicular to $\mathbf{B}_0$ For this case let $\mathbf{k} = k_x\mathbf{a}_x$ as in the previous example and let $\mathbf{E}_0 = E_1\mathbf{a}_x + E_2\mathbf{a}_y$. The matrix multiplying $\mathbf{E}_0$ is the same as for the first case, but the $\mathbf{E}_0$ vector has

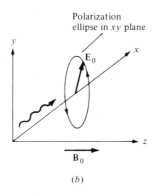

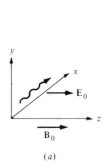

(a)

(b)

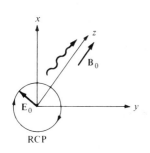

RCP

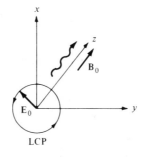

LCP

(c)

Figure 6.45 (a) Ordinary wave propagating perpendicular to magnetic field. (b) Extraordinary elliptically polarized wave propagating perpendicular to magnetic field. (c) Right and left circularly polarized waves propagating parallel to the magnetic field.

the components E_1, E_2, 0. The determinant set equal to zero gives

$$(k_x^2 - \kappa_1 k_0^2)[(k_x^2 - \kappa_1 k_0^2)\kappa_1 k_0^2 + \kappa_2^2 k_0^4] = 0$$

One solution is $k_x^2 = \kappa_1 k_0^2$ but requires $E_1 = E_2 = 0$. The other solution is

$$k_x = \sqrt{\frac{\kappa_1^2 - \kappa_2^2}{\kappa_1}} \, k_0 \tag{6.87}$$

For this solution we find that $-\kappa_1 k_0^2 E_1 + j\kappa_2 k_0^2 E_2 = 0$ or

$$\frac{E_2}{E_1} = -j\frac{\kappa_1}{\kappa_2} \tag{6.88}$$

This wave is elliptically polarized in the plane perpendicular to $\mathbf{B}_0$ and has a component of the electric field in the direction of propagation, as shown in Fig. 6.45b, which is a phenomenon that does not occur for plane waves in an isotropic medium. The solution described for this case is called the extraordinary wave.

Case 3: Propagation along B_0, E_0 perpendicular to B_0 For this last case to be considered, let $\mathbf{k} = k_z \mathbf{a}_z$ and $\mathbf{E}_0 = E_1 \mathbf{a}_x + E_2 \mathbf{a}_y$. The matrix equation becomes

$$\begin{bmatrix} k_z^2 - \kappa_1 k_0^2 & j\kappa_2 k_0^2 & 0 \\ -j\kappa_2 k_0^2 & k_z^2 - \kappa_1 k_0^2 & 0 \\ 0 & 0 & -\kappa_1 k_0^2 \end{bmatrix} \begin{bmatrix} E_1 \\ E_2 \\ 0 \end{bmatrix} = 0 \qquad (6.89)$$

The vanishing of the determinant gives

$$k_z = k_1 = k_0\sqrt{\kappa_1 - \kappa_2} = k_0\sqrt{1 - \frac{\omega_p^2}{\omega(\omega - \omega_c)}} \qquad (6.90a)$$

$$k_z = k_2 = k_0\sqrt{\kappa_1 + \kappa_2} = k_0\sqrt{1 - \frac{\omega_p^2}{\omega(\omega + \omega_c)}} \qquad (6.90b)$$

with the last forms being the solutions when $\nu = 0$. There are two solutions for k_z. For the $k_z = k_1$ solution the electric field is

$$\mathbf{E} = E_1(\mathbf{a}_x - j\mathbf{a}_y) e^{-jk_1 z} \qquad (6.91a)$$

since $E_2 = -jE_1$. This is a right-circular polarized wave. The other solution has

$$\mathbf{E} = E_1(\mathbf{a}_x + j\mathbf{a}_y) e^{-jk_2 z} \qquad (6.91b)$$

which is a left-circular polarized wave. The right-circular polarized wave has an electric field that drives the electron in its natural direction of rotation about the magnetic field, and this shows up in the solution for k_1, which has the resonance denominator term $\omega - \omega_c$. When collisions are included we get

$$k_1 = k_0\sqrt{1 - \frac{\omega_p^2}{\omega(\omega - j\nu - \omega_c)}}$$

which has a large imaginary part at the cyclotron frequency with a consequent high absorption of the wave. The left-circular polarized wave has an electric field that drives the electron in a direction opposite to its natural direction of rotation, and hence k_2 has $\omega + \omega_c$ as a denominator factor which does not exhibit a resonance effect.

Faraday Rotation

Consider an ionospheric layer l m thick along z. Let the incident plane wave be

$$\mathbf{E} = 2E_0 \mathbf{a}_x e^{-jk_0 z}$$

$$= E_0(\mathbf{a}_x + j\mathbf{a}_y) e^{-jk_0 z} + E_0(\mathbf{a}_x - j\mathbf{a}_y) e^{-jk_0 z}$$

after decomposition into left and right circularly polarized waves. This wave enters the ionospheric layer at $z = 0$ and propagates as two circularly polarized waves with different propagation constants. Thus at the exit plane the electric field is (we are neglecting reflections at each interface)

$$\mathbf{E} = E_0(\mathbf{a}_x - j\mathbf{a}_y)\, e^{-jk_1 l} + E_0(\mathbf{a}_x + j\mathbf{a}_y)\, e^{-jk_2 l}$$

We can rewrite this expression as

$$\mathbf{E} = E_0\, e^{-j(k_1+k_2)l/2}[\mathbf{a}_x(e^{j(k_2-k_1)l/2} + e^{-j(k_2-k_1)l/2}) - j\mathbf{a}_y(e^{j(k_2-k_1)l/2} - e^{-j(k_2-k_1)l/2})]$$

$$= 2E_0\, e^{-j(k_1+k_2)l/2}\left[\mathbf{a}_x \cos(k_2 - k_1)\frac{l}{2} + \mathbf{a}_y \sin(k_2 - k_1)\frac{l}{2}\right] \qquad (6.92)$$

which shows that the exiting wave is again a linearly polarized wave but with the direction of polarization rotated by an angle ϕ relative to the x axis. The angle ϕ is given by

$$\tan \phi = \frac{E_y}{E_x} = \tan(k_2 - k_1)\frac{l}{2}$$

so

$$\phi = (k_2 - k_1)\frac{l}{2} \qquad (6.93)$$

The phase delay is that associated with the average propagation constant $(k_1 + k_2)/2$. As noted previously, the rotation of the plane of polarization is called Faraday rotation. It is most pronounced when ω is close to ω_c, in which case k_1 and k_2 have the largest difference. At high frequencies k_1 and k_2 have almost the same value, so the amount of rotation is much smaller. The rotation angle depends on so many variables that it is generally not predictable and thus will lead to a loss in received signal power at the receiving antenna because of the resultant polarization mismatch.

6.7 MICROWAVE AND MILLIMETER-WAVE PROPAGATION

In the microwave and millimeter-wave region where the frequency ranges from 1 GHz ($\lambda_0 = 30$ cm) up to 300 GHz ($\lambda_0 = 1$ mm) the ionosphere is transparent, since ω is much greater than the plasma frequency ω_p and the cyclotron frequency ω_c. The propagation of waves in this frequency range is predominantly line-of-sight propagation. There will be interference phenomena from the ground-reflected wave, but it is not as pronounced as it is at lower frequencies because the roughness of the ground is much greater relative to the wavelengths involved. Thus the reflection from the ground is more diffuse with a weaker specular-reflected component. In those instances where a relatively smooth ground or water surface is present at the reflection point, the interference phenomena can be significant, and the interference pattern will exhibit a lobe structure with closely spaced lobes.

The most important factor to take into account at wavelengths of a few centimeters and shorter is attenuation and scattering by rain and snow, and for the millimeter-wave band attenuation, which can be very high, by fog, water vapor, and other gases in the atmosphere. In this section we will present an outline of the theory for predicting the attenuation and scattering by rain and also data on the attenuation caused by atmospheric gases. Other phenomena that affect the propagation of microwaves and millimeter waves are scattering by tropospheric irregularities in the index of refraction and ducting caused by inversions in the index-of-refraction profiles. The latter two topics are discussed in later sections of this chapter.

Attenuation by Rain

Radio waves propagating through rain are attenuated because of absorption of power in the lossy dielectric medium represented by water. There is also some loss in the direct transmitted wave because of scattering of some energy out of the beam by the rain droplets. The scattering loss is usually small relative to the absorption loss. The theory for rain attenuation and scattering is based on the calculation of the absorption and scattering cross sections of a single raindrop. This calculation is straightforward for the case of a spherical droplet of water having a radius no larger than $\lambda_0/10$. In this situation the low-frequency Rayleigh scattering theory can be applied. Since the radius of raindrops ranges from a fraction of a millimeter up to several millimeters, the Rayleigh scattering theory is generally valid down to wavelengths of order 3 cm or somewhat less. The assumption of spherical droplets is not valid since raindrops take on an oblate spheroidal or flattened shape under the influence of aerodynamic forces and pressure forces as they fall. However, at the longer wavelengths an equivalent spherical radius can be assumed. At millimeter wavelengths it is important to consider the drop shape, and the determination of the cross sections is then much more difficult and laborious. However, with modern computer facilities and techniques, the limitation is not in the computational aspect but in knowing the drop shape, which depends on drop size and the velocity with which the drop falls. We will only consider the case where Rayleigh scattering theory applies.

Consider a spherical drop of water with a radius a much smaller than the wavelength of the incident plane wave, as shown in Fig. 6.46. The drop is characterized as a dielectric sphere with a complex dielectric constant $\kappa = \kappa' - j\kappa''$. The incident electric field is chosen as

$$\mathbf{E}_i = E_0 \mathbf{a}_z \, e^{-jk_0 x}$$

Over the extent of the drop the incident field is essentially uniform and equal to $E_0 \mathbf{a}_z$. The polarization produced in the drop is thus the same as would be produced in a dielectric sphere under the action of a uniform static electric field. This boundary value problem is readily solved (see Prob. 2.7) and shows

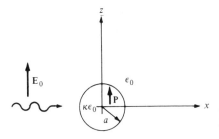

Figure 6.46 A plane wave incident on a spherical water drop.

that the dipole polarization **P** per unit volume in the drop is given by

$$\mathbf{P} = 3\frac{\kappa - 1}{\kappa + 2}\,\epsilon_0 E_0 \mathbf{a}_z \tag{6.94}$$

The total dipole moment of the water sphere is obtained by multiplying by the volume and is

$$\mathbf{P}_0 = \tfrac{4}{3}\pi a^3 \mathbf{P} = 4\pi a^3\,\frac{\kappa - 1}{\kappa + 2}\,\epsilon_0 E_0 \mathbf{a}_z \tag{6.95}$$

Since $a \ll \lambda_0$ the far-zone scattered field from the sphere is the same as that radiated by a small electric dipole of total strength $\mathbf{P}_0$.

A current element $I\,dl$ is equivalent to the time derivative of the dipole moment, so $j\omega \mathbf{P}_0$ may be used to replace $I\,dl$ in Eq. (2.29a) for the far-zone radiated field; thus

$$\mathbf{E}_s = -\omega Z_0 k_0 P_0 \sin\theta\,\frac{e^{-jk_0 r}}{4\pi r}\,\mathbf{a}_\theta \tag{6.96}$$

The scattering pattern of a small dielectric sphere is the same as the radiation pattern of a small electric dipole. The total scattered power is given by

$$P_s = \tfrac{1}{2}Y_0 \int_0^{2\pi}\int_0^{\pi} |\mathbf{E}_s|^2 r^2 \sin\theta\,d\theta\,d\phi = \frac{\omega^2 k_0^2 Z_0}{12\pi}|P_0|^2$$

When we substitute for $\mathbf{P}_0$ from Eq. (6.95) we obtain

$$P_s = \tfrac{4}{3}\pi a^2 (k_0 a)^4 Y_0 |E_0|^2 \left|\frac{\kappa - 1}{\kappa + 2}\right|^2 \tag{6.97}$$

for the total scattered power. This is the *low-frequency* or *Rayleigh formula* for the scattered power.

The scattering cross section σ_s is defined as the total scattered power divided by the incident power per unit area. Hence we find that

$$\sigma_s = \frac{P_s}{\tfrac{1}{2}Y_0|E_0|^2} = \tfrac{8}{3}\pi a^2 (k_0 a)^4 \left|\frac{\kappa - 1}{\kappa + 2}\right|^2 \tag{6.98}$$

The radar backscatter cross section σ_{BS} is defined such that if scattering occurred isotropically the same backscattered power would result. From Eq. (6.96) we find that the backscattered power per unit area is

$$P_{BS} = \tfrac{1}{2} Y_0 |E_s|^2 \bigg|_{\theta = \pi/2} = \frac{\omega^2 k_0^2 |P_0|^2 Z_0}{32\pi^2 r^2} = P_{inc} \frac{\sigma_{BS}}{4\pi r^2}$$

where P_{inc} is the incident power per unit area. This defining relationship shows that

$$\sigma_{BS} = 4\pi a^2 (k_0 a)^4 \left| \frac{\kappa - 1}{\kappa + 2} \right|^2 = \tfrac{2}{3} \sigma_s \tag{6.99}$$

The absorption cross section may be found by first evaluating the power P_a absorbed by the sphere. The polarization current density in the sphere is $\mathbf{J}_p = j\omega \mathbf{P}$ and is uniform. The total electric field $\mathbf{E}$ in the sphere is related to $\mathbf{P}$ by the equation $\mathbf{P} = (\kappa - 1)\epsilon_0 \mathbf{E}$. The time average absorbed power is given by

$$P_a = \tfrac{1}{2} \mathrm{Re} \int_0^a \int_0^{2\pi} \int_0^\pi \mathbf{E} \cdot \mathbf{J}_p^* r^2 \sin\theta \, d\theta \, d\phi \, dr$$

$$= \tfrac{2}{3}\pi a^3 \, \mathrm{Re} \, \mathbf{E} \cdot \mathbf{J}_p^*$$

$$= 6\pi a^3 k_0 Y_0 \left| \frac{\kappa - 1}{\kappa + 2} \right|^2 \frac{\kappa'' |E_0|^2}{(\kappa' - 1)^2 + (\kappa'')^2}$$

By dividing this equation by the incident power density we obtain the absorption across section σ_a, which is

$$\sigma_a = 12\pi a^2 (k_0 a) \left| \frac{\kappa - 1}{\kappa + 2} \right|^2 \frac{\kappa''}{(\kappa' - 1)^2 + (\kappa'')^2} \tag{6.100}$$

The ratio of the absorption cross section to the scattering cross section is

$$\frac{\sigma_a}{\sigma_s} = \frac{4.5}{(k_0 a)^3} \frac{\kappa''}{(\kappa' - 1)^2 + (\kappa'')^2} \tag{6.101}$$

As a typical example consider the case when $\lambda_0 = 3$ cm, $a = 0.1$ cm, $\kappa' = 65.3$, and $\kappa'' = 31.5$, for which we find that $\sigma_a = 3\sigma_s$. This shows that the absorption cross section is larger than the scattering cross section. For smaller drops the ratio is even larger because of the $(k_0 a)^3$ factor in the denominator.

The extinction cross section σ_e is the sum of the scattering and absorption cross sections; thus

$$\sigma_e = \sigma_s + \sigma_a = \left[\tfrac{8}{3}\pi a^2 (k_0 a)^4 + 12\pi a^2 (k_0 a) \frac{\kappa''}{(\kappa' - 1)^2 + (\kappa'')^2} \right] \left| \frac{\kappa - 1}{\kappa + 2} \right|^2 \tag{6.102}$$

The ratio σ_s/σ_e is called the *albedo* of the particle. The total power removed from the incident wave as scattered and absorbed power is given by the product of the incident power density per unit area with the extinction cross section σ_e.

When an electromagnetic wave propagates through rain it encounters a great many water droplets with different radii. Since σ_e is a strong function of the radius a it is necessary to take into account the drop size distribution. Let $N(a)\, da$ be the number of drops per unit volume with radii in the interval a to $a + da$. The total power removed from a wave with power density $P = \frac{1}{2} Y_0 |\mathbf{E}|^2$ by the drops in a volume element of unit cross-sectional area and thickness dz along z is (we now assume propagation to be in the z direction)

$$\frac{dP}{dz} = -\tfrac{1}{2} Y_0 |\mathbf{E}|^2 \int_0^\infty \sigma_e(a) N(a)\, da$$

$$= -P \int_0^\infty \sigma_e(a) N(a)\, da \tag{6.103}$$

As a result of this power loss the power flow decays at a rate 2α where

$$A = 2\alpha = \int_0^\infty \sigma_e(a) N(a)\, da \tag{6.104}$$

This equation defines A, the specific attenuation per unit length along the propagation path. From Eqs. (6.103) and (6.104) we have

$$\frac{dP}{dz} = -A(z)P$$

for which the solution is

$$P(z) = P(0)\, e^{-\int_0^z A(z)\, dz} \tag{6.105}$$

The drop size distribution may vary along the propagation path because of nonuniform rain, and hence A is a function of z, which accounts for the integral in the above equation.

The theory outlined above is generally found to be adequate to describe attenuation by rain. The theory does, however, require a knowledge of the extinction cross section of each drop, the drop-size distribution, and the dependence of the drop-size distribution function $N(a)$ on the rain rate R. Usually only the rain rate R in millimeters of water per hour can be easily measured. A light drizzle corresponds to a rain rate of 0.25 mm/h, light rain corresponds to $R = 1$ mm/h, moderate rain to 4 mm/h, heavy rain to 16 mm/h, and cloud bursts up to many centimeters per hour. The drop-size distribution is a function of the rain rate, with a greater concentration of large drops occurring for heavy rain. Marshal and Palmer proposed the following empirical distribution formula:

$$N(a) = N_0\, e^{-\Lambda a} \tag{6.106}$$

where $N_0 = 1.6 \times 10^4$ mm^{-1}/m^3

$\Lambda = 8.2 R^{-0.21}$/mm

with R being the rain rate in millimeters per hour. This model is widely used for the theoretical evaluation of attenuation. It is in close agreement with the distributions measured by Laws and Parsons.†

From the point of view of the communications engineer what is needed is a relatively simple formula relating specific attenuation to rain rate, frequency, and temperature. Fortunately such a formula exists, and it is of the form

$$A = aR^b \text{ dB/km} \tag{6.107}$$

where R is the rain rate in millimeters per hour and a and b are constants that depend on frequency and temperature of the rain. The temperature dependence is due to the variation of dielectric constant of water with temperature. A detailed review of the theory and experimental data has led to a compilation of the values of the two constants a and b by Olsen, Rodgers, and Hodge.‡ These authors established the following empirical formulas for the constants a and b at a temperature of 0°C:

$$a = G_a f^{E_a} \qquad f \text{ in gigahertz} \tag{6.108a}$$

where $G_a = 6.39 \times 10^{-5}$ $E_a = 2.03$ $f < 2.9 \text{ GHz}$

$G_a = 4.21 \times 10^{-5}$ $E_a = 2.42$ $2.9 \text{ GHz} \leq f \leq 54 \text{ GHz}$

$G_a = 4.09 \times 10^{-2}$ $E_a = 0.699$ $54 \text{ GHz} \leq f < 180 \text{ GHz}$

$G_a = 3.38$ $E_a = -0.151$ $180 \text{ GHz} < f$

and $$b = G_b f^{E_b} \qquad f \text{ in gigahertz} \tag{6.108b}$$

where $G_b = 0.851$ $E_b = 0.158$ $f < 8.5 \text{ GHz}$

$G_b = 1.41$ $E_b = -0.0779$ $8.5 \text{ GHz} \leq f < 25 \text{ GHz}$

$G_b = 2.63$ $E_b = -0.272$ $25 \text{ GHz} \leq f < 164 \text{ GHz}$

$G_b = 0.616$ $E_b = 0.0126$ $164 \text{ GHz} \leq f$

Some representative curves of attenuation in decibels per kilometer at frequencies of 10, 30, and 100 GHz as a function of rain rate were computed using Eqs. (6.107) and (6.108) and are shown in Fig. 6.47. At 10 GHz and below the attenuation due to rain is relatively small. For moderate rain (5 mm/h) it is only 0.074 dB/km at 10 GHz. The corresponding attenuation at 30 GHz is 0.85 dB/km, while at 100 GHz it is 3.42 dB/km. Since typical line-of-sight paths are 20 to 30 km in length, attenuation rates of 1 dB or more per kilometer can lead to large decreases in signal strength. This attenuation must be offset by

† A very good treatment of the theory of attenuation in rain can be found in Kerr, op. cit., Chap. 8. A recent review of the effects of hydrometeors on radio-wave propagation has been given by T. Oguchi, "Electromagnetic Wave Propagation and Scattering in Rain and Other Hydrometeors," *Proc. IEEE*, vol. 71, Sept. 1983, pp. 1029–1078.

‡ R. L. Olsen, D. V. Rodgers, and D. B. Hodge, "The aR^b Relation in the Calculation of Rain Attenuation," *IEEE Trans.*, vol. AP-26, March 1978, pp. 318–329.

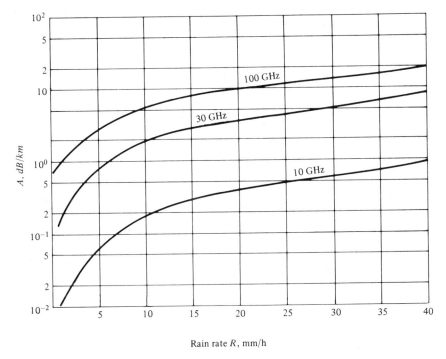

Rain rate R, mm/h

Figure 6.47 Attenuation by rain at 10, 30, and 100 GHz as a function of rain rate.

increased antenna gain or transmitter power, which is relatively expensive if a 1000-fold increase is required.

Attenuation by Fog

The attenuation of microwaves and millimeter waves by fog is governed by the same fundamental equations as attenuation by rain. The main difference is that fog is a suspended mist of very small water droplets with radii in the range 0.01 to 0.05 mm. For frequencies below 300 GHz the attenuation by fog is essentially linearly proportional to the total water content per unit volume at any given frequency. The upper level for water content is around 1 g/m^3, with the content usually considerably less than this for most fogs. A concentration of 0.032 g/m^3 corresponds to a fog that is characterized by an optical visibility of around 2000 ft. A concentration of 0.32 g/m^3 corresponds to an optical visibility range of around 400 ft. The attenuation by fog in decibels per kilometer as a function of frequency is shown in Fig. 6.48 for the two concentration levels mentioned above. At a frequency of 300 GHz the attenuation in the more dense fog is still only about 1 dB/km. Hence, for communication link designs with sufficient signal margin built in to overcome the attenuation by rain, the attenuation by fog will not be the limiting factor.

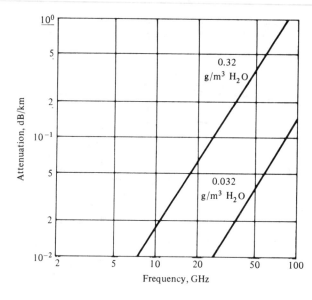

Figure 6.48 Attenuation in fog as a function of frequency for two different concentrations.

Attenuation by Snow and Ice

When water solidifies into snow and ice crystals there is a significant change in the complex dielectric constant $\kappa = \kappa' - j\kappa''$. For ice, κ' is nearly constant and equal to 3.17 for temperatures from $0°$ to $-30°C$ throughout the centimeter and millimeter wave bands. The imaginary part is very small, nearly independent of frequency in the microwave and millimeter wave bands, and drops from a value of approximately 3.7×10^{-3} at $0°C$ to 5.2×10^{-4} at $-30°C$.† The small value of the imaginary part indicates relatively little attenuation by dry ice crystals. However, snow and hail consist of a mixture of ice crystals and water in many instances, so the attenuation is strongly dependent on the meteorological conditions. Furthermore the shape of snow and ice crystals is so varied that the calculation of absorption by a single typical particle is a formidable task, if indeed a typical particle can even be defined.

Attenuation of microwaves in dry snow is at least an order of magnitude less than in rain for the same precipitation rate. However, attenuation by wet snow is comparable to that in rain and may even exceed that of rain at millimeter wavelengths.‡ Even in dry snow, measurements have shown that the attenuation of 0.96 mm radiation may be greater than in rain with the same precipitation rate. Measurements have shown an attenuation of around 2 dB/km at 35 GHz for wet snow and a precipitation rate of 5 mm/h. For dry snow the attenuation is two orders of magnitude less. Because of the many variables involved, in particular the relative water content, it is difficult to specify the attenuation in any simple form related to precipitation rate. Hence no further data on attenuation in snow will be presented here.

† See Kerr, op. cit., Table 8.18.
‡ Oguchi, op. cit.

Attenuation by Atmospheric Gases

Uncondensed water vapor and oxygen both have various absorption lines in the centimeter and millimeter wave regions. Consequently, there are frequencies where high attenuation occurs and which are separated by windows or frequency bands where the attenuation is much lower. Figure 6.49 shows the attenuation by oxygen and water vapor (uncondensed) at 20°C at sea level. The water content is 1 percent water molecules, which is typical in temperate climates. At frequencies greater than 300 GHz the attenuation by oxygen is negligible relative to that of water vapor. There are strong water vapor absorption lines at $\lambda_0 = 1.35$ cm and at 1.67 mm, as well as at shorter wavelengths. There is strong absorption by oxygen at $\lambda_0 = 0.5$ and 0.25 cm. At $\lambda_0 = 0.5$ cm, attenuation by oxygen alone exceeds 10 dB/km. The attenuation by oxygen and water vapor is additive. In those bands where the attenuation exceeds 10 dB/km the range over which communication can take place is severely restricted. By a proper choice of frequencies it is possible to achieve much less attenuation; for example, at $\lambda_0 = 1.33$ mm the attenuation is less than 1 dB/km. For frequencies above 300 GHz the minimum attenuation is still large, 6 dB or more per kilometer, and places a great restriction on the

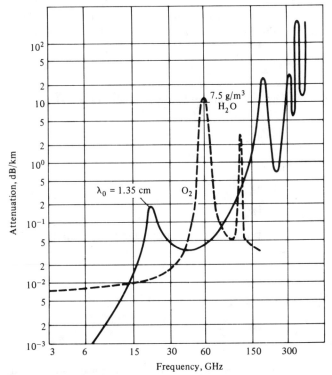

Figure 6.49 Attenuation by oxygen and water vapor at sea level. $T = 20°C$. Water content is 7.5 g/m^3.

application of millimeter- and submillimeter-wave radiation for terrestrial line-of-sight paths. However, various specialized applications such as short-range secure communication systems and satellite-to-satellite links are suited to the use of millimeter-wavelength radiation. The short wavelengths involved allow very compact high-gain antennas to be used, and this can compensate for some of the attenuation loss.

6.8 SCATTERING BY RAIN

The scattering of microwaves by rain is sufficiently high that radar can be used to detect the presence of rain cells. This is important for navigational purposes and in weather forecasting. Scattering by rain can also have a deleterious effect when, for example, a radar system is used to detect and track an aircraft and rain in the intervening space obscures the target. A simple theory for backscattering by rain can be constructed by using the expression derived earlier for the radar backscattering cross section of a spherical drop of water. This theory is developed in this section.

Consider a single drop of water located at a point defined by the spherical coordinates r, θ, ϕ, where r is the distance from the radar and θ and ϕ are the polar and azimuthal angles measured relative to the bore-sight direction of the radar antenna, as illustrated in Fig. 6.50. If P_t is the transmitted power then the incident power per unit area at the location of the water droplet is given by

$$P_{inc} = \frac{P_t G(\theta, \phi)}{4\pi r^2}$$

where G is the antenna gain. The backscattered power at the radar location is

$$dP_{BS} = P_{inc} \frac{\sigma_{BS}}{4\pi r^2}$$

and the received power dP_r will be

$$dP_r = \frac{\lambda_0^2}{4\pi} G(\theta, \phi) \, dP_{BS}$$

when we assume that there is no polarization or impedance mismatch at the

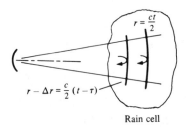

Rain cell

Figure 6.50 Volume of rain cell illuminated by a pulsed radar system.

antenna. The required cross section is given by Eq. (6.99), and since $|\kappa|$ is around 70 we can replace $(\kappa - 1)/(\kappa + 2)$ by unity with very little error. Hence the received power from a single drop is given by

$$dP_r = \frac{\lambda_0^2}{(4\pi)^3 r^4} P_t G^2(\theta, \phi) 4\pi a^2 (k_0 a)^4 \qquad (6.109)$$

Since the cross section depends on $(k_0 a)^4$ the scattering is very weak at the longer wavelengths. The cross section given by Eq. (6.109) is based on the Rayleigh scattering theory, which requires that $a \ll \lambda_0$. At the shorter wavelengths when the drop radius becomes comparable to the wavelength in size, the backscatter cross section approaches the geometrical cross section πa^2, and the resultant backscattered power is much greater.

In order to obtain an expression for the total received power from an extended volume of rain, a number of simplifying assumptions are usually made. The first of these is that the scattered field from the drops is very weak compared with the incident field, and thus the polarizing field acting on each drop is assumed to be the incident field only. In other words, multiple scattering is neglected. The second assumption is that the positions of the drops are random, so the phase of the scattered electric field from the various drops can be considered to be a random variable uniformly distributed over the interval 0 to 2π. For a drop located at $r = r_i$ the phase of the received voltage is determined by the two-way propagation factor $e^{-2jk_0 r_i}$, while for a drop at $r = r_j$ the corresponding factor is $e^{-2jk_0 r_j}$. The difference in phase angle is $2k_0(r_i - r_j)$, and when this is averaged over all drop locations the result is that there is no coherent in-phase addition of the scattered field at the radar site. Consequently the *average* received power is simply the addition of that contributed by each drop. It is, however, necessary to take into account the drop size distribution since the cross section is dependent on the drop radii. We again let $N(a)\,da$ be the number of drops per unit volume, with radii in the interval a to $a + da$. The average backscatter cross section per unit volume is thus given by

$$\langle \sigma_{BS} \rangle = \int_0^\infty 4\pi a^2 (k_0 a)^4 N(a)\,da \qquad (6.110)$$

in the Rayleigh regime.

The total backscattered power is obtained by multiplying the average cross section by $P_{\text{inc}}/4\pi r^2$ and integrating over the volume of rain illuminated by the radar. In general, the drop-size distribution $N(a)$ may not be the same throughout the whole rain cell, since the rain rate is not necessarily uniform. Consequently $\langle \sigma_{BS} \rangle$ should be regarded as a function of r, θ, and ϕ. On this basis we obtain

$$P_r = \frac{\lambda_0^2}{(4\pi)^3} P_t \int_V G^2(\theta, \phi) \frac{\langle \sigma_{BS}(r, \theta, \phi) \rangle}{r^2} \sin\theta\,d\theta\,d\phi\,dr \qquad (6.111)$$

where we have put $dV = r^2 \sin\theta\,d\theta\,d\phi\,dr$ for the element of volume.

In many radar systems the transmitted signal is a pulsed carrier tone of duration τ. In this instance the received power at any instant of time comes only from an interval in range of length $c\tau/2$, where c is the speed of light. This range-gating effect can be understood by reference to Fig. 6.50. Let the leading edge of the pulsed signal leave the radar at time $t = 0$. The return signal from drops at a range r comes at a time $2r/c$ later. The signal that leaves the transmitter at time t_1 will be returned at the same time $2r/c$ by drops located at a range $r - \Delta r = r - ct_1/2$, since the propagation delay must be $t_1 = 2\Delta r/c$ s shorter. The trailing edge of the pulse returns a signal from drops at $r - c\tau/2$ at the same time as the leading edge of the pulse returns signals from drops located at r. The range interval that returns signals at the same instant of time is thus $c\tau/2$ long. As time proceeds this range interval moves outwards to allow for the greater lapse in time. As a function of time the received power P_r is thus a sample of the return from drops in an interval $c\tau/2$ centered on the range $r_0 = ct_d/2$ where t_d is the time delay between when the pulse was transmitted and when the returned signal is being observed. This delay time can be chosen by the radar operator and thus allows various range increments of the rain cell to be explored.

For this particular case the integration over r in Eq. (6.111) can be replaced by a factor $c\tau/2$ and r can be replaced by r_0. The average received power from a single pulse transmission is thus

$$P_r = \frac{\lambda_0^2}{(4\pi)^3} P_t \frac{\langle \sigma_{BS} \rangle}{r_0^2} \frac{c\tau}{2} \int_\Omega G^2(\theta, \phi) \sin \theta \, d\theta \, d\phi \qquad (6.112)$$

where we have now assumed that $\langle \sigma_{BS} \rangle$ is uniform over the limited volume that is illuminated and the integration is over the solid angle of the antenna beam.

The range interval $c\tau/2$ is usually quite short; for example, for a 1-μs pulse it is 150 m long. Thus the attenuation of the incident and returned signals along the range increment is normally small. However, if the range interval that is being observed is located deep within the rain cell, it is necessary to take into account the two-way attenuation of the incident and returned signal in propagating through the depth d of the rain cell, where d is the distance from the nearest boundary of the rain cell to the range increment that is being observed. The expression for received average power as given by Eq. (6.112) should then be multiplied by e^{-2Ad}, where A is the one-way power-attenuation constant per unit distance.

An approximate value for the integral in Eq. (6.112) can be obtained by assuming that $G(\theta, \phi)$ is a constant equal to the on-axis gain $G(0)$ over the half-power beam widths of the antenna and is zero outside this interval. For a circularly symmetric pattern with a half-power beam width $2\theta_{1/2}$, we then obtain

$$\int_0^{2\pi} \int_0^{\theta_{1/2}} G^2(0) \sin \theta \, d\theta \, d\phi = G^2(0) 2\pi (1 - \cos \theta_{1/2})$$

$$\approx G^2(0) \pi \theta_{1/2}^2$$

for a high-gain antenna. The volume V of rain that is illuminated is given by

$$V = \frac{c\tau}{2} \int_0^{2\pi} \int_0^{\theta_{1/2}} r_0^2 \sin\theta \, d\theta \, d\phi$$

$$\approx \frac{c\tau}{2} r_0^2 \pi \theta_{1/2}^2$$

When V is introduced into Eq. (6.112) we obtain

$$P_r = \frac{\lambda_0^2}{(4\pi)^3} P_t G^2(0) \frac{\langle \sigma_{\text{BS}} \rangle}{r_0^4} V \qquad (6.113)$$

For rain cells that fill the antenna beam, the illuminated volume V is proportional to r_0^2, so the received power varies as the inverse distance squared, which is in contrast to the r^{-4} variation for the returned signal from a localized target. The effect of scattering by rain is thus more pronounced in obscuring the target signal at long distances.

Since raindrops are in motion, the returned signal fluctuates in time and has a noiselike characteristic. The theory presented above only gives the average received scattered power, it does not provide any information on the fluctuation of the received power. The latter has also been investigated but will not be dealt with in this text.†

An estimate of the average backscatter cross section as a function of rain rate may be obtained by using the drop size distribution given by Eq. (6.106) in Eq. (6.110). This results in

$$\langle \sigma_{\text{BS}} \rangle = \frac{2^6 \pi^5}{\lambda_0^4} N_0 \int_0^{\infty} a^6 e^{-\Lambda a} \, da$$

The integral can be integrated by parts successively to give $6!/\Lambda^7$. It is now found that by putting $N_0 = 1.6 \times 10^4 \text{ mm}^{-1}/\text{m}^3$ and $\Lambda = 8.2 R^{-0.21}/\text{mm}$,

$$\langle \sigma_{\text{BS}} \rangle = \frac{9.05 \times 10^{-14}}{\lambda_0^4} R^{1.47} \text{ m}^2/\text{m}^3 \qquad (6.114)$$

In this equation the numerical factor has been adjusted so that λ_0 is given in meters and R is the rain rate in millimeters per hour. The following example will illustrate the use of this formula.

Example 6.10 Radar return from rain A radar system has the following parameters:

> Transmitted power $P_t = 100 \text{ kW}$ peak
> Pulse length $\tau = 1 \mu s$
> Antenna gain $G = 30 \text{ dB}$ or 1000
> Wavelength $\lambda_0 = 3 \text{ cm}$
> Antenna half-power semi-beam width $\theta_{1/2} = 0.063 \text{ rad}$

† Kerr, op. cit., Chap. 6 and Appendix B.

We wish to determine the received power from a rain cell located 10 km away for which the rain rate is 10 mm/h. From Eq. (6.114) we find that $\langle\sigma_{BS}\rangle = 3.3 \times 10^{-6}\,m^2$ per unit volume. The illuminated volume is

$$V = \frac{c\tau}{2}r_0^2\pi\theta_{1/2}^2 = 1.87 \times 10^8\,m^3$$

By using Eq. (6.113) we obtain $P_r = 2.8 \times 10^{-9}\,W$. If the radar were observing a point target with a radar cross section of $5\,m^2$ at this same range the returned signal would be

$$P = \frac{P_t G^2 \lambda_0^2}{(4\pi)^3 r_0^4}\sigma = \frac{\sigma}{V\langle\sigma_{BS}\rangle}P_r = \frac{5}{617}P_r$$

$$= 2.27 \times 10^{-11}\,W$$

The target signal is more than 100 times weaker, since the total rain cross section $V\langle\sigma_{BS}\rangle$ equals $617\,m^2$ because of the large volume illuminated. ∎

Effect of Wave Polarization

The theory developed above for backscatter from rain made no reference to the polarization of the radar signal incident on the rain. At first thought it might be considered that the polarization of the incident field should not be an important factor. However, surprisingly it turns out that the polarization of the incident wave has a strong influence on the received power at the radar, even though it is not important in determining the total backscattered power. The reason for this is that when the drops are spherical or nearly spherical in shape and multiple scattering can be neglected, an incident circularly polarized wave is returned as a circularly polarized wave of the opposite sense and is not received by the radar antenna. A complete polarization mismatch between the antenna and the returned signal will occur. This phenomenon is used in practice to reduce the clutter interference produced by rain. The reflection from rain essentially returns a circularly polarized wave of the opposite sense to that being transmitted because of the rotational symmetry of a raindrop. A target such as an airplane will produce a strong returned signal in both polarizations because the complex shape of the target causes a large amount of oppositely polarized scattered fields to be generated.

The theory presented at the end of Chap. 5 is readily applied to determine the received open-circuit voltage produced by scatter from rain. By looking at the received open-circuit voltage instead of power, both polarization and phase effects can be included. Thus the formulation of the scattering problem presented below is more general than that given earlier.

Let the radar antenna be an aperture-type antenna. When the input current at the antenna terminals is unity let the far-zone radiated field be

$$\mathbf{E}(\mathbf{r}) = \frac{jk_0\cos\theta}{2\pi r}\mathbf{f}(k_x, k_y)\,e^{-jk_0 r} \tag{6.115}$$

where $\mathbf{f}$ is related to the Fourier transform of the aperture field as described in

Sec. 4.1. k_x and k_y are equal to $k_0 \sin \theta \cos \phi$ and $k_0 \sin \theta \sin \phi$, respectively. When the radar is transmitting let the input current be I. The radiated field is then given by Eq. (6.115) after multiplying by I. When multiple scattering effects are neglected the incident field on a drop located at r, θ, ϕ will be $I\mathbf{E(r)}$, where $\mathbf{E}$ is given by Eq. (6.115). In the Rayleigh regime the induced dipole moment in the water drop is given by Eq. (6.95) and is

$$\mathbf{P}_0 = 4\pi a^3 \frac{\kappa - 1}{\kappa + 2} \epsilon_0 I \mathbf{E(r)}$$

The equivalent current element is $j\omega \mathbf{P}_0$. The application of the reciprocity theorem now shows that the contribution to the open-circuit voltage from a single drop is

$$dV_{oc} = -j\omega \mathbf{P}_0 \cdot \mathbf{E(r)}$$
$$= \frac{jk_0^3 Y_0 \cos^2 \theta}{4\pi^2 r^2} I 4\pi a^3 \mathbf{f} \cdot \mathbf{f} \, e^{-2jk_0 r} \qquad (6.116)$$

where we have approximated $(\kappa - 1)/(\kappa + 2)$ by unity. When we express $\mathbf{f}$ in spherical coordinates we have

$$\mathbf{f} = \frac{\mathbf{a}_\theta(f_x \cos \phi + f_y \sin \phi)}{\cos \theta} + \mathbf{a}_\phi(f_y \cos \phi - f_x \sin \phi)\cos \theta$$

$$= f_\theta \mathbf{a}_\theta + f_\phi \mathbf{a}_\phi$$

where f_θ and f_ϕ are defined by this equation. For a circularly polarized antenna

$$f_\theta = e_\theta(\theta) \qquad \text{and} \qquad f_\phi = \pm j e_\theta(\theta)$$

and then

$$\mathbf{f} \cdot \mathbf{f} = f_\theta^2 + f_\phi^2 = e_\theta^2 - e_\theta^2 = 0$$

which shows the complete polarization mismatch between the antenna and the scattered field and leads to zero received voltage.

The approximation of using the incident field as the polarizing field acting on each drop is called the *Born approximation*. To this order of approximation the received open-circuit voltage from a volume of drops is obtained by summing Eq. (6.116) over all drops to get

$$V_{oc} = \frac{jk_0^3 Y_0 I}{\pi} \sum_i (\mathbf{f} \cdot \mathbf{f})_i \frac{\cos^2 \theta_i}{r_i^2} a_i^3 e^{-2jk_0 r_i}$$

The subscript i denotes the value of the corresponding parameter for the ith drop located at r_i, θ_i, ϕ_i at time t. The received power at time t when the antenna is impedance-matched to a load R_L is (V_{oc} is the RMS value of voltage)

$$\frac{V_{oc} V_{oc}^*}{4R_L} = \frac{k_0^6 Y_0^2 |I|^2}{4\pi^2 R_L} \sum_i \sum_j (\mathbf{f} \cdot \mathbf{f})_i (\mathbf{f}^* \cdot \mathbf{f}^*)_j \frac{\cos^2 \theta_i}{r_i^2} \frac{\cos^2 \theta_j}{r_j^2} a_i^3 a_j^3 \, e^{-2jk_0(r_i - r_j)}$$

$$(6.117)$$

The relative phase angle is $\Delta_{ij} = 2k_0(r_i - r_j)$. At a time Δt later than t the positions of all of the drops have changed by small random amounts, since the drops are in motion. Thus all the Δ_{ij} take on new values. The various drop configurations at successive time intervals Δt can be viewed as new realizations of an ensemble of drops. The *average* or *expected* received power is then obtained by averaging over the ensemble. We can consider the Δ_{ij} to be uniformly distributed over the range 0 to 2π with a probability density $1/2\pi$. The ensemble average of $e^{-j\Delta_{ij}}$ is given by

$$\langle e^{-j\Delta_{ij}} \rangle = \int_0^{2\pi} e^{-j\Delta_{ij}} \frac{d\Delta_{ij}}{2\pi} = 0$$

for $i \neq j$. For $i = j$ we have $\Delta_{ij} = 0$, so the ensemble average is 1. We now see that when we average Eq. (6.117) the effect is to reduce the double summation to a single summation; thus

$$P_r = \frac{\langle V_{oc} V_{oc}^* \rangle}{4R_L} = \frac{k_0^6 Y_0^2 |I|^2}{4\pi^2 R_L} \sum_i (\mathbf{f} \cdot \mathbf{f})_i (\mathbf{f}^* \cdot \mathbf{f}^*)_i \frac{\cos^4 \theta_i}{r_i^4} a_i^6 \qquad (6.118)$$

When there are a great many drops per unit volume and the volume is large, the sum can be replaced by suitable integrals. The sum over a unit volume is essentially the sum of the a_i^6, since r_i, θ_i, ϕ_i can be considered as constant over a unit volume element. The sum of a_i^6 over a unit volume can be replaced by the integral

$$\int_0^\infty N(a)a^6 \, da$$

where $N(a) \, da$ is the number of drops per unit volume with radii in the interval a to $a + da$. The remaining sum over the unit volume elements may be replaced by an integral over θ, ϕ, and r. Hence we obtain

$$P_r = \frac{k_0^6 Y_0^2 |I|^2}{4\pi^2 R_L} \int_V \int_0^\infty |\mathbf{f} \cdot \mathbf{f}|^2 \frac{\cos^4 \theta}{r^2} N(a)a^6 \sin \theta \, da \, d\theta \, d\phi \, dr \qquad (6.119)$$

In order to correlate this expression with Eq. (6.111) we note that when the antenna is linearly polarized $|\mathbf{f} \cdot \mathbf{f}|^2 = (\mathbf{f} \cdot \mathbf{f}^*)^2$, as can be verified by direct evaluation. The input power to the antenna when it is transmitting is $P_t = |I|^2 R_L$ so the gain function for the antenna is

$$G(\theta, \phi) = \frac{|I|^2 k_0^2 \cos^2 \theta \mathbf{f} \cdot \mathbf{f}^* Y_0}{4\pi^2 |I|^2 (R_L/4\pi)}$$

When this expression is introduced into Eq. (6.119) that equation becomes identical with Eq. (6.111). However, in general, Eq. (6.119) is valid under conditions for which Eq. (6.111) does not hold because it includes the effect of a polarization mismatch through the factor $\mathbf{f} \cdot \mathbf{f}$.

Bistatic Scattering from Rain

A rain cell will cause scattering to take place in directions other than in the backward direction. The theory for bistatic scattering can be developed using the differential scattering cross section of each drop. The differential scattering cross section is that cross section which, when multiplied by the incident power density, gives the scattered power in a given direction. The theory can also be developed as an extension of that used to describe polarization effects, and this approach is described in this section. Bistatic scattering is of interest in satellite communication systems, since it can cause cochannel interference to occur whereby the signal in one beam gets scattered and is received by a nearby antenna that is serviced by a second beam from the satellite.

Consider a single drop of rain located at r_1, θ_1, ϕ_1 relative to antenna number 1. The incident field from antenna 1 will produce an equivalent polarization current $j\omega\mathbf{P}_0$ in this drop given by

$$j\omega\mathbf{P}_0 = -k_0^2 Y_0 I_1 \frac{\cos\theta_1}{2\pi r_1} 4\pi a^3 \mathbf{f}_1(k_{x1}, k_{y1}) e^{-jk_0 r_1}$$

where the subscript 1 refers to antenna 1. In the above equation we have replaced $(\kappa - 1)/(\kappa + 2)$ by unity, since κ is very large in the microwave region. The received open-circuit voltage at a second antenna, as shown in Fig. 6.51, is given by the interaction of the field of this antenna, when it is radiating with unit input current, with the polarization current produced by antenna 1. There may, of course, also be direct coupling between the two antennas. However, we will assume that the antennas are positioned and oriented such that there is no direct coupling. The received open-circuit voltage produced by scattering from one drop is thus

$$dV_{oc} = -\frac{jk_0 \cos\theta_2}{2\pi r_2} e^{-jk_0 r_2} j\omega \mathbf{f}_2(k_{x2}, k_{y2}) \cdot \mathbf{P}_0$$

$$= jk_0^3 Y_0 I_1 \frac{\cos\theta_1 \cos\theta_2}{\pi r_1 r_2} a^3 \mathbf{f}_1 \cdot \mathbf{f}_2 \, e^{-jk_0(r_1 + r_2)} \tag{6.120}$$

The coordinates r_2, θ_2, ϕ_2 describe the location of the drop relative to antenna 2, as shown in Fig. 6.51.

All of the drops in the *common volume*, which is defined by the volume

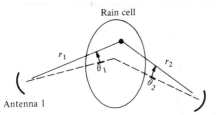

Rain cell

Antenna 1

Antenna 2   **Figure 6.51** Bistatic scattering from rain.

over which the two antenna beams overlap, will contribute to the received open-circuit voltage. The resultant open-circuit voltage is obtained by summing Eq. (6.120) over all drops in the common volume, as was done for the backscattering problem. When the expression for received power is formulated and an ensemble average is carried out, we again find that the average received power is the sum of that contributed by each drop. When the sum is replaced by appropriate integrals the final result is

$$P_r = \frac{k_0^6 Y_0^2 P_t}{4\pi^2 R_L^2} \int_V \int_0^\infty \frac{\cos^2 \theta_1 \cos^2 \theta_2}{r_1^2 r_2^2} |\mathbf{f}_1 \cdot \mathbf{f}_2|^2 a^6 N(a)\, da\, dx\, dy\, dz \qquad (6.121)$$

In this formula the variables x, y, and z describe the common volume, and r_1, r_2, θ_1, etc., must be expressed in terms of x, y, and z. When the rain cell is far away from both antennas, r_1 and r_2 are nearly constant throughout the common volume. Furthermore, for high-gain antennas the maximum values of θ_1 and θ_2 are small, so the cosine factors can be replaced by unity. For this situation Eq. (6.121) can be replaced by the simplified formula

$$P_r = \frac{k_0^6 Y_0^2 P_t}{4\pi^2 R_L^2 r_1^2 r_2^2} \int_V \int_0^\infty |\mathbf{f}_1 \cdot \mathbf{f}_2|^2 a^6 N(a)\, da\, dV \qquad (6.122)$$

where r_1 and r_2 are now the distances to the center of the common volume. In both Eq. (6.121) and Eq. (6.122) $|I_1|^2 R_L$ has been replaced by the total transmitted power P_t from antenna 1.

An important modification of Eqs. (6.121) and (6.122) must be included when the assumption of spherical drops is not valid. For irregular-shaped scatterers such as flattened drops, snowflakes, etc., the dipole moment $\mathbf{P}_0$ is generally not in the same direction as the polarizing electric field. We can express Eq. (6.95) in the form

$$\mathbf{P}_0 = \alpha_e \epsilon_0 E_0 \mathbf{a}_z$$

where $\alpha_e = 4\pi a^3(\kappa - 1)/(\kappa + 2)$ is called the *polarizability of the particle*. For irregular-shaped particles α_e must be replaced by a dyadic $\bar{\boldsymbol{\alpha}}_e$, and we then have

$$\mathbf{P}_0 = \epsilon_0 \bar{\boldsymbol{\alpha}}_e \cdot E_0 \mathbf{a}_z \qquad (6.123)$$

The polarizability will be a function of a size parameter a corresponding to a characteristic dimension of the particle. A formula such as Eq. (6.123) is valid only for small particles to which the Rayleigh scattering theory is applicable. With this generalization the factor $\mathbf{f}_1 \cdot \mathbf{f}_2 a^3$ in Eqs. (6.121) and (6.122) must be replaced by $\mathbf{f}_2 \cdot \bar{\boldsymbol{\alpha}}_e \cdot \mathbf{f}_1$. Nonspherical particles will in general produce cross-polarized scattered fields, and these will cause cochannel interference between communication links operating with orthogonal polarized beams in close proximity.[†]

† W. L. Stutzman and D. L. Runyon, "The Relationship of Rain-Induced Cross-Polarization Discrimination to Attenuation for 10 to 30 GHz Earth-Space Radio Links," *IEEE Trans.*, vol. AP-32, July 1984, pp. 705–710.

Bistatic scattering from rain and other hydrometeors will not be pursued beyond the theory outlined above. However, it is noted that the scattering from tropospheric fluctuations in the index of refraction and on which tropospheric scatter propagation is based is also described by equations similar to (6.121) and (6.122). This was one of the primary reasons for outlining this theory in the present section.

6.9 TROPOSPHERIC SCATTER PROPAGATION

An over-the-horizon tropospheric-scatter communication link is illustrated in Fig. 6.52. The two antenna beams overlap in a common volume located at considerable height above the surface of the earth (3 to 8 km). The scattering comes from the small random irregularities or fluctuations in the index of refraction of the atmosphere. These fluctuations are very weak, but when sufficiently high transmitted power is used a useful signal, in view of the large volume from which scattering occurs, is scattered in the direction of the receiving antenna. Tropospheric-scatter-propagation links operate in the frequency range of 200 MHz up to 10 GHz. Operation at lower frequencies is not attractive because of the cost of building antennas with sufficient gain. At higher frequencies the transmission loss becomes too large. There is considerable fading associated with tropospheric-scatter-propagation links, so some form of diversity is desirable for high reliability links. The typical distance involved in a tropospheric scatter link is a few hundred miles, usually not more than 400. At heights greater than 10 km the troposphere is too rarefied to produce sufficient scattering. If we assume an effective earth radius equal to four-thirds of the actual radius, then the maximum line-of-sight distance to a scattering point 20,000 ft above the earth (6 km) is 200 mi. The maximum horizontal range is 400 mi for this case.

There was considerable interest in tropospheric scatter propagation during the decade 1950–1960. With the development of satellite communication systems there is now less need for tropospheric scatter systems. A considerable amount of research has gone into the development of the theory and also the gathering of operational performance data for tropospheric scatter links. A special issue of the *IRE Proceedings* was devoted to this topic, and the reader is

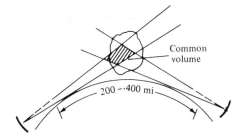

Figure 6.52 A tropospheric-scatter-propagation communication link for over-the-horizon transmission.

referred to this for further information.† The discussion in this text will be limited to that of the basic theory for tropospheric scattering.

The model that we will use to describe tropospheric scatter is that of an atmosphere in which at a fixed time t the dielectric constant κ consists of an average value κ_0 plus a small random component κ_1 that varies in an unknown manner from point to point. At a time Δt of the order of a few milliseconds or less, the variation of κ_1 with position has changed. This new system will be viewed as another realization of an ensemble of atmospheres. The average of a physical variable will be carried out as an ensemble average. In practice one carries out time averages, but if the random process is a stationary one and one assumes that it is also an ergodic process, then ensemble averages are equivalent to time averages. In essence we are neglecting the dynamic evolution of the dielectric constant with time, but since the time interval over which significant changes occur is very long compared with the period of the microwave field, and the time for propagation through the scattering volume, the effects are not significant and can be ignored as far as determining the average scattered power goes.

The index of refraction $n = \kappa^{1/2}$ for the atmosphere is given approximately by

$$(n - 1) \times 10^6 = \frac{a}{T}\left(p + \frac{be}{T}\right) \tag{6.124}$$

where $a = 79$ K/mbar, $b = 4800$ K, $T =$ temperature in kelvin, and $p =$ total pressure in millibars. For dry air at sea level $(n - 1) \times 10^6 \approx 270$ at °C. If we let $n^2 = \kappa_0 + \kappa_1 = (n_0 + n_1)^2 \approx n_0^2 + 2n_0 n_1$, where n_0 is the average value and n_1 is the fluctuating part, it is clear that we can approximate n_0 and κ_0 by unity. The fluctuations in κ_1 are typically only a few parts per million and are due to fluctuations in temperature and pressure.

Under the action of an electric field the polarization produced in a dielectric medium is given by

$$\mathbf{P} = (\epsilon - \epsilon_0)\mathbf{E} = \epsilon_0 \mathbf{E}(\kappa - 1) = \epsilon_0 \mathbf{E}(\kappa_0 - 1 + \kappa_1)$$

The fluctuating part that gives rise to scattering is $\kappa_1 \epsilon_0 \mathbf{E}$. Since κ is very close to unity, the polarizing field can be chosen to be the incident field from the transmitting antenna, which is antenna 1 (Born approximation). The random induced polarization current in the medium is $j\omega \mathbf{P} = j\omega \kappa_1 \epsilon_0 \mathbf{E}_{inc}$ or

$$\mathbf{J}_p = j\omega \mathbf{P} = \frac{-k_0^2 Y_0 I_1}{2\pi r_1} \cos \theta_1 \, e^{-jk_0 r} \mathbf{f}_1 \kappa_1$$

The interaction of the field of the receiving antenna with the polarization

† Special issue on scatter propagation, *Proc. IRE*, vol. 43, Oct. 1955. See also F. Villars and V. F. Weisskopf, "The Scattering of Electromagnetic Waves by Turbulent Atmospheric Fluctuations," *Phys. Rev.*, vol. 94, April 1954, pp. 232–240.

currents in the common volume gives the received open-circuit voltage; thus

$$V_{oc} = \frac{k_0^3 Y_0 I_1}{4\pi^2} \int_V \frac{\cos\theta_1}{r_1} \frac{\cos\theta_2}{r_2} \kappa_1(\mathbf{r}_1)\mathbf{f}_1 \cdot \mathbf{f}_2 \, e^{-jk_0(r_1+r_2)} \, dV \qquad (6.125)$$

The subscripts 1 and 2 refer to antennas 1 and 2, respectively. In this equation $\mathbf{f}_1$ is a function of $k_x = k_0 \sin\theta_1 \cos\phi_1$ and $k_y = k_0 \sin\theta_1 \sin\phi_1$, while $\mathbf{f}_2$ is a function of $k_x = k_0 \sin\theta_2 \cos\phi_2$ and $k_y = k_0 \sin\theta_2 \sin\phi_2$. We can regard r_2, θ_2, ϕ_2 as functions of $\mathbf{r}_1$, where $\mathbf{r}_1$ is the vector distance from antenna 1 to the volume element being considered, as shown in Fig. 6.53. For high-gain antennas, the maximum values of θ_1 and θ_2 are small enough that $\cos\theta_1$ and $\cos\theta_2$ can be replaced by unity with only a small error. Also, in practice, $\mathbf{r}_1$ and $\mathbf{r}_2$ do not change very much throughout the common volume, so these factors in the denominator can be replaced by the distances R_1 and R_2 to the center of the common volume from the two respective antenna sites. If, for simplicity, we assume that the antenna patterns have rotational symmetry, then $\mathbf{f}_1$ is a function of θ_1 alone, while $\mathbf{f}_2$ is a function of θ_2 only. With these simplifications Eq. (6.125) becomes

$$V_{oc} = \frac{k_0^3 Y_0 I_1}{4\pi^2 R_1 R_2} \int_V \kappa_1(\mathbf{r}_1)\mathbf{f}_1(\theta_1) \cdot \mathbf{f}_2(\theta_2) \, e^{-jk_0(r_1+r_2)} \, dV \qquad (6.126)$$

The average received power is given by the ensemble average of $V_{oc}V_{oc}^*/4R_L$ and is

$$P_r = \frac{\langle V_{ov}V_{oc}^*\rangle}{4R_L}$$

$$= \frac{k_0^6 Y_0^2 |I_1|^2}{64\pi^4 R_1^2 R_2^2 R_L} \int_V \int_V \langle \kappa_1(\mathbf{r}_1)\kappa_1(\mathbf{r}_1')\rangle$$

$$\times [\mathbf{f}_1(\theta_1) \cdot \mathbf{f}_2(\theta_2)][\mathbf{f}_1(\theta_1') \cdot \mathbf{f}_2(\theta_2')]^* \, e^{-jk_0(r_1+r_2-r_1'-r_2')} \, dV \, dV' \qquad (6.127)$$

In order to proceed further in the evaluation of this expression a number of additional simplifying assumptions will be made that do not seriously affect the accuracy of the final result. The first assumption we will make is that $\kappa_1(\mathbf{r}_1)$ is a

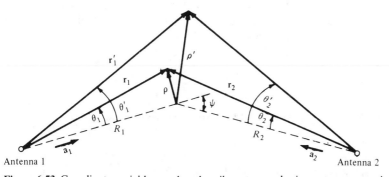

Figure 6.53 Coordinate variables used to describe a tropospheric-scatter-propagation system.

homogeneous random process for which the correlation function $\langle \kappa_1(\mathbf{r}_1) \kappa_1(\mathbf{r}_1') \rangle$ will then be a function of $\mathbf{r}_1 - \mathbf{r}_1'$, which we denote by $C(\mathbf{r}_1 - \mathbf{r}_1')$. Associated with the correlation function is a three-dimensional Fourier transform that gives the spatial spectrum $S(\boldsymbol{\beta})$; that is,

$$S(\boldsymbol{\beta}) = \int\int\int_{-\infty}^{\infty} C(\mathbf{r}_1 - \mathbf{r}_1') \, e^{j\boldsymbol{\beta} \cdot (\mathbf{r}_1 - \mathbf{r}_1')} d(\mathbf{r}_1 - \mathbf{r}_1') \tag{6.128}$$

The correlation function becomes small when $|\mathbf{r}_1 - \mathbf{r}_1'|$ is greater than 50 to 100 m in the troposphere, since the dielectric constant fluctuations become uncorrelated at distances of this order of magnitude; that is, $\kappa_1(\mathbf{r}_1)$ is unrelated to $\kappa_1(\mathbf{r}_1')$ when $\mathbf{r}_1$ and $\mathbf{r}_1'$ refer to points more than 50 to 100 m apart.

With reference to Fig. 6.53 we have

$$\mathbf{r}_1 = \mathbf{R}_1 + \boldsymbol{\rho}$$

so

$$r_1 = (R_1^2 + \rho^2 + 2\boldsymbol{\rho} \cdot \mathbf{R}_1)^{1/2}$$

$$\approx R_1 + \boldsymbol{\rho} \cdot \mathbf{a}_1$$

where $\mathbf{a}_1$ is a unit vector along $\mathbf{R}_1$. Similarly we have

$$r_1' \approx R_1 + \boldsymbol{\rho}' \cdot \mathbf{a}_1$$

$$r_2 \approx R_2 + \boldsymbol{\rho} \cdot \mathbf{a}_2$$

$$r_2' \approx R_2 + \boldsymbol{\rho}' \cdot \mathbf{a}_2$$

and

$$\mathbf{r}_1 - \mathbf{r}_1' = \boldsymbol{\rho} - \boldsymbol{\rho}'$$

$$r_1 + r_2 - r_1' - r_2' = (\boldsymbol{\rho} - \boldsymbol{\rho}') \cdot (\mathbf{a}_1 + \mathbf{a}_2)$$

When we introduce these variables, Eq. (6.127) becomes

$$P_r = \frac{k_0^6 Y_0^2 |I_1|^2}{64\pi^4 R_1^2 R_2^2 R_L} \int_V \int_V C(\boldsymbol{\rho} - \boldsymbol{\rho}')[\mathbf{f}_1(\theta_1) \cdot \mathbf{f}_2(\theta_2)]$$
$$\times [\mathbf{f}_1(\theta_1') \cdot \mathbf{f}_2(\theta_2')]^* \, e^{-jk_0(\boldsymbol{\rho} - \boldsymbol{\rho}') \cdot (\mathbf{a}_1 + \mathbf{a}_2)} \, d\boldsymbol{\rho} \, d\boldsymbol{\rho}'$$

The antenna patterns are almost constant over the small regions for which the correlation function has significant values. We can therefore replace θ_1 and θ_1' by the average "center-of-mass" coordinate $\theta_{1c} = (\theta_1 + \theta_1')/2$ and similarly for θ_2 and θ_2'. It is convenient to change to the center-of-mass and difference coordinate systems defined by

$$\boldsymbol{\rho}_c = \tfrac{1}{2}(\boldsymbol{\rho} + \boldsymbol{\rho}') \qquad \boldsymbol{\rho}_d = \boldsymbol{\rho} - \boldsymbol{\rho}'$$

This change of variables allows P_r to be expressed as

$$P_r = \frac{k_0^6 Y_0^2 |I_1|^2}{64\pi^4 R_1^2 R_2^2 R_L} \int_{V_c} |\mathbf{f}_1(\theta_{1c}) \cdot \mathbf{f}_2(\theta_{2c})|^2 \, d\boldsymbol{\rho}_c \int_{V_d} C(\boldsymbol{\rho}_d) \, e^{-jk_0 \boldsymbol{\rho}_d \cdot (\mathbf{a}_1 + \mathbf{a}_2)} \, d\boldsymbol{\rho}_d \tag{6.129}$$

where V_c and V_d are the new volumes that become defined by the change in the variables of integration. Since $C(\boldsymbol{\rho}_d)$ becomes very small for large values of $\boldsymbol{\rho}_d$ and V_d is a large volume, only a small error is made in extending the integral over $\boldsymbol{\rho}_d$ to an infinite three-dimensional space. We can then use Eq. (6.128) to evaluate this integral and thus obtain $S(-k_0\mathbf{a}_1 - k_0\mathbf{a}_2)$ for its value. Now $k_0\mathbf{a}_1$ is the propagation vector $\mathbf{k}_i$ for the incident field and $-k_0\mathbf{a}_2$ is the propagation vector $\mathbf{k}_s$ for the scattered field, so we have $S(\mathbf{k}_s - \mathbf{k}_i)$ for the value of the integral over $\boldsymbol{\rho}_d$.

The above result has the following physical interpretation. The spatial spectrum $S(\boldsymbol{\beta})$ describes the dielectric constant fluctuations as a spectrum of plane waves for which one plane-wave component is shown in Fig. 6.54. A plane wave with propagation vector $\mathbf{k}_i$ incident on this periodic gratinglike structure is scattered in that direction for which the Bragg scattering relation holds, that is, in that direction for which the scattering from the periodic array of peaks in the fluctuations add up in phase. Consider a dielectric medium with $\kappa = A\,e^{-j\boldsymbol{\beta}\cdot\mathbf{r}}$. An incident wave $\mathbf{E}_0\,e^{-j\mathbf{k}_i\cdot\mathbf{r}}$ will produce a polarization current $j\omega\epsilon_0(\kappa - 1)A\mathbf{E}_0\,e^{-j(\boldsymbol{\beta}+\mathbf{k}_i)\cdot\mathbf{r}}$ which will radiate a field with a propagation factor $e^{-j\mathbf{k}_s\cdot\mathbf{r}}$ that matches that of the polarization current. Hence $\boldsymbol{\beta} + \mathbf{k}_i = \mathbf{k}_s$, which is the *Bragg condition*.

The integral over the center-of-mass coordinate $\boldsymbol{\rho}_c$ in Eq. (6.129) is much more difficult to evaluate. The volume V_c is approximately that defined by the half-power beam widths of the antennas. At this point we will assume that the antennas are linearly polarized in the plane of R_1 and R_2, so that $\mathbf{f}_1 \cdot \mathbf{f}_2 = f_1 f_2 \cos \psi$, where ψ is the angle shown in Fig. 6.53. We will also assume that $\mathbf{f}_1$ and $\mathbf{f}_2$ are constant over the volume V_c defined by the half-power beam widths. We now find that

$$P_r = \frac{k_0^6 Y_0^2 |I_1|^2}{64\pi^4 R_1^2 R_2^2 R_L} |\mathbf{f}_1(0)|^2 |\mathbf{f}_2(0)|^2 S(\mathbf{k}_s - \mathbf{k}_i) V_c \cos^2 \psi$$

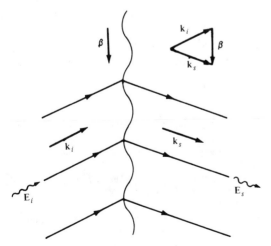

Figure 6.54 Illustration of the Bragg scattering condition.

If we also introduce the antenna gains

$$G_1 = \frac{k_0^2|\mathbf{f}_1(0)|^2 Y_0}{\pi R_L} \qquad G_2 = \frac{k_0^2|\mathbf{f}_2(0)|^2 Y_0}{\pi R_L}$$

and the transmitted power $P_t = |I_1|^2 R_L$, we obtain

$$P_r = \frac{P_t k_0^2 S(\mathbf{k}_s - \mathbf{k}_i)}{4\pi^2 d^4} G_1 G_2 V_c \cos^2 \psi \tag{6.130}$$

where we have also put $R_1 = R_2 = d/2$. Tatarski† gives the following expressions for S and the estimate of the common volume V_c (the antennas are assumed to be pointed along the horizontal direction):

$$S(\beta) = (32\pi^3)(3.3 \times 10^{-2} C_n^2)\beta^{-11/3} \text{ m}^3 \tag{6.131}$$

$$V_c = \frac{d^3 \theta_{1/2}^3}{\psi} \tag{6.132}$$

where $2\theta_{1/2}$ is the half-power antenna beam width, $\psi = d/a_e$, and a_e is the effective radius of the earth (5280 mi). The constant C_n is called the *structure constant* for the index-of-refraction fluctuations. The structure constant depends on temperature fluctuations and height above the earth. At a height of 1.5 km, C_n ranges from 5×10^{-7} to 2×10^{-8} m$^{-1/3}$.

The magnitude of $\mathbf{k}_s - \mathbf{k}_i$ is readily shown to be $2k_0 \sin \psi/2$. The final expression for the average received power becomes

$$P_r = 1.8 \times 10^{32} P_t k_0^{-5/3} G_1 G_2 C_n^2 \frac{\cos^2 \psi}{d^{17/3}} \theta_{1/2}^3 \tag{6.133}$$

when we replace $2 \sin \psi/2$ by ψ and put $\psi = d/a_e$. In Eq. (6.133) C_n is expressed as units of $m^{-1/3}$ and d and λ_0 are in meters. The range dependence comes from the behavior of the spatial spectrum $S(\mathbf{k}_s - \mathbf{k}_i)$. It should also be noted that at longer distances the scattering volume is at a greater height above the earth's surface, and C_n^2 will be smaller, which further decreases the received power with an increase in the distance d.

Fried and Cloud, based on data obtained by Hufnagel, give the following expression for C_n^2 as a function of the height h above the earth's surface‡

$$C_n^2 = 4.2 \times 10^{-14} h^{-1/3} e^{-h/h_0} \text{ m}^{-2/3} \tag{6.134}$$

---

† V. I. Tatarski, *Wave Propagation in a Turbulent Medium*, McGraw-Hill Book Company, New York, 1961, Chap. 4. Equation (6.131) differs from that given by Tatarski by a factor of $32\pi^3$. A factor of $8\pi^3$ comes from the definition of the Fourier transform that is used, and an additional factor of 4 comes from the fact that S is the spectrum of κ_1, and not that of n_1.

The formula for received power is sometimes called the *Booker-Gordon formula* after the authors who first examined tropospheric scatter. See H. G. Booker and W. E. Gordon, "Radio Scattering in the Troposphere," *Proc. IRE*, vol. 38, April 1950, pp. 401–412.

‡ D. L. Fried and J. D. Cloud, "Propagation of an Infinite Plane Wave in a Randomly Inhomogeneous Medium," *J. Opt. Soc. America*, vol. 56, Dec. 1966, p. 1667.

where $h_0 = 3200$ m. The range d is given by $d = 2\sqrt{2a_e h}$, so we can express C_n^2 in the form

$$C_n^2 = \frac{1.68 \times 10^{-13}}{d^{2/3} a_e^{-1/3}} e^{-d^2/8a_e h_0} \tag{6.135}$$

Consequently the rate of decrease of the average received power is expected to be greater than $d^{-6.3}$. At a height of 3.2 km, Eq. (6.134) gives $C_n = 3.2 \times 10^{-8}$ m$^{-1/3}$, while at a height of 6.4 km, $C_n = 1.73 \times 10^{-8}$ m$^{-1/3}$.

The result given in Eq. (6.133) for received power should only be regarded as an estimate. It is based on a particular form for the spatial spectrum S and a generally unknown and not easily determined structure constant C_n. However, the equation does focus on those parameters that govern the general behavior of tropospheric scatter. The example that follows will illustrate typical parameter values that are involved.

Example 6.11 Tropospheric-scatter-propagation link An over-the-horizon link with the following parameters is to be evaluated:

$$P_t = 10^3 \text{ W}$$

$$G_1 = G_2 = 10^5 \text{ (50 dB)}$$

$$d = 400 \text{ km}$$

$$\lambda_0 = 10 \text{ cm}$$

$$C_n = 10^{-8} \text{ m}^{-1/3}$$

If we assume that the antenna aperture efficiency is 0.5, we have $\pi D^2/8 = G_1 \lambda_0^2/4\pi$, so $D/\lambda_0 = \sqrt{20} \times 10^2/\pi$ and the required antenna diameter D equals 14.2 m (46.7 ft). We can estimate the half-power beam width from the relation $4\pi/\pi\theta_{1/2}^2 = 4/\theta_{1/2}^2 = G_1$, which gives $\theta_{1/2} = 6.3 \times 10^{-3}$. Since d is small relative to a_e, the angle ψ is small and $\cos \psi \approx 1$. From Eq. (6.133) we find that the received power is 8.15×10^{-13} W. We will compare this signal with that which would have been received under free-space propagation conditions. The latter is given by

$$\frac{P_t G_1 G_2}{(4\pi)^2 d^2} \lambda_0^2 = 6.33 \times 10^{-2} \text{ W}$$

The tropospheric scatter link has 109 dB more loss.

In order to compare the received signal with the receiver noise we will assume a bandwidth of 1 MHz and a system noise temperature of 600 K. The noise power is then

$$P_n = 1.38 \times 10^{-23} \times 10^6 \times 600 = 8.28 \times 10^{-15} \text{ W}$$

which gives a signal-to-noise ratio of 20 dB. The signal power needs to be increased by about 10 dB in order to be adequate to overcome the fading that will normally occur. If the range is reduced to 300 km, a gain of $(4/3)^{17/3}$, or 7 dB is achieved. If the antenna diameters are doubled, an additional gain of only 3 dB is obtained. (Why?) With a smaller range the common volume is lower, so C_n^2 could be expected to be 10 dB larger. All of these additional gains add up to 20 dB. Further improvement would require an increase in transmitted power and/or a reduction in bandwidth. However, an average signal-to-noise ratio of 40 dB should be more than adequate. ∎

Experimental Results

In order to compare the results predicted by the theoretical formula with results obtained in practice, we will summarize the results of one experiment that was carried out over a period of more than 1 yr.† The path loss that is in addition to the normal free-space transmission loss is obtained by dividing Eq. (6.133) by

$$\frac{P_t G_1 G_2 \lambda_0^2}{(4\pi)^2 d^2}$$

to obtain

$$L = \frac{7.2 \times 10^{32} k_0^{1/3} \theta_{1/2}^3 C_n^2}{d^{11/3}} \tag{6.136}$$

In the experiment 28-ft-diameter parabolic antennas were used with a gain of 31 dB at 505 MHz and 46 dB at 4090 MHz. The other parameters describing the systems used are summarized below.

Frequency, MHz	505	4090	505
Range d, km	300	300	512
P_t, W	500	10	500
$G_1 = G_2$, dB	31	46	31
Free-space loss, dB	135	153	140
Transmission-line loss, dB	1	2	2
Measured L, dB	Mar., 77	Dec., 90	June, 68
	Oct., 57	Nov., 84	Oct., 75
	June, 58	June, 77	

A comparison of the measured loss and computed loss using Eq. (6.136) and two values of C_n is tabulated below on the next page.

† K. Bullington, W. J. Inkster, and A. L. Durkee, "Results of Propagation Tests at 505 MHz and 4090 MHz on Beyond the Horizon Paths," *Proc. IRE*, vol. 43, Oct. 1955, pp. 1306–1316.

System, MHz	Measured L, dB	Computed L, dB	
		$C_n = 10^{-8}\,\mathrm{m}^{-1/3}$	$C_n = 5 \times 10^{-8}\,\mathrm{m}^{-1/3}$
505	58–77	70	56
4090	77–90	94.3	80.3
505	68–75	78.4	64.4
($d = 512$ km)			

This example clearly shows that the theory is generally in agreement with experimental results. However, the lack of knowledge of the structure constant C_n makes the theoretical predictions subject to at least a ± 10-dB uncertainty.

On the basis of experimental evidence Bullington et al. predict a decrease in received power by 18 dB for each doubling of the distance d in the range 50 to 300 mi. This corresponds to a range dependence of d^{-6}, whereas the theory presented above gives a dependence on d^{-1} with an exponent greater than 6.3. Part of the discrepancy is associated with the assumed dependence of S on the wave number β, which is not necessarily valid for very small values of β. If the modified von Karman spectrum

$$S(\beta) = \frac{32\pi^3 \times 3.3 \times 10^{-2} C_n^2\, e^{-(\beta l_i/2\pi)^2}}{[\beta^2 + (2\pi/l_0)^2]^{11/6}} \tag{6.137}$$

is used instead where l_0 and l_i are the outer and inner scales of turbulence, then the increase in S for small values of β is not nearly as rapid. This reduces the inverse dependence of the received power on d. However, in the troposphere l_0 is of order 100 m, so in most cases the effect of using the von Karman spectrum is very small. Whenever $\beta \gg 2\pi/l_0$ the von Karman spectrum becomes equal to that given by Eq. (6.131), provided also that βl_i is small. The inner scale of turbulence l_i is of order a few millimeters.

6.10 EXTREMELY LOW TO VERY LOW FREQUENCY PROPAGATION

The extremely low frequency band (ELF) is the band of frequencies from 30 to 300 Hz, with a corresponding wavelength of 10,000 km (6210 mi) at the low-frequency end and 1000 km (621 mi) at the upper-frequency end. Band 3 covers frequencies from 300 Hz to 3 kHz, while band 4, the very low frequency band, ranges from 3 to 30 kHz. The wavelength at the upper edge of the VLF band is 10 km. At frequencies in the above bands, the collision frequency ν in the ionospheric D layer is much greater than ω, and this makes the ionosphere behave like a conducting medium. The earth also behaves like a conducting medium. Although the conductivities are many orders of magnitude less than those of metals, they are sufficiently large to make the earth and the ionosphere act like reflecting boundaries, and thus provide a waveguide consisting of two spherical shells that guide the waves from the transmitting antenna to the receiving antenna. The confinement of the field between these two spherical shells results in considerably less attenuation due to wave spreading than occurs in free space. There is, of course, attenuation due to the poor conductivity of the earth and the ionosphere, but this attenuation is small enough that propagation in the earth-ionosphere waveguide over great distances is possible. At frequencies below 50 Hz the attenuation is less than 1 dB/1000 km, while at 20 kHz it is of order 5 to 15 dB/1000 km.

The earth-ionosphere waveguide provides a very stable propagation path, thus making low-frequency waves ideal for the transmission of time signals and for navigational purposes. For example, the Omega navigational system operates in the 10 to 13 kHz band. The two major disadvantages are the inefficiency of the antennas because of their limited size in terms of wavelength and the narrow bandwidth, and hence low data rate.

The D layer in the ionosphere is the layer closest to the earth. The height of the D layer is around 65 to 70 km at midday, rising to 85 to 90 km at midnight. The peak electron concentration is in the range 5×10^8 to 2×10^{10} electrons per cubic meter at midday, while that at nighttime is up to an order of magnitude less. A model layer at a height of 80 km and a density of 6×10^8 electrons per cubic meter has been proposed for propagation studies.†

The dielectric constant of the ionosphere is given by Eq. (6.68) and is

$$\kappa = 1 - \frac{\omega_p^2}{\omega(\omega - j\nu)}$$

When ω is much smaller than the collision frequency ν, we find that

$$\kappa = 1 - j\frac{\omega_p^2}{\omega\nu}$$

When this expression is used in Maxwell's equation

$$\nabla \times \mathbf{H} = j\omega\epsilon_0\kappa\mathbf{E}$$

we obtain

$$\nabla \times \mathbf{H} = j\omega\epsilon_0\mathbf{E} + \frac{\omega_p^2}{\nu}\epsilon_0\mathbf{E}$$

which shows that the conductivity σ of the ionosphere is given by

$$\sigma = \frac{\omega_p^2}{\nu}\epsilon_0 \tag{6.138}$$

Typical values for ω_p^2/ν in the D region range from 10^5 to 10^6, which gives a

† A. H. Waynick, "The Present State of Knowledge Concerning the Lower Ionosphere," *Proc. IRE*, vol. 45, June 1957, pp. 741–749.

conductivity in the range 10^{-5} to 10^{-6} S/m. The conductivity of the earth is larger, being of order 10^{-3} to 10^{-2} S/m.

In the ELF band, the free-space wavelength is so long that only the quasi-TEM mode of propagation is possible, since all higher-order modes are cut off. In the VLF band the guide height h, being around 80 km, is several wavelengths in height and thus allows many propagating modes to exist.

The most satisfactory theory for low-frequency propagation is the mode theory. The pioneering work in this field was done by Wait and also Budden.† The theory does take into account the feature that the waveguide consists of two spherical shells, as in Fig. 6.55a. However, for simplicity we will approximate the guide as a parallel-plate waveguide, as shown in Fig. 6.55b.

With reference to Fig 6.55b we will consider transverse magnetic waves (TM waves) propagating in the z direction and having only E_x, E_z, and H_y field components. For these waves E_x and E_z may be expressed in terms of H_y as follows:

$$\nabla \times \mathbf{H} = -\mathbf{a}_y \times \nabla H_y = j\omega\epsilon\mathbf{E} + \sigma\mathbf{E}$$

or in component form

$$(j\omega\epsilon + \sigma)E_x = -\frac{\partial H_y}{\partial z} \tag{6.139a}$$

$$(j\omega\epsilon + \sigma)E_z = \frac{\partial H_y}{\partial x} \tag{6.139b}$$

When we assume that the fields have a z dependence of the form $e^{-\gamma_z z}$, then we

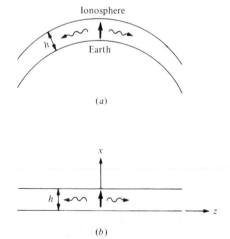

Ionosphere

h

Earth

(a)

x

h

z

(b)

Figure 6.55 (a) The spherical earth-ionosphere waveguide. (b) An approximate parallel-plate waveguide model.

† See the special VLF propagation issue, *Proc. IRE*, June 1957; and also
M. L. Burrows, *ELF Communications Antennas*, Peter Peregrinus, Ltd., London, 1978.

find that

$$\frac{E_x}{H_y} = \frac{\gamma_z}{j\omega\epsilon + \sigma} = Z_w \tag{6.140}$$

which is the mode impedance in the direction of propagation. In the guide σ is zero and $\epsilon = \epsilon_0$. Since H_y is a solution of Helmholtz' equation

$$\frac{\partial^2 H_y}{\partial z^2} + \frac{\partial^2 H_y}{\partial x^2} + k_i^2 H_y = 0 \tag{6.141}$$

where $k_i^2 = -(j\omega\epsilon_i + \sigma_i)(j\omega\mu_0) = \kappa_i k_0^2 - j\omega\mu_0\sigma_i$ with $k_0^2 = \omega^2\mu_0\epsilon_0$ and $\kappa_i = \epsilon_i/\epsilon_0$, we see that the x dependence is according to $e^{\pm\gamma_x x}$ and

$$\gamma_x^2 + \gamma_z^2 + k_i^2 = 0 \tag{6.142}$$

Let σ_1 be the conductivity of the earth and σ_2 be that of the ionosphere. The corresponding values of k_i will be denoted as k_1 and k_2. In the three regions $x < 0$, $0 < x < h$, and $x > h$ shown in Fig. 6.55b, γ_z has the same value. From Eq. (6.142) we obtain

$$\gamma_x^2 = \begin{cases} -k_1^2 - \gamma_z^2 = \gamma_1^2 & x < 0 \\ -k_0^2 - \gamma_z^2 = \gamma^2 & 0 < x < h \\ -k_2^2 - \gamma_z^2 = \gamma_2^2 & x > h \end{cases} \tag{6.143}$$

In the ionosphere $\epsilon = \epsilon_0$, while on the earth $\epsilon = \kappa\epsilon_0$. Suitable solutions for H_y in the three regions are

$$H_y = \begin{cases} A\, e^{\gamma_1 x - \gamma_z z} & x < 0 \\ B\, e^{-\gamma_1 x - \gamma_z z} + C\, e^{\gamma_1 x - \gamma_z z} & 0 < x < h \\ D\, e^{-\gamma_2 x - \gamma_z z} & x > h \end{cases} \tag{6.144}$$

where A, B, C, and D are amplitude constants.

For propagation in the x direction the mode transverse impedance is

$$-\frac{E_z}{H_y} = \frac{\gamma_x}{j\omega\epsilon + \sigma} \tag{6.145}$$

We will denote the mode transverse impedances by Z_1, Z, and Z_2 respectively, in the three regions according to the use of γ_1, γ, and γ_2 for γ_x and the appropriate values of ϵ and σ. In the transverse direction the waveguide may be modeled as a transmission line of length h, propagation constant γ, and characteristic impedance Z. The transmission line is terminated in impedances Z_1 and Z_2 at the two ends, as shown in Fig. 6.56. The propagation constant γ_z may be found by setting the determinant of the system of equations obtained for A, B, C, and D by requiring that H_y and E_z be continuous across the two boundaries at $x = 0$, h. The eigenvalue equation for γ_z can also be found from the transmission-line model by requiring that the impedance at $x = 0$ looking

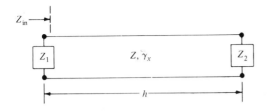

Figure 6.56 The equivalent transmission-line model of the parallel-plate waveguide transverse section.

towards Z_2 be equal to $-Z_1$. By using transmission-line theory we find that

$$Z_1 + Z_{\text{in}} = Z_1 + Z \frac{Z_2 + Z \tanh \gamma h}{Z + Z_2 \tanh \gamma h} = 0 \qquad (6.146)$$

The normalized values of the mode impedances are

$$\bar{Z}_1 = \frac{Z_1}{Z} = \frac{\epsilon_0 \gamma_1}{\epsilon \gamma} \frac{1}{1 - (j\sigma_1/\omega\epsilon)} \qquad (6.147)$$

$$\bar{Z}_2 = \frac{Z_2}{Z} = \frac{\gamma_2}{\gamma} \frac{1}{1 - (j\sigma_2/\omega\epsilon_0)}$$

We can solve Eq. (6.146) for $\tanh \gamma h$ to obtain

$$\tanh \gamma h = - \frac{\bar{Z}_1 + \bar{Z}_2}{1 + \bar{Z}_1 \bar{Z}_2} \qquad (6.148)$$

By using Eq. (6.143) we find that

$$\gamma_i^2 = \gamma^2 + jk_0^2 \frac{\sigma_i}{k_0 Y_0} - (\kappa - 1)k_0^2 \qquad i = 1, 2 \qquad (6.149)$$

where $\kappa = 1$ for $i = 2$. In the ELF band $\omega\epsilon_0$ is very small (of order 10^{-8}) compared with σ_1 and σ_2, so $\bar{Z}_1$ and $\bar{Z}_2$ are then small. For this case γh is also small and $\tanh \gamma h$ can be replaced by γh. If we use this approximation and neglect $\bar{Z}_1 \bar{Z}_2$ relative to unity, Eq. (6.148) reduces to

$$\gamma h = -(\bar{Z}_1 + \bar{Z}_2) \approx -j \frac{k_0 Y_0}{\gamma} \left(\frac{\gamma_1}{\sigma_1} + \frac{\gamma_2}{\sigma_2} \right)$$

$$\approx \frac{k_0}{\gamma} \left(\sqrt{\frac{-jk_0 Y_0}{\sigma_1}} + \sqrt{\frac{-jk_0 Y_0}{\sigma_2}} \right)$$

which gives

$$-\gamma^2 = k_0^2 + \gamma_z^2 = -\frac{k_0}{h} \left(\sqrt{\frac{-jk_0 Y_0}{\sigma_1}} + \sqrt{\frac{-jk_0 Y_0}{\sigma_2}} \right) = -q$$

In obtaining this result we have used $\gamma_i^2 \approx jk_0^2 \sigma_i / k_0 Y_0$. The above equation shows that $\gamma_z \approx jk_0$, since the term on the right-hand side is small. We can solve for γ_z to obtain

$$\gamma_z = (-k_0^2 - q)^{1/2} = jk_0\left(1 + \frac{q}{k_0^2}\right)^{1/2} \approx jk_0 + \frac{jq}{2k_0}$$

$$= jk_0 + \frac{1+j}{2h}\left(\sqrt{\frac{k_0 Y_0}{2\sigma_1}} + \sqrt{\frac{k_0 Y_0}{2\sigma_2}}\right) = j\beta + \alpha \tag{6.150}$$

As an example, consider the case when $f = 300$ Hz, $h = 80$ km, $\lambda_0 = 3 \times 10^6$ m, $\sigma_1 = 10^{-3}$ S/m, and $\sigma_2 = 10^{-6}$ S/m, for which Eq. (6.150) gives

$$\gamma_z = j2.09 \times 10^{-6} + (1+j)3.4 \times 10^{-7}$$

$$= j2.43 \times 10^{-6} + 3.4 \times 10^{-7}$$

The first-order correction to k_0 is about 17 percent, so the approximations are reasonably well justified. The calculated attenuation is 2.9 dB/1000 km. If we assumed that the conductivities were a factor of 10 larger, the correction to k_0 would be around 8 percent, and the attenuation would be only 0.9 dB/1000 km.

In the ELF band where the approximations made are valid, the field is very nearly a TEM wave with $H_y = B e^{-\gamma_z z}$, since the constant C turns out to be very small. The expression obtained for α has the same value as could be found using the standard waveguide power-balance approach to finding α (see Prob. 6.31).

If the TEM mode is excited by a vertical dipole in the earth-ionosphere waveguide, it will be a cylindrical TEM wave of the form

$$E_x = -\frac{k_0 Z_0}{4h} I \Delta l H_0^2[(\beta - j\alpha)\rho] \qquad \rho \gg h \tag{6.151}$$

where $I \Delta l$ is the strength of the vertical current element, $H_0^2[(\beta - j\alpha)\rho]$ is the Hankel function of the second kind, and ρ is the radial coordinate. In the spherical waveguide the main effect of the spherical-shell configuration is to change the spreading characteristics of the wave. Thus in place of Eq. (6.151) the field is more nearly like that described by the following equation:

$$E_r = -\frac{k_0 Z_0}{4h} I \Delta l \left(\frac{\rho_e}{a \sin \theta}\right)^{1/2} H_0^2[(\beta - j\alpha)\rho_e] \tag{6.152}$$

where a is the radius of the earth, E_r is the radial component of the field, the current element is located along the polar axis, and θ is the polar angle relative to the current element. In this equation ρ_e is the distance $(a + h/2)\theta$ measured along a great circle at the center of the guide, as shown in Fig. 6.57. The circumference of the wave front is $2\pi a \sin \theta$, and since the Hankel function behaves like $\rho_e^{-1/2}$ for large ρ_e, the correction in Eq. (6.152) amounts to replacing the circumference $2\pi\rho_e$ by $2\pi a \sin \theta$.

The expressions for the radiated field given by Eq. (6.151) or (6.152) show that in practice the coupling between a vertical antenna of practical length to the TEM mode in the spherical earth-ionosphere waveguide is very small, since

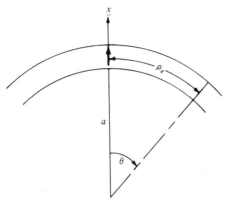

Figure 6.57 Illustration of the great-circle distance ρ_e in the spherical earth-ionosphere waveguide.

it is proportional to $\Delta l/h$. For an antenna 100 m long, this factor is 0.00125, which would give a coupling loss of almost 60 dB. A similar coupling loss would occur at the receiving antenna. The problem of exciting the TEM mode by a vertical antenna is further compounded by the extremely high input capacitive reactance of an antenna that is very short relative to a wavelength.

The TEM mode can also be excited by a horizontal antenna. The coupling to a horizontal current element is much weaker, but this can be offset by the practical realization of a much longer antenna, which also could be buried beneath the surface of the earth. The value of H_y at the surface of the earth can be used to estimate the horizontal component of the electric field, since $E_z = Z_1 H_y = E_x(Z_1/Z_w)$. The coupling to a horizontal antenna is reduced by the factor Z_1/Z_w, which is approximately equal to $(\omega \epsilon_0/\sigma_1)^{1/2}$, which numerically is a factor of around 10^{-3}. Thus a horizontal antenna needs to be at least a thousand times longer than a vertical antenna. The much longer antenna does provide for a large decrease in the input reactance also, so a significant further improvement in overall efficiency is obtained from this aspect alone.

In the spherical waveguide the field is refocused at a point diametrically opposite to that at which it was generated. At certain specific frequencies a condition of resonance will occur for which the total phase change for propagation around the earth once along a great-circle path equals $2\pi k_0 a = n(1 + n^{-1})^{1/2} 2\pi \approx 2n\pi + \pi$ for large n. These resonances are called *Schumann resonances* and have been observed experimentally.[†] The first three measured resonances occurred at 7, 14, and 21 Hz.

Higher-Order Modes

If the conductivities σ_1 and σ_2 were infinite the higher-order modes in the

[†] J. R. Wait, "Earth-Ionosphere Cavity Resonances and the Propagation of ELF Waves," *Radio Sci.*, vol. 69D, 1965, pp. 1057–1070.

J. Galejs, *Terrestrial Propagation of Long Electromagnetic Waves*, Pergamon Press, Oxford, 1972.

parallel-plate waveguide model would have a magnetic field

$$H_y = C_n \cos \frac{n\pi x}{h} e^{-\gamma_{zn} z}$$

for the nth mode where

$$\gamma_{zn} = \left[\left(\frac{n\pi}{h} \right)^2 - k_0^2 \right]^{1/2}$$

These modes are propagating modes for those values of n for which $n < 2h/\lambda_0$. At the upper edge of the VLF band where $\lambda_0 = 10$ km, we see that up to approximately 16 modes could propagate. When the wavelength is such that a given mode is well above cutoff, the wave is composed of obliquely propagating TEM waves that are incident on the air-earth and air-ionosphere boundary at a relatively small grazing angle, as shown in Fig. 6.58. As a consequence, the reflection coefficient magnitude at each boundary is close to 1, and little power penetrates into the ionosphere or the earth. Wait has calculated the attenuation constant for the first few higher-order modes, and some typical results based on that work are illustrated in Fig. 6.59. The results are for modes propagating in the spherical waveguide.† The conductivity of the ground has a relatively small effect, since the ionosphere with its much lower conductivity accounts for the major portion of the loss. At a frequency of 20 kHz the attenuation for the $n = 1$ and $n = 2$ modes is only a few decibels per 1000 km. Thus propagation over distances as large as halfway around the earth would result in an attenuation of order 40 to 80 dB only. In addition there is the attenuation due to the d^{-1} distance dependence as the power is spread out over a larger wave-front surface. In the VLF band the $n = 0$ or TEM mode attenuates quite rapidly because of penetration into the ionosphere.

6.11 PROPAGATION INTO SEAWATER

Communication with submerged submarines by means of radio waves is limited to the VLF band of frequencies or lower because of the large attenuation in

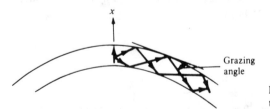

Figure 6.58 Higher-order mode propagation in the earth-ionosphere waveguide.

† J. R. Wait, "The Attenuation vs. Frequency Characteristics of VLF Waves," *Proc. IRE*, vol. 45, June 1957, pp. 768–771.

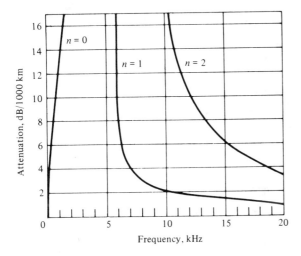

Figure 6.59 Attenuation as a function of frequency for the first three modes in the earth-ionosphere waveguide. $\sigma_1 = 2 \times 10^{-2}$ S/m, $\sigma_2 = 10^{-6}$ S/m, $h = 80$ km.

seawater brought about by the high conductivity. In the low-frequency bands seawater may be characterized as a lossy dielectric medium, with a relative permittivity ϵ/ϵ_0 or dielectric constant κ equal to 80 and an average conductivity σ equal to 4 S/m. It is readily established that the displacement current $j\omega\epsilon\mathbf{E}$ is much smaller than the conduction current $\sigma\mathbf{E}$. At 100 kHz the ratio is around 10^{-4}. The propagation constant k for seawater may thus be approximated as follows:

$$k = [-j\omega\mu_0(j\omega\epsilon + \sigma)]^{1/2} \approx (-j\omega\mu_0\sigma)^{1/2}$$

$$= \frac{1-j}{\delta_s} \tag{6.153}$$

where the skin depth δ_s is given by

$$\delta_s = \left(\frac{2}{\omega\mu_0\sigma}\right)^{1/2} \tag{6.154}$$

The skin depth is equal to 0.8 m at 100 kHz and 2.5 m at 10 kHz. In one skin depth the field will decrease by 8.68 dB, so clearly unless very low frequencies are used, the attenuation will be excessive at depths of 25 to 30 m. The attenuation per meter as a function of frequency is shown in Fig. 6.60.

The factors involved in the design of a receiving system and a transmitting system for a submerged submarine are quite different for the following reasons: Consider an incident signal wave along with the noise field coming from atmospheric noise sources. The noise field corresponds to a noise temperature of order 10^{14} K in the VLF band. If the signal field is 20 dB stronger, then as the noise field and signal field propagate into the seawater both are attenuated at the same rate, but the signal-to-noise ratio remains at 20 dB. If we now assume that the receiver equivalent input noise temperature is 1000 K and a total attenuation of 10^{-11} occurs, then at the receiver the total noise will be

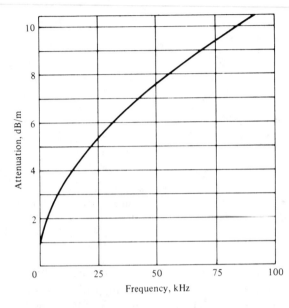

Figure 6.60 Attenuation in seawater; $\sigma = 4$ S/m.

equivalent to 2000 K, and the signal-to-noise ratio is degraded by 3 dB because of the addition of receiver noise. The interesting feature is that 100 dB or more attenuation can be tolerated without any significant degradation of the signal-to-noise ratio at the receiver. The attenuating quality of seawater diminishes the signal strength but at the same time shields the receiver from the high ambient atmospheric noise that exists above the sea.

On the other hand, for an antenna submerged in seawater the transmitted signal up to the air-sea interface would be severely attenuated. An attenuation of 100 dB would have a devastating effect on the power requirements of the transmitter. When it is desirable to transmit a signal, the submarine would normally be required to be located very close to the air-sea interface in order to radiate a useful amount of power into the region above.

The large value of the conductivity σ relative to $\omega\epsilon$ causes an electromagnetic wave incident at a finite angle on the air-sea boundary to be strongly refracted toward the interface normal. Consequently the field will propagate nearly vertically downwards. The propagation between two submerged anten-

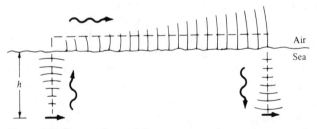

Figure 6.61 Propagation path between two submerged antennas in seawater.

nas is loosely described as up, over, and down, as illustrated schematically in Fig. 6.61.

The smallest rate of attenuation for the surface-wave field over seawater is obtained with vertical polarization, as is the case for propagation over a lossy earth. However, this does not mean that the antennas should be vertically polarized. It turns out that the high refraction of the field at the interface results in stronger coupling to a horizontal antenna submerged in seawater. From another point of view a horizontally polarized wave propagating vertically upwards will couple to a vertical polarized wave because of the boundary conditions that must hold at the air-sea boundary.

Many of the concepts that apply to an antenna radiating into a lossless medium do not apply when the antenna radiates into a lossy medium.[†] For one, the integration of the Poynting vector over a sphere of radius r surrounding the antenna will not give the total radiated power, since some of this power is dissipated within the sphere because of dissipation in the lossy medium. A second effect is that the radiation pattern, which is a plot of the relative field strength as a function of direction on a sphere of constant radius, will depend markedly on the choice of origin for that sphere. This is because of the strong attenuation of the field with distance, as caused by the lossy media. The reader wishing to explore some of the properties of antennas in lossy media is directed to read the tutorial paper by Moore.

In this section we will present a summary of the analysis of the field produced by a horizontal dipole source in a lossy medium such as the sea. The results are based on the work by Hasserjian and Guy.[‡] The analysis neglects the effects of the ionosphere and assumes that the field of interest above the air-sea boundary is that of the surface wave. For propagation over very long distances the effect of the ionosphere should be included, using the earth-ionosphere waveguide model treated in the previous section.

A vertical dipole antenna submerged several skin depths below the surface makes a very inefficient radiator.[§] The field strength directly above the dipole is very small because of the directional characteristics. At an offset point the slant distance to the surface is larger, and the high rate of attenuation causes the field at some horizontal distance away from the point directly above to be small also. In addition, the reflection coefficient at the air-sea surface is close to unity because of the large difference in the intrinsic impedance of air and seawater. These factors combine in such a manner that a horizontal dipole couples more efficiently to the vertical polarized surface wave field than a vertical dipole does.

A horizontal current element $I\,dl$ at a depth h is shown in Fig. 6.62. For

[†] R. K. Moore, "Effects of a Surrounding Conducting Medium on Antenna Analysis," *IEEE Trans.*, vol. AP-11, May 1963, pp. 216–225.

[‡] G. Hasserjian and A. W. Guy, "Low-Frequency Subsurface Antennas," *IEEE Trans.*, vol. AP-11, May 1963, pp. 225–231.

[§] R. K. Moore and W. E. Blair, "Dipole Radiation in a Conducting Half Space," *J. Res. NBS*, vol. 65D, Nov. 1961, pp. 547–563.

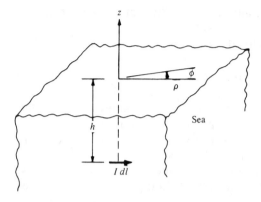

Figure 6.62 A horizontal current element radiating into a sea environment.

this source the *far-zone* radiation field above the surface at distances $\rho > \lambda_0$ is

$$E_z = \frac{jk_0 Z_0 I \, dl}{2\pi\rho} \frac{\gamma_0}{\gamma_1} F(p) \, e^{-\gamma_0\rho - \gamma_1 h} \cos\phi \qquad (6.155a)$$

$$E_\rho = \frac{jk_0 Z_0 I \, dl}{2\pi\rho} \left[\left(\frac{\gamma_0}{\gamma_1}\right)^2 - \frac{G(v)}{F(p)} \right] F(p) \, e^{-\gamma_0\rho - \gamma_1 h} \cos\phi \qquad (6.155b)$$

$$E_\phi = \frac{jk_0 Z_0 I \, dl}{2\pi\rho} G(v) \, e^{-\gamma_0\rho - \gamma_1 h} \sin\phi \qquad (6.155c)$$

where ϕ = angle measured from the dipole axis

$\gamma_0 = j\omega\sqrt{\mu_0\epsilon_0} = jk_0$

$\gamma_1 = (1+j)/\delta_s$ (propagation constant in seawater)

$F(p), G(v)$ = Norton surface-wave attenuation functions

$v = (\gamma_1/\gamma_0)^4 p$

$p = -(\gamma_0\rho/2)(\gamma_0/\gamma_1)^2$ = numerical distance

The radial distance along the surface is ρ, as shown in Fig. 6.62.

For the problem of interest the frequency will be below 100 kHz, so the wavelength λ_0 is greater than 3000 m and the skin depth δ_s is of order 1 m. The distance ρ is normally small enough so that the numerical distance p is much less than unity in magnitude. For this condition $|G| \ll |F|$ and $E_\rho = (\gamma_0/\gamma_1)E_z$, so $|E_\rho| \ll |E_z|$. For a vertical dipole located at the surface but above the sea the radiated fields are given by

$$E_z = \frac{jk_0 Z_0 I \, dl}{2\pi\rho} F(p) \, e^{-\gamma_0\rho} \qquad (6.156a)$$

$$E_\rho = \frac{\gamma_0}{\gamma_1} E_z \qquad (6.156b)$$

This latter result shows that E_z for a submerged horizontal current element differs from that for a vertical dipole at the surface by the directional factor $\cos \phi$, the refraction term γ_0/γ_1, and the depth attenuation factor $e^{-\gamma_1 h}$. Thus for $\phi = 0$ the coupling factor at the sea-air interface is simply the factor $\gamma_0/\gamma_1 = (1 + j)\delta_s \pi/\lambda_0$, which is quite small. The loss due to this coupling factor is shown in Fig. 6.63.

The attenuation function $F(p)$ for small numerical distance $|p|$ is given by

$$F(p) \sim 1 + \frac{\gamma_0}{\gamma_1}\left(\frac{\rho}{\lambda_0}\right)^{1/2}\pi \qquad (6.157)$$

Since $\lambda_0 \gg \delta_s$ and ρ/λ_0 will not be large, $F(p)$ can be set equal to unity with little error. E_z then has a value twice that if radiation occurred in free space apart from the coupling loss and depth attenuation. The numerical distance p has a magnitude given by $(\pi\rho/\lambda_0)(\omega\epsilon_0/\sigma) = 1.45 \times 10^{-19}f^2\rho$. For $f = 50$ kHz the numerical distance equals unity for $\rho = 3.1 \times 10^8$ km. This distance is much greater than that for which the flat-earth attenuation formulas hold and also much greater than the propagation distances normally of interest. For practical calculations Eq. (6.157) is acceptable and in most instances $F(p)$ can be set equal to unity since $|\gamma_0/\gamma_1| = (\omega\epsilon_0/\sigma)^{1/2}$ is a small factor. The following example will illustrate the evaluation of the received power in a horizontal receiving antenna when the transmitting antenna is a vertical monopole located at the surface.

Example 6.12 Communication system involving a submerged antenna Figure 6.64 shows a vertical monopole antenna transmitting to a submerged horizontal receiving antenna a distance ρ away. It will be as-

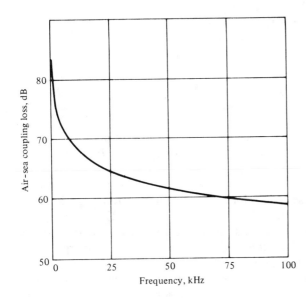

Figure 6.63 The sea-air interface coupling loss $20 \log|\gamma_1/\gamma_0|$.

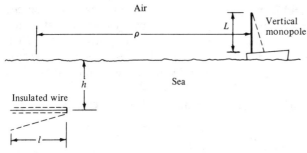

Figure 6.64 A communication link over seawater.

sumed that the submerged vehicle antenna is an insulated wire of length l equal to 25 m. The transmitting antenna is assumed to be a monopole of length L. The frequency is very low in order to avoid prohibitive attenuation in the sea. Thus both l and L are very small relative to a free-space wavelength. Under these conditions the current distribution on the antennas can be taken as triangular, as shown in Fig. 6.64.

The received open-circuit voltage V_{oc} is given by

$$V_{oc} = -\frac{1}{I_0} \int_0^L I(z) E_z(z) \, dz$$

where $I(z)$ is the current on the transmitting antenna and $E_z(z)$ is the field radiated by the wire antenna of length l when it is used for transmitting with an input current I_0. By using Eq. (6.155a) and assuming triangular current distributions, we obtain

$$V_{oc} = \frac{jk_0 Z_0 I_0 l}{4\pi \rho I_0} \frac{I_{in} L}{2} \frac{\gamma_0}{\gamma_1} e^{-\gamma_1 h - \gamma_0 \rho}$$

so

$$|V_{oc}| = \frac{k_0^2 Z_0 l L \delta_s}{8\sqrt{2}\pi\rho} e^{-h/\delta_s} I_{in} \qquad (6.158)$$

When the receiving antenna is matched to its load termination, that is, $Z_L = Z_{in}^*$, the received power will be $P_r = |V_{oc}|^2/4R_{in}$, where R_{in} is the input resistance of the receiving antenna.

In order to determine the signal-to-noise ratio at the receiver input, the contribution of the lossy sea at temperature T_1 and the atmospheric noise at temperature T_2 to the received noise must be found. The atmospheric noise and the sea noise are uncorrelated, so the received noise from these two sources may be added together. When the antenna is submerged to a depth of a few meters the power it would radiate is almost entirely absorbed in the seawater. The principle of detailed balancing then shows that the antenna-noise temperature due to the lossy sea is T_1. The error made in using this assumption is negligible if the path attenuation up to the surface is greater than 20 dB. Even for an attenuation of 10 dB the error is no greater than 10 percent.

The contribution of the atmospheric noise to the received noise can be determined approximately on a comparative basis. When the antenna is located in free space it would have an antenna noise temperature equal to T_2. The noiselike electromagnetic field incident on the air-sea interface from all directions above the sea is partially reflected at the surface. The remainder is transmitted down to the antenna and undergoes considerable attenuation in the process. The minimum reflection coefficient at the surface occurs for normal incidence. The reflection coefficient at normal incidence is

$$\Gamma = \frac{(j\omega\mu_0/\sigma)^{1/2} - Z_0}{(j\omega\mu_0/\sigma)^{1/2} + Z_0} \approx -1 + 2\frac{(j\omega\mu_0/\sigma)^{1/2}}{Z_0}$$

The transmission coefficient is $1 + \Gamma \approx 2(j\omega\mu_0/\sigma)^{1/2}/Z_0 = 2(j\omega\epsilon_0/\sigma)^{1/2}$. The power transmission coefficient is $4\omega\epsilon_0/\sigma$. The least amount of attenuation of the noise-field power incident on the receiving antenna is $4(\omega\epsilon_0/\sigma)\,e^{-2h/\delta_s}$. Thus the maximum possible contribution to the antenna-noise temperature from atmospheric noise is

$$T_2' = 4T_2\left(\frac{\omega\epsilon_0}{\sigma}\right)e^{-2h/\delta_s} \tag{6.159}$$

The effective antenna-noise temperature T_A equals $T_1 + T_2'$. In the VLF band T_2 is of order 10^{14} K, while T_1 is close to 273 K. If the total attenuation due to the low interface coupling and high path attenuation exceeds 120 dB, then atmospheric noise can be neglected. A more accurate expression for the noise temperature contributed by the atmospheric noise field would require a consideration of the integrated effect of all the incident noise fields over all angles.

If we assume that $f = 50\,\text{kHz}$, $h = 10\,\text{m}$, and $T_2 = 10^{14}$ K we find that $T_2' = 23.2$ K, which is negligible.

In order to proceed further with the evaluation of this communication link we must know the input resistance of the receiving antenna and the properties of the transmitting antenna. An insulated wire submerged in seawater may be viewed as a length of open-circuited lossy coaxial transmission line. On this basis its input impedance may be calculated.† When $l \ll \lambda_0$ then

$$R_{\text{in}} = \frac{40\alpha\beta l}{\epsilon_r k_0}\ln\frac{b}{a} \tag{6.160a}$$

$$X_{\text{in}} = \frac{-60}{\epsilon_r k_0 l}\ln\frac{b}{a} \tag{6.160b}$$

† A. W. Guy and G. Hasserjian, "Impedance of Large Subsurface Arrays," *IEEE Trans.*, vol. AP-11, May 1963, pp. 232–240.

where α and β are the attenuation and phase constants for the current wave on the insulated wire, a is the wire radius, b is the outer radius of the insulator, and ϵ_r is the dielectric constant of the insulator. If we assume that the antenna is made from 50-Ω coaxial cable by removing the outer conductor, then from Fig. 2 of the cited reference one finds that $\beta = 3.5\sqrt{\epsilon_r}k_0$, $\alpha = 0.09\sqrt{\epsilon_r}k_0$. Thus if we also use $\epsilon_r = 2.56$ we get

$$R_{in} = 105.5(l/\lambda_0) \tag{6.161a}$$

$$X_{in} = -4.97(\lambda_0/l) \tag{6.161b}$$

Note that R_{in} is very small and X_{in} is very large.

The above antenna requires an inductance of $0.066\,(\lambda_0/l)^2\,\mu H$ (microhenry) to tune it to resonance. For example, at 50 kHz an inductance of 3.8 mH is required. For an unloaded bandwidth of 300 Hz the coil Q should be $50,000/300 = 167$, and thus the coil resistance will be $R_c = (\omega L/Q) - R_{in} \approx 7.14\,\Omega$, which is much larger than R_{in} when $l = 25$ m and $\lambda_0 = 6$ km.

If the inductor is considered to be part of the antenna and the receiver is matched to $R_{in} + R_c = R$, then R must be used in place of R_{in} in the expression for received power to give

$$P_r = \frac{|V_{oc}|^2}{4R}$$

The loaded bandwidth of the receiver input circuit will be 600 Hz.

When the receiver-noise figure is F_n and the coil resistance is assumed to be at the temperature T_1, the total noise referred to the receiver input will be

$$P_n = (F_n - 1)KT_0\,\Delta f + k\,\Delta f\left(\frac{R_{in}(T_2' + T_1)}{R} + \frac{R_cT_1}{R}\right)$$

$$= (F_n - 1)KT_0\,\Delta f + kT_1\,\Delta f - k\,\Delta f\frac{R_{in}}{R}T_2'$$

$$\approx (F_n - 1)KT_0\,\Delta f + kT_1\,\Delta f \tag{6.162}$$

For $F_n = 4$, $\Delta f = 600$ Hz, $T_1 = 273$ K, we obtain $P_n = 9.71 \times 10^{-18}$ W.

The transmitting antenna input current will be found by assuming that the required signal-to-noise ratio is 10. By using Eq. (6.158), the expression for P_r, and Eq. (6.162) we find that

$$I_{in} = \frac{2 \times (80RP_n)^{1/2}\lambda_0^2\rho\,e^{h/\delta_s}}{\pi Z_0 lL\delta_s}$$

For a bandwidth of 600 Hz, $l = L = 25$ m, $h = 10$ m, $\rho = 10$ km, and the previously assumed parameters, we obtain $I_{in} = 4.6 \times 10^3$ A. Clearly this large input current cannot be realized very easily in practice. The large interface coupling loss (61.58 dB) and the depth attenuation loss (76.85 dB) increase the required input current by a factor of 8.35×10^6. Without this loss an input current of 0.55 MA would have sufficed.

The radiation resistance of a short monopole antenna is given by

$$R_a = 40\pi^2 \left(\frac{L}{\lambda_0}\right)^2 \tag{6.163}$$

The antenna will also exhibit a large input capacitive reactance. This reactance will depend on the diameter-to-length ratio of the monopole. An antenna with a large cross section will have a smaller reactance. An inductance is normally used to tune the antenna to resonance, and the antenna current is determined by the series resistance of this tuning coil when the radiation resistance is very small. This also means that the tuning coil must dissipate close to 100 percent of the transmitter power output, and the overall efficiency will be low.

If the antenna has an effective cross-sectional diameter d the approximate value of the input reactance is

$$X_{in} = -\frac{30}{\pi}\frac{\lambda_0}{L}\left(\ln\frac{4L}{d} - 1\right) \tag{6.164}$$

The antenna is assumed tuned to resonance, with a base loading coil with loaded quality factor Q and total series resistance $2R$. (This includes the generator resistance R_g, which we choose equal to R.) The tuning coil must provide an equal and opposite reactance. For a bandwidth of 600 Hz the loaded Q should be $f/600$, and the total series resistance $2R$ is given by $-X_{in}/Q$ or

$$2R = \frac{-X_{in}}{f}600$$

The efficiency is $R_a/(R + R_a) \approx R_a/R$ and is given by

$$\eta = \frac{80\pi^3}{60[\ln(4L/d) - 1]}\frac{f}{300}\left(\frac{L}{\lambda_0}\right)^3$$

If we use $L = 25$ m, then $R_a = 6.85 \times 10^{-3} \Omega$. For $d = 1$ m, $\eta = 1.382 \times 10^{-4}$, which is very small. The power in R_a is $I_{in}^2 R_a = 1.45 \times 10^5$, and the input power is a factor η^{-1} larger, or 1.04×10^9 W. This is a very unrealistic power level. The example has shown the great difficulty that exists in providing communication to a submerged antenna. The high attenuation of seawater requires the use of very low frequencies, and if the antennas are short in terms of the very large wavelength they are very inefficient; the result is a requirement of unrealistically large transmitter power.

If the frequency is reduced to 10 kHz, the interface coupling loss increases by 7 dB, but the depth attenuation decreases by a factor of

43.7 dB for a net gain of 36.7 dB. However, the antenna efficiencies would decrease by a significant amount unless their lengths were increased by a factor of 5. Consequently the use of lower frequencies helps, but the antenna size requirement remains a difficult problem. ∎

Near-Zone Fields

The expressions for the fields at the air-sea surface radiated by a horizontal current element are valid for a distance ρ greater than the free-space wavelength. At the low frequency that is often used, the wavelength is very long and instances occur where ρ is less than a wavelength. For short distances it is necessary to consider the near-zone fields as well. These include terms that vary like ρ^{-2} and ρ^{-3}. In the near-zone range the fields are given by†

$$E_z = \frac{jk_0 Z_0 I\,dl}{2\pi\gamma_1\rho^2}(1 + \gamma_0\rho)\cos\phi\,e^{-\gamma_1 h - \gamma_0\rho} \tag{6.165a}$$

$$E_\rho = \frac{jk_0 Z_0 I\,dl}{2\pi\gamma_1^2\rho^3}(1 + \gamma_0\rho + \gamma_0^2\rho^2)\cos\phi\,e^{-\gamma_1 h - \gamma_0\rho} \tag{6.165b}$$

$$E_\phi = \frac{jk_0 Z_0 I\,dl}{\pi\gamma_1^2\rho^3}(1 + \gamma_0\rho)\sin\phi\,e^{-\gamma_1 h - \gamma_0\rho} \tag{6.165c}$$

The notation is the same as that used in Eq. (6.155). These expressions become equal to those given by Eq. (6.155) at a range where ρ is comparable to λ_0 so that $\gamma_0\rho$ and $\gamma_0^2\rho^2$ become the dominant terms relative to unity. At a frequency of 10 kHz the near-zone field expressions must be used out to a distance of order 30 km.

6.12 ATMOSPHERIC DUCTS AND NONSTANDARD REFRACTION

The standard atmospheric model used in propagation studies is the one where the index of refraction decreases linearly with height. The decreasing value of the index of refraction causes the radio-wave rays to curve downward. The effect is accounted for by increasing the effective earth's radius by a factor of 4/3 and then assuming that there is no ray curvature for propagation over this larger earth. The standard atmospheric model does not always apply. In certain parts of the world it often turns out that the index of refraction will have a rate of decrease with height over a short distance that is sufficient to cause the rays to be refracted back to the surface of the earth. These rays are then reflected and refracted back again in such a manner that the field is trapped or guided in

---

† Hasserjian and Guy, op. cit.

a thin layer of the atmosphere near the earth, as shown in Fig. 6.65. This phenomenon is known as *trapping*, or *ducting*. The confined field will propagate over long distances with much less attenuation than for free-space propagation because of the guiding action, which is somewhat similar to that in the earth-ionosphere waveguide at low frequencies.

Ducts may form near the surface of the earth (surface duct) or at some height up to 5000 ft above the surface (elevated ducts). In order to obtain long-distance propagation, both the transmitting and receiving antennas must be located within the duct in order to couple effectively to the field in the duct. The thickness of the duct may range from a few feet to several hundred feet. In order to obtain trapping the rays must propagate in a nearly horizontal direction and thus, in order to satisfy the conditions for guiding within the duct, the wavelength has to be relatively small. Consequently ducting occurs primarily for frequencies above several hundred megahertz (UHF and microwave bands).

The formation of ducts is due primarily to the water vapor content of the atmosphere, since this has a stronger influence on the index of refraction than temperature gradients do. For this reason ducts most often form over large bodies of water such as in the trade-wind belt of the oceans. Ducting over land surfaces is much less common. In the trade-wind belt over the ocean there appears to be a more or less permanent duct about 1.5 m thick.

The simplified theory of propagation in ducts will be presented below and is based on the ray picture of propagation in a nonhomogeneous medium. The index of refraction of the medium is usually described in terms of the meteorological data by modified index of refraction curves. These curves are a plot of the modified index of refraction on a horizontal scale versus height. The modified index of refraction is the difference between the actual index of refraction and that which corresponds to refractive conditions in the atmosphere that would cause the rays to remain at a constant height above the curved surface of the earth.

Consider an atmosphere for which the index of refraction is a function $n(z)$ of the height z above the earth's surface. With reference to Fig. 6.66a, Snell's law, as discussed in Sec. 6.6 and illustrated in Fig. 6.40c, requires that $n(z) \sin \psi(z)$ be constant for a flat earth. For a spherical earth with a spherically stratified atmosphere Snell's law takes the form $(a + z)n(z) \sin \psi(z) =$ constant. (For a derivation see Prob. 6.34.) The derivative with respect to z

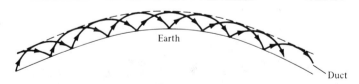

Figure 6.65 Ray paths for a surface duct.

gives

$$\sin \psi \frac{dn}{dz} + n \cos \psi \frac{d\psi}{dz} = -\frac{n}{a+z} \sin \psi$$

or

$$\frac{d\psi}{dz} = -\frac{\tan \psi}{n} \frac{dn}{dz} - \frac{1}{a+z} \tan \psi \qquad (6.166)$$

We can relate the rate of change of the angle of incidence ψ with respect to height to the rate of change of the angle θ, which measures angular distance along the earth's surface, as shown in Fig. 6.66b. From the figure it is seen that $dz = (a + z) \cot \psi \, d\theta$, and hence

$$\frac{d\psi}{d\theta} = -\frac{a+z}{n} \frac{dn}{dz} - 1 \qquad (6.167)$$

where a is the radius of the earth. If the initial angle of incidence at some height z_0 is 90°, the ray will propagate along a path parallel to the earth's

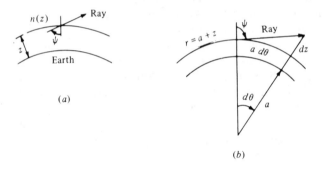

(a)

(b)

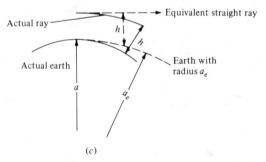

(c)

Figure 6.66 (a) Curved ray in an inhomogeneous atmosphere above the earth. (b) Ray height as a function of $d\theta$. (c) The equivalence of a straight ray above an earth with radius a_e and the actual ray above the earth.

surface, i.e., at constant height, provided $d\psi/d\theta = 0$. The required index of refraction gradient is

$$\frac{dn}{dz} = -\frac{n}{a+z} \approx -\frac{1}{a} \tag{6.168}$$

The average value of the index-of-refraction gradient for the standard atmosphere is smaller than this value and is given by

$$\frac{dn}{dz} = -\frac{1}{a_e} \tag{6.169}$$

where $a_e = 4a/3$. For the standard atmosphere the ray curves downward, and its height above the earth's surface is the same as that which a ray propagating along a straight line would have relative to an earth with an effective radius a_e, as shown in Fig. 6.66c. This is the basis for using an effective earth radius a_e and for assuming that above the surface of this equivalent earth the index of refraction is constant and the rays propagate along a straight-line path.

The integral of Eq. (6.168) gives

$$n(z) = n(0) - \frac{z}{a} \tag{6.170}$$

while for the standard atmosphere

$$n(z) = n(0) - \frac{z}{a_e} \tag{6.171}$$

With nonstandard refractive conditions the index of refraction may decrease with height less rapidly or more rapidly than according to Eq. (6.171). When the decrease is more rapid, the ray will curve downward at a greater rate and hence propagate to a greater distance without getting too far away from the earth's surface. For this reason the refraction is referred to as *superrefraction* for this case. When the index of refraction decreases less rapidly, there is less downward curvature, and we have *substandard refraction*.

The modified index of refraction N is equal to the difference between the actual index of refraction and that for the equivalent atmosphere over a flat earth. It is obtained by the subtraction of the term $-z/a$; thus

$$N(z) = n(z) + \frac{z}{a} \tag{6.172}$$

The gradient of the modified index of refraction is

$$\frac{dN}{dz} = \frac{dn}{dz} + \frac{1}{a} \tag{6.173}$$

and can be either positive (substandard refraction) or negative (superrefraction) with respect to that for the standard atmosphere. The modified index of refraction is used to study ray propagation over a flat earth, since the effect of the curvature of the earth's surface has been removed. The actual index of refraction for the standard atmosphere decreases with height, but the modified index N will increase with height, since

$$\frac{dN}{dz} = \frac{1}{a} - \frac{1}{a_e} = \frac{1}{4a}$$

Since the index of refraction differs from unity by approximately 300 parts in a million, it is a common practice to describe it in terms of m units given by

$$m = (n-1)\times 10^6 \qquad (6.174a)$$

and for the modified index of refraction in terms of M units given by

$$M = (N-1)\times 10^6 \qquad (6.174b)$$

The height-versus-M profiles or curves are often plotted as a function of the meteorological parameters in order to show superrefraction, substandard refraction, and ducting conditions. Similar N profiles may be plotted. Typical N profiles are shown in Fig. 6.67. For the standard atmosphere the N profile is a straight line with constant positive slope. When the slope is less we have substandard conditions, while a greater slope indicates superrefraction. An inversion in the profile, such as that shown in Fig. 6.67d, e, and f, indicates the presence of a surface duct or elevated duct.

Ray Trajectories in a Surface Duct

We will assume that the modified index of refraction is given by

$$N(z) = N_0 + N_1 z(h - z) \qquad 0 \le z \le h \qquad (6.175)$$

A typical value for the constant N_1 is $1.3 \times 10^{-7}/\text{m}^2$. This parabolic index profile represents the medium within the ducting region, which extends from the surface up to a height h. Consider a ray that leaves a transmitter at height $h/2$

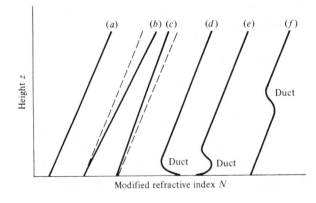

Figure 6.67 Modified index of refraction profiles; (a) standard atmosphere; (b) substandard refraction; (c) profile for super-refraction; (d) profile for surface duct; (e) profile for near-surface duct; and (f) profile for elevated duct.

at an angle ψ_i, as shown in Fig. 6.68. At a height $z > h/2$ the angle ψ is given by Snell's law (since $N(z)$ is used the flat earth formula must be used) as

$$N(z) \sin \psi = N(h/2) \sin \psi_i \qquad (6.176)$$

At the turning point $\psi = \pi/2$ and from Eq. (6.176) we obtain $N(z) = N(h/2) \sin \psi_i$. By using Eq. (6.175) we can solve for $z = z_t$ at the turning point to obtain

$$z_t = \frac{h}{2} \left[1 + \left(1 + \frac{4N_0}{h^2 N_1} \right)^{1/2} (1 - \sin \psi_i)^{1/2} \right] \qquad (6.177)$$

If the initial angle of incidence ψ_i is too small, the ray will penetrate through the duct and not be trapped. The critical angle ψ_c is that angle which makes the turning point occur at $z = h$. From Eq. (6.177) we readily find by setting $z_t = h$ that

$$\sin \psi_c = \frac{1}{1 + (h^2 N_1 / 4N_0)} \qquad (6.178)$$

As an example let $N_0 = 1$, $N_1 = 1.3 \times 10^{-7}/\text{m}^2$ and $h = 20 \text{ m}$, for which the critical angle is 89.708°. This result is a typical one and shows that only those rays that propagate in an almost horizontal direction can become trapped. When $\psi_i > \psi_c$ the turning point is at $z_t < h$, and the ray trajectory is like that shown in Fig. 6.68. In Fig. 6.68 the angle of incidence is shown to be much less than $\pi/2$ at the midpoint for clarity.

The ray picture suggests that all rays with $\psi_i < \psi_c$ are trapped. While this is true, only certain angles that depend on frequency correspond to guided modes in the duct. The waveguiding action of a duct is very similar to that of a dielectric slab. A dielectric slab waveguide is shown in Fig. 6.69. For this guide we will consider a TM mode with field components E_z, E_x, and H_y. For H_y we will assume a solution of the form

$$H_y = \begin{cases} A[e^{-jkz \cos \psi_i} + e^{jkz \cos \psi_i}] e^{-jkx \sin \psi_i} & -\dfrac{h}{2} < z < \dfrac{h}{2} \\ B e^{-jk_0|z| \cos \psi_t - jk_0 x \sin \psi_t} & |z| > h/2 \end{cases}$$

where $k = \sqrt{\kappa} k_0$ and A and B are constants. In order to match the tangential

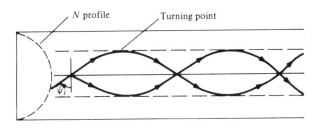

Figure 6.68 Ray trajectories in a duct with a parabolic profile for the modified index of refraction.

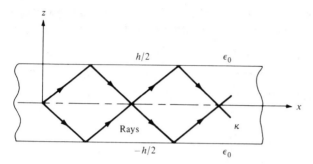

Figure 6.69 A dielectric-slab waveguide model for a duct.

field across the surfaces $z = \pm h/2$ for all values of x we require that

$$k_0 \sin \psi_t = \sqrt{\kappa} \, k_0 \sin \psi_i$$

which is Snell's law. We have assumed upward and downward propagating waves that form a standing-wave solution in the z direction within the slab. Such a solution is possible only if there is complete reflection at each dielectric-air interface. This requires that the angle ψ_i be greater than the critical angle given by $\sqrt{\kappa} \sin \psi_c = 1$, which makes $\psi_t = \pi/2$ and results in complete reflection at each air-dielectric interface. When $\psi_i > \psi_c$ we see that $\cos \psi_t = (1 - \sin^2 \psi_t)^{1/2} = (1 - \kappa \sin^2 \psi_i)^{1/2}$ will be pure imaginary. Thus the field outside the slab will be evanescent. For convenience let $k \sin \psi_i = \beta$, $k \cos \psi_i = \gamma = (k^2 - \beta^2)^{1/2}$, and $jk_0 \cos \psi_t = \alpha = (\beta^2 - k_0^2)^{1/2}$. The solution for H_y can then be expressed in the form

$$H_y = \begin{cases} 2A \cos \gamma z \, e^{-j\beta x} & -\dfrac{h}{2} < z < \dfrac{h}{2} \\[3mm] B \, e^{-\alpha|z| - j\beta x} & |z| > \dfrac{h}{2} \end{cases} \qquad (6.179)$$

The x component of the electric field is given by

$$j\omega\epsilon E_x = -\frac{\partial H_y}{\partial z}$$

Hence

$$E_x = \begin{cases} \dfrac{2\gamma A}{j\omega\epsilon_0 \kappa} \sin \gamma z \, e^{-j\beta x} & -\dfrac{h}{2} < z < \dfrac{h}{2} \\[3mm] \dfrac{\alpha B}{j\omega\epsilon_0} e^{-\alpha z} \, e^{-j\beta x} & x > \dfrac{h}{2} \end{cases} \qquad (6.180)$$

When we make H_y and E_x continuous at $z = h/2$ we find that a solution for A and B is possible only if

$$\gamma \tan \gamma \frac{h}{2} = \kappa \alpha \qquad (6.181)$$

This characteristic equation, along with the relationship $\gamma^2 = \kappa k_0^2 - \beta^2 =$

$\kappa k_0^2 - (\alpha^2 + k_0^2)$ or $\gamma^2 + \alpha^2 = (\kappa - 1)k_0^2$, determines the allowed values of γ and β that will correspond to guided modes in the slab. As an example, let the dielectric constant $\kappa = 1.002$ and $\lambda_0 = 10$ cm and assume that $\alpha = 2.75$. We then obtain $\gamma = 0.5772$, and from Eq. (6.181) we find that the required slab thickness h equals 4.72 m. For this mode $\psi_i = 89.47°$. The higher-order modes require a larger value of h.

The propagation of a guided mode in a duct is similar to that in a dielectric slab but is more difficult to analyze because the dielectric constant is not uniform along the cross section of the guide. There will be an evanescent field beyond the turning point in the duct just like there is beyond the boundary in the dielectric slab guide. The characteristic values of ψ will be very close to $90°$ because the index of refraction is very close to unity. A first approximation to the solution could be obtained by assuming that the duct is equivalent to a dielectric slab of thickness h and having a dielectric constant equal to $N^2(h/2)$.

As long as $(\kappa - 1)(k_0 h/2)^2 \ll 1$, then $\gamma h/2$ is also very small, and Eq. (6.181) gives

$$\alpha = \frac{\gamma^2 h}{2\kappa} \tag{6.182}$$

We then find from the relation $\gamma^2 + \alpha^2 = (\kappa - 1)k_0^2$ that

$$\gamma^4 \left(\frac{h}{2\kappa}\right)^2 + \gamma^2 = (\kappa - 1)k_0^2 \tag{6.183}$$

which is readily solved for γ. The required value of ψ_i may be found from

$$\cos \psi_i = \frac{\gamma}{\kappa^{1/2} k_0} \approx \frac{\gamma}{k_0} \tag{6.184}$$

For $N_1 = 1.3 \times 10^{-7}/\text{m}^2$, $N_0 = 1$, $\lambda_0 = 10$ cm, and a duct thickness $h = 50$ m, we find that $\psi_i = 89.77°$.

PROBLEMS

6.1 A line-of-sight communication link operating at 50 MHz has the transmitting antenna at a height of 20 m. The distance to the receiving site is 15 km. Use the flat-earth interference formulas to determine the height of the receiving antenna for maximum received signal.

6.2 A communication system operates at 100 MHz and has its transmitting antenna at a height of 50 m. Construct a flat-earth coverage diagram for this system. Plot the first two lobes for free-space range parameters of 5, 10, and 20 km. See Eq. (6.6a) and (6.6b).

6.3 A 3-cm radar has its antenna located 3.9 m above ground ($\nu = 0.25$). Plot the relative received signal strength returned from an aircraft flying towards the radar at a height of 156 m by using the coverage diagram given in Fig. 6.19. See Example 6.2.

6.4 A communication link operating at 300 MHz has its transmitting antenna at a height of 25.5 m. For a receiving antenna at a height of 255 m plot the relative received signal power as a function of d for d in the range of 5 to 25 mi.

6.5 A microwave relay link is to be designed such that the signal power level will not be less than what it would be under free-space propagation conditions. The frequency of operation is 10 GHz. The antenna heights at each terminal are 30 m. Determine the maximum distance that can be used between stations.

6.6 In a communication link the antenna heights are 40 and 60 m. The distance between terminals is 30 km. Find the point at which reflection from the ground occurs. Assume standard refraction occurs. Find the path-gain factor for this system when $\lambda_0 = 1$ m. Assume a reflection coefficient of -1.

6.7 An FM station operating at 100 MHz with a transmitted power of 5 kW has its transmitting antenna at a height of 70 m. Find the field strength in microvolts per meter at a receiving site a distance of 60 km away. The receiving antenna is located 10 m above the ground. The gain of the transmitting antenna is 5. If the receiving antenna is raised to a height of 20 m, what is the new value of field strength? See Figs. 6.28 and 6.29.

6.8 When $h_c = -\infty$ show that Eq. (6.33) gives $(E_0 e^{jk_0 d}/d)$ for the field at the center of the receiving antenna. Use the approximations $R_1 \approx d_1$, $z \approx d_2$. This is the expected result in view of Eq. (6.29), which was chosen for the transmitted field.

6.9 A range of hills 50 m high exists midway between the terminals of a microwave relay link operating at 1 GHz. The distance between the terminals is 15 km. Determine the required antenna heights in order to keep the diffraction loss less than 6 dB when substandard refraction occurs such that the effective earth radius is 0.7 of the actual earth radius ($a_e = 2770$ mi). What should the antenna heights be in order to keep $H_c = 0.8$ under substandard refraction conditions? How much lower could the antenna heights be if $a_e = 5280$ mi and $H_c = 0.8$? *Hint*: Plot the path profile above an earth with radius a_e using straight-line ray paths.

6.10 An AM broadcasting station operates on a frequency of 700 kHz with a transmitter power of 50 kW. The antenna gain is 2. Find the distance at which the surface-wave field will provide a field strength of 10 mV RMS/m. Assume that $\kappa = 15$ and $\sigma = 10^{-2}$ S/m. For a similar station operating at 1.5 MHz, what is the corresponding distance for the same field strength? *Hint*: Find the field strength for $d = 100$, 125, and 150 km and extrapolate between these values.

6.11 A ship-to-shore communication system operates on a frequency of 300 kHz. At what distance will the signal level be 20 dB below its free-space value? Assume that $\kappa' = 80$ and $\sigma = 4$ S/m for seawater. See Fig. P6.11 for $|A_s|$.

6.12 A small portable AM radio receiver uses a ferrite-core antenna with an effective permeability $\mu_e = 10$. The cross section of the ferrite-rod core is 2 cm². The antenna consists of a coil of 50 turns with an inductance of 250 μH. The Q of the coil is 300. The receiver has an overall noise figure of 8. An AM broadcasting station operating on a frequency of 1.5 MHz with a power of 20 kW and an antenna gain of 2 is to be received. If the antenna-noise temperature is 10^9 K and the receiver bandwidth is 10 kHz, what is the signal-to-noise ratio at a distance of 80 km (about 50 mi)? Assume $\sigma = 10^{-2}$ S/m and $\kappa' = 12$.

6.13 Determine the distances at which the signal power will be 20 dB below its free-space value for the following conditions:

(a) $f = 50$ MHz, $\kappa' = 15$, $\sigma = 10^{-3}$ S/m
(b) $f = 50$ MHz, $\kappa' = 80$, $\sigma = 4$ S/m (over seawater)
(c) $f = 10$ MHz, $\kappa' = 15$, $\sigma = 10^{-3}$ S/m
(d) $f = 100$ MHz, $\kappa' = 15$, $\sigma = 10^{-3}$ S/m

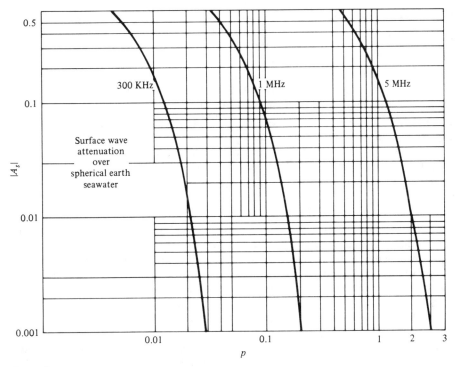

0.5

300 KHz

1 MHz

5 MHz

0.1

$|A_s|$

Surface wave
attenuation
over
spherical earth
seawater

0.01

0.001

0.01

0.1

1 2 3

p

Figure P6.11

6.14 Two individuals use walkie-talkies operating at 50 MHz in a rural environment where the ground constants are $\kappa' = 10$, $\sigma = 5 \times 10^{-3}$ S/m. The antenna gains are equal to unity. The transmitted power is 4 W. The receiver bandwidth is 5 kHz. The receiver-noise temperature is 1200 K, and the antenna-noise temperature is 10^4 K. Determine the signal-to-noise ratio at distances of 5, 10, and 20 km assuming surface-wave propagation. If propagation took place under free-space conditions, what would the signal-to-noise-ratio be at 20 km?

6.15 Compare the surface-wave attenuation for vertical and horizontal polarization for $f = 1$ MHz, $\kappa' = 10$, $\sigma = 5 \times 10^{-3}$ S/m, and $d = 60$ km.

6.16 The electron concentration at a height of 300 km is 10^{11}/m³. What is the maximum angle of incidence ψ_i that can be used at a frequency of 10 MHz? What is the horizontal skip distance if the maximum angle ψ_i is used?

6.17 A short-wave broadcasting service is to be established covering a distance of 6000 km in three skips, each 2000 km long. Assume that reflection takes place at a height of 250 km and that the electron density is 5×10^{11}/m³. What frequency and angle of incidence should be used? What is the maximum usable frequency?

6.18 A plane wave at a frequency of 10 MHz propagates through a distance of 200 km in the ionosphere. The average electron density is 5×10^{10}/m³, and the cyclotron frequency $\omega_c = 8 \times 10^6$ rad/s. Find the amount of Faraday rotation produced. Assume that collisions are negligible.

6.19 A plane wave propagates along $\mathbf{B}_0$ in the ionosphere with $f_c = 1.4\,\text{MHz}$. The frequency of the plane wave is 1.5 MHz. The electron density is $10^{10}/\text{m}^3$ and the collision frequency $\nu = 10^4$. Find the attenuation constants for the left and right circularly polarized waves. Repeat for $f = 2\,\text{MHz}$.

6.20 By using Eq. (6.96) show that the scattered power from a spherical water drop in a plane $\theta = \pi/2$ is the same as the backscattered power per unit area. Thus the radar bistatic scattering cross section is the same in this plane as the backscattering cross section.

6.21 Use Eqs. (6.107) and (6.108) to calculate the attenuation in decibels per kilometer for a microwave signal with $f = 20\,\text{GHz}$ and moderate rain of 6 mm/h. What is the attenuation at a heavy rain rate of 20 mm/h?

6.22 A microwave relay system uses terminals spaced 10 mi apart. The frequency of operation is 10 GHz. What additional signal margin is required to offset attenuation by rain for a rain rate of 10 mm/h along the whole path?

6.23 A 60-GHz millimeter communication system uses antennas (parabolic) that are 40 cm in diameter and have an efficiency of 0.65. The transmitter power is 2 W. The receiver bandwidth is 200 kHz, and the system-noise temperature is 500 K. What is the maximum free-space range for a signal-to-noise ratio of 15 dB? What is the maximum range possible when attenuation by oxygen and water vapor is taken into account?

6.24 Two microwave relay systems have their paths at right angles to each other (see Fig. P6.24). The antenna gains are equal to 30 dB, and the half-power beam widths are 7°. The frequency is 10 GHz. Rain at a rate of 10 mm/h occurs in the region where the two antenna beams cross, as shown in Fig. P6.24. Estimate the common volume to be a cube with sides of length $r \times \text{BW}$, where BW is the half-power beam width and $r = 5\,\text{km}$ is the distance to the rain cell. Find the average scattered power received by antenna 2 when the power transmitted by antenna 1 is 5 W. *Hint*: See Prob. 6.20.

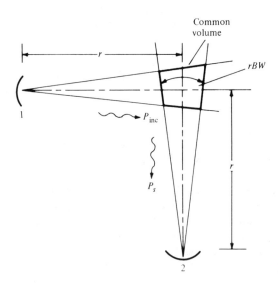

Figure P6.24

6.25 For a tropospheric scatter link show that $|\mathbf{k}_s - \mathbf{k}_i| = 2k_0 \sin \psi/2$. *Hint*: Consider $(\mathbf{k}_s - \mathbf{k}_i) \cdot (\mathbf{k}_s - \mathbf{k}_i)$.

6.26 Under the conditions stated in the text, why is $\mathbf{f}_1 \cdot \mathbf{f}_2 = f_1 f_2 \cos \psi$?

6.27 Assume that the antenna beams have square cross sections, as shown in Fig. P6.27. Let $2\theta_{1/2}$ be the half-power beam width so that H in the figure will be equal to $d\theta_{1/2}$. Show that the common volume is BH^2 and find B in terms of H and ψ. Assume $\sin \psi \approx \psi$. How is ψ related to the angle α and the elevation angle γ of the two antennas? *Answer:* $\psi = \alpha + 2\gamma$.

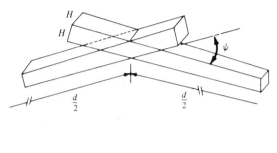

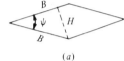

(a)

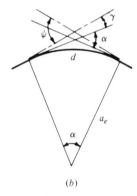

(b)

Figure P6.27

6.28 In a tropospheric scatter link the antennas are beamed $0.25°$ above the horizon. The range d is 250 km. What is the height above the earth of the common volume from which scattering occurs? What are the values of the angles α and ψ? Assume an effective earth radius of $a_e = 5280$ mi to account for standard refraction. How should the expression (6.133) be modified when α and ψ are not equal? Note that $\alpha = d/a_e$ and ψ is the angle between $\mathbf{k}_i$ and $\mathbf{k}_s$, as in Fig. P6.27. See also Prob. 6.27.

6.29 For the tropospheric link described in Prob. 6.28 the antenna gains are 50 dB, the transmitted power is 2 kW, and the frequency is 2 GHz. If $C_n = 5 \times 10^{-8} \, \text{m}^{-1/3}$, what is the received power? *Hint:* See Example 6.11.

6.30 For the 505-MHz tropospheric scatter link described in the text find the received power for $d = 300$ km. Assume $\theta_{1/2} = 2/\sqrt{G}$ and $C_n = 3 \times 10^{-8} \, \text{m}^{-1/3}$.

6.31 Assume that the magnetic field of the TEM mode in the ideal parallel-plate earth-ionosphere waveguide is given by $H_y = B e^{-jk_0z}$. The earth and the ionosphere can be treated as surfaces, with a surface impedance given by $Z_s = (j\omega\mu_0/\sigma)^{1/2} = (1+j)(\omega\mu_0/2\sigma)^{1/2} = (1+j)/(\sigma\delta_s)$, where δ_s is the skin depth. The power loss per unit area in one surface is given by $|H_y|^2/(2\sigma\delta_s)$. Find the power loss P_l per unit length in the parallel-plate waveguide and find the attenuation α from the power-balance equation $-dP/dz = 2\alpha P = P_l$, where P is the power flow for the TEM mode. Show that α found by this method agrees with that obtained from Eq. (6.150).

6.32 An atmospheric duct is modeled as a dielectric slab of thickness $h = 25$ m and with a dielectric constant $\kappa = 1 + 1.5 \times 10^{-6}$. Find the critical angle ψ_c. When $\lambda_0 = 20$ cm, what is the value of the angle ψ for a guided mode in the slab?

6.33 Derive the characteristic equation (6.181).

6.34 Derive Snell's law as used in the derivation of Eq. (6.166). *Hint*: From Eqs. (IV.19) and (IV.21) show that

$$n\frac{ds}{ds} = \mathbf{n}_p \mathbf{n}_p \cdot \nabla n$$

The directional derivative of n along s is

$$\frac{dn}{ds} = \mathbf{s} \cdot \nabla n$$

From these relationships show that

$$\frac{d n\mathbf{s}}{ds} = (\mathbf{n}_p \cdot \nabla n)\mathbf{n}_p + (\mathbf{s} \cdot \nabla n)\mathbf{s} = \nabla n$$

Now consider

$$\mathbf{r} \times \frac{d n\mathbf{s}}{ds} = \mathbf{r} \times \nabla n = r\frac{\partial n}{\partial r}\mathbf{a}_r \times \mathbf{a}_r = 0$$

Expand $d(\mathbf{r} \times s n)/ds$ to obtain $-n\mathbf{s} \times d\mathbf{r}/ds = 0$ since $d\mathbf{r}/ds$ is along $\mathbf{s}$. Hence $|\mathbf{r} \times sn|$ is constant along the ray. Thus $rn \sin\psi = $ constant where ψ is the angle between the position vector $\mathbf{r}$ and the unit tangent $\mathbf{s}$ to the ray. When r is set equal to $a + z$ the required law is obtained.

USEFUL VECTOR RELATIONSHIPS

VECTOR ALGEBRA

Let vectors **A** and **B** be expressed as components along unit vectors $\mathbf{a}_1$, $\mathbf{a}_2$, and $\mathbf{a}_3$ in a right-hand orthogonal coordinate system. Then

$$\mathbf{A} \pm \mathbf{B} = (A_1 \pm B_1)\mathbf{a}_1 + (A_2 \pm B_2)\mathbf{a}_2 + (A_3 \pm B_3)\mathbf{a}_3 \tag{I.1}$$

$$\mathbf{A} \cdot \mathbf{B} = |\mathbf{A}|\,|\mathbf{B}| \cos\theta = A_1 B_1 + A_2 B_2 + A_3 B_3 \tag{I.2}$$

where θ is the angle between **A** and **B**.

$$\mathbf{A} \times \mathbf{B} = \mathbf{a}_1(A_2 B_3 - A_3 B_2) + \mathbf{a}_2(A_3 B_1 - A_1 B_3) + \mathbf{a}_3(A_1 B_2 - A_2 B_1) \tag{I.3a}$$

$$|\mathbf{A} \times \mathbf{B}| = |A|\,|B| \sin\theta \tag{I.3b}$$

$$\mathbf{A} \cdot \mathbf{B} \times \mathbf{C} = \mathbf{A} \times \mathbf{B} \cdot \mathbf{C} = \mathbf{C} \times \mathbf{A} \cdot \mathbf{B} \tag{I.4}$$

$$\mathbf{A} \times \mathbf{B} = -\mathbf{B} \times \mathbf{A} \tag{I.5}$$

$$\mathbf{A} \times (\mathbf{B} \times \mathbf{C}) = (\mathbf{A} \cdot \mathbf{C})\mathbf{B} - (\mathbf{A} \cdot \mathbf{B})\mathbf{C} \tag{I.6}$$

VECTOR OPERATIONS IN COMMON COORDINATE SYSTEMS

Rectangular Coordinates (Fig. I.1)

$$\nabla\Phi = \mathbf{a}_x \frac{\partial\Phi}{\partial x} + \mathbf{a}_y \frac{\partial\Phi}{\partial y} + \mathbf{a}_z \frac{\partial\Phi}{\partial z} \tag{I.7}$$

$$\operatorname{div} \mathbf{A} = \nabla \cdot \mathbf{A} = \frac{\partial A_x}{\partial x} + \frac{\partial A_y}{\partial y} + \frac{\partial A_z}{\partial z} \tag{I.8}$$

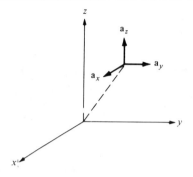

Figure I.1 Rectangular coordinate system.

$$\text{curl } \mathbf{A} = \nabla \times \mathbf{A} = \mathbf{a}_x \left(\frac{\partial A_z}{\partial y} - \frac{\partial A_y}{\partial z} \right) + \mathbf{a}_y \left(\frac{\partial A_x}{\partial z} - \frac{\partial A_z}{\partial x} \right) + \mathbf{a}_z \left(\frac{\partial A_y}{\partial x} - \frac{\partial A_x}{\partial y} \right) \quad \text{(I.9)}$$

$$\nabla^2 \Phi = \frac{\partial^2 \Phi}{\partial x^2} + \frac{\partial^2 \Phi}{\partial y^2} + \frac{\partial^2 \Phi}{\partial z^2} \quad \text{(I.10)}$$

$$\nabla^2 \mathbf{A} = \mathbf{a}_x \nabla^2 A_x + \mathbf{a}_y \nabla^2 A_y + \mathbf{a}_z \nabla^2 A_z \quad \text{(I.11)}$$

Cylindrical Coordinates (Fig. I.2)

$$\nabla \Phi = \mathbf{a}_r \frac{\partial \Phi}{\partial r} + \mathbf{a}_\phi \frac{1}{r} \frac{\partial \Phi}{\partial \phi} + \mathbf{a}_z \frac{\partial \Phi}{\partial z} \quad \text{(I.12)}$$

$$\nabla \cdot \mathbf{A} = \frac{1}{r} \frac{\partial}{\partial r} r A_r + \frac{1}{r} \frac{\partial A_\phi}{\partial \phi} + \frac{\partial A_z}{\partial z} \quad \text{(I.13)}$$

$$\nabla \times \mathbf{A} = \mathbf{a}_r \left(\frac{1}{r} \frac{\partial A_z}{\partial \phi} - \frac{\partial A_\phi}{\partial z} \right) + \mathbf{a}_\phi \left(\frac{\partial A_r}{\partial z} - \frac{\partial A_z}{\partial r} \right) + \mathbf{a}_z \left[\frac{1}{r} \frac{\partial (r A_\phi)}{\partial r} - \frac{1}{r} \frac{\partial A_r}{\partial \phi} \right] \quad \text{(I.14)}$$

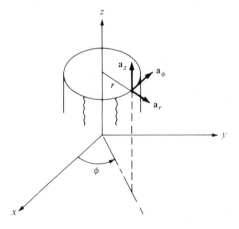

Figure I.2 Cylindrical coordinate system.

$$\nabla^2 \Phi = \frac{1}{r} \frac{\partial}{\partial r} \left(r \frac{\partial \Phi}{\partial r} \right) + \frac{1}{r^2} \frac{\partial^2 \Phi}{\partial \phi^2} + \frac{\partial^2 \Phi}{\partial z^2} \tag{I.15}$$

$$\nabla^2 \mathbf{A} = \nabla \nabla \cdot \mathbf{A} - \nabla \times \nabla \times \mathbf{A} \tag{I.16}$$

Note that $\nabla^2 \mathbf{A} \neq \mathbf{a}_r \nabla^2 A_r + \mathbf{a}_\phi \nabla^2 A_\phi + \mathbf{a}_z \nabla^2 A_z$ since $\nabla^2 \mathbf{a}_r A_r \neq \mathbf{a}_r \nabla^2 A_r$, etc., because the orientation of the unit vectors $\mathbf{a}_r$, $\mathbf{a}_\phi$ varies with the coordinates r, ϕ.

Spherical Coordinates (Fig. I.3)

$$\nabla \Phi = \mathbf{a}_r \frac{\partial \Phi}{\partial r} + \mathbf{a}_\theta \frac{1}{r} \frac{\partial \Phi}{\partial \theta} + \frac{\mathbf{a}_\phi}{r \sin \theta} \frac{\partial \Phi}{\partial \phi} \tag{I.17}$$

$$\nabla \cdot \mathbf{A} = \frac{1}{r^2} \frac{\partial}{\partial r} (r^2 A_r) + \frac{1}{r \sin \theta} \frac{\partial}{\partial \theta} (\sin \theta \, A_\theta) + \frac{1}{r \sin \theta} \frac{\partial A_\phi}{\partial \phi} \tag{I.18}$$

$$\nabla \times \mathbf{A} = \frac{\mathbf{a}_r}{r \sin \theta} \left[\frac{\partial}{\partial \theta} (A_\phi \sin \theta) - \frac{\partial A_\theta}{\partial \phi} \right] + \frac{\mathbf{a}_\theta}{r} \left(\frac{1}{\sin \theta} \frac{\partial A_r}{\partial \phi} - \frac{\partial}{\partial r} r A_\phi \right)$$

$$+ \frac{\mathbf{a}_\phi}{r} \left(\frac{\partial}{\partial r} r A_\theta - \frac{\partial A_r}{\partial \theta} \right) \tag{I.19}$$

$$\nabla^2 \Phi = \frac{1}{r^2} \frac{\partial}{\partial r} \left(r^2 \frac{\partial \Phi}{\partial r} \right) + \frac{1}{r^2 \sin \theta} \frac{\partial}{\partial \theta} \left(\sin \theta \frac{\partial \Phi}{\partial \theta} \right) + \frac{1}{r^2 \sin^2 \theta} \frac{\partial^2 \Phi}{\partial \phi^2} \tag{I.20}$$

$$\nabla^2 \mathbf{A} = \nabla \nabla \cdot \mathbf{A} - \nabla \times \nabla \times \mathbf{A} \tag{I.21}$$

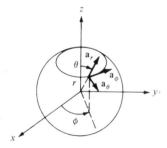

Figure I.3 Spherical coordinate system.

VECTOR IDENTITIES

$$\nabla (\Phi \psi) = \psi \nabla \Phi + \Phi \nabla \psi \tag{I.22}$$

$$\nabla \cdot \psi \mathbf{A} = \mathbf{A} \cdot \nabla \psi + \psi \nabla \cdot \mathbf{A} \tag{I.23}$$

$$\nabla \cdot (\mathbf{A} \times \mathbf{B}) = (\nabla \times \mathbf{A}) \cdot \mathbf{B} - (\nabla \times \mathbf{B}) \cdot \mathbf{A} \tag{I.24}$$

$$\nabla \times \psi \mathbf{A} = \nabla \psi \times \mathbf{A} + \psi \nabla \times \mathbf{A} \tag{I.25}$$

$$\nabla \times (\mathbf{A} \times \mathbf{B}) = \mathbf{A} \nabla \cdot \mathbf{B} - \mathbf{B} \nabla \cdot \mathbf{A} + (\mathbf{B} \cdot \nabla) \mathbf{A} - (\mathbf{A} \cdot \nabla) \mathbf{B} \tag{I.26}$$

$$\nabla(\mathbf{A} \cdot \mathbf{B}) = (\mathbf{A} \cdot \nabla)\mathbf{B} + (\mathbf{B} \cdot \nabla)\mathbf{A} + \mathbf{A} \times (\nabla \times \mathbf{B}) + \mathbf{B} \times (\nabla \times \mathbf{A}) \qquad (I.27)$$

$$\nabla \cdot \nabla \Phi = \nabla^2 \Phi \qquad (I.28)$$

$$\nabla \cdot \nabla \times \mathbf{A} = 0 \qquad (I.29)$$

$$\nabla \times \nabla \Phi = 0 \qquad (I.30)$$

$$\nabla \times \nabla \times \mathbf{A} = \nabla \nabla \cdot \mathbf{A} - \nabla^2 \mathbf{A} \qquad (I.31)$$

If $\mathbf{A}$ and Φ are continuous functions with at least piecewise continuous first derivatives in V and on S (or on S and the contour C bounding S) (Fig. I.4),

$$\int_V \nabla \Phi \, dV = \oint_S \Phi \, d\mathbf{S} \qquad (I.32)$$

$$\int_V \nabla \cdot \mathbf{A} \, dV = \oint_S \mathbf{A} \cdot d\mathbf{S} \qquad \text{divergence theorem} \qquad (I.33)$$

$$\int_V \nabla \times \mathbf{A} \, dV = \oint_S \mathbf{n} \times \mathbf{A} \, dS \qquad d\mathbf{S} = \mathbf{n} \, dS \qquad (I.34)$$

$$\int_S \mathbf{n} \times \nabla \Phi \, dS = \oint_C \Phi \, d\mathbf{l} \qquad (I.35)$$

$$\int_S \nabla \times \mathbf{A} \cdot d\mathbf{S} = \oint_C \mathbf{A} \cdot d\mathbf{l} \qquad \text{Stokes' theorem} \qquad (I.36)$$

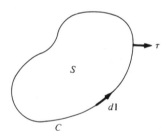

Figure I.4 Surface S with contour C.

RELATIONSHIP BETWEEN UNIT VECTORS IN RECTANGULAR AND SPHERICAL COORDINATES

$$\mathbf{a}_x = \mathbf{a}_r \sin \theta \cos \phi + \mathbf{a}_\theta \cos \theta \cos \phi - \mathbf{a}_\phi \sin \phi \qquad (I.37)$$

$$\mathbf{a}_y = \mathbf{a}_r \sin \theta \sin \phi + \mathbf{a}_\theta \cos \theta \sin \phi + \mathbf{a}_\phi \cos \phi \qquad (I.38)$$

$$\mathbf{a}_z = \mathbf{a}_r \cos \theta - \mathbf{a}_\theta \sin \theta \qquad (I.39)$$

$$\mathbf{a}_r = \mathbf{a}_x \sin \theta \cos \phi + \mathbf{a}_y \sin \theta \sin \phi + \mathbf{a}_z \cos \theta \qquad (I.40)$$

$$\mathbf{a}_\theta = \mathbf{a}_x \cos \theta \cos \phi + \mathbf{a}_y \cos \theta \sin \phi - \mathbf{a}_z \sin \theta \qquad (I.41)$$

$$\mathbf{a}_\phi = -\mathbf{a}_x \sin \phi + \mathbf{a}_y \cos \phi \qquad (I.42)$$

SUMMARY OF TRANSMISSION-LINE THEORY

Figure II.1 shows the distributed parameter-equivalent network model of a differential length dz of a two-conductor transmission line. By applying Kirchhoff's law to this network we can write, to first order in dz,

$$v - \left(v + \frac{\partial v}{\partial z}\, dz\right) = \left(iR + L\,\frac{\partial i}{\partial t}\right) dz$$

$$i - \left(i + \frac{\partial i}{\partial z}\, dz\right) = \left(vG + C\,\frac{\partial v}{\partial t}\right) dz$$

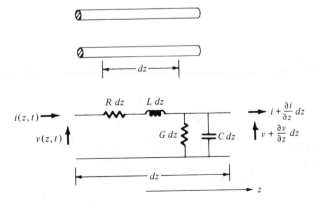

Figure II.1 Equivalent circuit for a section of transmission line.

or
$$\frac{\partial v}{\partial z} = -\left(iR + L\frac{\partial i}{\partial t}\right) \tag{II.1a}$$

$$\frac{\partial i}{\partial z} = -\left(vG + C\frac{\partial v}{\partial t}\right) \tag{II.1b}$$

where R is the series resistance per meter, L is the series inductance per meter, G is the shunt conductance per meter, and C is the shunt capacitance per meter.

For the sinusoidal steady state we can use phasor analysis to obtain

$$\frac{dV}{dz} = -(R + j\omega L)I \tag{II.2a}$$

$$\frac{dI}{dz} = -(G + j\omega C)V \tag{II.2b}$$

By forming d^2V/dz^2 and using Eq. (II.2b) to replace dI/dz we obtain

$$\frac{d^2V}{dz^2} = (R + j\omega L)(G + j\omega C)V \tag{II.3}$$

This equation has the following solution:

$$V = V^+ e^{-\gamma z} + V^- e^{\gamma z} \tag{II.4}$$

where

$$\gamma = j\beta + \alpha = \sqrt{(R + j\omega L)(G + j\omega C)}$$

The coefficients V^+ and V^- are the complex amplitudes of waves propagating in the $+z$ and $-z$ directions, respectively. For most transmission lines, $R \ll \omega L$ and $G \ll \omega C$ so that

$$\gamma \approx j\omega\sqrt{LC}\left[\left(1 + \frac{R}{2j\omega L}\right)\left(1 + \frac{G}{2j\omega C}\right)\right]$$

$$\approx j\omega\sqrt{LC} + \frac{1}{2}(R\sqrt{C/L} + G\sqrt{L/C}) \tag{II.5}$$

LOSS-FREE LINE

When $R = G = 0$ we have $\gamma = j\beta = j\omega\sqrt{LC}$. This also equals $j\omega\sqrt{\mu_0\epsilon_0} = j\omega/c = jk_0$ for an air-filled line. From Eq. (II.2a) we find that

$$I = \frac{V^+}{Z_c}e^{-j\beta z} - \frac{V^-}{Z_c}e^{j\beta z} \tag{II.6}$$

where $Z_c = \sqrt{L/C}$ and is called the *characteristic impedance* of the transmission line. For a coaxial line and a two-wire line, as shown in Fig. II.2, Z_c is given by the formulas shown in the figure.

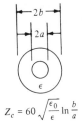

$$Z_c = 60 \sqrt{\frac{\epsilon_0}{\epsilon}} \ln \frac{b}{a}$$

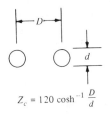

$$Z_c = 120 \cosh^{-1} \frac{D}{d}$$

Figure II.2 Two common transmission lines: (*a*) a coaxial line and (*b*) a two-conductor line.

TERMINATED TRANSMISSION LINE

Figure II.3 shows a transmission line with characteristic impedance Z_c terminated in a load impedance Z_L. The voltage and current waves on this line are given by Eqs. (II.4) and II.6); thus

$$V = V^+ e^{-j\beta z} + V^- e^{j\beta z}$$

$$I = V^+ Y_c e^{-j\beta z} - V^- Y_c e^{j\beta z} \qquad Y_c = \frac{1}{Z_c} = \sqrt{C/L}$$

At $z = 0$, the load end, we must have

$$V = V_L = V^+ + V^-$$

$$I = I_L = V^+ Y_c - V^- Y_c = \frac{V_L}{Z_L}$$

These terminal relations can be solved for the ratio V^-/V^+, that is, the amplitude of the reflected wave relative to that of the incident wave. This ratio is called the *load voltage reflection coefficient* and is given by

$$\Gamma_L = \frac{V^-}{V^+} = \frac{Z_L - Z_c}{Z_L + Z_c} \tag{II.7}$$

If $Z_L = Z_c$, then Γ_L is zero and the load is said to be matched to the transmission line. When Γ_L is nonzero, we will have a partial standing wave on

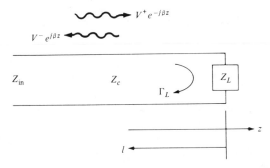

Figure II.3 A terminated transmission line.

the line. This manifests itself as a variation in the magnitude of the voltage along the line. The maximum voltage on the line will be $|V^+| + |V^-|$, while the minimum voltage on the line will be $|V^+| - |V^-|$ and occurs when the incident and reflected voltage waves add in phase or out of phase, respectively. The voltage standing wave ratio (VSWR) is given by

$$\text{VSWR} = \frac{|V^+| + |V^-|}{|V^+| - |V^-|} = \frac{1 + |V^-/V^+|}{1 - |V^-/V^+|} = \frac{1 + |\Gamma_L|}{1 - |\Gamma_L|} \qquad \text{(II.8)}$$

At a distance l from the load, that is, where $z = -l$, the line voltage and current are given by

$$V(l) = V^+ e^{j\beta l} + V^- e^{-j\beta l}$$

$$= V^+ (e^{j\beta l} + \Gamma_L e^{-j\beta l})$$

$$I(l) = V^+ Y_c (e^{j\beta l} - \Gamma_L e^{-j\beta l})$$

The reflection coefficient at this point on the line is

$$\Gamma(l) = \frac{V^- e^{-j\beta l}}{V^+ e^{j\beta l}} = \Gamma_L e^{-2j\beta l} \qquad \text{(II.9)}$$

The ratio $V(l)/I(l)$ gives the input impedance Z_{in} looking toward the load and is

$$Z_{in} = \frac{1 + \Gamma}{1 - \Gamma} Z_c = \frac{1 + \Gamma_L e^{-2j\beta l}}{1 - \Gamma_L e^{-2j\beta l}} Z_c \qquad \text{(II.10}a\text{)}$$

which can also be expressed in the form

$$Z_{in} = Z_c \frac{Z_L + jZ_c \tan \beta l}{Z_c + jZ_L \tan \beta l} \qquad \text{(II.10}b\text{)}$$

by using Eq. (II.7) to replace Γ_L in terms of Z_L and noting that $e^{-j\beta l} = \cos \beta l - j \sin \beta l$.

CYLINDRICAL DIPOLE ANTENNA MODELS

The purpose of this appendix is to examine briefly various mathematical models that are used to represent a dipole antenna and the transmission-line feed system. The objective is to introduce a mathematical model that is easier to analyze than the real physical system is and yet will give reasonably accurate results for the input impedance, current distribution, and radiation field.

Figure III.1*a* through *d* shows four different ways of connecting a dipole antenna to a transmission line. The first arrangement is the use of a two-conductor transmission line. The electric field lines of the TEM mode on the transmission line are also shown. This applied field is highly concentrated near the center of the dipole antenna. The induced current on the antenna will produce a scattered electric field that cancels the tangential component of the applied field along the assumed perfectly conducting surface of the antenna. The antenna current flows from the two halves of the antenna onto the transmission-line conductors at the feed points.

In Fig. III.1*b* the antenna is the continuation of the center conductor of a coaxial transmission line above a ground plane. In the absence of the antenna the applied electric field is again highly concentrated near the input to the antenna, as shown in the figure.

In Fig. III.1*c* the dipole antenna is excited by a source and coaxial line feed that is placed internally to the dipole outer surface. The fringing electric field at the gap opening constitutes the applied electric field.

In Fig. III.1*d* the dipole antenna is coupled to the transmission line by mutual inductance. A variation of this feed system is to connect the antenna, which is a continuous rod, directly to the transmission line as shown. For impedance-matching purposes the transmission line may be flared into a delta section or a tee section which gives rise to the so-called delta-match and tee-match feed systems.

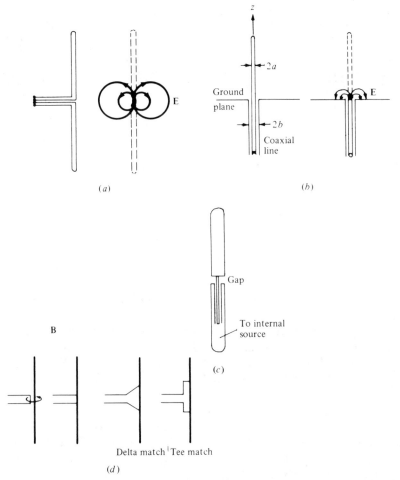

Figure III.1 Various methods of coupling a dipole antenna to the transmission line: (*a*) two-conductor transmission line; (*b*) coaxial-line-driven monopole antenna; (*c*) internal-coaxial-line-driven antenna; (*d*) inductive coupling, including the delta-match and tee-match feed systems.

The various arrangements described above have the general property that the applied electric field is highly concentrated near the center of the antenna and that there is a path for the antenna current on each half of the antenna to flow either onto the feed line itself or continuously along the antenna, as in the inductive coupling arrangements. A mathematical model of the dipole antenna should preserve these two general features.

From a practical point of view the antenna input impedance is the input impedance measured on the transmission line several half-wavelengths away from the antenna, so that the voltage and current on the line are those due to the incident and reflected TEM modes. This impedance is generally somewhat different from the ratio of the voltage across the transmission line to the current on the transmission line at the feed point because of the perturbation of the TEM mode fields caused by the antenna. The mathematical models that are used to replace the antenna and feed line by an antenna excited by means of some other simpler source or an idealized applied field do not take this perturbation of the field into account.

The arrangement shown in Fig. III.1b is readily formulated as a boundary-value problem that can be solved to as high a degree of accuracy as desired. The unknown radial electric field at the coaxial line opening can be thought of as equivalent to a magnetic current sheet $\mathbf{J}_{ms} = -\mathbf{a}_z \times \mathbf{a}_r E_r$ in the coaxial line aperture. By using image theory the field above the ground plane can be found from the electric currents flowing on the full antenna as excited by the disk of magnetic current $2\mathbf{J}_{ms}$ located at the center, as shown in Fig. III.2a. The field in the coaxial line can be expanded in terms of the incident and reflected TEM modes, plus higher-order TM modes in the coaxial line. The amplitudes of

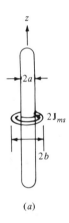

(a)

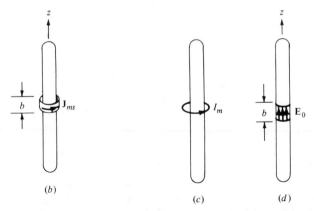

(b)

(c)

(d)

Figure III.2 (a) Equivalent dipole antenna excited by a disk of magnetic current. (b) Antenna excited by a short cylinder of magnetic current. (c) Antenna excited by a single-turn magnetic current loop. (d) Antenna excited by a uniform applied electric field.

these modes can be expressed in terms of the magnetic current $\mathbf{J}_{ms}$. The unknown electric current $\mathbf{J}_{es}$ on the antenna is determined by solving an integral equation obtained by setting the tangential electric field obtained from $\mathbf{J}_{es}$ equal to the negative of that produced by the magnetic current $\mathbf{J}_{ms}$ on the antenna surface. An integral equation for $\mathbf{J}_{ms}$ can be obtained by requiring that the total magnetic field H_ϕ above the ground plane be equal to that in the coaxial line at the aperture opening. These two integral equations are coupled. In order to simplify the problem it is usually assumed that the higher-order modes in the coaxial line have a negligible amplitude. In this case the field in the coaxial line is that of the TEM mode alone and at the opening has the form $E_r = V/(r \ln b/a)$, where V is the total voltage and a and b are the inner and outer radii, respectively, of the coaxial transmission line. With this assumption the magnetic current $\mathbf{J}_{ms}$ is known, and the resultant mathematical model is that of a continuous antenna rod driven by a disk of known magnetic current $2\mathbf{J}_{ms}$. The electric field produced by the magnetic-current disk-shaped loop can be calculated as though the current acts in free space and is highly concentrated along the center of the antenna.

The electric field produced by the induced antenna currents $\mathbf{J}_{es}$ on the antenna is made to cancel the tangential component of the applied field along the surface of the antenna. The imposition of this boundary condition leads to the integral equation for $\mathbf{J}_{es}$. The integral equation is often simplified by neglecting the current on the end caps of the antenna and by assuming that the current is concentrated along the axis. These approximations are not necessary, although they are often useful and valid for the case of thin antennas. The antenna impedance is taken as the ratio of V to the total antenna current at the center, and V is equal to I_m, the total magnetic current on the disk. This is an approximate value for the impedance, since it does not include the effects of the higher-order modes in the coaxial line. A thorough investigation of the effects of these higher-order modes on the antenna impedance does not seem to have been carried out even though this would not be very difficult to do with the currently available high-speed, high-capacity computers.

The theory shows that the computed antenna impedance is not sensitive to the actual nature of the applied field as long as it is concentrated over a small region near the center of the antenna. Thus, instead of a disk of magnetic current, a short cylinder of magnetic current of length b or even a single loop of magnetic current coaxial along a circle, as shown in Fig. III.2b and c, could be used as a source to excite the antenna. The applied field from these loops of magnetic current is very nearly the same as that from the disk of magnetic current. The total magnetic current I_m is considered equal to the applied voltage, as in the case of the disk of magnetic current.

A further simplification is obtained by assuming that the antenna is excited by an applied electric field that is uniform and in the axial direction and acts along the surface of the antenna over a band of length b at the center, as shown in Fig. III.2d. If E_0 is the applied electric field, then the applied voltage is bE_0. This model has the advantage that the applied field itself is specified, so the step of calculating the applied field from a magnetic current loop is eliminated. The disadvantage of the model shows up if the band length b is made vanishingly small and the applied field is assumed to be a delta-function field $V\delta(z)$, since the integral equation will then give a current with a logarithmic singularity at the source point if the integral equation is solved exactly. However, as long as b is kept finite, this model is just as valid as those based on magnetic current loops and gives essentially the same values for the antenna impedance. The uniform applied field model is the one used in the text in Chap. 2.

Some care must be exercised in formulating the integral equation for the induced current on the antenna so that it conforms with the model being analyzed. For example, with the antenna driven by a cylinder of magnetic current of length b and adjacent to the antenna surface, as in Fig. III.2b, the total tangential electric field equals J_{ms} over the region $-b/2 \le z \le b/2$ on the exterior of the magnetic current sheet and equals zero along the remaining surface of the antenna. The total electric field is produced by $\mathbf{J}_{ms}$ and the induced electric current $\mathbf{J}_{es}$ flowing on the antenna. Thus it is incorrect to impose the above boundary condition on the partial electric field produced by $\mathbf{J}_{es}$ alone. If the latter is done, the resultant integral equation applies to the model in which the excitation of the antenna is due to an applied uniform electric field of strength $-J_{ms}$ and acting over a band of length b. This model, as noted earlier, is acceptable, but it is not that of an antenna driven by a cylinder of magnetic current.

Some authors model the dipole antenna as an antenna with a physical gap of length b, as shown in Fig. III.3. It is then assumed that somehow a uniform applied electric field can be made to act across this gap, say, $-E_0\mathbf{a}_z$. The applied voltage is $V = bE_0$. This is a well-posed boundary-value problem, since it corresponds to knowing the tangential electric field everywhere on a closed surface S adjacent to and surrounding the antenna. This field is zero everywhere on the perfectly conducting antenna surface, and, on the cylindrical

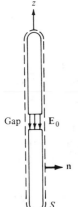

Figure III.3 A dipole antenna with a specified electric field applied across the gap.

surface of the gap, it equals the given applied field. The problem is now that of solving for the total electric field subject to these boundary conditions and a radiation condition at infinity. The problem has a unique solution.

The tangential magnetic field at the antenna surface is related to the induced electric current $\mathbf{J}_{es}$ by the relation $\mathbf{n} \times \mathbf{H} = \mathbf{J}_{es}$, where $\mathbf{n}$ is a unit normal directed away from the antenna surface. At the gap, $\mathbf{n} \times \mathbf{H}$ has some value which cannot in general be related to an electric current, which, of course, cannot flow across the gap.

If a vector potential function $\mathbf{A}_e$ is found in terms of the tangential values of $\mathbf{H}$ by means of the usual formula ($\mathbf{n} \times \mathbf{H}$ is equivalent to a current source)

$$\mathbf{A}_e(\mathbf{r}) = \frac{\mu_0}{4\pi} \oint_S \mathbf{n} \times \mathbf{H}(\mathbf{r}') \frac{e^{-jk_0|\mathbf{r}-\mathbf{r}'|}}{|\mathbf{r}-\mathbf{r}'|} \, dS'$$

a corresponding electric field may be found using

$$\mathbf{E}(\mathbf{r}) = -j\omega \mathbf{A}_e(\mathbf{r}) + \frac{\nabla\nabla \cdot \mathbf{A}_e(\mathbf{r})}{j\omega\epsilon_0\mu_0}$$

If the boundary conditions on the surface enclosing the antenna and gap are imposed on this electric field, then the resultant integral equation for the tangential values of $\mathbf{H}$ (induced current) is not the correct one for the postulated model. The integral equation is, in fact, that for a solid rod to which an applied electric field $E_0\mathbf{a}_z$ has been imposed over a cylindrical band of length b.

The electric field can be found in terms of its tangential values on the closed surface S by first finding an appropriate Green's dyadic function that is a solution of the equation

$$\nabla \times \nabla \times \bar{\mathbf{G}} - k_0^2\bar{\mathbf{G}} = -\bar{\mathbf{I}}\delta(\mathbf{r}-\mathbf{r}')$$

where $\bar{\mathbf{I}}$ is a unit dyadic and $\bar{\mathbf{G}}$ satisfies the radiation condition at infinity and the boundary condition $\mathbf{n} \times \bar{\mathbf{G}} = 0$ on S. The solution is given by†

$$\mathbf{E}(\mathbf{r}) = -\oint_S \mathbf{n} \times \mathbf{E}(\mathbf{r}') \cdot \nabla' \times \bar{\mathbf{G}} \, dS'$$

The determination of $\mathbf{G}$ is difficult, except for special situations such as when the surface S is a spherical surface. In this case $\bar{\mathbf{G}}$ can be found in terms of an eigenfunction expansion involving vector wave solutions in spherical coordinates.

The field-equivalence principle states that the field outside S can be found in terms of equivalent currents $\mathbf{J}_{es} = \mathbf{n} \times \mathbf{H}$ and $\mathbf{J}_{ms} = -\mathbf{n} \times \mathbf{E}$ placed on the closed surface S and radiating in free space. This problem can be formulated and the

---

† R. E. Collin, *Field Theory of Guided Waves*, McGraw-Hill Book Company, New York, 1960, Chap. 2, Eq. (70).

unknown quantity $\mathbf{n} \times \mathbf{H}$ must then be determined by solving an integral equation obtained by requiring that $\mathbf{n} \times \mathbf{E}$ satisfy the prescribed values on the closed surface S. But this problem is now fully equivalent to that of a solid antenna rod driven by a cylinder of magnetic current, so the physical gap originally postulated has no real relevance to the boundary-value problem as posed. The specified total electric field across the gap can be viewed as being maintained by a cylinder of magnetic current placed just outside a solid continuous antenna rod. A model with a real physical gap present requires some condition or statement to be made about the nature of the field within the gap volume. An example of an antenna that presents a gap structure is that shown in Fig. III.1c. The field from the coaxial line feed within the gap would have to be included if the physical effects of the gap are to be properly taken into account. When the electric field across the gap at the outer radius is specified a priori, then the existence of the gap is irrelevant. The author is of the opinion that the gap should not be introduced at all since it tends to confuse the mathematical nature of the boundary-value problem that is being posed.

Wu and King develop a mathematical model that is equivalent to exciting the antenna by a concentrated loop of magnetic current, as in Fig. II.2c. However, they express the electric field from the magnetic current loop in terms of the field produced by an equivalent disk of uniform z-directed electric current elements.† The equivalence of these two sources is demonstrated below.

Consider a disk of radius a and thickness b in which a uniform distribution of z-directed electric current $J_e \mathbf{a}_z$ exists, as in Fig. III.4a. The electric field outside the source region can be expressed in terms of the vector potential $\mathbf{A}_e$

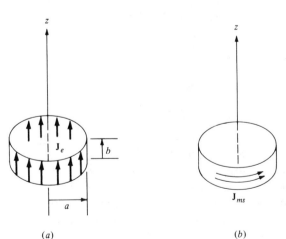

z

z

J_e b

a

J_{ms}

(a) (b)

Figure III.4 (a) A disk of uniform z-directed electric current. (b) Equivalent cylinder of magnetic current.

† J. J. Wu and R. W. P. King, "The Thick Tubular Transmitting Antenna," *Radio Science*, vol. 2, 1967, pp. 1061–1065.

by means of the relation

$$j\omega\epsilon_0\mu_0\mathbf{E}(\mathbf{r}) = \nabla \times \nabla \times \mathbf{A}_e(\mathbf{r})$$

Hence we have

$$j\omega\epsilon_0\mu_0\mathbf{E}(\mathbf{r}) = \nabla \times \int_V \nabla \times \mathbf{J}_e(\mathbf{r}')g(\mathbf{r}, \mathbf{r}')\, dV'$$

where

$$g = \frac{e^{-jk_0 R}}{4\pi R} \qquad R = |\mathbf{r} - \mathbf{r}'|$$

Now

$$\nabla \times \mathbf{J}_e(\mathbf{r}')g = -\nabla' \times g\mathbf{J}_e(\mathbf{r}') + g\nabla' \times \mathbf{J}_e(\mathbf{r}')$$
$$= -\nabla' \times g\mathbf{J}_e(\mathbf{r}')$$

since $\nabla' \times \mathbf{J}_e(\mathbf{r}') = 0$ because $\mathbf{J}_e$ is constant. We now find that

$$j\omega\epsilon_0\mu_0\mathbf{E}(\mathbf{r}) = -\nabla \times \int_V \nabla' \times g\mathbf{J}_e(\mathbf{r}')\, dV'$$

$$= \nabla \times \oint_S g\mathbf{J}_e \times \mathbf{n}\, dS'$$

by using a standard vector integral transformation. When we compare this expression with the electric field from a surface layer of magnetic current, that is,

$$\mathbf{E}(\mathbf{r}) = -\nabla \times \oint_S g\mathbf{J}_{ms}(\mathbf{r}')\, dS'$$

we see that the field outside the source region is the same, provided

$$\mathbf{J}_e \times \mathbf{n} = -j\omega\mu_0\epsilon_0\mathbf{J}_{ms}$$

For the postulated current $\mathbf{J}_e$ we find that $\mathbf{J}_e \times \mathbf{n} = 0$ on the two faces and equals $J_e\mathbf{a}_\phi$ along the outer cylindrical surface, as shown in Fig. III.4b. Hence a cylinder of azimuthally directed magnetic current is equivalent to a disk of uniform z-directed electric current. There is a surface of positive and negative electric charge that terminates the current $\mathbf{J}_e$ on the two faces. This double layer of charge gives rise to the discontinuity of the scalar potential in the Wu-King theory. When the above equivalence is taken into account the Wu-King theory can be interpreted as that of an antenna excited by a magnetic current loop.

GEOMETRICAL OR RAY OPTICS

Ray tracing and the transport of the electric and magnetic fields along ray tubes are important concepts in the analysis of waves propagating in an in-homogeneous atmosphere or ionosphere and also in determining approximate values for the aperture field in reflector- and lens-type antenna systems. Geometrical optics is generally a valid approximation when the index of refraction changes very little over a distance that is large compared with the wavelength and when the antenna apertures are many wavelengths in size. Geometrical or ray optics theory can be derived from Maxwell's equations as an asymptotic solution obtained in the limit as the frequency approaches infinity. The theory is developed by assuming that the fields can be expanded as a power series in inverse powers of the radian frequency ω. The basic elements of this theory are presented in this appendix. For a more detailed treatment, the book by Kline and Kay is recommended.[†]

RAY OPTICS FORMULAS IN ISOTROPIC MEDIA

We assume that a monochromatic field has an asymptotic series expansion in terms of inverse powers of ω as follows:

$$\mathbf{E}(\mathbf{r}) = \sum_{m=0}^{\infty} \frac{\mathbf{E}_m(\mathbf{r})}{(j\omega)^m} e^{-jk_0 L(\mathbf{r})} \qquad (IV.1a)$$

$$\mathbf{H}(\mathbf{r}) = \sum_{m=0}^{\infty} \frac{\mathbf{H}_m(\mathbf{r})}{(j\omega)^m} e^{-jk_0 L(\mathbf{r})} \qquad (IV.1b)$$

[†] M. Kline and I. W. Kay, *Electromagnetic Theory and Geometrical Optics*, Interscience Publishers, John Wiley & Sons, Inc., New York, 1965.

where $k_0 = \omega \sqrt{\mu_0 \varepsilon_0}$ but the medium is allowed to have electrical parameters ϵ, μ which are functions of x, y, and z. Maxwell's equations $\nabla \times \mathbf{E} = -j\omega\mu\,\mathbf{H}$, $\nabla \times \mathbf{H} = j\omega\epsilon\,\mathbf{E}$, $\nabla \cdot \mathbf{D} = 0$, $\nabla \cdot \mathbf{B} = 0$ give

$$\sum_{m=0}^{\infty} \left[\frac{\nabla \times \mathbf{E}_m}{(j\omega)^m} + \frac{jk_0 \mathbf{E}_m \times \nabla L}{(j\omega)^m} \right] e^{-jk_0 L} = \sum_{m=0}^{\infty} \frac{-j\omega\mu\,\mathbf{H}_m}{(j\omega)^m} \tag{IV.2a}$$

$$\sum_{m=0}^{\infty} \left[\frac{\nabla \times \mathbf{H}_m}{(j\omega)^m} + \frac{jk_0 \mathbf{H}_m \times \nabla L}{(j\omega)^m} \right] e^{-jk_0 L} = \sum_{m=0}^{\infty} \frac{j\omega\epsilon\,\mathbf{E}_m}{(j\omega)^m} \tag{IV.2b}$$

$$\sum_{m=0}^{\infty} \left[\frac{\epsilon\nabla \cdot \mathbf{E}_m}{(j\omega)^m} - \frac{jk_0\epsilon\,\mathbf{E}_m \cdot \nabla L}{(j\omega)^m} + \frac{\mathbf{E}_m \cdot \nabla\epsilon}{(j\omega)^m} \right] e^{-jk_0 L} = 0 \tag{IV.2c}$$

$$\sum_{m=0}^{\infty} \left[\frac{\mu\nabla \cdot \mathbf{H}_m}{(j\omega)^m} - \frac{jk_0\mu\,\mathbf{H}_m \cdot \nabla L}{(j\omega)^m} + \frac{\mathbf{H}_m \cdot \nabla\mu}{(j\omega)^m} \right] e^{-jk_0 L} = 0 \tag{IV.2d}$$

We now equate coefficients of like powers in ω. From Eq. (IV.2a) the equations obtained by equating the terms in ω and the constant terms are

$$k_0 \mathbf{E}_0 \times \nabla L = -\omega\mu\,\mathbf{H}_0 \tag{IV.3a}$$

$$\nabla \times \mathbf{E}_0 + \frac{k_0}{\omega} \mathbf{E}_1 \times \nabla L = -\mu\,\mathbf{H}_1 \tag{IV.3b}$$

The corresponding terms obtained from Eq. (IV.2b) are

$$k_0 \mathbf{H}_0 \times \nabla L = \omega\epsilon\,\mathbf{E}_0 \tag{IV.4a}$$

$$\nabla \times \mathbf{H}_0 + \frac{k_0}{\omega} \mathbf{H}_1 \times \nabla L = \epsilon\,\mathbf{E}_1 \tag{IV.4b}$$

while from Eq. (IV.2c) we obtain

$$-jk_0\epsilon\,\mathbf{E}_0 \cdot \nabla L = 0 \tag{IV.5a}$$

$$\epsilon\nabla \cdot \mathbf{E}_0 - \frac{k_0}{\omega}\epsilon\,\mathbf{E}_1 \cdot \nabla L + \mathbf{E}_0 \cdot \nabla\epsilon = 0 \tag{IV.5b}$$

Similarly Eq. (IV.2d) gives

$$-jk_0\mu\,\mathbf{H}_0 \cdot \nabla L = 0 \tag{IV.6a}$$

$$\mu\nabla \cdot \mathbf{H}_0 - \frac{k_0}{\omega}\mu\,\mathbf{H}_1 \cdot \nabla L + \mathbf{H}_0 \cdot \nabla\mu = 0 \tag{IV.6b}$$

The 0th order equations describe the geometrical optics field. These are

$$\mathbf{E}_0 \times \nabla L = -\frac{\omega\mu}{k_0} \mathbf{H}_0 \tag{IV.7a}$$

$$\mathbf{H}_0 \times \nabla L = \frac{\omega\epsilon}{k_0} \mathbf{E}_0 \tag{IV.7b}$$

$$\mathbf{E}_0 \cdot \nabla L = 0 \tag{IV.7c}$$

$$\mathbf{H}_0 \cdot \nabla L = 0 \tag{IV.7d}$$

The vectors $\mathbf{E}_0$, $\mathbf{H}_0$, and ∇L are mutually perpendicular. The phase fronts are given by the surfaces $L = \text{constant}$, if L is real, and by $\text{Re } L = \text{constant}$ for complex L.

The complex Poynting vector is given by [we use Eq. (IV.7a) for $\mathbf{H}_0$]

$$\mathbf{E}_0 \times \mathbf{H}_0^* \, e^{-jk_0(L-L^*)} = \mathbf{E}_0 \times \left(-\frac{k_0}{\omega\mu^*} \mathbf{E}_0^* \times \nabla L^* \right) e^{-jk_0(L-L^*)}$$

$$= \frac{k_0}{\omega\mu^*} (\mathbf{E}_0 \cdot \mathbf{E}_0^*)\nabla L^* \, e^{-jk_0(L-L^*)} \tag{IV.8}$$

and is in the direction of $\mu \nabla L^*$. The power flow is in the direction of ∇L when L is real and this is the ray direction. For lossy media let $\epsilon = \epsilon' - j\epsilon''$, $\mu = \mu' - j\mu''$, and $L = L_r - jL_i$. Then the real part of Eq. (IV.8) is

$$\text{Re } \mathbf{E}_0 \times \mathbf{H}_0^* = \frac{k_0}{\mu\mu^*} (\mathbf{E}_0 \cdot \mathbf{E}_0^*) \, e^{-2k_0 L_i}(\mu' \nabla L_r - \mu'' \nabla L_i) \tag{IV.9}$$

which serves to define the ray direction in lossy media. From Eq. (IV.7a),

$$\nabla L \times (\mathbf{E}_0 \times \nabla L) = (\nabla L \cdot \nabla L)\mathbf{E}_0 - (\nabla L \cdot \mathbf{E}_0)\nabla L$$

$$= (\nabla L \cdot \nabla L)\mathbf{E}_0 = -\frac{\omega\mu}{k_0} \nabla L \times \mathbf{H}_0 = \frac{\omega^2\mu\epsilon}{k_0^2} \mathbf{E}_0$$

upon using Eq. (IV.7c) and (IV.7b). Hence

$$\nabla L \cdot \nabla L = n^2 = \frac{\mu\epsilon}{\mu_0\epsilon_0} \tag{IV.10}$$

This is called the *eikonal equation*, and L is called the *eikonal function*. A solution of Eq. (IV.10) determines the eikonal function and hence the ray directions and the wave fronts.

The transport equations for $\mathbf{E}_0$, $\mathbf{H}_0$ cannot be found from Eq. (IV.7); these lead only to the eikonal equation. The equation for $\mathbf{E}$ is obtained as follows:

$$\nabla \times \nabla \times \mathbf{E} = \nabla\nabla \cdot \mathbf{E} - \nabla^2\mathbf{E} = \nabla \times (-j\omega\mu\mathbf{H})$$

$$= -j\omega\mu \nabla \times \mathbf{H} + j\omega\mathbf{H} \times \nabla\mu = \omega^2\epsilon\mu\mathbf{E} + j\omega\mathbf{H} \times \nabla\mu$$

$$= n^2 k_0^2\mathbf{E} + \frac{\nabla\mu}{\mu} \times \nabla \times \mathbf{E}$$

or

$$\nabla^2\mathbf{E} - \nabla\nabla \cdot \mathbf{E} + n^2 k_0^2\mathbf{E} + \nabla \ln \mu \times \nabla \times \mathbf{E} = 0 \tag{IV.11}$$

We now use the expansion (IV.1) and equate coefficients of like powers of ω.

We then get

$$\nabla^2 \mathbf{E} = \nabla \cdot \nabla \mathbf{E} = \sum_{m=0}^{\infty} \left\{ -jk_0 \nabla L \cdot \left[-jk_0 \nabla L \frac{\mathbf{E}_m}{(j\omega)^m} + \frac{\nabla \mathbf{E}_m}{(j\omega)^m} \right] \right.$$

$$\left. - jk_0 \nabla^2 L \frac{\mathbf{E}_m}{(j\omega)^m} - jk_0 \nabla L \cdot \frac{\nabla \mathbf{E}_m}{(j\omega)^m} + \frac{\nabla^2 \mathbf{E}_m}{(j\omega)^m} \right\} e^{-jk_0 L}$$

$$\nabla\nabla \cdot \mathbf{E} = \sum_{m=0}^{\infty} \left\{ -jk_0 \nabla L \left[-jk_0 \frac{\nabla L \cdot \mathbf{E}_m}{(j\omega)^m} + \frac{\nabla \cdot \mathbf{E}_m}{(j\omega)^m} \right] - \frac{jk_0}{(j\omega)^m} \nabla(\nabla L \cdot \mathbf{E}_m) \right.$$

$$\left. + \frac{\nabla\nabla \cdot \mathbf{E}_m}{(j\omega)^m} \right\} e^{-jk_0 L}$$

and $\nabla \times \mathbf{E}$ is given by the left-hand side of Eq. (IV.2a). By using these expansions in Eq. (IV.11) we find that the terms in ω^2 give

$$-k_0^2(\nabla L \cdot \mathbf{E}_0)\nabla L - k_0^2(\nabla L \cdot \nabla L)\mathbf{E}_0 + n^2 k_0^2 \mathbf{E}_0 = 0$$

or

$$\nabla L \cdot \nabla L = n^2$$

while the terms in ω yield the result

$$\frac{jk_0^2}{\omega}(\nabla L \cdot \nabla L)\mathbf{E}_1 - jk_0 \nabla L \cdot \nabla \mathbf{E}_0 - jk_0 \nabla^2 L \mathbf{E}_0 - jk_0 \nabla L \cdot \nabla \mathbf{E}_0 - \frac{jk_0^2}{\omega} \nabla L \nabla L \cdot \mathbf{E}_1$$

$$+ jk_0 \nabla L \nabla \cdot \mathbf{E}_0 + jk_0 \nabla(\nabla L \cdot \mathbf{E}_0) - \frac{jn^2 k_0^2}{\omega} \mathbf{E}_1 + jk_0 \nabla \ln \mu \, (\mathbf{E}_0 \times \nabla L) = 0$$

By using Eq. (IV.5b) this expression can be written as

$$\tfrac{1}{2}\mathbf{E}_0 \nabla^2 L + \nabla L \cdot \nabla \mathbf{E}_0 - \tfrac{1}{2}\nabla \ln \mu \times (\mathbf{E}_0 \times \nabla L) + \tfrac{1}{2}\mathbf{E}_0 \cdot \nabla \ln \epsilon \nabla L = 0$$

which may also be written in the form

$$(\nabla L \cdot \nabla)\mathbf{E}_0 + \tfrac{1}{2}(\nabla^2 L)\mathbf{E}_0 + (\mathbf{E}_0 \cdot \nabla \ln n)\nabla L - \tfrac{1}{2}(\nabla L \cdot \nabla \ln \mu)\mathbf{E}_0 = 0 \quad \text{(IV.12)}$$

upon using $\nabla \ln \mu \times (\mathbf{E}_0 \times \nabla L) = (\nabla \ln \mu \cdot \nabla L)\mathbf{E}_0 - (\mathbf{E}_0 \cdot \nabla \ln \mu)\nabla L$ and $\nabla \ln \mu + \nabla \ln \epsilon = \nabla \ln n^2 = 2\nabla \ln n$. In a similar way we find that $\mathbf{H}_0$ satisfies the equation (replace $\mathbf{E}_0$ by $\mathbf{H}_0$ and μ by ϵ)

$$(\nabla L \cdot \nabla)\mathbf{H}_0 + \tfrac{1}{2}(\nabla^2 L)\mathbf{H}_0 + (\mathbf{H}_0 \cdot \nabla \ln n)\nabla L - \tfrac{1}{2}(\nabla L \cdot \nabla \ln \epsilon)\mathbf{H}_0 = 0 \quad \text{(IV.13)}$$

Later on we will cast these equations into a more meaningful form.

From this point on we will call the direction of ∇L the ray direction, even though in lossy media it may not coincide with the direction of the Poynting vector. We now define a unit vector $\mathbf{s}$ by

$$\frac{\nabla L}{\sqrt{\nabla L \cdot \nabla L}} = \frac{\nabla L}{n} = \mathbf{s} \quad \text{(IV.14)}$$

From Eq. (IV.7a) we then find that

$$\mathbf{H}_0 = \frac{k_0}{\omega\mu} n\mathbf{s} \times \mathbf{E}_0 = Y\mathbf{s} \times \mathbf{E}_0 \qquad Y = \sqrt{\frac{\epsilon}{\mu}} \tag{IV.15}$$

Thus the geometric optics field satisfies the usual plane-wave relationship between $\mathbf{E}$, $\mathbf{H}$, and $\mathbf{s}$, since from Eqs. (IV.7c), (IV.7d), and (IV.14) we also have $\mathbf{s} \cdot \mathbf{E}_0 = \mathbf{s} \cdot \mathbf{H}_0 = 0$. However, in lossy media $\mathbf{s}$ may be complex.

In the preceding derivations we have assumed that ϵ and μ are not functions of ω. In physical media this is not true. We can circumvent this difficulty by replacing the physical medium by a fictitious medium having constant (ω independent) values of ϵ, μ, with the latter chosen to have values corresponding to those for the physical medium in the vicinity of the frequency ω, for which we are evaluating the geometrical optics field.

RAY OPTICS FORMULAS IN HOMOGENEOUS, ISOTROPIC, LOSSLESS MEDIA

For homogeneous, isotropic, lossless media the equations to be solved are

$$\nabla L \cdot \nabla L = n^2 = \frac{\epsilon\mu}{\epsilon_0\mu_0} \tag{IV.16a}$$

$$(\nabla L \cdot \nabla)\mathbf{E}_0 + \tfrac{1}{2}(\nabla^2 L)\mathbf{E}_0 = 0 \tag{IV.16b}$$

$$\mathbf{H}_0 = Y\mathbf{s} \times \mathbf{E}_0 \tag{IV.16c}$$

where $\mathbf{s} = \nabla L/n$. For lossless media

$$\mathbf{E}_0 \times \mathbf{H}_0^* = \frac{k_0}{\omega\mu}(\mathbf{E}_0 \cdot \mathbf{E}_0^*)\nabla L = Y(\mathbf{E}_0 \cdot \mathbf{E}_0^*)\mathbf{s}$$

Now $\nabla L \cdot \nabla = n(\nabla L/n) \cdot \nabla = n\mathbf{s} \cdot \nabla = n d/ds$ is the directional derivative along the ray. Hence Eq. (IV.16a) and (IV.16b) become

$$\frac{dL}{ds} = n \tag{IV.17a}$$

$$n\frac{d\mathbf{E}_0}{ds} + \tfrac{1}{2}(\nabla^2 L)\mathbf{E}_0 = 0 \tag{IV.17b}$$

The integration of Eq. (IV.17) along the ray path gives

$$L(s) = L(s_0) + \int_{s_0}^{s} n\,ds = L(s_0) + n(s - s_0) \tag{IV.18a}$$

$$\mathbf{E}_0(s) = \mathbf{E}_0(s_0)\exp{-\tfrac{1}{2}\int_{s_0}^{s} \frac{\nabla^2 L}{n}\,ds} \tag{IV.18b}$$

From Fig. IV.1, we find by similar triangles that

$$\frac{|ds|}{ds} = \frac{ds}{\rho}$$

so

$$\frac{ds}{ds} = \frac{\mathbf{n}_p}{\rho} = \mathbf{s} \cdot \nabla \mathbf{s} \tag{IV.19}$$

where ρ is the ray radius of curvature and $\mathbf{n}_p$ is a unit inward normal to the ray path. Consider $\mathbf{s} \times (\nabla \times \mathbf{s})$ and use $\mathbf{A} \times (\nabla \times \mathbf{B}) = \nabla_B(\mathbf{A} \cdot \mathbf{B}) - \mathbf{A} \cdot \nabla \mathbf{B} = \frac{1}{2}\nabla \mathbf{A}^2 - \mathbf{A} \cdot \nabla \mathbf{A}$, when $\mathbf{A} = \mathbf{B}$ to obtain $\mathbf{s} \times (\nabla \times \mathbf{s}) = \frac{1}{2}\nabla \mathbf{s} \cdot \mathbf{s} - \mathbf{s} \cdot \nabla \mathbf{s} = -\mathbf{s} \cdot \nabla \mathbf{s}$, since $\mathbf{s} \cdot \mathbf{s} = 1$. Thus

$$\frac{\mathbf{n}_p}{\rho} = -\mathbf{s} \times (\nabla \times \mathbf{s}) \tag{IV.20}$$

which shows that $\mathbf{n}_p$ is perpendicular to $\mathbf{s}$. We also have

$$\frac{\mathbf{n}_p}{\rho} = -\mathbf{s} \times \left(\nabla \times \frac{\nabla L}{n}\right) = -\mathbf{s} \times \left(\nabla \frac{1}{n} \times \nabla L\right) = -\mathbf{s} \times \left(\frac{\nabla L}{n} \times \nabla \ln n\right)$$

$$= -(\mathbf{s} \cdot \nabla \ln n)\mathbf{s} + \nabla \ln n$$

Consequently, since $\mathbf{n}_p \cdot \mathbf{s} = 0$, we get

$$\frac{1}{\rho} = \mathbf{n}_p \cdot \frac{ds}{ds} = \mathbf{n}_p \cdot \nabla \ln n \tag{IV.21}$$

This equation shows that when n is constant $1/\rho = 0$; that is, the rays have zero curvature (are straight lines).

Evaluation of $\nabla^2 L$

At each point of the surface $L = $ constant there are two principal radii of curvature R_1, R_2. The gaussian curvature K is given by $K = 1/R_1 R_2$ for the

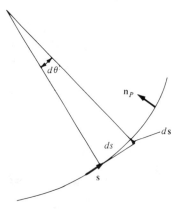

Figure IV.1 Illustration for determining the ray curvature.

surface, with **s** the unit normal. Consider two closely spaced constant-phase surfaces $L = L_1$ and $L = L_1 + \Delta L_1$, as in Fig. IV.2. For the ray tube illustrated the elements of area on the two surfaces are $dA_1 = R_1 R_2 \, du \, dv = 1/K_1 \, du \, dv$ and $dA_2 = (R_1 + \Delta R_1)(R_2 + \Delta R_2) \, du \, dv = 1/K_2 \, du \, dv$, where u and v are angular measures.

Consider the vector $\mathbf{F} = kn\mathbf{s}$ for which

$$\oint_A \mathbf{F} \cdot d\mathbf{A} = \mathbf{F} \cdot \mathbf{s}|_{L_1 + \Delta L_1} \, dA_2 - \mathbf{F} \cdot \mathbf{s}|_{L_1} \, dA_1 = 0$$

where A is the surface bounded by the sides of the ray tube and the surfaces L_1 and $L_1 + \Delta L_1$. Since $\oint_A \mathbf{F} \cdot d\mathbf{A} = \int_V \nabla \cdot \mathbf{F} \, dV = 0$ we conclude that $\nabla \cdot \mathbf{F} = 0$. Thus $\nabla \cdot Kn\mathbf{s} = 0 = Kn\nabla \cdot \mathbf{s} + \mathbf{s} \cdot \nabla Kn$ or

$$\nabla \cdot \mathbf{s} = \frac{-1}{Kn} \frac{dKn}{ds} = -\frac{d \ln nK}{ds}$$

Now $\nabla^2 L = \nabla \cdot \nabla L = \nabla \cdot n\mathbf{s} = n\nabla \cdot \mathbf{s}$ for n constant, so

$$\nabla^2 L = -n \frac{d \ln nK}{ds} = -n \frac{d \ln K}{ds} \qquad \text{(IV.22)}$$

Our equation for $\mathbf{E}_0$ becomes

$$\mathbf{E}_0(s) = \mathbf{E}_0(s_0) \exp -\tfrac{1}{2} \int_{s_0}^{s} -\frac{d \ln K}{ds} \, ds$$

$$= \mathbf{E}_0(s_0) \sqrt{\frac{K(s)}{K(s_0)}} \qquad \text{(IV.23)}$$

The power density in a ray tube at s_0 is

$$P(s_0) = \frac{|\mathbf{E}_0(s_0)|^2}{2Z}$$

while that at s is

$$P(s) = \frac{|\mathbf{E}_0(s)|^2}{2Z}$$

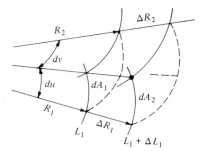

Figure IV.2 A flux tube.

which upon using Eq. (IV.23) is also seen to be equal to $P(s_0)[K(s)/K(s_0)]$. Since the cross-sectional area of the flux tube varies as $1/K$ we find that the total power flow in a flux tube is conserved. Our final result is

$$\mathbf{E}_0(s) = \mathbf{E}_0(s_0) \, e^{-jk_0 L(s_0) - jk_0(s - s_0)} \sqrt{\frac{K(s)}{K(s_0)}} \qquad (IV.24)$$

RAY OPTICS FORMULAS IN LOSSLESS, ISOTROPIC, NONHOMOGENEOUS MEDIA

Ray Trajectories

Let $s = s(\tau)$ where τ is a parameter that establishes points along the ray, with s being the arc length along the ray. Then $x(\tau)$, $y(\tau)$, $z(\tau)$ are coordinates of a point on the ray. The components of the tangent along the ray are proportional to $dx/d\tau$, $dy/d\tau$, $dz/d\tau$ and also to $\partial L/\partial x$, $\partial L/\partial y$, $\partial L/\partial z$. Hence we must have

$$\frac{dx}{d\tau} = \lambda(\tau) \frac{\partial L}{\partial x} = \lambda L_x \qquad \frac{dy}{d\tau} = \lambda L_y \qquad \frac{dz}{d\tau} = \lambda L_z \qquad (IV.25)$$

where λ is a proportionality constant that may be a function of τ. Now

$$\frac{d}{d\tau} \frac{1}{\lambda} \frac{dx}{d\tau} = \frac{dL_x}{d\tau} = \frac{\partial L_x}{\partial x} \frac{dx}{d\tau} + \frac{\partial L_x}{\partial y} \frac{dy}{d\tau} + \frac{\partial L_x}{\partial z} \frac{dz}{d\tau}$$

$$= \lambda(L_{xx}L_x + L_{xy}L_y + L_{xz}L_z) = \tfrac{1}{2}\lambda \frac{\partial}{\partial x}(L_x^2 + L_y^2 + L_z^2)$$

$$= \tfrac{1}{2}\lambda \frac{\partial n^2}{\partial x}$$

by using the eikonal equation. We now see that the equations for the rays are

$$\frac{d}{d\tau} \frac{1}{\lambda} \frac{dx}{d\tau} = \tfrac{1}{2}\lambda \frac{\partial n^2}{\partial x} \qquad \frac{d}{d\tau} \frac{1}{\lambda} \frac{dy}{d\tau} = \tfrac{1}{2}\lambda \frac{\partial n^2}{\partial y} \qquad \frac{d}{d\tau} \frac{1}{\lambda} \frac{dz}{d\tau} = \tfrac{1}{2}\lambda \frac{\partial n^2}{\partial z} \qquad (IV.26)$$

along with the condition

$$\left(\frac{dx}{d\tau}\right)^2 + \left(\frac{dy}{d\tau}\right)^2 + \left(\frac{dz}{d\tau}\right)^2 = \lambda^2 n^2 \qquad (IV.27)$$

obtained by squaring and adding the equations in Eq. (IV.25).

Since τ is still arbitrary we can choose it so as to make $\lambda(\tau) = 1$; then the ray equations become

$$\frac{d^2\mathbf{r}}{d\tau^2} = -\nabla(-\tfrac{1}{2}n^2) \qquad (IV.28)$$

where **r** is the position vector along the ray. This equation is the same as that for a unit point mass moving in a potential field $-\frac{1}{2}n^2$.

Example IV.1 Ray trajectories in an inhomogeneous medium Let the ray enter a medium having the index of refraction $n^2 = n_0^2 \pm n_1 x$ at the origin with an angle θ_0, as in Fig. IV.3. Our equations are

$$\frac{d^2x}{d\tau^2} = \pm \frac{1}{2}n_1 \qquad \frac{d^2y}{d\tau^2} = \frac{d^2z}{d\tau^2} = 0$$

which yield

$$x = \pm n_1 \frac{\tau^2}{4} + A\tau + B$$

$$y = C\tau + D$$

$$z = E\tau + F$$

At the point of entry let $\tau = 0$, then $B = D = F = 0$. Also at $\tau = 0$, $dz/d\tau = 0$, so $E = 0$. Also $(dy/d\tau)/(dx/d\tau) = \tan \theta_0 = C/A$ at $\tau = 0$. Hence $x = \pm (n_1/4)\tau^2 + A\tau$ and $y = A\tau \tan \theta_0$. To determine the constant A we use Eq. (IV.27) to obtain

$$\left(\pm \frac{n_1}{2}\tau + A \right)^2 + A^2 \tan^2 \theta_0 = n^2 = (n_0^2 \pm n_1 x)$$

$$= \left[n_0^2 \pm n_1 \left(\pm \frac{n_1}{4}\tau^2 + A\tau \right) \right]$$

or $A = n_0 \cos \theta_0$. Consequently

$$x = n_0\tau \cos \theta_0 \pm \frac{n_1}{4}\tau^2$$

$$y = n_0\tau \sin \theta_0$$

$$z = 0$$

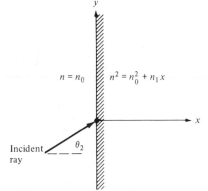

Figure IV.3 An inhomogeneous medium in the half space $x \geqslant 0$.

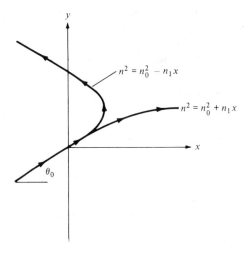

Figure IV.4 Ray trajectories in an inhomogeneous medium with $n^2 = n_0^2 \pm n_1 x$.

specifies the ray path. From these equations $dx/d\tau = n_0 \cos \theta_0 \pm (n_1/2)\tau$ and equals zero for $n_0 \cos \theta_0 = n_1\tau/2$ when the lower sign is used. For this case the ray turns around and emerges on the $x < 0$ side. For the other case (upper sign) the ray path eventually becomes parallel to the x axis, as in Fig. IV.4. ∎

Fermat's Principle

Consider two points P_1 and P_2 and a family of possible ray paths connecting these points, as in Fig. IV.5. Fermat's principle states that the actual path taken by the ray will be that which makes the optical path length an extremum (usually a minimum). Thus we have

$$\delta \int_{P_1}^{P_2} n \, ds = 0 \tag{IV.29}$$

We may describe each possible curve in parametric form as $x = x(\tau)$, $y = y(\tau)$, $z = z(\tau)$. Then $n = n[x(\tau), y(\tau), z(\tau)]$ and $ds = (ds/d\tau)d\tau = [(dx/d\tau)^2 + (dy/d\tau)^2 + (dz/d\tau)^2]^{1/2} \, d\tau$, so Eq. (IV.29) becomes

$$\delta \int_{P_1}^{P_2} n[x(\tau), y(\tau), z(\tau)] \left[\left(\frac{dx}{d\tau}\right)^2 + \left(\frac{dy}{d\tau}\right)^2 + \left(\frac{dz}{d\tau}\right)^2 \right]^{1/2} d\tau \tag{IV.30}$$

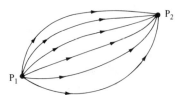

Figure IV.5 A family of possible ray paths.

which is of the form $(x' = dx/d\tau, \text{ etc.})$

$$\delta \int_{P_1}^{P_2} F(x, y, z, x', y', z') \, d\tau = 0$$

By a Taylor series expansion

$$\delta F = \frac{\partial F}{\partial x} \delta x + \frac{\partial T}{\partial x'} \delta x' + \cdots$$

so

$$\delta \int_{P_1}^{P_2} F \, d\tau = \int_{P_1}^{P_2} \left(\frac{\partial F}{\partial x} \delta x + \frac{\partial F}{\partial y} \delta y + \frac{\partial F}{\partial z} \delta z + \frac{\partial F}{\partial x'} \delta x' + \frac{\partial F}{\partial y'} \delta y' + \frac{\partial F}{\partial z'} \delta z' \right) d\tau$$

$$= \left(\frac{\partial F}{\partial x'} \delta x + \frac{\partial F}{\partial y'} \delta y + \frac{\partial F}{\partial z'} \delta z \right) \Big|_{P_1}^{P_2} + \int_{P_1}^{P_2} \left[\left(\frac{\partial F}{\partial x} - \frac{\partial}{\partial \tau} \frac{\partial F}{\partial x'} \right) \delta x \right.$$

$$\left. + \left(\frac{\partial F}{\partial y} - \frac{\partial}{\partial \tau} \frac{\partial F}{\partial y'} \right) \delta y + \left(\frac{\partial F}{\partial z} - \frac{\partial}{\partial \tau} \frac{\partial F}{\partial z'} \right) \delta z \right] d\tau$$

upon integrating by parts once. Since all possible paths under consideration are constrained to begin at P_1 and end at P_2 we have $\delta x = \delta y = \delta z = 0$ at P_1 and P_2. Hence in order for the variation in the integral to vanish for arbitrary and independent variations δx, δy, δz we must have

$$\frac{\partial F}{\partial x} - \frac{\partial}{\partial \tau} \frac{\partial F}{\partial x'} = 0 \qquad \frac{\partial F}{\partial y} - \frac{\partial}{\partial \tau} \frac{\partial F}{\partial y'} = 0 \qquad \frac{\partial F}{\partial z} - \frac{\partial}{\partial \tau} \frac{\partial F}{\partial z'} = 0$$

which are the usual Euler-Lagrange equations from the calculus of variations. Now $\partial F/\partial x = \partial n/\partial x$, etc., so the ray equations become

$$\frac{d}{d\tau} \frac{nx'}{\sqrt{x'^2 + y'^2 + z'^2}} = \sqrt{x'^2 + y'^2 + z'^2} \, \frac{\partial n}{\partial x}$$

and similarly for the other two equations. We now let $\lambda(\tau) = \sqrt{x'^2 + y'^2 + z'^2}/n$, which is the same condition as Eq. (IV.27), and then obtain

$$\frac{d}{d\tau} \frac{1}{\lambda} \frac{\partial x}{\partial \tau} = n\lambda \frac{\partial n}{\partial x} = \tfrac{1}{2}\lambda \frac{\partial n^2}{\partial x}$$

and so forth, the same as Eq. (IV.28). Hence Fermat's principle is an equivalent statement of the ray equations. It corresponds to the principle of "least action" in mechanics.

Transport Equations for E_0 and H_0 in Inhomogeneous, Lossless, Isotropic Media

The equation for E_0 is [note that $\nabla L \cdot \nabla E_0 = n(dE_0/ds)$]

$$n \frac{dE_0}{ds} + \tfrac{1}{2}\nabla^2 L E_0 + \nabla L E_0 \cdot \nabla \ln n - \tfrac{1}{2}E_0 \nabla L \cdot \nabla \ln \mu = 0$$

Introduce $\sqrt{\epsilon}\,\mathbf{E}_0$ and note that

$$\frac{d}{ds}(\sqrt{\epsilon}\,\mathbf{E}_0) = \mathbf{E}_0\frac{d\sqrt{\epsilon}}{ds} + \sqrt{\epsilon}\,\frac{d\mathbf{E}_0}{ds} = \mathbf{E}_0\frac{\nabla L \cdot \nabla \sqrt{\epsilon}}{n} + \sqrt{\epsilon}\,\frac{d\mathbf{E}_0}{ds}$$

since $\nabla L \cdot \nabla = n(d/ds)$. We now obtain

$$\frac{d}{ds}(\sqrt{\epsilon}\,\mathbf{E}_0) + \tfrac{1}{2}(\nabla \cdot \mathbf{s})(\sqrt{\epsilon}\,\mathbf{E}_0) + (\sqrt{\epsilon}\,\mathbf{E}_0)\cdot\nabla \ln n\,\mathbf{s} - \tfrac{1}{2}(\mathbf{s}\cdot\nabla \ln n)(\sqrt{\epsilon}\,\mathbf{E}_0) = 0$$

$$\text{(IV.31)}$$

since $\nabla^2 L = \nabla \cdot \nabla L = \nabla \cdot n\mathbf{s} = n\nabla \cdot \mathbf{s} + \mathbf{s}\cdot\nabla n$. The vector $\sqrt{\mu}\,\mathbf{H}_0$ also satisfies this equation. Now introduce two new vectors

$$\mathbf{P} = \sqrt{\frac{\epsilon}{2W}}\,\mathbf{E}_0 \qquad \mathbf{Q} = \sqrt{\frac{\mu}{2W}}\,\mathbf{H}_0 \qquad\qquad \text{(IV.32)}$$

where $W(s)$ is still to be specified. We now use

$$\frac{d\mathbf{P}}{ds} = \frac{1}{\sqrt{2W}}\frac{d}{ds}(\sqrt{\epsilon}\,\mathbf{E}_0) + \sqrt{\epsilon}\,\mathbf{E}_0\frac{d}{ds}\frac{1}{\sqrt{2W}}$$

to obtain

$$\frac{d\mathbf{P}}{ds} + \mathbf{P}\left(\frac{d}{ds}\ln\sqrt{2W} + \tfrac{1}{2}\nabla \cdot \mathbf{s} - \tfrac{1}{2}\mathbf{s}\cdot\nabla \ln n\right) + (\mathbf{P}\cdot\nabla \ln n)\mathbf{s} = 0 \qquad \text{(IV.33)}$$

Let us choose W so that

$$\frac{d}{ds}\ln\sqrt{2W} = \frac{d}{ds}\ln\sqrt{W} = -\tfrac{1}{2}\nabla \cdot \mathbf{s} + \tfrac{1}{2}\mathbf{s}\cdot\nabla \ln n$$

or equivalently

$$\frac{d}{ds}\ln\frac{W}{n} = -\nabla \cdot \mathbf{s} \qquad\qquad \text{(IV.34)}$$

The latter gives

$$\frac{W(s)}{n(s)} = \frac{W(s_0)}{n(s_0)}\,e^{-\int_{s_0}^{s}\nabla\cdot\mathbf{s}\,ds} \qquad\qquad \text{(IV.35)}$$

and Eq. (IV.33) becomes

$$\frac{d\mathbf{P}}{ds} + (\mathbf{P}\cdot\nabla \ln n)\mathbf{s} = 0 \qquad\qquad \text{(IV.36)}$$

The vector $\mathbf{Q}$ satisfies this equation also. Since $\mathbf{E}_0\cdot\nabla L = 0$ we must have $\mathbf{P}\cdot\mathbf{s} = 0$. A scalar product of Eq. (IV.36) with $\mathbf{P}$ gives

$$\mathbf{P}\cdot\frac{d\mathbf{P}}{ds} = \tfrac{1}{2}\frac{d\mathbf{P}\cdot\mathbf{P}}{ds} = \tfrac{1}{2}\frac{d|\mathbf{P}|^2}{ds}$$

and hence $|\mathbf{P}|$ does not change along the ray. Consequently we can choose $|\mathbf{P}| = |\mathbf{Q}| = 1$.

The energy density in the field is

$$U_e + U_m = U = \frac{\epsilon}{4}|\mathbf{E}_0|^2 + \frac{\mu}{4}|\mathbf{H}_0|^2$$

Since $|\mathbf{H}_0| = |Y\mathbf{s} \times \mathbf{E}_0| = Y|\mathbf{E}_0|$ we find that $U_e = U_m$, so $U = |\mathbf{E}_0|^2\epsilon/2$. Hence with $|\mathbf{P}| = 1$ the normalizing factor W is

$$W = \frac{\epsilon}{2}|\mathbf{E}_0|^2 = U \qquad\qquad \text{(IV.37)}$$

To further simplify the equation for $\mathbf{P}$ and $\mathbf{Q}$ note that

$$\nabla(\nabla L)^2 = \nabla n^2 = 2n\nabla n = \nabla(L_x^2 + L_y^2 + L_z^2)$$

$$= 2L_x\nabla L_x + 2L_y\nabla L_y + 2L_z\nabla L_z = 2\left(L_x\frac{\partial}{\partial x} + L_y\frac{\partial}{\partial y} + L_z\frac{\partial}{\partial z}\right)\nabla L$$

since

$$\nabla L_x = \nabla\frac{\partial L}{\partial x} = \frac{\partial}{\partial x}\nabla L$$

Hence

$$n\nabla n = (\nabla L \cdot \nabla)\nabla L = n\frac{d}{ds}\nabla L$$

or $\nabla n = (d/ds)\nabla L$. Therefore Eq. (IV.36) becomes

$$\frac{d\mathbf{P}}{ds} = -(\mathbf{P}\cdot\nabla\ln n)\mathbf{s} = -\frac{1}{n}\mathbf{P}\cdot\nabla n\mathbf{s} = -\frac{1}{n}\mathbf{P}\cdot\frac{d\nabla L}{ds}\mathbf{s}$$

But

$$\frac{d\nabla L}{ds} = \frac{dn\mathbf{s}}{ds} = n\frac{d\mathbf{s}}{ds} + \mathbf{s}\frac{dn}{ds}$$

and since $\mathbf{P}\cdot\mathbf{s} = 0$ we obtain

$$\frac{d\mathbf{P}}{ds} + \mathbf{P}\cdot\frac{d\mathbf{s}}{ds}\mathbf{s} = 0 \qquad\qquad \text{(IV.38)}$$

Frenet's formulas for a space curve are (see Fig. IV.6)

$$\frac{d\mathbf{s}}{ds} = \frac{\mathbf{n}_p}{\rho} \qquad \rho = \text{principal radius of curvature}$$

$$\frac{d\mathbf{n}_p}{ds} = -\frac{\mathbf{s}}{\rho} + \frac{\mathbf{n}_b}{T} \qquad T = \text{torsion (more corectly called the radius of torsion)}$$

$$\frac{d\mathbf{n}_b}{ds} = -\frac{\mathbf{n}_p}{T}$$

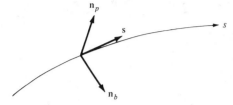

Figure IV.6 Orientation of unit tangent, unit principal normal, and unit binormal vectors along a ray.

$\mathbf{s}$ = unit tangent vector

$$\mathbf{n}_p = \frac{d\mathbf{s}/ds}{|d\mathbf{s}/ds|} = \text{unit principle normal}$$

$\mathbf{n}_b = \mathbf{s} \times \mathbf{n}_p$ = unit binormal

Note that for any unit vector $\mathbf{a}$ defined on $\mathbf{s}$, $d\mathbf{a}/ds$ is perpendicular to $\mathbf{a}$ because

$$\mathbf{a} \cdot \frac{d\mathbf{a}}{ds} = \tfrac{1}{2}\frac{d\mathbf{a}\cdot\mathbf{a}}{ds} = 0$$

since $\mathbf{a}\cdot\mathbf{a} = 1$. The third formula above follows from

$$\frac{d\mathbf{n}_b}{ds} = \frac{d}{ds}\mathbf{s}\times\mathbf{n}_p = \mathbf{s}\times\frac{d\mathbf{n}_p}{ds} - \mathbf{n}_p\times\frac{d\mathbf{s}}{ds} = -\frac{\mathbf{n}_p}{T}$$

upon using the first two formulas for $d\mathbf{s}/ds$ and $d\mathbf{n}_p/ds$.

Since $\mathbf{P}$ is a unit vector perpendicular to $\mathbf{s}$ we can write $\mathbf{P} = \mathbf{n}_p \cos\theta + \mathbf{n}_b \sin\theta$. The equation for $\mathbf{P}$ then gives

$$\mathbf{n}_p\frac{d\cos\theta}{ds} + \cos\theta\frac{d\mathbf{n}_p}{ds} + \mathbf{n}_b\frac{d\sin\theta}{ds} + \sin\theta\frac{d\mathbf{n}_b}{ds} + \frac{1}{\rho}\cos\theta\,\mathbf{s} = 0$$

Using Frenet's formulas and noting that $d\cos\theta/ds = -\sin\theta\,d\theta/ds$, etc., and equating vector components we find that $d\theta/ds = -1/T$. Hence

$$\theta = \theta_0 - \int_{s_0}^{s}\frac{ds}{T} = \theta_0 - \hat{\theta} \tag{IV.39}$$

Thus if $\mathbf{P}(s_0) = \mathbf{n}_p\cos\theta_0 + \mathbf{n}_b\sin\theta_0$ we have

$$\mathbf{P}(s) = \mathbf{n}_p\cos(\theta_0 - \hat{\theta}) + \mathbf{n}_b\sin(\theta_0 - \hat{\theta}) \tag{IV.40}$$

The vector $\mathbf{Q}$ is given by (see Fig. IV.7)

$$\mathbf{Q} = \mathbf{s}\times\mathbf{P} \tag{IV.41}$$

The angle of rotation of $\mathbf{P}$ away from $\mathbf{n}_p$ is given in terms of the torsion of the ray path by Eq. (IV.39).

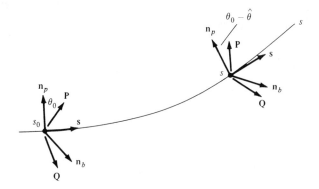

Figure IV.7 Illustration of rotation of the vectors **P** and **Q** along a ray with torsion.

Evaluation of $\nabla \cdot \mathbf{s}$

The polarization property of the field is determined by the torsion of the ray in that it causes **P** and **Q** to rotate about s. The intensity of the field is determined by the function $W(s)$ introduced earlier [Eq. (IV.35)] since

$$\mathbf{E}_0 = \sqrt{\frac{W}{2\epsilon}}\,\mathbf{P} \qquad \text{and} \qquad \mathbf{H}_0 = \sqrt{\frac{W}{2\mu}}\,\mathbf{Q}$$

The evaluation of $W(s)$ requires us to find $\nabla \cdot \mathbf{s}$.

Frenet's formulas for a space curve may be written in the form

$$\frac{d\mathbf{s}}{ds} = \boldsymbol{\delta} \times \mathbf{s} \qquad \frac{d\mathbf{n}_p}{ds} = \boldsymbol{\delta} \times \mathbf{n}_p \qquad \frac{d\mathbf{n}_b}{ds} = \boldsymbol{\delta} \times \mathbf{n}_b$$

by introducing the Darboux vector $\boldsymbol{\delta} = \mathbf{s}/T + (\mathbf{n}_b/\rho)$. With reference to Fig. IV.8 let the point P move along the ray with unit speed. Then the motion of the trio of vectors $\mathbf{s}$, $\mathbf{n}_p$, $\mathbf{n}_b$ can be described as a rotation about some axis. The form of Frenet's equations written above shows that $\boldsymbol{\delta}$ is the angular velocity of the vector trio as it moves along the ray.

Consider now a curve drawn on a surface and let $\mathbf{s}$, **N**, and **B** be the unit tangent, principal normal, and binormal to the curve. Let **n** be a unit inward normal to the surface and let $\mathbf{p} = \mathbf{s} \times \mathbf{n}$, as in Fig. IV.9. Let the angle between **N** and **n** be θ. As the point P moves on the curve the motion of the trio $\mathbf{s}$, **n**, **p** is that of the trio $\mathbf{s}$, **N**, **B**, plus an additional rotation about the common vector $\mathbf{s}$. Hence the angular velocity of the trio $\mathbf{s}$, **n**, **p**, as P moves with unit speed along

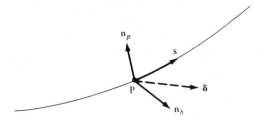

Figure IV.8 Illustration of the Darboux vector $\boldsymbol{\delta}$.

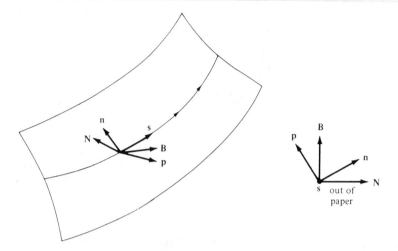

Figure IV.9 Curve located on a surface.

s, is

$$\omega = \delta + \frac{d\theta}{ds}\, s$$

Now $\mathbf{B} = \mathbf{n}\sin\theta + \mathbf{p}\cos\theta$, so we can also write

$$\omega = \left(\frac{1}{T} + \frac{d\theta}{ds}\right)\mathbf{s} + \frac{\sin\theta}{\rho}\,\mathbf{n} + \frac{\cos\theta}{\rho}\,\mathbf{p}$$

$$= t\mathbf{s} + \gamma\mathbf{n} + k\mathbf{p}$$

where t, γ, k are defined by this equation and called the *geodesic torsion*, *geodesic curvature*, and *normal curvature*, respectively. As P moves on s we can now write

$$\frac{d\mathbf{n}}{ds} = \omega \times \mathbf{n} = t\mathbf{p} - k\mathbf{s}$$

With reference to Fig. IV.10 let s_1 and s_2 be two arbitrary curves intersecting at right angles on a surface. Let ω_1 and ω_2 be the associated angular velocity vectors. Also let s_3 be a curve perpendicular to the tangent plane to the surface at the point of intersection P. In the orthogonal curvilinear coordinate system we have thus constructed, the divergence of a vector field $\mathbf{f}$ is given by

$$\nabla \cdot \mathbf{f} = \mathbf{s}_1 \cdot \frac{d\mathbf{f}}{ds_1} + \mathbf{s}_2 \cdot \frac{d\mathbf{f}}{ds_2} + \mathbf{s}_3 \cdot \frac{d\mathbf{f}}{ds_3}$$

If we let $\mathbf{f} = \mathbf{s}_3$, the unit tangent to s_3, then since $d\mathbf{s}_3/ds_3$ is perpendicular to $\mathbf{s}_3$

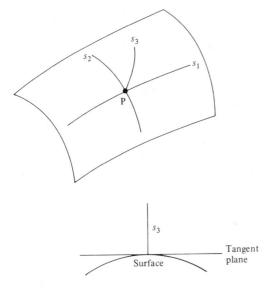

Figure IV.10 Two curves on a surface.

we have

$$\nabla \cdot \mathbf{s}_3 = \mathbf{s}_1 \cdot \frac{d\mathbf{s}_3}{ds_1} + \mathbf{s}_2 \cdot \frac{d\mathbf{s}_3}{ds_2} = \mathbf{s}_1 \cdot \boldsymbol{\omega}_1 \times \mathbf{s}_3 + \mathbf{s}_2 \cdot \boldsymbol{\omega}_2 \times \mathbf{s}_3$$

$$= k_1 + k_2$$

where we have assumed that $\mathbf{s}_3$ corresponds to the outward normal to the surface. Since $\nabla \cdot \mathbf{s}_3$ is an invariant quantity we see that the sum of the normal curvatures for two orthogonal directions on a surface is a constant. If we rotate $\mathbf{s}_1$ and $\mathbf{s}_2$ about $\mathbf{s}_3$ at P, one of the curvatures will take on a maximum value and the other must then be a minimum. Hence $\nabla \cdot \mathbf{s}_3 = k_{max} + k_{min} =$ sum of principal curvatures. The surface curves which yield k_{max} and k_{min} are characterized by having zero geodesic torsion t.

Our final result for Eq. (IV.35) is

$$\frac{W(s)}{n(s)} = \frac{W(s_0)}{n(s_0)} e^{-\int_{s_0}^{s} (1/R_1 + 1/R_2) \, ds} \tag{IV.42}$$

where R_1 and R_2 are the principal radii of curvature of the eikonal surface $L =$ constant.

This equation is obtained by letting the surface be the eikonal surface $L =$ constant for which $\mathbf{s}_3$ is then the unit vector $\mathbf{s}$ along the ray that intersects the surface at right angles to it. When the eikonal surface is convex, the principal radii of curvature are positive, and the field intensity decreases as it propagates along the ray because of the diverging characteristic of the rays. A knowledge of the eikonal function L is needed in order to determine the principal radii of curvature, and from these the function $W(s)$. If the family of rays and their unit tangent $\mathbf{s}$ have been found and expressed in terms of the coordinate variables and unit vectors in a suitable coordinate system, then $\nabla \cdot \mathbf{s}$ can also be found directly without knowing the eikonal function. Equation (IV.35) may be used to find $W(s)$, and Eq. (IV.42) serves to provide a physical interpretation of that equation.

Example IV.2 Plane wave incident on an inhomogeneous medium This example will illustrate the application of some of the formulas derived above. Consider a medium in $z \geq 0$ for which $n^2 = n_0^2 + n_1 z$. A plane wave $E_0 \mathbf{a}_y e^{-jk_0(x \sin \theta_i + z \cos \theta_i)}$ is incident on the interface at $z = 0$ from below. This incident wave launches a field in $z > 0$, with all rays having an initial angle θ_0 with respect to the z axis, where (see Fig. IV.11) $n_0 \sin \theta_0 = \sin \theta_i$. The ray trajectories may be found as in Example IV.1 and are given by

$$z = \tau n_0 \cos \theta_0 + \tau^2 \frac{n_1}{4}$$

$$x = x_1 + \tau n_0 \sin \theta_0$$

The initial point $x = x_1$, $z = 0$ determines each ray in the family of rays. At $z = 0$ the eikonal function L is given by $L(0) = n_0 x \sin \theta_0$. All the rays are plane curves with zero torsion. Hence the electric field remains polarized along the y axis as the field propagates along the ray.

The phase of the field at a distance z above the interface is given by Eq. (IV.18a) as

$$L(s) = L(0) + \int_0^s n(s)\, ds = n_0 x_1 \sin \theta_0 + \int_0^\tau n(\tau) \frac{ds}{d\tau}\, d\tau$$

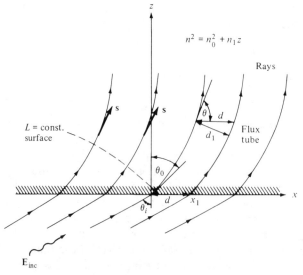

Figure IV.11 A plane wave incident on an inhomogeneous medium in $z > 0$.

for the ray beginning at $x = x_1$, $z = 0$. From Eq. (IV.27) we have $dx^2 + dy^2 + dz^2 = ds^2 = n^2\,d\tau^2$, and hence $ds/d\tau = n$ and

$$L(\tau) = L(0) + \int_0^\tau n^2\,d\tau$$

When we substitute the expression for z in terms of τ into the expression for n^2 and carry out the integration we obtain

$$L(\tau) = n_0 x_1 \sin\theta_0 + n_0^2\tau + n_1 n_0 \frac{\tau^2}{2}\cos\theta_0 + \frac{n_1^2\tau^3}{12}$$

A given value of τ determines a corresponding value of z, which may be used to determine L as a function of z.

The amplitude of the field is determined by the function $W(s)$. In order to evaluate $W(s)$ we must first find $\nabla \cdot \mathbf{s}$. The unit vector along a ray is given by

$$\mathbf{s} = \frac{\mathbf{a}_z(dz/dx) + \mathbf{a}_x}{[1 + (dz/dx)^2]^{1/2}}$$

We can eliminate the parameter τ in the parametric equations for x and z to obtain

$$z = (x - x_1)\cot\theta_0 + \frac{n_1}{4}(x - x_1)^2\csc^2\theta_0$$

$$= a(x - x_1) + b(x - x_1)^2$$

where a and b are defined by this equation. From this equation we get

$$\frac{dz}{dx} = a + 2b(x - x_1)$$

From Fig. IV.11 it is seen that the unit tangent vector is a function of z only, since all rays are similar. We can express $x - x_1$ in terms of z to obtain

$$x - x_1 = \frac{a}{2b} + \sqrt{\frac{a^2}{4b^2} + \frac{z}{b}}$$

and

$$\frac{dz}{dx} = \sqrt{a^2 + 4bz}$$

When we substitute this expression into the equation for $\mathbf{s}$ we have an expression for $\mathbf{s}$ that applies for all values of x and z. The divergence is readily evaluated to give

$$\nabla \cdot \mathbf{s} = \frac{2b}{(a^2 + 4bz)^{1/2}(1 + a^2 + 4bz)^{3/2}}$$

Equation (IV.35) gives $W(s)$, which we can express as a function of z in the form

$$\frac{W(z)}{n(z)} = \frac{W(0)}{n(0)} e^{-\int_0^z \mathbf{\nabla \cdot s}(ds/dz)\, dz}$$

Now

$$\frac{ds}{dz} = \left[1 + \left(\frac{dx}{dz}\right)^2\right]^{1/2} = \frac{[1 + (dz/dx)^2]^{1/2}}{dz/dx}$$

so we obtain

$$\mathbf{\nabla \cdot s}\frac{ds}{dz} = \frac{2b}{(a^2 + 4bz)(1 + a^2 + 4bz)} = 2b\left(\frac{1}{a^2 + 4bz} - \frac{1}{1 + a^2 + 4bz}\right)$$

The integral of this expression is readily carried out to give

$$\int_0^z \mathbf{\nabla \cdot s}\frac{ds}{dz}\, dz = -\ln\left[\frac{(a^2 + 4bz)(1 + a^2)}{a^2(1 + a^2 + 4bz)}\right]^{1/2}$$

We now find that

$$\frac{W(z)}{n(z)} = \frac{W(0)}{n_0}\left[\frac{a^2(1 + a^2 + 4bz)}{(1 + a^2)(a^2 + 4bz)}\right]^{1/2}$$

We can show in a more direct way that this is an expected result. With reference to Fig. IV.11 it can be seen that for two rays with a spacing d along x at $z = 0$ the perpendicular spacing d_1 at a height z is given by

$$d_1 = d \sin \theta = \frac{d \tan \theta}{(1 + \tan^2 \theta)^{1/2}}$$

The conservation of power in a flux tube requires that $n_0|E_0(0)|^2 d_1(0) = n(z)|E_0(z)|^2 d_1(z)$, and hence upon using $\tan \theta = dz/dx$ we get

$$\frac{|E_0(z)|^2}{|E_0(0)|^2} = \frac{n_0}{n(z)}\left(\frac{1 + a^2 + 4bz}{1 + a^2}\frac{a^2}{a^2 + 4bz}\right)^{1/2} = \frac{W(z)}{n^2}\frac{n_0^2}{W(0)}$$

in agreement with the earlier result. Note that $(W/2n^2\epsilon_0)^{1/2}$ gives the magnitude of the electric field as shown by Eq. (IV.37). ∎

BIBLIOGRAPHY

Antennas: Introductory and Intermediate Level

Balanis, C. A.: *Antenna Theory, Analysis, and Design*, Harper & Row Publishers, Inc., New York, 1982.

Blake, L. J.: *Antennas*, John Wiley & Sons, Inc., New York, 1966.

Elliott, R. S.: *Antenna Theory and Design*, Prentice-Hall, Inc., Englewood Cliffs, N.J., 1981.

Jordan, E. C., and K. G. Balmain: *Electromagnetic Waves and Radiating Systems*, Prentice-Hall, Inc., Englewood Cliffs, N.J., 1968.

Kraus, J. D.: *Antennas*, McGraw-Hill Book Company, New York, 1950.

Schelkunoff, S. A., and H. T. Friis: *Antennas: Theory and Practice*, John Wiley & Sons, Inc., New York, 1952.

Silver, S. (ed.): *Microwave Antenna Theory and Design*, M.I.T. Radiation Laboratory Series, McGraw-Hill Book Company, New York, 1949.

Stutzman, W. L., and G. A. Thiele: *Antenna Theory and Design*, John Wiley & Sons, Inc., New York, 1981.

Weeks, W. L.: *Antenna Engineering*, McGraw-Hill Book Company, New York, 1968.

Wolff, E. A.: *Antenna Analysis*, John Wiley & Sons, Inc., New York, 1966.

Antennas: Advanced

Collin, R. E., and F. J. Zucker (eds.): *Antenna Theory*, vols. I and II, McGraw-Hill Book Company, New York, 1969.

King, R. W. P.: *Theory of Linear Antennas*, Harvard University Press, Cambridge, Mass., 1956.

Schelkunoff, S. A.: *Advanced Antenna Theory*, John Wiley & Sons, Inc., New York, 1952.

Antennas: Special Topics

Amitay, N., V. Galindo-Israel, and C. P. Wu: *Theory and Analysis of Phased Array Antennas*, John Wiley & Sons, Inc., New York, 1972.

Bahl, I. J., and P. Bhartia: *Microstrip Antennas*, Artech House, Inc., Dedham, Mass., 1980.

Brown, J.: *Microwave Lenses*, Methuen & Co., Ltd., London, 1953.

Burrows, M. L.: *ELF Communications Antennas*, Peter Peregrinus, Ltd., London, 1978 (IEE publication).

Galejs, J.: *Antennas in Inhomogeneous Media*, Pergamon Press, New York, 1969.

Hansen, R. C. (ed.): *Microwave Scanning Antennas*, Academic Press, Inc., New York; vol. I, 1964; vols. II and III, 1966.

Harper, A. E.: *Rhombic Antenna Design*, D. Van Nostrand Company, Inc., New York, 1941.

Haykin, S.: *Array Processing Applications to Radar*, Dowden, Hutchinson & Ross, Stroudsburg, Penn., 1980.

Hudson, J. E.: *Adaptive Array Principles*, Peter Peregrinus, Ltd., London, 1981 (IEE Publication).

James, J. R., Hall, P. S., and C. Wood, *Microstrip Antenna Theory and Design*, Peter Peregrinus, Ltd., London, 1982 (IEE publication).

Jasik, H. (ed.): *Antenna Engineering Handbook*, McGraw-Hill Book Company, New York, 1961.

Jull, E. V.: *Aperture Antennas and Diffraction Theory*, Peter Peregrinus, Ltd., London, 1981 (IEE publication).

Kiely, D.G.: *Dielectric Aerials*, Methuen & Co., Ltd., London, 1953.

King, R. W. P., R. B. Mack, and S. S. Sandler: *Arrays of Cylindrical Dipole Antennas*, Cambridge University Press, London, 1968.

Love, A. W. (ed.): *Electromagnetic Horn Antennas*, IEEE Press, New York, 1976.

———: *Reflector Antennas*, IEEE Press, New York, 1978.

Ma, M. T.: *Theory and Application of Antenna Arrays*, John Wiley & Sons, Inc., New York, 1974.

Monzingo, R. A., and T. W. Miller: *Introduction to Adaptive Arrays*, John Wiley & Sons, Inc., New York, 1980.

Popovic, B. D., M. B. Dragovic, and A. R. Djordjevic: *Analysis and Synthesis of Wire Antennas*, Research Studies Press, John Wiley & Sons, Inc., New York, 1982.

Rhodes, D. K.: *Synthesis of Planar Antenna Sources*, Clarendon Press, Oxford, London, 1974.

Rudge, A. W., K. Milne, A. D. Olver, and P. Knight. (eds.): *Handbook of Antenna Design*, Peter Peregrinus, Ltd., London; vol. I, 1982; vol. II, 1983 (IEE publication).

Rumsey, V. H.: *Frequency Independent Antennas*, Academic Press, Inc., New York, 1966.

Rusch, W. V. T., and P. D. Potter: *Analysis of Reflector Antennas*, Academic Press, Inc., New York, 1970.

Steinberg, B. D.: *Principles of Aperture and Array System Design*, John Wiley & Sons, Inc., New York, 1976.

Walter, C. H.: *Traveling Wave Antennas*, McGraw-Hill Book Company, New York, 1965.

Wood, P. J.: *Reflector Antenna Analysis and Design*, Peter Peregrinus, Ltd., London, 1980 (IEE publication).

Radio-Wave Propagation

Al'pert, Ya.: *Radio Wave Propagation and the Ionosphere* (Russian translation), Consultants Bureau, New York, 1963.

——— and D. S. Fligel: *Propagation of ELF and VLF Waves Near the Earth* [J. S. Wood (trans.), J. R. Wait (ed.)], Consultants Bureau, New York, 1970.

Banos, A.: *Dipole Radiation in the Presence of Conducting Media*, Pergamon Press, New York, 1966.

Bremmaer, H.: *Terrestrial Radio Waves*, Elsevier Publishing Company, New York, 1949.

Budden, K.: *Radio Waves in the Ionosphere*, University Press, Cambridge, 1961.

———: *The Wave-Guide Mode Theory of Wave Propagation*, Prentice-Hall, Inc., Englewood Cliffs, N.J., 1961.

Burrows, C. R., and S. S. Attwood (eds.): *Radio Wave Propagation*, Academic Press, Inc., New York, 1949. (Consolidated summary technical report of the Committee of Propagation of National Defense Research.)

Davies, K.: *Ionospheric Radio Propagation*, National Bureau of Standards Monograph 80, 1965. (Available from U.S. Government Printing Office, Washington, D.C.)

Galejs, J.: *Terrestrial Propagation of Long Electromagnetic Waves*, Pergamon Press, Oxford, 1972.

Hall, M. P. M.: *Effects of the Troposphere on Radio Communication*, Peter Peregrinus, Ltd., London, 1979 (IEE publication).

Kerr, D. E.: *Propagation of Short Radio Waves*, McGraw-Hill Book Company, New York, 1951.

Livingston, D. C.: *The Physics of Microwave Propagation*, Prentice-Hall, Inc., Englewood Cliffs, N.J., 1970.

Mathews, P. A.: *Radio Wave Propagation, VHF and Above*, Chapman & Hall, London, 1965.

Picquenard, A.: *Radio Wave Propagation*, John Wiley & Sons, Inc., New York, 1974.

Saxton, J. A. (ed.): *Radio Wave Propagation in the Troposphere*, Elsevier Publishing Company, New York, 1962.

Wait, J. R.: *Electromagnetic Waves in Stratified Media*, Pergamon Press, New York, 1962.

——: *Wave Propagation Theory*, Pergamon Press, New York, 1981.

NAME INDEX

SUBJECT INDEX

Adaptive array, 150–151
Albedo of scatterer, 404
Antenna in seawater, 439–443
Antenna array (*see* Array)
Antenna gain (*see* Gain, antenna)
Aperture antenna:
  circular, with uniform field, 171–173
    beam width, 172
    radiation pattern for, 172
  and field-equivalence principle, 179–182
  Fourier transform method for, 164–175
    asymptotic evaluation of, 284–286
  radiated power from, exact equations for, 215–216
  rectangular, with linear phase variation, 173–174
    beam width for, 173
  rectangular, with tapered field, 174–175
  rectangular, with uniform field, 169–171
    beam width for, 171
  (*See also* Horn antenna; Paraboloidal reflector)
Aperture efficiency for paraboloidal reflector, 201–210, 225–227
Aperture field:
  for microwave lens, 196–199
  for offset paraboloidal reflector, 248–249

Aperture field (*Cont.*):
  for paraboloidal reflector, 201, 212–215
Appleton-Hartree equation, 398
Array:
  adaptive, 150–151
  and array polynomial, 124–128
  binomial, 123–124
  Chebyshev, 128–139
  feed networks for, 139–141
    and Butler matrix, 141–143
  line, broadside, 111–115
    beam width for, 112
    directivity for, 112–115
  line, end-fire, 115–118
    beam width for, 116
    directivity for, 117
    Hansen-Woodyard condition for, 117–118
  line, uniform, 109–111
    field pattern for, 110
  log-periodic, 146–148
  parasitic, 143–145
    Yagi-Uda, 143–145
  pattern-multiplication principle for, 108–109
  phased, 119, 148
  retrodirective, 148–150
  superdirective, 133–134
  synthesis of: with Chebyshev polynomials, 128–139
    with Fourier series method, 121–123

Heterick Memorial Library
Ohio Northern University

	DUE	RETURNED	DUE	RETURNED
1.			13.	
2.			14.	
3.			15.	
4.			16.	
5.			17.	
6.			18.	
7.			19.	
8.			20.	
9.			21.	
10.			22.	
11.			23.	
12.			24.